Byron

Byron

THE FLAWED ANGEL

Phyllis Grosskurth

A Peter Davison Book

HOUGHTON MIFFLIN COMPANY

BOSTON · NEW YORK

1997

For information about permission to reproduce selections
from this book, write to Permissions, Houghton Mifflin Company,
215 Park Avenue South, New York, New York 10003.

For information about this and other Houghton Mifflin trade and
reference books and multimedia products, visit
The Bookstore at Houghton Mifflin on the World Wide Web
at http://www.hmco.com/trade/.

Library of Congress Cataloging-in-Publication Data
Grosskurth, Phyllis.
Byron : the flawed angel / Phyllis Grosskurth.
p.   cm.
Includes bibliographical references (p.   ) and index.
ISBN 0-395-69379-9
1. Byron, George Gordon Byron, Baron, 1788–1824 —
Biography. 2. Poets, English — 19th century — Biography.
I. Title.
PR4381.G67 1997
821'.7 — dc21   96-54044   [B]   CIP

Printed in the United States of America

QUM 10 9 8 7 6 5 4 3 2 1

To my three Byron friends

ELIZABETH LONGFORD, WILLIAM ST CLAIR,
AND THE LATE
IAN SCOTT-KILVERT

Contents

List of Illustrations   ix

The Byron Family Tree   xi

Map of Byron's Eastern Journeys   xii

Introduction and Acknowledgements   xiii

Prologue   1

1   The Byrons – Impetuous, Bad and Mad   5

2   A New Life Begins, 1798–1803   21

3   School Days, 1803–5   36

4   Cambridge, 1805–8   52

5   Bitter-Sweet Departure, January–July 1809   71

6   The Great Adventure, July–December 1809   84

7   Athens, Constantinople, January–July 1810   99

8   Reluctant Return, 1810–11   116

9   Encounters with Death, 1811   129

10   The London Whirligig, 1812   147

11   Compulsive Thraldom, 1812–13   166

12   A Dangerous Passion, 1813–14   180

13   Uneasy Commitment, 1813–14   198

14   The Fatal Marriage, 1814–15   214

15   Annus Horribilis, 1815   229

16   Vengeful Women, 1816   241

17   Escape, 1816   260

Contents

18	Exile, August–September 1816	273
19	To Italy, 1816	292
20	Anteroom to the East, 1816–17	302
21	A New Life, 1817–18	316
22	Decadence in Venice, 1818–19	328
23	Next-to-Last Love, 1819	340
24	Opera Bouffa, 1819–20	353
25	Limbo in Ravenna, 1820	364
26	The Reluctant Departure, 1821	377
27	The Singing Birds, 1821–2	392
28	The Wren, the Eagle, and the Skylark, 1822	405
29	Genoa, 1822–3	415
30	Cephalonia, 1823	433
31	Missolonghi, 1824	446
32	Death in Greece, 1824	464
Epilogue		471
References		479
Index		493

List of Illustrations

Section One
Mrs Byron, Byron's mother
View of Newstead Abbey by J.C. Barrow (1793)
Mary Chaworth
John Fitzgibbon, 2nd Earl of Clare, after J. Slater
Byron in his Cambridge robes
Byron by George Sanders (1809)
Lady Caroline Lamb by Mary Anne Knight
Caroline Lamb's cartoon of Lady Holland
Annabella Milbanke
An engraving (after James Holmes) of Byron in 1815
Lady Melbourne, heliogravure after John Hoppner
Augusta Leigh by Sir John Hayter
Lady Byron's wedding dress
G.H. Harlow's engraving of Byron, 1815
Piccadilly Terrace in 1815
Lady Milbanke by James Northcote

Section Two
Dr Stephen Lushington
John Hanson by James Halls
John Cam Hobhouse by Charles Turner
Napoleon's coach captured at Waterloo, 1815
Lady Noel Byron engraved by William Henry Mote
Claire Clairmont by Amelia Curran
Thomas Moore
Countess Teresa Guiccioli
Count Alessandro Guiccioli
Percy Bysshe Shelley by E.E. Williams
Leigh Hunt
Edward John Trelawny by Joseph Severn
Douglas Kinnaird
Lord Byron in Pisa by William Edward West, 1822
Byron drawn by Count D'Orsay, 1823
Byron and Teresa Guiccioli
Byron's house at Missolonghi

The Byron Family Tree

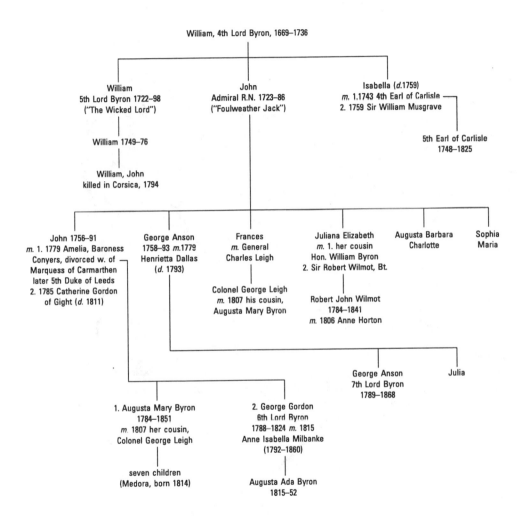

William, 4th Lord Byron, 1669–1736

William
5th Lord Byron 1722–98
("The Wicked Lord")

John
Admiral R.N. 1723–86
("Foulweather Jack")

Isabella (d.1759)
m. 1.1743 4th Earl of Carlisle
2. 1759 Sir William Musgrave

5th Earl of Carlisle
1748–1825

William 1749–76

William, John
killed in Corsica, 1794

John 1756–91
m. 1. 1779 Amelia, Baroness
Conyers, divorced w. of
Marquess of Carmarthen
later 5th Duke of Leeds
2. 1785 Catherine Gordon
of Gight (d. 1811)

George Anson
1758–93 m.1779
Henrietta Dallas
(d. 1793)

Frances
m. General
Charles Leigh

Juliana Elizabeth
m. 1. her cousin
Hon. William Byron
2. Sir Robert Wilmot, Bt.

Augusta Barbara
Charlotte

Sophia
Maria

Colonel George Leigh
m. 1807 his cousin,
Augusta Mary Byron

Robert John Wilmot
1784–1841
m. 1806 Anne Horton

George Anson
7th Lord Byron
1789–1868

Julia

1. Augusta Mary Byron
1784–1851
m. 1807 her cousin,
Colonel George Leigh

2. George Gordon
6th Lord Byron
1788–1824 m. 1815
Anne Isabella Milbanke
(1792–1860)

seven children
(Medora, born 1814)

Augusta Ada Byron
1815–52

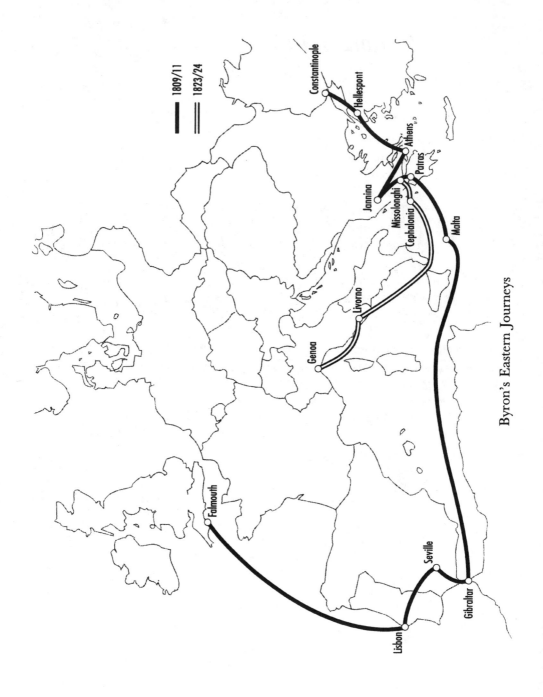

1809/11
1823/24

Constantinople
Hellespont
Athens
Patras
Jannina
Missolonghi
Cephalonia
Malta
Livorno
Genoa
Falmouth
Seville
Gibraltar
Lisbon

Byron's Eastern Journeys

Introduction and Acknowledgements

We all assume that we know what Byronic means, but do we know what Byron, the elusive man, was really like? Professor Leslie Marchand in his magisterial three-volume life of Byron (1957) and Doris Langley Moore in her fascinating essays, *The Late Lord Byron* (1961) and *Lord Byron: Accounts Rendered* (1974), have provided us with plentiful material about his life. Above all, Byron has told us much about himself in his marvellous letters (edited by Professor Marchand) and in his self-revealing poetry (also superbly edited by Jerome McGann).*

What we have not been given is the Byron who was known by those closest to him – his wife, Annabella Milbanke, and his sister, Augusta Leigh. Their views are to be found in the massive archive known as the Lovelace Papers now housed in the Bodleian Library, Oxford. These papers, and many others relating to the Byron separation, were passed down through Lady Byron's family, and are owned by the present Earl of Lytton. After months of immersion in this correspondence, I began to feel that I was meeting Byron for the first time, and in the course of this dawning recognition I was forced to discard many preconceived notions associated more with Byronic mythology than with fact. No marital separation in history has been so extensively documented as that of Byron and his wife. Much of his life reads like a picaresque novel; but a surprising amount of it, particularly after the publication of *Childe Harold*, could have been lifted out of the pages of *Les Liaisons Dangereuses*. This aspect of his life unfolds itself in the Lovelace Papers; and for access to these and for permission to quote from them I thank the Earl of Lytton. I have endeavoured, in light of conflicting material and biased observers, to present Byron as honestly as possible, but of course any biographical portrait will inevitably be shaped by the eyes of the limner. It is also a frustrating fact that the seeker after truth must inevitably accept inconclusive answers to many inaccessible areas of someone else's life.

The Lovelace Papers reinforced the view I had gradually been absorbing as I traced the troubled trajectory of Byron's life: namely, that from birth

* All quotations from Byron's letters and poetry are taken from the Marchand and McGann editions.

he was an Outsider, someone who viewed himself as different from other people. His deformed foot set him apart from normal children, and his shame about his lameness – which he greatly exaggerated – coloured his relationships, fuelled his anger, and exacerbated his defensiveness. The Calvinism he had absorbed from his nurse made his foot a visible reminder of his ostracism from the elect. Byron was obsessed by the conviction that he was a fallen angel, and in his wilder moments talked of being foredoomed to evil. His title was an unexpected acquisition, and since it was not accompanied by either wealth or influential connections, Byron experienced an uneasy feeling that there was something slightly spurious about it. As a consequence, he over-prized and flaunted his rank to assure himself and others of its importance. Paradoxically, it was this very "difference" from others that was to prove Byron's main attraction for his fascinated admirers.

All his life Byron lacked what for most of us is a fundamental need – a home. By "home" I mean not simply a physical dwelling, but some significant degree of nurturing, security, comfort, consistency, and familiarity. His feckless father deserted him and his mother when he was three. Mrs Byron represented the closest person to incorporate many of the qualities associated with "home", but once they moved from Scotland to England, Byron began to develop a feeling of shame about her vulgar excesses. In rejecting her, Byron rejected the deepest need of his heart, and its demands refused to be stifled. As a consequence of his denial of his parent, he sought aspects of her in a series of maternal figures (particularly in Lady Melbourne and his half-sister, Augusta). Then, in turn denying his need of these particular women, he slipped into a pattern of pleasureless promiscuity.

The inheritance of the Byron title was a mixed blessing. The romantic estate was encumbered by debt, and Byron was forced to let others live in the abbey. He was not to know financial security until nearly the end of his life. His rank forced him to live beyond his meagre income, and his only escape from the anxiety of his debts was in fantasy and self-destructive behaviour. Unless he had married a rich heiress, any marriage he entered into would have been doomed. As it was, the woman he found himself united to lacked both fortune and humour. During their brief marriage Byron was almost driven mad by money worries, and in a rented mansion the marriage dissolved into a nightmare. The separation proceedings revealed the fragility of Byron's acceptance by his social class. The fickle public which had once fought for introductions to him now evaporated into a hostile Chorus. Byron was condemned to banishment as the symbolic scapegoat of a dissolute and corrupt society, whose hypocritical cant he would later mock.

Poetry was always to prove a cathartic release in the sheer physical energy of writing, but Byron was overly dependent on the response of his readers. In his first foray into verse, he was almost crushed by the sneering contempt of his youthful pretentiousness. The later sudden success of *Childe Harold* in 1812 caught him unawares. Having created a persona of the attitudinising anti-hero, he felt compelled to adopt the posture of a scornful alien. This role actually helped him to adapt to his final exile in 1816 when he found himself caught in a series of situations in which he could find only momentary way-stations as he moved reluctantly from place to place in Italy.

Nevertheless, those seven years in Italy were to be the most creative period of his life despite the comic operatic nature of his actual situation. As he distanced himself from his countrymen, gradually learning to ignore their attitude towards his work, Byron found his true poetic voice.

In his final days in Greece the comic opera developed into true tragedy. The poetic voice was stilled. Caught in a desperate situation which was beyond any man's capabilities to control, he was eventually crushed by a fate beyond his understanding. In death he found the release and peace that had eluded him all his life. Byron was a basically decent man who was destroyed by the expectations and projections of an incomprehensible world into which fate had thrust him.

The quest for Byron has been a rich adventure, and I shall be for ever grateful to William St Clair for the suggestion that I write this book and for help in innumerable ways. With Elizabeth Longford I have had hours of intense discussions about Byron and his associates. In addition to William St Clair and the Countess of Longford who read the original manuscript in its entirety, I am indebted to Ruth Rendell and Steven Marcus for reading and commenting on portions of it. Professor Marcus, with his usual generosity, helped to extricate me from a particularly difficult predicament. Professor Marchand was kind enough to answer my many queries.

Ruth and Don Rendell extended their warm hospitality to me. One evening in Paris, while dining at La Coupole, Mavis Gallant presented me with her treasured first edition of Trelawny's *Recollections*. Timothy Gorman uncovered all sorts of esoteric material. My gratitude also goes to Armando Pajalich; Rosella Zorzi; Anthony Johnson; Annette Peach; Professor Ernest Gidday; Michael Holroyd; Roger Lloyd-Jones; Maureen Crisp; Peter Graham; Elma Dangerfield; Michael Mees; Claire Tomalin; Susan Normington; Timothy d'Arch Smith; Margot Strickland; Lord Brocket;

Larissa and Francis Haskell; Sarah Fox-Pitt; Phyllis Rose; Deirdre Bair; Aileen Ward; Betty Bennett; Jonathan Gross; Jerome McGann; Benita Eisler; John McMullan; Richard Holmes; Marion K. Stocking; Charles Robinson; Peter Graham; Robert Silvers; Edward Shorter; Stephen Waddams; Martin Friedland; Heather Robertson; the late Robertson Davies; Milton Wilson; Laura Pietropaulo; David Mason; Janice Kulyk Keefer; Jane Millgate; Austin Clarkson; Lord Ravensdale; the Hon. Shaun Mosley; Ivo Mosley; Ron Bloore; John Polanyi; J.E. Chamberlin; Anthea Mander Lahr. Many people have helped me with the assembly of the illustrations, and I should particularly like to thank Peter Cox of the National Portrait Gallery, London, and Anne-Marie Ehrlich.

Francesca Valente, director of the Istituto Italiano di Cultura in Toronto, opened doors for me in Italy. Signora Donatella Asta allowed me to roam through the Palazzo Mocenigo in Venice. Donatino Domini and Claudia Giuliani were immeasurably helpful in the Biblioteca Classense in Ravenna. Christine Pennison in the civic archives in Pisa was also most kind. Haidee Jackson, the curator of Newstead Abbey, has shared her encyclopaedic knowledge with me and helped me in innumerable ways. I owe a special thanks to Colin Harris and Nicky Pound of the Department of Western Manuscripts in the Bodleian Library, and to Peter Hunter, the Librarian of Harrow School. I wish also to thank the staffs of the British Library; the Pforzheimer Library; Mrs Penelope Ruddock and Mrs Geraldine Marchand of the Museum of Costume in Bath; the Hertfordshire Record Office; the Berg Collection of the New York Public Library; the Pierpont Morgan Library; the Fisher Rare Book Room of the Robarts Library, University of Toronto; the Huntington Library; the Harry Ransom Humanities Research Center of the University of Texas; the William Andrew Clark Memorial Library, University of California; Keele University Library; and Mrs Virginia Murray for allowing me access to the Murray Archives, and John Murray for permission to quote from Byron's letters. Dr David Sutton of the WATCH Project at the University of Reading has given me invaluable advice on copyright law. For permission to quote unpublished material I thank Lord Kinnaird and Sir Charles Hobhouse.

The Social Sciences and Humanities Research Council, the Canada Council, and the Toronto Arts Council extended much-needed financial help. My agents, Jacqueline Korn and Georges Borchardt, have been towers of strength. My editors, Peter Davison and Roland Phillips, have helped to make this a much tighter manuscript than it was originally, and I am grateful for all their suggestions. My first editor, John Curtis, has remained my supportive and encouraging friend. My Canadian publisher, Jan Walter, has always been there when I needed her. Morag Lyall has been the indispensable copy editor. Douglas Matthews kindly compiled the Index.

My assistant, Peter Shklanka, has had to learn all sorts of odd things, and I hope he has enjoyed the experience as much as I have appreciated what he has done for me. My grandson, Alan Grosskurth, has helped me with the maps, and my nephew, Scott Rogers, has computerised Byron's journeys as well as the Byron family tree. My children would not allow me to be discouraged. My husband, Bob McMullan, has read every word innumerable times and has offered incisive suggestions and criticism. I cannot imagine how this book could have been written without him.

Prologue

The great lumbering Napoleonic coach had always attracted attention. Now, travelling along that dusty road between Imola and Bologna, on a late afternoon in October 1821, it was somewhat the worse for wear with its chipped green paint. Nevertheless, its doors still carried a nobleman's crest, and as it swayed forward a carriage travelling in the opposite direction was forced to cower at the side of the road until it passed. Nowadays the highway from Imola to Bologna is crammed with *autocarri* bearing fruit from the orchards of Emilia-Romagna to the gastronomic centre of Italy. The road, which runs along the foothills of the Apennines, was narrower in 1821 but just as dusty as it is today.

On this particular afternoon, Lord Byron, the occupant of the coach, had reluctantly abandoned his familiar routine in Ravenna to make his way across Italy. He was on his way to rejoin his mistress, whose family had been expelled for their subversive politics and were living in a palazzo in Pisa that had been found for them by the renegade poet Shelley. All of them – the Gambas, the Shelleys, Byron and the other assorted exiles in Pisa – were transients, expatriates, marginal people at odds with society. These were the people with whom Byron had cast his lot.

The coach from Ravenna was about to pass a carriage travelling from Bologna. Certainly those travelling towards Imola must have craned their necks for a glimpse of the owner of that slightly ridiculous, grandiloquent conveyance. Whether it was Byron who first caught sight of Lord Clare we shall never know. What we do know is that both men sprang to the ground and fell into a deep, almost wordless embrace. Their meeting lasted five minutes at most, but for Byron they were the five most impassioned minutes of his life.

Only his swim across the Hellespont in 1810 received as much attention in his letters to numerous correspondents. After his arrival in Pisa, on November 5, in his journal he recorded the encounter with Clare, "after not having met for seven or eight years".

He was abroad in 1814 – and came home just as I set out in 1816 – This meeting annihilated for a moment all the years between the present time and the days of *Harrow* – It was a new inexplicable feeling like rising from the grave to me. Clare too was much agitated – more – in *appearance* – than even myself – for I could feel his heart beat to the fingers' ends – unless indeed – it was the pulse of my own which made me think so. – He told me that I should find a note from him left at Bologna – I did. – We were obliged to part for our different journeys – he for Rome – I for Pisa – but with promise to meet again in Spring. – We were but five minutes together – and in the public road – but I hardly recollect an hour of my existence which could be weighed against them . . . Of all I have ever known – he has always been the least altered in every thing from the excellent qualities and kind affections which attracted me to him so strongly at School. – I should hardly have thought it possible for Society – (or the World as it is called) to leave a being with so little of the leaven of bad passions.[1]

Clare's travelling companions impatiently urged him to climb back into their coach to continue their journey to Rome. In the emotion of the moment, Byron seemed unaware of anyone else. Usually he avoided other British tourists who shunned or gawked at the exiled poet with his unsavoury reputation. As it was, on Clare's journey home from Rome the following year he was able to spare only a single day to slip down from Genoa to visit Byron at Montenero, south of Livorno, where he had rented a villa to escape the summer heat. If Byron found Clare unaltered in every respect, Clare later reported to Byron's half-sister, Mrs Leigh, that his old friend seemed to have shrunk into himself.

At Harrow Clare had been one of a coterie of younger boys who vied with each other for Byron's exclusive attention. There were passionate quarrels – one with Clare was soon resolved, but Lord Delawarr never became fully reconciled to him. On the eve of Byron's departure for the East in 1809, he asked Clare to spend the afternoon with him and was deeply hurt when Clare airily replied that he had promised to accompany his mother and sisters on a shopping expedition. Nevertheless, in the first will he ever made, Byron left his entire library to his young favourite. He always said that he never heard Clare's name without a wild beating of the heart.

Byron noted that Clare was abroad in 1814 and returned in 1816 just before Byron had gone into exile. Clare, then, was not in England during 1815, that tumultuous year of Byron's ill-fated marriage to Annabella Milbanke, and he must have returned at a time when the newspapers and every London party buzzed with rumours and speculations about the causes of Byron's separation after only a single year of marriage. Clare later told Thomas Moore, Byron's official biographer, that he had destroyed all Byron's letters. This was curiously suspect as almost everyone else saved every letter received from the poet. But Byron never forgot him. One of the last letters he wrote during his final illness in Greece in 1824 was addressed to his "Dearest Clare". "I hope," he wrote from Missolonghi, "that you do not forget that I always regard you as my dearest friend – and love you as when we were Harrow boys together."[2]

There – on that road running along the edge of the Apennines – Byron saw again only that Harrow boy with his delicate features, a fresh unmarked face shining with a trusting innocence. Any slight, any disagreement from the past was erased. Clare represented a golden period from childhood, he reminded Byron of the only time he had believed himself truly happy. Now jaded, weary, and restless, Byron was shunned by the respectable English world which had once fought for introductions to him. Clare was the embodiment of a paradise lost and seemingly regained in those magical moments at the side of a foreign road.

I

ooooooooooooooo

The Byrons –
Impetuous, Bad and Mad

George Gordon Byron could not be considered fortunate in the parents fate had allotted him. He might boast – as he often did – of his ancient lineage, but he would be hard-pressed to name any ancestors of distinction. There were plenty of rakes, spendthrifts, melancholics, eccentrics and brutes, but no statesmen, notable warriors, philanthropists or enlightened landowners. The first artist in his family, Byron was to all intents and purposes a self-made man – apart, that is, from the burden that his ancestry had imposed upon him.

The Byrons claimed descent from Ralph du Burun, who arrived in England with William the Conqueror and who is mentioned in the Doomsday Book as holding extensive lands in Nottinghamshire. Later these were augmented by family estates in Derbyshire; and in the reign of Edward I, they acquired property in Rochdale, Lancashire, and in Norfolk. Many other families with similar histories made wise use of their properties and became wealthy landowners, but this was not the case with the Byrons. Upon the dissolution of the monasteries, Henry VIII for the sum of £810 disposed to "our beloved servant John Byron of Colwyke all the house and site, ground and soil, of the late Monastery and Priory of Newstede within the Forest of Sherwode in our said County of Nottingham". The Priory of Newstead (founded by Henry II around 1170) had been dedicated to God and the Virgin as the house of the Canons Regular of the Augustinian Order. John Byron, knighted by Queen Elizabeth in 1579, converted the monastic quarters around the cloister into an impressive mansion where he maintained an extravagant style of life, including a resident troupe of players.

Not surprisingly, the Byrons were ardent Royalists during the Civil War. Seven brothers were said to have served under King Charles I; and one of them, John, was knighted for having raised his own regiment of horse for the king. In 1643 he was raised to the peerage as Baron Byron of Rochdale. To this day his portrait stares imperiously from a canvas hanging in Newstead Abbey, bearing the sort of arrogance often associated with stupidity. He received his title just before the Battle of Marston Moor. Lord Byron's contribution to the battle was largely responsible for the defeat of the Royalists in what was possibly the most significant battle of the Civil War. Far outnumbered by the parliamentary troops, Byron had received strict instructions to hold the right wing of the Royalist forces. He was not to move until the Roundheads had been slowed down in marshy ground between the opposing troops. But once Cromwell's forces started to move, Byron could not maintain his patience. His cavalry and musketeers, rather than Cromwell's men, struggled ineffectually through the marsh, and were mowed down by musketry, thus opening up the entire right wing of the army. As a result of Byron's impetuosity, Charles lost the whole north of England. It was not a story that the poet was known to repeat to his friends.

In the middle of the seventeenth century the Byrons married into the Chaworth family, owners of the adjoining estate of Annesley Hall. The Chaworth line is thought to have accentuated the eccentric and extravagant strain in the Byrons, although habitual intermarriage must have played an even greater part. William, born in 1722, became known as "the Wicked Lord". His brother John, born the following year, was later to become an admiral and is chiefly remembered as the grandfather of the poet.

The Wicked Lord epitomised the profligacy and irresponsibility of the Byrons. After succeeding to the title, he neglected the property but held lavish parties in a miniature castle he built in the woods of Newstead. He also erected two forts by the lake where he staged naval engagements with small cannon, aided by a servant, Joe Murray (who lived on to serve our Lord Byron).

The Wicked Lord's extravagance came to an end when he was in his early forties. A group of Nottinghamshire landowners had formed a London dining club in the Star and Garter tavern in Pall Mall. On January 26, 1765, Lord Byron and his cousin and neighbour, William Chaworth (who seems to have been equally irascible), quarrelled over the best way to hang game. In order to settle the dispute, they retired to an empty room lit only by a single candle. Here Byron plunged a sword through Chaworth's belly. The latter lingered on until the next day, bitterly regretful that he had been stupid enough to fight in a darkened room. A coroner's jury returned a verdict of wilful murder and Byron was lodged in the Tower to stand trial before his peers in the House of Lords. The verdict this time was more favourable: four peers voted "Not guilty" and 119 voted "Not guilty of murder, but guilty of manslaughter". Under a statute of Edward VI Byron was able to be discharged simply by paying a fee and retiring to Newstead. He kept the sword with which he had killed Chaworth in his bedroom at the abbey. Because of the scandal he grew into a recluse, travelling to London only through necessity and then under the name of Waters. His wife left him, and he took as mistress one of the servants, a Mrs Hardstaff, known as "Lady Betty", by whom he had an illegitimate son.

Burdened by debt as he was, his only hope of escaping from his impasse was the marriage of his son William to an heiress. However, William wasn't particularly happy with the young woman selected to repair the fortunes of the family: on the eve of the wedding the defiant young man eloped with his first cousin, the daughter of Admiral John Byron. His furious father swore that he would leave him a burdened inheritance. Partly out of bitterness, partly in order to keep his creditors at bay, the Wicked Lord began a systematic spoliation of the estate. He cut down the great stands of timber, and 2,007 deer were slaughtered and sold at the nearby Mansfield market. For a paltry sum he allowed the illegal lease of the coal mines in Rochdale, the return of which was to preoccupy the sixth lord, the poet, for many years. In old age the Wicked Lord became increasingly eccentric. He kept a menagerie of crickets which were said to have left the abbey in swarms after his death in 1798. As it was, his own son died before him in 1776; and in turn his grandson, also named William, was killed in action at the Battle of Calvi in 1794, thus leaving a little boy living in Aberdeen as heir to the impoverished estate.

How this little boy came to be heir brings us back to the Wicked Lord's younger brother, John, Admiral Byron, one of the many irresponsible rakes who embellished the family tree. In addition to his notorious amours, he became distinguished for a turbulent naval career, particularly for the storms he weathered, thus bringing him the sobriquet "Foulweather Jack". He published an account of his early adventures (including a shipwreck Byron later used in *Don Juan*) in *The Narrative* in 1768. "He had no rest at sea, nor on shore," his grandson later commented.

Foulweather Jack's son, John (known as "Mad Jack"), distinguished himself by his total disregard of public opinion. Born in 1756, he was educated at Westminster and later at a French military academy. After his father bought him a commission in the Guards, he saw some service in the American War of Independence, but he soon abandoned the army for a life of dissipation in London.

Here he entered into a much publicised affair with Amelia, the enchanting wife of the Marquis of Carmarthen (later Duke of Leeds). In 1779 the marquis obtained a divorce, and on June 9 the marriage of Captain John Byron and Lady Amelia d'Arcy took place. A month later, on July 19, a daughter was born (she subsequently died). Although Amelia had a substantial income in her own right, it was insufficient to pay for their extravagant style of living. In order to escape their creditors they moved to France; and on January 26, 1784, Amelia's only surviving child, Augusta Mary, was born in Paris. Amelia did not survive the birth, and Augusta seems to have been cared for by her uncle, Captain George Anson Byron, who had married Henrietta Dallas, and was living at Chantilly, outside Paris.

Amelia's annual income of £4,000 ceased with her death and Mad Jack returned to England to repair his fortunes. He headed for Bath, where heiresses resorted not for the waters so much as to secure suitable husbands. John Byron was not exactly suitable, but he was, as his son later described him, "an extremely amiable and joyous character". (He could also be petulant and short-tempered but that is not how Byron chose to remember him.) As Byron put it, he was "a very handsome man which goes a great way".[1] He had to go a great way in a very short time in order to keep ahead of his creditors, and he set his sights in a calculated way on the most vulnerable young woman he could find.

She was not beautiful but she had a tolerable fortune; she was not graceful but she loved to dance, and in no time at all the handsome Jack had swept her off her feet. Catherine Gordon, heiress of Gight, was a large ungainly girl with a strong Scottish burr. She was good-natured, and very headstrong. It would have been useless for her relatives to try to dissuade her from this impetuous match and on May 13, 1785, the marriage took place in St Michael's Church, Bath. By marrying on the thirteenth day of the month Catherine deliberately flouted superstition even though she herself was very superstitious, and the gossips of Aberdeenshire predicted that her new husband would soon run through her fortune. Curiously enough, less than a year before, she had attended the Theatre Royal in Edinburgh to watch a performance by Mrs Siddons in *The Fatal Marriage*. As Isabella, Mrs Siddons brought audiences to a state of nervous prostration when Isabella learns that her first husband, Biron, is still alive. On the night Miss Gordon of Gight attended the play she was carried out of her box in hysterics, screaming, "Oh, my Biron! My Biron!" Sir Walter Scott was one of the witnesses to record this strange behaviour.

Catherine was the eldest (and only survivor) of the three daughters of

George Gordon, twelfth Laird of Gight. She had been born in the shire of Aberdeen in 1764 and had been brought up in the Castle of Gight. The castle, now a complete ruin, had been sacked and restored many times. In Catherine's day it was habitable and situated on a beautiful site, perched on a rocky promontory above the valley of the River Ythan.

Catherine frequently boasted that she was directly descended from Jean Stewart, a daughter of King James I of Scotland. Her family history was filled with bloody and treacherous deeds, and it also contained deep strains of depression. Catherine's father was of a melancholy cast of mind. His death by drowning in the Bath Canal in 1779 was clearly suicide, and his own father had died by drowning in the River Ythan in 1760. Byron later told his publisher, John Murray, that he had inherited his melancholy temperament from his maternal grandfather: "I had always been told that in *temper* I more resembled my maternal Grandfather than any of my *father's* family – that is in the gloomier part of his temper – for he was what you call a good natured man, and I am not."[2]

The Byron marriage, like their son's after them, was nasty, brutish, and short. Among Catherine's relatives and neighbours there was a good deal of disapproval that she had not married a Scot, and tongues wagged as they witnessed the wild carousing that took place after the couple moved into the castle. Byron was soon repeating the same pattern of behaviour he had displayed with his first wife's inheritance. The trustees of the estate tried to resist his demands, but they had limited control, and within a year the new husband had run through most of his wife's fortune of over £22,000. The Gight lands were sold off bit by bit. Forests were chopped down and the timber disposed of. Eighteen months after the marriage the estate had to be sold to Lord Aberdeen, and almost all the money was paid to Captain Byron's creditors. Mrs Byron was left with the income from £4,200, out of which she had to pay an annuity to her grandmother, who did not die until 1801. In July 1785 Jack Byron was seized for debt and taken to the King's Bench Prison. His tailor was the only person who would post bail for him. Catherine's high spirits began to sink into bitterness. She was still infatuated enough to be unable to deny her husband anything, so she asked the trustees if a settlement could be made on her in such a way that Captain Byron could not get his hands on her funds.

Finally the only way they could elude the creditors was to flee back to France. At Valenciennes Mrs Byron took over the care of her husband's daughter Augusta and nursed the child through a serious illness which she reminded her of many years later. On October 18, 1801, Catherine wrote: "I still recollect with a degree of horror, the many sleepless nights and days of agony I have passed at your bedside drowned in tears, while you lay insensible and at the gates of death. Your recovery certainly was wonderful, and thank God I did my duty."[3] This effusive letter did little to sway Augusta, whom Mrs Byron had handed over to the care of her grand-mother, Lady Holderness, and she was raised with her half-brothers and -sisters by her mother's first husband, the Duke of Leeds. Augusta grew up with an impression of her stepmother as a vulgar, loud-mouthed woman whom she later blamed as responsible for some of the poet Byron's meretricious traits. Nothing could have been more different than the households in which Byron and Augusta were raised.

Towards the end of 1787, Catherine settled temporarily in London to await the birth of her child. She rented a furnished room at No. 16 Holles Street (which runs between Oxford Street and Cavendish Square) on a site now occupied by the John Lewis department store. Her husband could not visit her lest he be arrested for debt, and she was left totally alone without friends or relatives during her confinement. Her Scottish agents helped her financially as much as they could. To James Watson in Edinburgh she wrote: "I don't want much and if there was large sums it would only be thrown away as it was before."[4]

The trustees had learned exactly what to expect from this ne'er-do-well. Mad Jack had no intention of keeping his promise to pay off his debts when the estate was sold, and now in France he was left without a guinea. One of the agents, Becket, reported: "After such an incident, and many other similar, I am afraid that discharging the present debts would only be paving the way to the accumulation of new ones."[5] An MP for Edinburgh, concerned about Catherine's plight, introduced her to a young London lawyer, John Hanson, of No. 6 Chancery Lane. His wife, who had given birth recently, was able to recommend a midwife or *accoucheuse*. In later years Byron was often impatient with his lawyer's procrastination, but in this instance he had every reason to be grateful to the Hanson family for providing the wherewithal for his birth.

It was long-drawn-out and difficult. On Tuesday, January 22, 1788, Catherine was delivered of a baby boy born with a caul over his head, which was usually considered a mark of distinction or good luck. It was given to Hanson's brother, a captain in the Royal Navy, to prevent him from drowning, but the superstition proved wrong as the captain drowned at sea twelve years later. One of the first references to the deformed foot with which Byron was born appears in a letter of February 19, 1791, from his father to his sister Frances Leigh. It is apparent that Captain Byron was far more agitated about his sister's sending him some money than the welfare of his wife and son: "For my son, I am happy to hear he is well; but for his walking 'tis impossible, for he is club-footed."[6]

Byron later attributed his deformity to his mother's false delicacy in wearing corsets. At the time of his birth women were still wearing tight lacing, but surely the *accoucheuse* would have insisted that she loosen the corset. It is also unlikely that his mother would have told him that she was the cause of his deformity. Where, then, did he pick up this idea? The most likely possibility is from one of the maids. It was a story he chose to believe because he needed to have someone to blame for what he considered the greatest disaster of his life.*

Catherine had no clear idea of what the future held for her and her baby. A month after the birth she wrote to James Watson in Edinburgh, her letter summarising her fears about her situation:

> there will be still more debts coming in & more demands for money. I am sorry he is getting a new carriage the money Mr Leslie gave me is not sufficient to clear all my expenses but I will let you know exactly what I shall want in a few days and what I shall want to keep me in London for two months longer as I have taken a House for that time at two Guineas and a half a week which is just twenty guineas for two months. I would not have taken one till I had known Mr Byron's plans but the time I must have this is on Sunday and I could not get any for a shorter time and none so cheap. I will not go to Bath as I don't keep a carriage and have got to travel Mr Byron will have got a house in some cheap country whether Wales or the North of England. I want money to be sent me while in town and I must have it as if Mr Byron gets it it will be thrown away in some foolish way or other and I shall be obliged to apply for more. I don't want more than is necessary but I will let you know exactly in a few days. I will live as cheap as I can but it was impossible till now as there was a great many expences that could not be avoided direct for me No 2 Baker Street Portman's Square my little boy is to be named George don't show Mr Byron this.[7]

There was no way she could ever let James Watson or anyone else know "exactly" what her plans were. On March 25 she told Watson: "Leave this House I must in a fortnight from this day so there is no time to be lost and if

---

* By 1824 he told Millingen, one of the doctors at Missolonghi, that the condition of his foot was due to "the unskilful treatment of a sprained ankle" (Millingen, p.143).

they will not remit the money before that time I don't know what I shall do and what will become of me."[8] She never did move into the house in Portman Square, probably because it was cheaper to stay in Holles Street. On February 29 – her husband still being absent in France – she took the baby to Marylebone Parish Church to be christened. The decision about his name seems to have been entirely hers. She called him George Gordon after her own father and chose as sponsors the Duke of Gordon and her cousin, Colonel Robert Duff of Fetteresso.

Within days of her son's birth Catherine called in John Hunter, a Scottish surgeon then living in London, to examine his deformity and inoculate the child against smallpox. The inoculation, but not the examination of the foot, appears in Hunter's surviving case books. Perhaps it did not seem sufficiently important to Hunter to necessitate an entry. Professor Leslie Marchand believes that it was undoubtedly a club foot, but it is unlikely that a club foot would have fitted into a fragile Turkish slipper that survives from Byron's period at Missolonghi. What we do know is that his right foot inclined markedly to its inner side through a shortening of the tendon. Through the years extremely painful measures were taken to straighten it. These early memories would probably have enhanced his sense from the beginning of his life that he was different from other people.

It seems appalling that Catherine should find herself so alone in these circumstances. She had shunned the disapproving Scottish relatives after her marriage and, stubborn as she was, she would not turn to them now. As for her husband's relatives, Jack Byron would not go near them unless there was a chance of dunning them for money. His own mother, the widow of the admiral, he ignored since he knew nothing was to be had from her. George Gordon Byron never set eyes on any of his grandparents. To all intents and purposes, this was a single-parent family – with all its attendant problems.

Jack Byron returned briefly early in March, apparently little interested in his new son and heir. He seems to have been far more affected by the death of his sister, Juliana, Lady Wilmot, and to Frances he wrote: "My Father and now my Sister dying within a few years really makes me reflect that it will [be] my turn soon, and I am quite depressed."[9] His own situation was unbearably gloomy: "My income is but small and what there is of it is settled on Mrs Byron and the Child, therefore I am obliged to live in a narrow circle which I need not have done, if those Rascals had not cheated me of a great deal by a law Suit I have in Edin[burgh] and I am obliged to pay the Jointure of a grandmother of Mrs Byron, who is as tough as possible." In his total self-absorption he may actually have believed this, but in a rare flash of insight he admits his fear that he might "run into extravagance . . . by buying horses and perhaps hounds, in short I cannot answer for myself".

Although Catherine intended leaving Holles Street earlier, she was still there by the middle of April. Then she suddenly disappeared – only to reappear in Aberdeen in August. The decision must have been thrust upon her by desperation, an anxiety to be back among her own people and the knowledge that in Scotland she would not be left destitute. When her husband followed her there it was simply because she was the only possible remaining source of funds.

Byron's passion for the sea may have been awakened by a childhood spent in a seaport. Aberdeen is situated on the North Sea on the estuaries of the Dee and the Don. Here whalers set out for the Arctic, and the port was generally filled with ships from Europe and America. Aberdeen was also the central market town of Deeside, within easy reach of the Cairngorm Mountains, which Byron would recall in one form or another in many nostalgic descriptive passages.

Apart from the charged emotional atmosphere of his home, Byron seems to have had a relatively happy childhood. He had cousins, his early schooling was lacking in trauma, and while there was little enough money, the family could live without real shame in Aberdeen. His father was a somewhat disturbing presence until Byron was about two and a half. Even from that early age he remembered the constant quarrels between his parents so vividly that they instilled in him a lifelong aversion to marriage.

Jack Byron joined them when Mrs Byron took up lodgings in Queen Street, but the domestic broils impelled him to move to rooms at the other end of the street. He was always more interested in Augusta than in little George, possibly because he had been genuinely in love with her mother, Amelia, or because he felt aversion for a child born with a deformity. He once took the boy for a night but he howled so lustily that his father returned him hurriedly the next morning. Still, many years later, Byron was to write lines of excessive sentimentality about his loss:

> Stern Death, forbade my orphan youth to share,
> The tender guidance of a Father's care;
> Can Rank, or ev'n a Guardian's name supply,
> The Love, which glistens in a Father's eye?
> For this, can Wealth, or Title's sound atone,
> Made, by a Parent's early loss, my own?
> ("Childish Recollections", 1806, I, 219–224)

In September 1790 Jack Byron left for France to join his sister Frances, now separated from her husband, at her house in Valenciennes. Catherine Byron was never to see or hear from her husband again except for a brief refusal to help her.

The widow of Admiral Byron died in Bath on November 12, 1790. Frances, who seems to have been as self-centred as her brother, set off for England immediately to ascertain whether she had benefited from her mother's death. Jack Byron could not follow her because of his debtors, but Frances promised to look out for his interests. It never occurred to either of them to erect a tablet to her memory.

The letters exchanged between brother and sister during this period reveal that they undoubtedly had an incestuous affair while sharing the house in Valenciennes. "There is no person I love as well as you and that I wish you were here every minute," he told her (December 12). In letters of unadorned coarseness he tells his "dearest Fanny" of his relationships with local prostitutes: "As for La *Henry* she told me that I did it so well, that she always *spent* twice every time. I know this will make you laugh, but she is the best piece I ever . . . [sic]"[10] The only fatherly feeling he exhibited was to ask Fanny to enquire through a maid how Augusta was faring.

Meanwhile Catherine Byron, desperate for money, also turned to Fanny after she heard of the death of her mother, hoping that possibly there might be a legacy.

> Some time ago I wrote to Mr Byron telling him I had not farthing in the world nor could I get any at present, and begging him to ask you to lend him thirty or forty pounds to send to me, to which he returned for answer that he could not think of asking you as you had been so good to him but that he had wrote to a person that he hoped would send it to me . . . I only say this to let you know what situation I am in and that me nor my child have not at present a farthing nor know where to get one . . . The reason I trouble you with this letter is to beg you will have the goodness to lend me thirty or forty pounds. I will pay you honestly in May next . . . I beg an answer as soon as possible.[11]

When her husband heard of this pathetic letter, he responded peevishly: "What can the Correspondence of Mrs Byron be? I hope not for money, as she has quite enough & never would give me a farthing."[12] At all costs Fanny must not be persuaded to divert any money from himself to his wife and child. In order to reinforce this point he wrote again on February 19:

"With regard to Mrs Byron I am glad she wrote to you. She is very amiable at a distance; but I defy you and all the apostles to live with her for two months for, if anybody could live with her it would be me."[13]

In order to divest herself of the responsibility of her brother, Fanny suggested that Catherine rejoin her husband in France. This Catherine refused to do. She was far more concerned about doing something about little George's foot and begged her sister-in-law to contact the surgeon, Mr Hunter, who had examined the foot when the boy was an infant. She wanted an adequate shoe to correct his problem: "I am perfectly sure he would walk very well in time if he could have a proper shoe."[14]

There is no indication that Fanny did anything about getting in touch with Mr Hunter; and it is possible that Byron's foot might have been improved were it not for lack of money. If Byron was to blame anyone for the neglect of his foot, it should have been his father for leaving his mother without the means to correct it.

Meanwhile Jack Byron's plight in France was becoming desperate and his letters to his sister increasingly plaintive. By April 13, 1792, he was at the end of his tether: "I dare not go out as everybody points at me. For God's sake come if possible, as it is impossible for me to remain here longer. The man [the bailiff] threatens to take the furniture away every minute, and I shall not have a bed to sleep on – no person will give me credit for a sous, & I live absolutely on mere Bread."[5] On June 21, 1792, he dictated his will to two French notaries, leaving his penniless son of four responsible for his debts and funeral expenses. Six weeks later he was dead of consumption. Frances had joined her brother again; and feeling very righteous, she informed Catherine of his death, adding the insensitive comment that she doubted if his wife would be sorry to hear of his end. On August 28 Catherine replied:

> My dear Madam, You wrong me very much when you suppose I do not lament Mr Byron's death. It has made me very miserable and the more so that I had not the melancholy satisfaction of seeing him before his death . . . notwithstanding all his foibles for they deserve no worse name I most sincerely loved him and believe my Dear Madam I have the greatest regards and affection for you for the very kind part you have acted to poor Mr Byron . . . did he ever mention me was he long ill and where was he buried be so good [as] to write all these particulars and also send me some of his hair as to money matters they are perfectly indifferent to me I only wish there may be enough to pay his debts and to pay you the money that was laid out on his

account I wish it was in my power to do all this but a hundred and fifty pounds a year will do little which is all I have . . . George is well I shall be happy to let him be with you some time but at present he is my only comfort and the only thing that makes me wish to live. I hope if anything should happen to me you will take care of him.[16]

Fond deluded woman! In her lucid or angry moments she recognised what an irresponsible cad her husband was, but she undoubtedly loved him. The rest of her life was spent in anxious devotion to the interests of her son; and when she saw him repeating his father's pattern of impetuous behaviour she was driven to distraction.

The uncertain peripatetic life was over and Catherine had to think of managing as best she could in Aberdeen. She moved into larger quarters at 54 Broad Street, the principal street in the town. Here she and her son with their maid, Agnes Gray, occupied the entire first floor. By now George was walking, and he must have become aware, from his mother's anxious expression, of his handicap. When a tactless lady remarked on how handsome he was but what a pity he had to limp, he lashed at her with his little whip. "Dinna speak of it." Nevertheless, he was very swift in his movements and was in constant mischief.

In the autumn of 1792 Mrs Byron enrolled the boy in a school in Long Acre where a Mr Bowser took in boys and girls for a guinea a year. Mrs Byron told Bowser that she was sending George to him that he might be "kept in about" – that is, in order physically and morally. Many years later, with time on his hands in Ravenna in 1821, Byron began to keep a journal in which he recorded his memories of Mr Bowser's school.

I learned little there – except to repeat by rote the first lesson of Monosyllables – "God made man – let us love him" by hearing it often repeated – without acquiring a letter – Whenever proof was made of my progress at home – I repeated these words with the most rapid fluency, but on turning over a new leaf – I continued to repeat them – so that the narrow boundaries of my first year's accomplishments were detected – my ears boxed – (which they did not deserve – seeing it was by *ear* only that I had acquired my letters) – and my intellects consigned to a new preceptor. He was a very decent – clever – little Clergyman – named Ross – afterwards Minister of one of the Kirks . . . under *him* – I made an astonishing progress – and I recollect to this day his mild manners & good-natured painstaking – The moment I could read – my grand passion was *history* . . .[17]

He was reading fluently by the time he was five, which would have delighted his mother who read every book and newspaper she could lay her hands on. From a very early age she took him to old St Paul's Episcopal Chapel. The poet Samuel Rogers was told by an old lady that she recalled sitting in the same pew and watching young George pricking his mother's plump arm with a pin as she prayed.

The next seven years seem to have been relatively tranquil. After her husband's death Catherine made peace with her grandmother and often took her son to stay in Banff, a pleasant town on the north-east coast, where she had many happy memories of her carefree youth. Byron was also taken to Ballerich, forty miles from Aberdeen, to recover from scarlet fever. Here he developed his great love of the Highlands, and for several years his mother returned there with him for holidays when he probably learned to swim in Highland streams.

The earliest picture we have of Byron survives from this period in Banff in a portrait by John Kay of a remarkably feminine boy with long curling hair holding a bow and arrow. Since Byron was always supposed to be chubby, the slight figure is probably a highly idealised version of the boy, but it would have pleased his doting mother. It is from Banff that the first stories of his teasing, stubborn nature survive. "The little devil Georgie Byron" someone called him; and sometimes indeed he seemed possessed of the devil in his sullen moods or ferocious tempers. Most children are mischievous, but in Byron the devilment could be imaginative and witty, a streak that survived throughout his life. Once when a doctor was about to bleed him he threatened to pull his nose and threw the medicine out of the window. On another occasion, when his mother was sitting with her relatives in the drawing room, he slipped upstairs and dressed a pillow with his coat and hat, flinging it out of the window with a shriek, to the terror of the assembled ladies.

Byron was enrolled at the Aberdeen Grammar School in 1794. He was not renowned for his academic achievement and was never one of the pupils who received a prize on Visitation Day. Scottish education has always been impressive, and Byron would have received a good grounding, especially in Latin. We know nothing about how he managed in the playground: children can be very cruel, and undoubtedly he was taunted about his foot. It is possibly significant that in his recollections he does not mention any playmates.

A deeply emotional child, before he was eight he had fallen passionately in love with a cousin, Mary Duff, whom he met at dancing school. Nineteen years later in "Detached Thoughts" he recollected this intense attachment:

How the deuce did all this occur so early? where could it originate? I certainly had no sexual ideas for years afterwards; and yet my misery, my love for that girl were so violent, that I sometimes doubt if I have ever been really attached since. Be that as it may, hearing of her marriage several years after was like a thunder-stroke – it nearly choked me – to the horror of my mother and the astonishment and almost incredulity of every body. And it is a phenomenon in my existence (for I was not eight years old) which has puzzled, and will puzzle me to the latest hour of it; and lately, I know not why, the *recollection* (*not* the attachment) has recurred as forcibly as ever. I wonder if she can have the least remembrance of it or me? or remember her pitying sister Helen, for not having an admirer too? How very pretty is the perfect image of her in my memory – her brown dark hair and hazel eyes; her very dress! I should be quite grieved to see *her now*; the reality, however beautiful, would destroy, or at least confuse, the features of the lovely Peri who then existed in her and she still lives in my imagination, at the distance of more than sixteen years.[18]

Catherine Byron was an emotional, sentimental and volatile woman. She shouted at her son and often slapped him when he bit his nails. In the charged atmosphere she created around her, Byron would have been accustomed to tears, for none of her feelings was bottled up. Repeatedly he heard her curse the whole Byron connection. As a child his emotions were over-developed, as was his longing to love and to be loved. Again and again throughout his life he was subject to sudden, violent attachments. While he says that no one ever engaged him again the way Mary Duff did, the facts of his life indicate something far different. There was also a strong rational strain in the boy. His mother took him to see a performance of *The Taming of the Shrew* when he was nine. At the point when Petruchio contradicts Katherina with the statement, "I swear it is the blessed sun", the boy jumped up and shouted, "But I say it is the moon, Sir!"

From time to time Catherine continued to correspond with her sister-in-law, Mrs Frances Leigh. However, relations cooled between them when Catherine learned that Frances, through their kinsman Lord Carlisle, had obtained a pension for the orphaned children of her other brother George Anson Byron but had done nothing for little George. Coolness turned to anger when she learned that her son had become heir to the Wicked Lord of Newstead Abbey and that Frances had not bothered to inform her that William Byron, the heir of the fifth lord, had been killed at the Battle of Calvi on July 31, 1794. "I should have supposed," Catherine wrote on

November 23, 1794 "you would have wrote before now to have enquired about your Newphew [sic]. He is a fine Boy and very well and walks and runs as well as any other child."[19]

Fiercely protective of her beautiful child, and hearing from Frances that the Wicked Lord was wasting the estate, she was anxious that something be done for him, particularly as her hands were tied when she lived so far away. On December 8 she tried to enlist Frances's aid: "You know Lord Byron. Do you think he will do anything for George, or be at any expense to give him a proper education; or, if he wish to do it, is his present fortune such a one that he could spare anything out of it? You know how poor I am, not that I mean to ask him to do anything for him, that is to say, to be of any expense on his own account."[20]

The Wicked Lord, interested only in his crickets and perhaps his mistress, would not have wasted a thought on this little stranger in Aberdeen. He lingered on in bad health until May 19, 1798. By now Mrs Byron had been in touch with Mr Hanson who had treated her so kindly when her child was born. He produced her marriage certificate, necessary for the legality of her son's right to the title, but he had more difficulty in finding the money to bury the old man, who wasn't lowered into his final resting place until June 16, when Mrs Byron managed to raise the funds to pay for the burial by selling her furniture. Attentive to certain proprieties, she also insisted that the servants be dressed in black.

Even though he was only ten years old, George Gordon was certain that something momentous had happened to him from the excited way everyone around him was behaving. His mother – whom he later described as "haughty as Lucifer" – was carried away by his expectations. He asked her whether she perceived any change in him since he had become a lord, for he perceived none himself. At school the Headmaster called him into his study and offered him cake and wine. When his name was read out in roll-call as Georgeus Domines de Byron he burst into tears.

It was a confusing time for the child. Of course it was pleasant to be fussed over and made to feel important. But, in human terms, it was a disaster for him. He might have had a reasonably contented existence had he continued to live in somewhat restricted circumstances in Aberdeen. He had not – nor ever would have – the funds to sustain the exalted station to which fate had suddenly elevated him. Nor did he have the family or extended network of connections to which other young men in his station could turn.

By cutting herself off from her family, Catherine had also cut off the possibilities for her son's future. What if he had not inherited the title? If he had gone into the Church, he would have had to seek an appointment or a "living" from a landowner. In any case, he was surely not suited by temperament for the ministry. Nor did he have a wealthy relative who could purchase a commission for him in the army. His foot might have been an impediment although he did become an excellent rider. Finally, it is difficult to imagine him as a short-tempered schoolmaster. The options were extremely limited given his birth, station, and the historical moment.

It is also problematic whether Byron would have become a poet if he had not become the sixth lord. He might have written poetry, but would an audience have been ready to listen to him had he not been a handsome aristocrat? It is hard to separate Byron the poet from Byron the man and from the life he led. And without an aristocratic background could he have written *Childe Harold* or *Don Juan*? The adventures he experienced, the turbulence he felt, the anxiety he suffered, the humiliation of his deformity – all these were to become an intrinsic part of his work.

2

ooooooooooooooo

A New Life Begins,
1798–1803

In early August 1798 Mrs Byron, the new lord, aged ten, and his nanny, Mary (May) set out for their new home. Only May was ever to see Scotland again. It was still dark when they departed. Any sort of travel was prohibitively expensive, and they would have taken a stagecoach as the cheapest form of transportation. It involved frequent changes of horses and overnight stops at inns so that Mrs Byron's limited resources were exhausted by the end of the trip.

As they passed down the side of lovely Loch Leven Mrs Byron regaled them with the story of one of the Gordons of Gight who had tried to escape across the loch and was subsequently beheaded for his loyalty to Mary Queen of Scots. "I recollect Loch Leven as though it were yesterday," Byron later told his publisher, John Murray.

> My Mother, who was as haughty as Lucifer with her descent from the Stuarts and her right line, from the *old Gordons, not the Seyton Gordons,* as she disdainfully termed the Ducal branch, told me the story, always reminding me how superior *her* Gordons were to the southern Byrons, – notwithstanding our Norman, and always masculine descent, which has never lapsed into a female, as my mother's Gordons had done in her own person.[1]

Despite the discomforts of a three-day journey, the sense of intense anticipation mounted as they approached the ancestral property at Newstead. As Thomas Moore recounts it, when they arrived at the tollgate Mrs Byron, in a teasing mood, asked if there was not a nobleman's estate nearby.

"Yes."

"To whom does it belong?"

"It was Lord Byron's, but he is dead."

"And who is the heir now?"

"They say a little boy that lives at Aberdeen."

"This is he, God bless him," exclaimed May Gray, the nurse, turning and kissing the child on her lap.[2]

They drove down the long sandy road, seemingly unaware that where they saw bracken and bushes, magnificent trees had once stood, and the thousands of deer, once part of the forest, had all been slaughtered. They swept around a bend, and there before them lay the magnificent ruin of the abbey with its lovely lake. The wide stone sweep of the building and the soaring arches of the ruined monastery delighted the romantic Byrons. Their lawyer, Mr Hanson, had arrived from London, and Joe Murray, factotum to the previous lord, was there to greet them. Almost all the furniture was gone, the east wing was open to the sky, and the refectory was being used to store hay. Mother and son had eyes only for the beauty of the place.

For one happy month Byron roamed the grounds, explored the picturesque ruins, and planted an oak tree close to the abbey where he could watch it grow. (It eventually withered away, and Byron was to identify it symbolically with his own fortune.) His bedroom was on the first floor of the abbey from where he had a magnificent view of the lake which he was to describe nostalgically in Canto 13 of *Don Juan*, written in 1823 in Genoa before his last great adventure in Greece. In this section of the poem Juan joins a house party at the seat of Sir Henry and Lady Amundeville, and here Byron was to bring his powers of total recall to his description of the scene.

57

Before the mansion lay a lucid lake,
  Broad as transparent, deep, and freshly fed
By a river, which its soften'd way did take
  In currents through the calmer water spread
Around: the wild fowl nestled in the brake
  And sedges, brooding in their liquid bed:
The woods sloped downwards to its brink, and stood
With their green faces fix'd upon the flood.

58

Its outlet dash'd into a steep cascade,
   Sparkling with foam, until again subsiding
Its shriller echoes – like an infant made
   Quiet – sank into softer ripples, gliding
Into a rivulet; and thus allay'd
   Pursued its course, now gleaming, and now hiding
Its windings through the woods; now clear, now blue,
   According as the skies their shadows threw.

59

A glorious remnant of the Gothic pile,
   (While yet the church was Rome's) stood half apart
In a grand Arch, which once screened many an aisle.
   These last had disappear'd – a loss to Art:
The first yet frowned superbly o'er the soil,
   And kindled feelings in the roughest heart,
Which mourn'd the power of time's or tempest's march,
   In gazing on that venerable Arch.

The placid lake had witnessed the absurd sea battles waged by the Wicked Lord; but Byron was most impressed with tales of the ghosts of friars who were supposed to haunt the Gothic ruin, a building once enthusiastically described by Horace Walpole. The taste for the Gothic was then at its height in works ranging from *The Castle of Otranto*, through Beckford's *Vathek*, to parodies of its excesses in Thomas Love Peacock's *Nightmare Abbey* and later Jane Austen's *Northanger Abbey*.

Within his own family history there were stories enough to intrigue the boy, especially that of the duel of the fifth lord with William Chaworth. Shortly after their arrival at Newstead, John Hanson took Mrs Byron and her son to nearby Annesley Hall to meet Byron's distant cousin, Mary Chaworth, her mother, Ann Clarke, and her stepfather, the Reverend William Clarke. Mary was two years older than Byron and exceedingly pretty, but Byron did not particularly notice her. At this point he was far more interested in the fact that his great-uncle had killed her great-uncle, and he imagined that the portrait of her ancestor gazed down at him with hatred.

Hanson teased him about Mary. "Here is a pretty young lady, you had better marry her," to which Byron replied, "What, Mr Hanson, the Capulets and the Montagues intermarry?"[3] Nevertheless, he gradually began to form the notion that he and Mary were spiritually united, only to be eternally separated by a river of blood.

Hanson returned to London to secure the legal documents necessary for the Byrons to gain possession of the abbey. The estate had been neglected so long that there was no way of knowing whether they could live there. Hanson should have advised caution more strongly – certainly until the amount of the necessary repairs was ascertained – but he could not check Mrs Byron's enthusiasm. Commonplace details were the last thing she wanted to think about in that first magical month. Rank meant entitlement. The expectation was that the money would be raised by one means or another, and who could resist such a wonderfully interesting dwelling after the cramped quarters in which the Byrons had been living? From the moment she heard of the old lord's death, Mrs Byron was determined that the abbey was to be her son's home, and she assiduously set about making the main object of her life the promotion of his interests.

The 3,200 acres of the Newstead property included sixteen farms which were supposed to yield an annual income of between £1,200 and £1,500, but these revenues were drained by debts and legal fees. There was no money at all to administer the estate which was in desperate need of attention. Mrs Byron had only £150 a year income; and in early June the first steps were taken to make Byron a Ward of Chancery so that he would be given an income as a minor. On August 30 Hanson wrote to her Scottish lawyer, James Farquhar:

> I have seen Mrs Gordon [Mrs Byron] and I find she has a great wish to live at Newstead – I doubt very much the prudence of it at least at first, it strikes me it would be better for her to take a House or Lodgings in or near London till the affairs are arranged and it is known what she is to have allowed her. The Young Lord is a fine sharp Boy not a little spoiled by indulgence but that is scarcely to be wondered at.[4]

There was not even enough money to retain old Joe Murray. Eventually, through the kind intervention of Byron's half-sister Augusta, a position was found for him in the household of the Duke of Leeds, but he was miserable until Byron was able to bring him back to the abbey after he had come of age. Meanwhile Hanson hired Owen Mealey as steward to the abbey, installing him opposite the main gate in the lodge from which Mealey sent regular grumbling reports to London.

Hanson was able to impress on Mrs Byron that it would be impossible for them to continue living in the abbey once the cold weather set in and they moved to Nottingham for the winter of 1798–9. Here she and her son lived first with the late lord's widow, the Hon. Frances Byron, and her sister, Mrs Ann Parkyns, in Griddlesmith Gate (now renamed Pelham Street). They later moved into lodgings at No. 76 St James's Street. Mrs Byron continued to spend a great deal of time in Newstead supervising the renovations while Byron stayed on in Nottingham where serious attention was finally given to treating his foot.

Byron's malformation was confined to the right leg; it was, according to modern medical opinion, congenital, and no form of treatment even today could improve it – though some doctors who examined it at that time believed that it might have been improved if measures had not been left so late. The abnormally thin leg and small foot were indications of a failure to develop properly, a condition known medically as dysphasia.* The long narrow foot curved inwards, so stiff that it impeded the movement of the ankle. This accounted for the sliding gait which many observers noticed about Byron's walk.

Mrs Byron became obsessed with making her son perfect, and he in turn submitted stoically to various forms of torture, aware that there must be something seriously wrong with him, that he was different from normal people. During those early months he spent in Nottingham he was put in the hands of a quack called Lavender, a truss-maker at the local hospital, who only succeeded in subjecting the boy to unnecessary pain.

Mrs Byron did not seem to take the same interest in her son's education. She had refused the suggestion that Byron attend a day school conducted by Drummer Rogers, an American loyalist, which was attended by the daughters of Mrs Parkyns. Her objection seemed to be that it was not fashionable enough for him. At eleven, Byron had more sense than his mother; and on March 13 from Nottingham he sent a letter of expostulation to Newstead Abbey:

> I am astonished you do not acquiesce in this scheme which would keep me in mind of what I have almost entirely forgot, I recommend this to you because if some plan of this kind is not adopted I shall be called or rather branded with the name of dunce which you know I could never bear. I beg you will consider this plan seriously & I will lend it all the assistance in my power.[5]

---

* The most persuasive argument I have found is that in "The Problem of Byron's Lameness" by Denis Browne, F.R.C.S. *Proceedings of the Royal Society of Medicine*, 1966.

His mother was persuaded by his pleas, and Mr Rogers taught him Virgil and Cicero for several months in 1799. When his teacher expressed concern about the obvious discomfort that Byron was suffering from Lavender's ministrations, Byron responded with extraordinary dignity: "Never mind, you shall not see any signs of it in me again." Byron, however, took his own form of revenge on Lavender. One day he set down various letters of the alphabet in random order but grouped in such a way that they looked like words. Byron asked Lavender what language it was and when he replied, "Italian," the cunning boy collapsed with laughter.

When it was apparent that there was no improvement in the foot, Mrs Byron decided to send him to London to seek more expert advice. Hanson had already called on Lord Carlisle, Byron's kinsman by marriage, to persuade him to act as the boy's guardian. He agreed on the condition that his role would be confined only to advice. Carlisle and his wife had been very good to Augusta who often stayed with them at Castle Howard, but Carlisle seemed less than happy about taking on this child whose mother he had never met – and from what he had heard of her, had no wish to. Nevertheless, he had a family obligation. He was the son of Admiral Byron's elder sister who had married the fourth Earl of Carlisle, thus making him the first cousin of Byron's father, Mad Jack.

On July 9, 1799, Mrs Byron wrote to Lord Carlisle about her son's projected visit to London. The wording of this letter strongly suggests that parts of it were dictated by Hanson. Both of them were placing enormous importance on Lord Carlisle's kindly intervention. What is interesting are the disclaimers about Byron's deformity lest Lord Carlisle be prejudiced against him for that reason. The combination of the sudden title and the importance that was now being attached to his foot might at this point have made Byron more sensitive about it than he had been in Aberdeen. He began to regard it as worse than it was because it detracted from his appearance as a peer. It was only natural for Mrs Byron to turn to Carlisle for help in her situation; and had she not subsequently behaved very foolishly, he might have continued to take an active interest in the boy's welfare.

In her long rambling letter Mrs Byron constantly reiterated that her son's foot was receiving the best possible treatment. Above all, she emphasised that it was necessary for Byron to be made a Ward of Chancery. Could Lord Carlisle possibly secure some small pension for her in her reduced circumstances?

When Byron arrived in London, he was welcomed into the Hanson family of four boisterous children in their comfortable home in Earls

Court. These children had heard a great deal about the young lord. The youngest, Newton, later wrote an account of the meeting. One of his sisters, after scrutinising the chubby boy with his head of curly chestnut hair, declared very gravely, "Well, he is a pretty boy, however."

Dr Matthew Baillie and a Dr Maurice Laurie examined Byron's foot. A specialist bootmaker in the Strand was instructed to make an appliance for it. At one point, Mrs Byron complained to Laurie about the exorbitant sum of £150 he was charging. (While it is impossible to compare this price with today's currency, it might be helpful to think of it as an amount equal to her total net income for a year.) In reply to her complaint, she was told that Baillie believed that "if the proper means had been taken at the first in Infancy the malformation might have been brought round . . . but little could be done after the lapse of ten or twelve years."[6]

Hanson, accompanied by Dr Baillie, took Byron to report on the examination to Lord Carlisle in his town house in Grosvenor Square. The boy became embarrassed under the examination to which he knew he was being subjected, and tugged at Hanson: "Let us go!" Lord Carlisle, however, seemed favourably impressed with him.

Unlike Byron's mother, Lord Carlisle was more interested in Byron's formal education than in the improvement of his foot. He recommended that he be placed in Mr Glennie's Academy in Dulwich at the end of the summer. In the meantime Mrs Byron was busy with further negotiations to secure her son's future. She laid her radical political sympathies to one side in asking Lord Carlisle to solicit the Duke of Portland for a civil pension. He agreed to speak to the king; and as a result her income was augmented by £300 a year, although it was to be paid very erratically. When her grandmother died in 1801 she inherited the sum of £1,200. She also received £500 a year from the Court of Chancery for her son's education during his minority, but this meant a reduction in her own pension. Life continued to be difficult for her since the rents at Newstead were often unpaid. She was also responsible for the payment of taxes, and Hanson's annual retainer.

She was disturbed, too, by another matter. Hanson (in whom Byron confided) informed her that while she had been occupied at Newstead, May Gray had been associating with low company. Worse still, she had not only beaten Byron but had been climbing into his bed and initiating the boy's sexual education.

"I should be mortified in the highest degree," Hanson wrote indignantly, "to see the honorable feelings of my little fellow exposed to insult by the Inordinate Indiscretions of any Servant. He has Ability and Quickness of

Conception, and a correct Discrimination that is seldom seen in a youth, and he is a fit associate of men, and choice indeed must be the Company that is selected for him."[7] Perhaps Mrs Byron had difficulty in crediting the truth of the matter, for even though Hanson wrote to her in September, May was not sent back to Scotland until November. The sentimental Catherine gave her a parting gift of the early miniature of Byron as an archer. If May had maltreated him as he claimed, it is a little puzzling that Byron also gave her a watch. Could it have been that he was deliberately causing mischief? Perhaps he dropped heavy hints and Hanson inferred worse than had actually occurred.

During the period 1799–1801 when Byron attended school in Dulwich, his fond mother took lodgings in Sloane Terrace in order to be near him, although she continued to pay frequent supervisory visits to Newstead. Byron got into the habit of spending most of his holidays with the Hansons, where he was treated as one of the family. On one occasion the cook, infuriated by his constant teasing, chased him in a rage, roaring, "You a lord – indeed you a lord, I wonder who the d—l ever made you a lord."

In the summer of 1800 Byron stayed in Nottingham where he fell in love for the second time, on this occasion with his cousin Margaret Parker who inspired the first poetry he ever wrote. While compiling his "Detached Thoughts" in Ravenna in 1821, he wrote: "I have long forgotten the verses – but it would be difficult for me to forget her – Her dark eyes! – her long eye-lashes! her completely Greek cast of face and figure!"[8] Margaret was about a year older, one of a series of female figures older than himself who stirred his deeply emotional nature. Later, at Harrow, he learned that she had died of consumption. Still later he tried to write an elegy to her memory which he described as "a very dull one."

> I do not recollect scarcely anything equal to the *transparent* beauty of my cousin – or to the sweetness of her temper – during the short period of our intimacy – she looked as if she had been made out of a rainbow – all beauty and peace – My passion had its effects upon me . . . it was the torture of my life – to think of the time which must elapse before we could meet again – being usually about *twelve hours* of separation! – But I was a fool then – and am not much wiser now.[9]

His foolish mother did not have the sense to leave him in uninterrupted study at Dr Glennie's, repeatedly arriving to take him away for long weekends. She and Dr Glennie had heated words that embarrassed Byron in front of his schoolfellows. Dr Glennie made no secret of his contempt for her, and he was particularly concerned about the type of companions to whom she was exposing her son. At some point in the autumn of 1800 she became involved with a dancing-master and began laying plans to take Byron away with them to France. Glennie complained to Lord Carlisle, and Mrs Byron's access to her son at weekends was terminated. She made such a scene about this to the headmaster that one of the boys remarked to Byron, "Byron, your mother is a fool," to which he replied philosophically, "I know it." Not only was she eroding her son's respect for her, but her indiscretion was enough to forfeit forever the confidence of the Byron relatives, particularly Lord Carlisle, to the hazard of Byron's future.

When compiling his biography of the poet, Thomas Moore interviewed Dr Glennie who spoke disparagingly of his fellow countrywoman: "Mrs Byron was a total stranger to English society and English manners; with an exterior far from prepossessing, an understanding where nature had not been bountiful, a mind almost wholly without cultivation and the peculiarities of northern opinions, northern habit and northern accent."[10] Glennie considered her the worst possible person to raise her son. Nevertheless, she *was* Byron's mother, and always – apart from this single time when she succumbed to an impetuous infatuation – she disregarded her own comfort for his. Byron, too, was fond of his mother; but since arriving in England at an impressionable age he began to notice the unfortunate effect she had on other people. Like many Scots before and after him, he made a conscious effort to shed his Scottish accent and was always to be disturbed if people detected any evidence of it in his speech. He was to embrace his identity as a Byron more than a Gordon, and it is perhaps significant that he never revisited Scotland even when the opportunity presented itself.

During these early years John Hanson was to come as close as anyone in serving as a father-substitute for Byron. On his numerous visits to the Hanson home, the attorney began to respect Byron's integrity; he found himself growing attached to him and concerned about his future. Shortly after Byron had spent Christmas of 1800 with the family, Hanson requested an interview with Lord Carlisle, who acceded to his suggestion that Byron be sent to Harrow. Then on January 21, 1801, Hanson made a trip to Harrow to discuss the matter with Dr Joseph Drury, the Headmaster. Hanson admitted frankly that the boy's education had been neglected but that he thought there was "a *cleverness* about him". Hanson was also concerned that there did not seem to be much improvement in Byron's foot. The practical care of the foot had been turned over to Dr Maurice Laurie although still under the supervision of Dr Baillie. A kind of brace around the ankle was constructed in an attempt to straighten the foot, but Byron found it so uncomfortable that he wore it as little as he possibly could. His friend John Cam Hobhouse was later told that once he threw it into a pond.

On December 7, 1801, Laurie reported, after examining Byron:

> I found his foot in a much worse state than when I last saw it, – the shoe entirely wet through and brace round his ankle quite loose; I much fear that his extreme Inattention will counteract every exertion on my part to make him better. I have only to add that with proper care and bandaging, his foot may still be greatly recovered; but any delay further than the present vacation would render it folly to undertake it."

Byron was delighted when he heard in February 1801 that Lord Carlisle had agreed that he should transfer to Harrow. Situated twelve miles north-west of London,* the school had been granted a charter in 1571 by Queen Elizabeth. It was originally intended as a free grammar school for local boys, but was soon allowed to take boarders and charge fees.** During the nineteenth century, with the broadening of the curriculum beyond Latin and Greek, it developed into one of the great public schools which were beginning to be patronised by the aristocracy late in the eighteenth century, and during the Victorian period were to become the training ground of the middle-class intelligentsia. It will be remembered that as early as 1811, in *Sense and Sensibility*, Edward Farrars is thought to have suffered because, unlike his brother, he had not attended a public school. Numbers fluctuated during the early part of the nineteenth century, but in Byron's time about 200 boys were enrolled at Harrow.

Hanson escorted him there in late April 1801. They rode up the steep curving village street to a high brick building with pointed gables behind which stood the fourteenth-century church of St Mary, in the graveyard of which Byron was to spend many reflective hours reclining on a tomb. He must have been bewildered by the mass of boys in broad-brimmed black hats, frock tailcoats and tight-fitting trousers. Dr Drury immediately realised how shy he was – "a wild mountain colt" – and gently tried to

---

* Measured from the tollgate at Hyde Park Corner.
** Byron's fees at Harrow were four guineas a year in addition to his board and lodging. Like Harrow, Shrewsbury and Rugby were also based on sixteenth-century grammar schools, while Winchester, Eton and Westminster developed from monastic foundations.

draw him out: "there was Mind in his eye . . . His manner and temper soon convinced me that he might be led by a silken string to a point rather than by a cable – on this principle I acted." Byron was always to be devoted to this kindly man whom he later described as the worthiest friend he had ever possessed.

At thirteen, Byron was older than most boys who entered Harrow; many of them were only ten when they arrived, and the youngest boy was six and a half. Realising the embarrassment Byron would suffer if placed with boys younger than himself, Dr Drury assigned his own son Henry to bring him up to the level of boys of his own age. Proud and sensitive, Byron's four years at Harrow were to prove crucial in his development. For the first time in his life he was to be surrounded by contemporaries on a day-to-day basis, and at first it was a bewildering experience. The first year was particularly difficult. While he had longed to leave Dulwich, his hatred of Harrow did not soften into love until his final year. Only the magical alchemy of memory would later transform the school into an idyllic paradise.

He stayed with Henry Drury, the son of the Headmaster, until February 1803, transferring then to Evans's House. Finally, in January 1805, Byron moved into the Headmaster's House so that he spent his last term, the summer of 1805, with the new headmaster, Dr George Butler. On a typical day he would rise shortly after six to attend First School between seven and nine, followed by breakfast. Second School lasted till noon, Third from three to four, and Fourth from five to six. The school was locked up at eight-thirty in summer and at six in winter. Tuesday was a holiday and Thursday and Saturday half-holidays. All the classes were crammed together in the Old School House, where Byron, according to tradition, carved his name in numerous places in the oak panelling.

Despite the fact that all the staff were clerics, there was no formal religious instruction, the boys attending St Mary's Church where they sat in galleries, since removed, and indulged in notoriously rowdy behaviour. The syllabus until the middle of the nineteenth century was exclusively classical, mainly Virgil and Horace. Horace's satirical bent seems to have left a strong impression on Byron. Harrow was unusual in including Greek in its curriculum so that Byron became familiar with the great tragedies, which were to enhance his knowledge of Greece during his first visit to the country. It was the regular practice for the boys to write free translations of the classical poets. In December 1804 Byron wrote his first translation of a chorus from Aeschylus which, he recalled, Dr Drury received "but coolly":

Great Jove! to whose Almighty throne,
Both Gods and mortals homage pay,
Ne'er may thy soul thy power disown,
Thy dread behests ne'er disobey.

Byron, who was addressed as "Birron", was probably teased about his Scottish accent, and his infirmity was the cause of some humiliating pranks: once he woke up to find his bad leg in a tub of water. His poems about Harrow paint an idyllic picture of roaming around the Middlesex countryside with his friends, but the truth was somewhat different. Sometimes he swam in the duck puddle, but he preferred a bathing pool almost two miles away. In order to reach it he had to hire a pony because it was too far for him to walk. In a day when the boys habitually bathed naked one wonders what Byron did about his withered leg, for when he was an adult he always wore trousers when swimming.

On May 1, 1821, Edward Noel Long, who was to become one of his most intimate friends, wrote to his father about the new boy: "There is another, Lord Byram [sic] a lame fellow just come he seems a good sort of fellow."[12] But on the whole during his first year Byron was exceedingly unpopular, and in fact he quickly acquired a reputation as a bully. At first he kept very much to himself and it is possible that he developed the habit of stretching out on a tomb known as the Peachey Stone in St Mary's graveyard in order to avoid the other boys.

He hated the daily grind of school exercises but on occasion could do prodigious feats of work. By the end of June he had made such remarkable progress that he was placed in the fourth form together with Long and Robert Peel, the future statesman. In later years Byron was generous about Peel's outstanding abilities:

As a scholar, he was greatly my Superior: as a declaimer and actor, I was reckoned at least his equal. As a school-boy *out* of school, I was always *in* scrapes, and *he never*: and *in School* he always knew his lesson, and I rarely; but *when* I knew it, I knew it nearly as well. In general information, history, etc. etc. I think I was *his* superior, as also of most boys of my standing.[13]

When holidays arrived the other boys went off to their family homes, but Byron moved from place to place with his mother, interspersed with welcome visits to the Hansons. The first summer his mother was staying at No. 16 Piccadilly with a Mrs Massingberd, an association that was to bode no good for the future. Later in the summer they travelled to Cheltenham and visited the Malvern Hills. For the first time he saw a part of England that reminded him of the Scottish Highlands. In a note to *The Island* he recalled his reaction to the hills: "After I had returned to Cheltenham, I used to watch them every afternoon at sunset, with a sensation which I cannot describe.* This was boyish enough; but I was then only thirteen years of age, and it was in the holidays."[4]

It may have been during this visit to Cheltenham that Mrs Byron visited a fortune-teller who told her that she had a lame son who would be married twice, the second time to a foreign lady. Possibly it was this woman who told her that her son would experience some terrible misfortune in his twenty-seventh year. Both mother and son were very superstitious and Byron later identified the misfortune as his marriage which occurred when he was just short of twenty-seven.

In 1802 he spent the Christmas holidays with his mother at No. 16 Henrietta Street in Bath. Mrs Byron, by taking him to fashionable places such as Cheltenham and Bath, was doing her best to introduce him into polite society. In Bath, influenced by *The Arabian Nights*, he attended a fancy-dress ball dressed as a Turk with a diamond crescent in his turban.

Then on January 19, 1803, Mrs Byron wrote to Hanson:

"Byron *positively* refuses to return to Harrow to be Henry Drury's *Pupil* as he says he has used him *ill* for some time past."[5] Hanson apparently persuaded him to return, but trouble broke out again the following year. In May, in an impassioned letter, he complained to his mother that Dr Drury's brother Mark had also taunted him about his lack of fortune, abused him to another boy, and threatened to have him expelled. Byron's letter is remarkably sensible and spirited for a boy of sixteen:

> if my fortune is narrow, it is my misfortune not my fault. But however the way to *riches* to *Greatness* lies before me, I can, I will cut myself a path through the world or perish in the attempt. – others have begun life with nothing and ended Greatly. And shall I who have a competent if not large fortune, remain idle, No, I will carve myself the passage to Grandeur, but never with Dishonour.[16]

On the other hand, one must remember how violently he had already reacted to Henry Drury. One wonders if the humiliations were actually as acute as he described them.

---

* This was a rare lapse in Byron's memory, for this would have been a physical impossibility.

Hanson sent on the complaint to the Headmaster, and Dr Drury replied on May 15, apologising for his brother's behaviour. He described Byron as possessing "a mind that feels, and that can discriminate reasonably on points on which it conceives itself injured . . . I feel particularly hurt to see him idle, negligent and apparently indifferent."[7] Dr Drury was being absolutely sincere about his appreciation of Byron. In an interview with Lord Carlisle he reported Byron's progress: "He has talents, my lord, which will add lustre to his rank." An astonished Carlisle replied, "Indeed!" He would have been even more astonished if he had known that this chubby boy would become the most celebrated poet of the century.

Byron was subsequently transferred to Mr Evans's House, and after he left Harrow, he and Henry Drury became fast friends. Indeed in 1822 Drury conducted the funeral service for Byron's illegitimate daughter Allegra in the churchyard after the vicar refused to have it held within the church.

Tired of moving from place to place, Mrs Byron set about looking for a house in the neighbourhood of Newstead. In October of 1802 the abbey had been lent temporarily to two sisters, Launders by name, and it was not long before trouble with Mrs Byron erupted. A young gentleman, Lord Grey de Ruthyn, was eager to rent the abbey for £50 a year on a five-year lease, also agreeing to be responsible for the taxes and repairs. The ladies claimed that they had understood they could keep the abbey until Byron was twenty-one, and refused to budge. They spread stories about Mrs Byron's open activities on behalf of the Whig candidate in a county that was overwhelmingly Tory. So great was the animosity between the two parties that families of different persuasions would cut each other dead. At first Lord Grey was accommodating with the stubborn sisters but his patience began to be taxed beyond endurance, particularly as Hanson did little to clarify matters. Lord Grey finally moved in on July 31, 1803, after the Miss Launders decamped leaving unpaid bills.

In the meantime, Mrs Byron found exactly what she wanted in Burgage Manor, situated in the pleasant town of Southwell only twelve miles from Newstead. It was a comfortable house overlooking the green, and she filled it with family portraits. Her neighbours seemed agreeable and she looked forward to welcoming her son to a conventional home. But a conventional home was not what Byron wanted. There was plenty of excitement in Bath, Cheltenham, or London, but what was there to do in a provincial village, which Byron described as the resort of "old parsons and old Maids"?[18] The abbey offered space and grandeur – even if derelict – and he refused to be confined to an ordinary house. So he made off for Newstead where he persuaded the grumbling Owen Mealey to put him up at the lodge. Apparently he approached Lord Grey as well, for in early August Grey informed Hanson that Byron was welcome to visit the abbey whenever he liked but he simply didn't have the wherewithal to put him up.

All this happened soon after Mrs Byron had begun to congratulate herself that Byron was finally settling down in Harrow. In June he had written to her that he actually wanted Sheldrake, the bootmaker, to fit him with a proper brace, "as I want one rather I have been placed in a higher form in this school to day and Dr Drury I go on very well write soon my dear Mother."[9]

But his thoughts were to be totally diverted from school that summer by a passion, the memory of which was never to be extinguished.

3

ooooooooooooooo

School Days, 1803–5

That summer of 1803, Byron again met his Annesley Hall neighbour, Mary Chaworth. While staying in the lodge (opposite the present gate) with the surly Owen Mealey, he was happy to accept the invitation of her mother, Mrs Clarke, to visit the family. They soon made him feel very much at home even though he still feared that the portraits of the Chaworths were glaring down at him because of the circumstances of the duel. Mary had grown into a young woman of delicate beauty, and in no time at all he was wildly infatuated with her.

His adoration for her grew despite the fact that she was in love with a man of whom her parents strongly disapproved. This was a dashing neighbour, Jack Musters, who seemed to excel at everything he did from the hunting field to the ballroom – everything, indeed, that Byron could not do. Jack, however, had a reputation for wildness, and the Clarkes also suspected he was a fortune-hunter. Since Mary was only sixteen, Mrs Clarke applied to the Lord Chancellor, Lord Eldon, to have her daughter made a Ward of Court, and Jack was forbidden to see or correspond with her. The lovers managed to elude the interdiction. Every day Mary and her cousin Ann Radford would ride to a wooded hill on the estate which Byron was later to call the Diadem and there they would leave letters for each other in a secret hiding place.

Byron became aware of these assignations because he was persuaded to move into Annesley Hall after claiming that on riding back to Newstead one night he had encountered "a bogy" – a Scottish word for ghost. This sounds rather like a ruse on his part. Mary behaved playfully towards him, perhaps even a little flirtatiously, since it was so apparent how smitten he was with her. The Clarkes must have been very indulgent towards him, as they allowed him to stand in the door firing his pistol towards the terrace.

He sulked when Mary refused to give him a lock of her hair. It is possible that he was being encouraged as a more suitable husband than Musters; and he was in sheer heaven when the Clarkes proposed that he join them on an excursion to Matlock in Derbyshire.

Many years later, in "Detached Thoughts", he recollected the high point of their visit:

> When I was fifteen years of age – it happened that in a Cavern in Derbyshire – I had to cross in a boat – (in which two people only could lie down) a stream which flows under a rock – with the rock so close upon the water – as to admit the boat only to be pushed on by a ferryman (a sort of Charon) who wades at the stern stooping all the time. – The Companion of my transit was M.A.C., with whom I had long been in love – and never told it – though *she* had discovered it without. – I recollect my sensations – but cannot describe them – and it is as well.[1]

They also attended a ball at Malvern, and Byron stood against the wall, glaring balefully as Mary whirled around the room. Whatever fantasies Byron had about her, he was disabused when he heard that Mary's maid had been teasing her about his attachment, and she had exclaimed, "Do you think I should care anything for that lame boy?"[2] According to Thomas Moore, when Byron heard this "it was like a shot through his heart".[3] It was late at night and Byron rushed from the house, never stopping until he found himself back at Newstead. Mr Clarke, however, soon followed and fetched him back to Annesley.

The holidays came to an end, yet still Byron remained either at Annesley or sometimes in the lodge with Mealey. Dr Drury was writing to Hanson to enquire as to his whereabouts. His mother pleaded with him to return to Harrow. In mid-September she sent her servant William to bring him back to Southwell. On September 15 Byron wrote her an agonised letter:

My Dear Mother–
I have sent Mealey to Day to you, before William Came, but now I shall write myself, I *promise* you upon my *honour* I will come over tomorrow in the *afternoon*. I was not wishing to resist your *Commands*, and really seriously intended, Coming over tomorrow, ever since I received your Last letter, you know as well as I do it is not your Company I dislike, but the place you reside in. I know it is time to go to Harrow. It will make me *unhappy*, but I will *obey*; I only *desire*, *entreat*, this one day, and on my *honour* I will be over tomorrow, in the evening

or afternoon. I am Sorry you disapprove my Companions, who however are the first this county affords, and my equals in most respects but I will be permitted to Chuse for myself, I shall never interfere in yours, and I desire you will not molest me in mine; if you Grant me this favour, and allow me this one day unmolested you will eternally oblige your

unhappy Son

Byron

I shall attempt to offer no excuse as you do not desire one. I only entreat you as Governor, not as a Mother, to allow me this one day. Those that I most Love live in this county, therefore in the name of Mercy I entreat this one day to take leave, and then I will Join you again at Southwell to prepare to go to a place where – I will write no more it would only incense you, adieu. Tomorrow I come.[4]

Knowing that they would soon be parted for ever since Mary was determined to marry Jack, even a single additional day with her was precious. In 1817, by then an exile, Byron recalled all those feelings of hopeless love in "The Dream".

> she was his life,
> The ocean to the river of his thoughts,
> Which terminated all: upon a tone,
> A touch of hers, his blood would ebb and flow,
> And his cheek change tempestuously – his heart
> Unknowing of its cause of agony.
>
> (2, 56–61)

In August 1803 Lord Eldon summoned the Chaworth and Musters families to an interview to reassess the situation. He agreed that the young couple might see each other again, thus paving the way for their engagement. By now Byron, understandably, was feeling absolutely desperate.

In the many allusions to her to his friends or in the numerous poems he wrote about Mary he never once referred in any way to the existence of Jack Musters. He describes the Diadem as the hill on which he and Mary were supposed to have had a tender parting, knowing full well that it had sentimental associations for the lovers.

Mrs Byron could not help feeling pity for her son. On October 30 she told Hanson:

He has no indisposition that I know of, but love, desperate love, the worst of all maladies in my opinion. In short, the Boy is distractedly in love with Miss Chaworth . . . it has given me much uneasiness. To prevent all trouble in future, I am determined he shall not come here again until Easter; therefore I beg you will find some proper situation for him at the next Holydays. I don't care what I pay. I wish Dr Drury would keep him.[5]

He may have left Annesley, but he still was not seen in Southwell. Lord Grey, who had been in Yorkshire during the summer, returned to Newstead in October. A personable young bachelor of twenty-three, he provided Byron with mindless distractions, taking him around the estate shooting while Mealey sent off urgent complaints to Hanson about how they were wasting the game and Grey was doing nothing to improve the grounds: "I hope to God you will come down very soon to put things to rights here. The most of all me time has been taken up waiting of Lord Byron since the 1st of August. When I tell him that you will blame me not to attend to the work he says he [does not] Care that he must be waited on."[6]

Byron's relationship with Lord Grey is one of the most puzzling episodes in his life. In November Byron moved into the abbey with Grey and apparently intended to stay until his birthday on January 22. Surprisingly Mrs Byron agreed to this arrangement, postponing his return to Harrow even longer. Perhaps she thought Grey might be a good influence on Byron. She herself began to make frequent visits to the abbey. Grey flattered her and, silly woman that she was, despite the more than ten years' difference in age between them, she became rather infatuated with him. Byron was infuriated by her foolish behaviour.

He might have resented Mrs Byron's intrusion into a situation where he regarded Grey as his special friend. There are various possibilities to be considered to account for Byron's sudden break with Lord Grey. If he resented the presence of his mother, he could have left Newstead abruptly out of pique. Byron frequently lied or insinuated something dire in order to heighten the drama of a situation. There was clearly no dramatic parting. Byron simply returned to Southwell and a puzzled Lord Grey tried to extract from him the reason for his sudden coolness. Only a couple of months later Byron hinted at something diabolical about Grey to Augusta. This would be less shaming than to say he was sulking because his mother seemed to be taking over his friend. One may speculate that in time he came to believe the more dramatic version and later succeeded even in pulling the wool over the eyes of the usually sceptical Hobhouse, who had been convinced by Byron that Grey was responsible for some sexual trauma in his life.

Four years later (August 7, 1808) Byron had occasion to write to Grey on a business matter and the wording of his conclusion is ambiguous: "Circumstances, which though now long past, and indeed difficult for me to touch upon, have not yet ceased to be *interesting* [italics mine] – Your Lordship must be perfectly aware of the very peculiar reasons that induced me to adopt a line of conduct, which however painful, and painful to me it certainly was, because unavoidable."

This brings us to the second hypothesis. The views of John Cam Hobhouse are probably the most reliable source we have to substantiate the generally accepted view. In his biography of Byron, Thomas Moore wrote that "an intimacy . . . soon sprung up between (B) and his noble tenant."[7] By "intimacy" Moore probably means kissing and caressing, which would fall within Byron's view of a "pure relationship" – that is, one that did not progress to full sexual relations. In Hobhouse's copy of Moore's biography he wrote in the margin: "A circumstance occurred during [this] intimacy which certainly had much effect on his future morals." This would suggest that Grey had attempted to sodomise him. In "Detached Thoughts", written in 1821, Byron confessed: "My passions were developed very early – so early – that few would believe me – if I were to state the period – and the facts which accompanied it."[8] He is probably referring to Mary Gray, but it is possible that he is also thinking of the relationship with Lord Grey.

Grey's reply to Byron's letter of August 7 indicates total bewilderment about his ambiguous insinuations.

> As you seem to suppose me so well acquainted with the cause of your sudden secession from our former friendship, I must beg leave to assure you that, much as I have reviewed every circumstance and given to each its most full and weighty import, still I am now at a loss to account for it. We parted in 1804 the best of Friends, your letters were afterwards most affectionate . . . and therefore under all these counts you cannot wonder at my being somewhat surprised. You say the break was painful to yourself, I need not say to you who know I have not the power to command my feelings when deeply wounded what my sensations were.[9]

The fact that Byron's affectionate letters have never turned up does not necessarily mean that Byron did not write them. Grey's reply would indicate that Byron did not reject his advances at the time. Indeed, he might willingly have concurred; and later felt deep shame at the recognition of some secret urges that he didn't want to acknowledge. By denying his part in the episode, Byron could thus throw the entire blame on Lord Grey. Byron's uneasiness about their activities might have increased after he returned to Harrow. Possibly his dislike of the school stemmed in part from its depravity. It is difficult to believe that the moral atmosphere had deteriorated significantly in arriving at the situation John Addington Symonds described fifty years later:

> Every boy of good looks had a female name, and was recognized either as a public prostitute or as some bigger fellow's "bitch". Bitch was the word in common usage to indicate a boy who yielded his person to a lover. The talk of the dormitories and the studies was incredibly obscene. Here and there one could not avoid seeing acts of onanism, mutual masturbation, the sports of naked boys in bed together. There was no refinement, no sentiment, no passion; nothing but animal lust in these occurrences. They filled me with disgust and loathing. My school-fellows realised what I had read in Swift about the Yahoos.[10]

Until Byron's last two years at Harrow he disliked the school intensely, perhaps for the same reasons as Symonds. He didn't make many close friends until his final year. It is possible that he used to retire to a tomb in St Mary's churchyard because he felt isolated and perhaps rejected. Some boys found it difficult to accept his sullen, menacing silences and his strange outbursts of passion. While he was an extremely handsome boy he may not have been courted by the older boys because of his deformity. By the time he returned in late January 1804 he had reached an age when he found himself in a position of power. He now gathered around him a group of adoring young acolytes, all of them vying fiercely for his attention. Later he repeatedly emphasised the "purity" of these relationships, which must have been difficult to maintain considering that it was the custom for boys to share a bed.

Byron had a propensity all his life for assigning blame to other people. His mother was responsible for his deformity. Mary Gray and Lord Grey corrupted him sexually. What Byron wanted was uncritical adoration. Hobhouse, by far the best friend he ever had, a sensible Horatio to a posturing Hamlet, was never listed among those whom he considered the dearest of his friends because Hobhouse had no hesitation in teasing him when he took himself too seriously. With no father to hold him in check and an over-indulgent mother who was frustrated in her attempts to discipline him, Byron grew up to be thoroughly self-indulgent. Nevertheless it was his mother who recognised the basically sterling nature of his character: "God only knows, he is a turbulent, unruly Boy that wants to be emancipated from all restraints, his sentiments are however noble."[11]

Most teenagers rebel against their parents, but Byron seemed to develop a real animus against his mother in the period following the disintegration of his friendship with Lord Grey. That she continued friendly with the tenant at the abbey we know from Mealey's reports to Hanson. On March 26, 1804, he wrote: "He [Lord Grey] is very thick with Mrs Byron and Lord Byron is displaised [sic] at it, he [Grey] has been setting Mrs Byron against me."[12] Again, on July 30: "Mrs Byron and him is greater than ever, he has dined with her several times since you left here and whatever he says is right with her, when he writes to her it is 'My dear Mrs Byron'." Mrs Byron was so dazzled by Grey's charming ways and their shared Whig sympathies that she seemed oblivious to his shocking neglect of the estate or aware that their conduct was making them the gossip of the county. She was constantly exhorting her son to mend the quarrel which only made Byron all the more stubborn in his antagonism.

Our knowledge of Byron's attitude towards Grey and his growing attachment to a group of younger boys at Harrow can be gained mainly through his correspondence with his half-sister Augusta Leigh. When they first actually met again is not altogether clear, although it was probably in 1802. When Augusta's grandmother Lady Holderness died in 1801, Mrs Byron wrote to her, partially in the hope of learning whether she had inherited sufficient income to help her brother. At the least she hoped that Augusta might aid him in gaining entrée into the aristocratic world. The tactless woman was unable to restrain her bitterness against Lady Holderness, and the condolence letter she wrote on October 18, 1801, was scarcely worded in a way to ingratiate herself with the young woman: "As I wish to bury what is past in oblivion I shall avoid all reflections on a Person now no more, my opinion of yourself I have suspended for some years. The time is now arrived when I shall form a very decided one." She then goes on to remind her of the devoted care she had bestowed on her when she lay ill as a motherless infant in France. Finally: "Your brother is at Harrow school and if you wish to see him I now have no desire to keep you asunder."[13]

Augusta spent a good part of each year with the Carlisle family; and after Lord Carlisle became Byron's nominal guardian she heard a good deal about him and his vulgar mama. A regular correspondence between the brother and sister developed in 1802. It is understandable that they were drawn together as the only surviving siblings. Byron needed a confidante and Augusta was willing to fulfil the role of a wise older sister whom she perceived he badly needed since she regarded his mother as an unfortunate influence. In addition to being united by ties of blood, as the letters passed between them they discovered that they shared an ironical sense of humour and a love of laughter. Above all, Byron needed affection and this Augusta provided in abundance since she was genuinely concerned about his welfare.

In mid-February 1803, Hanson received a letter from Augusta enquiring if he knew the reason why Byron had not returned to Harrow from Bath where he was spending his holidays with his mother. Again, the following year on March 12, she asked Hanson if he would call on her at 60 Lower Grosvenor Street where she was staying with the Duchess of Leeds. She told him that she was "particularly anxious" to have some conversation with him about Lord Byron whom she had not seen for over a year. Hanson contacted Byron about his sister's concern, and on March 22, 1804, he wrote to her from Southwell:

Although, My ever Dear Augusta, I have hitherto appeared remiss in replying to your kind and affectionate letters; yet I hope you will not attribute my neglect to a want of affection, but rather to a shyness naturally inherent in my Disposition. I will now endeavour as amply as lies in my power to repay your kindness, and for the Future I hope you will consider me not only as *a Brother* but as your warmest and most affectionate *Friend*, and if ever Circumstances should require it as your *protector*. Recollect, My Dearest Sister, that you are *the nearest relation* I have in *the world both by the ties of Blood* and *Affection*. If there is anything in which I can serve you; you have only to mention it; Trust to your Brother, and be assured he will never betray your confidence. When You see my Cousin and future Brother George Leigh tell him that I already consider him as my Friend, for whoever is beloved by you, my amiable Sister, will always be equally Dear to me . . . Also remember me to poor old Murray, tell him that I will see that something is to be done for him, for *while I live he shall never be abandoned In his old Age*. Write to me Soon, my Dear Augusta, And do not forget to love me, In the meantime I remain more than words [can] express, your ever sincere, affectionate

Brother and Friend
Byron

P.S. Do not forget to Knit the purse you promised me, Adieu my beloved sister.[14]

What sister would not have been touched by the tenderness, sincerity, and gentleness of this letter? Augusta herself was in particular need of sympathy, for George Leigh's parents were opposed to the possibility of marriage to a young woman who had inherited only £350 a year. George's father had purchased a commission for him in the 10th Dragoon Guards in which Beau Brummell was a fellow officer.* The Prince of Wales, the colonel-in-chief of the regiment, had secured an appointment for George at his stud farm at Six Mile Bottom near Newmarket. As an equerry, a charming sporting young man, George Leigh spent his time travelling around to race meetings where he stayed at great country houses. Naturally his parents hoped that he would meet an heiress in the grand company he kept.

On March 26, in response to a letter from Augusta, Byron again wrote:

> Ah, How unhappy I have hitherto been in being so long separated from so amiable a Sister, but fortune has now sufficiently atoned by discovering to me a relation whom I love, a Friend in whom I can confide. In both these lights my Dear Augusta I shall ever look upon you, and I hope you will never find your Brother unworthy of your affection and Friendship. I am as you may imagine a little dull here, not being on terms of even intimacy with Lord Grey I avoid Newstead, and my resources of amusement are Books, and writing to my Augusta, which wherever I am, will always constitute my Greatest pleasure, I am not reconciled to Lord Grey, *and I never will.* He once was my *Greatest Friend,* my reasons for ceasing that Friendship are such as I cannot explain, not even to you my Dear Sister (although were they to be made known to any body, you would be the first) but they will ever remain hidden in my own breast. – They are Good ones however, for although I am *violent* I am not *capricious* in my *attachments.* – My mother disapproves of my quarrelling with him, but if she knew the cause (which she will never know) She would reproach me no more. He Has forfeited all *title to my esteem,* but I hold him in too much *contempt* ever *to hate him.*[15]

This letter contains the strongest evidence that Grey had tampered with him sexually, and the fact that Byron spoke so strongly to Augusta probably left her in little doubt to what he was referring. Still, he was capable of creating the most plausible fabrications, sometimes out of a spirit of

* A large inheritance enabled Brummell to leave the army in 1798.

mischief, although mischief would not have been the motive force in this case.

It was not until later in April that Byron was actually back at the school, this time complaining about Mark Drury, the Headmaster's brother; his spirited letter (referred to in the last chapter) contains another attack on Lord Grey who continued to haunt his memory. He could only imagine that Drury, "this upstart Son of a Button-maker", had heard stories about his straitened circumstances from Hanson or "that officious Friend Lord Grey de Ruthyn, whom I shall ever consider my most inveterate enemy".[16]

Just before leaving for Harrow, Byron began to find Southwell more pleasing than he had originally considered it. In order to relieve his sense of tedium Mrs Byron arranged a party for him on April 9. He was overcome with shyness and did not create a very good impression. Even though he was handsome, he was fat and his hair was combed straight over his forehead in a very unattractive way. The next day his mother took him across the green to call on the Pigot family. When Thomas Moore interviewed Elizabeth Pigot while preparing his life of Byron, she recalled: "The conversation turned upon Cheltenham, where he had been staying, the amusements there, the plays etc. and I mentioned that I had seen the character of Gabriel Lackbrain very well performed. His mother getting up to go, he accompanied her, and I, in allusion to the play, said 'Good-by Gaby.' With this his face lit up with a broad grin. 'Come, Byron, are you ready?' his mother asked as she was about to make her departure." He replied that he would stay a little while longer; and soon the twenty-one-year-old Elizabeth Pigot had become another confidante – particularly about the increasing difficulties between himself and his mother whom she herself disliked.

Mrs Byron had good reports of Byron's progress during the summer term. On July 2 she wrote to a kinswoman, Miss Abercromby: "I long to see him, he is much improved in every respect. He is truly amiable and passes his time I am informed very differently from most young people, he writes a great deal [of] poetry."[17]

The longing for a reunion was not mutual. From Harrow Byron continued to write to Augusta on two subjects. The first was about his very particular friend, Lord Delawarr, considerably younger than Byron but "the most good tempered, amiable, clever fellow in the universe . . . remarkably handsome, almost too much so for a boy".[18] The other was his persistent grievance against his mother, although he was willing to admit that "I believe it is all my fault. I am rather too fidgety, which my precise mama objects to." But, despite his mother's liberality with him, unlike most boys he dreaded the holidays.

In former days she spoilt me, now she is altered to the contrary, for the most trifling thing, she upbraids me in a most outrageous manner, and all our disputes have been lately heightened by my one with that object of my cordial, deliberate detestation, Lord Grey de Ruthyn. She wishes me to explain my reasons for disliking him, which I will never do . . .[19]

He actually suspected that his mother was now in love with Grey, for when Grey called during the summer holiday Byron could not be cajoled out of his room even though "she threatened, begged, me to make it up". He pleaded with Augusta not to desert him. If she did, "I have nobody I can love but Delawarr. If it was not for his sake, Harrow would be a desert."[20] This was on November 2, 1804. Again on the 11th he voiced his suspicion that his mother fancied "that detestable Lord Grey". As Christmas approached he recoiled from having to meet his former friend "whom I detest" although he had to concede that his mother in some respects was "very kind, though her manners are not the most conciliating".[21] It does indeed look as though poor lonely Mrs Byron was totally smitten with Grey and that he continued cultivating her only in the hope of procuring a reconciliation with Byron. The following year Lord Grey spoke to Hanson of "the shyness that exists between Lord Byron and myself" to which a puzzled Hanson replied: "I am extremely sorry that any Shyness should exist between his Lordship and Lord Byron, the cause of which I never could learn."[22]

Augusta, alarmed by her brother's plight, wrote to Hanson (18 November, 1804), urging him to arrange for Byron to spend the next vacation with him so that he could evade his mother. She hoped that Lord Carlisle would then be able to give him some attention, as he was "the only relative who has the *Will* and *power* to be of use to him".[23]

In Byron's last year at Harrow the attractive Lord Clare was added to the list of his special favourites. There were jealous quarrels, and Delawarr became so angry (probably because of his attention to Clare) that he stopped speaking to him. Years later Byron recalled that "P. Hunter, Curzon, Long, and Tatersall, were my principal friends. Clare, Dorset, Go.Gordon, De Bathe[e], Claridge, and Jno. Wingfield, were my juniors and favourites whom I spoilt by indulgence."[24] Delawarr is significantly missing from the list. Byron spoke most warmly about Clare in his Ravenna Journal of 1821:

My School friendships were with *me passions* (for I was always violent) but I do not know that there is one which has endured (to be sure some have been cut short by death) till now – that with Lord Clare began one of the earliest and lasted longest – being only interrupted by distance – that I know of. I never hear the word "*Clare*" without a beating of the heart – even *now*, and I write it with the feelings of 1803–4–5 – ad infinitum.[25]

But there were occasions on which Clare felt slighted by Byron and in a letter of July 28, 1805, he expressed the hurt he felt at the way Byron had been treating him:

Since you have been so unusually unkind to me, in calling me names whenever you meet me, of late, I must beg an explanation, wishing to know whether you choose to be as good friends with me as ever. I must own that, for this last month, you have entirely cut me, – for, I suppose, your new cronies. But think not that I will (because you choose to take into your head some whim or other) – be always going up to you, nor do, as I observe certain other fellows doing, to regain your friendship; nor think that I am your friend either through interest, or because you are bigger and older than I am. No, – it never was so, nor ever shall be so. I was only your friend, and am so still, – unless you go on in this way, calling me names whenever you see me.[26]

Byron felt suitably remorseful and the breach was soon healed. Byron in turn was deeply affronted another time when Clare addressed him as "my dear" instead of "my dearest". On a number of occasions in Byron's life we shall see that in situations involving three people he rather delighted in playing favourites and arousing jealousy in one of the trio. He repeatedly seized opportunities where he could control the life around him.

While Byron later described these friendships as "passions", he clearly did not mean in a sexual sense – or at least the underlying sexuality was unacknowledged. Nevertheless, we cannot ignore the testimony of Hobhouse, who later travelled in the East with him and knew more about his personal life than anyone else. Moore tended to gloss over these friendships so that in the margin of his copy of the *Life* Hobhouse felt obliged to write: "Moore knows nothing, or will tell nothing of the principal cause & motive of all these boyish friend[ships]."[27] And in his diary of January 15, 1830, Hobhouse disagreed strongly with his insinuation that Byron had been corrupted by his Cambridge friends: "Certainly Byron had nothing to learn in the way of depravity either of mind or body when he came from Harrow nor was his Southwell recreation such as Moore pretends them to have been – I have Byron's own words for his *innocent* amusements there . . . He little knows the ground he treads –"[28]

Byron's attitude to William Harness was typical of the attitude he assumed towards those who were weaker and younger than himself. Harness, too, was lame. One day Byron encountered the boy, then just ten, standing apart from the noisy crowd. Byron immediately recognised him as the sort of victim who would be picked on by bullies. He approached him, telling him reassuringly: "Harness, if anyone bullies you, tell me, and I'll thrash him if I can."[29] Byron identified with this weaker, more vulnerable self and gave him the loving support he himself had desperately craved. Harness of course became Byron's devoted disciple. Almost all these boys were of higher rank than himself except Harness and Long; and Byron did not become really friendly with Long until they found themselves at Cambridge together. Byron always felt slightly uncomfortable with peers of his own age and generally made friends with those towards whom he might have some slight reason for feeling superior.

Certainly there was a homo-erotic tinge to his Harrow friendships, yet most scholars feel that none of them became explicitly sexual. If this is so – given the general moral atmosphere of the public school at the time and the fact that it is a period when boys are disturbingly aware of pressing sexuality – we would have to assume that Byron and his group stood apart from other boys of their age.

For two years Byron had been evading Harrow, and Dr Drury had repeatedly written anxiously enquiring about his whereabouts. Suddenly, in December 1804, it appeared that he was no longer welcome at the school. After a discussion with Byron, Dr Drury wrote frankly to his mother that he thought the boy should be removed from the school. Hanson in turn requested that the Headmaster be more specific about the reasons, but his reply was evasive:

> During his last residence at Harrow his conduct gave me much trouble and uneasiness – and as two of his Associates were to leave me at Christmas, I certainly suggested to him *my wish* that he might be placed under the care of some private Tutor previously to his admission to either of the Universities. This I did with no less than a view to the forming of his mind and manners, than to my own comfort.[30]

Dr Drury believed that if he left immediately they might still "entertain affectionate dispositions towards each other". What does this ambiguous statement mean? Was Byron's behaviour totally unruly? The reference to "two of his Associates" is interesting. It is possible that Dr Drury disapproved of the coterie of boys Byron had gathered around him, uneasy about what he considered his pernicious effect on them. He obstinately displayed a bust of Napoleon on his desk, which would have been displeasing at a time when England was at war with France. From remarks Byron later made it was clear that he was becoming incorrigible and threatening the discipline of the school.

Byron was greatly distressed because he viewed Dr Drury's fiat as tantamount to an expulsion. He had set his heart on taking part in the summer Speech Day. Dr Drury, who was soon due to retire, was persuaded to concede and Byron was back at Harrow in February 1805. But trouble erupted again. This time he and a group of other boys violently objected to the choice of the new Headmaster, Dr George Butler. Although Byron lived in Dr Butler's House, he did everything he could to defy and annoy him. His behaviour was so violent that Dr Butler was to say that he was an unfit companion for the other boys. He ripped down the blinds in the hall, and when sharply rebuked by Butler this seventeen-year-old began to blubber like a child. It is possible that his rebelliousness was an outlet for the resentment he was unable to vent against Lord Carlisle. Certainly he had a great deal of aggression which he was later able to channel into his poetry.

Despite his fractiousness, his last term at Harrow was to prove unusually happy, so happy, in fact, that it coloured all his eventual recollections of his school. No longer did he brood Hamlet-like on the Peachey Stone. He was now either involved in cricket or carousing in the local inn. He pleaded with Augusta to come to hear him deliver the highly dramatic lines of Zanga over the body of Alonzo in Young's tragedy *The Revenge*. He would have been humiliated if his schoolfellows had caught a glimpse of his vulgar mother. After Augusta had received an intemperate letter from her, he commented: "She is as I have before declared certainly mad (to say she was in her senses, would be con-demning her as a Criminal,) her conduct is a *happy* compound of derangement and Folly."[31] Byron is showing rare understanding of the fact that she was a deeply disturbed woman. Her behaviour was undoubtedly that of a manic depressive; and when he too exhibited the same symptoms as he grew older, his wife found him as difficult to live with as he had found his own mother. Mrs Byron, by now forty, would have been entering the menopause, and her erratic tantrums could have been closely linked to her physical condition.*

Byron was deeply disappointed when Augusta failed to put in an appearance at the Speech Day on July 4 for which he had carefully memorised a passage from King Lear's address to the storm. He was so wrung out from the exertion of his declamation that he had to leave the room afterwards. He was ambitious to improve his speaking skills, aware that it would not be long before he would be taking his seat in the Lords, which he had attended in early May to hear the debate on the Catholic Question. Nevertheless, he wanted to prolong those last school days into a timeless zone of contentment, fearful of what lay beyond in a world that demanded responsibility, choice, and maturity. In an effort not to fall behind the other boys, he set about learning to swim proficiently. By now he was no longer wearing a brace around his ankle but a corrective inner shoe so that his shoes looked like everyone else's. He even played in the cricket match against Eton that took place in Dorset Square on August 2, although someone else had to run for him.** Later the boys all went off and kicked up a convivial row in the Haymarket Theatre. Without any real family of his own, Harrow – and particularly his close friends – became his surrogate family, where he could play the role of both protector and irresponsible child.

Byron had no alternative but to spend part of the summer of 1805 in Southwell. Relations with his mother continued to be as stormy as ever. Her lack of tact displayed itself towards the end of August in an incident recorded by Moore, probably gained from Elizabeth Pigot:

> His mother said, "Byron, I have some news for you –" "Well, what is it?" – "Take out your handkerchief first, for you will want it." "Nonsense!" – "Take out your handkerchief, I say." He did so, to humour her – "Miss Chaworth is married." An expression, very peculiar, impossible to describe, passed over his pale face, and he hurried this handkerchief into his pocket, saying, with an affected air of coldness and nonchalance "Is that all?" – "Why, I expected you would have been plunged in grief!" He made no reply, and soon began to talk about something else.[32]

* I am indebted to Professor Edward Shorter for directing me to an article, "Changing Age at the Menopause" by D.J. Frommer, *British Medical Journal*, 8 August. 1964, 349–51, for a discussion on the earlier age of the menopause in the early nineteenth century.

** Thomas Lord laid out his original cricket ground in Dorset Square in 1787. The MCC was established the same year.

Some months previously Mrs Byron had broken the news of the marriage of his Scottish cousin Mary Duff. On that occasion he had nearly had convulsions. Did all the people to whom he gave his heart desert him? Possibly this number included Lord Grey. The possessive, passionate way he attached himself to his Harrow favourites indicates a terror of desertion. Let us remember that for no apparent cause whatever, he pleaded with Augusta not to desert him because then his only friend would be Delawarr – who actually did desert him finally.

Elizabeth Pigot's cousin, the Reverend J.T. Becher, also took a great interest in the boy and was concerned by the frequent depressions into which the boy would lapse. In an endeavour to lift him out of his low spirits, he talked to him about how fortunate he was to be endowed with a superior mind, to which Byron replied: "Ah, my dear friend, if *this* [placing his hand on his forehead] places me above the rest of mankind, *that* [pointing to his foot] places me far far below them."[33]

But the summer passed pleasantly enough. Elizabeth's brother John Pigot, who was home from medical school in Edinburgh, would go swimming with Byron in the local river, the River Greet, which Byron later recalled as "that rippling surge". Young ladies would try to time their visits to the hour when they expected to find Byron in the Pigot home, but he was still so shy that he jumped out of the window to avoid them. Byron later felt sufficiently comfortable with Elizabeth that one day, when they were reading Burns together, he confessed to her that he wrote poetry also. Inspired by Richard Gall's "Farewell to Ayrshire" (attributed at the time to Burns) his sorrow over his lost Mary was poured into lines written shortly after he heard of her marriage.

> Hills of Annesley, bleak and barren,
>   Where my thoughtless childhood stray'd,
> How the northern tempests, warring,
>   Howl above thy tufted shade!
>
> Now no more, the hours beguiling,
>   Former favourite haunts I see;
> Now no more my Mary smiling
>   Makes ye seem a Heaven to me.
>
>   (*Works*, I, p.3)

The remembrance of Mary was a compound of devotion and humiliation, emotions which were to haunt him all his life. Fortunately he had the poetic talent to utilise, if not to exorcise, his inner demons.

4

Cambridge, 1805–8

W hy Byron attended Cambridge rather than Oxford, which he claimed was his preference, has never been made clear. He was so indifferent to going to university at all that it seemed a matter of little consequence. On April 4, 1805, he spoke to Augusta of his "idle disposition". In the same letter, he talked of his future plans: "Mr H[anson] Recommends Cambridge, Ld. Carlisle allows me to choose for myself, and I must own I prefer Oxford. But, I am not violently bent upon it, and whichever is determined upon, will meet with my concurrence."

There was a curious strain in Byron's character of allowing events to bear him along, of deferring decisions to whatever happened to turn up. By the time he realised that most of his Harrow contemporaries – particularly Lord Clare – were going to Christ Church, Oxford, there were no places left; so on July 1, 1805, he travelled to Cambridge to enrol at Trinity, the largest of the colleges. In a sense he was right that it did not matter all that much. For a young man of Byron's rank the universities were regarded as a playground rather than as serious places of learning. For Byron the next three years were in a sense a repetition of the Harrow years, with the same pattern of frequent absences. The significant difference was that, despite the flash and the frivolity, he was beginning to garner and focus his talent.

There wasn't much that Cambridge had to teach him and by Elizabethan statutes, as a peer he was not required to sit any examinations. His general reading was probably far greater than most undergraduates. Like Dr Johnson, he "tore the heart out of a book". He read while he ate, he read in bed, he read when stretched out on the Peachey Stone. At Harrow he possessed – and displayed – so much general knowledge that it was suspected that he had culled it from reviews. In a memorandum book dated November 30, 1807, he listed his reading: biographies, historical works, the English classics, Rousseau's *Confessions*, most of the modern poets, especially Alexander Pope, whom he had loved since he first encountered his work in 1803, possibly enhanced by the fact that Pope was crippled. By the time Byron was fifteen he claimed to have read about 4,000 novels. The sceptical Hobhouse wrote in the margin of Moore's *Life*: "As Lord Byron says he read these volumes I am inclined to believe the fact, but it is certain he never gave any sign of this knowledge afterwards."[1]

One of the consolations of Southwell was the library of Mrs Byron's landlord, Mr Falkner. Here Byron discovered the *Autobiography* of Lord Herbert of Cherbury, whose views had influenced Locke and the eighteenth-century Deists and now were to have an impact on Byron, who was looking for a point of view that differed from unquestioned orthodoxy. He was particularly impressed with Herbert's view of revealed religion as the invention of a certain hierarchy, a relativist position that was to be reinforced for Byron in his travels in the Near East.

With the encouragement of Agnes and Mary Gray, he had read through the Old Testament before he was eight. He was never attracted to the New Testament, but he loved dramatic stories with characters such as Cain and Abel. Much, perhaps too much, has been made of his imbibing Calvinism at an early age from the Gray sisters. The idea of predestination was reinforced by his discovery of a semi-Gothic novel *Zeluco* (1786) by John Moore in which the misanthropic hero is fated to perform evil deeds. Undoubtedly Byron recognised something of himself when he read that Zeluco had lost his father at a very early age and "very soon after his death, he indulged, without control, every humour and caprice; and his mistaken mother applauding the blusterings of petulance and pride as indications of spirit, his temper became more and more ungovernable, and at length seemed as inflammable as gunpowder, bursting into flashes of rage at the slightest touch of provocation."[2] The fact that Byron was lame as well marked him as different from other men, and his youthful imagination was caught up by the idea that he was fated to repeat the excesses of his ancestors.

His dramatic imagination was balanced from an early age by a sardonic and sensible side to his character. He liked the image of the worldly, deistic Herbert of Cherbury: adventurous, studious, urbane. But as yet his persona fluctuated among experimental selves. Added to this was his perplexity about his wavering sexual identity. As a young man of seventeen, about to enter Cambridge, he was uncertain what role to play. He was certainly determined to cut a dash; and, as he had told his mother after Mark Drury insulted him about his lack of fortune, "I will carve myself the passage to Grandeur."

Cambridge would prove the milieu in which to stand out from the crowd; but the quiet of Southwell was to nourish his budding poetic genius. On October 24, 1805, he arrived at Cambridge at the last possible date to take up residence. He was still feeling dejected about leaving Harrow, for parting from it seemed like parting with his youth: "it was one of the deadliest and heaviest feelings of my life to feel that I was no longer a boy," he wrote in his "Detached Thoughts". "From that moment I began to grow old in my own esteem – and in my esteem age is not estimable."[3]

To his surprise he found himself delighted with his quarters in the south-east corner of the Great Court of Trinity. (The precise location is often disputed.) Next door to him was his tutor, the Reverend Thomas Jones, whom he met on his first evening, together with William Bankes and the brilliant and handsome Charles Skinner Matthews. Both Bankes and Matthews were enchanting companions, and both were homosexual. Byron was attracted by Bankes's capacity for mischief and dazzled by Matthews's beauty.

It is often suggested that all his best friends had gone on to Oxford, but who were they apart from Clare? Byron had a talent for being dissatisfied wherever he was; and when he complained that he would have preferred to have been at Oxford, it was only because he was elsewhere. At Trinity he had his one close Harrow contemporary, Edward Noel Long. Together they rode, read, and had musical evenings with Byron listening to Long play his flute. Most enjoyable of all, they swam in the Cam, diving for plates, eggs and even shillings. With Long he was still a boy without the stress of having to show off.

But college life demanded something else. Byron became very self-important as only a young man of that age can be, strutting about in his nobleman's gown with its elaborate gold embroidery. He boasted that he received more invitations than he could accept. To Hanson he despatched orders for four dozen bottles of wine and elaborate furnishings for his rooms. When Hanson protested that there was not sufficient money to pay for all this extravagance, he replied loftily: "not even the Shadow of dishonour shall reflect on *my* name, for I will see that the Bills are discharged; whether by you or not is to me indifferent, so that the men I employ are not the victims of my Imprudence or your duplicity."[4] It was very high-handed of him to take this tone with Hanson since he did not trouble himself with how little money was actually available, choosing to believe that there would be unlimited resources once he came of age. His doting mother had stinted herself by handing over to him his educational income of £500 per annum, and as a result her own pension was considerably reduced so that she could no longer keep a carriage. It never occurred to Byron to appreciate her generosity. To Augusta he complained: "I need scarcely inform you that I am not in the least obliged to Mrs B for it, as it comes off of my property, and She refused to fit out a single thing for me from her own pocket."[5]

Mrs Byron was determined not to get into debt; but this was impossible to avoid while Byron kept three horses and purchased a carriage. Eager for him to live according to his rank, she enabled him to have one of the best incomes in the college. But neither Byron nor his mother deserve blame. Both were victims of institutionalised extravagance. Moneylenders were on hand because aristocrats were expected to live beyond their means. But when Byron's excesses soon became apparent, his mother threatened to descend on Cambridge; to which Byron warned Hanson: "the instant I hear of her arrival, I quit Cambridge, though *Rustication* or *Expulsion* be the consequence."[6] He began to be seen more often at the theatre in London than in Cambridge, and Hanson warned him that the Court of Chancery might cut off his allowance if he did not return to the university.

Byron was entering the world of *Vanity Fair*, plunging rapidly into the financial maelstrom in which young men like Thackeray's Honourable George Boulter floundered. The language of the time was filled with terms such as "bolting", "doing a bolt", "doing a Levant"; and many young men decamped to the continent where they were either immune from arrest for debt or could negotiate with their creditors as Becky Sharp did with Rawdon's creditors. Naturally Byron fell into the hands of the money-lenders, many of them Jewish (hence the term "doing a Levant"). On March 4, 1806, his distraught mother wrote frantically to Hanson:

> He knows I am doing everything in my power to pay his Debts and he writes to me about hiring Servants and the last time he wrote to me was to desire me to send him £25:0:0, to pay his Harrow Bills which I would have done if I had had as much as he has – three hundred – God knows what is to be done with him. I much fear he is already ruined; at eighteen!!! Great God I am distracted I can say no more.[7]

This was the public side of his life which was confusion enough; but within two weeks of his arrival in Cambridge he had fallen in love with a chorister younger than himself by two years to the day. As Byron later wrote of this period, he did not join in the general dissipation of the undergraduates, "for my early passions, though violent in the extreme, were concentrated . . . I could have left or lost the world with or for that which I loved."[8] He and John Edelston met every day; and he insisted of course that it was "a violent, though *pure*, love and passion", which apparently did not exclude kisses and caresses.

The question again arises: what did Byron mean by "pure"? Professor Marchand believes that "Stanzas to Jessy", written in the summer of 1807, was addressed to Edelston.

> There is a bosom all my own,
> 	Has pillow'd oft this aching head,
> A mouth, which smiles on me alone,
> 	An eye, whose tears with mine are shed.
>
> There are two hearts whose movements thrill
> 	In unison so closely sweet,
> That pulse to pulse responsive still,
> 	They both must heave, or cease to beat.

These lines suggest that anything short of sexual congress constituted "purity".

Elizabeth Pigot was to become his confidante about this infatuation. Byron told her, "He is nearly my height, very thin, very fair complexion, dark eyes, and light locks":[9] precisely Byron's picture of ideal beauty. Again: "He certainly is perhaps more attached to me than ever I am in return":[10] Byron's preferred sort of adulation. He refers to himself as Edelston's "patron", so it seems highly likely that Byron lavished gifts on him. On July 5, 1807, Byron describes his emotions as "a Chaos of hope and sorrow" at the prospect of parting from Edelston who had to leave for work in London. The very fact that he wrote so openly about him to Elizabeth Pigot would seem to rule out a sexual relationship but not a homo-erotic one. "I certainly love him more than any human being." Did he, then, let Edelston disappear from his life? In a state of total fantasy, he talked about their planning to live together like the ladies of Llangollen, famous lesbians of the time. Edelston left Cambridge in October and Byron was in London from January until mid-June of 1808. Is it too much to surmise that it was partly Edelston who drew him there?

In 1805 he had begun to mention bouts of melancholy. These had started at Harrow but were to become more severe in his late teens, a common pattern with manic depression although the temper tantrums in childhood were a warning signal. Kay Redfield Jamison has presented a brilliant case for Byron as a manic-depressive rather than a schizophrenic.[11] She bases her argument on the fluctuating nature of his disease, with pronounced oscillations of mood, whereas with schizophrenia the condition is chronic, most notably characterised by the inability to reason clearly.

The constant movement, the different levels on which he was living, provided distractions from himself, but it was poetry that was to provide the most sustaining means of controlling his black moods. While he might rail histrionically against Southwell, it was in this sleepy little town that his latent talent was nourished by the encouragement and practical help of the Pigot family.

Byron had started writing poetry at Harrow, inspired by one of his young votaries, William Harness. In his innocent bravado he thought the world would be interested in the details of his life since they were those of a young peer under twenty-one. This combination, he believed, would prove his entrée to fame. To his kinsman, Robert Charles Dallas, he wrote on January 20, 1808: "The events of my short life have been of so singular a nature, that though the pride, commonly called honour, has, and I trust ever will prevent me from disgracing my name by a mean or cowardly action, I have been already held up as a votary of Licentiousness and the Disciple of Infidelity." Byron had an instinctive knowledge of how to market himself.

With the encouragement of Elizabeth Pigot's cousin, the Reverend J.T. Becher, he took his poems to a well-known printer, John Ridge, in the nearby town of Newark, at the beginning of August 1806. A furious row with his mother occasioned his flight from Southwell soon afterwards so that a good many of the instructions about their publication had to be despatched through Elizabeth's brother, John Pigot, while Byron was staying near his friend Long at Littlehampton on the south coast. More poems were added to the collection in October; and they were finally issued anonymously in November as *Fugitive Pieces*. It was indeed a miscellany: some poems on Newstead; love poems addressed to a mysterious "Caroline"; Dr Butler was ridiculed as "Pomposus" in "On a Change of Masters at a Great Public School". The Reverend Becher was outraged by the frankly erotic "To Mary" which had been inspired by Thomas Moore's *The Poetical Works of the Late Thomas Little* (1801):

> Now, by my soul, 'tis most delight
>   To view each other panting, dying,
>   In love's *ecstatic posture* lying,
> Grateful to *feeling*, as to *sight*.

Byron had gone too far, even naming a number of young ladies in the town. He had flirted with one in particular, Julia Leacroft, with whom he participated in local theatricals. Her family felt that he had been acting irresponsibly with her; and in the revised version she was transformed into "Lesbia". He might profess to despise Southwell but he was certainly not going to lose its good opinion over his work, which he took very seriously indeed. On November 26 he ruefully went around collecting all his presentation copies and burned the lot (four escaped, including Becher's copy).

It says much for Byron's determination that he immediately set about compiling a revised version. "To Mary" was suppressed. He fictionalised the names of the other young ladies, making the volume "vastly correct and miraculously chaste", as he described it to John Pigot. The most significant omission was "L'Amitié Est L'Amour Sans Ailes" with its paean to Lord Clare ("My Lycus") and the reference to the quarrel with Delawarr:

> In one, and one alone deceived,
> Did I my error mourn?
> No – from oppressive bonds relieved,
> I left the wretch to scorn.

This was not to be published until after his death.

By March he was working on yet another collection, *Hours of Idleness*, which was published in June 1807. This excessive haste was due to his compulsion to appear in print before he had reached his majority. The Preface is particularly interesting for its attempt to divert possible criticism. Byron announces himself immediately as a young man "who has lately completed his nineteenth year". Some of the poems had been written, he admitted disingenuously, "during the disadvantages of illness, and depression of spirits". They had been printed, he avows, at the request of a partial social circle. He assures his readers that poetry is not his "primary vocation". While he had passed his childhood as a careless mountaineer in the Highlands of Scotland, he had long been away from his natural haunts and hence had been deprived of the inspiration of genuine bards. This volume, he promised, was to be his first and last attempt at poesy. Was ever a Preface so silly, so callow, or so touching!

As for the poems, they were clearly written by a young man who takes himself very seriously, particularly as he is aware that the best of life is behind him. He romanticises himself as the descendant of a noble race. There are the usual laments to lost love, in his case Mary Chaworth. His very special friends at Harrow receive tributes: this time he softens his complaints about Delawarr in the hope of a reconciliation, "That both may be wrong, and that both should forgive." Nevertheless, he realises that these friendships were "too romantic to last". In the poems to Newstead Abbey and in "Lachin Y Gair" we have the sentimentalist lamenting a past that can never be recovered, and a longing for a time when he can return to a wild nature where he can recover his true self. More important, we have the first instance of Byron creating a poetic persona, "A being more intense" (*Childe Harold*, III, 6) than other men.[12]

There are also references to his present life, particularly in the poems clearly addressed to Edelston. In "To E. –" he begs him to disregard their inequality of rank; and "The Cornelian" is a gushing effusion about a stone the blushing youth had given him. He urged Long not to divulge the identity of "The Cornelian" and was distressed when he learned that he had shown a copy of the volume to William Bankes whose acerbic tongue he feared. Bankes, however, sent him a letter of measured but appreciative criticism. In reply Byron expressed the inevitable anticlimax following the publication of the work, complaining of his low spirits and his determination to leave Cambridge for good. Actually a return to Cambridge was impossible because by now his debts had mounted to frightening heights.

Byron seemed totally incapable of handling the freedom that life at Cambridge had suddenly offered him. If one traces his life from early 1806 until his departure from England in 1809, it is understandable why flight would seem the only alternative open to him. His letters chart a wavering course of mood swings, alternating between states of hyperactivity, a sense of omnipotence and wild spirits, followed by paranoia and prolonged periods of inactivity, sadness, and despair.

At the beginning of 1807 Augusta expressed her concern about his sinking spirits; and in reply to her anxious questions he assured her (January 7, 1806) that his health was fine and that he had no problems in love. In short, he did not know the cause of his depression. He admitted that he was already deeply in debt and asked her if she would act as guarantor to a loan. Perplexed, she went to Lord Carlisle for advice and asked Hanson to come and discuss the situation with her. When Byron heard this he flew into a fury. Regarding her action as a betrayal by the person he most trusted, he broke off all communication with his sister for the next two years. He managed to borrow several hundred pounds from a moneylender at a ruinous rate of interest:* "I happen to have a few

---

* This he was able to do through his London landlady, Mrs Massingberd, who stood surety for him. The proprietor of his London hotel, Mr Dorant, acted as co-signer. Mrs Massingberd profited from this arrangement. Byron later introduced Scrope Davies to her and they used her Piccadilly boarding-house as a rendezvous with usurers (Burnett, p.75).

hundreds in ready Cash lying by me," he airily informed his mother (February 26, 1806). The university had nothing to teach him, he declared, and he had decided that he would learn more if he spent a couple of years abroad. His mother's hysterical reaction was predictable, and one cannot help feeling pity for the anguish she expresses in a letter to Hanson (March 4, 1806):

> That Boy will be the death of me, and drive me mad! I will never consent to his going Abroad. Where can he get Hundreds? Has he got into the hands of Moneylenders? he has no feeling, no Heart. This I have long known; he has behaved as ill as possible for years back. This bitter Truth I can no longer conceal; it is wrung from me by heart-rending agony.[3]

The plans for going abroad were abandoned during the rest of 1806 as he plunged into the arrangements for the publication of his poems. Temporarily subdued by the Southwell reaction to the first volume, on February 6, 1807, he complained to Lord Clare about his depressed spirits, adding, 'for my attentions have been divided amongst so many *fair damsels*, and the drugs I swallow are of such variety in their composition, that between Venus and Aetsculapius [sic] I am harassed to death." Bankes also heard about his depression (March 1807). He describes himself as "a solitary animal, miserable enough, and so perfectly a Citizen of the World, that whether I pass my days in Great Britain, or Kamchatka, is to me, a matter of perfect Indifference."[4]

Byron believed himself destined never to be happy. "I am an isolated Being on the Earth, without a Tie to attach me to life, except a few School-fellows, and a *score of females*."[5] Religion offered him no consolation. Life meant so little to him, he claimed, that death held no fears. At the same time he was taking drastic measures to re-create himself. By now immensely fat – at five feet eight inches he weighed over fourteen stone – he was intent on losing weight with manic intensity. To Hanson he described his daily regimen (April 2, 1807):

> I wear *seven* Waistcoats, & a great Coat, run and play at Cricket in this Dress, till quite exhausted by excessive perspiration, use the hot Bath daily, eat only a quarter of [a] pound [of] Butchers meat in 24 hours, no Suppers, or Breakfast, only one meal a Day, drink no malt Liquor, [only?] little Wine, take physic occasionally, by these means, my *Ribs* display Skin of no great Thickness, & my

Clothes, have been taken in nearly *half a yard*, do you believe me now?

In the following months his friends were informed of *exactly* how much weight he was shedding, and how people were amazed at the transformation in him. At the same time he was busily preparing a new volume of poems. He was madly in love with Edelston. His debts were by now so pressing that he could not possibly return to Cambridge. There were references to gambling. He plunged into the world of boxing and the demi-monde, boasting of having two mistresses, yet they seemed to afford him little pleasure. He professed himself pleased by a review of *Hours of Idleness* although he knew perfectly well that it appeared in a journal owned by his bookseller. He made plans for a journey to Scotland and immediately abandoned them. He swam three miles down the Thames.

What are we to make of all this? He could not change his foot but he *could* control his body. The marathon swim – the first of many – was a triumph over his deformity. Perhaps he could escape destitution by seizing fame. These were months of mania. Apparently having raised enough money to pay off some of his debts, by October Byron was back at Cambridge, this time accompanied by a tame bear, and he was proud to report that he had wittily announced that the animal was to sit for a Fellowship (to Elizabeth Pigot, October 26, 1807). He had written 214 pages of a novel. Bitterly stung by a review in the *Satirist*, he was already planning his revenge in a poem that would eventually appear as *English Bards and Scotch Reviewers*. At the same time he was making plans for a long sea voyage with his cousin, George Bettesworth, "to the Mediterranean, or to the West Indies, or to the Devil".

Then he decided to stay on at Cambridge, having made some new friends. He renewed his acquaintance with Charles Skinner Matthews who in turn introduced him to John Cam Hobhouse. Hobhouse had initially avoided him since he regarded him as a rather silly, affected young man who "wore a *white hat*, and a *grey* coat, and rode a *grey* horse".[16] Hobhouse, a basically serious chap, was inclined to look more kindly on him now that Byron had already published some poetry. He himself had recently brought out an imitation of one of Juvenal's satires. Another new literary acquaintance was Francis Hodgson, a tutor at King's. Seven years older than Byron, he impressed Byron because his father was a friend of William Gifford, whose satires, *Maeviad* and *Baviad*, Byron greatly admired. Hodgson was a fussy, pedantic clergyman, also given to depressions;

and he quickly became devoted to Byron whose mortal soul he was intent on saving. He was determined to persuade him to give up gambling.

Hobhouse introduced Byron to other members of his set, an interesting group of young men who considered themselves wildly dissolute. Matthews, whom he had already met, had occupied Byron's rooms during his absence, and had been amused by Jones, Byron's tutor, warning him to be careful not to cause any damage because Lord Byron was "a young man of *tumultuous passions*". Byron's life of dissipation continued with his new friends but they were not altogether frivolous as they had formed a Whig Club of which Byron soon became a member. One of its members was Douglas Kinnaird who later became Byron's banker and staunch friend. All these young men were lifelong Whigs who had supported Charles James Fox until his death in 1806. They shared Byron's enthusiasm for Napoleon whom they saw as ushering in a new age of freedom against ancient oppression.

These companions, not his Harrow acolytes, were to form the core of a devoted group of lifelong friends. They were worldly and intelligent. Their protectiveness and loyalty to Byron through all the vicissitudes of his life give us a sense of the generosity, vivacity and integrity they recognised in him despite the posturing, the melancholia, and swift changes of mood. "Vain, overbearing, conceited, suspicious and jealous", Scrope Davies once described him.[7] Byron would often moan, "I shall go mad"; to which Davies would retort in his charming stammer, "Much more like silliness than madness." But there was an honest directness to Byron also, and clearly he radiated a charisma that we can only imagine from the way others described him.

By Byron's twentieth birthday in January 1808 he was in debt to the tune of £5,000. He told Hanson semi-facetiously that he was thinking of converting his title into cash although, since he was only a baron, he didn't expect that it would fetch much. He could not return to Cambridge without paying his college bills. Thus, a good part of the year was spent in London working on his new poems and cavorting with the amusing Scrope Berdmore Davies, who directed most of his own intelligence into his gambling. Davies also introduced Byron to the world of the dandies who would be influential in forming his public persona.

Scrope, five years older than Byron, impressed him with his wit and steady nerve, marks of a true dandy. He had been a friend of Beau Brummell from their Eton days together. Like Brummell, he constructed *bons mots*. (When asked if he ever ate vegetables, Brummell replied, "Madam, I once ate a pea.") Scrope's insouciance and simple elegant

clothes served as much as a role model for Byron as any of his contemporaries. Like Brummell, he drew attention to himself not by flam-
boyance, but by the restraint of his dress, his spotless linen, a cravat
impeccably folded, highly polished boots. The dandy was a rebel armed
with invincible self-assurance, a Mr Darcy who scorns the vulgar crowd.

To Hobhouse Byron reported that he and Davies were now members of
the Cocoa Tree Club "and next week the dice will rattle – My worldly
affairs are not over flourishing, but that is a common case."[18] We have no
way of knowing how much Byron lost in gambling, but excess led to excess.
Scrope won and lost fortunes overnight, and eventually had to flee to the
continent. Unlike Byron, without a title he had no alternative to debtors'
prison except flight. Scrope's most famous exploit occurred the night his
intoxicated friends left him in despair at the gaming table. The next day,
when they visited him, they found him asleep with the chamber pot stuffed
with notes – and with no recollection of how he had won them. Byron, who
lived for sensation, admired this coolness immensely; and years later in
"Detached Thoughts" wrote reflectively:

I have a notion that Gamblers are as happy as most people – being
always *excited* – women – wine – fame – the table – even Ambition –
sate now & then; but every turn of the card & cast of the dice – keeps
the Gambler alive – besides one can Game ten times longer than one
can do any thing else.[19]

With Byron's appetite for sensation it is interesting that he did not
become a compulsive gambler. Scrope was a risk-taker, like all gamblers;
and Byron, who lived on the edge in other ways, could recognise the manic
intensity of the addict. His own feverish excitement was a mask for the
anger and humiliation he experienced from two unfavourable reviews of
Hours of Idleness, particularly disturbing after an initially favourable
response. The first appeared in the *Monthly Monitor* in January 1808. It
was suggested by the anonymous reviewer that perhaps these poems were
school exercises for which the author deserved to have been whipped.
Byron considered challenging the reviewer to a duel. His next response was
flight. To his old Harrow schoolfellow, James de Bathe, he suggested not
the usual Grand Tour but a voyage to the eastern Mediterranean
(February 2, 1808), the first time he had considered the actual locale
where he would eventually travel.

Worse was to come. Nothing had prepared him for the sheer vitriol of
the *Edinburgh Review* in May, even though he had wind of it weeks before its

appearance. Byron suspected the author to be Francis Jeffrey (a member of the Holland House set), but it was actually Henry Brougham, one of the founders of the *Review*, who was to continue his animus against Byron in later years. In Italy Byron told Thomas Medwin that when he first saw the review of *Hours of Idleness*, he was in such a rage as he had never experienced since. His fury can be imagined as he read: "The poesy of this young lord belongs to the class which neither gods nor men are said to permit. His effusions are spread over a dead flat, and can no more get above or below the level, than if they were so much stagnant water." The writer had a merry time with the disclaimers Byron had made about his youth, in the hope that his age would allay criticism. Byron was in a puzzled rage as to why a Whig journal (which *should* have known he was a Whig, he naïvely argued) would attack him. He petulantly threatened to resign from the Cambridge Whig Club, and of course soon changed his mind. But revenge he was determined to have.

His immediate reaction was to plunge into "an abyss of Sensuality" (February 27, 1808) in order to forget that his little fabric of fame had been "completely demolished". Two days later he was "as miserable in mind & Body, as Literary abuse, pecuniary embarrassment, and total enervation can make me. – I have tried every kind of pleasure, and it is 'Vanity'."[20] He retired to his room at Durant's Hotel to console himself with laudanum.

Scrope meanwhile had returned to Cambridge with news of Byron. A disturbed Hobhouse lectured him like a Dutch uncle: "Those nightly vigils & daily slumbers, that habit of agitating your mind & body in the pernicious exercise of midnight gambling, were they not enough, together with that total want of air & healthy exercise which you experienced, to weaken and exhaust your frame to the very last extremity?"[21] He had been relieved, at least, to hear from Scrope Davies that Byron had given up gambling.

How, Byron wondered, would his mother feel about the attacks on him? Her pride in him meant more than Byron would ever acknowledge. Through Becher he sent her a despondent letter announcing that he was going to renounce poetry for ever. Her very sensible response was "God help him if he is so easily discouraged."[22]

Of course he had no intention of renouncing poetry since he was already at work on the new volume that would comprise *English Bards and Scotch Reviewers*. According to Jerome McGann, he had initially started the poems while flushed with the early success of *Hours of Idleness*, but Brougham's attack effected a change from aloof satire to fierce invective. His fury was not diminished in May when Hewson Clarke, editor of the *Satirist*, printed caustic passages of reviews of *Hours of Idleness* from the *Eclectic*, the *Monthly Mirror*, and the *Edinburgh Review*. These reviewers had been quick to pick up on the vulnerability of the self-protective tone he had adopted to ward off criticism. Perhaps in an effort to divert him, Scrope Davies and Hobhouse persuaded him to accompany them to Brighton in July. Byron took with him his latest whore dressed as a boy. They all lost at gaming. After a plunge in the sea, Scrope and Hobhouse quarrelled violently and Hobhouse stabbed Scrope; but the next day the incident was put behind them. Hobhouse was the most sensible man in the set; but it is not to be wondered at that his father, a prosperous merchant with political ambitions, strongly disapproved of his son's way of life and his questionable associates.

During that summer of 1808 Byron renewed his ties with Harrow. This was done with reluctance through prodding from Henry Drury. Byron felt embarrassed about confronting Dr Butler after the impertinent verses he had written about him. Nostalgic memories eventually drew him back, and once again he saw his old comrades Wingfield, Harness, and also Delawarr with whom he seems to have made his peace. He was greeted like a hero by the younger boys who loved the cheek with which he had twitted Butler as "Pomposus".

However, some sort of reconciliation seems to have taken place between him and the headmaster because on February 11 he wrote to Ridge, his printer, that he must suppress "Childish Recollections" from the second edition of *Hours of Idleness*: "It is better my Reputation should suffer as a poet by the omission, than as a man of honour by the Insertion."[23] As a result, he felt comfortable enough to make several excursions to the school during the spring and summer.

His relationship with Cambridge was less tranquil. In "Thoughts Suggested by a College Examination" (1806) he had ridiculed the ponderous dons:

> Vain as their honours, heavy as their Ale,
> Sad as their wit, and tedious as their tale,
> To friendship dead, though not untaught to feel,
> When Self and Church demand a Bigot zeal.

The stipulations for residency applying to noblemen were notoriously lax, but at the least peers were required to pass nine terms there to obtain their BA. Byron had spent at the most three full terms and made occasional appearances during part of two others. Nevertheless, he was determined to get his degree. On February 29 he told Hobhouse: "It is not very probable that I shall again appear at Cambridge till my degree is granted, and *that* is very problematical." However, by sheer persistence the university was persuaded to grant him an MA on July 4, 1808.

Lord Grey's lease on Newstead finally expired in June 1808. Byron had spent little time in the abbey since his arrival in 1798, yet now it was fully his – indebted, neglected, and as romantic as ever. He had occasionally told Hanson that he considered selling it to pay off his debts, but once he actually saw it again, nothing would induce him to part with it. Early in September he moved in, accompanied by his pet bear. Willam Fletcher, the son of one of his tenants, who had been his groom now became his valet, and Joe Murray was happy to return as the head retainer. Byron was sad to see that the oak tree he had planted had withered away, but he installed a plunge bath where he cavorted with his bear.

The roof was leaking and workmen were engaged to carry out makeshift repairs, as Byron began to make ambitious plans to entertain his friends. He installed a large four-poster in his bedroom, covered the walls with pictures of his boxing companion, "Gentleman" Jackson, and views of Cambridge and Harrow. A local boy, Robert Rushton, had become his page and occupied a small room leading off the main bedroom.

One person who was not welcome was his mother. In August Mrs Byron – exhausted by worry – began to feel seriously ill. She never seems to have fully recovered and it is possible she was suffering from some form of stomach or colon cancer. Whether Byron knew anything about this or not is not known. Preoccupied with his own affairs, he never enquired after her health. On October 7 he wrote in reply to an attempt at a reconciliation, in which Mrs Byron must have tried to flatter him by telling him that she thought he resembled Jean-Jacques Rousseau. He used the opportunity to establish a distance between them very firmly.

I have no ambition to be like so illustrious a madman, but this I know, that I shall live in my own manner, and as much alone as possible, when my rooms are ready, I shall be glad to see you, at present it would be improper, & uncomfortable to both parties – You can hardly object to my rendering my mansion habitable, notwithstanding my departure for Persia in March (or May at farthest) since *you* will be the *tenant* till my return, and in case of any accident (for I have already arranged my will to be drawn up the moment I am twenty-one) I have taken care you shall have the house and manor for *life*, besides a sufficient income. – So you see my improvements are not entirely selfish.[24]

If not "entirely selfish", they were totally unrealistic. It is also possible that Mrs Byron preferred her quiet life in Southwell to the multitude of vexations that Newstead would impose upon her.

On October 12, 1808, Byron and Hobhouse attended the Infirmary Ball in Nottingham, and here for the first time since Mary Chaworth's marriage to Jack Musters three years before, they met again. Byron was no longer a pudgy callow youth but now slender, handsome, with wavy chestnut hair. Mary, who was already beginning to be disenchanted with Jack for his infidelities, was in a vulnerable emotional state.

The two young men were invited to a dinner party at Annesley Hall. Hobhouse was puzzled by the fact that Byron and their hostess sat there in embarrassed silence. When Mary's little daughter was brought in, Byron's discomfiture was complete. Byron knew Hobhouse would laugh at his emotions but to Francis Hodgson he recounted (November 3) the awkwardness of the incident: "What fools we! We cry for a plaything, which like children we are never satisfied till we break it open, though like them, we cannot get rid of it, by putting it in the fire." He also sent Hodgson some stanzas (November 27) – "Hobhouse hates everything of the kind" – "Well! Thou Art Happy" and "To Mrs Musters on being asked my Reasons for Quitting England in the Spring". In the first he poured out his painful feelings:

> When late I saw thy favourite child,
>   I thought my jealous heart would break;
> But when th' unconscious infant smil'd,
>   I kiss'd it, for its mother's sake.
>
> I kiss'd it, and repress'd my sighs
>   Its father in its face to see;
> But then it had its mother's eyes,
>   And they were all to love and me.
>   ("Well! Thou Art Happy", 3–4)

The title of the second was later to be changed to "Stanzas to a Lady on Leaving England" with its refrain:

> And I must from this land begone,
> Because I cannot love but one.

Hobhouse might scoff, but he was later to publish it in a miscellany of poems he collected which included some of his own rather pedestrian efforts.

Byron spent three more months at Newstead. Always a lover of animals, he was greatly distressed when his beloved Newfoundland dog, Boatswain, died of rabies while cradled in his arms: "I have now lost everything except Old Murray."[25] The dog was buried close to the abbey; Byron expressed the wish to be buried in a tomb which was eventually built for the dog for whom he wrote the following epitaph:

> Near this spot
> Are deposited the Remains of one
> Who possessed Beauty without Vanity,
> Strength without Insolence,
> Courage without Ferocity,
> And all the Virtues of Man without his Vices.
> This Praise, which would be unmeaning Flattery
> If inscribed over human ashes,
> Is but a just tribute to the Memory of BOATSWAIN,
> a Dog . . .

A reconciliation with Augusta had gradually been developing. In a gesture of propitiation Byron had sent a copy of *Hours of Idleness* to Lord Carlisle when it was first published, with an obsequious dedication from "his obliged ward and affectionate kinsman". Carlisle replied courteously – urging him not to feel discouraged if he did not receive the praise he hoped for – and enclosing some of his own poems. But there was no communication with Augusta who had finally married George Leigh in August 1807 and they had settled in a rambling house, Six Mile Bottom, near the Prince of Wales's stud farm at Newmarket.

George had been sent off to Spain in the British expeditionary force under Sir John Moore; and, after Madrid was retaken by Napoleon in December, he was part of the bitter winter retreat over the mountains of northern Spain to Corunna. He was far from home when his first child, Georgiana, was born on November 4, 1808. On November 30 Byron wrote to his now once more "dearest Augusta" to congratulate her on making him an uncle, "but the next must be a nephew". He was living alone at Newstead and reverted to the grievance she had heard so any times in the past – namely, his mother. "I can never forgive that woman, or breathe in comfort under the same roof. I am a very unlucky fellow, for I think I had naturally not a bad heart; but it has been so bent, twisted, and trampled on, that it has now become as hard as a Highlander's heel-piece." If this were so, it was because the poor silly woman had indulged him to the point of breaking under the strain of the burden of her indulgence.

Byron, caught on the upswing of one of his over-optimistic periods, painted an unrealistically favourable picture of his finances for his sister. Good old Hanson would attend to all the tiresome details, such as the prolonged negotiations for untangling the affairs of the Rochdale property. On November 15 Byron dismissed them: "As to myself, I have no great curiosity in the business." A pity, because if he had shown some interest, he would have had a more realistic perception of how matters stood.*

The grandiose plans for the Eastern trip continued to occupy his mind. On November 18 he was contemplating India. His letter sounds almost responsible in part; and Hanson must have been astonished when he read: "I am young, tolerably vigorous, abstemious in my way of living, and I am determined to take a wider field than is customary with travellers." He saw this journey as a maturing process which would prepare him for politics. To travel abroad for about six months would be far less expensive than to maintain an establishment in London, especially as he would leave his mother in Newstead – "there is one great expense saved". After this series of sage observations, he issued commands:

> You honour my debts; they amount to perhaps twelve thousand pounds, and I shall require perhaps three or four thousand at setting out, with credit on a Bengal agent. This you must manage for me. If my resources are not adequate to the supply I must *sell*, but *not Newstead*. I will at least transmit that to the next Lord. My debts must be paid, if possible, in February.[26]

If Hanson let out an oath of incredulity on learning – so casually – that Byron's debts had more than doubled within a year, one can sympathise with him. Most of Byron's admirers have accepted his view of Hanson as dilatory; but what is puzzling is why Hanson simply didn't wash his hands of the whole insoluble mess. When he told Byron that the tangle over the Rochdale estates had not yet been resolved, Byron replied (December 17): "I suppose it will end in my marrying a *Golden Dolly* or blowing my brains out, it does not much matter which, the Remedies are nearly alike." His mother repeatedly told the agent that she could see no solution to his

---

* These were the estates that had been sold illegally by the fifth lord. If Hanson had exerted himself more, Doris Langley Moore believes that Byron might have been a rich man because they comprised immensely productive quarries and coal mines.

problems except a good marriage. Nevertheless, earlier in the year he had made a bet of a hundred guineas that he would never marry. Matrimony would be a last resource, associated only with ruin.

The cold winter of 1808–9 settled in. Byron exercised his *droit de seigneur* and one of the servant girls, Lucy, became pregnant. (He had already at least one child by a London whore.)* Byron instructed Hanson to pay an annuity of £100 to the girl (January 17, 1809). According to Professor Marchand he altered his will only a month later, reducing the sum to £50 for Lucy and £50 for the illegitimate child who was probably the subject of "To My Son"

> Why, let the world unfeeling frown,
> Must I fond Nature's claim disown?
> Ah, no – though moralists reprove,
> I hail thee, dearest child of love . . .

Surely even curiosity prompted him to hold the child in his arms? But Lucy disappeared from the scene – as most servant girls were supposed to do when heavy with embarrassment.

Christmas he spent entirely alone at Newstead after various friends had pleaded other engagements. "I am a mighty scribbler," he told Augusta. This scribbling was the careful polishing of *English Bards and Scotch Reviewers*, intended to wreak vengeance on his critics in the coming year.

* Thomas Moore includes an interesting anecdote which he probably obtained from Elizabeth Pigot. While at Harrow some girl became pregnant and claimed Byron as the father. He wrote to his mother that the child was Curzon's who had recently died, but asked her if she would look after it. She agreed; but it was said to have died in infancy (I, p. 104).

5

ooooooooooooooo

Bitter-Sweet Departure,
January–July 1809

Byron's predominant feeling as his twenty-first birthday drew near
was of embarrassment. From an abnormally early age he had
dreaded the eventuality of ageing. He would have preferred to have
stayed fifteen for ever. In addition, he realised that a peer was supposed to
celebrate the occasion with great *éclat* and he simply did not have the funds
to do it in style. He planned to stay away from Newstead because his
presence would be like 'a Corpse of the Funeral solemnized in its honour".[1]

Hanson was told to expect him in London on January 19, 1809; and on
his birthday – the 22nd – the tenants would celebrate with roast oxen, a
sheep, and plenty of ale. Hanson urged him to dine with his family in their
new home in Chancery Lane on the great evening, but he declined.
Hanson then agreed to represent him at Newstead for the festivities which,
Joe Murray grumbled, were falling far short of the wild carousing when the
fifth lord came of age. Byron's only concession to the occasion was to dine
on his favourite food – bacon and eggs and a bottle of ale – which he
usually avoided because it disagreed with him.

When Hanson also congratulated Mrs Byron, she replied: "I hope my
son will *conduct* himself thro' life in a way to do honour to *both* the great
families from whom he is descended and that he will be of *service* to his
country. Of his talents there can be *no* doubt."[2]

Both mother and son were aware at last, in their own ways, of the
seriousness of the financial situation. Now that he was twenty-one, Byron's
creditors began to descend on him in earnest, and he complained to
Hanson that he was "*dunned* from Morn till Twilight".[3] He began to
question petty details like the cost of a mustard pot and a cup he had
ordered made from a skull found on the property. He asked Hanson if the
tenants' rents could be raised and wanted the servants put on "board

wages" – that is, they would cater for themselves so that they could not run up extravagant bills. The staff was cut to a minimum and wages reduced.

Mrs Byron saw only ruination through the cost of running Newstead, for there was no possibility of those Rochdale coal mines being alchemised into gold. No, like many young men before him, he would have to marry for money. Remembering her own situation, she declared that "love matches is all nonsense." Hanson asked him to consider selling Newstead. To his mother Byron expostulated dramatically:

> *Newstead* and I *stand* or fall together, I have now lived on the spot, I have fixed my heart upon it, and no pressure present or future, shall induce me to barter the last vestige of our inheritance; I have that Pride within me, which will enable me to support difficulties, I can endure privations, but could I obtain exchange for Newstead Abbey the first fortune in the country, I would reject the proposition.[4]

Byron had recently told Augusta that he would have nothing to do with his mother, but occasionally she served as a useful appendage. He urged her to obtain a loan for him from her inheritance. But Mrs Byron was afraid, she told Hanson, that he would leave the country with debts unhonoured: "There is some Trades People in Nottingham that will be *completely* ruined if he does not pay them which I would not have happen for the whole *World*. He must really impower you & me to act for him when he is abroad, which he talks of doing, but he is so *unsteady* and *thoughtless* with the *best heart* in the world."[5]

Early in the year his plans were to depart in May – this time for Sicily – with a new companion, a naval man, Lord Falkland. But there were two important events to be attended to first: his introduction into the House of Lords and the publication of *English Bards and Scotch Reviewers*. Enter the rather seedy figure of a relative, Robert Charles Dallas, thirty years his senior, and author of some less than minor novels. He had written to Byron to congratulate him on *Hours of Idleness* when it was published two years before. His claim of kinship was tenuous indeed since his sister had been married to Byron's uncle, George Anson Byron. The son of a physician in Jamaica, Dallas had moved between the West Indies, America, and France, and was always hard up.

Byron asked Dallas to call on him at Reddish's Hotel on his birthday. His main reason for seeing Dallas was to ask his advice on how to get his poem published. Byron was in one of his manic moods. He seemed gay at first, then launched into a bitter attack on the Earl of Carlisle. He had written to Carlisle as his nominal guardian asking him to present him in the House of

Lords. According to Byron, he had received a cool reply giving him the technical details of the procedures for entrance. As a result, Byron lashed out at Augusta and swore he would not speak to her again, and continued to rage against the *Edinburgh Review*. Mrs Byron shared her son's indignation when she heard about Carlisle's unwillingness. To Hanson she wrote: "Lord Carlisle just behaved as I expected. I wish he may live to see my Son as superior to himself in all respects as he is at present above him in talents as an author."[6] At this point Dallas could smell a possible opportunity, and eagerly offered his services in the search for a suitable publisher.

As a result of Carlisle's lack of cooperation, Hanson was obliged to look up records tracing Byron's legitimacy, a costly and humiliating procedure. Byron had initially written some complimentary prefatory lines to Carlisle, but he now altered them to the following:

> No Muse will cheer with renovating smile,
> The paralytic puling of CARLISLE:
> The puny Schoolboy and his early lay
> Men pardon, if his follies pass away;
> But who forgives the Senior's ceaseless verse,
> Whose hairs grow hoary as his rhymes grow worse?

Dallas advised against this insertion, fearing that it would reveal the identity of the anonymous author. He also suggested the title, "The Parish Poor of Parnassus", and sent along a number of poems of his own to be included with those of Byron. These Byron politely declined and suggested a title of his own – *English Bards and Scotch Reviewers* – by which title the volume was eventually to appear. Dallas's own publisher, Longman, turned it down, but finally Dallas came to an agreement with James Cawthorn for an edition of 1,000 copies, although Byron had the sense to realise this was an excessive number even for a poetry-reading public. Byron was infuriated by Longman's rejection; and when he later gave Dallas the copyright of *Childe Harold's Pilgrimage*, it was on condition that it not be published by this house.

Byron's life was never without incident. His old friend Edward Long was drowned early in the year when his ship, bound for the Peninsular War in Portugal, collided with another ship. It does not reflect well on Hobhouse that he laughed at what he considered Byron's excessive grief and made lampoons on the word "long". Hobhouse had begun to be possessive of his friendship with Byron and displayed real jealousy over anyone else to whom he seemed to be attached.

Then in early March another friend, Lord Falkland, was killed in a drunken duel. When Falkland's child was born after his death, Byron dropped £500 into the christening cup – a lordly gesture, but reckless considering the tradesmen who had not yet been paid. The widow took this as a gesture of affection, and was later to pursue Byron with unwelcome offers of love.

Because they were in almost daily contact over the details of publication, Dallas managed to create a sort of intimacy with Byron. Scholars have tended to reject Dallas's statements that he influenced Byron in altering certain lines, but from letters of his own that he published in *Recollections of the Life of Lord Byron*, it seems that this was frequently true because Byron regarded him as far more experienced than himself.

It is distressing to think that Dallas was the only person available to accompany Byron the day he entered the House of Lords. Byron had already told Hanson that he would "studiously avoid a connection with ministry. – I cannot say that my opinion is strongly in favour of either party" (January 15, 1809). He wasn't impressed with the views of any of them, he intended to speak seldom, and "As to *patriotism* The word is obsolete, perhaps improperly so, for all men in this country are patriots, knowing that their own existence must stand or fall with the Constitution." For someone who had had aspirations of becoming a great orator, he was quickly losing his nerve.

For all Byron's bravado, he was extremely agitated when Dallas encountered him just as he was about to enter his carriage on that fateful day, March 13, 1809. He asked Dallas if he would accompany him to the House. To mask his nervousness, he talked about the forthcoming poem. Dallas detected mortification and pride in his face. Paler than usual, he entered the chamber which was almost empty. The Chancellor, Lord Eldon, advanced towards Byron with a smile and extended his hand. Byron barely touched it with his fingers. What Eldon did not know was that he harboured a childish grudge against him for allowing Mary Chaworth and Jack Musters to marry. Byron flung himself carelessly on one of the empty benches to the left of the throne which were generally occupied by the opposition. After the oath had been taken, Eldon apologised for the delay to which he had been subjected, and Byron replied ungraciously, "You did your *duty*, and you did no *more*." When he left the chamber after a brief period, he remarked to Dallas who was waiting in the corridor: "I have taken my seat, and now I will go abroad."[7] His first appearance in public without any sponsor had been a humiliating experience. He relapsed into a deep depression, aroused only by discussions about the impending publication of the volume of poetry.

Numerous revisions were made to the poem as it was being printed. Dallas should have advised more caution about the changes, but he had nothing to lose and everything to gain. His silence on the content of the poem suggests that he welcomed a *succès de scandale*. Byron had nearly been tipped over the edge by Carlisle's humiliating treatment, which succeeded in reviving all his animus against Francis Jeffrey, the editor of the *Edinburgh Review*, whom he still believed the author of the critical review of *Hours of Idleness*.* Stringent libel laws had not yet been introduced; only the imputation of crime or social disease or aspersions on professional competence were punishable. As a result the newspapers could often be extremely virulent. The crown still had a good deal of power, however. The editor of the *Examiner*, Leigh Hunt, was thrown into jail for mocking the Prince Regent. By publishing anonymously – and also being afforded certain protection as a peer – Byron was able to give free expression to all his malice and misanthropy. One would have thought that his victims would be lining up to challenge him to a duel.

English Bards and Scotch Reviewers is one of the most unpleasant poems in the English language, and the fact that some of the poetry is excellent is not enough to excuse its sheer nastiness. Byron ostensibly modelled the poems on traditional satires of the evils of the time; but his major focus was on the sad state of contemporary English poetry and the worthless taste of the critics who admired it. Few figures escaped whipping. "Fools are my theme," he announced, "let Satire be my song." He seized every opportunity to castigate Carlisle and Jeffrey, and excused the dedication of *Hours of Idleness* to Carlisle as "dutiful" and written "more from the advice of others than my own judgement". Thomas Moore was criticised for his immorality (!) and accused of cowardice in a duel. Wordsworth was described as "The meanest object of the lowly group", an insult he was never to forgive. Scott was described as wasting his genius. Only Rogers and Campbell were commended for following Popean models.

The first edition was published in early March 1809; the identity of the author was quickly known; and by April Byron was revising a second edition which appeared in mid-May. In the Preface added to the second edition he declared: "I am not to be terrified by abuse, or bullied by reviewers with or without arms." In the Postscript he made a revealing

---

* For an interesting argument that Byron's reaction to the *Edinburgh Review* stemmed from his great admiration of Jeffrey, and that the opinions and tone of *English Bards and Scotch Reviewers* were much influenced by Jeffrey, see Muriel J. Mellown, "Francis Jeffrey, Lord Byron, and English Bards and Scotch Reviewers", *Studies in Scottish Literature*, ed. G. Ross Roy, vol. XVI, 1981, 80–90.

comment: "It may be said that I quit England because I have censured these 'persons of honour and wit about town,' but I am coming back again, and their vengeance will keep hot until my return." Third and fourth editions of the poem appeared when Byron was in the East. In 1812 he attempted to suppress the poem altogether, but pirated editions continued to proliferate. By July 1816, then an exile in Switzerland, Byron wrote: "The greater part of this Satire I most sincerely wish had never been written – not only on account of the injustice of much of the critical and some of the personal part of it – but the tone and temper are such as I cannot approve."[8]

If *Childe Harold* was to make him famous, *English Bards and Scotch Reviewers* made him infamous – and undoubtedly made his departure from England all the more expedient.

Augusta was so appalled by the viciousness of the attack on Carlisle, who had shown her nothing but kindness, that she stopped writing to her brother. The vitriol of the poem is ample evidence of the fierce aggression to which Byron could be roused when in the most pathological phases of his depression. Dallas informed him that the first reaction had been highly favourable, but admitted that some severe reviews were likely to follow: "I shall not repeat my own opinion to you; but I will repeat the request I once made to you, *never to consider me a flatterer*."[9]

Dallas may have been a Svengali but he has left us a vivid depiction of Byron's state of mind at the time. Sceptical, impious, misanthropic, Byron spoke of women with contempt and railed against family life. Dallas was convinced that he had no real friends, simply companions. He had commissioned miniatures to be painted of his close Harrow friends by the fashionable (and expensive) portrait painter George Saunders. Byron frequently spoke of the deep affection Clare had for him, but Dallas noticed that Clare's visits were becoming less frequent. Finally, on the day before Byron was to depart from England, Dallas discovered him in a state of indignation because Clare could not spare an hour for his friend as he had promised to accompany his mother and sisters on a shopping expedition. "Friendship!" Byron exclaimed. "I do not believe I shall leave behind me, yourself and family excepted, and perhaps my mother, a single being who will care what becomes of me."[10]

Yet in mid-April he gathered together his cronies at Newstead for the kind of house party he had always dreamed of: Hobhouse, Hodgson, Matthews and Wedderburn Webster, a bit of a buffoon. They dressed up in monks' costumes, roistering until the early hours of the morning, and there was some quarrelling, as well as a good deal of talk about the projected trip to the East. Hobhouse had agreed to act as a substitute for all the various travelling companions who had disappeared one by one; and much persuasion was exerted on Matthews to accompany them. On May 22 Matthews wrote to his sister: "And where do you think I am going next? To Constantinople! – at least, such an excursion has been proposed to me. Lord Byron and another friend are going thither next month, and have asked me to join the party; but it seems to be but a wild scheme, and requires twice thinking upon."[11]

Indeed it did. The main obstacle was that neither Hobhouse nor Byron had any money. On April 16 Byron told Hanson: "If the consequences of my leaving England were ten times as ruinous as you describe, I have no alternative, there are circumstances which render it absolutely indispensable, and quit the country I must immediately. – My passage is taken, and the 6th of May will be the day of my departure from Falmouth." The dark hints about some imperative need to leave the country were simply a device to exert pressure on Hanson to act; but also Byron wanted to be out of the country when the adverse reviews of *English Bards and Scotch Reviewers* appeared.

Byron was already more than £14,000 in debt, and he told Hanson he had only £5 in his possession. Then there was a small domestic crisis. In mid-May – for of course they had not been able to sail on May 6 as originally planned – Byron reported to his mother that he was sending young Rushton back to Newstead because he had discovered that Fletcher had taken the boy to prostitutes. Byron was returning him, he said, in order to keep him from "the *temptations* of this *accursed place*".[12] It would have seemed far more reasonable to have returned the older Fletcher, but of course he was more useful to Byron, whose concern for Rushton's future is expressed in a will he signed on June 14 in which he left £25 a year to his page. Byron's library was to go to the Earl of Clare, his lands and property to Hobhouse and Hanson, and £500 a year for life to his mother. He was to be buried in the vault at Newstead Abbey with "as little Pomp as possible – No Burial Service or Clergymen or any Monument or Inscription of any Kind", except the date of his death and his initials. We cannot dismiss the possibility that Byron had a sexual interest in Rushton and reacted in jealous anger to his amorous adventure. In the full-length portrait of Byron painted by Saunders at this time, a handsome Rushton secures the boat as Byron stands theatrically on a foreign shore. After many tears of remorse on the boy's part, Byron recalled him in time to accompany his master on the Eastern voyage.

Curiously, Scrope Davies was not named in the will. Usually unflappable, he was made extremely anxious by Byron's behaviour. Since the discovery of Scrope's trunk full of papers in a bank vault in 1981, we know a good deal more about the extent of Scrope's involvement in Byron's financial affairs. Scrope had often acted as a guarantor for Byron when he was a minor, especially over a large loan in 1808; and he was fearful that the creditors would pursue him in the event of Byron's death while out of the country. At the last minute a Colonel Sawbridge, a friend of Hanson's partner Birch, was induced to lend Byron £6,000 which enabled him to pay both his expenses and those of Hobhouse on the journey. Scrope, however, was still concerned about the earlier loan, especially as Hanson had told him there was no money to pay the interest on the outstanding annuities for which apparently Scrope had acted as guarantor. About June 20, he wrote to Byron, who by now had arrived in Falmouth: "In consequence of your permission, I opened your will, and, to my great disappointment, found no mention made either of me or the annuities, unless you include them in the word 'debts' – But how am I to substantiate my claim in the event of your death? I have no grounds at all on which I may proceed." Surely, Scrope asked, Byron could raise a loan on the security of his Rochdale estate? "For God's sake do not inflict murder on one who has been guilty of kindness only towards you – Under my present anxiety existence is intolerable – I cannot sleep – and much fear madness."[3]

Another of Scrope's letters has a drawing of a figure hanging from a gallows. Byron treated all these letters as though Scrope were merely joking in his usual fashion. But he did ask Hanson about finding the necessary money by Scrope's suggestion of raising a bond of indemnity. Hanson disagreed because there were so many other prior demands on outstanding loans.

Byron eventually added a codicil to his will. As T.A.J. Burnett has remarked: "Byron's departure abroad in 1809 with his affairs in such a condition were an act of considerable irresponsibility."[4] Scrope was still highly anxious; and the blame cannot be assigned entirely to Hanson's dilatoriness. Hanson warned his impetuous young client repeatedly that there was no money; and Hanson cannot be held responsible for the fact that the Rochdale estate was under litigation. If it had not been sold it was because no buyer had appeared. Hanson tried to raise a mortgage on Newstead Abbey, which no sensible investor would consider in light of Byron's dire finances. But Hanson did manage to sell the Norfolk property in 1810; and the subsequent difficulties in selling Newstead Abbey suggest that Rochdale was equally difficult to unload.

Byron's commentators have tended to accept Byron's evaluation of

Hanson. The law is notoriously slow, but Hanson does not appear to have been slower than most lawyers. He tried to warn Byron of the dangers of his extravagance, but Byron did not want to hear boring and unpleasant details. He wanted Hanson to produce money – as if by magic – whenever he needed it. He was under the delusion that Rochdale would yield a fortune and that eager buyers were waiting in the wings: it was only the difficult Hanson who was preventing their appearance.

It is indeed remarkable that Hanson persuaded Colonel Sawbridge to part with £6,000, although the latter prudently released only £2,000 before the young men sailed off to an adventure where they wouldn't have to bother with such sordid details as having to pay their debts, even to their friends. Indeed, Byron persuaded Hobhouse to write to Scrope on June 24 assuring him that Byron had just signed a codicil "by which a particular acknowledgement is addressed to the executors to see that the sum be properly discharged". There was to be no question, he went on, but that the interest would be paid regularly. As usual Hanson was made the scapegoat: "the agent either from peevishness or disappointment at this tour does not appear to have given you quite such satisfactory answers to your queries as you might have wished or expected."[5] This was the first of many occasions on which Hobhouse took on the role of sorting out Byron's financial affairs.

Scrope would have preferred a bond of indemnity. Just as their ship was about to sail, Byron dashed off a note to Hanson:

> The Codicil supersedes the necessity of a bond to Mr Davies who professes himself merely to be anxious for security in case of my demise, besides it is for £10,000 and Mr Ds only stands pledged for £6,000, it is true I offered to sign any satisfactory instrument for Mr Davies, but I think the codicil sufficient, without a Bond of Indemnity which shifts the responsibility completely, now as there must be a reliance either on my part upon Mr D. or on Mr D's upon me, I see no reason why it should not stand in its present state, as the annuities are fully intended to be redeemed the moment the estates are sold.[16]

Those golden ethereal estates of fantasy!

On June 26, 1809, Byron finally wrote to Scrope himself with an airy dismissal of his fears. He was in one of his manic states of excitement:

> & Since your epistle I have received a codicil from Hanson, which I trust will prevent the sad catastrophe of the triple suicide, yours,

Mrs and Miss Messingberd's – We are shortly to sail, and I hope by this time Hanson has prepared the cash requisite to suspend Your "ensuing insanity" (at least for the present) and I further trust that a few months will make you free . . . with renovated youth, and me independent. – Pray let me hear from you, your letters are always amusing, particularly the tragical ones. I hope I shall not behold any catastrophical paragraphs in the "Malta Mercury" – Seriously, dear Scrope, you are one of the few things in England I leave with regret & shall return to with pleasure, I hope God or the Devil (it matters not which if the end is the same) will prosper you at Newmarket, at the Union, the Racket's, at the Cocoa Tree, I am sure in my absence you will laugh when you think of me, I wish I may be able to do the same and to furnish you with many Oriental anecdotes wherewithal to astonish your gregarious audience at the various clubs of which you form so distinguished an ornament.[17]

Byron, however, failed to furnish Scrope with the laughter he promised when Scrope's thoughts reverted to his absent friend. A year later, on July 17, 1810, Scrope penned an anxious letter:

I was happy to hear from you, but should be more happy to see you – I not only am not relieved from responsibility, but am obliged to pay the Arrears – Your Agent must have concealed all these things from you, or I am sure, you would long since have returned to England. – I can say no more at present but that I am subject to arrest day after day and nothing but your return can still relieve me – God bless you.[18]

But even after receiving this anguished letter, Byron (who was moving back from Constantinople to Athens at the time) still made no preparations to return to England. He repeatedly told Hanson that nothing would persuade him to set foot in that cursed country again. During his absence, Hanson sent him regular detailed reports, yet Byron complained about never hearing from him without taking into consideration that he was constantly on the move. No letters from Byron have turned up asking if the interest on the loans for which Scrope was responsible were being paid. He wrote only to demand that money be sent to himself. Scrope was not repaid until 1814 when a prospective buyer for Newstead, Thomas Claughton, put down a deposit to buy the abbey.

Hobhouse and Byron were impatient at the delays in their departure, but both were in rip-roaring spirits. Why should they dwell on mortgages and bills of indemnity when the world lay waiting to be explored? A sense of liberation breaks through in the uninhibited way Byron begins to write to his friends. The correspondence between Byron and Matthews during this period of waiting for the Lisbon packet, after missing the ship they intended to take to Malta, gives an insight into the bisexuality that was never far below the surface with this group of friends. To Henry Drury, Byron promised to write a treatise on "Sodomy simplified or Paederasty proved to be praiseworthy from ancient authors and modern practice".[19] As for his travelling companion, Byron declares that "Hobhouse further hopes to indemnify himself in Turkey for a life of exemplary chastity at home by letting out his 'fair bodye' to the whole Divan."[20] To Matthews particularly he spoke obliquely but in a way which suggests a familiar banter among them: "I do not think Georgia itself can emulate in capabilities or incitements to the 'Plen. and optabil. – Coit.' the port of Falmouth & parts adjacent. – We are surrounded by Hyacinths and other flowers of the most fragrant [na]ture, & I have some intention of culling a handsome Bouquet to compare with the exotics we expect to meet in Asia."[21] Professor Marchand has revealed that "plenum et optabilem coitum" means "full and to-be-wished-for intercourse" and is taken from the *Satyricon* in which a boy was obtained by various tricks. Finally, Hodgson was told that on their way to Falmouth they changed horses at an inn where "the great Apostle of Paederasty, [William] Beckford! sojourned for the night".[22] Beckford, the author of *Vathek*, had to flee England in 1785 because of his intimacy with Lord Courtenay, twenty years younger than himself. With such excitement to occupy his mind, Byron did not have much time to fret over Bills of Indemnity. Such worries were left to Scrope and Mrs Byron.

Byron and his mother had parted on reasonably good terms. She had moved into Newstead to look after the abbey during her son's absence, meanwhile continuing to pay rent on her house in Southwell. On June 17, under the impression that Byron had already left England, she told Hanson: "The grief I feel at my son's going abroad and the addition of his leaving his affairs in so unsettled a state and not taking the thousand pounds on himself [a loan she had secured for him], I think altogether it will kill me."[23]

She was left to worry that fires could be maintained during the winter so that the furniture would not be spoiled or the wallpaper peel off. She would have enjoyed the gardens but there was no money to maintain them. The last letter she had received from Byron (June 22), did not contain news to cheer her:

> As to money matters I am ruined, at least till Rochdale is sold, & if that does not turn out well I shall enter the Austrian or Russian service, perhaps the Turkish, if I like their manners, the world is all before me, and I leave England without regret, and without a wish to revisit any thing it contains, except *yourself*, and your present residence. – – –

Hobhouse was equally negligent in failing to inform his estranged father that he was about to sail for parts remote and inaccessible. He intended to write a travel book on their adventures and had equipped himself with dozens of pens and reams of paper. Byron brought stacks of books. He was accompanied by Fletcher and a Prussian servant recommended by Dr Butler because he had been in the East, as well as Joe Murray, and Rushton, whom he intended to send home from Gibraltar.

On July 2 the Lisbon packet *Princess Elizabeth* finally caught a favourable wind and sailed out of Falmouth harbour. Two days before, Byron had sent Hodgson some roistering verses which caught the effervescent spirit of the party:

> Now at length we're off for Turkey,
>   Lord knows when we shall come back,
> Breezes foul, & tempests murkey,
>   May unship us in a crack,
> But since life at most a jest is
>   As Philosophers allow
> Still to laugh by far the best is,
>   Then laugh on – as I do now,
>   Laugh at all things
>   Great & small things,
> Sick or well, at sea or shore,
>   While we're quaffing
>   Let's have laughing
>   Who the Devil cares for more?
> Save good wine, & who would lack it?
> Even on board the Lisbon Packet.
>   (*Letters*, 1, p. 213)

Years later, by then subdued by life, he told Thomas Medwin: "My own master at an age when I most required a guide, left to the dominion of my passions when they were the strongest, with a fortune anticipated before I came into possession of it, and a constitution impaired by early excesses, I commenced my travels in 1809, with a joyless indifference to the world and all that was before me."[24]

6

∞∞∞∞∞∞∞∞∞∞

The Great Adventure,
July–December 1809

T his journey was to be a Grand Tour with a difference. During the
eighteenth century young English aristocrats would travel abroad
for a year or so with their attendant tutors (known as governors or
bear leaders) to further their education, to polish their manners, and to sow
their wild oats. Certain cities were considered essential for broadening the
mind: Paris, Florence, Venice, Rome and Naples. However, this pleasurable itinerary was changed for ever during the years 1793–1815 when
Britain was at war with France. British travellers as a consequence turned
their attention from their usual itinerary to the Near East,* stimulated by
oriental scholarship and a stream of books which emphasised the strange-
ness and excitement of these exotic regions. This travel literature was
produced by a group of professional travellers, far more concentrated in
their focus than the English milords.

Byron and Hobhouse were re-enacting their own variation of the Grand
Tour. Instead of being subsidised by wealthy parents, they were both
estranged from their families, and were living on borrowed money. Instead
of a bear leader, they had a Sancho Panza in the figure of the whining
William Fletcher, who had been a farmer until Byron took him into his
employ. Instead of a fixed itinerary, they travelled as chance and wind
propelled them with the vague destination of Greece and Turkey as their
goals. Hobhouse travelled to gain information that might prove helpful in a
political career. Byron travelled for new sensations and for escape into a
world of fantasy.

---

* An area defined by the eastern half of the Mediterranean to a line between the Caspian
Sea and the Persian Gulf – that is, Albania, Greece, Bulgaria, Turkey, Palestine, Persia,
Arabia, Abyssinia, Egypt, and Tripoli.

With pleasure drugg'd he almost long'd for woe,
And e'en for change of scene would seek the shades below.
(*Childe Harold*, I, 6, 53–4)

What is somewhat puzzling – at least before their departure – is their seeming lack of interest in the momentous events taking place on the continent. They had originally planned to sail directly to Malta; but having missed the Malta packet, they boarded ship for Lisbon, intending to spend a few days in the Portuguese capital and then take another ship to Gibraltar. Even a few days in Lisbon, given the naval and military situation, might seem hazardous, but perhaps the prospect added spice to the adventure. It is possible also that the two young men, both great admirers of Napoleon, were not all that concerned about what was taking place on the peninsula. It was almost as though they assumed that their admiration for Napoleon would protect them from any danger. The greater probability is that they had been so absorbed in raising money for the trip that they were unconcerned and even ignorant of events. As Whigs they would have concurred in the general abhorrence of the conduct of the war with France and distrusted the Tory general Wellesley.

The crossing took four and a half days and Byron confessed to Hodgson that he had been seasick "and sick of the sea" (July 16). But crowded on the deck that morning of July 7, 1809, as the *Princess Elizabeth* approached land they felt that their adventure had well and truly begun. Byron always remembered Lisbon as one of the most beautiful harbours he had ever seen, surrounded by steep terraces of gardens and orange groves rising in tiers beyond them.

Her image floating on that noble tide,
Which poets vainly pave with sands of gold . . .
(*Childe Harold*, I, 16, 217–18)

They slipped through the narrow eight-mile channel of the Tagus into the bay filled with vessels of the British fleet. The British presence was everywhere. More than 8,000 troops were in the city waiting to join the advance into Spain.[1] In August 1808, there had been a revolt against the French occupation, and Junot's army were forced to retreat eastward where they had been defeated at Vimeiro on August 24, 1808. At the moment that Hobhouse and Byron landed in Lisbon, Wellesley was close to Talavera, south-west of Madrid, where he was to defeat the French on July 28.

The magical city seemed less attractive on closer inspection. The young men had arrived with certain prejudices against the Portuguese, and these were soon confirmed. Immediately they set foot on shore they were assailed by the shouts of donkey boys as they pushed their way through aggressive beggars. They thought they were men of the world, but as inexperienced travellers they were constantly cheated and charged exorbitant exchange rates. Hobhouse professed disgust at the lascivious dancing in the theatres. The people were filthy and the clergy ignorant. Little wonder, they agreed, that Henry Fielding had called Lisbon "the nastiest city in the world".

Hobhouse recorded his indignation in his diary. Byron later made good use of the material for the early stanzas of *Childe Harold*. But they enjoyed themselves as tourists. They saw Fielding's grave. For three weeks they visited palaces, monasteries, and convents. Byron was in ecstasies over Cintra, the beautiful hill town fifteen miles from Lisbon. That world traveller described it to his mother: "it contains beauties of every description natural & artificial, Palaces and gardens rising in the midst of rocks, cataracts, and precipices, convents on stupendous heights . . . It unites in itself all the wildness of the Western Highlands with the verdure of the South of France."[2]

Never again was he to experience the freshness of that rapturous day at Cintra. He was also intrigued by the now deserted Moorish palace once occupied by the notorious William Beckford whose translation of *Vathek* was to have a profound influence on his own work. Beckford had lived there while in disgrace and exile. Byron wrote three stanzas on him for Canto I of *Childe Harold*, but wisely suppressed the third (which was later published in Moore's *Life*, much to Beckford's displeasure):

> Unhappy Vathek! in an evil hour
> ⟨By one fair form⟩ Gainst Nature's voice seduced to deed accurst,
> Once Fortune's minion, now thou feel'st her Power!
> Wrath's vials on thy lofty head have burst,
> In ⟨mind, in science⟩ wit, in ⟨talents⟩ genius, as in wealth the first
> How wondrous bright thy blooming morn arose
> But thou wert smitten with unhallowed thirst
> Of nameless crime, and ⟨round thee twining close⟩ thy sad day must close
> ⟨Scorn, Exile,⟩ To scorn, and Solitude unsought – the worst of woes.
>
> (*Works*, II, p.18)

At the time Byron wrote these lines, he had returned from Greece and his own rather mysterious life in Athens, so prudence probably dictated their suppression.

The most important event during their stay in Lisbon was Byron's swim across the Tagus from the old town to Belem Castle. While the crossing of the Hellespont has received far more attention because of its classical associations, this was a much more difficult feat, since it took two hours to struggle with the tide, the wind, and the counter-current.

The fighting in Spain had shifted for the time from the south to the north so they decided to ship Murray and the baggage by sea to Gibraltar.* Accompanied by Rushton and a Portuguese guide, Sanguinetti, they set out on July 20 to ride to Gibraltar by way of Seville and Cadiz. They galloped through vineyards and beautiful cork woods with glimpses of wild deer. But there were grim reminders of murders by the side of the road, and the first night Hobhouse recorded in his diary: "danger and fears by way of supper." They had no way of knowing whether Sanguinetti was cheating them. At towns they were obliged to show passports to officious guards. Hobhouse found the food spoilt by "stinking oil and salt butter". They often had to sleep on the floor and were attacked by fleas. Nevertheless, the horses were excellent and the roads splendid. They travelled seventy miles a day, and Byron had never felt better in his life.

At the frontier town of Elvas they followed tradition by bathing in the little stream that separated the "rival realms":

> But these between a silver streamlet glides,
> And scarce a name distinguisheth the brook,
> Though rival kingdoms press its verdant sides.
> (*Childe Harold*, I, 33, 369–71)

Written in retrospect, in *Childe Harold* Byron has his hero enter Spain with a rousing exhortation to its people to resist their oppressors. The great Battle of Vimeiro had taken place very close to Elvas, but the travellers seemed unaware of it at the time. In the poetical account there is a description of the Battle of Talavera, although they heard the news of it only after reaching Cadiz. On they rode over the rugged Sierre Morena range where they began to meet people sporting red cockades in their hats in loyalty to the deposed King Fernando VII. They also encountered the wounded and homeless, from whom Byron developed a lasting horror of war.

---

* At Falmouth Byron had dismissed the Prussian servant.

Descending into the plain, as they approached Seville, they entered a grim landscape recently fought over by the Spanish and French. The usually tranquil city was bursting at the seams because the Grand Junta of the British and Spanish allies had chosen it as their headquarters. Eventually the travellers found accommodation, but went supperless to bed.

The following day (July 26) they called on the British ambassador, John Hookham Frere, whose mock-epic poem *The Monks and the Giants*, published under the pseudonym "Whistlecraft", would later serve as the model for Byron's boisterous experiment *Beppo*, a style he was to perfect in *Don Juan*. At this point Byron was less interested in poetry than in the beauty of the Spanish women whom he celebrated in *Childe Harold*, I, 57:

> Yet are Spain's maids no race of Amazons,
> But form'd for all the witching arts of love:
> Though thus in arms they emulate her sons,
> And in the horrid phalanx dare to move,
> 'Tis but the tender fierceness of the dove,
> Pecking the hand that hovers o'er her mate: . . .

He told his mother that "Intrigue here is the business of life."[3] He resisted the invitation to bed the daughter of his landlady, who bestowed on him a three-foot hank of her hair on parting. The experiences in the city left such an impression on him that his ultimate anti-hero became Don Juan, a native of Seville.

The road from Seville to Cadiz wound through beautiful country, but the travellers were filled with compassion for the plight of the peasants whose crops had been devastated by the retreating French. While Byron did not know it at the time, his topographical/military/reflective poem would capture the general imagination at exactly the moment when the public was passionately interested in the Peninsular War.* By the time they reached Cadiz, they had ridden over 300 miles, an impressive feat.

Cadiz delighted Byron even more than Seville. Once he had reached Gibraltar he exclaimed: "Cadiz, sweet Cadiz, – it is the first spot in the

---

* Yet as John Galt would later remark: "Considering the interest which he afterwards took in the affairs of Greece, it is remarkable that he should have passed through Spain at the period he has described, without feeling any sympathy with the spirit which then animated that nation. Intent, however, on his travels, pressing onward to an unknown goal, he paused not to inquire as to the earnestness of the patriotic zeal of the Spaniards, nor once dreamt, even for adventure, of taking a part in their heroic cause" (p. 56).

creation."[4] At Cadiz they attended a bullfight. Hobhouse records in his diary that they were disgusted by the carnage, but Byron must have been intrigued as well, for he devoted eleven stanzas to it in *Childe Harold*.

Part of its attraction lay in meeting the lovely señoritas who made a great fuss over the handsome Englishmen. One evening at the play, Hobhouse was put in another box, and rather sourly commented in his diary: "Whilst Byron was in a box with Miss Cordova, a little mad and apt to fall in love . . . I went out."[5] On August 1 they were present when Lord Wellesley was greeted by a thunderous cannon salute when he arrived to assume his new post as Envoy Extraordinary to the Supreme Junta. To these observers of the colourful scene this was all merely spectacle.

Byron was too busy to write letters while travelling, and from the entries in Hobhouse's diaries we can assume that so far their relationship went smoothly. When exposed to new experiences and in a state of constant movement Byron did not have time to brood. He wanted to go to Africa but was prevented by a contrary wind. He dined at Algeciras with Lady Westmoreland at whose London house he was to meet Caroline Lamb three years later. He had already ordered an expensive uniform "as a court dress indispensable in travelling". Gibraltar he described as "the dirtiest most detestable spot in existence".[6] While he was detained waiting for the servants to arrive by sea with the baggage, we catch our first glimpse of Byron's darker side. He was observed by a fellow Scot, John Galt, a prolific writer of novels and travel books. Galt was sitting reading in the garrison library and his attention was immediately drawn by the entrance of a fashionable young man who sat down opposite him. Galt's interest in Byron never wavered from that minute.

> His physiognomy was prepossessing and intelligent, but ever and anon his brows lowered and gathered; a habit, as I then thought, with a degree of affectation in it, probably first assumed for picturesque effect and energetic expression; but which I afterwards discovered was undoubtedly the occasional scowl of some unpleasant reminiscence: it was certainly disagreeable – forbidding – but still the general cast of his features was impressed with elegance and character.[7]

Galt attributes the gloomy cast of Byron's mind to his background in the Highlands. It was a common enough belief at the time, particularly fostered by the Romantics, that climatic conditions affected character. Galt ignores the high spirits of *Don Juan*; but he does make some interesting observations – like Wilson Knight after him – about the absence of sensual imagery in Byron's work. He actually speculates that "something morbid" was induced in Byron at Harrow. Whether he suspected anything in Byron's relationship with Rushton and noticed his depression when the lad was sent back to England with Murray is open to question. On August 13 Byron informed Hanson: "I have sent Robert Rushton home, because Turkey is in too dangerous a state for boys to enter, & I beg he may still be considered as my servant, so that in case of my death he may be entitled to his legacy." From his wide reading on the subject, Byron knew precisely what the sexual temptations ahead of him would be.

On August 16 they boarded the packet *Townshend* for Malta. Galt was one of the passengers and he continued to observe Byron closely with a mixture of fascination and distaste, fuelled by the haughty way Byron treated him as someone not worthy of his attention. This was confirmed by Byron himself in conversation with Lady Blessington in Genoa in 1823 when he admitted candidly that he had been offended because Galt had not treated him with sufficient deference.

Hobhouse made himself at ease with everyone immediately, always cheerful and full of droll stories. Byron stood apart, and Galt noticed that he addressed Fletcher in a petulant manner. He "held himself aloof, and sat on the rail, leaning on the mizzen shrouds, inhaling as it were, poetical sympathy, from the gloomy rock, then dark and stern in the twilight".[8]

In a day or so Byron tired of his brooding isolation and became as playful as a boy. He initiated shooting competitions and was always the winner. Several times a boat was lowered; and Byron caught a turtle and also hooked a shark. Nevertheless, in the evenings he sat out on the deck alone. This behaviour aroused Galt to heights of poetic prose, written, let it be remembered, by the time Byron's mysterious persona had become established.

> He was often strangely rapt – it may have been from his genius; and, had its grandeur and darkness been then divulged, susceptible of explanation; but at the time, it threw, as it were, around him the sackcloth of penitence. Sitting amidst the shrouds and rattlings, in the tranquillity of the moonlight, churming an inarticulate melody, he seemed almost apparitional, suggesting dim reminiscences of him who shot the albatross. He was as a mystery in a winding-sheet, crowned with a halo.[9]

On the evening they arrived in Cagliari, the capital of Sardinia, they attended the opera. In the audience was a figure rehearsing for a Byronic role – a nobleman who had been outlawed for murder. Byron was extremely pleased when the ambassador, Mr Hill, took him to a private box as befitting his rank. When they parted Byron made him an eloquent speech of appreciation. Hobhouse was much amused by this performance and began to tease Byron, who had been under the impression that he had acquitted himself with immense dignity. Byron took offence, and Hobhouse strode on ahead of the others. Byron's bad foot made walking on the rough pavement difficult; and in a very human gesture, he took Galt's arm, and asked him earnestly if he thought he had exceeded the demands of courtesy. Galt actually agreed with Hobhouse, but assured Byron that it was entirely appropriate. From then on Byron treated him with more civility.

Byron, probably in a sulk, did not appear until the next evening; and Hobhouse confided to Galt that it was necessary to humour him like a child. They must have become reconciled because the following day he was overflowing with good spirits as they sailed along the coast of Sicily. They reached Malta on August 28. The island was of great strategic importance and had been through tumultuous times in the past decade. For long a stronghold of the Knights of Malta, the island was seized by Napoleon in 1798 on his way to Egypt but it was retaken by the British in 1800, and the dispute over its possession led to renewed war with France. Again, Byron seemed oblivious of this background, viewing it simply as a stepping-stone to the more glamorous Levant.

More important to him was the fact that the guns of Valetta did not give him the salute he believed his rank merited. But soon the young men were enjoying themselves immensely. Byron bought an Arabic grammar and began taking lessons. There were many indications that the world of adventure was near: they heard horror stories of Ali Pasha, the dreaded warlord of western Greece; and they were also told of the depredations Lord Elgin was making on the Parthenon.

On September 6 Hobhouse noted in his diary that they were prepared to take a cutter bound for Constantinople the following day. Byron even made a bet with a Mr Wherry that he could get into the female slave market. However, there was an abrupt change of plans because of Byron's involvement with a Mrs Constance Spencer Smith, whom Hobhouse described as "a tall pretty woman with fat arms well made". On September 10 he noted: "Lord Byron galanting at Mrs Fraser's."[10]

The lady was born in Constantinople, the daughter of Baron Herbert, the Austrian ambassador to the Porte, where she met her future husband, John Spencer Smith, the British minister. Smith had created difficulties for himself because of his resentment of Elgin's appointment as ambassador. He was then posted to Württemberg as British minister and again ran into trouble when the French tried to plant documents on him implicating him in an attempt to assassinate Napoleon,[11] and he had to make a hurried retreat to England.

At any rate Mrs Spencer Smith's past was eventful and seemed most romantic to Byron. She had been arrested by the French in Venice in 1805 and escorted to the Italian border, after which she was to be incarcerated in Valenciennes. At Brescia she was rescued by a Count Salvo who transported her across Lago di Garda in boy's clothes. Her husband was now in England where she was supposed to join him. Byron described her to his mother as "very pretty, very accomplished, and extremely eccentric" (September 15), a type that always appealed to him. The lady may have been an adventuress and a liar, but the relatively inexperienced Byron was totally captivated by the first worldly woman he had ever encountered. He gave her a diamond ring, and she urged that they elope together to her mother's house in the Friuli north of Venice.

Byron later told Lady Melbourne:

> I was seized with an *everlasting* passion considerably more violent on my part than this [Caroline Lamb] has ever been – every thing was settled – & we . . . were to set off for the Friuli; but lo! the Peace spoilt every thing, by putting this in possession of the French, & some particular occurrences in the interim determined me to go on to Constantinople.[12]

All Byron's passions tended to be "everlasting", and the "particular occurrences" which separated them seems to have been the lure of the East. Possibly the presence of her two small sons was also a deterrent. He was a very long time getting to Constantinople despite his promise to meet his beloved again in a year's time.

Before leaving Malta he almost had a duel with an officer who had made what he considered an insulting gesture about their relationship.* Hobhouse quickly settled things and bundled Byron on to the ship; "& so I escaped murder and adultery", Byron later told Henry Drury.[13] Nevertheless he made use of this "*everlasting*" passion to write a number of poems to the "sweet Florence": once during a thunderstorm in northern Greece, and another while sailing through the Ambracian Gulf.

On September 19 the two accidental travellers boarded the *Spider*, which was to accompany a convoy of British merchant vessels to Patras and then

---

* Byron often threatened duels, but never participated in one.

on to Prevesa. Again, they seemed unfazed by the fact that they were in the middle of a war zone. The Ionian Islands, a chain of seven islands off the south-western coast of Greece, had passed from the control of one power to another. The Venetians had ruled the islands for nearly 300 years; and they had recently been seized by the French who still occupied them as the *Spider* made for Greece, but were to be taken by the British a month later. En route they experienced a couple of minor skirmishes with boats whose main cargo seems to have been currants. This was as close as they were to being actually involved in the war.

Hobhouse was absorbed in re-reading Homer, and on the 23rd they caught a glimpse of Ithaca as they left the channel between Cephalonia and Zante. When the ship dropped anchor briefly at Patras, they went ashore to touch the ground of Greece, even if it meant only practising pistol-shooting in a vineyard. Sailing up the west coast towards Prevesa they passed Missolonghi (Messolongion). Thus Byron was to have on his first day in Greek waters a premonitory glimpse of his last destination. On the 29th they landed in Prevesa, the southernmost point in what was known as Albania. Unfortunately they arrived during a violent storm and their impressive "regimentals" were soon soaked through. The filthy muddy streets, disgusting latrines, and their miserable quarters left them thoroughly disheartened. "Never afterwards," Hobhouse recalled, "during our whole journey, did we feel so disheartened, and inclined to turn back, as at this instant."[4] But the sun emerged and they rode out to the ruins of Nicopolis which Octavian (later Emperor Augustus) had founded as a triumphal city after the Battle of Actium (31 BC) at which he had defeated Mark Antony. Now all that remained was the fragmented theatre with its silence broken only by the sound of crickets. Here they sat and contemplated the distant bay which seemed so minute in comparison with the outcome of the battle. The scene had a kind of melancholy grandeur that never failed to move Byron:

> Look where the second Caesar's trophies rose!
> Now, like the hands that rear'd them, withering:
> Imperial Anarchs, doubling human woes!
> GOD! was thy globe ordain'd for such to win and lose?
> (*Childe Harold*, II, 45, 402–5)

On October 3, from the town of Arta, they headed northward for their real adventure, an excursion into Albania, the least accessible part of Europe. Only William Martin Leake, the British Resident at Jannina, had so far penetrated what was undoubtedly *terra incognita* ruled by the infamous

Ali Pasha. Albania, still technically a province of Turkey (comprising the northern area of Greece and Illyria), was separated from the rest of Greece by the rugged mountains of northern Epirus. The vizier, Ali Pasha, was cunningly playing the French and British against each other. Hobhouse and Byron were fortunate at this particular moment in history that the British had just seized the Ionian Islands so that they were relatively safe in their attempt to visit the country ruled by the tyrant. There was always the danger of *banditti*, but, like a Mafia chief, Ali managed to keep even these under control.

The intrepid band set out with ten horses, four of which carried the heavy baggage including three beds. They took along two Albanian soldiers as guards. The journey took them through country of picturesque beauty, crowned on October 5 by their first sight of Jannina and its famous lake, "houses, domes, and Minarets, glittering through gardens of orange and lemon trees, and from groves of cypresses – the lake spreading its smooth expanse at the foot of the city – the mountains rising abruptly from the banks of the lake."[5] But as they entered the town they were sickened by the sight of a man's arm hanging from a tree. They later learned that it had belonged to a Greek patriot who had plotted an uprising against the Albanian despot.

News of their imminent arrival had preceded them; and Byron received the sort of reception that always pleased him. The vizier had put a comfortable house at their disposal and had left word that unfortunately he was unable to greet them himself as he was temporarily engaged in a "*petite guerre*" to the north. Nevertheless, he would provide them with an escort to accompany them to Tepelene, his birthplace, about seventy-five miles north of Jannina.

They travelled on through breathtaking mountain passes to the Greek monastery of Zitza: "the most beautiful Situation (always excepting Cintra in Portugal) I ever beheld," Byron told his mother (Nov. 12, 1809). Here they were struck by a fearsome storm and Byron and Fletcher became separated from the rest of the party. Hobhouse fretted for nine hours until they were reunited. Fletcher was terrified of robbers, but Byron found a graveyard where he calmly squatted down and penned lines to the "fair Florence":

> Clouds burst, skies flash, oh, dreadful hour!
>   More fiercely pours the storm!
> Yet here one thought has still the power
>   To keep my bosom warm.
>
>   (*Works*, I, p.276)

Now that they didn't have debts to quarrel over, Byron sent Mrs Byron the most informative and interesting of his letters from the East. To her he described the exciting spectacle of arriving at Tepelene at sunset. Nothing can exceed his own description:

> I shall never forget the singular scene on entering Tepaleen at five in the afternoon as the Sun was going down, it brought to my recollection (with some change of *dress* however) Scott's description of Branksome Castle in his lay, & the feudal system. – The Albanians in their dresses (the most magnificent in the world, consisting of a long *white kilt*, gold worked cloak, crimson velvet gold laced jacket & waistcoat, silver mounted pistols & daggers,) the Tartars with their high caps, the Turks in their vast pelises & turbans, the soldiers & black slaves with the horses, the former stretched in groups in an immense open gallery in front of the palace, the latter placed in a kind of cloister below it, two hundred steeds ready caparisoned to move in a moment, couriers entering or passing out with dispatches, the kettle drums beating, boys calling the hour from the minaret of the mosque, altogether, with the singular appearance of the building itself, formed a new & delightful spectacle to a stranger.[16]

When Hobhouse expressed surprise at the pleasurable reception they were being accorded, Byron, he noted in his journal, "gave me a lecture about not caring enough for *the English nobility*'.[17]

The following afternoon they had their first interview with Ali Pasha, by then a white-bearded gentleman in his late sixties. He congratulated them on the British capture of the Ionian Islands. Instead of the monster whom they had been hearing about for weeks, a courtly host greeted them. Hobhouse had the impression that he "looked a little benignly" at Byron. The vizier asked him how he had the heart to leave his mother, admired his small ears and delicate hands, and begged him to visit him, with a suggestion that the evening would be more convenient. For his part Byron found the Albanian men "the most beautiful race in point of countenance in the world". They were turned away from a bath-house that contained "belli ragazzi".[18]

In his journal Hobhouse recorded that he was told that pederasty was openly practised; and assured that it was to be found among any large body of men living without women. Shortly after this Byron showed a shocked Hobhouse a journal he had been keeping which Hobhouse persuaded him to burn. It was his first attempt to censor Byron's work. But it is curious that a page of Hobhouse's own journal covering the period they stayed at Tepelene has been torn out.* Hobhouse did include, however, an account of a performance they witnessed of copulation enacted by young boys: "nothing could be more beastly – but Ld. B tells me that he has seen puppet shows in England as bad, and that the Morris dances in Nottingham are worse."

One can only speculate whether Byron succumbed to Ali Pasha but he was fascinated by the contrast in his character between courtliness and cruelty. He certainly used him as the model for Pasha Giaffir in *The Bride of Abydos* and for the pirate Lambro in *Don Juan*, "the mildest mannered man/ That ever scuttled ship or cut a throat". On their return to Jannina they met Ali's grandsons, "the prettiest little animals I ever saw", Byron described them despite their elaborate make-up. On October 31, Hobhouse made a puzzling entry in his journal: "Lord Byron broke the only remaining tea cup on purpose being suspicious that this little individual might be the cause of war – this was what he said but I suspect another reason."[19]

Hobhouse also added: "Byron is writing a long poem in the Spenserian stanza." This was the first canto of *Childe Harold's Pilgrimage* that he was deliberately modelling on Spenser's *Faerie Queene* which he found in an anthology of poems he had brought with him from England. The poem was started while he was in a jubilant frame of mind: "I have no desire to return to England, nor shall I unless compelled by absolute want and Hanson's neglect," he told his mother, and again: "I have no one to be remembered to in England, & wish to hear nothing from it but that you are well, & a letter or two on business from Hanson."[20]

In order to avoid the bandits said to be roaming the mountains they accepted the vizier's offer of a galiot to convey them back to Prevesa. A strong wind blew up, and the crew was thrown into a frenzy at the prospect of being driven on to the headland of Sante Maura, still held by the French. Byron laid his Albanian capote on the deck "to wait the worst". Bandits would be preferable to these hysterical seamen, so when the ship turned back to port the two friends decided to travel overland to Prevesa, accompanied by a large Albanian escort.

They spent their first night on Greek soil at Utraikee on the Gulf of

* Louis Crompton has speculated that Hobhouse, as well as Byron, were part of a Cambridge bisexual set (*Byron and Greek Love*, London: Faber, 1985, p.129). Cecil Y. Lang surmises that Hobhouse made Byron destroy it because they both had some sexual experience in Tepelene ("Narcissus Jilted: Byron, *Don Juan*, and the Biographical Imperative", *Historical Studies and Literary Criticism*, ed. Jerome J. McGann, Madison, WI: University of Wisconsin Press, 1985).

Actium where robbers had murdered and plundered a few days before. Their companions were a group of Suliotes, mountain warriors (all former banditti) who, after roasting a goat, spent the night dancing and singing around a great fire. Hobhouse would have preferred some sleep, but for Byron it was natural, wild, and free.

> . . . bounding hand in hand, man link'd to man,
> Yelling their uncouth dirge, long daunc'd the kirtled clan
> (*Childe Harold*, II, 71, 638–9)

On November 20 they reached Missolonghi where they paid off their Albanian escorts. They were only too happy to be out of the dank, swampy place, with its huts propped up by poles against the malodorous tides. The longed-for destination, Athens, was now within reach. At Vostitza Byron shot an eagle, and felt so reproached by the bird's dying eyes that he resolved never to shoot another. He wrote movingly of the episode in his 1814 Journal: "The last bird I ever fired at was an *eaglet*, on the shore of the Gulf of Lepanto, near Vostitza. It was only wounded, and I tried to save it, the eye was so bright; but it pined, and died in a few days; and I never did since, and never will, attempt the death of another bird."[21]

It was at Vostitza on the southern coast of the Gulf of Corinth that Byron first learned of the profundity of the Greek hatred of their Turkish masters. Here they stayed with the twenty-year-old Andreas Londos, a Greek who served as Ali Pasha's first minister in the Morea (as the Peloponnese was then called). He regaled them with stories of the Greek patriot, the poet Rhigas, who had been murdered by the Turks in 1798. One evening while he and Hobhouse were playing chess, on hearing Rhigas's name, Londos "jumped suddenly from the sofa, threw over the board, and clasping his hands, repeated the name of the patriot with a thousand passionate exclamations, the tears streaming down his cheeks".[22] Up until this time Hobhouse's journal had been filled with comments about the order Ali Pasha had brought to Epirus and to the Morea under his son Veli Pasha. His reaction was similar to that of many tourists to the modern wonders Mussolini brought to Italy in the 1930s. These few brief days spent with Londos were to make an enormous difference in their thinking. It is very important to our story to know that both Hobhouse and Byron had their eyes opened at the same time. Order they found, yes; but at the cost of the smouldering resentment of a once proud people.

Both travellers longed to visit Delphi, especially as by now they could see snow-capped Parnassus to the north-east. They were rowed across the gulf to the northern shore and from Itea followed a tortuous path, so steep that they had to dismount from their horses. Byron had an ecstatic view of a flight of birds – the number increased with the passing years – which he took to be eagles although Hobhouse assured him that they were vultures. Undeterred by Hobhouse, he wanted to believe that they were a sign from the muses on Parnassus who were bestowing a blessing on his new poem. But he could not hide his disappointment at the rubble of the as yet unexcavated Delphi. They found two marble pillars bearing the names "H.P. Hope, 1799" and "Aberdeen, 1803" to which they added their names just as countless other tourists have defaced ancient monuments.

After they descended into the Boetian plain, the villages became clusters of dirty huts and miserable poverty. Byron cut off the head of a goose with his sword in order to provide dinner one night. On Christmas Eve they stayed in the worst hovel of their entire journey. The following day – Christmas 1809 – the guide cried out: "*Affendi, Affendi, to chorio*" – "Sir, sir, the Town!" It was the most glorious prospect of Byron's life: through the fir trees rose the Acropolis, almost a mirage floating in the sky.

This was the apex of a six-month journey, and this last autumnal adventure had exceeded his most romantic dreams. The physical rigours he had survived had been a triumph over his disability. The breathtaking vistas, the exotic customs, the feeling of living a *natural* life, the sense of adventure that accompanied each waking moment – never, never, could this be duplicated. All life that succeeded it was an anticlimax, a constant struggle to mitigate boredom.

7

oooooooooooooooo

Athens, Constantinople,
January–July 1810

As with Lisbon, a distant view lent enchantment to the vista. Athens had long since degenerated into a shanty town. Something over a thousand houses struggled up the northern and western slopes of the Acropolis divided by narrow muddy lanes. On the pinnacle rose the gleaming marble ensemble of the Parthenon, in its magnificent ruination, true, yet seemingly disdainful of the squalor below. Unaware of the passing of time, it still stood as a monument of Pericles's great record of public works built between 447 and 432 BC. The Acropolis, ironically, had been built as a tribute to Athene, goddess of wisdom, and once the presiding deity of the city.

Although French and British antiquarians had already descended on the city, soon to be followed by tourists diverted from the war in Europe, there were no inns to accommodate travellers, who had to be put up in private dwellings. Byron and Hobhouse took over the house of Mrs Tarsia Macri, the widow of the former British vice-consul. Their lodgings consisted of two bedrooms and a sitting room that opened on to a courtyard with lemon trees. This last was vital, for they had brought with them a considerable retinue, consisting of Fletcher, two Albanian servants and Andreas, a boy whom they had picked up in Patras to help them with the language. They now added a Greek, Demetrius Zograffo, who acted as local guide and gossip. This group slept outdoors while the widow Macri and her three young daughters were confined to the kitchen and what appeared to be a single small room.

They soon learned something of the political climate and of the tensions dividing the inhabitants of the town. The Greeks seemed subdued and passive under their Turkish masters who had reigned supreme since the seventeenth century. Athens was ruled by a waiwode to whom they paid tribute, and the administration was in the hands of certain Greeks whose extractions from their own people made them far more hated than the Turks. The city was occupied by Greeks, Turks, Albanians, and a scattering of Franks or Europeans. As a tributary of Turkey, the city remained neutral territory during the Napoleonic Wars.

Naturally Byron and Hobhouse were anxious to ascend to the Parthenon, the shining white ruin beleaguered by the petty factions squabbling below. The sordid acquisition of its sculptures had become an extension of the periodic changes in fortune during the war and it was no longer possible to wander freely around the summit of the citadel.

The two major protagonists in the struggle for its treasures were the French agent, Louis François Sebastian Fauvel, and Giovanni Battista Lusieri, a Neapolitan landscape painter. In 1783 Comte de Choiseul-Gouffin had been appointed French ambassador to the Porte. Having already visited Athens where he was struck by the possibility of gaining its treasures for Paris, he appointed Fauvel to draw and make preliminary casts of the marbles. Ten years later Lusieri arrived as the agent of Thomas Bruce, Lord Elgin, the British ambassador to the Porte. It is ironical that, prior to Lusieri's arrival, the previous British ambassador had protested to the waiwode about the vandalism by the French. Lusieri had entered Elgin's employ in Naples where he had been painting local antiquities for another avid collector, Lord Hamilton, and he was soon sharing Elgin's eager acquisitiveness. Both Fauvel and Lusieri competed feverishly in bribing the Turkish officials for access to the marbles on the Acropolis. In the Notes to *Childe Harold* Byron would describe Lusieri as "the agent of devastation".

Lord Elgin was later to tell a select committee of parliaments in 1816, "it was no part of my original plan to bring away anything but my models."[1] These models were intended to educate British taste in the beauty of original Greek statuary in contrast to feeble Roman imitations. As time passed, Elgin realised that if he did not act swiftly to remove them they were bound to be destroyed by Turkish indifference. A striking example was the Propylae, the great ceremonial gateway which had been used to store gunpowder until wrecked by lightning and by French acquisitiveness. With Britain in the ascendancy after the victory in Egypt, Elgin managed to gain permission to erect scaffolding and make plaster casts; and gradually he pushed the Turkish government, in exchange for payment, to allow him to remove some of the friezes and statues for shipment to England.

Elgin's first shipment arrived in England in 1807 when he built a large shed behind a house in Park Lane in order to display the collection to the public. The Society of Dilettanti, headed by Payne White, denounced the marbles as ugly and misshapen in contrast to the Italian works in English collections upon which he had bestowed much praise. Like the rest of the fashionable world, Byron visited the marbles. Ignorant young man that he was, in *English Bards and Scotch Reviewers* he joined in the general mockery. In a footnote he even made cruel fun of Elgin's face which had been eaten away by a fever contracted in Constantinople, hinting that it was the result of syphilis.

Throughout their travels, Byron and Hobhouse had been hearing stories of Elgin's looting. Hobhouse's journals record his indignation at what Elgin was doing. Even Fletcher had something to say on the subject: he decried Elgin's "rapacity", yet confessed "he should wish for no better thing than to make his fortune by the marble".[2]

Lusieri paid them a visit the day after their arrival. He told them that the rivalrous French were doing everything in their power to foil his attempt to send a second shipment to England in order to procure it for themselves. "Is this not a good excuse for my Lord's barbarous love of these antiques!" Hobhouse exclaimed.[3] Lusieri at the time was feverishly stripping the Parthenon of the metopes, the panels in high relief with their scenes of conflicts between gods and giants, as well as the frieze depicting the procession of the Great Panathenaea which encircled the entire building. Hobhouse had also heard "scandalous tales" of Lusieri from their guide Demetrius. A man close to sixty, he was cohabiting with two young women, giving each to believe that he intended to marry her. If Lusieri was such an unsavoury character, why then did the young men almost seem to cultivate him? Initially it would appear that when it was apparent that they could not gain immediate access to the Parthenon, Lusieri seemed the man who might be helpful to them.

They first had to send gifts of tea and sugar to the disdar, the military commander of the citadel. Until permission was granted they were reduced to exploring their immediate squalid surroundings. Byron spent most of the time indoors working on Canto II of *Childe Harold*. Hobhouse picked up further gossip from Demetrius and also reported that he could walk around the walls of the town in forty-seven brisk minutes. On January 8 they received permission to tour the Acropolis with Lusieri acting as their guide. Byron was appalled by the contrast between the glory that was Greece and the sad spectacle of neglect and spoliation that met their eyes. He began to view the controversy in a new light. By now Elgin's second shipment was being loaded in a ship in the Piraeus. It has often been said that the Greeks were indifferent or eager to sell ancient artefacts to foreigners, but

Hobhouse reports that some of them refused to load Lord Elgin's crates because they believed the statues contained spirits wailing in lament at leaving their fellow statues behind on the Acropolis.

While Byron was storing up impressions and memories which he would eventually use in *Childe Harold,* our only real knowledge of this period comes from Hobhouse's journals on which he was to draw for *A Journey through Albania and other provinces of Turkey in Europe and Asia to Constantinople* (1813). There is only one extant letter of Byron's written during this first ten-week stay in Athens. In Prevesa he had already written his mother a long account of his Albanian tour. He felt too indolent to write letters, he claimed, and he especially begrudged one he had been obliged to write to his lawyer, Hanson, on the eve of his departure for Constantinople. He was probably impelled to write because a post had arrived the previous day with only a single letter from Francis Hodgson. "I have written often,"* he told Hanson, "in vain, neither letters nor (what is of more importance) further remittances have arrived."4 He assumed that income should have been coming from the estates in Norfolk, from the sale of Rochdale, and the rents from Newstead. Byron never could grasp that no news from Hanson meant no good news. He reiterated his intention of never returning to England until he absolutely had to.

There was enough to distract him in exploring the area south of the city; as Byron said, they "topographized Attica". At first they made forays to accessible sites such as Eleusis to the west, and to the east Mount Hymettus and Mount Pentelicus where they saw the actual cave where the marble for the Parthenon had been quarried. On January 19 they set off on an expedition to the rocky promontory of Sounion, on the south-east tip of Attica (Byron always referred to it as Colonna). On January 22, 1810 – Byron's twenty-second birthday – they reached Kartea where they were held up by heavy rains. They climbed nearby Mount Parne to explore a cave. Here, armed with torches, they penetrated the interior, only to discover that they had entered a vast labyrinth. Their guide finally admitted he was lost – just as their torches flickered to extinction. While Byron might laugh ruefully about it later, there were a few minutes of sheer terror until they miraculously found themselves at the entrance.

The white columns of Sounion, with its temple set high on a cliff above the sea, were to retain a special place in Byron's memory. He even did a small act of barbarism of his own by carving his name on one of the columns that made up the ruin of the ancient Temple of Poseidon. A large wolf loping

* There seem to have been only two letters, from Prevesa and Patras.

through the shadows added to the savage romanticism of the scene. The following day, after turning their horses northwards, they reached Marathon, whose glory Byron would celebrate so frequently in his verse.*

The stirring scene of the Athenians warding off their Persian invaders in 490 BC he finally immortalised in perhaps the most famous lines he ever wrote to stir the flagging Greek spirit:

> The mountains look on Marathon –
>   And Marathon looks on the sea;
> And musing there an hour alone,
>   I dream'd that Greece might still be free;
> For standing on the Persian's grave,
> I could not deem myself a slave.
>   (*Don Juan*, III, 86, 701–6)

In February, Byron did not accompany Hobhouse on a five-day trip to Negroponte. That Hobhouse missed his company is revealed in a comment in *Journey*: "You will attribute any additional defects in the narration of this short tour, to the absence of a companion, who, to quickness of observation and ingenuity of remark, united that gay good humour which keeps alive the attention under the pressure of fatigue, and softens the aspect of every difficulty and danger."[5]

One might wonder why Byron decided to stay behind. Perhaps an entry in Hobhouse's journal for February 14, 1810, reveals the reason: "Byron riding out with Nicolai to Phyle." This was Nicolas Giraud, supposedly the brother of Lusieri's "wife". He was about fifteen or sixteen and very comely. Since, according to Demetrius, Lusieri was not married to either of the women with whom he was living, we might conjecture that he was Lusieri's son. Whatever the relationship, it was close enough that it could account for the fact that Byron continued to cultivate Lusieri despite the fact that he secretly despised him.

Nicolas's presence might also account for the fact that within three weeks of his arrival in Athens, Byron wrote his final farewell to Constance Spencer Smith: "The Spell is Broke, the charm is flown!" In addition to Hobhouse, there was another witness to Byron's proclivity for nubile young men. On February 21 their old travelling companion John Galt arrived in Athens, and in his biography of Byron, Galt makes indirect but pointed allusions to Byron's bisexuality.

* In a footnote to *Childe Harold* Byron says that the plain was offered to him for £900!

Scholars have loved the idea of a sentimental attraction of Byron to Theresa, the twelve-year-old daughter of his landlady.

> Maid of Athens, ere we part,
> Give, oh give me back my heart!

Is it not possible that these lines were actually addressed to Nicolas? Galt says he doubts whether Byron had any sincere attachment to her, "though he spoke of buying her from her mother" – probably one of his momentary impulses.* When he returned to Athens in July, Byron possibly let the flirtation get out of hand just as he had done with Julia Leacroft with whom he had flirted in the boring days at Southwell. His friendship with the family deteriorated when it became clear that he had no intention of either marrying or buying the girl. This seems to have precipitated his move to the Capuchin convent, for he was far more interested in spending time with Nicolas than with Theresa.

The first period in Athens was drawing to a close. Suddenly – as always – Byron decided to move on to the next destination after being offered a berth on a ship the following day. On March 4, he and Hobhouse made hasty preparations to board an English man-of-war, the *Pylades* which was sailing for Smyrna. Hobhouse says the parting from Athens was painful so they galloped swiftly towards the Piraeus to put Athens behind them as quickly as possible. "I like the Greeks," Byron told Henry Drury in a letter written from Constantinople, "who are plausible rascals, with all the Turkish vices without their courage – However, some are brave, and all are beautiful."[6] And in a footnote to *Childe Harold*, he wrote: "The Greeks will never be independent; they will never be sovereigns as heretofore, and God forbid they ever should! but they may be subjects without being slaves."[7] In time he was to encourage them to reignite their courageous spirit.

A particularly interesting aspect of this voyage upon which they were about to embark is that the *Pylades* was the British warship Lord Elgin had persuaded the government to send as an escort for the second shipment of the marbles.** Moreover, Lusieri had enlisted Galt as an ally. When the *Pylades* returned to Athens to pick up the cargo later in March, Galt took passage on the ship as far as Hydra. He also wrote to his banker in Malta

* The sisters seem to have served as models for the odalisques who were attracted to Don Juan.

** The chance of a berth for Byron and Hobhouse occurred because there was a delay in the arrival of the firman granting permission for the release of the marbles.

instructing him to buy up the marbles if Elgin's bankers proved unco-operative. As William St Clair remarks: "What fate a collection of 'Galt' Marbles might have suffered is anyone's guess. If he had found it profitable, Galt would have dispersed them without hesitation."[8] There is no evidence as to whether Byron knew about these plans at the time.

The *Pylades* arrived in Smyrna, the chief trading port of Asia Minor, on March 6. Our travellers were anxious to press on to Constantinople, but were forced to wait until almost the end of the month for a ship to convey them. They were put up in "two fine rooms" in the home of the British consul, Mr Francis Wherry, whose patience was to be taxed by the extended visit of the uninvited guests.

Smyrna itself offered little of interest. The stalwart Albanians in their retinue were taken to be slaves and the young Greek, Andreas, as their master, for he was asked if he would consider selling them. In a coffee-house the travellers witnessed lascivious dancing by whirling dervishes. On the 13th they set off to view the ruins of Ephesus, once the chief Roman city in Asia. Before its destruction by the Goths in AD 262 its Temple of Artemis had been one of the seven wonders of the world.

Travelling south from Smyrna they passed caravans of camels and marshy plains where they were almost deafened by the croaking of frogs. A ride of two days brought them to Ephesus which proved a disappointment; and Byron declared that "the temple has almost perished, and St Paul need not trouble to epistolize the present brood of Ephesians, who have converted a large church built entirely of marble into a Mosque, and I don't know that the edifice looks the worse for it."[9] He was struck more than anything else by the mournful wail of jackals among the ruins. Perhaps even a month earlier Byron might have meditated on the contrast between the mighty city and the ruins almost effaced by time.

None of this he used as background material for *Childe Harold*, the second canto of which he finished while stranded at Smyrna. However, he did use the terrain as background to two works written in Switzerland in 1816, both highly autobiographical. One was an unfinished novel written as a ghost story to while away rainy evenings with the Shelleys and which Polidori, his attendant physician, later appropriated for *The Vampyre*. The other was the poem "The Dream", remembered mainly for its evocation of his hopeless longing for Mary Chaworth.

During their last week in Smyrna they were joined again by John Galt. Galt and the travellers had enjoyed each other's company while in Athens, but the perceptive Scot noticed that Byron had fallen into one of his ill humours. At table one night he held forth in an authoritative way on politics and when contradicted by Bathurst, the captain of the recently arrived sloop *Salsette*, he relapsed into sullen silence. Galt's basic hostility to Byron resurfaced. "I never in the whole course of my acquaintance," Galt recalled, "saw him in so unfavourable a light as on that occasion."[10]

Byron's uncertainty about what to do with his life is reflected in some letters he managed to write to his mother despite his general lethargy. To her he probably wrote in the hope that she might stir Hanson to some kind of action. He told her that once he arrived in Constantinople he would decide whether or not to proceed to Persia "or return, which latter I do not wish if I can avoid it". He assured her that he had written to her and Hanson out of a sense "of duty and business rather than of Inclination" (March 19, 1810); and on April 10, the day before he sailed, he again wrote in the assurance that she was enjoying living in Nottinghamshire, "at least my share of it".

Byron never enquired about her health or seemed to have the slightest curiosity about how she was managing to cope with his tangled affairs. In furnishing Newstead, he had run up a bill of £2,100 with an upholsterer in Nottingham of which £1,600 was still owing. The bailiffs had posted a summons on the door of the abbey and Mrs Byron was frightened that they might seize the belongings that she had brought from Southwell. She knew the whole county would be gossiping about it. When she wrote to her son on March 9 she cried: "Good God, where are you? . . . I hope & trust in God you are safe. Neglect no opportunity of writing if you have any regard for my peace – God bless and protect you prays your affectionate and unhappy Mother – unhappy on your account."[11] But Mrs Byron spared him any complaint about the upholsterer's bill or the bailiffs. The affectionate and concerned woman would have been more helpful to him if she had explained the financial situation clearly and insisted that he return immediately to deal with his responsibilities. Not unreasonably she expected there would be some income from *English Bards and Scotch Reviewers*, now in its second edition, unaware that Byron had snobbishly allowed his publisher, Cawthorne, to keep the profits.

In late April 1810 she received Byron's letter written from Prevesa on November 12, 1809, with its wonderful account of his adventures in Albania. In reply she told him that three heiresses had been married: "They will all be gone before you return,"[12] and communicated the news that Augusta's husband, George Leigh, was in disgrace with his employer, the Prince of Wales, because he had pocketed some of the money from the sale of a horse belonging to the prince. Early in May the bear which she had been looking after died (Byron felt so remote from all concerns in England that he hadn't even enquired about his pet).

At Newstead, Mrs Byron found that she had to lay off some servants to reduce expenses. Yet she was concerned about how Byron was managing, and on May 25 told Hanson: "I hope Lord Byron has remittances sent as it would not be convenient to starve in a strange country."[13] Hanson had problems of his own about Byron's finances. He had managed to sell the estate in Norfolk but there was not enough income to meet all the annuities.

Meanwhile Mr Wherry was becoming restive under his guests' prolonged stay, particularly as his wife didn't conceal her infatuation for Byron. On March 18 Hobhouse recorded in his journal: "began to have a suspicion Dominus Wherry is tired of us."[14] And the following day: "Dominus Wherry is certainly tired – so we scheme."[15] Fortunately for all, Bathurst, the captain of the *Salsette* which had been sent to escort the British ambassador, Robert Adair (who had obtained the firman for Lord Elgin), back to England offered them passage to Constantinople. Mrs Wherry was in tears at parting from Byron. She had cut off some of his hair – Hobhouse suspected it was pubic – "pretty well at fifty six years at least".[16]

The voyage took longer than they expected. They could not enter the Dardanelles without official permission and for two weeks they lay at anchor off Cape Sigeum at the entrance to the straits. This was not at all irksome to Byron who, with Pope's *Iliad* at hand, had leisure to explore the windy north-western promontory of Asia Minor known as the Troad. At this time a dispute, led by Jacob Bryant, was raging about the authenticity of the site. (It wasn't until late in the nineteenth century that Heinrich Schliemann identified the modern Hissarlik as the site of ancient Troy.) Byron refused to credit the scepticism of "the blackguard Bryant":

> I still venerated the grand original as the truth of *history* (in the material *facts*) and of *place*. Otherwise, it would have given me no delight. Who will persuade me, when I reclined upon a mighty tomb, that it did not contain a hero? – its very magnitude proved this. Men do not labour over the ignoble and petty dead – and why should not the *dead* be *Homer's* dead?[17]

He was certain that the great barrow he could see from his cabin window was the tomb of Antilochus. And there was the River Scamander and Mount Ida in the distance to excite a sense of wonder in the travellers. Years later Byron was to drop Don Juan here on his way to the slave market in Constantinople.

As always, water revived him. He spent hours diving for land turtles which he had tossed into the sea. Byron's low spirits disappeared in perhaps the most engaging adventure of his life which presented itself only because of the ship's prolonged detention at the mouth of the Dardanelles. No one had yet proved the possibility of Leander's swim across the Hellespont to his inamorata Hero but he, Byron, whom people had despised for his deformity, would prove that it could be done. With Lieutenant Ekenhead from the ship, he wagered that he could reach the opposite shore first. Competition always whetted Byron's spirit of adventure. On April 16 they made their first attempt from the European side,* but had to give up an hour after they entered the water because it was still frigid from melting snow, nor could they battle the strength of the current which carried them upstream. They finally had to be pulled out of the water by the boat that was following them, exhausted and so numb that they were unable to stand.

Hobhouse shared in the excitement of the second attempt. In his journal he recorded:

> This instance 3 May 10 a.m. write this in the Dardanelles at anchor. Byron and Ekenhead gone to swim. Now swimming across the Hellespont – Ovid's Hero and Leander open before me. Mr Ekenhead performed this in one hour and five minutes setting off two miles above Europe castle and coming out a mile at least before Dardanelles, Lord Byron in one hour ten minutes, got under weigh [sic] – wind – only drifted further below where anchored.[18]

After they reached Constantinople on May 25 Byron, still exultant in his triumph, wrote in Hobhouse's journal: "The whole distance Ekenhead and myself swum was more than four miles the current very strong and cold, some large fish near us when half across, we were not fatigued but a little chilled. Did it with difficulty." Byron wore long pants as he always did when swimming, but Ekenhead was probably naked. They both would have used the breast stroke as the crawl didn't come into fashion until later in the century. If subsequent swimmers made the crossing in less time one must remember that with the breast stroke one cannot achieve the same speed.

Byron's mood had never been so manic. He suddenly started writing to his friends and for the next two months his letters were filled with

* Leander had swum from the Asiatic shore before making his return journey.

descriptions of the exploit. It had indeed been a trial of endurance because while the actual distance is only about a mile, the current was so strong that the swimmers were obliged to swim almost four miles before reaching the opposite shore. Byron also celebrated it in a lively poem "Written after Swimming from Sestos to Abydos"; and in *Don Juan*, he writes of his antihero:

> A better swimmer you could scarce see ever,
> He could, perhaps, have pass'd the Hellespont,
> As once (a feat on which ourselves we prided)
> Leander, Mr Ekenhead, and I did.
> (II, 105, 837–40)

Finally, on May 13, the myriad minarets of Constantinople rose up before them as they rounded Seraglio Point. The travellers had leaned over the railings of ships to view the harbours of Lisbon and Valetta; they had glimpsed the green shore of Greece welcome after the white wastes of Malta; and now finally they had reached the most eastern and exotic of their destinations. Perhaps Byron had become a little jaded, for his letters from Constantinople lack the freshness and the excitement first experienced after their landing in Portugal. A world-weariness, a restless purposelessness and irritability settled over him, relieved only by constant sightseeing or riding. Hobhouse had decided to return to England in about a month, but Byron's plans changed from day to day. Without the expectation of Hobhouse as an anchor, he began to feel totally alienated and adrift.

He could not complain about their accommodation. They first put up at an inn in Pera at a crossroads which Hobhouse described "as bad as Wapping" (May 14), but their rooms were good, and on their first night they had the best dinner since leaving London. The day after their arrival they called on the First Secretary of the embassy, Stratford Canning, who had played for Eton in the cricket match in Dorset Square in which Byron had participated. Hobhouse described him as a "pleasing young man with a vulgar voice".[9] The ambassador, who was ill in bed, was anxious to see them. They found Robert Adair ill and pale but he roused himself enough to voice his detestation of the Turks. He offered them accommodation in his own quarters but they preferred a house of their own into which they moved for the duration of their visit.

Constantinople comprised two distinct cities, divided by the Golden Horn: on the one side the ancient and still mysterious city of Stamboul and on the other the Frank quarter consisting of the suburbs of Galata and Pera. Only the Turks were allowed to live in the old city and at that time no bridge crossed the Horn.

There was much to occupy them in Constantinople and for the next six weeks they were to see a great deal of the city and its environs, memories of which were stored in Byron's memory to use when he came to write some of the oriental tales and *Don Juan*. The Seraglio was totally forbidden territory and any intention of penetrating it was deterred by heads of criminals hanging on its gates, with the bodies flung on to dung heaps. There was no social intercourse between Turks and Franks (that is, the Europeans), but in wine houses they saw Turkish boys engaged in lustful dancing which Hobhouse described as "indescribably beastly". Then there were the whirling dervishes who danced themselves into a state of sexual ecstasy. What Byron thought of all this is not recorded.

They travelled up the Bosphorus as far as the Black Sea, delighted by the gaily painted wooden villas of the wealthy Turks lining the banks. Eventually permission was granted to visit the mosques but Byron was unmoved by their beauty and declared that San Sophia could not be compared with St Paul's. But nothing excelled the four-mile ride around the ivy-covered triple walls of the Seraglio with its 218 towers and the Turkish burial grounds on the other side of the road, "the loveliest spots on earth," Byron told his mother, "full of enormous cypresses, I have seen the ruins of Athens, of Ephesus, and Delphi, I have traversed great [sic] part of Turkey and many other parts of Europe and some of Asia, but I never beheld a work of Nature or Art, which yielded an impression like the prospect on each side, from the Seven Towers to the End of the Golden Horn."[20]

It was in dealing with other people that Byron ran into trouble. Some of the diplomatic community wondered if he were perhaps mad. His childish behaviour at a ceremonial event was eccentric enough to cause tongues to wag. On May 28 Bruce was to present his parting credentials to the Caimacan who represented the Grand Vizier now away fighting the Russians. Byron arrived in his scarlet regimentals and an elaborate feathered hat, fully expecting to be granted precedence in the procession. On learning that he had to fall behind Canning, he flew into a rage. Adair tried to make him understand that the Turks would only acknowledge persons belonging to the embassy. When Byron continued to make a fuss, Adair referred him to the Austrian authority on diplomatic etiquette, the internuncio, who strongly supported Adair.

Byron then stalked off in a pique and when Hobhouse returned he found him making arrangements to travel back to Smyrna by land. When Fletcher protested about the hardships of such a journey, Byron exploded, discharging him on the spot, and wrote impulsively to Bathurst to enquire whether he could be replaced by one of the sailors from the *Salsette.*

Hobhouse simply recorded the incident in his journal without any comment and calmly continued with his own sightseeing. On May 30 he went by boat around the city. When he arrived back "Byron asked me how I did – and then turned sulky and so went to bed."[21] On June 1 Hobhouse was surprised to receive a letter "from a friend" deploring his partnership with Byron.* By the 3rd, Byron had emerged from his black mood and within a few days had succumbed to Fletcher's pleas to let him accompany him back to Greece.

Before leaving England, Hobhouse had put in the hands of the printer a miscellany of poems, including a few of Byron's. On July 6 he recorded in his journal: "messenger arrived from England bringing a letter from Hodgson to Byron – tells news that the *Collection* is accused of indecency."**[22] Because of its slight pruriency, the politically ambitious Hobhouse later greatly regretted that his miscellany ever saw the light of day; but at the time Byron generously urged all his correspondents to read the volume.

Byron was sufficiently repentant of his behaviour to write to Adair shortly before the projected visit to the sultan on the eve of their departure. It was not like him to make a formal apology but he did have sufficient grace to admit that "On all occasions of this kind one of the parties must be wrong, at present it has fallen to my lot, your authorities (particularly the *German*) are too many for me. – I shall therefore make what atonement I can by cheerfully following not only your excellency, 'but your servant or your maid your ox or your ass or any thing that is yours!'"[23] A joke was the best he could muster, and perhaps that was for the best for everyone's sake. He went on to say that "I am never very well adapted for or very happy in society, and I happen at this time from some particular circumstances to be ever less so than usual." The "particular circumstances" – like the mysterious circumstances which impelled him to leave England – were fantasies of his own whims and paranoia.

---

* Hobhouse's discretion, even in his journal, is apparent because he knew full well who the "friend" was, and he answered him in pencil. Was it Canning?

** Unfortunately Leslie Marchand misread *Collection* as "Edleston", thus causing certain confusion in subsequent hypotheses arising from the error.

The temptation of an audience with the sultan himself was too much even for Byron's *amour propre*. Always a late riser, it must have been difficult for him to appear at half past four in the morning at the ambassador's palace. Again dressed in his ceremonial garb, this time he was charming and good-natured. A large party was rowed across the harbour to the Seraglio palace (now the Topkapi), with the guns of the *Salsette* saluting them.

On arriving at the residence they were escorted through various courts to the presence of the Vice-Vizier. Here they sat down to a banquet of twenty-two dishes. After dining they were instructed to attire themselves in fur robes for the ceremonial presentation to the sultan. Mahmoud II, a young man still under thirty, was sitting on a dazzling silver throne encrusted with pearls. He remained immobile with a hand on each knee, rolling his eyes from side to side as the British ambassador expressed the wish that the friendship between England and Turkey would continue in its tranquil course. The sultan in turn handed the ambassador a letter to deliver to George III.

It is curious that Byron never used the sultan as a figure in his poetry. An older, more flamboyant figure such as Ali Pasha was more to his liking than a young man his own age with the wealth, rank, and power that he himself would have liked to possess. Later the sultan asserted that the handsome creature he had beheld with his red regimentals visible under the fur robes was really a woman. This was the same sultan against whom Byron was to be pitted at the side of the Greeks when he returned to help them in their struggle for independence, and Mahmoud would then denounce him as an official enemy of the Porte.

In reality – and reality was the last thing Byron wanted to think about – he was an impoverished aristocrat who strutted about as though he were the Duke of Devonshire. In this instance he was saved by £500 that finally arrived from Hanson. By now Byron had abandoned the plan for travelling on to India, for perhaps without Hobhouse as companion the idea did not appear so attractive. While Byron might make fun of Hobhouse's complaints of fleas, and the like, in point of fact Hobhouse was a far more independent and curious traveller than Byron. In the next few years he was to travel on his own over a great part of Europe but could not persuade Byron to accompany him even as far as Paris. And so, at this juncture, Byron settled on returning to the familiarity of Athens for the rest of the summer – and perhaps the winter as well. "My stay depends so much on my caprice," he told Drury, "that I can say nothing of its probable duration. I have been out a year already, and may stay another; but I am quicksilver, and say nothing positively" (June 17, 1810).

What he did know was that he wanted to postpone his return to England as long as possible. "I left the land without regret, I shall return without pleasure." While his inclination was to be a "citizen of the world" he feared that "some indispensable affairs will soon call me back".[24] That these affairs were financial he could not bear to put into words, although he did instruct Hanson that whatever happened to him, the lawyer was not to allow his mother "to suffer any unpleasant privation" (May 3).

That he had begun to think of the inevitability of his return and to accept that his future lay in England is apparent in a spate of letters he suddenly began to write from Constantinople. He renewed his literary association with Robert Charles Dallas, asking him to instruct Murray not to bring out a collected edition of his works before his return and expressing disappointment that *English Bards and Scotch Reviewers* was only in its third edition due to Cawthorn's initial mistake of printing too many copies. With Dallas he reverted to the bitter feelings he had experienced when Lord Clare had refused to spend Byron's last day in England with him. "The only person whom I expected to have grieved took leave of me with a coolness which, had I not known the heart of the man, would have surprised me; I should have attributed it to offence, had I ever been guilty in that instance of any thing but affection."[25]

He had begun to think again of Newstead with fondness and with a renewed sense of the responsibilities it entailed. He told his mother that the walls of the Seraglio reminded him of those surrounding the grounds of the abbey. He had heard from her that Miss Rushton (probably the sister of his favourite, Robert) had been made pregnant by one of the tenants who refused to marry her.

> It is my opinion that Mr Bowman ought to marry Miss Rushton, our first duty is not to do evil, but alas! that is impossible, our next is to repair it, if in our power, the girl is his equal, if she were his inferior a sum of money and provision for the child would be some, though a poor compensation, as it is, he should marry her. I will have no gay deceivers on my Estate, and I shall not allow my tenants a privilege I do not permit myself, viz – *that*, of debauching each other's daughters. – God knows I have been guilty of many excesses, but as I have laid down a resolution to reform, and *lately* kept it, I expect this Lothario to follow the example, and begin by restoring this girl to society, or, by the Beard of my Father! he shall hear of it.[26]

In the past he had informed his mother that he was writing only out of a sense of duty, but he now expressed the wish that she was well and happy.

To another correspondent, Edward Ellice, he confessed to be saddened by the news that Augusta had been distressed by his caustic lines on Lord Carlisle in *English Bards and Scotch Reviewers*. As for any friends who expected him to be crushed by the attacks on his work, he assured Ellice: "I mean to live a long time in defiance of pens and penknives" (July 4).

Publishers, tenants, debts – soon, soon, dear God, but not quite yet. Lest Hanson deceive himself that he could relax his vigilance in keeping an eye on all his affairs, he assured him: "I shall not return to England for two years at least (from this date) except in case of war" (June 30). On July 2 the two friends drank a glass of wine to their having adventured a year together. Byron was to accompany Hobhouse to the island of Zea (Kea) off Cape Sounion where he would leave the ship and make for Greece. On the 14th the *Salsette* slowly sailed out of the harbour of Constantinople and Byron must have been pleased that a salute rang out in his honour.

Byron coped with Hobhouse's return with blasé assertions about how tiresome it was to be with one person for too long. "I have known a hundred instances of men setting out in couples, but not one of a similar return," he exaggerated to Hodgson (July 4, 1810). Hobhouse might have irritated him at times, but he was seldom judgemental, he accepted Byron's mercurial moods as a matter of course, he was stalwart ballast. A part of Byron resented the fact that Hobhouse was concerned with settling his troubled affairs in England as Byron himself should have been doing. In a sense Hobhouse was also deserting him, leaving him to a freedom he didn't know how to handle on his own.

Throughout his life Hobhouse's attentiveness to Byron's welfare and concerns was remarkable, particularly as Byron usually accepted all that he did for him simply as a matter of course in the way a child takes for granted the attentions of a parent. Undoubtedly Byron elicited a nurturing, protective side of Hobhouse's character. Hobhouse shared the same steadfast, possessive affection as Byron had for his friends, but without the wayward, volatile, and sometimes treacherous streak. Byron in turn provided his stolid English nature with a frisson of glamour, and of course snobbery played a part in the attraction.

Thomas Moore, in his life of Byron, relates that Adair noticed that Byron seemed particularly dejected during the voyage from Constantinople to Zea. He gives an anecdote of Byron picking up a small Turkish dagger on the deck and being heard to mutter, "I should like to know how a person feels, after committing a murder."[27] Incidents like these contributed to the legend of the dark Byron which was beginning to be established even before the publication of *Childe Harold*.

On July 17 the friends parted at the port of Zea, off the coast of Greece. Hobhouse wrote in his journal: "Took leave, *non sine lacrymis*, of this singular young person, on a little stone terrace at the end of the bay, dividing with him a little nosegay of flowers, the last thing perhaps I shall ever divide with him."[28] Byron later scoffed at his friend's sentimentality, but it would have been surprising if he did not also wipe away a tear that day.

8

ooooooooooooooo

Reluctant Return, 1810–11

Byron's second period in Greece – spanning eight months – was altogether different from the previous exploratory tour with Hobhouse. Where there had been adventure and novelty, there was now reassuring familiarity. His last view of the *Salsette* was of the ship tossing listlessly on the waves waiting for a favourable wind to lift her sails. With a determined shrug of his shoulders, he set off for the mainland and within ten hours was back in Athens on July 18, 1810.

He had declared himself "woefully sick of travelling companions", yet almost immediately he was making plans with an old Cambridge acquaintance, Lord Sligo, to journey together into the Morea. Sligo had just arrived in the Piraeus in command of a brig, and was now eager to see something of Greece. The heat was overpowering, yet within three days of Byron's return he started off with Sligo, a retinue of retainers, and twenty-nine horses carrying their baggage. Since his posture had been that all he wanted at this point was to be alone, he had perforce to explain his conduct to Hobhouse to whom he reiterated that he was "already heartily disgusted with travelling in company" (July 29, 1810). In truth he had grown very dependent on Hobhouse, both for his company and for his willingness to handle the practical details of travel; and his precipitancy in joining Sligo was an indication of a dependency he would never admit.

Yet there had to be some excuse for this journey in the sweltering heat. To Hobhouse and other correspondents he mentioned vaguely some urgent "business" he had to transact with the British consul, Strane, in Patras. Sligo *would* insist on accompanying him, nuisance as it was, although at Corinth they parted, Sligo for Tripolitza, Byron eventually for Patras.

On one occasion they bathed together in the Gulf of Corinth. According to Thomas Moore, Byron pointed to his lame foot and exclaimed:

Look there! – it is to her [my mother's] false delicacy at my birth that I owe that deformity; and yet, as long as I can remember, she has never ceased to taunt and reproach me with it. Even a few days before we parted, for the last time, on my leaving England, she, in one of her fits of passion, uttered an imprecation upon me, praying that I might prove as ill-formed in mind as I am in body![1]

Sligo also told Moore that Byron bathed without "trowsers", but this was contradicted by Fletcher, when the story was repeated to him. According to him no one except doctors and Fletcher saw his bare foot and he always wore "nankeen trowsers" when bathing. However, something must have been said to Sligo about Mrs Byron, possibly to cover his embarrassment and shame. It is, however, doubtful that he was telling the truth. It would have been ludicrous to attribute his deformity to his mother's false modesty. It is also unlikely that she constantly taunted him with it, although in a moment of anger she may have screamed something like this. What Byron was trying to do was to divert his friend's attention from his foot to the monstrosity of his mother. Whatever the truth, shortly after this incident was supposed to have taken place, he was writing a teasing, affectionate letter to Mrs Byron.

On the 25th he reached Vostitza where he and Hobhouse had stayed with Andreas Londos – the emotional patriot – the previous year. Here he again encountered a nubile youth, Eustathios Georgiori (was this the "business" he had to attend to?). Despite his professed dislike of travelling companions, Eustathios joined the entourage; and Byron was so fascinated by him that he sent Hobhouse a long descriptive letter marked by a tone of mock exasperation. It was clear that he was totally infatuated with the boy. With his curls hanging down his back, and carrying a parasol to protect his complexion from the sun (much to Fletcher's amusement), Eustathios set off with the group for Patras.

Next day he went to visit some accursed cousin and the day after we had a grand quarrel, Strané said I spoilt him, I said nothing, the child was as froward as an unbroken colt . . . I think I never in my life took so much pains to please any one, or succeeded so ill, I particularly *avoided* every thing which *could possibly give* the *least offence* in any *manner*, somebody says that those who try to please will please, this I know not; but I am sure that no one likes to fail in the attempt.[2]

Byron was compelled to tell – in part confess – everything to Father Hobhouse, to describe the boy, even to relate his jealousy when he disappeared to visit a "cousin". Obsession gained over pride, and he reverted to the kind of agitated feelings of Harrow days. He also begged Hobhouse to relate it all to Matthews whom Hobhouse called "the pederast" and Byron privately coded "the Citoyen". While he could put this down on paper to Hobhouse, at the same time he teased him, "You cannot conceive what a delightful companion you are now you are gone" – especially as Hobhouse would have acted as a restraining influence on his amours. He would have known, too, that all this would have aroused Hobhouse's jealousy.

They next set off for Tripolitza to visit Veli Pasha, the son of Ali Pasha, and ruler of the Morea. Veli, who was about to leave on an expedition against the Russians, in turn became infatuated with Byron, presented him with "a very pretty horse" and begged Byron to join him in Larissa. "He said he wished all the old men . . . to go to his father, but the young ones to come to him, to use his own expression, 'vecchio con vecchio, Giovane con Giovane'."[3] Veli put his arm around his waist and squeezed his hand in public which Byron claimed to find embarrassing, but he was really quite giddy from the erotic atmosphere. Eustathios, however, had one tantrum too many and was sent home to Tripolitza, although Byron promised to bring him to Athens – a vow that was never kept.

When Byron returned to Athens, either because of strained relations with the Macri family or because he wanted an all-male milieu, he moved into the Capuchin convent at the foot of the Acropolis. This served as a school for Frank boys and as a hostelry which had been used by Galt during his stay in Athens. For Byron it was to be a re-creation of his most carefree days at Harrow or the high jinks of house parties at Newstead.

There was to be no more striving for precedence, simply the uninhibited boisterousness of childhood. Byron had always feared losing it and now that the inevitability of return to England loomed ever nearer, he lost all reserve, romping with the "ragazzi", and renewing his intimacy with Nicolo Giraud who was a pupil at the school. "I am his 'Padrone' and his 'amico'," he told Hobhouse, "and the Lord knows what besides, it is about two hours since that after informing me he was most desirous to follow *him* (that is me) over the world, he concluded by telling me it was proper for us not only to live, but 'morire insieme.' "[4] This was the kind of blind devotion Byron craved. And Lusieri he now described as "a new ally of mine". His spoliation of the Parthenon apparently counted for little when compared to the proximity of his relationship with Nicolo. Byron described their antics as "too good to last".

During these *carpe diem* early months in Athens he reverted to the manic hoydenism of an adolescent let off the leash. His sexual activities were by no means confined only to boys. Indeed, it was one of those recurrent periods of rampant promiscuity that seized him from time to time throughout his life.

He was in the habit of riding most days, accompanied by Nicolo, to the Piraeus for a long swim. As they were returning to Athens one afternoon he found himself involved in an incident which he never forgot for the rest of his life. They encountered a group of Turkish soldiers surrounding a horse bearing a sack which turned out to contain the body of a living woman whom they were about to cast into the sea, on the waiwode's orders, for having had illicit sex during Ramadan. Byron drew his pistol and talked the leader of the party into returning to the waiwode. Probably with the help of baksheesh he persuaded the ruler to release the girl on the condition that she live outside Athens, and Byron took on the responsibility of settling her in Thebes.

The truth of Byron's involvement in the affair has always been murky. That he could have been the person with whom the girl had sexual relations cannot be ruled out, although he would never say that he had any personal interest in the case. He was always quick to help the oppressed and he never recalled the incident without shuddering. He used the material in 1813 (for him all life eventually became "material") as the pivotal incident for his oriental poem, *The Giaour*. What is curious is that at the time of the publication of the poem he asked Lord Sligo to write an account of what he remembered the current story to be at the time. By asking for Sligo's corroborative version he seemed to be making an attempt to absolve himself of any responsibility in the affair. Years later he told Thomas Medwin that the incident was one "in which I was nearly and deeply interested" – one of those provocative Byronic innuendos. Hobhouse believed that the girl was Byron's servant. Hobhouse only knew what Byron told him, and neither he nor any of Byron's other correspondents were informed of the incident at the time. Not only was the occurrence horrifying in itself but it would have been doubly so if he had in any way been involved in the girl's predicament. Certainly Byron hinted at being engaged in many intrigues: "I have been employed the greater part of today in conjugating the verb 'ασπαζω' [embrace] . . . I assure you my progress is rapid, but like Caesar 'nil actum reputans dum quid superesset agendum,' I must arrive at the pl & opt . . ."[5]

During this same period – early September – while Byron was diving in the Piraeus a ship sailed into the harbour carrying the eccentric traveller Lady Hester Stanhope and her companion, Michael Bruce. They had just arrived from Corinth with Lord Sligo, who persuaded Byron to dress and join them. Later in her life Lady Stanhope was to settle in an abandoned Syrian fortress where the local Bedouins worshipped her as a goddess. Her charisma failed to charm Byron. He loathed intellectual women and Lady Stanhope, well aware of this, taxed him repeatedly for his low opinion of her sex. Byron took refuge in silence, and said of her to Hobhouse: "I have discovered nothing different from other she-things, except a great disregard of received notions in her conversation as well as conduct."[6] Lady Stanhope did not like Byron any better. She found him self-absorbed and moody, even discovered "a great deal of vice in his looks – his eyes set close together, and a contracted brow".[7]

Lady Stanhope naturally heard all the gossip concerning Byron's involvement in the bizarre incident in the Piraeus. Byron loathed being the subject of gossip; and claiming that he had urgent "business" in the Morea, he and Nicolo disappeared for several weeks. It was not the most propitious of journeys. In the Gulf of Corinth they were driven ashore by high winds. Byron was seized by a fever (probably malaria) and by the time they reached Patras had become very ill indeed. Nicolo also succumbed to the fever. Alternating between chills and a soaring temperature, Byron was never fully to shake off the infection.

While in some moods he jested about his condition, he also felt very forlorn. To Francis Hodgson he complained:

> As for England, it is long since I have heard from it, every one at all connected with my concerns, is asleep, and you are my only correspondent, agents excepted. – I have really no friends in the world, though all my old school companions are gone forth into the world, and walk about in monstrous disguises, in the garb of Guardsmen, lawyers, parsons, fine gentlemen, and such other masquerade dresses. – So I have shaken hands and cut with all these busy people, none of whom write to me, indeed I asked it not, and here I am a poor traveller and heathenish philosopher, who hath perambulated the greatest part of the Levant, and seen a great quantity of very improveable land and sea, and after all am no better than when I set out, Lord help me.[8]

Always obsessed by his weight, by the time he returned to Athens in the middle of October he was skeletal. Byron was delighted by his appearance. Sligo one day found him admiring himself in front of a looking-glass. Byron remarked that he should like to die of consumption. His bewildered friend asked why, eliciting the reply that the ladies would all say, "Look at that poor Byron, how interesting he looks in dying." Determined to retain this interesting shape, Byron frequented the Turkish baths daily, and with the extremity with which he pursued everything, began to confine his diet to vinegar, water, and a little rice.

Byron had constantly badgered Hanson for letters and now at the beginning of November he finally heard that his situation was so desperate that Hanson believed the only recourse was to sell Newstead. This unsettling news did nothing to impel him to return to salvage what he could of the situation. He might be ruined, but Newstead, he averred, would never be sold. It was the only place in the world which he had ever regarded as in any sense "home". If he lost it, he would be totally adrift. "I am some thousand miles from home with few resources, and the prospect of their daily becoming less, I have neither friend nor counsellor."[9] He was sending Fletcher home and his situation was "forlorn enough for a man of my birth and former expectations". To return Fletcher was a half-gesture in re-establishing links with England.

Hobhouse wrote that Scrope Davies was in a state of anxiety about being held responsible for the debt for which he had signed a promissory note to enable Byron to go on his travels. "Tell Davies, in a very few months I shall be at home to relieve him from his responsibility which he would never have incurred so long, had I been aware of the law's delay and the (not Insolence) but 'Indolence of office'" (November 26, 1810). Scrope had not been repaid, not because of the law's delay but because there was no money. Byron continued to reiterate his determination not to sell Newstead, and how he intended to repay Scrope is not clear since in the same letter he admitted that "My affairs are greatly embarrassed, and I see no prospect of their ever being better."

Meanwhile Mrs Byron was fretting that Brothers, the Nottingham merchant, would have to go to prison or be bankrupt because of the unpaid upholsterer's bill. "This is a very disagreeable business, as my Son will be represented as the cause of the Man's ruin whether it be true or not," she told Hanson (February 13, 1811).[10] But none of this she revealed to Byron. He twitted her playfully for being a "vixen" and hoped that she was getting along with her neighbours (October 4, 1810). She had received the expensive portrait of Byron (with Rushton in the background) for which he had paid Saunders an enormous sum before his departure, and found it "very like". She continued to withhold disturbing money problems from him, only disclosing them with her usual refrain that all the heiresses would be snatched up if he didn't return soon. She commended him for his determination not to sell Newstead (March 16, 1811), assuring him that she would share her last farthing with him. She had raised the rents of the tenants and she held out the possibility of potential riches from the coal mines of Rochdale, and "you will be rich again." And so continued this tragic *folie à deux*.

There was much in Greece to occupy Byron's attention. The political situation in the western part of the country – Epirus – was far different from what it had been the previous year when the two young travellers had anticipated the possibility of robbers as a great lark. Ibraham Pasha had retaken Berat (captured by Ali Pasha while Byron and Hobhouse were riding towards Tepelene) and Albania was torn by "carnage and cutting of throats".

Athens, where there had been only an occasional English visitor, was now "infested with English people" (October 4, 1810). Byron wasn't sure he liked this new situation. Even by January 10 Byron declared himself "very undecided in my intentions"." He supposed he would have to drag himself back to England in the spring to cope with his affairs, but in the meantime he was beginning to enjoy himself with the English visitors, who turned out to be more congenial than he expected. There were also various sophisticated Scandinavians and Germans who had arrived to pursue cultural and archaeological investigations.

The day of the dilettante was past. This new group included Charles Cockerell who was to discover the Aegina marbles and became a distinguished architect; John Foster, another architect; John Friott, an eminent collector and man of science who was an original member of the Royal Astronomical Society; and the scholar-antiquary, John Nicholas Fazakerly. Among the various Europeans whom Byron began to see regularly were Karl Haller van Hallerstein, architect to Prince Louis of Bavaria; Peter Bronsted and George Koes, both archaeologists at the University of Copenhagen; and numerous others who were preparing scholarly books on Greece.

Most of these scholars – unlike Lusieri and Fauvel – were outraged by the depredation and humiliation to which the Greeks had been subjected by their Turkish masters. While Byron still deplored the cunning of the Greeks, he began to see that they might shake off their chains with the enthusiastic and practical support of the Franks. He now began a serious study of demotic Greek under the guidance of a Greek patriot, Marmaratouri.

Still he lingered on, but by January 14 in a letter to his mother he mentioned that he *might* be returning in the spring. His absence he justified in that it had been invaluable in saving him from the narrow prejudices of his countrymen. As for his future, "I have done with authorship," he declared, adding that on his return he hoped to lead "a quiet, reclusive life". Such a life would never be possible for Byron, and he himself did most to bring turbulence to it. Despite his momentary impulse to abandon writing, by the middle of March he had completed a good portion of another long satire against his countrymen and also nearly 200 lines of *The Curse of Minerva*, a searing indictment of Lord Elgin, even though he continued to be on the same companionable terms with Lusieri.

Byron deliberately set out to model his *Hints from Horace*, written in heroic couplets, on both Pope's *Satires and Epistles of Horace* and his *Essay on Criticism*. It lacks, however, Pope's mordant bite, and while it was not published until after Byron's death, it is interesting as a key to his state of mind in the early spring of 1811. Knowing that his inevitable return to England was fast approaching, his paranoia about the reception of *English Bards and Scotch Reviewers* – and anything else he might write – was rekindled. Still under the delusion that Francis Jeffrey was responsible for the hostile piece in the *Edinburgh Review*, he taunted him for never replying to his counter-attack in *English Bards and Scotch Reviewers*.

> "Dear d—d contemner of my schoolboy songs,
> Hast thou no vengeance for my Manhood's wrongs?
> If unprovoked thou once could bid me bleed,
> Hast thou no weapon for my daring deed?
>
> (*Works*, I, p.319)

These lines, the most personal in the poem, he later removed. Critics have generally regarded the poem as mediocre, but it remained one of Byron's favourite works, probably because it was an enunciation of his own neo-classical view that poetry must please, improve, and imitate life as closely as possible.

The Curse of Minerva was something else altogether. Byron started writing it in the Capuchin convent in March 1811, but the major part of it was not completed until November after his return to England. The poem opens with an exquisite description of the sun setting over Attica, then moves on to an entirely different note: an intemperate attack on Lord Elgin whom Byron compares to Alaric in his depredations, ascribing his actions to the influence of his homeland Scotland (Caledonia), "land of meanness, sophistry, and mist". Finally, he ends by representing Elgin as symbolic of the general imperialistic foreign policy of Britain.

Here were the deeds that taught her lawless son
To do what oft Britannia's self had done.

(Works, I, p.327)

Minerva, the patron saint of Athens, pronounces a curse on Elgin and all his sons. The poem might have been excessively virulent, but his indignation had aroused Byron from his youthful indifference to anything that did not directly concern him.

As usual he continued to dither about his plans. He secured a firman to visit Syria and Egypt, and on February 1 applied to Hanson for an immediate remittance – "as I have nearly finished my credit" – forgetful, apparently, of Hanson's warning that he was close to ruin. By the end of February he reluctantly conceded the possibility of losing Newstead. If such a disaster occurred, he was determined, he told his mother, to spend the rest of his life in the East: "I feel myself so much a citizen of the world, that the spot where I can enjoy a delicious climate, & every luxury at a less expense than a common college life in England, will always be a country to me, and such are in fact the shores of the Archipelago. – This then is the alternative, if I preserve Newstead, I return, if I sell it, I stay away."[12]

It had indeed been a delightful winter with balls, expeditions to Sounion, and general socialising with the European community. But with the arrival of spring his new friends were gradually beginning to slip away to further antiquarian investigations. On March 19 Byron gave a dinner party, which was in fact his own farewell party. In April he was packing up his possessions. He decided to take with him two of his Albanian servants, Demetrius and Andreas, and the one who was left behind, Dervish, was inconsolable at being parted from his master. It is a measure of Byron's attractiveness that those who served him became absolutely devoted to him.

On April 21 he boarded the transport ship *Hydra*. Three of his scholarly acquaintances – Cockerell, Foster, and Linckh – saw him aboard. The following day as the group headed for the excavations at Aegina, they found Byron's ship still in the harbour of the Piraeus. They set off in a small boat to surprise him with a serenade. The delighted Byron invited them on board where they shared a comradely glass of port until called by their own pilot. The next day from the Temple of Jupiter they could still see the becalmed *Hydra* which was not able to get away until the 24th. The reluctance of wind and sail reflected Byron's own unwillingness to leave his Lotus Land where his major decisions had been limited to where he would take his daily ride.

On the same ship, headed for Malta, was Lusieri, conveying the second shipment of marbles on its way to Lord Elgin. These were the large objects that had had to be left behind from the first shipment, as well as everything Lusieri had collected in the past five years. Byron carried with him the half-written *Curse of Minerva*, whose existence was probably unknown to Lusieri. Also accompanying them was Nicolo who was going to attend school in Malta.

Undoubtedly some of Byron's reluctance to leave Athens was the expectation of having to meet Constance Spencer Smith again in Valetta. The previous September she wrote to say that if his feelings were the same as he had professed in September 1809, "then set out for Malta on the very first opportunity, as I cannot stay here longer without injuring my interests. But if you have changed your mind, if you are not in the same intention you was, then send me back this letter with your answer immediately."[3] Byron cannot have given her an entirely unambiguous answer for again on March 3, 1811, she wrote: "Recollecting our conversation in September, 1809, I thought myself bound to talk to you on that subject, and my being obliged to leave this place early in the spring makes me fearful of missing you if you do not come soon. Malta is rather more brilliant than it was, and you would perhaps like it.[4] The wistful final sentence almost suggests that she suspected:

> The Spell is broke, the charm is flown!
> Thus is it with life's fitful fever.
>   (*Works*, I, p.279)

Byron was still feeling unwell, and when he was depressed his symptoms were always more acute. His mood was decidedly glum as he viewed Valetta from the deck of the *Hydra* when the ship sailed into harbour on April 30. How on earth was he going to handle the ardently anxious Constance Spencer Smith?

Byron's ardours tended to be fervent and short-lived. Constance's letters suggest that she had fallen genuinely in love with him but soon realised that his passion had cooled. A year later he laughingly recounted a version of their meeting to Lady Melbourne. He had heard that the lady was in Vienna writing her Memoirs and he realised that "I shall cut a very indifferent figure", which suggests that he wasn't particularly proud of his behaviour. At any rate, he airily dismissed the former object of his great passion, since he now claimed that she was "a woman perfectly mistress of herself & every act of intrigue, personal or political, not at all in love, but very able to persuade me that she was so, & sure that I should make a most *convenient* & complaisant fellow-traveller."[5] The month he passed in Malta is shrouded in ambiguity.

The harbour was filled with British ships, triumphant after having defeated a French and Italian squadron off Lissa, on the Dalmatian coast. Byron had been promised a berth to England on the *Volage* as soon as necessary repairs had been completed. He was anxious to escape from his erstwhile love, but he also dreaded the return to England. His mood at departure was far different from two years before as attested by "Farewell to Malta" written on May 22:

> I go – but God knows when, or why,
> To smoky towns and cloudy sky,
> To things (the honest truth to say)
> As bad – but in a different way. –
>
>   (*Works*, I, p. 339)

The same day he jotted down "Four or Five reasons in favour of a Change", although before he was through he had added two more to the list.

> 1st At twenty three the best of life is over and its bitters double.
> 2ndly I have seen mankind in various Countries and find them equally despicable, if anything the Balance is rather in favour of the Turks.
> 3rdly I am sick at heart

> > Me jam nec *faemina* . . .
> > Nec *Spes animi credula mutui*
> > Nec *certare* juvat *Mero*.*

> 4thly A man who is lame of one leg is in a state of bodily inferiority which increases with years and must render his old age more peevish & intolerable. Besides in another existence I expect to have *two* if not *four* legs by way of compensation.

---

* Byron was misquoting Horace's lines:
> me nec faemina nec puer
> > iam nec spes animi creduli mutui
> nec certare juvat mero
> > nec vincire novis tempora floribus

5thly I grow selfish & misanthropical, something like the "jolly Miller" "I care for nobody no not I and Nobody cares for me"
6thly My affairs at home and abroad are gloomy enough.
7thly I have outlived all my appetites and most of my vanities aye even the vanity of authorship.[16]

The curious friendship with Lusieri was compounded by the fact that the Italian gave him a letter to deliver to Lord Elgin on his return. If Lusieri had known about Byron's detestation of Elgin – something more than the odd semi-jocular remark – would he have entrusted Byron with this commission? One can only speculate that Byron felt that his private feelings need not disturb the temporary nature of their relationship.

His feelings were decidedly mixed because it was extremely painful to part from Nicolo, the only being, he believed, who loved him unconditionally. Byron made him a gift of a considerable sum of money; and on his return to England added a clause to his will leaving Nicolo £7,000. Nicolo kept his word to write regularly. On January 1, 1815, the young man wrote from Athens: "It is now almost three years that I am at Athens; and have sent you many letters, but I have not received any answer . . . I pray your excellency to not forget your humble servant who so dearly & faithfully loves you."[17] Byron by now was married, and Nicolo was the last person he would have wanted to hear from.

Byron was bored and unhappy during the long voyage home. His fever flared up intermittently; he was suffering from piles; and he had a dose of the clap. He whiled away the time writing long letters, mainly to Hobhouse. These were almost like a journal since he could not post them until he arrived in England. He had managed to salvage some marble remnants Hobhouse had left behind in Greece. His own interest lay in bizarre curiosities, so he was bringing back four tortoises and four skulls he had found in an ancient sarcophagus. As to what lay ahead, "I shall first endeavour to repair my irreparable affairs" (June 19). He urged his friend not to be discouraged by the cool reception of the *Miscellany* and generously told him to blame it on friends such as himself who had been one of the contributors.

These letters – and the sequence in which they were written – are interesting as a reflection of Byron's state of mind during a period in which he felt totally isolated. While he professed to prefer solitude, this sort of solitude was one in which he was captive. A letter to his mother (June 25) radiates thoughtfulness. He requested her to prepare his apartments, "but don't disturb yourself on any account, particularly mine, nor consider me in any other light than as a visitor." As a partner in misfortune, he supposed "we shall wrestle through life like our Neighbours."

To Hodgson (June 29) he claimed that his only desire to see England was because he was utterly bored with the long voyage. "I am returning *home*, without a hope, and almost without a desire." As soon as his irreparable affairs were settled, he planned to be off again, either to the East or to join the campaign in Spain. Hobhouse he wanted to meet as soon as possible after he landed. There was a ridiculous fellow passenger, "and the worst of it is, I have no friend with me to laugh at the fellow." In the first positive plan he had considered, he suggested that perhaps, in collaboration with Matthews, they might start a periodical journal together (July 2).

Then, only two days later, he informed Hanson that he planned to join the army in Spain (despite his admiration for Napoleon and dislike of Wellington!). He had made up his mind "to bear the ills of Poverty", but in the meantime he needed £20 or £30 to enable him to travel to London. The tedious journey was prolonged still further by the ship being diverted from Portsmouth to the Nore. He finally landed at Sheerness on July 14, 1811, just two years after his giddy departure.

He returned sober and thoughtful. He had departed with the sense that the world lay all before him; and now the best seemed behind him for ever. In these two years abroad he had undergone all manner of privation and met all manner of men. His views about English convention and morality were irrevocably changed. Years later he told Trelawny that the air of Greece had made him a poet, but he was speaking in hindsight. When he arrived back he had not an inkling of the fame that would be thrust upon him within a year. The East had matured him, yes, but it had also confirmed in him a sense that he did not belong anywhere. In future years Greece would represent escape, a haven about which he could always fantasise as offering a way to leave the world behind.

9

oooooooooooooo

Encounters with Death, 1811

T here are some experiences, exotic and unusual, that make for worldliness and sophistication. There are others that are shared by the vast commonality of men – death, above everything else – that are so disturbing that they reach a depth of feeling that can be touched in no other way. Byron returned from the East as a clever and self-absorbed young man, complacent in the belief that his adventures had set him apart from his contemporaries. Within two months of his return he was to be devastated by a series of deaths, so baffling and humbling to him that we begin to encounter a man approaching real maturity rather than a narcissistic youth trying to prolong the period of immaturity beyond its normal limits.

As soon as his ship docked at Sheerness on July 14, 1811, he was off to London where he installed himself at Reddish's Hotel in St James's Street.* His first letter was to Hobhouse, promising to join him in Sittingbourne, Kent, within a couple of days. Hobhouse had made peace with his father who had agreed to repay his debt to Byron for the expenses of the Eastern trip (for which Hobhouse had kept meticulous records), but he extracted a heavy price. Hobhouse had to join the militia and he agreed to this stipulation with a heavy heart. He, too, was having his own problems with growing up.

On Byron's first night in town he dined with Scrope Davies who got drunk – as he often did – but mainly because he was relieved to see Byron alive and well. The creditors had to be dealt with – which meant persuading them to hold off a little while longer – and Byron's signatory, Mrs Massingberd, had

---

* He had told people that he was going to stay as usual at Dorant's in Albemarle Street, but he still owed money to Mr Dorant as co-signer of a bond he had not been able to repay.

to be pacified that "measures" were under way. Literary matters had to be attended to as well. The day after his arrival Robert Charles Dallas hurried eagerly to the hotel in his impatience to seize the manuscript of the Horatian satire of which Byron had alerted him. As Dallas read through it that evening he was devastated with disappointment. Any second-rate talent could have produced it "in the smoky atmosphere of London, whereas he had been roaming under the cloudless skies of Greece".[1]

This was what Dallas had to say years later, but at the time he could see that the tone, much milder than *English Bards and Scotch Reviewers*, would arouse little publicity. Surely Byron had also spoken of something "in Spencer's [sic] measure"? He had indeed; but he was reluctant to present it first lest the critics ridicule the patently autobiographical protagonist. His hesitation had been reinforced by Hobhouse's unenthusiastic reaction when he read the first two cantos just after Byron had completed them. Byron realised that Hobhouse also aspired to be a poet and that his reaction might have been tinged with envy, yet he also had a high opinion of Hobhouse's good sense. It is quite possible that Hobhouse was repelled by the self-conscious theatricality of the then *Childe Burun*.

Dallas was so anxious for a literary and financial success that he enlisted the opinion of Walter Wright. His reason for consulting Wright was fairly sound. Wright had been consul-general of the Ionian Isles and had published a poem, *Horae Ionicae*, which was one of the few productions praised in *English Bards and Scotch Reviewers*. He told Dallas bluntly that there was no possibility of the satire selling but he felt certain that the Spenserian poem would be a success. This opinion weighed strongly with Dallas since Byron, with his usual rash generosity, was handing over the copyright to him.

Dallas assured him that "You have written one of the most delightful poems I ever read."[2] However, he believed that publication was possible only if Byron agreed to some alterations and omissions. Left to ponder this reaction, Byron went off to rejoin Hobhouse for two days which they spent in visiting Canterbury and catching up on each other's news. Hobhouse recorded in his journal, "I left Canterbury on the 19th, after having parted with my dear friend."[3] Despite Byron's lamentations at sea that he would return friendless to his native land, old comrades flocked to see him. Francis Hodgson even wrote a poem in his honour:

> Return, my Byron; to Britannia's fair,
> To that soft pow'r which shares the bliss it yields;
> Return to Freedom's pure and vigorous air,
> To Love's own groves and Glory's native fields.

And within ten days of his return he was at Harrow visiting Henry Drury, who had become a father during his absence. On the 23rd, Byron wrote his mother a note that he would pay her a brief visit as soon as Hanson was ready to travel north with him to visit the coalfields of Rochdale, adding a courteous but curious comment: "You will consider Newstead as your house not mine, & me as only a visitor." On receiving this letter, Mrs Byron is said to have turned to her maid: "If I should die before Byron comes what a strange thing it would be." For three years she had been complaining about her health, but never to Byron. It is possible that she had cancer; and as she lay looking out on the south lawn, she longed to see once more the son whose interests she had put above everything else in life.

Still in her mid-forties, Catherine Byron had been a bouncy, cheerful girl who had grown careworn in the service of two selfish spendthrifts. History has not been kind to her, but perhaps "history" should be questioned if it has been manipulated in the service of a mythology created around Byron as hero. Catherine may have been a provincial with pretensions about her noble ancestry, but she was also highly intelligent, well-read, had a good sense of humour, and a store of common sense. Her temper has been held against her, but perhaps it indicated a certain spirit when she rebelled against being used only as a milch-cow by father and son. Her servants loved her dearly and remained with her for years. Possibly they were the only real friends she had for she always remained a stranger in a strange land, and they alone were there to offer comfort in her last days.

In London Byron was totally preoccupied with Dallas's search for a suitable publisher for the new poem. That Byron was also highly ambitious for its success is attested by his rejection of the obvious choice of Cawthorn as not sufficiently prestigious. He also loftily rejected the possibility of Longman because they had refused *English Bards and Scotch Reviewers*. He suggested Miller (whose long-standing bill had just been paid), but Miller declined it because of the attack on Lord Elgin, one of his best customers. Dallas then approached his own publisher, the Scot, John Murray (the son of the founder), who at that time had a shop in Fleet Street. Dallas's light novels were not among the shining lights of Murray's literary galaxy, but he listed among his authors Walter Scott, Robert Southey, Isaac D'Israeli and soon Jane Austen, whose *Sense and Sensibility* was published in 1811. Murray had also founded the *Quarterly Review* in 1808, and its first editor was William Gifford upon whom Byron had lavished praise in *English Bards and Scotch Reviewers*.

While Murray was reflecting on his decision, other vexatious matters began to plague Byron. Soon after his return he had ordered a *vis-à-vis*, which he immediately exchanged for a carriage belonging to his old drinking companion, James Wedderburn Webster. Webster found himself dissatisfied with it and demanded the return of his coach; Byron then complained that the lining was torn out when his was returned to him.* As for accepting an invitation to visit Webster and his wife: "I am infinitely obliged to you for your invitations, but I cant pay so high for a second hand chaise to make my friends a visit. – The Cornet will not *grace* the '*pretty Vis*' till your tattered lining ceases to dis*grace* it."[4]

Far more serious than this silly comedy was a personal attack on Byron in a new periodical, *The Scourge*. Those whom he had attacked with such savage glee in *English Bards and Scotch Reviewers* had come back to haunt him. When a Cambridge don, Hewson Clarke, had written critically of *Hours of Idleness*, Byron in turn wrote some cruel lines about his lowly birth in his satire. Clarke's riposte had appeared in March 1811, but only now came to Byron's attention.

> It may be reasonably asked [Clarke wrote] whether to be a denizen of Berwick-on-Tweed, be more disgraceful than to be "the illegitimate descendant of a murderer", whether to labour in an honourable profession . . . be less worthy of praise than to waste the property of others in vulgar debauchery, whether "to be the offspring of parents whose only crime is their want of title, be not as honourable as to be the son of a profligate father, and a mother whose days and nights are spent in the delirium of drunkenness".[5]

Byron widely publicised the fact that he was suing for libel, but by October the case was dropped on the advice of Sir Vickery Gibbs that a jury might consider Byron's own attack on Clarke as a provocative and extenuating circumstance.

Hobhouse, on hearing that his regiment was to be posted to Ireland, pleaded with Byron to visit him, but the latter replied: "I really have not money to carry me to Dover and back" (July 31). The reality principle was setting in with a vengeance. On August 2 he suddenly received a note from a local physician at Newstead: "My Lord, It is with concern I have to inform you that on my visit to Mrs Byron this Morning, I have found her considerably worse, so as to make me apprehensive of for [sic] the Event –

---

* It is possible that the lining was slightly torn. One should never forget Byron's habitual exaggerations. Why would Webster have ripped the lining out?

She is perfectly sensible and enquires about you – I am expecting Dr Marsden every minute from Nottingham."[6]

Mrs Byron actually died the very day on which this was written – August 1 – while Byron was rushing about trying to raise the money to travel to Newstead. Hanson was not at home but his wife lent him £40. By the time he reached the coaching inn at Newport Pagnell, less than halfway to his doleful destination, a messenger arrived with the news that his mother was dead. On August 2 he wrote to John Pigot, his old friend from Southwell days:

> My poor mother died yesterday! and I am on my way from town to attend her to the family vault. I heard *one* day of her illness, the *next* of her death – Thank God her last moments were most tranquil. I am told she was in little pain, and not aware of her situation. – I now feel the truth of Mr Gray's observation, "That we can only have *one* mother. – " Peace be with her!

He arrived at the abbey to find her servants overcome with grief. He went directly to her room. To Hobhouse (August 10) he wrote: "There is to me something so incomprehensible in death, that I can neither speak or think on the subject. – Indeed when I looked on the Mass of Corruption, which was the being from whence I sprang, I doubted within myself whether I *was*, or She *was not*." He had abused her so consistently to his friends that he was unable to speak of the depth of his sorrow, and they found themselves in the embarrassing situation of not knowing how to commiserate with him. To one of the servants who found him sitting forlornly beside her bed, he is said to have sighed, "Oh, Mrs By, I had but one friend in the world and she is gone!"

At first there were the funeral arrangements to prevent his dwelling on his loss. Mourning clothes – black hatbands, gloves, and coats – for himself and the servants had to be ordered. A notice was inserted in the *Morning Herald*. On her coffin Mrs Byron was described as "Mother of George Lord Byron the lineal descendant of the Earl of Huntley and Lady Jean Stuart, daughter of King James 1st of Scotland, obit in the 46th year of her age, August 1st, 1811." Identified only by her birth and progeny, no words of devotion or sorrow.

Byron's behaviour in the weeks following her death displayed a pattern of manic denial. His mother had in effect been his only parent. The most superficial explanation for his passion for younger boys would be that they were a creation of the ideal father–son relationship; and is it not equally possible that the tantrums and passionate reconciliations were a re-enactment of the relationship with his mother? The histrionic rows between mother and son during his adolescence, often provoked by him, were an attempt to break the bond binding him to her, just as Catherine fought fiercely to keep him. His manic dieting, which began during this period, was a manoeuvre to disclaim any identification with his corpulent parent. He had to go away as far as possible to find freedom, yet she was the recipient of the most delightful of his letters. His fear of engulfment and terror of separation revealed themselves in the bravado with which he reacted to Hobhouse's departure the previous year. Caught between these conflicting anxieties, what he too often confronted within himself was a yawning emptiness, expressed either in depression or ennui.

Byron had fled from home, secure in the knowledge that his mother was keeping Newstead in readiness for him. How could she possibly abandon him to face the future without devoted support? His grief was an ambivalent compound of anger, bewilderment, loss, and guilt. He tried to elude his inner feelings in exaggerated activity in order to assure himself that he could continue leading a normal life without her.

He was scrupulous about adhering to all the funeral proprieties, yet instead of accompanying the sombre cortège to the family vault at Hucknall Torkard* he stood at the entrance of the abbey until the procession was out of sight. He then ordered Rushton to fetch his boxing gloves for their usual morning routine, but after a desultory round or two he retired to his room. The curious nature of this behaviour cannot be denied. Was he afraid that he might break down in tears that would acknowledge his need for her? Consciously he could have justified his absence from the funeral in that he simply did not believe in all that Christian clap-trap. Lord Sligo has left on record the monstrously exaggerated remarks Byron made at Corinth when he attributed his deformity to her false modesty and accused her of taunting him about it. Nevertheless, John Galt, not one of Byron's most sympathetic biographers, has written: "Notwithstanding her violent temper and other unseemly conduct, her affection for him had been so fond and dear that he undoubtedly returned it with unaffected sincerity and from casual and incidental expressions which I have heard him employ concerning her, I am persuaded that his filial love was not at any time even of an ordinary kind."[7]

He had brought back gifts of attar of roses and exquisite shawls which she would never receive. In sorting through her possessions, he found all

---

* There was a large crowd of local people at the church, but no one of any rank.

the letters he had written to her as well as a bound volume of every review of his work with her marginal comments. Misguided as she was in the way she indulged him, no mother could have been fonder or prouder; and this he knew full well.

Even the possibility of grieving adequately for her was denied to him. While her body was still lying in the abbey he heard that Charles Skinner Matthews had died a most horrible death, enmeshed in the reeds of the Cam where he had been bathing alone. Matthews was Hobhouse's particular friend, closer to him than even Byron. "Alas, alas," Hobhouse lamented in his journal, "who is there left?"[8] But Byron's excessive reaction to Matthews's death was a marked contrast to the suppression of grief for his mother. "Some curse hangs over me and mine," he told Scrope Davies. Death and bereavement come to all men but for Byron it appeared as some special visitation from the fates reserved for him. He begged Scrope to join him at Newstead: "I want a friend."[9] This simple declaration was the closest he came to expressing his sense of loss over his parent. He had already heard of John Wingfield's death at the Battle of Coimbra, but Matthews's death was particularly horrifying in that it had occurred in water, the element which he perceived as his own. Not only Matthews but his first Harrow friend, Edward Noel Long, had drowned in 1809 on his way to join the Peninsular War when his transport collided with another ship in the night. All Byron's Celtic superstition was aroused.

Matthews had undoubtedly been a clever young man, but in death Byron exalted him to a pinnacle of excellence, in phrases he had never used when he was alive. "In ability, who was like Matthews? How did we all shrink before him?"[10] He kept dwelling on the fact that he had received a letter from Matthews on the very day of his death – but then he had also received a letter from Newstead on the day his mother died. Even to an acquaintance like Dallas, he cried (August 25), "At three and twenty I am left alone, and what more can we be at seventy? It is true, I am young enough to begin again, but with whom can I retrace the laughing part of my life?" Whatever the laughing part of his life had been, Matthews had played only a peripheral part in it.

Hobhouse told him that they must bury their dead and get on with their lives. "I cannot bear to read such melancholy letters from you. You should keep your spirits to enable you to go through . . . your Rochdale concerns" (August 2). August was a dreadful month for Hobhouse, isolated in Ireland with his regiment, but he had the sense to plead with Byron to temper his excessive grief by occupying himself with his writing. "To hear frequently from you will be one of my chief delights in this solitude, but do not my dear Byron, do not write so sadly, every line of your last wrings my very soul – I strive to forget my lamented friend, do you do the same."[11]

Such a letter was written in response to Byron's description of his emotional state (August 10):

I am very lonely, & should think myself miserable, were it not for a kind of hysterical merriment, which I can neither account for, or conquer, but, strange as it is, I do laugh & heartily, wondering at myself while I sustain it – I have tried reading & boxing, & swimming & writing, & rising early & sitting late, & water, & wine, with a number of ineffectual remedies, & here I am, wretched.

He seemed almost to wallow in morbid reflections as he sat gazing at his skulls. He was prompted to draw up his own will, one of several prepared in the course of his life. Newstead was to be left to his cousin John Anson Byron (son of his father's younger brother). Nicolo Giraud was to receive £7,000 when he reached the age of twenty-one and the former favourite, Robert Rushton, £50 per annum for life, the same sum to go to Fletcher, Joe Murray, and Demetrius Zograffo. Scrope Davies's debts were to be honoured. Finally, his body was to be buried not in the church at Hucknall Torkard but in the garden vault at Newstead and Boatswain's body was not to be removed. (Even in death was he trying to sever the cord to his mother?) If these latter instructions were disregarded "from bigotry or otherwise", he reminded his Nottingham solicitor, Samuel Bolton, that he was referring to "*consecrated* ground", and his estate should then revert to his half-sister, Augusta Leigh. His executors were to be Hobhouse and Davies; in case of their demise, the Reverend J. Becher and Dallas. Bolton left blanks for the Christian names of the executors. Byron wrote in the margin: "I forget the Christian name of Dallas – cut him out." Bolton informed him that Davies could not be an executor because if there were any outstanding debts owing to him, he had the right to indemnify himself without consulting his co-executors. Byron replied: "So much the better – if possible, let him be an executor."[12]

The death of Mrs Byron provided Byron and Augusta with an opportunity to re-establish contact. Unfortunately we do not have the first consolatory letter from Augusta, undoubtedly awkward in view of the fact that she had heard more than anyone else about Byron's problems with his mother. On August 27 she prattled on about her darling children. Scrope Davies had told her that her oldest, Georgiana, was "exactly the sort of child *you* would delight in".[3] Byron replied in mock horror (August 30): "I don't know what Scrope Davies meant by telling you I liked Children, I abominate the sight of them so much that I have always had the greatest respect for the character of *Herod*. – But as my house here is large enough for us all, we should go on very well, & I need not tell you that I long to see *you*." For the first time he talked about the possibility of marriage. If he could persuade "some wealthy dowdy to ennoble the dirty puddle of her mercantile Blood, – why – I shall leave England & all it's clouds for the East again, – I am very sick of it already."[4] In other words, he had begun to think of a convenient replacement for his mother as the custodian of the abbey while he was away enjoying his freedom. This was not simply hyperbole on Byron's part, but a recurring fantasy. Augusta hoped that he was serious about the idea of marriage, "PROVIDED *her Ladyship* was the sort of person who would suit you; and you won't be angry with me for saying that it is not EVERY *one* who would; therefore don't be too *precipitate*."[5]

She asked him if he planned to amuse them with any more satires. "Oh, *English Bards*! I shall make you laugh (when we meet) about it."[6] This was a great relief to Byron who had heard that she had been greatly offended by his lines on Lord Carlisle, and she was "perhaps the only person whom I did *not* want to *make angry*".[7] And here of course was the person sent to him to help him "retrace the laughing part of my life".

Augusta had hinted at financial embarrassments (due mainly to George's gambling debts as well as his loss of favour with the Prince Regent). Byron hastened to assure her that "at all events, & in all Situations, you have a brother in me, & a home here" (August 30). He urged her to visit him and even the "brats" would not be underfoot in the immensity of the abbey. He assured her that she was "probably the only being on Earth *now* interested in my welfare". The implication was that his mother had been the other person interested in his welfare; but in the very next sentence he reverted to mother-blaming: "You must excuse my being a little cynical, knowing how my *temper* was tried in Non-Age, the manner in which I was brought up must necessarily have broken a meek Spirit, or rendered a fiery one ungovernable, the effect it has had on mine I need not state." Augusta had awakened the tug of infantilism in him.

The earnest Francis Hodgson returned to his campaign to convince Byron of immortality. Byron replied that "we are miserable enough in this life, without the absurdity of speculating upon another." He then made a statement about his religious position, one from which he was never to deviate throughout his life:

I am no Platonist, I am nothing at all; but I would sooner be a Paulician, Manichean, Spinozist, Gentile, Pyrrhonian, Zoroastrian, than one of the seventy-two villainous sects who are tearing each other to pieces for the love of the Lord and the hatred of each other. Talk of Galileeism? Show me the effects – are you better, wiser, kinder by your precepts? I will bring you ten Mussulmans shall shame you in all good-will towards men, prayer to God, and duty to their neighbours.[18]

Hodgson was not the only person worried about Byron's defiantly unorthodox opinions. John Murray, who had been persuaded to publish the poem that was now referred to as *Childe Harold*, was concerned about his outspoken views on the scandalous British flabbiness at the Convention of Cintra* that "do not harmonize with the general feeling". As for the sniping at orthodox religion, Murray reminded him that this might result in the loss of readers: "I hope your Lordship's goodness will induce you to obviate them, and, with them, perhaps, some religious feelings which may deprive me of some customers amongst the Orthodox."[19]

Byron replied (September 5):

With regard to the political & metaphysical parts, I am afraid I can alter nothing, but I have high authority for my Errors in that point, for even the *Aeneid* was a *political* poem & written for a *political* purpose, and as to my unlucky opinions on Subjects of more importance, I am too sincere in them for recantation. – On Spanish affairs I have said what I saw, & every day confirms me in that notion of the result formed on the Spot.

Dallas offered another argument: "Mr Murray thinks that your sceptical stanzas will injure the circulation of your work. I will not dissemble that I am *not* of his opinion – I suspect it will rather sell the better for them: but I am of the opinion, my dear Lord Byron, that they will hurt *you*; that they will prove new stumbling-blocks in your road to life." Dallas predicted a great future for him if he gave more consideration to winning the good opinion of his countrymen: "Yield a little to gain a great deal; what a foundation may you now lay for lasting fame, and love, and honour!"[20]

---

* Although the British defeated the French at Vimeiro in 1808 they allowed the enemy soldiers to return to France in British ships.

Dallas's motives were in part pecuniary,* but he must be given credit for recognising the potential greatness and effect of the poem. Eventually Byron agreed to soften both the political diatribes and even the irreligious views, deleting the lines "Frown not upon me, churlish Priest! that I/Look not for Life, where life may never be . . ." Indeed, Dallas in his *Recollections of the Life of Lord Byron* has documented extensive revisions made at his suggestion; and it would appear that Byron was wise to heed his advice. For the six months prior to its publication the poem was in process of revision, alteration, and addition.

Byron had also insisted that Murray was not to show the manuscript to William Gifford because he did not want any special favours; and he was furious when he learned that Murray had ignored his injunction. "I am not at all pleased with Murray for showing the MS," he fumed to Dallas. "It is anticipating, it is begging, kneeling, adulating – the devil! the devil! the devil! and all without my wish, and contrary to my desire."[21] Nevertheless, despite his angry fulminations, it is probable that it was Gifford's favourable opinion that ultimately induced Murray to publish the poem.

There was also the issue of anonymity which Byron insisted on at the beginning. While the fact that the hero was originally called "Childe Burun" revealed beyond a doubt that the poem was autobiographical, Byron changed it in the feeble hope that it might deceive the reviewers. He was still smarting from the earlier attacks and fearful of another onslaught. Repeatedly he told Dallas that if he acceded to Murray's insistence that his name appear on the title-page, his old enemies would have a wonderful opportunity to humble him thoroughly. Nevertheless, he finally gave way, possibly influenced by the fact that he would be found out in any case and if the poem were a great success it would be more to his advantage to be directly associated with it.

His life during these months was not altogether taken up with the poem. He tried to play lord of the manor, even exercising his seigneurial rights by bringing the provocative Lucy back into the household. "I have just issued an edict for the abolition of caps; no hair to be cut on any pretext; stays permitted, but not too low before."[22] Scrope came for an all too short visit and a former Harrow favourite, John Claridge, came for an all too long one. After the companionship of worldly friends such as Davies and Hobhouse, Byron found extensive contact with the young man unbelievably tiresome. To Hobhouse he complained: "Now here is a good man, a handsome man, an honourable man, a most inoffensive man, a well

* He was given £600 for the copyright.

informed man, and a *dull* man, and this last damned epithet undoes all the rest."²³

Finally at the end of September he and Hanson made the long-planned visit to Rochdale. Just what the purpose of the trip was to be is unclear because the situation remained as muddled as ever. A great shock was awaiting Byron on his return. This was a letter from Ann Edelston, the sister of the chorister with whom Byron was infatuated at Cambridge. John Edelston had died of consumption the previous May but Byron only now heard the news. To Hodgson, among others, he poured out his sense of devastation: "I heard of a death the other day that shocked me more than any of the preceding, of one whom I once loved more than I ever loved a living thing, & one who, I believe, loved me to the last."²⁴ To Elizabeth Pigot in Southwell he wrote requesting the return of a cornelian that Edelston had given him. Whether he had entrusted the stone to her for safekeeping or had given it to her as a gift is unclear.

Again Byron was plunged into wild self-pity. Dallas, who was serving as something of a father-figure, was told: "It seems as though I were to experience in my youth the greatest misery of age. My friends fall around me, and I shall be left a lonely tree before I am withered."²⁵ What is puzzling is that there is no evidence that Byron had written to Edelston when he was in the East or that he had attempted to contact him since his return.* To Hobhouse (October 13) he confessed that "though I never should have seen him again (& it is very proper that I should not) I have been more affected than I should care to own elsewhere; Death has been lately so occupied with every thing that was mine, that the dissolution of the most remote connection is like taking a crown from a Miser's last Guinea." While undoubtedly Edelston's death aroused tender memories of the past, his death was additional proof to Byron that he was a figure doomed to suffering beyond the lot of normal men. With Edelston, Wingfield, Long, and Matthews – all gifted or beautiful young men – Byron was indulging in projective identification. In his excessive empathy, each of these deaths became *his* death. Hence developed the Byronic persona of hero as man of untold sorrows. It was a role Byron in some measure learned to slip in and out of, returning from role-playing to the everyday self whom his friends found so delightful. Lord Holland had something of this in mind when he made the sage remark to Thomas Moore that Byron had the ability to make his readers feel what he himself did not truly feel.

* Apparently he had received a letter from Edelston in Malta.

His moods could alter with startling rapidity. He was stirred out of the ennui of which he had complained since his return to Newstead by a ludicrous incident that occurred after he took himself off to London again at the end of October. The pious Hodgson had agreed to watch out for the welfare of a strumpet for his friend Robert Bland while he was away serving as chaplain in Holland. Hodgson became enamoured of her, begged her to marry him, and was refused in favour of a cavalry officer, thus plunging both Bland and Hodgson into a state of despair. "I saw this *wonder*, & set her down at seven shilling's worth," Byron told Hobhouse.[26] Worldly as these gallants might consider themselves, they were still in fact very, very young.

Once Byron had abandoned the gloom of Newstead his spirits rose appreciably. His nomination to the Alfred Club (the Savile of the day), which included literary figures such as William Gifford, was a source of enormous pride. His entry into wider literary circles was effected in a curious way. During Byron's absence in the East a letter was sent to him via Francis Hodgson from Thomas Moore (dated January 1, 1810). Sensing that it might be a challenge to a duel, the protective Hodgson had withheld the letter from him. He had reason to be apprehensive since he knew that Moore was offended because Byron had taunted him with cowardice in *English Bards and Scotch Reviewers*.

Briefly, the facts were these. The Irish poet, who had made his reputation with an English version of the *Anacreon*, had been attacked by Francis Jeffrey in 1806 for his *Odes, Epistles, and Other Poems*. Moore then challenged him to a duel; but just as it was about to take place the police arrived and hauled them off to Bow Street. The story got about that Jeffrey's pistol was not loaded, but Byron transposed it to Moore who demanded an apology.

In October, while visiting Davies in Cambridge, Byron received a second letter from Moore, almost apologetic in light of his bereavement, assuring him that the spirit in which he addressed him was "neither revengeful nor ungenerous".[27] Byron hastened to assure him that he had never received the first letter, and certainly any thoughts of vengeance were directed towards someone else (Jeffrey), but left it to Moore to pursue the matter more pugnaciously if he wished to.

Moore did not so wish. The son of an affluent Dublin grocer, Moore was a rather endearing little snob and his journals record his delight in mixing with the powerful and well connected. He was a welcome addition at the dinner parties of Lord Holland and Lord Lansdowne who were charmed by his vivacity. It would be pleasant, Moore reflected, to add another lord to his repertoire. The first letter would never have been sent had he known Byron was on a "distant ramble" (October 29)[28] and he found Byron's reply "as satisfactory as I could expect".[29] Byron intimated that he would not be averse to making his acquaintance if that were agreeable to Moore. Moore replied magnanimously (November 1): "*I* think the sooner we shake hands in amity the better."[30] Moore's friend, the poet, Samuel Rogers, was the means of bringing about the reconciliation.

And so they met at a dinner held at Rogers's home at 22 St James's Place. Rogers was just as snobbish as Moore. The son of a wealthy unitarian banker, he had the means to furnish his house with exquisite works of art, to help impecunious artists (and Moore was generally impecunious), and to entertain lavishly. He was regarded as one of the leading poets of the time (Byron admired *The Pleasures of Memory*), but his poetry barely survived him. Cadaverous in appearance, he was a sardonic conversationalist who took care to polish his epigrams; but one needed to stay on his good side lest a malicious story enliven one of his famous literary breakfasts. Rogers defended his sharp tongue with the witticism: "I have a very weak voice; if I did not say ill-natured things no one would hear what I said."[31] Count Gronow compared him to "one of those velvety caterpillars that crawl gently and quietly over the skin, but leave an irritating blister behind".[32] Many of the malicious anecdotes later circulating about Byron originated with Rogers.

The poet Thomas Campbell dropped in on Rogers on the morning of November 4 to find him and Moore discussing the prospect of the evening ahead. Campbell (who had also been spared in *English Bards and Scotch Reviewers*) insisted on being present. They were all consumed with curiosity to meet this remarkable young person who had pilloried most of their literary contemporaries and was rumoured to be about to bring out another long and mysterious poem. Rogers orchestrated the evening with great care. Moore and Campbell were to wait in another room until Rogers had had a few minutes alone with Byron. They then entered and were immediately charmed by the young man's courteous manners, soft voice, and handsome appearance heightened by his black mourning clothes.

Dinner got off to a rather awkward start when Rogers asked Byron if he would have some soup. No, he never took soup. Fish? No, he never partook of fish. Mutton? No, alas. But wine surely? No, he never tasted it. Well, then, what *did* he eat? Hard biscuits and soda water. Since Rogers did not have either, Byron finally agreed to settle for mashed potatoes doused in vinegar. The gentlemen exchanged puzzled glances, but an amiable

1. Mrs Byron, Byron's foolish but doting mother (*Courtesy of Newstead Abbey*)

2. View of Newstead Abbey from the west by J.C. Barrow (1793). The bay window next to the ruined west wall of the priory church was of Byron's bedroom from which he could view the lake (*Newstead Abbey*)

3. *Above* Mary Chaworth, Byron's
first passionate love, artist unknown
(Newstead Abbey)

4. *Above right* John Fitzgibbon, 2nd
Earl of Clare, after J. Slater (*Victoria
and Albert Museum*). The man Byron
said he loved above all others

5. Byron at his most arrogant in his
Cambridge robes

6. George Sanders's (1774–1846) portrait painted in 1809, just before Byron's departure for Greece. The romantic background was purely imaginary, but his mother believed the painter had caught a remarkable likeness of Byron
(© *Her Majesty Queen Elizabeth II/ Royal Collection Enterprises*)

7. Lady Caroline Lamb by Mary Anne Knight (*Newstead Abbey*), a mad, bad, and dangerous woman to know

8. Caroline Lamb's mischievous cartoon of Lady Holland summoning Byron to one of her literary salons (*Courtesy of the Earl of Lytton*)

9. Annabella Milbanke as a romantic ingenue, miniature, artist unknown (*Courtesy of the Harrow School Trustees*)

10. Byron in 1815, the year of his marriage, engraving after James Holmes (*National Portrait Gallery*)

11. Lady Melbourne, Byron's adored confidante, heliogravure after John Hoppner (*NPG*)

12. Hon. Augusta Leigh, Byron's beloved half-sister, by Sir John Hayter (© *British Museum*)

13. A rare glimpse of the petulant Byron, 1815, engraving G.H. Harlow (*Harrow School Trustees*)

14. Lady Byron's wedding dress which soon must have seemed to her like a shroud (*Courtesy of Museum of Costume, Bath*)

15. Piccadilly Terrace in 1815. Byron had rented Number 13, despite his superstitious nature

16. Lady Milbanke (later Lady Noel), Byron's vindictive mother-in-law, by James Northcote

atmosphere was soon re-established as the conversation turned to the merits of Walter Scott and Joanna Baillie.*

These men were all literary idols to Byron. Rogers was the oldest, twenty-five years Byron's senior; Campbell was thirty-four and Moore thirty-two. The enchantment was mutual. Byron reported to Hobhouse that he was leading "a most *poetical* life" (November 9) and that he and Moore were now on "the best of terms" (November 16). As for Rogers, he was "a most excellent & unassuming Soul, & Moore an Epitome of all that's delightful" (November 16). Hobhouse was interested but not altogether delighted: "I see you are beginning to feel the effects of notoriety; I foretold you would when we met at Sittingbourne" (November 12).[33] By the middle of December Byron was on such friendly terms with Rogers that the latter took him off to attend a current sensation, one of Coleridge's famous lectures on Shakespeare. He also renewed his passion for the theatre and was enchanted by both Mrs Siddons and Kemble as Coriolanus: "he was glorious & exerted himself wonderfully."[34]

But diversions did not dispel money problems. On the same day that Byron attended Coleridge's lecture, he wrote to Hanson in response to several anguished pleas from Mrs Massingberd: "I must take the securities on myself, & request you will arrange with the Jews on ye subject. – There is nothing else left for it, I cannot allow people to go to Gaol on my account, it is better they should tear my property to pieces, than make me a scoundrel . . . do something for the poor old Soul immediately."[35] Hanson tried unsuccessfully to raise a loan for him; and for the moment the possibility of selling Newstead was deferred.

Christmas was always a gloomy time. Byron tried to entice Moore to Newstead, but occasionally Moore would forgo his social round to spend time with his young wife. Byron did manage to collect Hodgson and the lame William Harness whom he had befriended at Harrow. At Newstead

---

* Years later, when Rogers had become very envious of Byron's fame, he recorded in his *Table-Talk*: "Some days after, meeting Hobhouse, I said to him, 'How long will Lord Byron persevere in his present diet?' He replied, 'Just as long as you continue to notice it.' – I did not then know, what I now know to be a fact, – that Byron, after leaving my house, had gone to a Club in St James's Street and eaten a hearty meat-supper." This anecdote is totally fictitious. Hobhouse was with his regiment in Ireland at the time. Moreover, Byron's letters reveal that he was still continuing with his stringent diet and chewing mastic gum to assuage the pangs of hunger. The following year Henry Long met him on the street, and reported to his father: "Lord Byron is grown so exceedingly thin that it is not every body that would recognise him – his hand felt like that of a skeleton when I shook hands with him" (July 3, 1812, Berg Collection).

Harness encountered something far different from what he anticipated. Snow was on the ground when they arrived and night fell early. Harness found the sparsely furnished abbey ponderously gloomy. Instead of the boisterous rowdyism he had heard about in the past, the three friends settled down to sedentary pursuits. Hodgson was writing a review for a literary magazine; Harness was reading for his degree; and Byron was correcting the proofs of *Childe Harold*. In the evenings they would sit late discussing literature and religion. Harness was impressed by the way Byron surreptitiously handed a glass of wine over his shoulder to the devoted Joe Murray. Hodgson would never abandon his pursuit of Byron's salvation, and sometimes he argued so passionately that his eyes were filled with tears.

Byron reserved his passion for late nights when he crept up to the chamber of the Welsh housemaid, Susan Vaughan. He became so enamoured of her that when he left for London on January 11 he sent her loving notes from every stop on the road, and even a locket in which to keep strands of his hair. Susan was equally smitten with her "dearest friend": "when you say you believe I love you, that you have tried everything to win my heart Shall I tell you my heart was yours, entirely long – long before you gave me any proof of your *Love?*"[36] When Washington Irving visited Newstead after Byron's death, he was told by an ancient housekeeper that Susan had had pretensions of becoming lady of the manor. She certainly aroused the envy of the former favourites, the other maid, Lucy, and the page, Robert Rushton, whom she caught frequently whispering together. Rushton hinted to Byron that Susan was being unfaithful; a tearful Susan claimed total devotion. Byron's paranoid jealousy is apparent in his encouragement to tattle on Susan. "I am *sure*," he told Rushton, "*you* would not deceive me, though *she* would" (January 25, 1812).[37] In actual fact, it was Rushton who had become the object of Susan's affection. Under pressure from Byron, he confessed that she had been pursuing him. When Hodgson heard of it, he wrote (January 31, 1812):

> he is wont to obey you – but more! he is attached to you – I honour his unfeigned affection – As to the manner in which he has shown it, on my soul it is beautiful – no mischief-making – no malice *forced* from him in his own defence . . . Your rival lover he could not bear to be – Oh what a blackhearted wretch must she have been to try to make it so, at the very moment she was writing the letters you show'd me.[38]

For two weeks Byron had been in agony with the symptoms of kidney stones, caused by the wrenching agony of suspicions about Susan. He chose to believe Rushton's version of the story; and Susan was dismissed. Miraculously his ailment disappeared. To Hodgson, whom he had mocked for his devotion to a prostitute, he cried in a rare moment of utter truth: "I do not blame her, but my own vanity in fancying that such a thing as I could ever be beloved."[39] This he sincerely meant; when anyone showed him affection, he would rush impulsively into a relationship, but was only too anxious to prove that it was illusory.

His thoughts again reverted to Edelston in one of the "Thyrza" poems: "And thou art dead, as young and fair." To Hodgson he wrote (February 16, 1812):

> I believe the only human being, that ever loved me in truth and entirely, was of, or belonging to, Cambridge, and, in that, no change can now take place. There is one consolation in death – where he sets his seal, the impression can neither be melted nor broken, but endureth for ever.
>
> Yours always,
B
>
> P.S. I almost rejoice when one I love dies young, for I could never bear to see them old or altered.

Or faithless. By dying Edelston could create for Byron the image of perfect fidelity never to be found among the living.

Had there also been a fantasy that the devoted Susan might become the custodian of Newstead? In actual fact he does not seem to have been much attached to Newstead as a home. There are no nostalgic letters from Greece about his longing for it, simply his reluctance ever to return to "your country" (whomever the recipient might be). He had insisted on retaining the abbey despite Hanson's cautionary advice because he needed a pivotal centre, but he did not have the means or the inclination to take a real interest in its upkeep. He was not given the opportunity to enjoy it because it stood as a tangible reproach for unpaid bills, merchants threatened with jail, recurrent humiliations. By the beginning of 1812 Byron's finances were so desperate that he was making preparations to sell the furniture in the abbey. It was very pleasant to have a country seat to which he could invite his friends, but despite his contention that he adored solitude, his depressions were worse when he was isolated there with his gloomy thoughts for company, and it is telling that he escaped to London as often as possible. Just before Christmas he wrote to Hobhouse that he was going "to Notts to be sulky for a fortnight".[40] Too restless to be buried in the country, for him Newstead was more an idea (and an unwelcome reminder) than a dearly loved home, and the amount of time he actually spent there was very limited. It had to exist because there had to be somewhere from which he could flee.

10

ᴏᴏᴏᴏᴏᴏᴏᴏᴏᴏᴏᴏᴏᴏ

The London Whirligig, 1812

Just before Byron left for his 1811 Christmas visit to Newstead, he wrote to Hobhouse (December 17, 1811): "I leave town tomorrow (19th) for Notts where the weavers are in arms & breaking of frames. Hodgson thinks *his frame* will be broken amongst the rest. – I hope not." The subject is serious, the tone semi-jocular, a tone Byron often used in addressing close friends, who learned to penetrate the frivolous to what was fundamental concern.

It was a time of economic unrest when British exports to Europe were closed off by Napoleon's continental blockade, and now also to America by the impending war with Britain. In order to make a quick and easy profit, the textile manufacturers had discarded the traditional narrow stocking frames for wider frames which required fewer hands. The workers in the Midlands revolted against this development which was resulting in both widespread unemployment and inferior products. Supported by local public opinion, the frames, placed in workers' cottages by the employers, were being systematically destroyed by masked "Luddites".*

By Christmas nearly 2,000 troops had been sent to Nottingham, resulting in violent clashes between the army and the workers. Byron's early mentor, the Reverend John Becher of Southwell, was angered by the distress of his parishioners, and Byron accompanied him on a tour of the neighbouring villages where he saw for himself the plight of the unemployed.

In January Byron returned to London, deeply preoccupied both with

---

* The origin of the term is disputed. The general view traces the appellation to "Ned Ludd", or "King Lud", a mythical figure living in Sherwood Forest in whose name the protesters issued proclamations.

his impending maiden speech in the House of Lords and with the imminent publication of *Childe Harold*. The juxtaposition of these two major events in his life cannot be overlooked. A career in politics would be a natural choice for a young aristocrat. Byron was aware of this when he attended debates at the House of Lords while still at Harrow. But he was a Whig, and the Whigs' brief hope of attaining power again had been snuffed out by what they regarded as the perfidy of the Prince Regent. When George III descended into madness his son, the Prince of Wales, was made regent in January 1811. For some years he had gathered around him a group of Whigs, led by Charles James Fox and Richard Brinsley Sheridan, the playwright, leading them to believe that he would support them once he was in power. His friend Fox (who many think would undoubtedly have become Prime Minister) had died in 1806, but it was widely believed that his nephew, Lord Holland, would head the next government. However, the prince began to see things differently after becoming regent. Many of his old friends (some of them, like Holland, supporters of Napoleon) were urging him to sue for peace with France, but he began to cast himself in the role of Napoleon's greatest antagonist. Deciding that the liberal tendencies of the Whigs were detrimental to a strong centralist government, he first suggested a coalition between the moderate Whigs and the Tories, a government that he must have realised would be totally unacceptable to the Whigs. He then asked the Tories, under Spencer Percival, to remain in office, in the belief that he could rely on the Tories to win the war. The Whigs continued to be exiled from power during all Byron's lifetime. At a banquet at Carlton House on February 22, 1812, the regent abused his former friends so brutally that his daughter, Princess Charlotte, burst into tears. Byron stored away the incident for later poetic use.

Byron was scheduled to give his maiden speech at the end of February, but at the beginning of the month he was still undecided about its topic. He considered the question of Catholic Emancipation, an issue supported by the Whig leaders but detested by the Prince Regent. Finally, further disturbing reports from Nottinghamshire about Luddite frame-breakers and clashes with the army changed his mind.

His resolve that he had chosen the right subject was reinforced on February 14 when the Frame Work Bill was introduced, by which the punishment for frame-breaking was changed from transportation to the death penalty. He began to prepare his speech on the causes of the riots at the same time as he was correcting the final proofs of *Childe Harold*. While he was eager to voice his indignation, the prospect of exposing himself on so many fronts sent him into a panic and he began to think of flight. On February 16, 1812, he announced to Hodgson:

> In the spring of 1813 I shall leave England for ever. Every thing in my affairs tends to this, and my inclinations and health do not discourage it. Neither my habits nor constitution are improved by your customs or your climate. I shall find employment in making myself a good Oriental scholar. I shall retain a mansion in one of the fairest islands, and retrace, at intervals, the most interesting portions of the East. In the mean time, I am adjusting my concerns, which will (when arranged) leave me with wealth sufficient even for home, but enough for a principality in Turkey. At present they are involved, but I hope, by taking some necessary but unpleasant steps, to clear every thing.

Despite this total fantasy, the more responsible and concerned part of him continued to press forward in the preparation of his speech. On the suggestion of Moore, he sought a meeting with the leading Whig, Lord Holland. (That Holland consented to see him was to his credit since Byron had attacked him unfairly in *English Bards and Scotch Reviewers* under the impression that he was partially responsible for the unfavourable critique of *Hours of Idleness* in the Whig *Edinburgh Review*.) Sensing correctly that Holland did not share his outrage over the bill, after listing the reasons for his opposition in a letter of February 25, Byron added a postscript: "I am a little apprehensive that your Lordship will think me too lenient towards these men, and *half a framebreaker myself.*"

When Dallas came to write his *Recollections* he had long since been estranged from Byron so that the tone is decidedly catty, but we cannot ignore his account of Byron's preparations for his debut since he saw a great deal of him during this period. Byron had memorised his speech, and would rehearse it to Dallas in a voice altered from its usual mellifluous tone into "a formal drawl". Undoubtedly his artificial delivery had something to do with the muted reception of his impassioned declamation on February 27.

Michael Foot is right that a good case can be made that the speech was greater than the poem he was about to publish.[1] Bringing all his acting ability to the fore, he literally smouldered with indignation. He had seen with his own eyes, he declared, "the most unparalleled distress", and he argued that only extreme poverty could have driven these hard-working people into acts of violence. This so-called "mob" were human beings who were being treated as more nefarious than British enemies abroad. People must not be sacrificed to the economic gain of the privileged. He then lapsed into hyperbole which was unlikely to win his audience: "I have traversed the seat of war in the peninsula, I have been in some of the most oppressed provinces of Turkey, but never under the most despotic of infidel governments, did I behold such squalid wretchedness as I have seen since my return in the very heart of a Christian country."[2]

As if to reinforce his point, no member of the government bothered to reply. In his *Memoirs* Holland described the speech as not "at all suited to our common notions of Parliamentary eloquence. His fastidious and artificial taste and his over-irritable temper would, I think, have prevented him from ever excelling in Parliament."[3] Holland did support him in his objections to the excessive use of force to quell the rioters; but he was a member of the established oligarchy, and behind the obfuscation of his comments on Byron was the suspicion that this was a man who might betray class solidarity.

Byron had intended to make a sensational event of the occasion. He was in such an elated state at the end of his delivery that he failed to notice the tepid reaction of Lord Holland and others, although he admitted to Hodgson that his delivery was "perhaps a little theatrical" (March 5, 1812).

Byron wanted desperately to be admitted into the Whig establishment but with an extraordinary want of judgement he sent off to the Whig *Morning Chronicle* an anonymous poem, "An Ode to the Framers of the Frame Bill", far more provocative than his speech, and also "Sympathetic Address to a Young Lady Weeping", based on Princess Charlotte's reaction to her father's attack on the Whigs at the famous Carlton House dinner. In time the author was bound to be recognised, thus marking him as a demagogue and effectively destroying his future in politics. His impetuous behaviour was almost a death wish to place himself on the periphery of society just at the moment he most wanted to enter it.

Malcolm Kelsall has argued that the maiden speech was delivered without any hope of changing anything.[4] Byron was undoubtedly sincere, but he could compartmentalise the issues which concerned him. His own financial worries led him to ask Hobhouse for an IOU for his share of the expenses of the Eastern trip. Benjamin Hobhouse repaid his son's loan (with interest) of £1,323 on March 17. Also, in the very month in which Byron was delivering the Frame Work Bill speech, he allowed Hanson to double the rents of his Newstead tenants.

Through Moore, Byron learned that Lord Holland would be grateful if no further editions of *English Bards and Scotch Reviewers* appeared. Moore must have told him that a fifth edition was being prepared. Byron's recklessness was replaced with prudence. He ordered Cawthorn to cease publication, although Cawthorn proceeded just the same with spurious editions, possibly as many as fifteen. To his publisher's dismay, Byron also ordered him not to print *Hints from Horace* and the attack on Lord Elgin, *The Curse of Minerva*. The latter placed him in a certain predicament. He had delivered Lusieri's letter to Elgin. Elgin had subsequently made a number of attempts to meet him, all of which Byron evaded. He did, however, write to warn Elgin that he planned to attack him in *Childe Harold*, and he could not refrain from distributing a number of privately printed copies of *The Curse of Minerva* which were to cause Elgin irreparable harm.

Childe Harold's Pilgrimage, A Romaunt was first published in an expensive quarto format in an edition of 500 copies at the beginning of March 1812. Byron and Murray had both given away copies in order to create interest but sales of the book exceeded all expectations. Within a short time the quarto edition had been sold out, and the book was being reprinted in a less expensive octavo. There is no record of the exact number of copies sold in the ten editions which were issued before the publication of *Childe Harold's Pilgrimage, Canto the Third* in 1816; but *Childe Harold's Pilgrimage, Canto the Fourth* in 1818 caused readers to demand the whole poem be printed together as a single book. William St Clair estimates that a total of 15,000 to 20,000 were printed.[5] In quarto the book cost a guinea and a half, and about forty or fifty shillings when bound. When Byron woke up to find himself famous, as William St Clair has shown, it was fame among a small group of wealthy aristocratic readers.

Besides the first two cantos of the main poem, *Childe Harold's Pilgrimage, A Romaunt** included a number of shorter poems which were added in subsequent editions at the back of the volume. These shorter poems, which included some on love and separation, addressed to Thyrza, were as much a part of Byron's personal appeal as the poem itself. They had originally been addressed not to a woman as most readers assumed but to Robert Edelston.

Byron the poet appeared at a time when the long verse romance, made popular by Sir Walter Scott, was a favourite type of reading mainly among the aristocracy. The dominance of the novel which can be said to have begun with *Waverley*, published anonymously by Scott in 1814, still lay

---

* The title deserves comment. In the days of chivalry "Childe" denoted a noble youth who was a candidate for knighthood. In the choice of Harold, probably prompted by Harold Harefoot, the illegitimate son of Canute, Byron was thus working in his ancient lineage, his sense of himself as an outsider, and his deformed foot.

ahead. The great period of Trollope, Dickens, and George Eliot was synonymous with the rise of a middle-class reading public. Now cultivated people discussed the latest poetry; and the poem of the season was undoubtedly *Childe Harold*.

The twenty-year-old Miss Annabella (Anne Isabella) Milbanke, down from Durham for her second London season, dined with her relatives, the Melbournes, on March 15. She recorded in her journal: "Julius Caesar, Lord Byron's new poem, and politics were the principal themes in conversation."[6] Her journal entry for March 24 records her reaction to the new poem: "Have finished Lord Byron's Childe Harold, which contains many passages in the best style of poetry. He is rather too much of a *mannerist* . . . He excels most in the delineation of deep feeling, and in reflections relative to human nature."[7]

The following morning she actually saw the poet at Lady Caroline Lamb's waltzing party where she observed him with close attention. In the long description that she transcribed in her journal she notes that "His mouth continually betrays the acrimony of his spirit. I should judge him sincere and independent. *Sincere* at least so far as he can be while dissimulating the violence of his scorn."[8]

What was there about the poem that within two short weeks after its publication that it should propel Byron into high society so that young ladies would be writing about him in their diaries? Byron and the recently introduced new German dance, the waltz, had become the rage at precisely the same time. Byron's subsequent behaviour indicated that he resented the waltz, not only because he could not participate in it, but because it detracted from the attention that might have been concentrated exclusively on him.

The still notorious *English Bards and Scotch Reviewers* had created a mood of anticipation for the poem. Also, apart from curiosity about what the author was up to this time, *Childe Harold* appeared at a moment when there was an enormous interest in the areas Byron had visited, particularly the Levant, which had been aroused by the spate of travel books on the East. Byron emphasised the immediacy of the background by his opening words in the Preface: "The following poem was written, for the most part, amidst the scenes which it attempts to describe. It was begun in Albania; and the parts relative to Spain and Portugal were composed from the author's observations in those countries." It was a clever touch of Byron's to place Albania first since, of all the countries he describes, it was still the most exotic and inaccessible.

Moreover, the Peninsular War was very much on people's minds. As

Childe Harold traverses Spain, he meditates on the humiliation of the Convention of Cintra: "Britannia sickens, Cintra! at thy name!" The Childe crosses the plain of Talavera (site of the battle in 1809) and reaches Seville which had been under siege for the last two years. Then on April 6, 1812, shortly after the publication of the poem, Wellington captured Badajos, one of the most brilliant achievements of the Peninsular War, and on July 22 Cadiz was liberated as a result of Wellington's victory at Salamanca. These events undoubtedly helped to prolong the topical value of the poem.

In the Preface, after a brief discussion of the background of the poem, Byron turns immediately to the protagonist:

> A fictitious character is introduced for the sake of giving some connexion to the piece . . . It has been suggested to me by friends, on whose opinions I set high value, that in this fictitious character, "Childe Harold," I may incur the suspicion of having intended some real personage; this I beg leave, once for all, to disclaim – Harold is the child of imagination . . .

It was not to be "once for all" because no one believed him.

In an Addition to the Preface (in the seventh edition, published in mid-September), Byron reiterated more strongly that Childe Harold was a character in his own right. In a half-hearted attempt to distance himself from his protagonist, he expressed a positive distaste for his creation. The poet's intention was actually to draw a moral, "to show that early perversion of mind and morals leads to satiety of past pleasures and disappointment in new ones, and that even the beauties of nature, and the stimulus of travel (except ambition, the most powerful of all excitements) are lost on a soul so constituted or rather misdirected".

Years later his bitter estranged wife wrote out some reflections in which she made a number of comments on the disclaimers in the Preface. As for Childe Harold being the "child of the Imagination", "In this as in many other instances within my knowledge – the author's real intentions are those which he disclaims."[9] This should be a warning to the unwary reader, she continued:

> the necessity of concealment, increasing in every year of his life, has induced habits of falsehood and duplicity, with all the "crooked policy" which constitutes the highest perfection of cunning. The dissipation to disburthen himself of that which "weighs upon the

heart" seems to be indulged only in poetry – where the character of Fiction can be employed to disguise the Truth – Truth which – whilst he cannot suppress – he is anxious to disown.

This caustic analysis was written very much in hindsight because at the time Annabella Milbanke, like many other young women, was intrigued by this fascinating self-portrait in which the protagonist virtually cried out for understanding, compassion, and absolution. A self-confessed rake, he had "spent his days in riot most uncouth". Immediately undercutting any pretensions at fiction, the narrator cannot resist describing his lineage as ancient, albeit stained by the deed of one of his ancestors (the fifth lord's murder of his Annesley neighbour). He departs from his noble pile (which bears a striking resemblance to Newstead), driven by self-hatred.

> For he through Sin's long labyrinth had run,
> Nor made atonement when he did amiss,
> Had sigh'd to many though he lov'd but one,
> And that lov'd one, alas! could ne'er be his.
> Ah, happy she! to 'scape from him whose kiss
> Had been pollution unto aught so chaste;
> Who soon had left her charms for vulgar bliss,
> And spoil'd her goodly lands to gild his waste,
> Nor calm domestic peace had ever deign'd to taste.
>
> (I, 5)

He finds a measure of peace in solitude, especially among the sublime and terrifying aspects of nature, craggy mountains, crevasses, wide plains, storm-tossed seas, but

> What Exile from himself can flee?
>   To Zones, though more and more remote,
> Still, still pursues, where-e'er I be,
>   The blight of life – the demon, Thought.
>
> ("To Inez", I, 857–60)

The impression of the Childe as a being apart is intensified by the dual narrative voice. At one moment Harold speaks out of his misery, at another we hear a disembodied commentator who is in fact another version of himself that Byron chose to project into his poetry. Both Harold and the commentator reveal their basically noble natures in pleas to the Spaniards and the Greeks to throw off their shackles and in the barely disguised attack on Lord Elgin for his plunder of the Parthenon. And who, the reader might ask, was the mysterious "more than friend" whose death had snatched away all possibilities of joy? Occasionally the poet realises that Harold has disappeared. After fifteen stanzas deploring the woes of Greece, he suddenly asks, "But where is Harold?" (II, 16). The confusion between poet and hero was compounded by the appended Notes in which Byron speaks unabashedly in his own voice.

The creation of Childe Harold, the projection of a persona, posturing yet idealistic, was a poetic figure entirely new in literature. He is a compound of the eternal Wanderer, the gloomy egoist, and man of feeling who is grieving for a lost love; he is also the philanthropist concerned with the suffering caused by war and oppression. The Childe was to become the prototype of the guilt-haunted hero who would capture the imagination of Europe and leave his imprint on the literature of an entire generation.

From the moment the Childe, the high-born youth, emerged from the pages, Byron and his poetic persona were indissolubly linked. The poem departed from the usual topographical genre in that concentration was focused on the Childe's reactions to scenes and events rather than on what was witnessed. The necessity to penetrate the hero's façade, to reach the sensitive heart that undeniably throbbed beneath the austere exterior became the determined purpose of every young woman who copied passages into her commonplace book. He might still be saved by a pure woman. Who, people wondered, was the "sweet Florence"? Hobhouse, who had returned from Ireland, reported to Byron: "Your *Florence* is found out, although I told a large party of women yesterday a tremendous lie in your behalf."[10] *Childe Harold* became something of a *roman à clef* to keep society speculating.

London was a small world that thrived on gossip. Geographically its area was confined within a startlingly small space. The western border was Tyburn Turnpike, beyond which lay the nursery gardens of Bayswater. North of Portland Place the city dissolved into meadows and pastures. The great houses that lined Piccadilly came to an abrupt end at Hyde Park where cattle and deer grazed under the trees. Bloomsbury was beginning to be established by merchants who had made their fortunes from India and the West Indies.

Belgravia was not to be created until 1825. Leicester Square was still privately owned. Bond Street was the fashionable shopping street and those who patronised it lived in Mayfair or St James's, east of the parks which had not yet been landscaped. When not in the city, they visited each other at their great stately country houses or frequented the fashionable watering places of Cheltenham, Bath, or Brighton.

Gas lighting had replaced whale oil in Pall Mall in 1807. The street was dominated by the regent's opulent residence, Carlton House, the centre of fashion and political patronage. In 1811 John Nash began to build Waterloo Place, with the grand design of making a roundabout at Piccadilly Circus and then swinging two curves of arcaded buildings to a noble avenue leading up to what would eventually become Regent's Park. The beauty of London (what has remained after the depredations of war and developers) is due to the grandiosity of the Prince Regent, who saw himself as ruler of a noble city.

In its preoccupation with amusing itself, Byron's little world turned its eyes inward away from the horrors of the slums around Westminster Abbey and the area now occupied by Trafalgar Square. Death by starvation was common. In her wonderful book, *The Dandy*, Ellen Moers has stressed the *exclusivity* that marked Regency society. Its clubs, in St James's, were all within easy hailing distance of each other. The most celebrated were White's, Boodle's, and Brooks's. White's was the most difficult to join, and it is significant that Byron was never made a member of any of the leading clubs. If he had been proposed, he would undoubtedly have been blackballed for his frame-breaking speech. There was also Watier's, the dandies' club, of which Beau Brummell was president for a time. Byron boasted that he was one of the few literary men to be a member. The club was supposed to have been founded by the Prince Regent's chef, a Frenchman by the name of Watier, after members of White's and Brooks's complained about the quality of their food.

Then there were the great Assembly Rooms of Almack's, a *sine qua non* for evening parties to which access was granted only by the condescension of a despotic patron like Lady Jersey. At the weekly ball men were required to wear knee breeches; and it must have been agony for Byron since he could not dance and was painfully conscious of his abnormally thin right leg.

People made their calls by carriage, *vis-à-vis*, or sedan chair. The amount of food and drink consumed was prodigious. Count Gronow's *Recollections* give us a list of what would be considered *de rigueur*.

> Mulligatawny and turtle soups were the first dishes placed before you; a little lower, the eye met with the familiar salmon at one end of the table, and the turbot, surrounded by smelts, at the other. The first

course was sure to be followed by a saddle of mutton or a piece of roast beef; and then you would take your oath that fowls, tongue and ham, would assuredly succeed as darkness after day, etc. etc."

The custom of women withdrawing after the meal had not yet come into vogue.

Gambling was the chief pastime, usually for very high stakes. The lavishly extravagant Prince Regent himself was deeply in debt to the money-lenders. It was very much a man's world, yet formidable power was exerted by the great hostesses led by Lady Melbourne and Lady Holland, whose residence, Holland House, was the centre of Whig activity. Lady Holland, who had left her husband, Sir Godfrey Webster, for Lord Holland, held despotic sway over her nightly dinners although few women attended them because of the scandal she had created by her divorce and remarriage. The priggish Annabella Milbanke assured her parents: "If I am asked to be introduced to Lady Holland's acquaintance, I shall certainly decline, but I think you will agree with me that no one will regard me as corrupted by being *in the room* with her."[12]

People attended opera at His Majesty's Theatre in the Haymarket once a week where they walked about during the performance visiting their friends. Again, the patronesses of Almack's were in control of the allocation of boxes and tickets. The two great London theatres were Drury Lane and Covent Garden. People flocked to see the Kembles, Mrs Siddons, and Edmund Kean in highly dramatic performances. It was acceptable for young men to jostle together in the pit, but once one was established in society, it was necessary to hire a box. Nevertheless, the theatre was not the fashionable rendezvous that the opera was because tickets were more readily available.

Hyde Park was another place to be seen. Here dandies displayed their elegant attire, and beautiful carriages conveyed marriageable daughters. There was a marked insularity about this society, cut off as it was by war from the continent. Only a few families such as the Hollands continued to travel around Europe. When people spoke of *the world*, they meant their own society within a universe marked off by Pall Mall, St James's Street, Piccadilly, and Whitehall.

In many ways it was a philistine society. Good music was almost non-existent and served only as a background to social occasions. The Dulwich Gallery, opened in 1814, was the first gallery accessible to the public, and was the collection which first aroused Ruskin's aesthetic sensibilities. There were annual (private) exhibitions at the Royal Academy where in 1812

Turner exhibited his magnificent *Snowstorm: Hannibal and his Army crossing the Alps* with its theatrical Byronic quality, although there is no evidence that Byron ever saw it. He was totally illiterate about art and music and did not really encounter great works (except for the Parthenon) before he went to Italy.

Yet conversation was of a high order, and one had to be *au courant* with all the latest gossip. A great deal of time was spent simply *sitting*, so one had to devise every means possible for avoiding boredom. London at that time had sixteen daily newspapers, the contents of which were constantly discussed. People met in drawing rooms with high ceilings and often the newly fashionable long windows now opened into a garden. Regency households had begun to import the products of the iron mills for graceful patterns of wrought-iron balconies. Furniture was simple and elegant, curved so that ladies could lounge gracefully.

Fashion was taken very seriously, as it has been in all affluent societies. The true dandy took immense trouble over his attire, the cut of his coat, the shape of his cravat. The aim was to look as though one hadn't taken such pains since the effect was to be simple and well groomed. Beau Brummell set the tone by replacing breeches with trousers and he was the first man to wear black for evening wear, a fashion Byron capitalised on. If anyone was to serve as a model for Byron it was Brummell with his insouciance, witty turn of phrase, and seemingly total disdain for most people.

Women attempted to look subtly seductive. Their dresses were usually of soft, clinging, and totally impractical materials such as muslin, although the lushness of velvet was also becoming popular. Skirts were now above the ankle, and a new over-garment, the pelisse, had recently been introduced. *Décolletage* was very much *à la mode* and indeed the fashions reflected the frivolity and general licentiousness of the period. Married couples generally went their own way. The tone was set by the Prince Regent who banished his German wife to another household as soon as their daughter was born.

The one rule necessary for preserving the fragile code of a world in which liaisons were taken as a matter of course was discretion. Lady Melbourne was a case in point. By 1812 she was sixty-two, and even though she had grown fat she was still enormously attractive with penetrating eyes, an air of mature understanding, and free from tiresome affectations. She came from an old Yorkshire family and after marrying a dull man at nineteen, she had a succession of lovers, including, it was said, the Prince Regent. Possibly all her six children were illegitimate. Her second son, William, who was to become Victoria's first Prime Minister, was generally believed to be the son of Lord Egremont.

Lady Melbourne's place in society was a reflection of the rise of a new parvenu aristocracy quite distinct from the ancient landed families. She and her brother, Sir Ralph Milbanke, were minor county gentry, not wealthy but well-connected. She had married Sir Peniston Lamb whose great wealth came from moneylending, and who had received his Irish peerage as late as 1770. Nevertheless, largely through the charisma of Lady Melbourne, Melbourne House in Whitehall had become one of the great Whig centres to which people felt privileged to be invited.

This was the world which Byron could never have penetrated by his title alone. Lord Carlisle had refused to act as his sponsor in the House of Lords because of his contempt for his vulgar mother. However, with a single poem Byron had achieved a sort of celebrity and attention beyond his wildest dreams. During his years at Cambridge Byron had donned and discarded various personae. Now, by some extraordinary coincidence he had touched a nerve, particularly with his female readers. The Man of Feeling was already becoming a stock character portrayed in such works as Laurence Sterne's *A Sentimental Journey through France and Italy* (1765). To the figure of heightened sensibilities, Byron added the frisson of erotic diabolism. When one balances that with humanitarianism and sensitivity to nature, the appeal extended far beyond squealing females to a European awareness that this figure represented a rebellion against the old order of decorum, restraint, privilege, and absolutism. Byron, more than any other single individual, contributed to the birth of a new sensibility. For a good part of the century European literature was to be dominated by the noble isolated hero who stands aloof from the petty preoccupations of the bourgeoisie while at the same time representing defiance of traditional attitudes. All that a bewildered Byron knew at the time was that he was the lion of the moment. The Duchess of Devonshire told her son, "The subject of conversation, of curiosity, of enthusiasm almost, one might say, of the moment, is not Spain or Portugal, Warriors or Patriots, but Lord Byron!"[3] Carriages arrived at 8 St James's, bearing more invitations than he could accept. Young ladies wrote him agitated love letters. Rogers was also besieged – so long as he promised to bring Byron with him. It is not surprising that Byron's head was turned. "Never," says Dallas, "was there such a sudden transition from neglect to courtship."[4] Dallas began to notice a marked change in him. "Though flattery had now deeply inoculated him with its poison, he was at first unwilling to own its effects even to himself"[5] Byron had always declared that he loathed society, but as the party invitations accumulated, he confessed: "I begin to like them."[16]

He was even tempted to disregard his Whig principles. At a gathering in

June he was presented to the prince, with whom he had a long conversation about literature. Indeed he was so carried away that he was dressed and ready to attend the prince's next levée but it was cancelled at the last moment. In his changeable state he was soon calling upon the prince's estranged wife and his embittered daughter, Princess Charlotte. The man who had professed that the hum and throb of cities was torture to him found that he actually enjoyed being the centre of attention. However, he did not know how to conduct himself with ease and was always conscious that people might be looking at his foot. It is doubtful if he had ever entered a fashionable drawing room before the publication of his poem, and he had a whole breviary of etiquette to master. To hide his unease, he adopted a defensive expression of furrowed brow and disdainful smile. The ladies were enraptured because that was precisely the demeanour of Childe Harold. Byron as a person became absorbed into a world even stranger than Albania, and the Byron we now meet is often the blurred projection of other people's fantasies. Women were forming a circle around him; and as the ring tightened, it is sometimes hard to catch more than a glimpse of him.

Miss Milbanke recorded every nuance of his expression. Byron noticed her as well. Compared to the other women, she was unfashionably dressed and not particularly comfortable in society. Byron enquired of Moore if she was someone's companion. Moore whispered that she was actually Lord Wentworth's heiress in town for the season and that he had better set his sights on her in order to retain Newstead. Taking note of this, he made sure to fan her interest in him by remarking to Lady Melbourne in her hearing, "I have not a friend in the world." Annabella's reaction was, "I consider it as an act of humanity and a Christian duty not to deny him any temporary satisfaction he can derive from my acquaintance – though I shall not seek to encrease [sic] it. He is not a dangerous person to me."[7] Her letters for the next weeks were so filled with praise of Byron that her parents became alarmed. Occasionally he would make remarks to her over which she would ponder, theatrical statements such as an observation that "there was scarcely one person who on returning home dared to look into themselves."

Annabella might have been a country mouse but she actually had plenty of suitors during that season. One was Augustus Foster, son of the Duchess of Devonshire, who warned him that she found Annabella "cold, prudent, and reflecting". Then there was a childhood friend, George Eden, and also General Pakenham, both of whom she rejected. She was irritated by the attentions of Byron's old Cambridge friend, William Bankes, who was bisexual yet genuinely attracted to her, but she found him a great pest who prevented her from making a real acquaintance of Lord Byron.

She was quick to notice other women who caught his eye. The great heiress, Miss Mercer Elphinstone, was lively and self-confident with him, and Annabella found her "incomprehensible", meaning that she disliked her immensely. At first she had no suspicions of Caroline Lamb, the wife of her cousin, William Lamb. The Lambs and their small retarded son lived in an apartment above his parents in Melbourne House. Caroline was the daughter of Lady Bessborough, and the niece of the Duchess of Devonshire, reputedly the greatest beauty of her time, and once the mistress of the Prince Regent. Caroline's mother had been the mistress of Richard Brinsley Sheridan as well as of Lord Granville to whom she married a niece. As a child Caroline had spent much time abroad. She was well-read and intelligent, but unstable and subject to nervous attacks.

Caroline was so charming and vivacious that her wilfulness and volatility were ascribed to an endearing eccentricity; and she was given nicknames such as Ariel, Sprite, and the Young Savage. When William Lamb married her in 1805 he was genuinely in love with her, but she was provocatively flirtatious and it was not long before she entered into an affair with Sir Godfrey Webster, the former husband of Lady Holland, an episode tolerated by her indulgent, indolent husband. Her worldly mother-in-law did not take so relaxed an attitude, and scolded her severely: "Your behaviour last night was so disgraceful *in its appearance* [italics mine] and so disgusting from its motives that it is quite impossible it should ever be effaced from my mind."[18]

Neither Caroline nor Annabella was a beauty. Annabella had a lovely figure but a snub face with bulging, pippin-like cheeks. Caroline was very thin, almost androgynous, with large dark eyes and a mop of short curls. She spoke with a sort of lisp – the Devonshire drawl – which Annabella found extremely irritating. On a visit to Brocket, the Melbournes' Hertfordshire estate, Annabella complained to her parents: "Lady Caroline baa-a-a-a's till she makes me sick."[19]

Annabella was the complete opposite of Caroline: reserved, pedantic, and humourless. She had grown up as an only child who was born to her mother when she was over forty. Her parents doted on her and encouraged her to think highly of her own opinions. Her provincial background was a total contrast to the licentious world in which Caroline shimmered, a world to which Annabella's parents were dubious about exposing their treasure.

Caroline, of course, had far more opportunities of cultivating Lord Byron than her country cousin. Rogers lent her his advance copy of *Childe*

Harold. As soon as she had read it she summoned him to Melbourne House with the demand that he introduce her to the poet. Rogers warned her that he was lame and bit his nails. Caroline was not to be deterred. "If he is as ugly as Aesop, I must see him!"

But first she wrote him an ecstatic letter urging him to be happy, to dispense with gloom and regrets. The letter was anonymous but she gave an address to which he could reply. Byron could not resist the bait; and, according to Dallas, was soon totally preoccupied in the exchange of letters. He probably suspected the identity of the mysterious woman. The first time they laid eyes on each other had been at a ball at Lady Westmoreland's. Caroline approached, saw that Byron was surrounded by adoring females, and then turned abruptly on her heel. Byron's curiosity was piqued. Caroline later told Lady Morgan that her first impression of him was that he was "Mad, bad, and dangerous to know"; such epithets applied far more appropriately to her than to Byron, but the combination was lethal. While he was always impulsive, had Byron's head not been turned by success he would never have allowed himself to be so swept away.

Their first real meeting was an introduction by Lady Holland, and immediately they began to banter flirtatiously. The next day, again after riding, Caroline was sitting in Melbourne House talking to Rogers and Moore when Byron was announced. Immediately she flew out of the room to tidy herself up. Rogers, who was becoming increasingly disgruntled by Byron's celebrity, remarked, "Lord Byron, you are a happy man. Lady Caroline has been sitting here in all her dirt with us, but as soon as you were announced she flew to beautify herself." He sent her a rose and a carnation, remarking sardonically: "Your Ladyship, I am told, likes all that is new and rare, for a moment." Caroline replied: "Lady Caroline does not plead guilty to this most unkind charge, at least no further than is laudable, for that which is rare and distinguished and singular ought to be prized and sought after than what is commonplace and disagreeable."[20]

It is difficult to describe the electricity between this pair without lapsing into romantic verbiage. If *Childe Harold* had been a sensation, within a month their affair was even more sensational. To some extent they were playing to the gallery, but Byron's success had thrown him into such a heightened state of exhilaration that it was predictable that he would fasten on an object as manic and narcissistic as himself.

Discretion was thrown to the winds, and soon all London was talking of their affair. What is curious is that Annabella makes absolutely no reference to the relationship in her journal. In early April (before it would have developed), she sent to Byron through Caroline some of her own poems for him to read. He found himself impressed by them; and, for fear he was developing an interest in her country cousin, Caroline implied that Annabella was "promised" to George Eden. Annabella was given some vague version of Byron's reaction, and she then made a strange entry in her journal: "Went in morning to Lady Caroline Lamb's, and undeceived her by a painful acknowledgement . . . Received Lord B's opinion of my verses."[21] Does this mean that Caroline wormed out of her that she was really in love with Byron? Caroline warned her to beware of genius and heroic sentiments in the corrupt world of London.

Annabella's journal continues with sightings of Byron, but her comments about him begin to reveal a new, critical streak. On June 16 she writes of a dancing party: "Ld B was there. I think he has a propensity to coquetry – there is certainly less simplicity in his manner towards women than towards men – Yet at times he seems to scorn himself for being influenced by female attention – I staid till sunrise!!!"[22] Her London season was drawing to a discontented close; and in mid-August she discontinued her journal until the following year. Late in September Byron heard that her father had been ruined by election expenses in Durham.

Meanwhile Byron's romance with Caroline was disintegrating after only four feverish months. Years later in Italy Byron told Medwin that he had tried to believe himself in love, but his behaviour at the time suggests that he was totally infatuated. He was violently jealous of her husband, William Lamb, and forbade her to continue waltzing because he could not bear to see her in the arms of another man. They quarrelled constantly. If he was at a party to which she was not invited, Caroline would hang about outside until he emerged. The gossip-mongers had a merry time; and once Rogers was appalled to see her hanging through the window of Byron's carriage talking to him.

With such distractions Byron neglected his parliamentary duties. He attended the House only twice in March and three times in April. He contributed to the Roman Catholic Claims debate on April 21 in a speech that expressed sincerity but also revealed a new, show-off streak in Byron. He reminded the government that its treatment of the Catholics must be applauded by Napoleon: "So grateful must oppression of the Catholics be to his mind, that doubtless . . . the next cartel will convey to this country cargoes of seve-china [sic]."[23] Hobhouse recorded in his journal (was Byron the only person in England who didn't keep a regular journal?) that he had stayed up all night to hear the debate and that Byron had "kept the House in a roar of laughter".

Hobhouse's presence on the scene was essential in order to prevent Byron from making a total fool of himself. Caroline's mother, Lady Bessborough, concerned about her daughter's scandalous disregard of the consequences of her actions, consulted Hobhouse about asking Byron to leave town. On July 29 he was instrumental in preventing an elopement when Caroline arrived in Byron's rooms dressed as a boy, and then took off in a hackney coach to Chelsea where Byron and Hobhouse tracked her down. This seems to have been some kind of hysterical ploy to persuade Byron to run away with her; and he confessed to Hobhouse that he would have done so if his friend had not intervened. On August 9 Caroline sent Byron some of her pubic hair and a passionate note: "I will kneel & be torn from your feet before I will give you up – or sooner be parted with."[24] Three days later – after a tumultuous scene at Melbourne House – she ran away again, causing her mother to have a slight stroke.

All this emotional turbulence was being played out against the backdrop of possible financial disaster. Hobhouse had been persuaded by Hanson that Byron's affairs were so hopeless that Newstead had to be sold. Byron began to long for freedom, peace, and order. Yet his conflicting feelings for Caroline were expressed in a letter probably written, Marchand suggests, on August 12, the day Caroline created one of the worst of her scenes in which she threatened to run off:

> My dearest Caroline – If tears, which you saw & know I am not apt to shed, if the agitation in which I parted from you, agitation which you must have perceived through the *whole* of this most nervous *nervous* affair, did not commence till the moment of leaving you approached, if all that I have said & done, & am still but too ready to say & do, have not sufficiently proved what my real feelings are & must be ever towards you, my love, I have no other proof to offer; God knows I wish you happy, & when I quit you, or rather when you from a sense of duty to your husband & mother quit me, you shall acknowledge the truth of what I again promise & vow, that no other in word or deed shall ever hold the place in my affection which is & shall be most sacred to you, till I am nothing I never knew till *that moment*, the *madness* of – my dearest & most beloved friend – I cannot express myself – this is no time for words – but I shall have a pride, a melancholy pleasure, in suffering what you yourself can hardly conceive – for you do not know me. – I am now about to go out with a heavy heart, because – my appearing this Evening will stop any absurd story which the events of today might give rise to – do you

think *now* that I am *cold & stern, & artful* – will even *others* think so, will your *mother* even – that mother to whom we must indeed sacrifice much, *more* much more on my part, than she shall ever know or can imagine. – "Promises not to love you" ah Caroline it is past promising . . .²⁵

The Prince Regent himself was drawn into the affair after Lord Melbourne complained to him about Caroline and the fact that Byron was confiding in his wife.* The prince replied that "Ld Byron had bewitch'd the whole family Mothers & Daughters & all & that nothing would satisfy us but making a fool of him as well as of ourselves . . . I never heard of such a thing in my life – taking the Mother for confidante! What would you have thought of my going to talk to Ly Spencer [Lady Bessborough's mother, at the time when he was having an affair with her daughter, the Duchess of Devonshire] in former times!"²⁶ Even the licentious monarch was shocked by the total lack of decorum in the situation.

Caroline was finally persuaded to accompany her mother and husband to Ireland in early September, and Byron made his separate way to Cheltenham, under the delusion that at least his financial affairs were being settled. On August 14 Newstead was put up for auction at Garraway's Coffee House.** Despite the fact that a nervous Hobhouse kept raising the bids, the final bid did not meet Byron's reserve of £120,000. (Hobhouse said that at the time he had only one pound one shilling and sixpence in the world!) The following day Thomas Claughton made an offer of £140,000: £25,000 was to be paid as a deposit, £60,000 as a three-year mortgage, and the remainder by Christmas. While Claughton eventually reneged on the arrangement, for the moment Byron had some expectations of ready cash, although still far from enough to meet his debts. However, by mid-October Claughton had not yet made the first payment, and Byron's creditors were now pressing harder than ever in the belief that Newstead had been sold.

In Cheltenham Byron continued to be besieged by tearful hysterical letters from Caroline in Ireland who would threaten immediate return if her lover's interest appeared to be waning at all. But it was. Within a period of only six months he had been propelled into fame and notoriety. Away from the frenzy of London society, he was beginning to see things in perspective. How was he to extricate himself from this tiresome entanglement?

* The prince was godfather to Caroline's son Augustus.
** At the beginning of the nineteenth century auctions were generally held in taverns.

II

ooooooooooooooo

Compulsive Thraldom, 1812–13

For Byron the attraction of the affair with Caroline lay in its heightened excitement. She was unpredictable, imaginative, and outrageous. He loved the thrill of living on the edge, but another part of him craved acceptance, respectability, and a quiet, indolent life. The very qualities that had once intrigued him had now come back to haunt him. A diet of vertigo has its limitations; and the slightly acrid waters of Cheltenham proved a welcome change to endless scenes.

Letters from a desperate Caroline exiled in Ireland interrupted the tranquillity of this existence with disturbing regularity. Fortunately for Byron he had found an understanding ear to whom he could confide his conflicting feelings. Caroline's mother-in-law, Lady Melbourne, was one of the most attractive people he had ever encountered and he fell a little in love with her. This older woman was by no means unaware of his infatuation and allowed him to flatter her with pleas to tell him exactly what to do with their troublesome female. She in turn reassured him: "I certainly am indebted to Caroline for the continuance of your *countenance* – and this cancels all her libels and larcenies."[1] He had come to the right person. Lady Melbourne was a born meddler; and besides, she disliked her son's wife intensely.

On September 10, 1812 – only a month after he had been tempted to elope with Caroline – he told his worldly mentor: "It is not that I love another, but loving at all is quite out of my way; I am tired of being a fool, and when I look back on the waste of time, and the destruction of all my plans last winter by this last romance, I am – what I ought to have been long ago." Caroline's mother, Lady Bessborough, wrote from Ireland to Lady Melbourne, "for heaven's sake do not lose your hold on him", a plea repeated to Byron, who of course begged, as she knew he would, for Lady

Melbourne to regulate him. Then, after telling her only three days before this that loving wasn't really his style, he confessed that he was actually attached to another. In a long, rather incoherent letter the astonished woman – and it took much to astonish her – heard that the young lady in question was her own niece, Annabella Milbanke. Indeed, Byron assured her that he would have proposed to her if this unfortunate affair with her daughter-in-law, Caroline, had not intervened. (He implied that he was the passive partner in something called "an affair" which had been more or less thrust upon him.) He had heard, he went on, that Lady Melbourne's brother, Sir Ralph Milbanke, had been ruined, but that was of little consequence because once Newstead was disposed of, he would have more than enough for them to live on. This was sheer fantasy; but, as always, he retreated to fantasy when life became tiresome. It was now up to Lady Melbourne to extricate him from this mess.

Lady Melbourne replied: "As a friend I say flirt as much as you please but do not get into a serious scrape before you are free from the *present* one."[2] She was understandably sceptical of the depth of his feelings, even though he assured her of his *esteem* for Annabella; and knowing her prudent niece as she did, she doubted that she would consider this erratic man for a husband. If Lady Melbourne had not possessed such a taste for intrigue, she would have discouraged him very firmly from the outset.

Since Byron was desperately seeking escape, what other alternatives were open to him? He could leave for the East, but that would require a great deal of money and energy, and in both he was entirely depleted. What about the attractive and very wealthy Miss Mercer Elphinstone who had recently invited him to Tunbridge Wells? Even Walter Scott had heard that their engagement was imminent. The problem was that Miss Mercer Elphinstone, as well as having a great deal of self-confidence, had entirely too much money – an intimidating amount, apparently – and there was every chance that her family would prevail against a match with a penniless title. Besides, if he proposed, he would actually have to exert himself, whereas with Annabella, everything might be arranged through Lady Melbourne.

The great advantage to marrying Annabella would be that he could then call Lady Melbourne "Aunt", but he hastened to add that he didn't in any sense regard her as a surrogate mother, a "*Mamma*, from whom I have already by instinct imbibed a moral aversion" (September 21). It is possible to interpret his bizarre conduct over the next year as an unconscious search for the nurturing he had lost with his mother's death.

He admitted candidly that in order to break with Caroline, "all I have left is to take some steps which will make her hate me effectually."[3] Three months was the limit for any of his romances, "except in one solitary instance" (Mary Chaworth). He spoke with condescending disdain of his dalliance in Malta with Constance Spencer Smith. There was no mention of Annabella until his next letter when he responded to Lady Melbourne's query as to whether he was sure of what he was doing: "I answer – no – but *you* are, which I take to be a much better thing."[4] He then turned to his immediate situation which he compared to a gulf in which he would sink unless he swam fast. It was a far easier feat to cross the Hellespont.

The proposal was then broached by Lady Melbourne in early October. Annabella did not take long to send off her rejection and also gave her aunt a Character of Byron which she had just written, both of which Lady Melbourne passed on to the unsuccessful suitor. As to the Character, Byron replied that it was "much *too indulgent*", but "in some points . . . very exact".[5] Lady Melbourne in turn also gave Annabella censored versions of Byron's reaction to her refusal of his hand.

In her rejection letter of October 12, Annabella wrote: "Believing that he never will be the object of that strong affection which could make me happy in domestic life, I should wrong him by any measure that might even indirectly, confirm his present impressions."[6] What she was really saying was that she doubted whether Byron would ever entertain an enduring affection for her. She could not have failed to have known about his tumultuous relationship with Caroline; and the indirect and tentative manner of the strange proposal was hardly flattering.

Byron disguised his humiliation with bravado. He was never enamoured, he declared; and besides, his main consideration in the choice of Annabella as a wife was the fact that he might remain close to his beloved non-judgemental mentor. If he had married Annabella, "That would have been but a *cold collation*, & I prefer hot suppers."[7] Yet his bitterness breaks through when he refers to Annabella as "my Princess of Parallelograms"; and he was more prescient than he knew when he said that "we are two parallel lines prolonged to infinity side by side but never to meet." Nevertheless, he still had to find a means of escaping from Caroline, and besides, "I cannot exist without some object of love."

After the proposal had been rejected, his intermediary wrote to Annabella asking her what qualities she would require in a husband. Annabella replied that she herself had defects of temper, but "I am never irritated except when others are so, and then I am too apt to imitate them. I am never sulky, but my spirits are easily depressed, particularly by seeing anybody unhappy." As for the qualities she desired in a husband, she enumerated them in a list:

> He must have consistent principles of Duty governing strong & *generous* feelings, and reducing them under the command of Reason.
>
> Genius is not in my opinion *necessary*, though desirable, *if united* with what I have just mentioned.
>
> I require a freedom from suspicion, & from *habitual* ill-humour – also an equal tenor of affection towards me, not that violent attachment which is susceptible of sudden increase or diminution from trifles.
>
> I wish to be considered by my husband as a *reasonable adviser*, not as a guide on whom he could *implicitly* depend . . . I would have fortune enough to enable me to continue without embarrassment in the kind of society to which I have been accustomed. I have no inclination to extravagance, and should be content to practise economy for the attainment of this object.
>
> Rank is indifferent to me. *Good intentions* I think an important advantage.
>
> I do not regard *beauty*, but I am influenced by the *manners of a gentleman*, without which I scarcely think that any one could attract me.

As almost an afterthought, she added, "I would not enter into a family where there is a strong tendency to Insanity."[8]

To this last reservation Lady Melbourne replied: "This I think a very wise determination, as it may prevent a thousand disagreeable occurrences you may be liable to." She added bluntly that "it appears to me that it is almost impossible while you remain on ye Stilts on which you are mounted, that you should ever find a person worthy to be your husband."[9] After all, she reminded her, marriage was a sort of lottery and one could never be sure in advance about the person one was marrying.

Until the matter of the proposal was settled, Byron had been vacillating between accepting invitations from either an old Harrow friend, Lord Harrowby, or Lord Oxford. Now – as if by intuition – he accepted the Oxfords' invitation to visit their family in Hereford. Lady Oxford had clearly had her eye on him, but his attraction to her did not fully express itself until he found himself in close proximity to her. She was forty but still an immensely attractive and highly intelligent woman. A rector's daughter, she had made what was considered a brilliant match with Edward Harley, fifth Earl of Oxford, but her husband proved very dull, and, like other women of her class, she took a series of lovers so that her various children were referred to as the "Harleian Miscellany". Byron was enchanted by her calm disposition and ripe charms; but Lady Melbourne was not quite as enchanted with the situation, and Caroline Lamb was beside herself with rage.

Caroline berated Lady Oxford herself, whereupon Byron wrote to her:

> Lady Caroline – our affections are not in our own power – mine are engaged. I love another – were I inclined to reproach you I might for 20 thousand things, but I will not. They really are not cause of my present conduct – my opinion of you is entirely alter'd, & if I had wanted anything to confirm me, your Levities your caprices & the mean subterfuges you have lately made use of while madly gay – of writing to me as if otherwise, would entirely have open'd my eyes. I am no longer yr. lover – I shall but never be less than your friend – it would be too dishonourable for me to name her to whom I am now entirely devoted & attached.[10]

Hobhouse was delighted: "I congratulate you most sincerely on your release from one who was not the Lamb of God which taketh away the sins of the world."[11]

Byron's letter was brutal, and Caroline utterly went to pieces when she perceived that it had Lady Oxford's seal affixed to it. Perhaps the lady herself had dictated it? This was the letter which Caroline was later to incorporate into her novel *Glenarvon*. In her extremity Caroline then turned to Lord Clare who was visiting in Ireland. Byron had felt embittered towards him ever since he had cancelled the plan for spending Byron's last day together before Byron sailed for the East in 1809. Aware of Byron's underlying affection for Clare, in her muddled state Caroline hoped that she might reach Byron through his former favourite. With some trumped-up story of having left some miniatures for Byron to be repaired, she attempted to induce Clare to secure one for her. She then went into a long account of her grievances.

> I can not but I can never make you guess what I feel – that he should have changed was natural – that he should set Lady Oxford above me & make her taunt me & betray me to her – tho' ungenerous was yet to be borne – but that Byron [him] self after all the love he once felt should in every light Company in his letters to others, make me the

object of his ridicule his mirth – you do not no man can tell what I have & must feel.[12]

In any event, Caroline's interference seemed to effect some kind of reconciliation between the two former friends.

Byron managed to tear himself away from the arms of his experienced mistress at the end of November to deal with pressing business concerns in London. On November 5, 1812, Claughton, the purchaser of Newstead, finally paid £5,000 of the deposit money; but not till March 1813 was the interest on the 1809 loan from Scrope Davies paid (£244.10), and the full amount owing to him was not cleared until March 28, 1814. By late 1812 Hanson had managed to persuade Byron that drastic economies in his way of life were necessary. All Byron could think of was to dismiss his groom and give up his horses.

Byron's writing had suffered because of his amatory preoccupations. During this late autumn of 1812 he visited Murray in his new premises at 10 Albemarle Street where they discussed how to deal with *Waltz*, a 200-line poem he had written denouncing the depravity of the dance. Byron was obsessional about the new craze: its swirling movement made him only too aware of his physical limitations. His poem contained several rude personal references to the Prince Regent who was one of its great enthusiasts. It was a provocative and unnecessary diatribe, and Murray was understandably reluctant to publish it. It was not set in type (and then anonymously, issued under the imprint of Sherwood, Neely, and Jones, Paternoster Row) until February 1813; but naturally there was speculation that Byron had written it, an act that would not endear him to the Tory establishment.

The only other literary work he had undertaken during the Caroline imbroglio was an address for the reopening of the Drury Lane Theatre which had been destroyed by fire on February 24, 1809. Lord Holland at first asked him to enter a competition but Byron refused because, as he told Lady Melbourne frankly, he could not bear rivalry. However, when the sub-committee (which Byron was to join in 1815) rejected all the entries, Lord Holland then turned to Byron with the explicit understanding that he alone was being commissioned. Annabella Milbanke was present when a leading actor, Robert Elliston, read the address on the opening night, October 10, 1812.

Byron did not want to tarry in the city too long lest he encounter Caroline who had by now returned from Ireland and was not going to take her dismissal lightly. She was staying in the country at Brocket where she staged a most ludicrous scene. Gathering a group of young girls from the neighbouring village of Welwyn, she dressed them in white and had them dance around a fire into which she cast copies of Byron's letters while a page recited some lines she had written for the occasion. After receiving an account of the event from Caroline, Byron told Lady Melbourne: "I begin to look upon her as actually mad or it would be impossible for me to bear what I have from her already" (December 31, 1812). No one could understand William Lamb's tolerance of his wife's behaviour. Actually he was beginning to be as tired of her as Byron was. Byron always spoke admiringly of his forbearance, but Lamb disliked Byron intensely; and years later when he was Prime Minister (as Lord Melbourne), he told Queen Victoria that Byron was "treacherous beyond conception . . . he dazzled everybody and deceived them."[3]

The Oxfords were talking about travelling to Sicily and the idea seemed to offer a delightful means of escaping all the troublesome things with which Byron associated England. He returned to the country to rejoin Lady Oxford just before Christmas. At Eywood he could revert to being a child by playing blind man's buff and other childish amusements. It was especially agreeable as a contrast to Caroline's bizarre behaviour of having the buttons on her servants' livery inscribed with "*Ne*, 'Crede B'". By forging Byron's name on a message to Murray, she managed to hoodwink him into surrendering a miniature of the poet to her. Byron was thrown into a fury since it was one of his favourite portraits which he had wished to give to Lady Oxford.

By the end of January 1813 Lady Oxford persuaded Byron to accompany her back to London. The Oxfords moved into their town home, Mortimer House, while Byron rented rooms at 4 Bennet Street, off St James's. Lady Oxford was a close friend of the Princess of Wales, and Byron found himself joining the circle of the other court at Kensington Palace. It was noted that while in some moods he could be gay and charming, he could also be petulant and morose, and Lady Oxford was sometimes seen in tears. The fact of the matter was that the relationship with Lady Oxford was not as tranquil as it had been in the past. Sicily did not promise escape from Caroline now so much as servitude to another woman; and in the months preceding the Oxfords' departure in June, Byron cast about desperately from one alternative destination to another.

Lady Oxford, who was extremely interested in politics, still had enough influence over him to persuade him to attend some of the sessions at the House of Lords where he found himself totally bored by the interminable speeches. On June 1, 1813, he made his own final speech in which he was almost the sole supporter for the abolition of "rotten boroughs" and greater proportional representation. These were mild demands compared to the measures of the Reform Bill of 1832 and subsequent legislation; but Byron was speaking during the last days of an oligarchy, whose policy of entrenchment was more marked because it sensed itself threatened.

As early as March 25 Byron wrote to Lord Holland: "The fact is that I can do no good anywhere – & am too patriotic – not to prefer doing ill in any country rather than my own. – Where I am going – I cannot positively say – & it is no great matter – 'there is a world beyond Rome'* and all parts of it are much the same to a personage with few friendships & no connections." He could not exist, he continued, without some occupation: "travel therefore is the only pursuit left me." Then the self-pity was undercut by the self-mockery of an added comment: "I have some notion of taking orders."

After the enormous impact of *Childe Harold*, he was nervous about appearing before the public in print again lest he fail to match his earlier success. In Cheltenham during the previous September he had begun a poem in couplets based on the incident near Athens in 1811 when he had encountered Turkish soldiers about to fling a woman into the sea. None of his poems ever received so much rewriting. Only fifteen copies were printed in March 1813 and distributed privately. *The Giaour* (that is, the infidel) was the first of his oriental tales, and its fragmentary nature reflects Byron's uncertainty about what he came to describe as "a snake of a poem".

Again he was to present a mysterious and remorseful Gothic protagonist. In appearance the Venetian hero resembles Harold with his pale complexion, gloomy expression, and bitter smile. He feels no guilt for the murder of a villain, but suffers silent grief for his responsibility in the death of a woman who loved him. In Jane Austen's *Persuasion* (1818) Anne Elliot and Captain Benwick discuss the correct pronunciation of Giaour (like "hour"), and Captain Benwick repeated "the various lines which imaged a broken heart, or a mind destroyed by wretchedness". Austen is probably referring to lines 937–42:

> If solitude succeed to grief,
> Release from pain is slight relief;
> The vacant bosom's wilderness
> Might thank the pang that made it less.
> We loathe what none are left to share –
> Even bliss – 'twere woe alone to bear;

---

* Byron may have been misquoting *Coriolanus*, Act III, scene 3, line 135: "There is a world elsewhere!"

Despite Byron's anxiety about the poem, after it was published publicly in May 1813 it became extremely popular and ran through fourteen editions by 1815. Byron's relief about its reception had much to do with cooling his enthusiasm for abandoning England. The enthusiasm also rekindled his decision to continue writing. To Lord Holland, who had received one of the privately printed copies, he wrote (April 3): "If I push forward to Greece or Persia it is not improbable that the want of better employment may lead me on to further scribbling."

Nevertheless, the early months of the year were a period of anxiety as he continued in a state of constant apprehension about what Caroline would do next. In addition to her stream of letters, he began to be inundated by a flood from the widow of Lord Falkland, his friend who had been killed in a duel in 1809 and to whose children Byron had contributed £500 in an act of rash generosity. Lady Falkland had become convinced that she was the "Thyrza" of *Childe Harold* and that Byron was leaving England because he did not believe his love was returned. Was ever a man so bedevilled?

He was back in the world again, he was not stagnating so long as he was meeting interesting people; yet he returned to Eywood on March 28; and on April 19 he told Lady Melbourne that his planned departure from England in May might be delayed because of "a slight perplexity owing to an event which certainly did not enter into my calculation – what it is – I leave to your own ingenious imagination . . ." This would certainly suggest that they feared an addition to the Harleian Miscellany. The crisis seemed to be ill-founded because Byron was back in town on his own by April 25 and rejoined by his mistress for a few short days before she and her husband set off for Sicily early in June.

The people Byron enjoyed seeing did not include Charles Dallas who was, he had decided, as he told Hobhouse, an excruciating bore, "a *damned nincom* – assuredly –" (January 17, 1813). For the time being there was no more talk of handing over copyrights to him. Byron was not good at disguising his feelings; and as Dallas began to feel excluded his antipathy towards his former protégé began to feed upon itself, resulting finally in his viperish book of recollections published after the deaths of both men.

Rogers, another man of whom Byron should have been more wary, he saw frequently. Byron was on affectionate terms with Thomas Moore, a relationship which the possessive Hobhouse viewed with disapproval because he regarded the Irishman as a smooth-talking social climber; Moore wasn't any fonder of Hobhouse, one of the group of Cambridge cronies whom he considered inferior to Byron. Actually Rogers and Moore were the only literary men with whom Byron felt comfortable because he realised that there was no scope for conversation with men like William Sotheby beyond praising their latest work. He much preferred the wit and style of the dandies although, despite his friendship with Scrope Davies, he never penetrated beyond the periphery of that rarefied circle.

In June 1813 Byron also met Madame de Staël, probably the most celebrated woman in Europe. Her father, the Swiss banker Jacques Necker, had been Louis XVI's minister of finance. During the revolution she had supported a limited monarchy similar to that in England. Napoleon exiled her from Paris in 1803 and she retired to her father's estate, Coppet, near Geneva, where she wrote *De l'Allemagne,** after travelling in Germany where she met all the great figures of the Romantic movement. This book, with its praise of German poetry, did much to arouse ardent nationalism against Napoleon. Increasingly hounded by Napoleon's agents, in 1813 she fled to England where she became the sensation of the drawing rooms for the next six months. At Lord Lansdowne's, people stood on tables and chairs to see her. She had replaced Byron as the current celebrity in this society eager for new sensations. Even though Byron detested intellectual women, he claimed that he found himself amused by her sense of authority on all subjects. He baited her about the immorality of her novels *Corinne* and *Delphine*. The virtuous characters were far too boring, he lectured her. Furiously she tried to interrupt: "*Quelle idée!*" "*Mon Dieu!*" "*Ecoutez donc!*" "*Vous m'impatientez!*" Byron was carried along by the egregiousness of himself as the most scandalous figure of the day delivering a sermon on morality.

Another sensation of the time were the Hunt brothers, John and Leigh, the editors of the free-spoken *Examiner*. For some years they had been closely watched by the government; but they went too far in 1812 when, in response to an obsequious article on the Prince Regent in the *Morning Post*, they described him as "a libertine over head and ears in debt and disgrace, a despiser of domestic ties, the companion of gamblers and demireps, a man who has just closed half a century without one single claim on the gratitude of the country or the respect of posterity." Earlier Henry Brougham had managed to get them off when they were taken to court for protesting against brutal beating in the army; but this time their offence was too serious, and in December 1812 they were fined heavily and sentenced to two years in separate jails.

In Surrey jail, Leigh Hunt was visited by all those with libertarian

* Murray bought *De l'Allemagne* for 1,500 guineas and when it was published in October it sold out in three days.

sympathies. On May 20, 1813, Moore took Byron to meet him. Hunt was only four years older than Byron, and they took an immediate liking to each other. A few days later Byron returned laden with books on Italy to help with the long poem Hunt was then writing, *The Story of Rimini*. Hunt told his wife Marianne, "It strikes me that he and I shall become *friends*, literally and cordially speaking; there is something in the texture of his mind and feelings that seems to resemble mine to a thread; I think we are cut out of the same piece, only a different wear may have altered our respective naps a little."[4] Marianne Hunt expressed scepticism because she had heard some of the scandalous stories about his past. Hunt replied, "You must make allowances for the early vagaries of Lord B . . . I am persuaded that his heart is an excellent one, and I am sure that his understanding is."[5]

These various contacts undermined Byron's original intention to flee Caroline's persecutions. His anxiety that she might turn up in his rooms disguised as a page at an awkward moment or commit some unforeseen piece of outrageousness took up a disproportionate amount of attention. While he was enclosed in the hothouse atmosphere of his amatory pursuits, Lady Melbourne was the only stable element in his life. "As you say," she wrote on March 25, 1813, "Caroline certainly prevents my dropping your Acquaintance, tho' I beg once and for all to state that if there was no Caroline in your World – it is your very last acquaintance I should wish to drop – and never will unless I am drop'd [sic]."[6]

The shifting climate of his feelings is reflected in the constant change of plan for a journey abroad. In January 1813 he was urging Hanson to do something about selling Rochdale because he intended to go abroad in May. On February 27 Hanson was told to make some arrangement with Claughton because he was planning to go abroad "almost immediately". On March 6, "no power on earth shall make me remain six weeks longer." Then on March 18 he wrote to Lady Melbourne:

> I believe I leave town next week – in the meantime I am in the agonies of three different schemes – the first you know [Sicily] – the 2nd is Sligo's Persian plan – he wants me to wait till Septr. set off & winter at Athens (our old headquarters) & then in the Spring to Constantinople (as of old) & Bagdad & Tahiran. – This has its charms too & recalls one's predilections for gadding, – then there is Hobhouse with a Muscovite & Eastern proposal also – so that I am worse off than ever Ass was before to which bundle of hay I shall address myself.

On March 24 Hanson was told, "I want to go abroad immediately – it is utterly impossible for me to remain here," and at this point his destination was Sardinia and then on to the Levant. By March 26 he was telling his sister Augusta: "I am going abroad again in June." On April 19 Lady Melbourne was informed that he didn't think he would accompany the Oxfords on the same ship, but would sail "nearly at the same time", unless Greece should prove too tempting. Then on April 20 Caroline heard that she would be responsible for driving him from the country in June. On May 24 he wrote despairingly to Lady Melbourne, "I am utterly ruined in fortune – not very brilliant in reputation – sans plan – or prospect of any kind – but of getting out of ye. country – with nothing to *hope*."

During the greater part of 1813 he ran up enormous bills for splendid uniforms in which to visit foreign potentates and for magnificent gifts with which to impress them. This wild spending went on even though Hanson was arguing that Claughton should be taken to court for failing to make his Newstead payments, and creditors were pressing from all sides. Byron suggested that they consider doubling the Newstead rents yet once more so that he could leave the country. The constant change of plan, the erratic behaviour and manic thought processes reflect a man without a fixed centre, someone who could find stability only in intense attachments to a series of mother-figures.

Meanwhile, Hobhouse's *Travels in Albania* was finally published on May 23, 1813, and two days later he had departed for an eight-month tour of the European capitals not in Napoleon's hands. Byron spent the evening before his departure with his friend; and then wrote sadly and dramatically to Lady Melbourne that it was not very probable that he would see him again: "he is ye. oldest – indeed – ye. only friend I have – & my regrets are equally *social & selfish* – for if I have [sic] had attended to his advice – I should have been anything but what I am – & in parting with him I lose 'a guide philosopher & friend' I neither *can* nor *wish* to replace."[7] All too seldom Byron expressed an appreciation of Hobhouse's true worth. Possibly if Hobhouse had not gone to the continent Byron might not have become embroiled in the biggest mistake of his life.

Yet Hobhouse had been unsuccessful in helping to extricate him once and for all from the entanglement with Caroline. She had demanded a lock of Byron's hair in exchange for the disputed portrait. Byron gleefully sent off a lock of Lady Oxford's chestnut tresses which were the same colour as his own. But Caroline continued to insist on a meeting. Byron finally agreed – so long as Lady Oxford was present.

Lady Melbourne was furious that she had not been included. Byron tried to mend the situation in an incoherent and unconvincing letter: "My wish that Ly. O should be the third person was to save you a scene – & I confess also – odd as it may seem – that it would have been less awkward for me – you will wonder why – & I can't tell you more than that she might make some brilliant harangue to which – [Lady Oxford] would be a less embarrassed listener than you could possibly be."[18] There seems a strong possibility that Lady Oxford herself had insisted on this stipulation, and that she was every bit as jealous of Byron's relationship with Lady Melbourne as Caroline was.

The meeting was postponed until early May; and Byron was uncharacteristically silent about it as he sometimes was when he was not in control of a situation. Somehow Lady Oxford was persuaded to stay away; and in their solitary and undoubtedly emotional meeting, Byron apparently broke down in tears. The following day Caroline wrote him an impassioned letter under the impression that Byron was about to sail off with Lady Oxford.

> One only word. You have raised me from despair to the joy we look for in Heaven. Your seeing me has undone me for ever – you are the same, you love me still. I am sure of it – your eyes, your looks, your manners, words say so. Oh God, can you give me up if I am so dear? Take me with you – take me, my master, my friend. Who will fight for you, serve you, in sickness and health, live but for your wishes and die when that can please you – who so faithfully as the one you have made yours bound to your heart of hearts? Yet when you read this you will be gone. You will think of me, perhaps, as one who gave you suffering – trouble. Byron, my days are passed in remembering what I once was to you. I wish you had never known me or that you had killed me before you went. God bless and preserve my friend and master.
>
> Your Caro[19]

One of the strangest developments in the story was the friendship being forged between Caroline and John Murray, who was becoming her confidant. Byron seems to have known nothing about the fact that they were communicating. It was a very indecorous – if not disloyal – role for his publisher to play, but like Byron in the early stages of his infatuation for Caroline, Murray seems to have been flattered and intrigued by this grand and yet fragile vixen.

Neither the lock of hair nor the interview prevented further disturbance from Caroline. One evening Byron attended a soirée at Lady Heathcote's where Caroline's famous stabbing scene occurred. Actually nothing much at all happened, but the newspapers blew it into a spicy piece of gossip. Caroline, encountering Byron, asked him if he had any objection to her waltzing *now*? He replied that she could do whatever she pleased; she was seen seizing a knife; some ladies took alarm and rushed after her; in the scuffle she cut herself slightly and there was some blood on her dress.

This incident occurred shortly after the departure of Lady Oxford. There had been a series of tearful farewells between Byron and his mistress. On May 26 Byron had written to Lady Melbourne: "Ly. O arrives in town tomorrow – which I regret – when people have once fairly parted – how do I abhor those partings! – I know them to be of no use – & yet as painful at the time as the first plunge into purgatory." Lady Oxford had offered a temporary home and a nurturing breast. Byron was feeling a little despondent about the void her departure would leave in his life, yet resentful of her demands on him, something of a re-enactment of his relationship with his mother. He would have felt truly desperate if Lady Melbourne had not provided a thread of continuity on which he could hang his amours.

12

·oooooooooooo·

A Dangerous Passion, 1813–14

Over four years had passed since Byron had seen his half-sister Augusta. Before he sailed for the East in 1809 he was angry with her for what he regarded as interference when she contacted Hanson in her concern over his extravagance. Then, after the publication of *English Bards and Scotch Reviewers*, he was nervous about having offended her by his insulting remarks about Lord Carlisle. On his return it was a great relief to learn that she bore him no grudge; but now that she was finally married to her feckless cousin, George Leigh, Byron made no attempt to travel to Newmarket to see her.

By 1813 George's gambling debts had created a situation almost as desperate as Byron's own crisis. It was sometimes difficult even to pay the servants at Six Mile Bottom, the smallish house that was becoming increasingly smaller as Augusta produced a child almost every year. She wrote to Byron – probably in early March 1813 – hinting at financial "embarrassments" in the hope that her now famous brother might be able to relieve them of some of their difficulties. Byron replied on the 26th, apologising for his delay in writing to her with the explanation that he had been hoping that Claughton would pay the instalment on his purchase of Newstead, but the payment had not appeared and "your brother consequently not less embarrassed than ever". He was planning to go abroad in June since there was nothing to hold him in England. He had no fortune with which to marry and no inclination for parliamentary life: "I hate the thing altogether." It must have been disturbing to Augusta that her brother's spirits were as low as they had been when his mother was alive, and to hear that he was "not happy nor even comfortable and I am a fool & deserve all the ills I have met or may meet with."[1]

At the time Caroline Lamb was still plaguing his life and even his liaison with Lady Oxford had not provided sufficient refuge. There was another hiatus of three months in the correspondence until shortly before the Oxfords sailed for Sicily in late June. Since we do not possess all the letters between brother and sister we can only surmise that in early June Byron had written to Augusta suggesting that she join him in London at a time that would prevent his having to suffer a final tedious parting with his mistress.

While in London Augusta stayed with Lord and Lady Harrowby in Berkeley Square, not far from from Byron's lodgings in Bennet Street. For both of them the reunion was an ecstatic revelation. Byron was no longer an obstreperous youth but a handsome, slender, self-assured adult, the sort of man she idealised her father, Wicked Jack, to have been. The four-year age difference now seemed as nothing, particularly after Byron's affair with the forty-year-old Lady Oxford. In Augusta he saw the mother he wished had been his, a reincarnation of the lovely Lady Carmarthen. Augusta seemed a female version of himself: the large eyes, chestnut hair falling in curls over her forehead, the full chin and expressive mouth. More than anything else, he saw a happy version of himself in Augusta's love of laughter, her gift for mimicry, and her appealing shyness. They were meeting as if for the first time, certainly for the first time as grown-ups, yet with the sense that they had always belonged together.

For the next three weeks London society, which had become accustomed to the self-consciously aloof Byronic pose, now suddenly saw a devoted brother bending over his sister in constant affectionate attention. Annabella Milbanke glimpsed them whispering and laughing together on a sofa at a reception one evening. There has been much speculation about when the relationship between Augusta and Byron developed into something more passionate and more dangerous than fraternal affection. It would seem to have occurred within a remarkably short time, possibly less than a month. What one must remember is that Byron really believed he was about to set off for the East almost immediately. The relationship could not have started in this rapturous way and be left unfinished. A few days after Augusta left for home, Byron suddenly took off in pursuit of her. Not only did they probably go to bed on this visit to Six Mile Bottom, but Byron succeeded in persuading the enraptured woman to accompany him on his travels. That he knew he was moving through dangerous waters can be gauged from the fact that he did not write to Lady Melbourne for almost a month, and Byron (who could never keep a secret) finally confessed to her on July 30 that Augusta had forbidden him to confide in "la tante".

Lady Melbourne was annoyed and apprehensive. Early in August Byron brought Augusta back to London, this time to stay with an older friend, Mrs Teresa Villiers, in Knightsbridge, still close to Bennet Street. On August 5, he confided to Lady Melbourne that Augusta was going abroad with him. Byron was several times on the point of divulging more. On August 11 he blurted out, "I should have been glad of your advice how to untie two or three '*Gordian* knots' tied round me." Again, "When I don't write to you, or see you for some time you may be very certain that I am about no good" (August 20, 1813). The next day he informed her that although he and Augusta wanted to go off together, the plague raging through the East was a deterrent, and equally difficult was Augusta's anxiety to take at least one of her children with her. In Byron's view, children certainly would not have contributed to the romance of the situation.

Unwanted children were very much on his mind. The following day he sent Thomas Moore a rambling letter with a postscript: "I perceive I have written a flippant and rather cold-hearted letter; let it go, however. I have said nothing, either, of the brilliant sex; but the fact is, I am, at this moment, in a far more serious, and entirely new, scrape than any of the last twelvemonths, – and that is saying a good deal. * * * It is unlucky we can neither live with nor without these women."*[2] The asterisks probably indicate a passage that Moore had suppressed, one that might have told us something very specific about the situation.

By now Augusta probably suspected that she was pregnant. Lady Melbourne was not slow to guess the truth; and she warned Byron that he was on the edge of a precipice, and in danger of ruining their reputations. Byron was sulking because Augusta, shocked into a sense of responsibility, refused to leave her family. He reacted like a spoiled child, although when he finally confessed the complete truth to Lady Melbourne, he pleaded with her to hold him completely responsible for plunging them into this predicament. In lines added to *The Gaiour*, he wrote:

> I grant *my* love imperfect – all
> That mortals by the name miscall—
> Then deem it evil – what thou wilt—
> But say, oh say, *hers* was not guilt!
>
> (1141–4)

---

* Moore maintained that the asterisks indicated actual blanks in Byron's manuscript, but since the manuscript no longer exists, there is no way of verifying his contention.

Commenting on these lines to Lady Melbourne on September 28, he pleaded for her understanding: "you – who know how my thoughts were occupied when these last were written – will perhaps perceive in parts a coincidence in my own state of mind with that of my hero – if so, you will give me credit for the feeling, though on the other hand I lose in your esteem." Yet by October 13, in a long letter written from the Websters' home where he was visiting, he discusses the speed with which he could move from one intense attachment to another. He was now pursuing the timid Lady Frances Webster: "You who know me & my weakness so well – will not be surprised when I say that I am totally absorbed in this passion – that I am even ready to take a *flight* if necessary – & as she says – 'we *cannot* part' – it is no impossible denouement." In other words, in little over a year he had suggested elopement with Caroline Lamb, Lady Oxford, Augusta, and now Frances Webster.

In order to forget Augusta, Byron attempted to plunge into another grand passion. If he got himself into a scrape it was Augusta's fault, he told his sister, since she had refused to accept the Websters' invitation to Aston Hall. Nevertheless, Lady Frances would prove only a passing fancy, and in early October 1813 he revoked his will of 1811, this time leaving half his estate to Augusta, the other half to his heir, George Byron.

Both Augusta and Byron shared an ability to compartmentalise and rationalise their behaviour. Augusta was constantly invoking the Scriptures in her letters, but basically she was cheerfully amoral. As time passed Byron increasingly saw himself as a man inevitably doomed whatever he did. Augusta had apparently slept with her husband after Byron's visit to Six Mile Bottom. George Leigh then could have no suspicion that the child his wife was carrying was possibly not his.

In the meantime Byron took flight from his new perplexity. For over a month he ceased communicating with Augusta, but occupied a good part of his time writing long letters to Lady Melbourne detailing his silly attempts to seduce his hostess. His worldly correspondent humoured him in this pastime as a means of diverting his attention from Augusta, but he began to be bored by the game. By late November he was confessing, "I am much afraid that that perverse passion was my deepest after all."[3] The need to confess was profoundly compulsive. Poetry had always provided a release for his pent-up emotions and now it did so more than ever. He started a new oriental tale, *The Bride of Abydos*. On November 4 he wrote to Lady Melbourne that "my mind has been from *late* and *later* events in such a state of fermentation that as usual I have been obliged to empty it in rhyme." The original title of the poem was *Zuleika* but before publication in late November he changed not only the title but the leading characters from brother and sister to cousins. At Holland House he was rash enough to remark to a shocked gathering that incest was not held in moral reprehension throughout the world.

On November 14 – for the second time in his life – he began to keep a journal. Byron eventually handed it over to Moore and sections of it have been replaced by asterisks. (It is hard to believe Moore's story of Byron's self-censure since the asterisks appear constantly in the letters to Moore that Moore quotes, but not in those to his other correspondents.) Nevertheless, there is sufficient remaining material to give us a view of Byron's emotional state, and the very fact that he turned to a journal revealed a need to confess. He started out by declaring that "At five-and-twenty, when the better part of life is over, one should be *something*; and what am I? nothing but five-and-twenty – and the odd months."[4] Here is no sense that he had achieved success at an incredibly young age. He describes himself as restless and bored, picking up books and throwing them down again. He believed that only the writing of *The Bride of Abydos* had kept him sane during this stressful period. He tried to write a comedy and a novel, but he found the material so close to the reality of his life that he threw them into the flames. He chose to believe that only in verse could he both reveal and conceal his inner turmoil.

He ground his teeth when he was asleep and was troubled both by insomnia and by nightmares. In late November, "I awoke from a dream! – well! and have not others dreamed? – Such a dream! – but she did not overtake me. I wish the dead would rest, however. Ugh! how my blood chilled, – and I could not wake – and – and – heigho!" Who could "she" be if not his mother? The next day he recorded: "No dreams last night of the dead nor the living."[5]

He discusses literary figures, friends, the vital importance of possessing money, his admiration of Napoleon; and by January 16, 1814, he announces: "A wife would be my salvation." Among all these disparate topics runs a real longing for Augusta. We do not possess the letters the journal reveals that they exchanged during this period but there exists a curl of Augusta's hair tied with white silk which she posted to him on November 29 with the message:

> Partager tous vos sentiments
> ne voir que par vos yeux
> n'agir que par vos conseils, ne
> vivre que pour vous, voilà mes
> voeux, mes projets, & le seul
> destin qui peut me rendre heureuse.

On the packet Byron wrote:

> La Chevelure of
> the *one* whom
> I most loved + *

On December 15 Augusta managed to get away from home to visit him in London. The journal entries of the 14th, 15th, and 16th contain only two sentences: "Much done, but nothing to record. It is quite enough to set down my thoughts, – my actions will rarely bear retrospection."[6] The journal ends on the 18th when he began to write *The Corsair*. On the 22nd brother and sister returned to Six Mile Bottom. Here Byron worked on the manuscript, and when he returned to the city on the 27th the first draft was completed. He now felt revitalised and full of plans for his projected visit to Newstead with Augusta in January.

What is one to make of this peculiar web of relationships during 1812 and 1813? Byron had been taken completely off guard by his sudden catapult to fame. He simply could not handle the unexpected success of *Childe Harold*. While it was flattering to be doted upon, it was also bewildering and like a little boy he ran to hide his head in the skirts of his surrogate mother, Lady Melbourne. How pleasant to have a worldly and non-judgemental mother to whom one could show the love letters that other women wrote to him! Indeed, instead of bringing the correspondence with Caroline to an abrupt halt, he continued answering her letters throughout 1813 as one means of cementing the friendship with his older friend. But some of his old resentment against his own mother also had to be played out with her. There was always the fear that she might desert him – as his mother had done by dying and his father had done by simply disappearing. He frequently spoke of the possibility of doing something that would necessitate the end of their correspondence. Hence, the series of intense but shallow relationships to prove that he was not totally dependent upon her. Lady Oxford was also clearly a mother-substitute, but the most appropriate figure yet was Augusta because they were really united by blood. It was inevitable that Byron would be ensnared by her seductive maternalism. The feelings she elicited were "a mixture of good & diabolical".[7] When one speaks of Byron's Don Juan complex, one is talking about a neurotic attachment from which Byron was never fully able to extricate himself. It is doubtful if he was even particularly highly sexed and his periods of

---

* Byron's secret symbol for Augusta. A series of crosses was to denote their relationship.

debauchery were sporadic. Sex he seemed to regard as an inevitable culmination of the more exciting foreplay of dangerous flirtation, such as writing notes to Lady Frances while her husband sat opposite him. Perhaps, too, in a society where other forms of permissiveness were possible, some of his relationships might have been bisexual, provided the object indicated sufficient affection to fill the emptiness of an aching heart. "I could not exist without some object of attachment,"[8] he acknowledged frequently during this stressful period when he had moments of extraordinary insight into his vulnerability.

Because he was a handsome celebrity, there would always be women ready to throw themselves at him. Annabella Milbanke, for one, began looking for an opportunity to reopen a communication between them. Just before returning to her home in Seaham with her parents, on July 18, 1813, she wrote to Lady Melbourne that she had heard an unpleasant rumour that Lord Byron had treated Mr Claughton, the purchaser of Newstead, with great harshness. Byron replied crossly (through Lady Melbourne) that if anyone had been treated harshly it was himself because Claughton had bought the property as a free agent, had reneged on his bargain, and now Byron and his agent had been forced to launch a Chancery suit against him.

Annabella then realised that she would have to make the first move. On August 22, 1813, she penned an extraordinary letter to Byron, so long and filled with so many ingenuous hints that a warier man would have been put on his guard. As Lady Melbourne warned him, he simply did not understand women. Annabella immediately tried to establish a mutual bond between them. He had once remarked on the serenity of her expression and she now assured him that she was not at all happy. "It is my nature to feel long, deeply and secretly, and the strongest affections of my heart are without hope."[9]

In her assumption that he was undoubtedly Childe Harold, the mythic man of sorrows, she assured him that she had suffered as he had suffered. She then proceeded to give him a sermon (and sermons were one of the reasons Byron never attended church!), advising him: "No longer suffer yourself to be the slave of the moment, nor trust your noble impulses to the chances of Life. Have an object that will permanently occupy your feelings and exercise your reason. Do good, etc. etc." She assured him that her parents were aware that she was writing to him (possibly), but she would prefer that Lady Melbourne not get wind of it.

Byron replied that Lady Melbourne had perhaps exceeded his intentions when she made a direct proposal on his part. Not that he was blaming her, of course, because she was quite correct in her assumption that he preferred Annabella above any other woman. Still, he had absorbed the disappointment "because it is impossible to impart one drop more to a cup which already overflows with the waters of bitterness".[10] Naturally he did not specify that at the moment he was deeply involved with Augusta and that his plans for their elopement had been thwarted. His departure from England was postponed for the moment, but "I must bend my course to some more accessible region – probably to Russia."

And so began a curious correspondence, both under the illusion that it was harmless: Annabella because it was assumed that she was protected by her attachment to another; Byron because he was always on the verge of sailing off over the horizon. In his next letter (August 31) he told her of the incident the previous winter when William Bankes had come to him in a dejected state because Annabella had just rejected him and Byron had laughed because their situations were so similar. This was a gloss on his comment at the time: "Is *that* all?"

Despite Annabella's request to keep their correspondence private, Byron could not resist sending on her letters to Lady Melbourne to whom he remarked on September 5: "She seems to have been spoiled – not as children usually are – but systematically Clarissa Harlowed into an awkward kind of correctness – with a dependence upon her own infallibility which will or may lead her into some egregious blunder." It was an amazingly prescient insight into an aspect of Annabella's character, a trait that would propel her into a disastrous marriage.

Could any man be less suited to a serious young woman than one who spoke passionately of the great object in life being sensation? The words fly across the page as Byron describes how one must "feel that we exist – even though in pain – it is this 'craving void' which drives us to Gaming – to Battle – to Travel – to intemperate but keenly felt pursuits of every description whose principal attraction is the agitation inseparable from their accomplishment" (September 6). Annabella in turn admonished him that his craving for excitement was caused by the lack of a fixed religious principle to guide his life.

In early October Annabella sent her aunt her reactions to the enlarged fifth edition of *The Giaour*:

> The description of Love almost makes *me* in love. Certainly he excels in the language of Passion . . . I consider his acquaintance as so desirable that I would risk being called a Flirt for the sake of enjoying it, provided I may do so without detriment to myself – for you know

that his welfare has been as much the object of my consideration as if it were connected with my own."[11]

Blissfully unaware that this Passion was inspired by Augusta – and to a degree by Lady Frances Webster – Annabella hoped that Lady Melbourne would pass on these suggestive comments to Byron. Preoccupied with his own affairs, Byron told Lady Melbourne that the correspondence was at an end. By November 3 Annabella could contain herself no longer: "I am not exacting an answer. I only request to be informed whenever my communications become unacceptable that I may discontinue them, and when you *partially* disapprove them pray tell me, that I may perceive my error."[12]

Byron had no recourse but to respond – and to enquire when she planned next to be in town: "I think we understand each other perfectly – & may talk to each other occasionally without exciting speculation . . . If I find my heart less philosophic on the subject than I at present believe it – I shall keep out of the way – but I *now* think it is well shielded – at least it has got a new suit of armour."[13]

How could she interpret this as anything but encouragement? "I cannot now have the least fear of your entertaining a wish for more of my regard than you possess"; and she assured him that she looked forward to their meeting in London in the spring "as one of the most agreeable incidents which my residence there can produce".[14]

If Byron had a confidante in Lady Melbourne, Annabella also had one in Lady Gosford. To her she poured out her longing to save Byron's soul. By now she was hopelessly and desperately in love. But how was she to convey to Byron that her heart was free? On December 5 she admitted her dilemma to her friend: she had led him to believe that she suffered from unrequited love, but she had to disabuse him of this idea – or "deception" as she called it – because in his last letter Byron had declared that "he shall never marry, for it is now too late, since the only woman to whom he could trust the happiness of his life *has disposed of her heart to another*."[15]

It has always been assumed that Annabella was telling the truth when she said that she initiated the correspondence with a lie. Yet it is possible that she rejected Byron because she had a more prudent match in mind. She might fully have expected that her friend Mary Millicent Montgomery's brother Hugh was going to propose to her. Certainly her letters to him have a playful, affectionate tone – almost flirtatious – that she seldom displayed. When she eventually confessed to Byron that Montgomery had bestowed his affections elsewhere, it is within the bounds of possibility that she was actually telling the truth. With prudence thwarted, her sexual longing was free to erupt. Frustrated and desperate, she fell ill after hearing a rumour that Byron had finally left England. Once she was reassured that he had not gone to Holland as she had been told, the correspondence was resumed in a desultory fashion during the next few months.

Meanwhile *The Bride of Abydos* proved to be an even greater success than *The Giaour*. Murray was so delighted that he offered to pay Byron 500 guineas for it. Byron recorded in his journal: "it is too much, though I am strongly tempted, merely for the *say* of it. No bad price for a fortnight's (a week each) what? – the gods know – it was intended to be called Poetry."[16] It did not occur to him that he could accept money to pay off some of his creditors such as Scrope Davies. He suggested that they wait a further six months to see whether Murray's optimism about its continuing sale was justified.

He sent copies of both poems to Leigh Hunt and apologised for his neglect of him by hinting vaguely about some personal affairs. Hunt he described in his journal as "an extraordinary character, and not exactly of the present age. He reminds me more of the Pym and Hampden times – much talent, great independence of spirit, and an austere, yet not repulsive, aspect."[17] Nevertheless, he made no further effort to visit Hunt in jail. He refused most of his many invitations, and by mid-December had plunged into the oriental tale which he took with him on his visit to Newmarket. *The Corsair* would prove to be even more revealing than anything he had yet written. Its motto was taken from Tasso's *Jerusalem Delivered*: "*I suoi pensieri in lui dormir non ponno*" – "Within him his thoughts cannot sleep." The poem was dedicated to Moore; and, curiously enough, he decided to give the copyright to Dallas, a man whom he had come to dislike. Dallas received £525 for it. The only explanation for this odd gesture is that Byron, preoccupied with his self-image, would be seen as a generous benefactor to a needy (if distant) relative, while the repayment of a debt to a tailor would be an altogether more tawdry matter. The greedy Dallas took umbrage at the fact that Byron hadn't turned over the copyrights of *The Giaour* and *The Bride of Abydos* to him as well.

As Byron and Augusta were preparing to leave for Newstead, a revenant suddenly appeared out of the past. All his later loves – even Augusta by now – had heard about the great unrequited passion of his life, Mary Chaworth. She had long since disappeared from his life when out of the blue he received a note, dated Christmas Eve, 1813: "My dearest Lord, if you are coming into Notts, call at Edwalton nr. Nottingham where you will find a *very old* and *sincere* friend most anxious to *see you*."[18]

Could this woman who described herself as "thin, pale and gloomy" – a creature he was told whom he would now scarcely recognise – be the lovely young woman who had broken his heart? Jack Musters's infidelities had become so flagrant that Mary was now about to separate from him. But this was one emotional entanglement Byron strenuously wanted to avoid; and on January 7 he told Augusta that he had heard from Mary again in *"all friendship – & really very simple and pathetic – bad usage – paleness – ill health – old friendship – once – good motive – virtue – & so forth."* To Lady Melbourne he sent on the letters from "my old love of all loves", telling her that he felt he ought to face the "melancholy interview", but needed her opinion.[19] For months he continued to be inundated with letters from Mary. If there was one thing Byron disliked, it was a supplicating female in pursuit – and this was particularly ironic in view of the fact that for so long she had been the unattainable one.

On January 17, 1814, brother and sister set off for Newstead although heavy snows had almost blocked the Great North Road. The Trent was frozen over and people were found frozen to death on the road. Once they had arrived at the abbey they stoked up the fires and settled into an oasis of laughter and intimacy from prying eyes. Never had he passed a birthday in a more contented state of mind. Augusta's condition made it possible to delay their return until February 6. It would have been possible to make a slight detour to visit Mary Chaworth Musters, but Augusta (despite Byron's disclaimers to Lady Melbourne) argued strongly against it. It actually took little to dissuade Byron from having his early dreams shattered.

Just before leaving for London Byron received a rapturous letter from Murray that he had sold 6,000 copies of *The Corsair* on the day of publication. Most of its popularity was due to the figure of the pirate Conrad, proud and bitter, with a mysterious past yet bearing the semblance of a fallen angel. He is something of the Hero of Sensibility in his chivalrous rescue of the Moslem tyrant's harem and in his devotion to his wife Medora. Medora is sweetly submissive yet deliciously nubile. After a long absence at sea Conrad returns only to tell Medora that he must set out again. She is the Penelope fated to keep the home fires burning while Conrad is destined for a life of adventure, sailing back from time to time, guided by a welcoming wisp of smoke. However, Conrad finally returns to find Medora dead of a broken heart. The poem on one level reflects Byron's conflict between a longing for companionable comfort and on the other his Ulyssean urge to pursue a life of untrammelled freedom.

The Harlequin Romance element of the poem was enough to maintain Byron's celebrity status, but he was not content with this. He insisted that Murray include the notorious "Lines to a Lady Weeping" which had been published anonymously in the *Morning Chronicle* in 1812. It was a deliberate affront to the Prince Regent, and the Tory press, led by the *Courier* and the *Morning Post*, erupted in indignation. It was almost as though Byron were deliberately seeking punishment and criticism. Murray removed the lines from the second edition but Byron insisted on his reinserting them: "I care nothing for consequences on this point – my politics are to me like a young mistress to an old man the worse they grow the fonder I become of them" (January 22, 1814).

Nevertheless, he was more sensitive to public opinion than he liked to admit. When a report was published that he had made a great deal of money from his poetry, he hinted broadly to Dallas that it would be helpful if he could make some kind of public statement that he had never accepted a penny for his work. Similarly, the previous September when Caroline Lamb was circulating stories that he was the figure portrayed in *The Giaour* he asked Lord Sligo to write out an account of the story as he remembered it when he was in Athens in 1810. This account he then sent on to Moore, Lord Holland, Lady Melbourne, and others. Ten lines of Sligo's report were blacked out to the point that they could not be read; and Byron gave the feeble excuse that they "contained merely some Turkish names, and circumstantial evidence of the girl's detection, not very important or decorous".[20]

Remarking on the attacks by the newspapers, he ended a letter to Lady Melbourne: "But all these externals are nothing to *that within* on a subject to which I have not alluded."[21] In his journal, which he had taken up again, he talked about a wife being his only salvation, but she must be a real companion (January 13, 1814). Only days before this (January 10) he complained of his inactivity, the sense that his life was being frittered away, whereas when he was in the East, "I was always in action or at least in motion – and except during Night – always on or in the sea – & on horseback – I am sadly sick of my present sluggishness – and I hate civilization." Yet by the time he had returned from his honeymoon interlude with Augusta in Newstead, the thought of parting from her was unbearable, "wined as she is round my heart in every possible manner – dearest & deepest in my hope & in my memory" (February 21, 1814). As Augusta's confinement approached, she longed to have Byron with her. George Leigh was going to Yorkshire; and although Byron had just moved into his new quarters in Albany on March 28, he set off for Newmarket on April 2 for five days. On April 15, nine months after Byron's first visit to Six Mile Bottom, Augusta gave birth to a daughter, Elizabeth Medora, who was christened on May 20, the sponsors being the Duchess of Rutland,

Mrs Wilmot – and Byron. To give the child such a name was a piece of unmitigated folly, and later the girl was known simply as "Libby".

Lady Melbourne asked him if his passion and all its attendant dangers were worth it (April 24). He replied unequivocally:

> Oh! but it is "worth while" – I can't tell you why – and it is *not* an "*Ape*"* and if it is – that must be my fault – however I will positively reform – you must however allow – that it is utterly impossible I can ever be half as well liked elsewhere – and I have been all my life trying to make some one love me – & never got the sort that I preferred before. – But positively she & I will grow good – & all that – & so we are *now* and shall be these three weeks & more too.[22]

There was absolutely no way Byron could be sure that he was the father of Augusta's baby. At the time he assumed this to be the case; but since he could never acknowledge the fact, he put her existence firmly out of his mind.

In the period since his return to London he had begun to see some of his old friends again. On February 8 Hobhouse returned from his continental travels with masses of anecdotes about Napoleon. With Hobhouse around, Byron felt he had firm ground under him; after a reunion at Covent Garden, Hobhouse wrote in his journal: "It is a long time since I have been so happy. I came home with my best friend, the most lively, and a man of the most startling talents extant."[23] On the 19th Francis Hodgson joined them for a performance of *Richard III* by the sensational new actor, Edmund Kean. Byron was ecstatic: "By Jove, he is a soul! Life – nature – truth – without exaggeration or diminution. Kemble's Hamlet is perfect; – but Hamlet is not Nature. Richard is a man; and Kean is Richard."[24] Constantly he talked about Kean and about Richard. His resemblance to Hamlet's wavering uncertainties was far more marked, but it is intriguing that he could see a reflection of himself in Richard's evil twisted self. On February 23 Hobhouse wrote in his journal that after dining with Byron he sat "hearing his confessions", followed by a long line.[25] What he was probably referring to was the incestuous relationship with Augusta.

Another identification was undoubtedly with Napoleon: even when only a boy at Harrow Byron had kept a bust of the man whom he regarded as a great emancipator, based on liberal sentiments he had imbibed from his mama. With Hobhouse and his other friends at Cambridge he had drunk a

---

* According to medieval belief, the child of an incestuous union would be an ape.

toast to Napoleon regularly at the Whig Club. He avidly followed the fortunes of his "little pagod". The attraction was understandable: here was another marginal man from the Marches whose accomplishments caused people to throw themselves at his feet in obeisance.

Napoleon's real downfall began with his retreat from Moscow on October 19, 1812, but Byron and his friends continued to hope that he might yet seize victory. Nevertheless, the following year, Russia, Prussia, Austria, and Sweden were closing round him, and Wellington was driving the French back across the Pyrennees. Finally, at Fontainebleau, Napoleon was forced to surrender; and after a farewell to his Guard, he departed for Elba, followed by the execrations of the populace who had so long adored him.

When the news of the abdication reached London on April 9, 1814, Byron pronounced himself "utterly bewildered and confounded". For some time he had been making theatrical pronouncements about his intention of giving up writing altogether, but now he shut himself away to compose his *Ode to Napoleon*. Reeling under what he considered Napoleon's shameful surrender, he described him as "a nameless thing", one who had once been miscalled the Morning Star, but now "Nor man nor fiend hath fall'n so far," and he deplored his failure to commit suicide in the high Roman fashion. When the poem was published anonymously on April 16, Murray did nothing to hide its authorship, and all London was soon talking about it. Despite the references to tyranny, it was enough to make the Tory press forget "Lines to a Lady Weeping". Byron failed to see that after Paris had fallen to the allies, Napoleon's own marshals insisted on his abdication. With his fierce allegiances, Byron seldom took cognisance of the complexities of a situation. Hobhouse did not share the extremity of Byron's new aversion and refused to allow the poem to be dedicated to him.*

Hobhouse was determined to reach Paris before Napoleon's departure; and one evening at the Cocoa Tree Club infected Byron with his enthusiasm for setting off on horseback for a last glimpse of the emperor. However, the next day (April 12, 1814), Byron sent him an unconvincing note: "I take the earliest opportunity of telling you that to my regret *my* Parisian scheme is knocked up – by some intelligence received in letters this morning on business & other concerns." Hobhouse felt some understand-

* I am grateful to both Professor Steven Marcus and Professor Austin Clarkson for the information that Arnold Schoenberg set the poem to music in 1942 as an anti-war piece ("String Quartet, Piano and Speaker, Opus 41").

able pique: "Byron goes not to Paris. He is a difficult person to live with."[26] The "intelligence" Byron had received was that the birth of Augusta's baby was imminent and he did not want to be far from her.

The fact that Byron had now moved into an apartment in Albany was a strong indication that he had no desire to travel abroad for the time being. This was the building in Piccadilly where the Melbournes had lived until 1789 when, as a favour to the Duke of York, they exchanged houses. It had now been converted into gentlemen's apartments and Byron had managed to secure one on the ground floor from Lord Althorp who was about to be married.* On March 28, the same day as he left his cramped quarters in Bennet Street, he dined with Scrope Davies at the Cocoa Tree where he finally discharged his debt of £4,800 by promissory notes on the vague premise that Claughton was about to pay another instalment.

Hobhouse had told him that he was turning into a *loup garou* – a solitary creature – but he began to accept the occasional invitation. We have a glimpse of him in paroxysms of stifled laughter at a solemn musical evening and another of his staggering home at dawn after a long night of drinking with his cronies. He could hold his liquor well but he suffered a recurrent kidney complaint as a result of his erratic eating habits. Late in April he was examined by a physician, Lord Stair, who seemed more concerned about the state of his mind, pronouncing him "horribly restless – and irritable".[27] Despite his joking tone, Byron was aware that the doctor suspected insanity.

Byron loved observing the human comedy, but he found society tedious and superficial. "I have no passion for circles," he told Moore (March 3, 1814), "and have long regretted that I ever gave way to what is called a town life." At the same time he believed that the Lake poets had been hindered in their development "by living in little circles and petty societies. London and the world is the only place to take the conceit out of a man."[28]

It is likely that Byron confided in Moore about Augusta. The meaning was only too clear in lines Byron wrote on May 4 in response to Moore's request for some lyrics to a song:

> I speak not – I trace not – I breathe not thy name,
> There is grief in the sound – there were guilt in the fame;
> But the tear which now burns on my cheek may impart
> The deep thought that dwells in that silence of heart.

* The Duke of York had sold the house to a builder who, in partnership with the architect Henry Holland, had converted it into gentlemen's apartments, a novel idea for its time. Byron's quarters were those entered by the second door to the left of the entrance.

Too brief for our passion, too long for our peace,
Were those hours, can their joy or their bitterness cease?
We repent – we abjure – we will break from our chain;
We must part – we must fly to – unite it again.

(*Works*, III, p.269)

Byron loved Moore's company and begged him to leave his domestic hearth in Derbyshire and join him in London. He was also absolutely sincere in his admiration of Moore's work and in his assertion that "I really have *no* literary envy; and I do not believe a friend's success ever sat nearer than yours do to my best wishes" (March 12, 1814). He was most comfortable in relaxed conversation with men, and while he often professed that he despised women's intellects, he also had to admit "There is something to me very softening in the presence of a woman" (February 27, 1814);[29] but often he was convinced that he was most content when alone with his books. God knows that Byron contained a multitude of contradictions, yet none of these feelings was incompatible.

Despite his disenchantment with Napoleon, he kept hoping that his little pagod would do something to redeem himself. On April 20 when Louis XVIII paraded down Whitehall in white cockades with the Prince Regent, Byron refused to leave his rooms. Murray offered him a seat at his window in Albemarle Street, but Byron told him that "I am a jacobin & could not wear white nor see the installation of Louis the gouty" (April 21, 1814). However, once Moore returned to London for a visit in May, for a few weeks he threw himself into the social scene with the impetuous abandon that marked his behaviour from time to time. (He had even started writing a sequel to *The Corsair* which he was to call *Lara*.) Naturally he had to take his friend to see Kean, and after a performance of *Othello*, they met him in the Green Room.* The following day, with typical magnanimous dash, he sent the actor £50.

After an unusual period of quietude, Caroline began to intrude into his life again. During June she managed to gain entry into Byron's rooms at all hours, probably by enticing Fletcher as she had done with Murray. On one occasion on finding Beckford's *Vathek* lying on a table, she dramatically scrawled on the first page "Remember me!" Byron, after finding this melodramatic message, under her admonition wrote the following lines:

---

* The waiting room for the performers near the stage was originally painted green to relieve the eyes from the glare of the stage lights.

Remember thee, remember thee!
   Till Lethe quench life's burning stream,
Remorse and shame shall cling to thee,
   And haunt thee like a feverish dream!

Remember thee! Ay, doubt it not;
   Thy husband too shall think of thee;
By neither shalt thou be forgot,
   Thou *false* to him, thou *fiend* to me!
                   (*Works*, III, p.84)

If we are to believe Caroline and the notes she wrote to him, during her visits in May and June Byron behaved tenderly towards her. The frequent expressions of detestation about her that he expresses to Lady Melbourne cannot always be taken at face value, although he might have believed them at the moment of writing. Caroline later claimed that at this time he showed her letters that destroyed her passion for him. If this was so, Byron's indiscretion would account for the terms he now applied to her, far more abhorrent than any he had used in the past. He was torn between his passion for Augusta and his anxiety that he might lose Lady Melbourne. Repeatedly he assured "la tante" that his affection for her was probably greater than for anyone else in the world and that she was indeed his greatest friend.

In May he gave his sister £3,000 to clear George's debts, at the same time advising her to "let him think well of some plan of regulating his expenditure" (June 24, 1814). At the time his own finances were desperate. The settlement with Claughton had not yet been finalised; and on July 19 he cried to Hanson that "it is the delay which drives me mad – I declare to God – I would rather have but ten thousand pounds clear & out of debt – than drag on the cursed existence of expectation & disappointment which I have endured for these last 6 years." Between the predicament over Augusta and the anxiety about money, it is not surprising that the physician had wondered if he were slightly deranged.

On June 10 Lady Melbourne sent him a note of strong disapproval of "the *easy* manner in which two people have accustom'd themselves to consider their situation quite *terrible* – but I shall not say more at present, as I see it is so useless."[30] A month later he was writing to Francis Hodgson in Hastings to find him a house large enough for Augusta, himself, her children, his cousin George Byron and their servants: "I don't much care about the price". (July 8, 1814). The need to get out of London quickly was precipitated by Mary Chaworth's announcement that she was coming to town.

Hodgson was in Hastings to be near his fiancée (the sister of Henry Drury's wife). Ironically, it was Byron's impetuous magnanimity that had allowed this happy union to take place. The young woman's mother had strongly objected to a match to a penniless parson, but had relented after Byron had galloped to Oxford to persuade her that he would take care of all his friend's debts. These various obligations were finally partially settled on August 3 when Claughton forfeited £25,000; and Newstead – with all its problems – was again in Byron's hands.

Hastings was a holiday of a kind, but one incident reveals the kind of tension Byron was suffering. One night Fletcher brought him a bottle of ink that was too full. As a result, Byron smeared his page, and in a fury threw the bottle out of the window so that the ink splattered all over a statue in the garden. Both Hodgson and Augusta were constantly talking to him about marriage. Hodgson's argument was that it would be a happy redemption for him; Augusta's urgent, though reluctant plea, was that it would be the only solution to their situation. Various prospects were discussed. Augusta was in favour of her friend Lady Charlotte Leveson-Gower; Hodgson, to whom Byron had shown one of Annabella's letters, pronounced that "*this* is the person to call out all the better parts of your character, & to assist you in subduing the worse."[31]

In August *Lara* appeared (published jointly with Rogers's *Jacqueline*) and was an immediate success. This time Byron accepted £700 for the copyright. On the 20th the final papers with Claughton were signed; and he departed for Newstead with Augusta and her children. Some sort of way out of their impasse was fast approaching. There seemed to be only a single option: marriage to a woman who would accept him.

13

ooooooooooooooo

Uneasy Commitment, 1813–14

After the initiation of the correspondence between Annabella and Byron in 1813, Byron began to refer to her in his letters to Lady Melbourne as "your A" and to his sister as "my A". The correspondence between Byron and Lady Melbourne is as strange in its way as that perplexing set of letters between the poet and the "Princess of Parallelograms". The latter correspondence is hesitant, obtuse, and exploratory, with the principals circling each other in wary appraisal. With Byron and his "tante" there is a continuing note of relaxed gaiety disturbed from time to time by Byron's discordant anxiety that he is going to lose this jewel among women. What is curious is that the subject-matter of their discussions is confined exclusively to Byron's amours: Caroline, Augusta, Lady Oxford, Annabella, and the various peripheral figures who flit across the stage as decorative supernumeraries. Despite promises of discretion to the women involved, Byron immediately showed Lady Melbourne all their letters, ostensibly for comment and advice. Lady Melbourne never suggested that there was something treacherous in their surreptitious complicity.

A profoundly collusive drama was being enacted as Byron brought his trophies to the feet of "La Tante", diverting all his longing and sexuality to her, thus creating an unconsciously Oedipal relationship. His obsession with his mentor could never be acted out, but it could find partial substitutes in incomplete and unsatisfying liaisons with other women. Unable – and unwilling – to break the bond with her, his other relationships were inevitably doomed. The women themselves – Caroline, Lady Oxford, Augusta, and Annabella – instinctively recognised Lady Melbourne's power and were apprehensive and jealous of her. Caroline later told Annabella that her mother-in-law was totally infatuated with Byron. Who knows to what degree this woman, once a *femme fatale*, envied the youth of her rivals? She basked in Byron's adoration; and while she urged on him the necessity to marry, none of the women involved met with her approval. She expressed her dissatisfaction when Byron acted independently without consulting her, and Byron ceased writing to her for periods when he knew that she would be angry with his defiant attempts at independence. Byron claimed that he considered Annabella as a wife in the first place only because the marriage would enable him to stay close to Lady Melbourne. He knew that she would be pleased by this constant reiteration of devotion; but it was she who, through her consuming obsession to control his life, took it upon herself to make the proposal to her niece.

The country mouse, in her secluded home in Durham, had altogether too much time on her hands to brood about Byron. After learning just after Christmas that he had not left England, she had to find a reason for his failure to answer a number of her letters. It must have been their discussion on religion, she concluded. On September 16, 1813, she had asked him for his views, assuring him that she had no "fancy" to convert him. On the 26th he replied in a good-natured way that his opinions were "undecided":

> I believe doubtless in God – & should be happy to be convinced of much more – if I do not at present place implicit faith on tradition & revelation of any human creed I hope it is not from a want of reverence for the Creator but the created . . . the *moral* of Christianity is perfectly beautiful – & the very sublime of Virtue – yet even there we find some of its finer precepts in earlier axioms of the Greeks. – particularly "do unto others as you would they should do unto you." – the forgiveness of injuries – & more which I do not remember.

In what way, then, could she have offended him? Carefully she scrutinised all his letters and the copies she had made of hers, analysing every sentence. Could the answer lie in a passage of November 29? In a long letter Byron assured her that he felt no pique over her rejection of his proposal. He reverted to his deep temptation for teasing: "I have but *2 friends* of your sex – yourself & Ly. M – as different in years as in disposition – & yet I do not know which I prefer – believe me a better-*hearted* woman does not exist – and in talent I never saw her excelled & hardly equalled – her kindness to me has been uniform."[1]

Had she then, Annabella asked herself, perhaps offended him in her first letter of August 22 when she had asked him not to tell Lady Melbourne of their correspondence? She had written, "we have little sympathy, & she is perhaps too much accustomed to look for design, to understand the plainness of my intentions."² Annabella now tried to rectify her blunder, and on February 10, 1814, she spontaneously opened the subject.

> I was sensible of many excellences in Lady Melbourne – Your opinion will induce me to look for more – I named her once in some ambiguous expression which I afterwards regretted, as likely to convey a meaning unfavourable to her Integrity . . . I meant only that from the habitual observation of vitiated morals, she might be disposed to see the *politics* of social life in the conduct of others – is the idea unfounded? You know her much better than I do."³

Ah, but for years Annabella had heard her mother, Lady Milbanke, inveighing against the lax morals of her worldly sister-in-law! Two days later Byron replied:

> I am not perhaps an impartial judge of Lady M. as amongst other obligations I am indebted to her for my acquaintance with yourself – but she is doubtless in talent a superior – a *supreme* woman – & her heart I know to be of the kindest – in the best sense of the word. – Her defects I never could perceive – as her society makes me forget them & every thing else for the time. – I do love that woman (*filially* or *fraternally*) better than any being on earth – & you see – that I am therefore unqualified to give an opinion.⁴

When one remembers what Byron's *fraternal* relationship was at the time, the language is highly charged as well as ambiguous.

But there still remained the awful blunder Annabella had committed in that first letter when she explained that her heart belonged to another who did not return her affection. In the same letter of February 10, after many alterations, she wrote the following:

> You have understood *me* at least as well as I understood myself. Both may have been partly deceived, though unwittingly by me; but I have found that Wisdom (often the most difficult Wisdom, Self-knowledge) is not less necessary than Will, for an absolute adherence to Veracity. How I may in a degree have forsaken *that* – and under an ardent zeal for Sincerity – is an explanation that cannot benefit either of us. Should any disadvantage arise from the original fault, it must be only

where it is deserved. Let this then suffice – for I cannot by total silence acquiesce in that which, if supported when its delusion is known to myself, would become a deception.[5]

Since her explanation was totally incomprehensible, Byron replied that he could not possibly understand why she felt that she had deceived him since she had done nothing to encourage him. He also mentioned the possibility of again meeting Mary Chaworth who had "once been deep in my heart".[6]

Annabella now realised that franker explanation was necessary lest Byron's feelings for Mary Chaworth be reignited.

I had certainly felt greater interest for the character I attributed to one man (with whom my personal acquaintance was comparatively slight) than for any other within my knowledge. In believing him deserving of happiness, I earnestly wished he might enjoy it; but he had never given me any reason to think I could bestow it, nor was my partiality discovered by himself or any other person. I indulged no hope, & had hope been offered, should have rejected it from regard to the views and wishes of others. Circumstances have since made it impossible for me even to dream of Hope . . . I have sometimes regretted that lost chance of domestic happiness – sometimes I have doubted if I should have possessed the characteristical happiness of married life, that of making happy.[7]

This woman, whom Byron was later to describe as a model of probity, was talking about two things at once: the "attachment" which had come to nothing, and the self-deception by which she had lost Byron. Perhaps the most sincere statement in the letter is her doubt that she had the capacity to make another person happy. For all the outward assurance of the pampered only child, she had turned down several proposals; and it cannot be ruled out that she might have had a profound suspicion that she was not truly lovable. It is only too easy to be critical of Annabella, but far more difficult to understand her insecurities.

Byron ignored the provocative hint, and, in his self-absorbed way, talked of "something or other – which will probably crush me at last".[8] Why, Annabella pleaded, did he not confide in her? And what comfort it would give him if he could bring himself to bow down before "the Chastener"! In a letter of March 3 for the first time he addressed her as "My dear Friend"; but as for her suggestion of turning to religion for comfort, "it is a source from which I never did – & I believe never can derive comfort." Annabella replied with an expression of steadfast faith in his salvation: "My interest for you will not be altered because at present you *cannot* be convinced – or by me. Despair not of yourself – I still hope the best for you, and whence soever it may come, though not through *my* means, it will add to *my* happiness."[9]

This was a month before the birth of Medora Leigh when Byron was in a state of great agitation. Was there actually a possibility that this self-righteous young woman could save him from damnation? On March 15 he cried impulsively, "You do not know how much I wish to see you"; and in his journal that night he remarked: "A letter from *Bella*, which I answered. I shall be in love with her again, if I don't take care." Hazlitt once faulted Byron for stimulating emotional states in himself; and in this case *he* was the one suffering self-deception when he could bring himself to believe that he had once before actually been in love with Annabella. Indeed, on March 22 he actually noted in his journal the possibility of marrying Lady Charlotte Leveson Gower, since "she is a friend of Augusta's, and whatever she loves I can't help liking." But Annabella's real attraction lay in the fact that she was not fun-loving like Augusta, nor worldly like Lady Melbourne, thus freeing him from his incestuous double-bind.

When Annabella read that he longed to see her, her heart leapt. She now asked timidly: "Am I mistaken in imagining you are disposed to visit us?"[10] She again emphasised that she did not want her aunt to know of their correspondence. Could this perhaps be avoided if Byron simply told her that he was making a trip to the north and had been invited to stop at Seaham on his way?

Byron as usual immediately turned to Lady Melbourne for advice (April 18). Possibly alluding to the birth of Medora, he wrote:

> Circumstances which I need not recapitulate may have changed *Aunt's* mind – I do not say that *Niece's* is changed – but I *should* laugh if their judgments had changed places & exactly reversed upon that point. – In putting this question to you – my motive is all due selfishness – as a word from you – could & would put an end to that or any similar possibility – without my being able to say anything but "thank you". – Comprenez vous?

On April 13 Annabella informed him that she too had revealed the possibility of his visit to her aunt, "which *I think she will be glad to learn*".[11] Byron, who kept the letter, underlined these words, adding, "*Will she?* credo di *No*."

By now Byron was discussing with Lady Melbourne the likelihood that Annabella had changed her mind (April 30). While La Tante pondered the situation Byron began to go about London "and (to please you) I am trying to fall *in* love."[12] *Lara* was written in intervals between balls held during the visit of the French king. On May 25 Lady Melbourne herself wrote guardedly to her Seaham relatives: "I was very glad to hear of my Brs. invitation to Ld.B – as should he accept it, I am sure you will be highly delighted with his Society, & I have no doubt you will all think me justified in the Character I have always given of him".[13]

This was Lady Melbourne's first great moral and tactical error. When she had taken it upon herself to suggest marriage initially, she did not stop to reflect sufficiently on how incompatible this ill-assorted pair would be. However, now that she knew the full extent of Byron's involvement with Augusta – and had been genuinely shocked at how easily they could accommodate themselves to the situation – it was reprehensible to present Byron as a model of rectitude. Her first priority, as she saw it, was to wean Byron away from Augusta; but to use her niece as an unwitting victim justified the fury later felt towards her by the Milbankes. Nevertheless, by now she was not encouraging a marriage as she considered Annabella far too much of a prig; but in her awareness of Byron's volatile state she should have done everything she could to discourage the visit to Seaham.

Despite Annabella's letter about the projected visit, almost two months passed without her hearing from Byron; and by June 19 she could contain herself no longer: "Pray write to me – for I have been rendered uneasy by your long silence, & you cannot wish me so."[14] The fact was that Byron had taken alarm. On June 10 he described Annabella to Lady Melbourne as "the most prudish & correct person I know". Basic courtesy demanded a reply to Annabella's cry of anguish; and he answered evasively that he would be glad to come to Seaham at her family's convenience. In other words, he wanted the decision to be taken out of his hands. He sent her no further letters before his departure for his holiday in Hastings on July 20. On August 1 he hedged his acceptance of her urgent invitation with the comment, "My memory is still retentive enough not to require the repetition that you are attached to another."

Meanwhile, Augusta and Hodgson were applying pressure on him to marry *someone*. Byron at this point was inclined to favour Lady Charlotte who had the attractive shyness of an antelope. Before the departure from Hastings some peculiar letters were exchanged with Annabella. In an attempt to induce him to some commitment, on August 6 she asked him to consider carefully whether he ought to accept the invitation to Seaham lest he "might still be in danger of feeling more than friendship towards me".[15] After returning to London on the 10th, Byron replied:

> I will answer your question as openly as I can. – I did – do – and always shall love you – and as this feeling is not exactly an act of will – I know no remedy and at all events should never find one in the sacrifice of your comfort. – When an acquaintance commenced – it appeared to me from all that I saw and heard – that you were the woman most adapted to render any man (who was neither inveterately foolish nor wicked) happy – but I was informed that you were attached if not engaged.

This was exactly how he imagined himself to have felt at the time.

He went on to suggest that he would have proposed had he not received this unhappy information. Then he learned that it was untrue: "the rest you know." What her own feelings were he realised that he had no right to enquire, but "you would probably like me if you could . . . You ask me how far my peace is – or may be affected by those feelings towards you? – I do not know – not quite enough to invade yours – or request from your pity what I cannot owe to your affection."

Three days later Annabella replied, carefully avoiding any discussion of her own feelings, except to say that while she did not doubt his capacity for domesticity, "you do not appear to be the person whom *I* ought to select as my guide, my support, my example on earth, with a view still to Immortality."[16] Had the voice of common sense suddenly asserted itself over the romantic girl's unreal fantasies? Or was it simply that she wanted to reassure him in order to lure him to Seaham, and then . . . who knows?

The correspondence was then resumed on more general topics, such as requests for recommendations of books that she should read, especially history which she knew to be his favourite subject. By now Byron and Augusta had arrived at Newstead where they were joined by Sophie Byron, their father's sister, and numerous family discussions took place as to whom he should direct his proposal to. Aunt Sophie had heard good reports about Annabella. For the time being Byron and Lady Melbourne were not writing because of her disapproval of the continued presence of Augusta on the scene, so she cannot be held responsible for any decisions taken at this point. Augusta was assiduously sounding out her friend Lady Charlotte who sounded well disposed. Then suddenly – on September 8 or 9 – an incoherent letter arrived from the timid antelope, breathlessly apologising that her family had other plans for her.

When Lady Charlotte was still the leading candidate, Byron informed Annabella that unfortunately he would not be able to make the journey to Seaham that year (August 18). He also pointed out that they "could hardly have met without some embarrassment" (September 7). This was intended as an oblique means of leaving one door open lest another was closed. With Lady Charlotte now ruled out, Byron turned helplessly to Augusta: "You see that, after all, Miss Milbanke is the person; – I will write to her." So far as we can reconstruct events, Byron sat down and wrote a rather odd letter asking her if there was any possibility that her original decision might be changed. Nervously he put it aside in his desk for a day. Augusta pleaded with him to consider his decision carefully, reminding him of Lady Melbourne's warnings about Annabella's character. According to what Augusta later told Annabella, during this stressful period he made a number of remarks about his determination to take revenge on Annabella for refusing him the first time, but Augusta believed he was indulging in his usual theatrical exaggerations.

He showed the completed letter to his sister, and after reading it, she made a comment about how well written it was and what a pity it would be if it weren't sent. Such a remark was indicative of Augusta's basic superficiality. On hearing her reaction, Byron exclaimed, "Then it *shall* go!" He immediately rang the bell, sealed the letter with great haste, and sent it off to the post so that there could be no risk of reclaiming it. During the next few days Byron was in a fever of agitation. He did not know what answer he desired. Each day he would sit on the steps of the abbey waiting for the arrival of the post.

While the letter was travelling between Newstead and Seaham, Annabella was involved in a hazardous experiment of her own. She had been intrigued by a recent incident when on a wager a man had walked blindfold from Sunderland to Seaham. Annabella thought that she might try the same stunt across the field behind the house, but instead of reaching the gate, she would have plunged into the horse-pond if not rescued just in time. Her encouragement to Byron had forewarned her of the consequences of her action, so that her behaviour was not simply coincidental. Would that someone had had the will to rescue her from the maelstrom into which she was about to be plunged!

Events occurred with eerie synchronicity. Even though Claughton had finally come to a settlement on his purchase of Newstead by paying a forfeit, Byron told Hanson (September 11): "This place I fully intend to dispose of – unless a wife – a legacy or a lottery ticket – (& I have put in for neither) induced me to retain it." One cannot rule out the possibility that

Byron's decision had been partly governed by his knowledge that Annabella was the heiress of her uncle, Lord Wentworth, who was (as Byron was aware) in frail health.

By September 14 Byron was beside himself with suspense. If Annabella refused him again, an alternative plan had to be ready. As usual, it would be flight from humiliation. Would Hobhouse consider a journey to Italy? With the forfeit paid by Claughton, he would be "pretty well in funds". As his letter to his friend proceeded, Italy increasingly took on a tangible existence. Byron assured Hobhouse that

> you are the only man with whom I could travel an hour except an "ιατρος" [physician] – in short you know my dear H – that with all my bad qualities – (and d—d bad they *are* to be sure) I like you better than any body – and we have travelled together before – and been old friends and all that – and we have a thorough fellow-feeling & contempt for all things of the sublunary sort . . .

Since he had already accumulated a great quantity of snuff-boxes and other gifts for Eastern potentates, they might even cross over to their old haunts again. He urged Hobhouse to study the map of Italy as he was doing. What he really wanted from Hobhouse was a commitment, although as yet he was not prepared to provide one himself. "I shall know tomorrow or next day – whether I can go – or not – & shall be in town next week – where I must see or hear from you – if we set off – it should be in October – & the earlier the better."

The same day Annabella received Byron's letter. He started out by reminding her of the question she had recently put to him. He now had one for her.

> Are the "objections" – to which you alluded – insuperable? – or is there any line or change of conduct which could possibly remove them? – I am well aware that all such changes are more easy in theory than practice – but at the same time there are few things I would not attempt to obtain your good opinion – at all events I would willingly know the worst – still I neither wish you to promise or pledge yourself to anything – but merely to learn a *possibility* which would not leave you the less a free agent.[7]

Without a moment's hesitation she sent off two letters, one to Newstead, and one to Albany accompanied by a note from her father. She assured him that she was almost too agitated to write:

but you will understand. It would be absurd to suppress anything – I am and have long been pledged to myself to make your happiness my first object in life. *If I can* make you happy, I have no other consideration. I will *trust* to you for all I should look up to – all I can love. The fear of not realizing your expectations is the only one I now feel. Convince me – it is all I wish – that my affection may supply what is wanting in my character to form your happiness. This is a moment of joy which I have too much despaired of ever experiencing – I *dared* not believe it possible, and I have painfully supported a determination founded in fact on the belief that you did not wish it removed – that its removal would not be for your good. There has in reality been scarcely a change in my sentiments. More of this I will defer. I wrote by last post – with what different feelings! Let me be grateful for those which I now acknowledge myself

Most affectionately yours.[18]

When her acceptance arrived at Newstead, Byron and Augusta were at dinner. During the meal the gardener brought in Mrs Byron's wedding ring, long since lost, which he had just dug up in the flowerbed under the window. Annabella's letter was then handed to him. Byron turned so pale that Augusta thought he was going to faint. He passed the letter across to her, remarking, "It never rains but it pours."

His letter in response was written with all the sincerity he felt at the moment:

Your letter has given me a new existence. It was unexpected, I need not say welcome – but *that* is a poor word to express my present feelings – and yet equal to any other – for express them adequately I cannot. – I have ever regarded you as one of the first of human beings – not merely from my own observation but that of others – as one whom it was as difficult *not* to love, as scarcely possible to deserve; – I know your worth – & revere your virtues as I love yourself and if every proof in my power of my full sense of what is due to you will contribute to *your* happiness – I shall have secured my own. – It *is* in your power to render me happy – you have made me so already.[19]

A decision had been made – his fate had been decided for him – and for the two final days they remained at Newstead he seemed in a remarkably tranquil mood. On the same day as he replied to Annabella, Byron wrote to Lady Melbourne with the news and expressed the hope that she would see him as soon as possible after he returned to town. There was no use pretending to her that he was overwhelmed by passion. All he asked for was her consent and "your friendship always". He could not face the world knowing about it yet so he begged her to keep the engagement a secret; and he assured her that he meant "to reform most thoroughly & become 'a good man and true' in all the various senses of these respective & respectable appellations".[20] They both knew exactly what he was referring to, but on the day brother and sister departed from Newstead – September 20, 1814 – they carved their interlocking names on an elm behind the abbey.

The betrothed pair had not seen each other for well over a year, and in their occasional meetings in London they had had only brief conversations. The letters had done little to deepen their knowledge of each other. In some ways they had a remarkable insight into aspects of the other's character – hardly a perceptive achievement. Both were lonely, self-absorbed narcissists. In a telling phrase in her letter of acceptance, Annabella had made a curious comment which she had underlined: "*if I can* make you happy". Neither of them knew what they wanted out of life or what they wanted from the other. Annabella might have been in love with the idea of love, but not with a real flawed being. Neither the letter of proposal nor that of acceptance exactly expressed enthusiastic affirmation. Byron had drifted into the situation more through indolence than anything else. He wanted money, companionship, and freedom from constraint. He didn't particularly like children and the image of Byron as a pater familias is risible. Annabella was not unaware that it would be a great prize to carry off the man over whom she had seen London belles making fools of themselves. The only thing the couple seemed to agree on completely was their alleged dislike of society. Annabella had frequently held out her hand as a staff to salvation and Byron now begged her to be "my Guide, Philosopher and friend"; but actually the reformer and the reformed were not roles either of them was particularly enthusiastic about assuming. "My ideas wait to be fixed by yours," she told him. She wanted a man who would dominate her, but such an urge was not part of Byron's temperament. "I am tired of having my own way."[21] Two strangers were about to unite, only to disunite again.

Gradually they tentatively informed their friends of what had taken place. After Hobhouse received Byron's letter proposing a trip abroad together, on September 18 his enthusiastic response was "To be sure I will go to Italy or any where with you."[22] On the 30th a terse entry appeared in his diary: "Lord B is going to be married I learn to Miss Milbanke.."*[23] There is no comment, but on October 1 he sent off a warm letter of congratulation. He had not yet met Annabella, but "If I had the pleasure of a personal acquaintance I should take the liberty of congratulating her on her approaching union with the person whom the trial of some varying years has made most dear to me, and whose qualities, as far as I am myself concerned, I would not exchange for those of any man living."[24] His devotion to Byron, his acceptance of him for exactly what he was, is a testament both to Hobhouse's generosity and to Byron's innate love-ableness. To Annabella Hobhouse wrote as well, and she told Byron that "One believes every word Mr Hobhouse writes because there is not a word too much – The good opinion of those who estimate *you* justly is on every account of great value to me."[25]

Hodgson was the only one of Byron's friends to react with unalloyed delight. Knowing Moore's opinion of Annabella as a strait-laced prig, Byron assured him that they had been mistaken about her. Besides, she had great expectations from her uncle, Lord Wentworth, a consideration Moore would understand since Moore had first alerted him to the fact. Byron was only half joking when he told him: "I must, of course, reform thoroughly . . . She is so good a person, that – that – in short, I wish I was a better."[26] But did he really want to be the better sort of person that would meet with Annabella's approval?

On September 24 Byron's publisher, John Murray, wrote excitedly to his wife in Edinburgh that Byron had conveyed the news to him in secret. "So here is news for you! I fancy the lady is rich, noble, and beautiful . . . Oh! how he did curse poor Lady Caroline as the friend who had interrupted all his projects, and would do so now if possible."[27] At the beginning of October, Murray journeyed up to Scotland, stopping off, out of curiosity, to visit Newstead. He was appalled to find it "crumbling into dust".[28]

Annabella's communications to her friends indicated a certain nervous defensiveness. To the straw-man suitor, Hugh Montgomery, she playfully announced that she could no longer correspond with "*handsome young bachelors*" and that she looked forward to "the most rational happiness" with the man who had been "greatly misconceived in the world" (September 22, 1814). Her old friend Selina Doyle hoped that Byron would appreciate "the Treasure" he had secured (September 24, 1814). Francis Doyle's sister-in-law, Emily Milner, frankly spoke of her "nervous anxiety on first hearing of the awful change

* Peter W. Graham, the editor of Hobhouse's letters, believes he heard the news through Scrope Davies.

about to take place in your situation". She herself had heard nothing negative about Byron beyond the fact that he possessed "a certain gloominess & despondency of disposition". Joanna Baillie referred cautiously to "the very extraordinary man to whom you are to be united" (October 3, 1814). To Lady Gosford, Annabella complained that "Nothing offends me so much as a doleful *hope* that I shall be happy." She also reconstructed a psychological history to account for Byron's depression: he had been so persecuted by the public and disappointed by her rejection that he had plunged into dissipation, but "stern and cruel experience" had given him the wisdom to control his passions.[29]

Annabella's mother, Lady Milbanke, was also busy with her pen. She cried sorrowfully to Hugh Montgomery: "what is to become of me when I lose my Darling I know not! It seems to me at this moment that every hour of my life will seem a doleful blank."[30] Turning to the man who was taking her Treasure from her, she assumed that he would be suited for domestic happiness since his "relatives" (?) adored him. This seemed to be confirmed, she believed, since after Annabella's acceptance, he had moved back into Newstead Abbey which would otherwise have been sold. Nevertheless, she was so upset by the prospect that she retired to her bed. She pulled herself together, however, to discuss the situation with Lady Melbourne from a worldly point of view. Her brother, Lord Wentworth, had given her every indication that Annabella was to be his heir. Then her fortune would be "*very considerable*". As for Annabella's feelings towards her affianced, "I have *always* thought that Ld Byron was the only Man who ever interested her – & I was right."[31] As for Annabella's own attitude towards Lady Melbourne, she could now tell Byron that "I do sincerely love her for her friendly conduct & feelings towards you."[32] Neither mother nor daughter said anything about Lady Melbourne's high regard for him being a strong recommendation in his favour.

Augusta did not write to Annabella until October 1 when she was settled back in Six Mile Bottom. She excused the delay: she had hoped that Byron would be there to supervise the letter. "If I could possibly express how deservedly dear my Brother is to me, you might in some degree imagine the joy I have felt in the anticipation of an event which promises to secure his happiness."[33] Byron was pleased to hear that the two women had exchanged letters and he assured Annabella that Augusta was "the least selfish & gentlest creature in being, – & more attached to me than any one in existence can be".[34] Annabella had the impression that she was shy, which Byron confirmed, describing her as "like a frightened hare – with new acquaintances".[35]

Annabella invited Augusta to join Byron on his anticipated visit to Seaham, but Augusta pleaded family duties. As a partial sister she defended her depiction of Byron as the dearest of men, "clever agreeable & good-natured, but to you who will soon love him, qualities much more *love-able*, I may venture to speak as I think."[36] She began to write more regularly than Byron; and in October 1816, after the separation, Annabella asked one of her confidantes: "Was I not likely to be influenced by such representations? – I should not now want him to know how much they prevailed with me to fulfil the Engagement."[37]

Lady Melbourne's jealousy of Augusta led her to see not the startled hare Byron described to Annabella, but a scheming woman who was responsible for preventing Byron from travelling immediately to Seaham. Using their private love sign, Byron defended his sister strenuously because she had been even more anxious for him to meet his intended than Lady Melbourne, as marriage would provide the only chance of redemption for both of them: "+ is the least selfish person in the world . . . you don't know what a being she is – her only error has been my fault entirely – & for this I can plead no excuse – except passion – which is none."[38]

He defended the engagement by telling her that "it is a match of *your* making." But he could not refrain from their usual joking tone with his old friend when he went on to wonder if he was stuck with one person for life. "I ask only for information." Lady Melbourne taxed him with flippancy about the marriage, and at that point he reverted to seriousness: "You very much mistake me if you think I am lukewarm upon it . . . if I think she likes me – I shall be exactly what she pleases – it is her fault if she don't govern me properly – for never was anybody more easily managed . . . *You* can't conceive how I long to call you Aunt."[39]

Naturally the Milbankes expected the love-struck Byron to visit his beloved at the first opportunity. Byron lingered on in London; but now he had the excuse that he could not leave until Hanson was ready to meet with the Milbankes' lawyer . . . and of course, Hanson had always been painted as notoriously dilatory. Newstead had to be sold in order for a settlement to be made on Annabella – indeed, for them to be able to manage at all. In any event, Byron's financial affairs were in such disarray that some intricate juggling was necessary before Hanson could have a meeting with the Durham lawyer.

The delay allowed the lovers to pour out some of their hitherto restrained feelings – at least, certainly on Annabella's part. Like all lovers, they recalled their first sight of each other. Byron had seen her standing apart at Caroline's waltzing party. He believed that she shared his contempt for the corrupt society, and she remained in his mind as a white virginal image. The attraction was that they were both "different". Annabella told him how in London he had always been depicted to her as a man of "mystery & mischief".[40] Her mother had shown her a bundle of letters she had written during that season of 1812 in which it was very clear that she was falling in love with him. She told him that George Eden and Hugh Montgomery had never been considered as serious suitors. Perhaps we hear the voice of complete truth when she confessed that she had turned him down in 1813 because she was convinced that she was not suitable for him.

Byron was not tempted to write as frequently as his beloved; and often she made the walk to the blacksmith's cottage where the post arrived only to be met with disappointment. Retracing her steps, she would compose her features into an expression of cheerfulness in order to reassure her concerned parents. Byron's erratic letters must have alerted her to a certain lack of ardour, a suspicion she tried to suppress. The urgent note that runs through all those that he did write expresses not passion but the need for redemption. He had his head examined by a phrenologist who found that "every thing developed in & on this same skull of mine has its *opposite* in great force so that to believe him my good & evil are at perpetual war – pray heaven the last don't come off victorious."[41] This interpretation exactly coincided with Byron's view of himself, but he might have been forewarned about Annabella's shaft of unforgiving steel when she told him of dismissing a maid who had become pregnant: "I believe she is a hardened sinner and whatever may be the present inconvenience, I must congratulate myself on the escape."[42]

As for congratulations, Lady Caroline wrote warmly to Byron: "God bless you – you may be very happy. I love and honour you from my heart as a friend may love – no wrong I hope – as a sister feels – as your Augusta feels for you."[43] Was there a barbed implication here? She made a number of catty remarks about Annabella to John Murray; and predicted that Byron would "never be able to pull with a woman who went to church punctually, understood statistics and had a bad figure".[44]

Byron was beginning to be terrified that the marriage would take place and just as terrified that it wouldn't. He was aware that George Leigh's friends at Newmarket were placing bets on it. He told Annabella that he doubted if he could spend more than a few days at Seaham. In mid-October Augusta was deputised to inform Annabella that it was imperative Newstead be sold. Augusta also tried to soften the effect of her brother's prolonged delay: "He writes me word that he hopes *very* soon to see you. It is most provoking that his departure to Seaham should have hitherto met with so many impediments."[45]

In this state of tremulous uncertainty Byron received a letter from Annabella that made him realise that action could no longer be delayed. Her rich uncle, Lord Wentworth, had travelled from Leicestershire to the Milbanke home particularly to meet the fiancé. It was humiliating to Annabella's parents to try to explain away the delay in his appearance. On October 22 she made the point very cleverly: "My uncle is obliged to leave us next week, and is in despair lest you should not arrive before he *must* go. It is odd that my task should be to pacify the old ones, and teach *them* patience. They are growing quite ungovernable, and I must have your assistance to manage them."*[46]

Byron immediately sent off a furious message to Hanson that he would never forgive him if he did anything to prevent the marriage. He asked Hobhouse if he would act as his groomsman. All the formalities connected with a wedding were anathema to him but he had to take the bit between his teeth. On October 29 he set off for the north, arranging with Hanson to proceed to Durham with all haste. He stopped off at Six Mile Bottom; and his dark mood deepened as he moved on. In this state his mind always reverted to flight. Perhaps, he brooded, perhaps he and Augusta should have run away a year ago after all? When he and Hanson had applied for the marriage licence, he had gravely asked the Doctor of the Commons: "Pray, sir, what is the proportion of those who come here first to make marriages and then afterwards to unmake them?"[47]

---

* Byron's dilatoriness might have persuaded Wentworth to leave his money to his sister rather than to Annabella direct.

14

ooooooooooooooo

The Fatal Marriage, 1814–15

O n that late November afternoon Annabella was sitting reading
in her room. Byron had been expected two days earlier (on
October 30), but, in order to prolong his journey, he stopped off
at Newstead. It was to be the last time he would see the abbey. When he
failed to appear, Sir Ralph and Lady Milbanke were in a fever of anxiety
which they had unsuccessfully tried to hide from their daughter. When they
eventually met Byron at the door, they ushered him into the drawing room.
Meanwhile, Annabella put out the candles and "deliberated what should
be done".[1]

She went downstairs and found Byron standing by the chimney-piece.
He did not move as she approached. She extended her hand which he
kissed. Both were choked with embarrassment. Finally Byron spoke almost
inaudibly: "It is a long time since we have met." At a loss for words,
Annabella ran from the room to fetch her parents.

The first evening they all made rather stilted conversation. Byron spoke
of his admiration of Kean's acting. Years later Annabella recalled that the
thought had crossed her mind that he was vain from the way he played with
his large watch-chain. The detail is too graphic for it to have been
imagined. She failed to attribute it to nervousness, but her long habit
of examining others fastened on such a detail. Writing in the third person,
she recalled her immediate impressions: "No sooner did she see him than
she felt most distinctly, 'he is coarser, sullied, since we last met' – it was like
a death-chill. In the animation with which we conversed, and in the
sentiments shewn towards herself, she however lost that impression. Still
there was a mysterious shadow, to which he made frequent and self-
reproachful allusions."[2]

Both mother and daughter knew that all was not well, but neither knew what to do about their instinct. Lady Milbanke was chagrined that the fiancé had not brought her darling an engagement ring or a single gift. That night in bed her good-natured husband tried to pooh-pooh her affronted feelings.

On parting for the night Byron enquired of Annabella at what hour she usually appeared in the morning. She replied about ten. But the next day she arose "early" – how early we do not know – and went directly to the library, hoping against hope that Byron would be eager to be there before her. Byron was always a late riser, and he would have been anxious to postpone the meeting as long as possible. Annabella waited for nearly two hours, and then went out for a walk, "hoping" that he would be there on her return. We are not told that he was, only that "later" she took him on her favourite walk along the cliff that faced the North Sea. She squeezed his arm. He was chilled to the bone, but his heart was colder still.

Byron, who was accustomed to chatterboxes like Caroline Lamb, found himself uncomfortable with her silences. He squirmed under her constant scrutiny. With the parents around, things were a little easier. Byron was determined to be pleasant. It was not hard to like the benevolent, unaffected father, and Sir Ralph was delighted when he listened attentively to his interminable stories. Judith Milbanke was all politeness, yet Byron sensed that she was suspicious of him. To Hugh Montgomery (and how she must have wished that he had been the suitor!), her reservations are apparent: "Ld.B. arrived here on tuesday. I am relieved that the first interview is over. Every thing so far is satisfactory to my feelings both in his manner and conduct, but I am in a state of agitation You would pity."[3]

To La Tante, Byron wrote: "I don't like Lady Mil. at all – I can't tell why – for we don't differ – but so it is – she seems to be every thing here, which is all very well – and I am & mean to be very conformable & dutiful but nevertheless I wish she & mine aunt could change places as far as regards me & mine."[4]

A pre-nuptial agreement was *de rigueur* among the upper classes. Each side had to be certain that their interests were protected, especially in cases where great fortunes were involved. In this instance the circumstances were embarrassing on both sides. Hanson finally arrived and a dowry of £20,000 was agreed upon, hardly a princely sum since Byron's debts alone amounted, by his own estimate, to at least £30,000.[5] Sir Ralph could raise only £16,000, and "covenanted" to pay the rest. Hanson, unwilling to divulge the extent of Byron's indebtedness, was inclined to promise a settlement on Annabella based on the sale of Newstead and Rochdale. By the laws of the time Annabella could not inherit Newstead which was destined to go to the heir, George Byron. "The die is cast," Byron remarked resignedly to Lady Melbourne; "neither party can recede . . . I shall become Lord Annabella."[6] Byron had known already that Sir Ralph was in financial difficulties, and while Annabella had expectations from Lord Wentworth, one could not by any stretch of the imagination describe her as an heiress. But Byron, in his usual casual way, had acquired no details as to what these "expectations" were. (Nor, apparently, had Hanson, for that matter.) These had the same sort of illusory value that Rochdale once possessed as a hope of financial salvation.

A fortnight passed in great uneasiness, although Byron seemed more relaxed in the evenings when he and Annabella sat talking before the fire, often about his poetry. He mentioned the mysterious "Thyrza" and the shock that "her" death had been to him. One of the most convincing reasons for believing in eternity, he remarked, was that we could never love enough in this life, that we could not mingle "soul in soul".[7] Annabella later believed that she had uncovered most of his secrets, but she never seems to have known anything about Edelston. Naturally they talked about Augusta. Byron told her that no one could ever have as much of his love as she had. Annabella, easily aroused to jealousy, felt a stab of pain which was never to be entirely assuaged.

All too frequently Annabella would retire to her room with attacks of nerves. Byron began to doubt that the marriage would take place. During her solitary sojourns Annabella did a great deal of thinking. Byron alluded often to the harm she had done by her rejection of his first proposal and the "revenge" he would have on her once they were married, when he half-jokingly said he would throw her out of the house. It is not surprising that after one of these diatribes Annabella decided to offer to break off the engagement. Was there, she asked him, anything on his mind that made him doubtful of the wisdom of their marriage? On hearing this, Byron fell back against the sofa in a state of violent shock. The poor girl was reassured that his reaction proved that he loved her, and she threw herself tearfully at his feet.

When she became agitated and weepy, Byron resorted to caresses. Annabella was totally inexperienced sexually, and Byron was surprised and somewhat alarmed by her passionate response. Fearing that they were exceeding the bounds of propriety, she finally told him that he must leave Seaham so that they could contain themselves until they were respectably married. The parents were bewildered by the sudden departure and Byron was extremely grumpy about his dismissal. On November 16, from Boroughbridge where he spent his first night at an inn, he wrote a slightly barbed letter: "My Heart – We are thus far separated – but after all one mile is as bad as a thousand – which is a great consolation to one who must travel six hundred before he meets you again. – If it will give you any satisfaction – I am as comfortless as a pilgrim with peas in his shoes – and as cold as Charity – Chastity or any other Virtue." Annabella, now calmer, tried to reassure him that only the tension of the circumstances had made her unlike her usual placid self.

Byron made for Cambridge where he ran into Hodgson whom he misled somewhat about the marriage settlement. To his fiancée, Hodgson wrote: "Oh! how I glowed with indignation at the base reporters of his *Fortune-hunting . . . entre nous* he is sacrificing a great deal too much."[8] As Hodgson understood it, Annabella's parents were putting Byron in a position where he had to sell Newstead: "His fortune is *not* large at present, but he settles £60,000 upon her. This he cannot do *without selling Newstead again*; and with a look and manner that I cannot easily forget he said: 'You know we must think of these things as little as possible.'"

From Cambridge Byron went to Six Mile Bottom for a few days. Here he berated Augusta for being responsible for his entanglement. He went as far as to write a letter breaking off the engagement, but his sister pleaded with him not to send it. The sole explanation one can find for Augusta's conduct is that she had determined that marriage would protect their reputations.

Byron returned to Cambridge on the 24th and saw Hodgson again. The latter wrote to Annabella to tell her how the students in the gallery had applauded her fiancé when he entered the Senate House to vote for Dr Clarke as professor of anatomy. Annabella was greatly relieved because her aunt, Lady Melbourne, had been taxing her with being responsible for the gossip that she had to deal with in London as a result of Byron's early departure from Seaham. On November 24 she wrote joyfully to Byron: "I shall be too happy – there will be no reverse – whilst you love me there cannot. Remember – I have done with doubts."[9] After the separation, in February 1816, while Annabella was staying at Mivart's Hotel, Byron returned this letter to her with a thick black line above and below the words: "There will be no reverse," and added the comment: "Prediction fulfilled, February 1816." He would never have had to return the letter had they only had the sense to reverse the decision at this point.

Once back in London, Byron's letters became brief and factual, Annabella's ever more pleading: "Come, come, come – to my heart" (November 26, 1814).[10] She could not understand why he was still delaying when the settlement seemed so straightforward. She herself began to worry about this aspect of things, however, since Sir Ralph could raise only £6,200 in cash (interest of 5 per cent to be paid on the remainder). Out of this Annabella was to have £300 pin money.*

Claughton had finally accepted the fact that he could not raise the money for Newstead, as he had hoped. This gave Byron an opportunity to ask Annabella if she would prefer to delay the marriage until a buyer could be found, since as things now stood they would find themselves in straitened circumstances. With Claughton's final removal from the scene, Byron told her that he would "leave it to you and yours to determine how far this may – will – or ought to cause any further delay in our marriage".¹¹ Indeed, both of them were constantly offering the other the opportunity to break off the engagement, but both lacked the resolve to act decisively and independently.

Annabella's reply is highly ironical in view of the situation she was walking into. "*I* can be as happy with little as with much, provided that little be not exceeded, and debt incurred. Of debt I have so great a horror that I should cheerfully make any exertions to avoid it."¹² She suggested that they keep only one house and one carriage and not to think of living in style. Annabella had no more idea than Byron himself of the basic cost of living for a married couple of their class.

December had now arrived and there seemed no possible cause for any delay of the marriage, yet Byron still tarried in his comfortable bachelor apartments. He knew that the wedding cake had been baked, and that Sir Ralph had composed an epithalamium, and when he heard that the bells in Sunderland had rung precipitously on the 12th, he snapped irritably, "I must say your Bells are in a pestilent hurry . . ." (Was he aware that he was also speaking of his betrothed?)

The same day Augusta wrote playfully:

My dearest B+
As usual I have but a short allowance of time to reply to your tendresses + but a few lines I know will be better than none – at least I find them so + It was very+ very+ very+ good of you to think of me amidst all the visitors &c.&c. I have scarcely recovered [from] *mine* of yesterday. La Dame did talk so, oh my stars! but at least it saved me a world of trouble. Oh, but she found out a likeness in your picture of Mignonne [Medora] who is of course very good humoured in

* Pin money was a woman's allowance for her personal expenditure. The term derived from the time when pins were very expensive.

consequence + I want to know Dearest B + your plans – when you come + when you go – umph! when the writings travel, when ye Cake is to be cut, when the Bells are to ring, &c &c&. By the bye, my visitors are acquainted with A & did praise her to the skies. They say her health has been hurt by studying &c&c&c.

I have not a moment more my dearest + except to say ever thine[13]

A desperate Annabella, meanwhile, used the same ploy by which she had managed to lure him to Seaham the first time: the "vexation of spirits to my father and mother". Byron replied that he had written to the Archbishop of Canterbury for a special licence allowing them to marry when and where they chose. Despite Lady Milbanke, he was determined not to marry in a church. Annabella was not to be put off by vague promises: what was the *latest* they could expect him? Well, then, he would leave London on the 23rd but, mind, this time there was to be a marriage and no tantrums.

On December 24 Hobhouse noted in his journal: "I rode up to London, and at twelve set off with Ld B on his matrimonial scheme."[14] At Chesterford they parted, Byron for Six Mile Bottom, Hobhouse for Cambridge. Christmas Day was spent miserably, with George Leigh complaining of the flu and Byron being persuaded yet again by his sister not to send a letter breaking off the engagement. Hobhouse's terse entries are evidence enough that the marriage was bound to end in disaster. On the 26th: "Byron did not arrive until three, when we set off and went three stages to Wansford . . . never was lover less in haste." On Tuesday: "The bridegroom more & more *less* impatient." At Thirsk on Thursday: "Indifference – almost aversion." Without any telephone to forewarn them, the Milbankes were in an even more agitated state than before Byron's earlier arrival.

Byron and Annabella met alone, and this time she threw her arms around his neck. Hobhouse's first impression of the bride-to-be was of dowdiness. "The lower part of her face is bad, but the upper expressive but not handsome – yet she gains by inspection."[15] He found her observations sensible and she obviously doted on Byron. The grooms-man soon made himself agreeable to the family with his fund of travel stories. On the 31st they were all in good spirits as the final settlements were signed. That evening they had a mock marriage ceremony, with Hobhouse acting as the bride. We are not told whether Byron took the role of groom or not. The next day was not quite so merry. Annabella was later told that Hobhouse talked earnestly to the Reverend Thomas

Noel (Lord Wentworth's illegitimate son), who was to perform the ceremony. Hobhouse expressed his concern about the marriage because of Byron's violent temper. Whether this was what he actually said – or whether this was a gloss Annabella put on it for her lawyers – we do not know. What Hobhouse probably said was that he didn't think Byron suited to marriage. At any rate, the clergyman replied that it was now too late to turn back. On parting that night, Byron said to his friend, "Well, Hobhouse, this is our last night – Tomorrow I shall be Annabella's (absit omen!!!)."

Byron awoke unseasonably early on his wedding day in the gloomiest of moods. When the marriage was about to take place at half past ten, the steward was sent out into the garden to fetch the groom, who was preoccupied with target practice. He joined Hobhouse who was surprised that he was wearing a black rather than the blue coat usually assumed on such occasions. They entered the drawing room where the parents and two clergymen were waiting. Kneeling mats were already in place for the victims. Annabella entered, accompanied by her former companion, Mrs Clermont (of whom much hereafter). On that cold January day she was dressed in a simple white muslin gown and jacket. During the ceremony she never took her eyes off Byron's face as she made her steady responses. When Byron came to the words, "With all my worldly goods I thee endow," he threw an amused glance at Hobhouse. He placed his mother's wedding band on the bride's finger. By eleven o'clock, January 2, 1815, their fates were sealed.

In his poem, "The Dream", Byron was later to write that during the ceremony his thoughts reverted to Mary Chaworth – but this detail might have been invented to insult his by then estranged wife. Did the groom kiss the bride or show any signs of affection? None that we are told of. Lady Milbanke was almost in hysterics, and Annabella's eyes filled with tears when she looked at her parents. There is no report of the stale wedding cake, baked more than a month earlier. Annabella retired to her room to change, and emerged in a soft grey satin travelling outfit. Byron seemed extremely calm, probably almost paralysed with shock. Where now could he flee? Was all hope of freedom taken from him?

Hobhouse's words are extraordinary: "I felt as if I had buried a friend."[16] He placed in the carriage his wedding present of a set of Byron's poems bound in yellow morocco. Just before twelve he handed Annabella into the carriage, wishing her many years of happiness. She replied, "If I am not happy it will be my own fault." And Byron? There was a melancholy parting. "He was unwilling to leave my hand, and I had hold of his out of the window when the carriage drove off."

There have been conflicting reports of what took placc in that small carriage on the ride of forty miles northwards through the snow-covered landscape to Halnaby, the country house which Lord Wentworth had lent them for the "treacle-moon". For Annabella it must have been a devastating experience. Even if she later coloured the situation, certain facts have the ring of truth. Byron was silent at first and then broke into a loud mournful song, probably the Albanian dirge the Shelleys would later hear on Lake Geneva. When they heard the bells of Durham pealing – for Sir Ralph had been a very popular member of parliament for the town – Byron made some bitter comment. Occasionally he read by the waning light. When they spoke, Byron told her what a fool she was to have married him, how she could have saved him from some nameless evil had she accepted his proposal in the first place, how much he disliked her mother and how this dislike was shared by Lady Melbourne. At one point he cried, "It *must* come to a separation!" Confined within a small space with the snow falling in the darkening world outside, it must have seemed like a journey through hell.

It was already night when they arrived at Halnaby. The servants were waiting on the steps with burning tapers. Byron limped off into the darkness on his own, and Annabella was left to assume as cheerful a face as she could muster. Various causes have been assigned to Byron's behaviour at this point. True, he was shy about meeting strangers and extremely self-conscious about his foot; but whatever construction one puts on it, it was cruel behaviour to his new bride.

Thomas Moore claimed that in the memoirs that were destroyed, Byron said that he "had" his new wife on the sofa before dinner. When they were about to retire, he told her that she could sleep with him if she wanted to, but he preferred to sleep alone. Annabella was startled by the fact that he placed a dagger and pistol beside the bcd. In thc middle of the night he awoke and, on seeing the reflection of the fire flickering on the red curtains, cried out, "Good God! I am surely in Hell!"

In the morning Annabella waited for her new husband's late appearance. His first words of greeting were, "It is too late now. It is done and cannot be undone." When he saw that she had tied a black ribbon around her wedding band, which was much too large for her finger, Byron's superstitious nature erupted in horror and he told her to take it off immediately. That first day he received a letter from Augusta. He read out parts to her, exulting in the intensity of his sister's affection. She addressed him as "Dearest, first, and best of human beings". She described her feelings at the moment when she knew the wedding was taking place as like "the sea trembles when the earth quakes."[7] This was the decisive moment when Annabella's real suspicions began to be aroused; and one can only regard the act of sending such a letter as not simply thoughtless but downright malicious. Perhaps Lady Melbourne was not altogether wrong in her estimation of Augusta as clever and wicked. Byron compounded the situation by telling his new wife that Augusta was the only person in the world who really understood him, a remark which Annabella repeated to her sister-in-law who replied in alarm that she couldn't think what he was talking about.

Nevertheless, Annabella turned to her sister-in-law for help. A day or so after their arrival she actually invited her to Halnaby to stay with them. Augusta found this impossible, but in reply to Annabella's confidences about Byron, told her to laugh away his extravagances. The bride received the same advice from her aunt, Lady Melbourne, who emphasised that Byron needed much affection and indulgence. And so Annabella tried to be calm and gentle as her puzzling bridegroom moved with terrifying rapidity from one mood to another. On one occasion when he was writing he told her that she was not to hover around him all the time. In the middle of the night he would pace frantically up and down the hall. Byron was feeling trapped and terrified, and what he was going through was akin to a psychotic breakdown. He reminded her of the list of qualities in a husband that she had noted down for Lady Melbourne almost two years before, and her stipulation that there should not be mental derangement in the family. He now mocked her with frightening stories of the madness on both sides of his family.

In that great house surrounded by snow, they were like two survivors on a raft who were clinging to different sides of their frail bark. But they spoke to each other, and there were certain topics of conversation that emerge from the various statements that Annabella later made to her lawyers. Byron at times would reproach her for the meagreness of her father's resources, and grow impatient at the vague replies he would receive in answer to his queries about the contents of Lord Wentworth's will.

From Seaham, Sir Ralph wrote that he was sorry to hear Lord Byron had a cold, and that they had found him "remarkably pleasant and agreeable". Lady Milbanke was much more reserved, retaining all her enthusiasm for Hobhouse, with whom the Milbankes had dined on the wedding evening. Byron's childish jealousy and sense of mischief were aroused. He told his wife that Hobhouse was consumed with envy of him, that he was the kind of man no decent woman would have anything to do with. At one point he said that all he seemed to have gained from this marriage was the loss of his friends; and Annabella's obtuseness is evident when she remarked that he seemed to regard them as "very burdensome". When she suggested that Hobhouse be invited to visit them, he replied "with an air of dread, 'no – God forbid'."[18]

Religion was bound to come up. "Now convert me!" Byron is supposed to have challenged his wife. He would respond sarcastically to all her arguments in favour of orthodox belief. But one cannot help feeling that he truly wanted to be converted, that he was testing her to the limit in every sense. He returned repeatedly to the nameless burden of guilt he was carrying around with him, and on several occasions seemed about to confess to her. At one point he told her he couldn't do so because it would mean betraying another person. When she asked him if Augusta knew about what was troubling him, he shuddered and told her never to mention the matter to *her*. He also told her that he had two illegitimate children, but she was not shocked since this was not regarded as a scandal at that time and even the clergyman who had performed the wedding ceremony was Lord Wentworth's natural son.

Then there was "Thyrza" about whom he talked at length. He said that the feelings that he had for "her" could never be rekindled. He described her beauty; and recalled how when they were to meet, he would walk up and down in a state of such excitement that he almost fainted. When he was on his return voyage from Greece in 1811, in Malta he had heard of Thyrza's well-being so that news of her death came as a shock on his return.

He also began to feel confident enough with her to speak about his malformed foot. Annabella was both skilful and compassionate in inducing him to speak directly about what he called almost tenderly his "little foot". He expressed anger towards his mother who, he insinuated, was in some way responsible for it. He recalled how, in one of her rages, she called him a "lame brat". He talked of people whose natures had been influenced by a physical defect and he hoped that some allowance would be made for him on the Day of Judgement. He had a notion of himself as some kind of fallen angel, and remarked that the devil was supposed to have cloven feet which he could never disguise. He described the Supreme Being as malignant, delighting in the sufferings of His creatures, and himself as one who was foredoomed to evil. Byron's avowed scepticism was clearly a defence against a deep-rooted terror.

Annabella noticed that he became intoxicated very easily, especially if he drank brandy. No doubt some of his ravings were the result of heavy drinking, but one cannot rule out the possibility that in this crisis in his life all the Calvinistic notions he had imbibed from May Gray had returned to haunt him. Where Augusta and friends such as Hobhouse had viewed his black moods as eccentricities, these three weeks at Halnaby reveal a man tortured by guilt about both his homosexuality and the incest with Augusta. As Annabella was later to remark perceptively, to him she was like the embodiment of a living conscience, welcome and yet dreaded. The refusal to be married in a church she now realised was not simply a mere whim on his part.

The nights were his worst time, but in the daylight hours, with the passing days, and as they had some contact with the outside world through the post, Byron's aversion towards his wife seemed to be tempered. Annabella discovered that her suspicions about his vanity were well founded. He would become greatly distressed if he found a grey hair and would examine and re-examine a slightly blemished tooth. He was also a terrible hypochondriac. He was constantly worried that he was coming down with some ailment; and Annabella would feel his pulse and reassure him. He seemed to enjoy this mothering. They began to discuss literature and there is no question that he found her intelligent and almost loveable. She copied out some of his poems in a fair hand. They started to address each other by pet names. Annabella's round cheeks elicited the name "Pip", and he became "Duck". It was probably in one of these more tranquil moods that he wrote to Lady Melbourne as early as January 7: "I have great hopes this match will turn out well – I have found nothing as yet that I could wish changed for the better – but Time does wonders – so I won't be too hasty in my happiness."

He did not want to return to Seaham. He suggested that he travel back to London on his own and would meet her later. Annabella had enough experience of him by now to put her foot down. After three weeks with no other company but themselves they travelled back to Seaham. They were supposed to return in time for Byron's birthday on the 22nd, but since that would mean travelling on a Friday, about which he had some superstitious dread, they had to leave on Saturday, the 21st. When they were in the carriage once more, Byron was in a surprisingly relaxed mood and remarked that he thought they would get along well enough since she now knew what subjects to avoid.

Annabella's pale appearance did not go unnoticed by Mrs Clermont and her concerned mother. But in a milieu surrounded by other people Byron had to restrain his wild moods. He found Sir Ralph's tedious stories more and more tiresome, but did his best to appear to listen politely. On hearing from Annabella that Byron had been involved in romping games and had pulled Lady Milbanke's wig from her head, Augusta wrote to her sister-in-law:

I have scarcely recovered the fit of laughing I was seized with on reading the account of your *frolic* – oh dear! I only wish some people whom I know & many others whom I *don't* know could have peeped in at the door – to have been convinced that *Owls* can frolic sometimes, & moreover that B can play the fool.

But pray how is Lady Milbanke – I fully expect to hear that she has at least a very bad cold in her *head*!¹⁹

It is difficult not to believe that Augusta was being very catty and hypocritical, and that Byron's snatching the wig was a piece of mischief against his disliked mother-in-law. At dinner one day he complained that he had just broken a tooth, to which his hostess snapped, "It's good for you!" Nevertheless, she made no objection to his strange habit of eating alone when the mood struck him.

Byron was reaching the point where he began to be bored beyond endurance. Moore heard most of his complaints. "Upon this dreary coast, we have nothing but country meetings and shipwrecks" (February 2, 1815). He told Moore that he had a plan of making a trip to Italy. Why didn't Moore join him? "If I take my wife, you can take yours; and if I leave mine, you may do the same" (February 10, 1815).

Despite himself, he was beginning to grow rather fond of Annabella. One night he almost choked with the fumes from his charcoal fire. He fell back on the bed gasping that his Patras fever was returning. He talked of the after-life with terror and shouted that he would defy his maker to the last with "impenitent remorse". Annabella patted his forehead with eau de cologne; and when she had calmed him, he said to her, "I have tried everything – I will try virtue, I think. Perhaps I shall go to heaven, holding by the hem of your garment."²⁰

At Seaham he heard of the death of one of his old Harrow favourites, Lord Dorset. He spoke to Moore of "the recollection of what I once felt, and ought to have felt now, but could not" (March 8, 1815). He was convinced that all feeling was dead in him. In memory of Dorset – and his once vibrant emotion – he wrote some of the most melancholy lines in his life:

> There's not a joy the world can give like that it takes away
> When the glow of early thoughts declines in feeling's dull
>   decay;
> 'Tis not on youth's smooth cheek the blush alone, which fades
>   so fast,
> But the tender bloom of heart is gone, ere youth itself be past.
>   ('Stanzas for Music', *Works*, III)

This was written by a man who had once traversed savage country and had sat around a great fire while wild Albanians danced and sang. In Seaham he was now reduced to playing provincial parlour games.

But he had to be dragged back out of melancholy self-indulgence to cope with everyday life. He and Annabella had to find a home of their own. Lord Wentworth offered to lend them Halnaby indefinitely, but neither of them wanted to return there. Byron made it clear that he had no desire to go to Newstead either, since it was imperative that another buyer be found. When Annabella made the sensible suggestion that a small house in town might be the best solution to their circumstances, Augusta assured her emphatically that Byron would not be content unless it was "a *great* one".[21] Since Byron refused to discuss the subject with her, Annabella turned to her aunt in desperation to ask her if he had confided any of his plans to her. Lady Melbourne firmly denied that she knew anything at all: "You are wrong when You Suppose that he has given me any information respecting yr future intentions, or about Newstead. I am in a total state of ignorance . . . His Letters to me are extremely merry & gay, but as to business, I don't think it is a Subject he is ever inclined to enter upon."[22] Annabella then asked her aunt if she would look out for a house for them in London.

After listening and absorbing the many ill-judged things Byron had told her at Halnaby, Annabella was tormented with jealousy and bombarded Augusta with probing questions. Augusta, who was beginning to sense real trouble, assured her that Byron had given her possibly only a couple of poems as gifts. She was hardly tactful when Annabella spoke of the way women flocked around him: "I can readily believe all you tell me of the melancholy state of female hearts, whenever B makes his appearance. I think I see him behaving very *prettily* – it *is* well indeed! you are not given to Jealousy."[23]

Byron took out his black moods on Annabella in private, which she tried to hide from her parents, but all of these were confided to her new confidante, Augusta. Her sister-in-law replied: "How sorry I am for the fit of vexation & all such fits! I think some remedy will be found ere long."[24] "I hope these minor calamities will soon cease" (February 5, 1815).[25] Augusta warned her to hide the brandy bottle. Then on February 13: "'Alas' indeed! 'naughty B'! as the children used to say when he affronted them. I am not many degrees removed from a fit of despair at his *untoward* ways."[26] She congratulated Annabella on her good influence in persuading him to get some fresh air. Could she not also persuade him to ride? And to eat normal meals and sleep through the night like other people? "I wonder my dearest A that you don't think me (but perhaps you *do*) the most troublesome creature on earth & forget all that I have said if it torments you – & attribute it to my anxiety & love for him, & then I think you will perhaps forgive me."[27] Despite the disturbing stories she was hearing, Augusta assured Hodgson:

> I really hope *most confidently* that all will turn out very happily. It appears to me that Lady B. *sets about* making him happy quite in the right way. It is true I judge at a distance, and we generally *hope* as we *wish*, but I . . . will own to you, what I would scarcely to any other person, that I HAD *many fears* and much anxiety founded upon many causes and circumstances which I cannot *write*.[28]

In early March Lady Melbourne discovered that the Duchess of Devonshire's house in Piccadilly Terrace would be available as the owner was planning to be in France. She was in "rather a fright" because of its size (and the cost that would entail), but "As Ld B wants Space I hope it will suit him."[29] Obviously Byron had never been frank with her about his finances or she would have discouraged them from taking such an expensive house. Lady Milbanke must have been extremely irritated that her disliked sister-in-law was managing the details of her darling's life.

Hobhouse, who had been engaged in trying to disentangle Byron's financial problems, arranged for the details of the lease of £700 a year. Incidentally, on February 27, Hobhouse, knowing that Annabella collected autographs, courteously sent her one of the diplomat and literary figure, the Prince of Ligne, which he had acquired on his continental tour; but Byron, after having perversely blackened Hobhouse to her, refused to allow her to write and thank him for it.*

Now that they had a concrete reason for leaving, Byron was all for setting off immediately for town, stopping on the way for a visit at Six Mile Bottom. Augusta went into a panic. The house was far too small even for her own family; Aunt Sophie would probably be staying with her at the

---

* Byron thanked him on Annabella's behalf on March 26, 1815.

time they proposed to come; and the Newmarket area itself was "miserable, desert country". She suggested that Byron rent a house in the vicinity, but he ignored the hint. He would stay with her just as long as it suited him. And Annabella was just as determined that he would not leave her there while he went off to town as he proposed.

They climbed into the carriage on March 9 to set out for their new life together. It was four months since Byron had first arrived at Seaham, and their lives were now set on an irrevocable course. As they were about to drive away, Judith called out anxiously, "Take care of Annabella!" Byron started to curse. What the devil did the meddlesome old woman mean?

His mood gradually brightened as they put the miles between them and Seaham. Yet he seemed in no hurry to reach Six Mile Bottom, and he repeatedly referred to his sister as "a fool". At Wansford where they spent the second night, he asked, "You married me to make me happy, didn't you? Well, then you *do* make me happy." It was in rare moments like these that Annabella almost wept with joy and relief. But he became increasingly agitated as they approached Six Mile Bottom and when they were within a few miles of their destination, he suddenly made a curious remark: "I feel as if I were just going to be married." At that moment, Annabella later recalled, "the blackness of his face was dreadful."[30] Yet in another statement she said that he then began kissing and caressing her, and was deterred only by the presence of the maid in the carriage.

If Augusta was nervous about the meeting, her anxiety was matched by that of Annabella who had already begun to nurse the most morbid suspicions about her and Byron.

Was this the beginning of the marriage, or the prelude to its terrible conclusion?

15

~~~~~~~~~~~~~~~

Annus Horribilis, 1815

Byron always felt uncomfortable unless he had plenty of space around him. A feeling of entrapment overwhelmed him during the first three months of his marriage: putting on a false self before the Milbankes: "I wonder how long I can keep up this role," he said to Annabella as they travelled off after the wedding; the confined carriage ride to Halnaby; the large Yorkshire house cut off from the world by snow; and now the cramped situation at Six Mile Bottom with these two problematic women seldom out of sight. He was like a crazed unbroken stallion, rearing, snorting, and kicking his captors.

He had never really wanted Annabella to visit his sister, and his nervousness almost approached hysteria as they drew closer to the house. When the carriage stopped, Byron told Annabella to wait until he roused Augusta. She was busy upstairs, and when Annabella entered, Byron was standing in the hall frowning over a disturbing letter about Newstead. Augusta flustered downstairs, smiling nervously as she took Annabella's hand. They both remembered seeing each other at Lady Glenbervie's party in 1813, and Annabella was again struck by the family resemblance: the same curling chestnut hair, the large hazel eyes, and the fine blue veins on the broad forehead, as well as a tendency to plumpness.

"What I suffered during this fortnight at S.M.B. is indescribable," Annabella later told her lawyers.[1] There is no reason to believe that this was an exaggeration. She was already consumed by apprehensive suspicions; Byron was nervous, yet this does not excuse his sadistic behaviour; and Augusta was at a loss as to how to contain the situation.

Most of what we know about this experience is derived from Annabella's recollections. A biographer creates a narrative from numerous documents, but the written word is not always reliable. It is particularly suspect when an angry, vindictive woman is drawing up statements incorporating recollections of maltreatment for the perusal of lawyers. Annabella's detractors – and there have been many – have pointed out that she had not only led a sheltered life but was also humourless and literal-minded, so that one has to allow for exaggerations. This I have tried to do, but when certain graphic details have the ring of truth I have usually presented them as part of the story. Undoubtedly Byron played on Annabella's gullibility, but it was a cruel game.

In Annabella's perception, on the first evening of their visit Byron made it clear that he preferred the company of his sister. When Annabella lingered in the drawing room, he sneered insultingly, "We don't want you, my charmer." It was two hours earlier than her usual bedtime, but she was being dismissed. Augusta looked uncomfortable, but said nothing.[2] When Byron came up to join her, he said, "Now I have *her*, you will find I can do without *you*." Annabella lay in bed night after night in a state of torment as she heard them laughing downstairs. (George Leigh was away at the time on a shooting party.) Augusta claimed that she was trying to control his drinking, but this was not her responsibility. Annabella was aware that Byron was not making love to her as much as usual, but undoubtedly it was in this house that she became pregnant.

Byron was devilishly clever in knowing how to embarrass Augusta and wound Annabella at the same time. He asked Augusta if she remembered when he had written the lines to her, "I speak not – I trace not – I breathe not thy name." He showed great fondness for Medora who he said was his daughter.* Annabella was struck by the child's extraordinary beauty. He alluded knowingly to Augusta's inflammable nature and to the fact that he knew she wore drawers.** If it were not true, how could Augusta contradict him? The affronts were endless; but worst of all was a parcel, delivered a couple of days after their arrival. It contained two gold brooches, one marked A, the other B, containing the hair of brother and sister, and three of those mysterious crosses on each. When Byron handed Augusta her gift, he remarked, "If *she* knew what these mean! Do you remember our signs at Newstead?" That Augusta was a "fool" was never more apparent than in her accepting – let alone wearing – this brooch, but perhaps she was stupid enough not to know what else to do. "There were moments when I could

* Those who do not believe that Byron was her father point out that he was her godfather.

** Drawers had begun to be worn about 1806. In 1811 Princess Charlotte raised eyebrows by showing her drawers. See *Dress and Undress. A History of Women's Underwear* by Elizabeth Ewing (London: B.T. Batsford, 1978).

have plunged a dagger through her heart, but she never saw them," Annabella recalled.

Indeed, Augusta's compassion for Annabella increased, and Annabella began to feel that she was her only protector against this strange creature to whom they were both united. When the two women were sitting alone together or out on walks, they began to form an intimate conspiracy of defence on how to handle his moods. Sometimes Annabella felt that Augusta was even more tormented than she was as he heaped insults on her as well.

Annabella was jealous, but she was confused also. At times when she expected Augusta to look very embarrassed, she would act as though she hadn't heard what Byron said. "Well, Guss, I'm a reformed man, ain't I?" Byron asked his sister, to which she replied in a flustered way that she noticed *some* improvement. He wickedly alluded to Lady Melbourne's disapproval of their visit. But what are we to think of the reports she sent to Francis Hodgson who had joined Augusta in urging Byron to marry? On March 18, 1815, she wrote:

> I've nothing but *agreeables* to communicate, on the subject of the greatest interest to you as well as to me. B. & Lady B. arrived here last Sunday . . . I hope they will stay some days longer with me, and shall regret their departure, whenever it takes place, as much as I now delight in their society. B. is looking particularly well, and of Lady B. I scarcely know how to write, for I have a sad trick of being struck dumb when I am most happy and pleased. The expectations I had formed could not be *exceeded*, but at least they are fully answered. I think I never saw or read of a more perfect being in mortal mould.'

Could it have been that Augusta at first was insensitive to Annabella's suffering, or is it possible that Byron's behaviour, always unpredictable, worsened the longer they stayed? Also it might have seemed to her that Annabella's patience with him would eventually tame him. She was relieved when they finally left after what seemed an interminable fortnight.

Once they had gone at the end of the month she wrote again to Hodgson:

> I am sorry to say his nerves and spirits are very far from what I wish them, but don't speak of this to him on any account. I think the uncomfortable state of his affairs is the cause; at least, I can discern no other. He has every blessing this world can bestow. I trust that the

Almighty will be graciously pleased to grant him those *inward* feelings of peace and calm which are now unfortunately wanting. This is a subject which I cannot dwell upon . . . I think Lady B. very judiciously abstains from pressing the consideration of it upon him at the present moment. In short the more I see of her, and feel how grateful I am and ought to be for the blessing of such a wife for my dear, darling B.[4]

Byron had always been a tease and a mischief-maker, but in his wilder moments he let this propensity deteriorate into savagery. But he really wanted Augusta and Annabella to like each other and was delighted when his sister found his wife pretty. While they were there Augusta received word that she had been appointed lady-in-waiting to Queen Charlotte, now in her seventies, and living in retirement in St James's Palace, while George III had retreated into a world of pitiful fantasy at Kew. In the Leighs' straitened circumstances, it was welcome news since it carried with it an annual income of £300. Augusta was touched too because she had been recommended by the Prince Regent even though George was in disfavour with him. Byron impulsively invited her to stay with them in London. Then, on March 28, waving his handkerchief to her "in the most passionate manner" (according to Annabella), they drove off for London. Byron remarked on how pleased he was that the women had become such friends.

Husband and wife were both delighted with their handsome house looking south over Green Park although the address, 13 Piccadilly Terrace, should have been a superstitious warning to Byron. Annabella remembered the ten days before Augusta's arrival as the happiest time in their married life. In a world in which madness had begun to seem the norm, she was elated by anything that approached normal behaviour. Byron was undoubtedly relieved to be back in London where he could again see his cronies and revert in large degree to his bachelor pursuits.

At first they occasionally went out to parties, and it was remarked how attentive Byron seemed to his wife, leaning over her chair and talking only to her. Mrs George Lamb told Annabella's former suitor, Augustus Foster, that "He appears very happy, and is very much improved by his marriage."[5] John Murray pronounced Annabella a delightful woman and remarkably sensible. Byron did not particularly want a child, but Annabella's condition provided him with an excuse for avoiding the tedious social round which had long since lost its appeal for him.

London was in a fever of excitement because Napoleon had escaped from Elba and landed near Cannes on March 1. Byron was chagrined that Napoleon had contradicted the final lines of his ode:

> He in his fall preserv'd his pride,
> And if a mortal, had as proudly died!

Hobhouse was anxious to get over to France during these stirring times, but until he heard from the indolent Byron he did not want to leave the country. On February 26 he wrote in his diary: "I am still undecided what to do . . . in a foolish state of apprehension with respect to Byron, my friend Byron, whose silence annoys me beyond what I can express." The following day he expressed his relief: "Heard from Byron: all my suspicions groundless." He called on the couple the day after their arrival in London, and noted that "he advises me not to marry though he has the best of wives."[6] Hobhouse left for the continent on April 1 and did not return until July so that he had little opportunity of getting to know Annabella.

Annabella had her own friends, chief of whom were Lady Gosford, Selina Doyle, and the playwright Joanna Baillie. She wrote to Augusta repeating Byron's invitation to visit them, an invitation which Augusta should have had the sense to decline, since she was provided with a small apartment in St James's Palace. On March 30 Augusta replied, "Dearest Sis I do not require your account of the view from yr Windows as an inducement to pay you a visit. You will perhaps be a better judge By & bye whether I shall be a plague – & you must tell me *truly* if I am likely to prove so – you know I should not be affronted."[7] Forgetting that it was he who had extended the invitation in the first place, Byron was extremely irritated when he heard that Annabella had urged Augusta to come; and shortly after the arrival of his sister, accompanied by her oldest daughter, he taxed his wife for her foolishness in inviting her: "You are a fool for letting her come to the house, and you'll find it will make a great difference to *you* in all ways."[8] He arranged to be out of the house when she arrived.

Byron had written little in the past months, and Murray was encouraging him to produce more. Samuel Coleridge wrote to ask for his help in getting a manuscript published by Murray, and Byron apologised for his immature strictures on the poet in *English Bards and Scotch Reviewers*. Murray's offices in Albemarle Street, just around the corner from Piccadilly Terrace, attracted distinguished men of letters and here Byron generally dropped in during the morning to chat with Campbell, D'Israeli, Gifford, Humphry Davy and others. The publisher's young son John was fascinated to meet the famous poet. It was clear that Byron took great pains over his dress. His fingers were covered in rings and *the* brooch was pinned to his shirt-front. He wore a black coat, an embroidered waistcoat, grey or nankeen trousers and a shirt open at the neck, a rather unconventional attire for a man of his rank. The boy of course knew about the foot and noticed that it was particularly apparent when he was on the stairs.

Murray had long been anxious for Byron to meet his other celebrity writer, Walter Scott, and the encounter finally took place on April 7. Even though Byron had criticised Scott for wasting his talents on romances, the older man (born 1771), with his usual magnanimity, wrote praising *Childe Harold* as soon as he had read it. Byron replied in a rather embarrassed way: "The satire [*English Bards and Scotch Reviewers*] was written when I was very young & very angry, & fully bent on displaying my wrath & my wit, & now I am haunted by the ghosts of my wholesale Assertions."[9] Byron had been entranced by Scott's 1814 novel *Waverley*; and in addition to mutual admiration, there was an immediate rapport between the two men. Byron's liking for him was probably enhanced by the fact that Scott also had a bad foot.

Scott's comments on Byron indicate a keen observer of men. He remarked on his love of mischief and mystification and his tendency to suspicion and deep depressions, although Scott was generous enough to attribute these qualities to his genius. He was also attracted by his generosity, and although Scott found him inordinately proud of his rank, he also found him free from affectation. Scott predicted that Byron some day might become a Catholic. They met frequently until the Battle of Waterloo on June 18,* after which Scott joined the stream of other British tourists who crossed the Channel to view the battlefield.

For the past two years Byron had sporadically been writing a series of lyrics to accompany Isaac Nathan's music and this compendium was brought out by Murray in April as *Hebrew Melodies*. It was immensely successful. The public bought 10,000 copies, under the impression that they were going to read some pious poems, only to discover that many of the poems followed the pattern of the opening lyric "She Walks in Beauty" which had been inspired by the sight of Byron's cousin, Mrs Wilmot, in a spangled black dress one evening in 1814. Only three stanzas long, it is one of the loveliest of his poems:

---

* On hearing of Napoleon's defeat, Byron exclaimed: "I'm d—d sorry to hear it!"

She walks in beauty, like the night
   Of cloudless climes and starry skies;
And all that's best of dark and bright
   Meet in her aspect and her eyes:
Thus mellow'd to that tender light
   Which heaven to gaudy day denies.

One shade the more, one ray the less,
   Had half impair'd the nameless grace
Which waves in every raven tress,
   Or softly lightens o'er her face;
Where thoughts serenely sweet express
   How pure, how dear their dwelling place.

And on that cheek, and o'er that brow,
   So soft, so calm, yet eloquent,
The smiles that win, the tints that glow,
   But tell of days in goodness spent,
A mind at peace with all below,
   A heart whose love is innocent!
             (*Works*, III, pp. 288–9)

In April Annabella's uncle, Lord Wentworth, became very ill, and Annabella moved into his London house until her mother arrived. On hearing that Lady Milbanke had reached town, Byron wrote: "Dearest – Now your mother is come I won't have you worried any longer – more particularly in your present situation which is rendered precarious by what you have already gone through. Pray – come home."[10] Annnabella later claimed: "I felt that death-bed scene a relief from the horrors of an incestuous home – for my suspicions were then at the height . . . I was almost mad – & to prevent myself from indulging in that tumultuous state of mind to substitute another – that of romantic forgiveness."[11] Annabella's suspicions, which had been temporarily assuaged, were once again alerted after returning to Piccadilly Terrace. She heard what sounded like conspiratorial laughter after she had retired early. Again her thoughts turned to Byron's dagger which she longed to pick up and plunge into Augusta's heart. It was an impulse that she often felt. Yet there was still the possibility, she conceded, that she was wrong in her suspicions. Nevertheless, she confided her fears to Selina Doyle and asked her to be on the alert for tell-tale indications of guilt.

Lord Wentworth died on April 17. Byron must have been dumbfounded when he heard the terms of the will. Lady Milbanke, not Annabella, had inherited her brother's estate at Kirkby Mallory and an income of £7,000 a year, from which Byron would benefit only after her death. Under the terms of the will the Milbankes were now obliged to assume the Wentworth family name of Noel. Sir Ralph received little help from the death of his brother-in-law because his own debts were so enormous. Byron's creditors were unaware of this; and in expectation that he was coming into money, became more pressing than ever. The expenses of the Piccadilly mansion were overwhelming; indeed, the marriage money was not enough to meet the rent and it remained unpaid for two years.

Yet in some ways the couple continued to go through the routines of everyday life. Lady Noel (as we must now call her) stayed in London until August. On one occasion Lady Melbourne came to call accompanied by Caroline Lamb and Mary Chaworth's mother-in-law, Mrs Musters. Caroline apparently sat silently throughout the visit. When Byron came in he looked aghast. It was the last time the former lovers were ever to lay eyes on each other. Annabella made little attempt to see Lady Melbourne of whom she was jealous because of her closeness to Byron. At one point Byron said to his sister, "Lady Melbourne doesn't like you, Guss." When she asked why, he whispered something in her ear, at which she looked embarrassed.

Byron found all Annabella's friends tiresome and refused to meet them. He kept up a constant rant about her parents and tried to avoid them. On Annabella's twenty-fourth birthday – May 17, 1815 – the Noels invited them to dine at Lord Wentworth's house where they were staying. Annabella pleaded illness on Byron's part. As they were sitting at dinner (which was served in mid-afternoon) they noticed Byron riding ostentatiously back and forth in front of the dining-room window. Her parents were as baffled as Annabella about how to handle this bizarre son-in-law.

But it was the presence of Augusta in the house that was most unsettling to Annabella and in mid-June she suggested that she leave for her own home. How she phrased this suggestion is unclear. Annabella claimed that she tried to stifle all her suspicions since it was so clear that Augusta felt great compassion for her patience in dealing with Byron's unpredictable moods. After Augusta's return home she resumed her affectionate correspondence with her sister-in-law.

During this period there are reports of Byron eating regular meals. (He never dined with his wife since he claimed that he could not bear to see women eating.) We also hear of him visiting Leigh Hunt (now out of prison) at his home in Maida Vale while Lady Byron went off to buy flowers at a local nursery. Annabella would often cuddle up on his knee, and they would engage in baby-talk. Not only this, but Byron was writing *The Siege of Corinth* which Annabella copied out for him in time for publication on November 2, and *Parisina* which they worked on together so that Murray received it the following month. The mysteries and contradictions of any marriage defy explanation, but this one is bafflingly complex.

Through Hobhouse's banker friend Douglas Kinnaird, Byron was invited in May to join a subcommittee for the new Drury Lane Theatre. Now he seldom returned home until the early hours of the morning. Byron's task was to read and select suitable plays for the theatre. He unsuccessfully tried to persuade Scott to write a drama. Only one play that he selected – Charles Maturin's *Bertram* – was accepted by the subcommittee, and it was to have a very successful run during 1816.

Hobhouse returned from Paris in late July and apparently almost persuaded Byron to accompany him back to the continent. One reason the scheme came to nothing was that things were now so desperate that immediate steps had to be taken to try to sell Newstead. On the 28th it was put up for auction at Garraway's coffee-house. An offer of 79,000 guineas was refused because it was not sufficient even to pay Byron's most pressing debts.

The following day Byron made what was to be his final will.* With the full knowledge of both women, the residue of Byron's estate, after his property was sold and the marriage settlement paid, was to go to Augusta and her children. Considering his finances at the time, it was a rather pitiful exercise. Hobhouse and Hanson were named as executors.

By now Annabella's parents had moved into Lord Wentworth's Leicestershire house, Kirkby Mallory, and they offered Seaham to Annabella for her confinement. It seemed an altogether sensible way of avoiding the financial pressures of London, which Annabella was coming to hate. To Augusta she exclaimed, "O that I was out of this horrid town, which makes me mad!"[12] Nevertheless she could not pull herself away from it.

If London was driving Annabella mad, it was having the same effect on Byron. By the end of August his temper and insulting remarks were making her life so miserable that she was relieved to see him leave for a visit to Six Mile Bottom. In London he had moved into another bed, but before his departure he asked his wife's forgiveness for the way he had been treating her. Then during the five-day visit, they exchanged playful, affectionate notes. Augusta told her that Byron missed her sorely. After his visit to Six

* A codicil was added in 1818, leaving £5,000 to his illegitimate daughter Allegra.

Mile Bottom Byron for a time became very affectionate with his wife, and spoke maliciously of his sister. In the carriage one day he suddenly said, "I shall break your heart and Augusta's after all." Annabella added, in her recollection of this incident, that it was "as if it were a fate which he was doomed to fulfil".

He had returned from the country in time for the opening of the season at Drury Lane, and was now absent from home more than ever. As the time for the birth grew near, Byron's behaviour became truly manic. At Halnaby he had told his young wife that he didn't want her to have any children because it would divert her attention and love from him. The baby she was carrying seemed like a rival, the last straw in his mounting burdens. The family retainer, Mrs Clermont, had joined her former charge. In her concern for Annabella, Mrs Clermont observed closely this strange man her darling had married. She was to testify later that he always treated her with perfect correctness.

Byron would tell Annabella constantly that marriage had destroyed him. By the end of the summer she was in such a state that she longed for Augusta's return. At Halnaby she had asked Augusta if she would be her *only* friend, and the irony of the situation was that in many ways this is how she appeared. It was strange indeed that her confidante should have been the cuckoo in the nest.

By October the situation had developed into a real crisis. Bailiffs threatened to enter the house, and Byron was beside himself that they would be there at the same time as the midwife. "For my part," Annabella told her mother, "it would probably be the time I should care least for them – but I care very much to see him in agony" (October 11, 1815).[13] Byron was drinking even more heavily than usual, and when drunk would smash valuable objects such as his favourite watch, although he never laid a hand on his wife. He spent a good deal of time in the Green Room at Drury Lane, and one of the minor actresses, Susan Boyce, became his mistress, a liaison of which he boasted to Annabella, even threatening to bring her home. He wanted to be sure that Augusta knew about the woman as well.

On November 1 Annabella wrote out an interpretation of his character for Augusta. A considerable portion of it should be quoted because it indicates that she had a remarkable insight into this strange man whom she had married.

His misfortune is an habitual *passion for Excitement*, which is always found in ardent temperaments, where the pursuits are not in some degree organized. It is the Ennui of a monotonous existence that

drives the best hearted people of this description to the most
dangerous paths, and makes them often seem to act from bad
motives when in fact they are only flying from internal suffering
by any external stimulus. The love of tormenting arises chiefly from
this Source. Drinking, Gaming &c. are all of the same origin. How far
it may depend on body or mind it is difficult to ascertain. I am
inclined to think that a vitiated stomach, particularly if arising from
habits of Excess, is a chief cause of the sensation of Ennui – and that
change of Scene, air & exercise are more efficient to its removal than
any efforts of Reason. As for seeking a cure in worldly dissipation, it is
adding to the evil – and for that reason I so much dread B's entering
into those pursuits of Fashion, whose votaries are always the victims of
this misery, in the intervals of their mischief-making occupations. At
the same time I would have his mind diverted from itself by every
possible means that would not lead to the accession of the Disease –
and so far from considering my own tastes, if I find that the disease is
making progress I will court Lady M's Society for him, or any thing in
the world to arrest its *fatal* course. I know in what it must end if it
encrease [sic] – and with such apprehensions will you wonder if I am
sometimes almost heart broken before my time. My dear, dear A, do
give me every opinion of yours on this, & don't mistrust your own
judgment. I will not blindly adopt it. Such were my waking reflections
last night.[14]

Shrewd as this assessment is, Annabella ignored the most vital element –
that the anxiety over money was driving him over the brink.

On the night of November 8 a bailiff slept in the house. The next day
Annabella expressed her agony to Augusta:

I have waited to the last in hopes of some change – but all is
inexorable pride & hardness. O Augusta, will it ever change for me –
I scarcely know what to say. Tho' I have been making the best of
things till yesterday when self-deception became impossible, I have
thought that since last Saturday (on which night he sat drinking with
Kinnaird's party till ½ past four in the morning) his *head* has never
been right – and he will add I fear more & more to the cause.[15]

One cannot help feeling great sorrow for the bewildered young woman.
The bailiff was "a sad brute" (November 10), and to add to her worries, her
father was being threatened with debtors' prison. On the 11th she pleaded

with Augusta to come to her aid. Ironically, that same day Hobhouse noted in his journal: "called on Byron and his Ladyship – he is unaltered in any respect, dear creature, but owns that marriage makes him selfish – 'I have not written to you, you see' – I forgive him – He does not dine with his wife – Well, he says – don't marry."[16] In one of her later statements to the lawyers, Annabella attributed the mounting excesses of Byron's behaviour to Hobhouse's reappearance on the scene, especially as Byron now began to talk of going abroad.

Despite the desperate situation, in the middle of November Byron refused an offer of a £1,500 advance from Murray. Augusta, who now shared Annabella's view that her brother was seriously deranged, arrived on the 15th. Lady Noel came to town the following day, but because she was seriously ill with a fever Annabella was not able to confide in her mother. Augusta arranged for their cousin, George Byron, to stay in the house because she had begun to fear for Annabella's safety.

On the night of December 9, after Annabella went into labour, Byron, who had been suffering from a raging thirst, made a fearful racket downstairs knocking off the tops of soda bottles. A daughter was born on December 10. When he was first shown the child he is supposed to have exclaimed, "Oh! what an implement of torture I have acquired in you!" Augusta wrote to Hodgson the day after the birth, "B. is in great good looks, and much pleased with his *Daughter*, though I believe he would have preferred a *Son*."[17] The child was named Augusta Ada.

Within a fortnight of her birth, everyone in the household was aware that Byron was treating his wife more savagely than ever. By then Annabella had determined to leave him. It was she, not Byron, who was fleeing from her gaoler.

16

ooooooooooooooo

Vengeful Women, 1816

The tragi-comedy was drawing to its inexorable close. Had Byron not been beset by money worries, he and Annabella might have struggled on in the sort of uncongenial arrangement that many other couples managed to accommodate. She would have pursed her lips when he blasphemed, and occupied herself with good works, attaining a sort of minor sainthood among her sympathetic friends to whom she would have continued to confide his infidelities. Byron might have managed to get away on extended trips abroad. The enormity of his debts, however, acted as a catalyst, making the end inevitable.

For the mother of a newly born child, Annabella was remarkably busy during the first week of January 1816. By now she had determined to join her parents at Kirkby Mallory, but whether she actually intended to leave her husband permanently at this point does not seem to have been entirely clear in her own mind, although in a very calculated way she took steps that would exonerate her from any charge of deserting him. Certainly the invitation by her parents provided her with an excuse to get away. Part of her anxiety to leave was the fear that she would become pregnant again once the baby was weaned. One of Byron's threats had been that he was going to father a male heir before he went abroad. He had told his wife that she was to wean the baby by February 10: "I think it is his intention about that time to join me *pour des raisons*," Annabella told Augusta, "and to go abroad as soon as there is a probability of having attained the object in view."[*]

Five or six bailiffs were now camped in the Piccadilly Terrace house, and there was an absolute necessity to break up the household, which could no

---

[*] It was widely believed that a woman could not get pregnant while she was nursing.

241

longer be maintained. Accordingly, on January 6, Byron – during one of the periods when they weren't speaking – sent Annabella a note asking her to decide on a date for her departure. She took umbrage at this communication – which she later described as a dismissal – but they made it up the next day.

Annabella began to plan her moves with great deliberation. First, on January 8 she consulted Dr Baillie (brother of Annabella's friend, the playwright Joanna, and the same doctor who had attended Byron's foot as a child). She told the doctor that Byron had given her to believe that he was guilty of some terrible crime – she suspected murder, but whether this was fact or the expression of a disordered mind she did not know. Dr Baillie suggested that she have her husband examined by Mr Francis Le Mann, the physician who had delivered her child and who was already attending Byron, then suffering from his recurrent liver complaint. She next made an appointment to talk to Hanson. With her she brought a medical journal (probably lent to her by Le Mann) in which she had marked passages which suggested to her that Byron might be suffering from hydrocephalus. The alarmed solicitor gathered that she was actually considering having her husband bound and restrained.

As she recited all the details which made her suspect insanity, Hanson recognised the eccentricities he had been familiar with since Byron was a child of eleven: the loaded pistols, his paranoid routine of looking under his bed, a rope ladder that he had once hung from his window in case of fire. The existence of a laudanum bottle did not surprise him. Hanson asked her if she was in any fear for her own personal safety, to which Annabella replied forcefully, "Oh, no, not in the least; my eye can always put down his!"

Mr Le Mann suggested that the country air would be good for her and the child, and promised to send her a report of his detailed examination. He also suggested that she not write anything that might upset him. On the eve of her departure – the 14th – Annabella, Byron and Augusta were in the drawing room. Byron, standing in front of the fireplace, asked rhetorically, "When shall we three meet again?" That night husband and wife made love as usual.

Byron was still asleep when she left in the morning. Annabella later recalled that she stood in front of his door torn by a strong impulse to throw herself on the mat on which the dog Boatswain had once lain, but she resisted and marched resolutely out the door. Such an impulse indicates that she feared she was leaving for ever. In addition to her child she was accompanied by Mrs Clermont, and by her maid Anne Rood, recently married to Byron's valet, William Fletcher. From Woburn, where she spent the first night, she sent the following note to Byron:

Dearest B –

The Child is quite well, and the best of Travellers. I hope you are *good*, and remember my medical prayers & injunctions. don't give yourself up to the abominable trade of versifying – nor to brandy – nor to any thing or any body that is not *lawful & right*.

Though I disobey in writing to you, let me hear of *your* obedience at Kirkby.

Ada's love to you with mine –

Pip[2]

That same evening she wrote a letter to her confidante, Selina Doyle, telling her that she "was desired to write from here a few lines in the usual form without any notice of serious subjects".[3] This note exonerates Annabella from the charge that was later made, namely, that her letter to her husband was so spontaneously affectionate that it proved that she had later been influenced by her parents. Her comments to Selina also reveal her deep concern about what the world would think of her deserting her husband if he were truly mentally deranged. The letter certainly provides evidence that at this point she had no intention of returning, although she hoped to postpone the final decision. But, she assured her friend, she had no alternative if her presence only exacerbated her husband's condition. Yet she was anxious. "How can such conduct be interpreted to my disadvantage? But were I now to take the final step, whilst the relations are possessed with this idea, they would desert me – and were the unhappy consequences which they apprehend to Ensue, what should I feel? Deeper regrets than under any other Circumstances."

Meanwhile Augusta, who had been living in Piccadilly Terrace since September, was packed and ready to move into her apartment in St James's Palace around the corner; but on the day of Annabella's departure she suddenly informed her sister-in-law that Le Mann thought it best if she remain at Piccadilly Terrace for a time to keep an eye on her brother. Augusta was probably not aware of her own motives, but during the next weeks, while sending daily reports of what Byron said, ate, did with his time, she was acting as a substitute wife. Annabella professed herself only too happy to have Augusta there. Augusta's presence relieved Annabella from the responsibility of looking after her husband, yet Augusta was also reinforcing the point that she could handle Byron far better than his own wife could. There is no doubt that she was genuinely grieved about Annabella, and Annabella responded gratefully to her concern. The day after Annabella's departure, Augusta told her: "I wish I could see you dearest I do miss you sadly."[4] Again, on the 20th: "I hope you are not tormenting yourself with repentance & scruples – for I do think your having gone will somehow be of use – & so does Le Mann."[5]

The events of the following month are confused and contradictory; and the quantity of evidence pertaining to the break-up of this marriage of a famous poet is overwhelming. His personality ceases to be the dominating perspective, submerged by the welter of letters passing from one woman to another. As in most divorces, the situation escalated to a point where people revealed their worst traits. Specific dates provide our most reliable guide. The day after her arrival at Kirkby, Annabella sent off a letter (one which seems genuinely affectionate), and which would later cause her many qualms lest it be used against her.

> Dearest Duck,
>
> We got here quite well last night and were ushered into the kitchen instead of drawing-room by a mistake that might have been agreeable enough to hungry people. Of this and other incidents Dad wants to write you a jocose account and both he and Mam long to have the party completed. Such a W.C.! and such a *sitting*-room or *sulking*-room all to yourself. If I were not always looking about for B, I should be a great deal better already for country air. *Miss* finds her provisions increased, & fattens thereon. It is a good thing she can't understand all the flattery bestowed upon her, "Little Angel". Love to the good goose, & every body's love to you both from hence.
>
> > Ever thy most loving
> > > Pippin . . . Pip – ip.[6]

On the 18th she told Augusta:

> My father & mother agree that in every point of view it would be best for Byron to come here . . . My dearest A, it is my great comfort that you are in Piccadilly . . . Tell me exactly how B. is affected by my absence, I conceive that in his morbid state of feeling he has no desire for the absent, & may feel relieved for a time as Le Mann expected. Make him write to me if you can because any manual exertion is good for him, since his active habits decrease with the progress of the disease, & to employ the powers diminishes the mental irritability.[7]

When, if, and how Annabella proposed to confide in her parents is unclear. After writing to Augusta on the 18th she received a letter from Selina Doyle (who had been privy to the whole domestic situation for months), in response to her note written from Woburn. Her mother asked to read it, and Byron's mental cruelty was revealed. Her parents were outraged: how could she have stayed with such a monster? Annabella was persuaded to write a long statement detailing her grievances against her husband which Lady Noel intended to show to a lawyer in London. The very act of putting everything down on paper energised Annabella's accumulated resentments, reinforced by the knowledge that the story had to be dramatic enough to carry conviction.

On the 20th her furious mother set off for London, bristling with righteous vengefulness. She had departed – and Annabella had made her statement – *before* Le Mann's letter arrived, the letter that was supposed to determine Annabella's future decisions. On January 21 (by which time Lady Noel had arrived in London) Annabella heard from Le Mann that while Byron was suffering from inflammation of the liver, he could find no indication of "settled lunacy";[8] and he suggested that Byron might now set off for Kirkby as soon as possible.

Once her parents had been apprised of her sufferings, and now that the wider world would be made aware of them as well, Annabella's state of mind changed dramatically, although there were periods when pity and compassion overwhelmed her briefly. There can be no doubt that she was in misery now that the die was cast. Her maid (who had married William Fletcher) reported that she was writhing on the floor in paroxysms of weeping. She wrote to the lawyer that she knew Byron would be generous about a settlement; and begged her mother not to gossip about the situation, a plea which might imply that she did not want to be forced into any irrevocable decisions. To Mrs Clermont, who had accompanied her mother, she wrote: "I hope you will keep my Mother sober. She will break my heart if she takes up this thing in *bitterness* against him" (January 21, 1816).[9] In this same letter she wrote: "I must never see him again – I shall wish otherwise when I am less sane – but let me be preserved from it by every means." Mrs Clermont had no intention of letting her weaken: "I have not the smallest doubt his real wish is that a separation should take place . . . He must feel himself a free man again and he will do it by some means or other even tho he should break your heart and have that upon his conscience ever after."[10] Annabella herself also feared that Byron was "playing a deep game to win over Augusta";[11] and she warned Lady Noel not to be taken in if she heard that he had spoken tenderly of her. By now her stubborn nature and her self-image of consistency were prevailing over any tender feelings.

Once Lady Noel had consulted a lawyer, there could be no turning back. Annabella's greatest fear seems to have been the publicity that would be aroused: "It would be a death-blow to me to be obliged to come forward publicly – & depend upon it the public will take his part warmly enough under any circumstances."[2] Meanwhile Byron was ignorant of the tumultuous emotions that were about to change his life. Augusta reported that he was in a quieter state than he had been for months. He was drinking less and eating more regularly. He spoke kindly of Annabella and their child; he puzzled over the strange expression in her first letter about "the abominable trade of versifying"; and each day he waited eagerly for the post.

One must also consider Annabella's suppressed envy of his fame and popularity. Annabella had long fancied herself as possessing genuine poetic powers; and while Byron had spoken favourably of her verses – once even telling her that she could be a poet – he had never taken them very seriously or given her any real encouragement. She was an avid reader of the novels of Maria Edgeworth and Jane Austen. She craved literary glory for herself, but the most she could expect was the reflected glow of marriage to a genius. Acting as an amanuensis for *The Siege of Corinth* and *Parisina* offered little reward. Now, with the removal of conventional restraints, her envy erupted into an obsession to destroy and deface both Byron's personal and professional reputation.

She found an eager accomplice in Dr Stephen Lushington, the legal figure her mother had consulted in London. Lushington had been recommended to her by Sir Samuel Romilly, who had been under retainer from Byron for many years. Romilly, renowned for his probity, on this occasion acted unprofessionally and unethically. Byron had every right to be outraged when he eventually learned that Romilly refused to act for him, using the insulting excuse that he had so many retainers that this one had slipped his mind. What Byron failed to take into consideration was that Romilly, an old friend of the Milbanke family, had placed his championship of Annabella over his professional obligation to Byron. The separation would prove indisputably the degree to which Byron was an outsider in his society.

Lady Noel's immediate aim was to gain advice on how Annabella might secure a legal separation. Lushington was known as a "civilian", that is, a lawyer or advocate practising in the ecclesiastical courts which, until 1858, held jurisdiction over matrimonial matters. There were only five or six of these civilians, all of whom had degrees from Oxford or Cambridge. The

London Consistory Court had the power to compel a wife to return to her husband or to live apart but supported by him. Divorce, in the modern sense of dissolution of marriage, did not yet exist.

At the time Lady Noel consulted him, Lushington, then only thirty-four years of age, was still a very junior member of his profession, but this case was to make him famous, and Lushington was quick to perceive its possibilities. He had to take into consideration the fact that any conduct that occurred before marriage would not be considered by the courts. Mental cruelty was not admissible unless the wife feared for her physical safety. Condonation of adultery would rule out the right to divorce; and hence Annabella's anxiety about the affectionate letters she had written after leaving London. As for property, everything belonging to the wife was vested in the husband during and after her lifetime. The father was also entitled to custody of any children, except in cases where the child was in physical or moral danger.

Lady Noel found Lushington "the most *gentlemanlike* & clear headed Man I ever met with";[13] and he endeared himself to her by declaring her sister-in-law Lady Melbourne "as infamous & wretched a woman as ever existed".[14] She confided to Mrs Clermont that Byron had told Annabella that in 1813 during his affair with Caroline Lamb he had sexual relations with La Tante (on her instigation) – obviously one of Byron's egregious attempts to shock his prim wife. Lady Noel was as intent on destroying her sister-in-law as she was on toppling Byron. While Annabella had begged that things be kept as quiet as possible, gradually more and more people were drawn into the proceedings so that the affair eventually resembled the Congress of Vienna. The most rational adviser seemed to be Selina Doyle's brother, Colonel Francis Doyle, and possibly also Hobhouse who was only gradually apprised of the true nature of the situation early in February.

Sir Samuel Romilly advised that at all costs Byron must be prevented from having access to the child. Lady Noel, more alive than ever in her life, after her return to Kirkby Mallory kept a gun with her lest an attempt be made to take the child by force. Selina Doyle reported that Lushington could not believe that a court would grant the child to such an unstable father.[15]

In the week that Lady Noel spent in London she visited Lushington several times. Based on Annabella's statement, he made a detailed memorandum of those points where he thought they had an advantage over Byron, but Annabella's case was weak, given the law at that time.*

---

* Lushington's notes are quoted in full in *Law, Politics and the Church of England, The Career of Stephen Lushington 1782–1873* by S.M. Waddams (Cambridge UP, 1992), pp.109–10.

However, Lushington's ability to seize any benefit is apparent in a comment made on January 25 when he suggested that, in view of Susan Boyce's reputation, Annabella was in danger of venereal disease if conjugal relations with her husband were resumed. Annabella was forbidden to see her husband under any circumstances since, Lushington argued, if they met this might strengthen Byron's case to demand from the courts the restitution of conjugal rights. Unfortunately for Byron, Hanson was to be no match for this wily advocate.

Meanwhile Augusta was reporting that Byron was puzzled and apprehensive when he heard that Lady Noel had come to town. His bizarre behaviour had begun to recur in statements such as his assertion that he was the greatest man alive; and, in reply to a laughing question from his cousin George Byron, he boasted that he was probably greater than Napoleon himself. He was always asking Augusta if she had heard from Annabella. "I think you had better send him a few lines I can show him – Fletcher says very uneasy when no letter when post arrives."[16] On the 28th Lady Melbourne asked him to come and see her. She questioned him about the rumours she had heard of a separation, and this seems to have been Byron's first knowledge of what was taking place.

Augusta at this point began strenuous efforts at peace-making. She pleaded with Annabella to pause and consider the consequences of a separation. She warned her that if Byron was not deranged he was entitled to custody of the child. Moreover, she knew that Lady Melbourne was trying to persuade him to act in a rational manner. Lady Noel was highly suspicious of Augusta who she suspected of supporting Byron because she would benefit by his will; but Annabella assured her that "She has been the truest of friends to me – & I hope you regard her, & *seem* to regard her as such, for I very much fear that she may be supposed the cause of separation by many, & it would be a cruel injustice."[17] At this point Annabella, in her dependence on Augusta, had pushed the suspicion of incest to the back of her mind.

On January 28 Lady Noel returned to Kirkby but continued to try to stiffen Annabella into a position of unremitting vengefulness. On January 29 Sir Ralph Noel, after consulting the lawyers, sent a letter to Byron proposing a separation. Alerted by Annabella, Augusta intercepted it and returned it unopened. Lady Noel was in a frenzy of indignation, and wrote to Augusta: "You have done infinite mischief, which if You really love and pity Annabella You will regret and lament – and for what reason do you imagine that a few days will *change his nature*? – or Why favour him at her Expense?"[18] This time it was Annabella who prevented her mother sending the letter.

Sir Ralph then travelled to London where a communication from him was delivered directly to Byron on February 2. In a short, cleverly worded note Sir Ralph announced that

Very recently, circumstances have come to my knowledge, which convinces me, that with your opinions it cannot tend to your happiness to continue to live with Lady Byron, and I am yet more forcibly convinced that after her dismissal from your house, and the treatment she experienced whilst in it, those on whose protection she has the strongest natural claims could not feel themselves justified in permitting her return thither.[19]

He hoped that Byron would agree to appoint a professional friend to discuss the terms of the separation.

Considering the suddenness of this startling letter and the volatility of Byron's temper, he responded in a surprisingly temperate way. He reminded Sir Ralph that his wife had in no way been dismissed from his home; although he admitted that

It is true – that previous to this period – I had suggested to her the expediency of a temporary residence with her parents: my reason for this was very simple & shortly stated – viz – the embarrassment of my circumstances, & my inability to maintain our present establishment. – The truth of what is thus stated may be easily ascertained by reference to Lady B. – who is Truth itself.

A note of sternness was injected when he reminded his father-in-law that Annabella was still his wife and the mother of his child, so that "until I have her express sanction of your proceedings – I shall take leave to doubt the propriety of your interference."[20] Augusta then wrote, on Byron's request, to ask Annabella if the idea of the separation had her concurrence. "I need not say with what grief I write on this subject. God bless you & dear little Guss."[21]

Byron, labouring under the delusion that Annabella would patiently endure any of his bizarre behaviour, simply could not believe that she would desert him voluntarily. It must have been the work of that damnable Mrs Clermont who had been placed in the house in order to spy on him. Mrs Clermont was certainly determined that no reconciliation should take place. Annabella, alarmed by Augusta's account of Byron's suffering, wrote: "Pray don't let me have his death to answer for

– if there should be *danger* – things must not be pursued too hastily – You *must* consult Le Mann on this."[22] Mrs Clermont immediately pooh-poohed his threats of suicide, assuring her that he was conducting his life as usual: "Pray do not be so weak as to mind Mrs Leigh's Oh's and Oh's . . . [it] is quite decisive as to its being his Pride that is affected and not his tenderer feelings."[23] Byron was so convinced that Annabella was under the sway of her parents that to elude their interception he sent one of his letters to her through Fletcher's wife. Annabella reacted with deep indignation to these "clandestine proceedings". In his letter Byron expressed his bewilderment and asked her to give him her explanation for her decision. He concluded: "Whatever may occur, it is but justice to you to say that you are exempt from all fault whatever – & that neither now nor at any time have I the slightest imputation of any description to charge upon you."[24] On this very day Annabella, who had been forbidden to write to Byron directly, was telling Augusta: "You are desired by your brother to ask if my father has acted with my concurrence in proposing a separation. He has."[25]

Two days later Hobhouse called at Piccadilly Terrace to find his friend more depressed than he had ever seen him. He was shown the "Dearest Duck" letter, and was as puzzled as Byron was by its affectionate tone. Byron eagerly accepted "Hob's" offer to write to Annabella on his behalf. But Byron himself, now thoroughly shaken out of his lethargy, wrote yet once more to his wife: "my errors – or what harsher name you choose to give them – you know – but I loved you, & will not part from you without your own express and *expressed* refusal to return to or receive me."[26] Annabella could not help being extremely agitated by these words of affection, but she continued adamant: "It is unhappily your disposition to consider what you *have* as worthless – what you have *lost* as invaluable. But remember that you believed yourself most miserable when I was yours."[27]

On this same day – February 6 – Hobhouse pleaded with her: "I am sure I *know the very worst of everything that can* be said against my friend, and in that very worst nothing is comprised which can bear out your friends in the extremity to which they seem inclined to proceed."[28] He also reminded her that as she left on her honeymoon she had said to him that if the marriage did not succeed, it would be her fault.

Annabella was outraged by Hobhouse's suggestion that others were making her decisions for her. She complained to Lushington of his insolence, particularly as he had seldom seen them together, and on those occasions Byron had disguised his bad temper. In a somewhat contradictory statement, she confided that she had for some time had reason to think that under the mask of friendship he was endeavouring Byron's ruin – & instigated *more* than anyone else the conduct which has disunited us – Ever since his return to England in the summer, there has been a decided change for the worse in B towards me . . . I *know* that Hobhouse has always represented my parents in an invidious light – The flattery to myself has been so gross & disgusting that it was evidently a *disguise.*[29]

Because of the outrageous lies Byron had told her about Hobhouse while they were still on their honeymoon at Halnaby, Byron had foolishly created a situation where his well-meaning friend could only make the situation worse. Hobhouse was gradually learning that there were things *he* did *not* know about Byron. When he called on the 12th both Augusta and George Byron opened his eyes to the sort of maltreatment Annabella had received. "Whilst I heard these things Mrs L. went out & brought word that her brother was crying bitterly in his bed room – poor poor fellow."[30]

Annabella was more impressed by the conciliatory tone of a letter written by Francis Hodgson who, incidentally, had travelled up to London at Augusta's request. Nevertheless, despite waverings from time to time she had grown into an inflexible rod of righteousness (particularly now that she was in regular communication with Lushington); and as to Byron's threats of suicide, she told her father that "the proposed intention of this sort is rather amusing."[31] Yet she had claimed that the danger of suicide was one of the reasons she had originally consulted the doctors.

At that time mental cruelty would not be considered cause for a wife to leave her husband, so that speculation swirled about every kind of monstrous sexual perversion. People were now talking openly about the incest between brother and sister. On February 17 Augusta sent Lady Byron a letter marked "*most* private". "There are reports abroad," Augusta wrote, "*of a nature too horrible to repeat* . . . [George Byron] yesterday sent for Hobhouse – who I found last night informed B of them – & *he* has desired me to inform you of them – of course this added considerably to his agitation – every other shrinks into nothing before this most horrid *one*. God alone knows what is to be the end of it all."[32] To this Annabella sent a disingenuous reply: "I have received your very painful letter – & am truly sorry that you should be so alarmed, though I think without cause – On the mysterious subject of which I am ignorant, I can only say – that if the report alludes to anything I know to be false – I will bear testimony to the falsehood."[33]

On the 15th Byron sent Annabella a third and final appeal. "And now – Bell – dearest Bell . . . I can only say in the truth of affliction – & without hope – motive – or end in again saying what I have lately but vainly repeated – that I love you: – bad or good – mad or rational – miserable or content – I love you – & shall do, to the dregs of my memory & existence." There is no reason to doubt that Byron had come genuinely to love his wife; so that he had actually believed that her love was as strong as his, and that she had come to him as a steadfast saviour, no matter what his offences were. To Lushington Annabella put a seemingly reasonable question: "if he laments so much to have made me 'the partner of his desolation' why is he so unwilling to release me?"[34] Lushington found it "really ludicrous to talk of receiving a person to his heart, whom he could for one instant suspect of abandoning him because of his embarrassments . . . I have unavoidably been led beyond the line of my professional duty."[35]

On the day following Byron's final appeal, Hobhouse sat up with him until one in the morning. He told Byron "the very worst I had heard against him which he received to my astonishment with very little discomposure – poor fellow".[36] Byron believed so implicitly that he was a doomed being that he had already accepted whatever fate had in store for him.

As far as Annabella was concerned, Augusta had served her purpose and it was now time to sacrifice her. On February 22 Annabella travelled to London, after writing to Lushington that there were things that he could understand only if they had a personal interview. She set up her headquarters in Mivart's Hotel. After hearing her suspicions about the incest, Lushington declared that there could be no possibility of reconciliation; and while he believed that such suspicions would not hold up in court, he had her put the reasons for her suspicions in a statement. She was to make many statements in defence of her continued friendship with Augusta despite her suspicions. In what appears to be a first draft she claimed that the desire to save both Augusta and her children had been her first object. She even quoted lines 120–1 from *The Giaour*:

that we had suffered together – and for each other – all this has made her dear to me, and for her sake I believe it right that I should treat her as if it were so – at the risk of being deemed too lax a moralist by those with whom

> Every fault a tear can claim
> Except an erring sister's shame –

Not that I mean to adopt the phraseology of B – with whom vice is folly, and crimes are faults."[37]

In a letter of February 28 to her mother, it is apparent that Annabella had by now confided her suspicions about the incest to her as well.

> I have been *perfectly* confidential with Dr L and so far from thinking that the *suspicions* could do any good for me . . . the slightest intimation of them having the appearance of malice would be altogether most injurious to *me* in a social view . . . Dr L *insists* that you write in a kind manner to Mrs Leigh as being most influential to my Justification whatever she may turn *out* – & that she be spoken of by us in a friendly manner.[38]

Nevertheless, Annabella had probably warned her not to confide even in Sir Ralph because it was not until March 16 that Lady Noel wrote to her husband: "I *now* know what was the report to be so shocking – it was that the Brother and Sister *forgot they were so*."[39]

All London of course was now talking; and rumours of incest, sodomy, and homosexuality were whispered as causes of the separation. Both *The Siege of Corinth* and *Parisina* were published in February, thus making Byron even more of a public figure.

Having accepted the fact that separation was probably inevitable, Hanson and Byron's other advisers started to take depositions from the servants at Piccadilly Terrace, and Fletcher was instructed to write to his wife to come to London to make a statement. The great fear in Annabella's party was that Byron would place the child in the custody of Augusta, even though Augusta had professed that she would never agree to such an arrangement. Sir Samuel Romilly advised making the child a Ward of Chancery in order to prevent Byron taking her away from her mother. Accordingly, at the beginning of March, Lushington told Annabella to cease all communication with her sister-in-law, thus leaving Augusta totally bewildered when Annabella refused to see her.

Lady Byron was determined to keep the case out of the courts if possible. When discussions about the actual settlement started, Annabella entered into the spirit of negotiations with the same intensity as her mother had shown. On March 4 a letter to her mother reveals the bellicosity of a nature that had hitherto seemed demure and composed:

> Well – nothing but war remains. An offer of amicable settlement has been refused – and perhaps when you know the terms *you* may not be sorry. Half the Noel property was offered, and only £200 per ann asked at present. It is a bad job – for I shall lose the cause, and can only

obtain present Security whilst the Suit lasts. They say I shall be justified to the World. The silence of my friends has been very *dis*advantageous to Lord B. in regard to opinion – since worse than the true causes are supposed, and from all accounts I find that there never was such unanimity of opinion on any subject, except at one house, and *that* is divided against itself – and if I were not a Spoiled Child *there*,* I might be something worse . . . Lamb warmly espouses my cause, Lady M. & Lady Cowper [Lady Melbourne's daughter] against me . . . My opinion of the best course to follow is this – to put in the strongest statement into Court, and then to delay proceedings, so as to tire him out – and we are at liberty to make use of his conduct during the suit, if it affords ground for adultery &c. So I don't think he can well escape – and yet he is so artful that I despond about it at times.[40]

Now that she was in London, Annabella's chief aim, in addition to securing custody of the child, was to gain public support for herself. Augusta's friend Mrs Villiers wrote to her, begging Annabella to refute the rumours that were circulating about Augusta. All Annabella would reply was that none of the reports had been sanctioned by her or any of her friends.[41] Thus began a long correspondence between the two women. On April 26 Annabella paid a visit to Mrs Villiers in which she managed to win the susceptible woman over completely. "She has been most strenuous in her endeavours to do away an impression so injurious to you in the world," Augusta was informed. "All that Lady B has said & done to you on this subject demands *your eternal gratitude*."[42] On this occasion Annabella had managed to convince Mrs Villiers of Augusta's guilt, and they were now allied in the endeavour to save the erring woman's soul.

Despite repeated requests from Byron, Annabella was not allowed to see him, but she did have a meeting with Augusta on March 5 (despite Lushington's disapproval) on the grounds that she was the sole person who could testify to her domestic virtues. Augusta was shocked by her extreme pallor and weird calmness of manner. It was around this period that Annabella's mother told her: "I neither do, or can expect that you should not *feel* and *deeply feel* – but I have sometimes thought . . . that Your mind is too *high wrought* – too much so for *this* World."[43] Augusta begged her at least to attempt a trial reconciliation, but came away from the interview in total despair.

* This was how Lady Melbourne had described Annabella to Byron, advising him that he must tame her.

When Caroline Lamb had first heard of the impending separation, she had written very sympathetically to Byron, pleading with him not to believe that the malicious stories had been spread by her; but it was not long before her devilish streak asserted itself. Shortly after Annabella arrived in London, she received one of a series of agitated letters from Caroline, this one traducing Lady Melbourne.

> She is infatuated about Lord B – she ever has been – & she is now more willing to think him Mad at times than wicked – besides which she has an idea that you have a *cold* character . . . therefore Dearest Lady Byron feel for yr Aunt – but never whilst you live let her think I have had any communication with you – burn these letters pray.
>
> One other word – Lady Melbourne has a good & kind heart – it is spoilt no doubt & she is infatuated by the specious character Lord Byron has ever assumed in her presence.[44]

The whole Melbourne household was divided against itself. The other "Caro", wife of George Lamb (William's younger brother), wrote to Augusta that although she knew nothing of the facts, "I only feel that *you* must be right – I have that confidence in your character."[45] When Lady Melbourne herself assured Annabella that she had never blamed Annabella for her conduct (indeed, she held Lady Noel responsible for Annabella's intransigence), Annabella tried to reassure her mother, who had been urging her to cut off all contact with her.

> I must beg that you hold your tongue. Lushington says the whole business might be undone, if Lord B. could trace any report of an unfavourable nature to us – my honour being pledged for silence till this arbitration is settled.
>
> The reports against Lord B. continue outrageous – and my conduct is much applauded in not endeavouring to encrease [sic] them.[46]

But Lady Melbourne was nervous and appealed to Hobhouse to try to retrieve her letters to Byron. Caroline was also extremely anxious that letters be returned to her, and Annabella agreed to meet Caroline at the home of Mrs George Lamb.* From Caroline she took a statement which

---

* Fortunately for us she failed to keep her promise to return the letters.

she sent off immediately to Lushington once the interview was over. The knowledge she had to impart was the following:

> That from the time Mrs L. came to Bennet St in the year 1813 – Lord B. had given her various intimations of a criminal intercourse between them – but that for some time he spoke of it in a manner which did not enable her to fix it upon Mrs L. thus – "Oh I never knew what it was to love before – there is a woman I love so passionately – she is with child by me, and if a daughter it shall be called *Medora*" – that his avowals of this incestuous intercourse become bolder – till at last she said to him one day, "I could believe it of *you* – but not of *her*."[47]

After he showed her some of Augusta's letters with the significant crosses, Caroline claimed that she never had any further intimacy with him. (What about her pursuit of him during the following year?) She also charged him with having "perverted" three of his Harrow friends as well as the page Rushton, and of having practised homosexuality "unrestrictedly" in the East. These were the kinds of insinuations with which Byron had tried to shock Annabella, and she now reproached Caroline for not trying to halt the marriage.

Caroline replied that she was miserable that she had not warned her, but would Annabella have believed her? She warned her again not to trust Lady Melbourne: "*his* influence over her is such that I feel secure *now* nothing can shake it – pray take care – above all let her not imagine what you know – for were you ever to confide, she would only try to disprove it – I fear nothing can change her."[48]

The woman scorned threw herself into the fray, sending Annabella several letters every day. In one she apologised for having written sympathetically to Byron, since now she felt nothing but disgust for him, especially if he threatened to take the child.

> I will tell that which if you merely menace him with the knowledge shall make him tremble – keep every one in the dark as to what you know . . . he made every promise of amendment man can make – but still I reproach myself that I did not fly before you & tell you all I know – all I had sworn never to reveal – to keep such oath was more scandalous than to have broken it – but I still loved Byron even then – & had he behaved to you as he said – I could not have hated & despised him as from my soul I now do & will – Lady Byron though

you are spotless & pure & I am all that is fallen & worthless yet hear me . . . trust no one – there are serpents round you who can smile on you & bite you to the heart.[49]

On hearing this incriminating information that Annabella had received from Caroline, Lushington replied, "I think it scarcely possible Lord Byron should now refuse to complete the Agreement, though he may evade it by a premature departure."[50] He heartily congratulated her on her escape from "such contamination". These scandalous disclosures of incest had come at a time when negotiations had become bogged down over a money settlement. The go-between in these matters was a pompous cousin of Byron's, Robert Wilmot, who seemed far more sympathetic to Annabella than to his own kin. At first Byron offered to give Annabella £1,000 per annum in addition to her pin money, but he indignantly refused to sign a statement dividing the Kirkby property on the death of Lady Noel. Annabella refused this additional allowance. On March 4 Byron, on hearing that Annabella herself had been involved in the negotiations, wrote bitterly to her that

> it appeared to me to be a kind of appeal to the supposed mercenary feelings of the person to whom it was made – "if you part with &c. you will gain *so much now,* – & so much – at the death of &c." – a matter of pounds, shillings & pence! – no allusion to my child – a hard – dry – attorney's paper: – Oh – Bell – to see you thus stifling and destroying all feeling all affections – all duties – (for they are your first duties – those of a wife & mother) is far more bitter than any possible consequences to me – –

Eventually it was agreed (on Byron's suggestion) that on the death of Lady Noel, Sir Samuel Shepherd, the Solicitor-General, would act as arbitrator on the division of the property. However, before Byron's friends would allow him to sign the agreement, they insisted that Annabella disavow all the ugly rumours about the incest or homosexuality that were circulating. All she would agree to say was that neither she nor any members of her family had spread any stories prejudicial to Byron's character. However, she now charged that Byron's friends had been repeating harsh comments he had made about her. On March 26 he sent her letters from Lord Holland, Samuel Rogers, and Douglas Kinnaird, strongly disputing this accusation. Rogers recalled Byron's saying that "wherever the Wrong lay, it did not lie with Lady Byron; – that Lady B.

had been faultless in thought, word, & in deed."[51] Kinnaird told him that he had "never heard you express yourself of Lady Byron but uniformly in the same tone of unqualified respect for her character".[52] Finally, Lord Holland told him that "you spoke of her judgment, her veracity, her character, and her conduct, with much respect."[53] If Byron did not include letters from Hobhouse and Scrope Davies, it was probably because he knew she would place no credence in them, although for her Kinnaird was also part of that "Piccadilly crew", which she associated with drinking, gaming, and licentiousness.

Byron was being absolutely truthful in his denials of never having traduced his wife – that is, until after the separation was actually effected. Thomas Moore expressed his grief at what had happened; and that marriage "instead of bringing you, as I expected, into something like a regular orbit, it has cast you off into infinite space, and left you, I fear, in a far worse state than it found you."[54] In an attempt to sympathise, Moore assured him that it was Byron's "choice" that was responsible for the tragedy. Byron contradicted him (March 8, 1816):

> The fault was *not* – no, nor even the misfortune – in my "choice" (unless in *choosing at all*) – for I do not believe – and I must say it, in the very dregs of all this bitter business – that there ever was a better, or even a brighter, a kinder, or a more amiable and agreeable being than Lady B. I never had, nor can have, any reproach to make her, while with me. Where there is blame, it belongs to myself, and, if I cannot redeem, I must bear it.

Nevertheless, Byron continued to be puzzled about the unstated grounds for the separation since he had never laid a finger on his wife. When Lady Noel got word of this, she expostulated that it was outrageous for a gentleman to make such a boast (March 19, 1816). "I think Byron is now so completely disgraced that only the Piccadilly committee will notice him."[55] Alas, it was only too true that his former society friends were beginning to avoid him and the word was that he would go abroad.

By now Augusta was close to collapse. Since Annabella was known to have broken off relations with her, fuel was added to the gossip. On March 14 Augusta wrote to Hodgson that she had stayed at Piccadilly Terrace

> while there was a *possibility* of reconciliation to do all I could towards it, I had better *now* go. You well know what it costs me to leave my dearest Brother, but indeed I CAN'T express one HALF of what I

suffer . . . One word more – all my fears of a *dreadful fatal event* have revived – the *dark hints* are again expressed *should any* charge be brought even without *proof* against him, that can blacken his character – he sometimes talks when viewing the subject in a fairer point of view of going abroad or Newstead . . .[56]

On April 3 she moved to her apartments in St James's Palace.

The following day Hobhouse joined his friend at Piccadilly Terrace. By now Byron was determined to go into exile.

17

Escape, 1816

In 1820 Byron wrote an article for *Blackwood's Magazine* in which he attempted to explain his decision to go into exile in April 1816. "I was accused of every monstrous vice by public rumour, – and private rancour; my name which had been a knightly or noble one since My fathers helped to conquer the kingdom for William the Norman, was tainted. – I felt that, If what was whispered and muttered and murmured was true – I was unfit for England, – if false – England was unfit for me."[1]

In this same article he quoted something Madame de Staël had said to him after his arrival in Switzerland: "You should not have warred with the World – it will not do – it is too strong always for any individual."[2] Madame de Staël was right: not only did he war with the world, but once it was apparent that the separation was inevitable, his behaviour became so defiantly imprudent that it simply confirmed the scandalous reputation that the world had assigned to him. He seemed driven by a death wish.

On the evening that Hobhouse moved in with him at Piccadilly Terrace – April 3 – Byron had a bachelor dinner with "Hob", Scrope Davies, and Leigh Hunt, who was again editing his weekly periodical, the *Examiner*. Hunt was struck by Byron's sickly appearance. The strain of the past months had been terrible, and his manic activities during the weeks before his departure were those of a man with little control over his judgement. Shortly after the initial separation agreement had been signed, on March 20 Byron sent a poem to his estranged wife in her inaccessible stronghold of Mivart's Hotel.

Fare thee well! and if for ever –
Still for ever, fare *thee well* –
Even though unforgiving, never
'Gainst thee shall my heart rebel. –

Would that breast were bared before thee
   Where thy head so oft hath lain,
While that placid sleep came o'er thee
   Which thou ne'er canst know again: . . .
Though my many faults defaced me,
   Could no other arm be found,
Than the one which once embraced me,
   To inflict a cureless wound! . . .
When our child's first accents flow –
   Wilt thou teach her to say – "Father!"
Though his care she must forego? . . .
All my faults – perchance thou knowest –
   All my madness – none can know . . .
Fare thee well! – thus disunited –
   Torn from every nearer tie –
Seared in heart – and lone – and blighted –
   More than this, I scarce can die.
             (*Works*, III, pp. 380–3)

With this he enclosed a note: "I send you the first verses that ever I attempted to write upon you, and perhaps the last I may ever write at all." It will be remembered that in the early days of her marriage, Annabella had questioned Augusta closely as to whether Byron had ever written any poetry to her. On his first visit to Seaham he had arrived without a single gift, and there is no evidence that he ever gave her any presents, although he lavished expensive baubles on an actress like Susan Boyce. This curious behaviour might express his unconscious expectation of Annabella as the provider and nurturer when perhaps she could have benefited from a little more nurturing from him and a little less from her parents. Byron had hoped that the poem might move her to thoughts of a reconciliation, but no acknowledgement was sent out from the impenetrable fortress of Mivart's Hotel. A fortnight later the poem was circulated among his friends. For a brief time it turned public sympathy towards Byron, and Annabella, so set on establishing her moral ascendancy, was fearful of its effect.

However, Byron lost any hold he had on general pity when his fearful temper drove him to abandon all caution and taste. Only a week after writing "Fare Thee Well", just after hearing that Sir Samuel Shepherd had delivered his judgement that Byron must be "bound" by the decision of the arbitrator about the eventual disposition of Lady Noel's property, he penned the most vicious lines of his life to Mrs Clermont, "A Sketch from Private Life". A few lines will convey the flavour of it:

> With eye unmoved, and forehead unabash'd,
> She dines from off the plate she lately wash'd.
> Quick with the tale, and ready with the lie –
> The genial confidante, and general spy –
> Who could, ye gods! her next exployment guess –
> An only infant's earliest governess!
> She taught the child to read, and taught so well,
> That she herself, by teaching, learn'd to spell.
>
> (*Works*, III, pp. 382–3)

Byron had chosen the wrong target. The vengeful harridan was not Mrs Clermont, but Annabella's mother, who was totally intent on destroying Byron, Augusta, and Lady Melbourne. Mrs Clermont had always been treated courteously by Byron yet he now saw her as the pawn of Lady Noel; but he would have been aware that to attack his mother-in-law would have been beyond the pale of civilised behaviour. Yet while Mrs Clermont supported Lady Noel that no reconciliation should be considered, she also tried to persuade her employer that Augusta had not the slightest intention of gaining custody of the child (Mrs Clermont was the only one who referred to Augusta Ada as "the babe" rather than as a piece of property, the Child). On March 9 she told her employer that while Annabella had had a lucky escape from a man who she now believed was an unredeemable monster, she had some kind words for Augusta. "I know she has acted weakly but I do firmly believe her intentions have been good – nor can I ever forget the kindness A: experienced from the latter part of the time she was in piccadilly [sic] even for her life I believe we may thank Mrs Leigh."[3]

Annabella herself assured Lushington that she was sure Augusta would sign a paper refusing any part in the custody of her godchild. As for "the Child's" fate, Lushington advised delay in making her a Ward of Chancery until Byron had signed the final agreement. On February 29 Mrs Clermont informed Lady Noel that it was possible to make Ada (as she was called) a Ward "by giving it any little property". Lushington had warned that it must be kept "a *profound secret* as it might have an ill effect if *he* knew it and is only a precaution to keep it out of the Court of King's Bench which is more determined as to paternal right than Chancery."[4]

Byron had fifty copies of both poems printed for private circulation, "inadvisedly", Hobhouse thought. On the evening of April 9 he attended a party at the Duchess of Somerset's where he found everyone staring and talking about his affairs. On his return to Piccadilly Terrace he and Hobhouse sat drinking until they parted for the night after a fierce quarrel – probably over the advisability of the publication. In his journal Hobhouse wrote: "Poor fellow, he came into my room next morning to ask how I was. He was very sorry and so was I, but our regrets originated from different causes."[5]

Caroline's proper sister-in-law, Mrs George Lamb, sent copies of the offensive poems to Annabella on the request of John Murray: "He says he could not as Ld. B's bookseller refuse to publish them, but hopes that you will believe that he did so with pain and reluctance"*[6]. Murray could certainly refuse to publish them – as he was to do with some of Byron's later poetry – but he undoubtedly should not have shown these or the "Stanzas to Augusta" to Caroline Lamb who immediately wrote to Byron, pleading with him not to publish the poem. The poem to his sister was probably written on April 12. He had written a poem of mournful loss, one of embittered venom, and now one of tender gratitude – the gamut of his attitudes to the three women involved in his fate.

> When Fortune changed – and love fled far,
>   And hatred's shafts flew thick and fast,
> Thou wert the solitary star
>   Which rose and set not to the last.
>
> Oh! blest be thine unbroken light!
>   That watched me as a seraph's eye,
> And stood between me and the night,
>   For ever shining sweetly nigh.
>
> (*Works*, III, pp. 387)

If Byron had wanted to protect his sister, he should have refrained from making a public announcement of his attachment to her, which only provided further morsels for the gossip-mongers.** What he was announcing to the world was that his sister, not his wife, knew all his weaknesses,

---

* According to Samuel Smiles, Murray printed but did not publish the poems on the advice of his solicitor that "The Sketch" was libellous. Constable was the publisher; but Murray's agent in Edinburgh, William Blackwood, refused to distribute the verses. On April 17, 1816, he wrote to Murray: "One cannot read 'Fare Thee Well' without crying. The other is 'vigorous hate', as you say. Its power is really terrible; one's blood absolutely creeps while reading it."

** He left instructions that the poem was not to be published until he left England. Augusta attempted to have it suppressed.

but she had love enough to bear with him, as he still proclaimed to Lady Blessington in 1823 when he described Augusta as his "only source of consolation in his troubles on the separation".[7]

The two poems (to Annabella and Mrs Clermont) were published in the Tory paper the *Champion* on April 14, planted there by Byron's implacable enemy, Henry Brougham,* who was one of the mediators in the separation, and the man whom Annabella described as her "warmest champion". The purpose of the publication was to discredit Byron and cast Lady Byron as a victim. On the 17th the *Morning Post* described "The Sketch" as "a base and unmanly attack upon a poor but worthy woman". The *Morning Chronicle* responded with a defence of Byron and "the conspiracy" against him. (It should be added that Hobhouse and the editor, James Perry, were on good terms.)

Sir Ralph Noel, furious on his daughter's behalf, demanded an interview with Perry. Perry reluctantly agreed to publish part of Sir Ralph's disclaimer that he "*knew* of no conspiracy". Sir Ralph continued to insist that there was no conspiracy whatever. Perry replied that if he published the entire letter, Byron would then have the opportunity to demand that the Noel party specify the charges against him. Annabella was in an even greater state of anxiety when Lady Caroline Lamb told her that in her opinion, "His verses are sure to affect many."[8] Annabella then wrote to Lushington asking if she should circulate Hobhouse's statement that she had authorised none of the defamatory statements about Byron "since with the publication of 'Fare Thee Well', the Tide of feeling has now turned against me". Lushington disagreed with her:

> Indeed I do not believe it – nay, I am perfectly satisfied it cannot be so – the feeling of all (with the exception of a very few who have no feelings at all) was unanimous in *your* favour, and I must doubt the magical effects you attribute to the "Fare Thee Well" . . . there are not twenty persons in London, who, though ignorant of the particulars, are not satisfied that the Separation has arisen from Lord Byron's gross misconduct.

He advised her against her proposal to avoid society, and suggested a little realism: "That all persons should think exactly of *you* as they ought is not profitable."[9]

Byron's activities at the Drury Lane Theatre also continued to generate

---

* Brougham was the anonymous reviewer who savaged *Hours of Idleness* in the *Edinburgh Review*.

gossip. He had dropped Miss Boyce, but another actress, Mrs Marden, with whom he was rumoured to be having a liaison, was insulted in the theatre. But in his vulnerable state Byron allowed himself to be seduced by a determined young woman who started to pursue him in March. Byron had received innumerable letters written in the same vein as her initial approach. "If a woman, whose reputation has yet remained unstained, if without guardian or husband to control she should throw herself upon your mercy, if with a beating heart she should confess the love she has borne you many years . . . could you betray her, or would you be silent as the grave?"[10]

The young woman, not yet eighteen, eventually revealed herself as the stepdaughter of the utopian philosopher William Godwin. At first Byron had ignored her; but on learning her identity, he was intrigued, fuelled by the fact that she told him she was writing a novel about a woman who had been brought up in wild nature and whose conduct was governed only by natural impulses.

Mary Jane Clairmont was known in her family circle as Jane, but later insisted on being called Claire.* She was the daughter of the woman Godwin had married after the death of Mary Wollstonecraft. Godwin's own daughter Mary had eloped with the notorious atheistic poet Percy Shelley, and Claire had accompanied them when they fled to the continent in 1814. Now back in England Shelley's Mary was tiring of this *ménage à trois*, and a restless Claire was avid for some excitement of her own. To whet Byron's appetite she sent him copies of *Queen Mab* and *Alastor*, and it is possible that this was the first time Byron had heard of Shelley or his work. An affair was begun. Claire brought her stepsister Mary to the Green Room to flaunt her far more famous lover. Mary found Byron much gentler than she expected. By April Claire was pregnant.

As for Shelley, having abandoned his wife and children, the Court of Chancery now ruled that he must lose custody of his children. While not as famous as Byron, he was the son of a baronet, and his situation was notorious enough that he felt forced to flee England. Claire persuaded him and Mary to allow her to settle with them in Geneva where Byron intended to spend some time. By now Byron was already tired of the intense young woman, but his allowing himself to become involved with her and the irregular Shelley household was almost a wilful need to identify himself with the banished and the scandalous.

---

* Despite her numerous names, I shall call her Claire since this was how Byron always referred to her.

During the first weeks of April the faithful William Fletcher was secretly preparing trunks for flight to the continent as soon as the final separation papers were signed. Byron told Moore candidly that "It is nothing to bear the *privations* of adversity, or, more properly, ill fortune; but my pride recoils from its *indignities*. However, I have no quarrel with that same pride, which will, I think, buckler me through every thing" (March 8, 1816). One of the "indignities" was the necessity of selling his books; and on that very day they were put up at public auction. His library (once bequeathed to Lord Clare in his first will) was painful to part with; and it was humiliating that the books fetched less than £800. Hobhouse bought some of them; and Murray secured others for Rogers and Mrs Leigh, as well as a screen covered with portraits of actors and pugilists which still stands in the Byron Room at Murray's offices in Albemarle Street. On March 28 Byron engaged a young physician, John Polidori, the son of an Italian exile, to accompany him into exile. Considering his persistent hypochondria, it is not surprising that he wanted a doctor with him as security in the unknown life that lay before him. Hobhouse immediately took a dislike to the cocky young man. Only twenty-four, Polidori had a medical degree from the University of Edinburgh, but he also had literary ambitions which he hoped to advance by joining Byron's entourage. Murray offered him £500 for the journal he was planning to keep during their travels. Byron's choice was partly governed by Polidori's ability to speak Italian fluently. It also had something to do with his identification with Napoleon, who had taken the *Bellerophon*'s surgeon, Barry O'Meara, with him to St Helena. Polidori was only another of Byron's unfortunate "choices" that were to complicate even further a life beset by bizarre complications.

Byron's general plan was to head for Venice, the "greenest island" – *his* St Helena – and then probably further to the freedom of the East. Sensing that he was about to do a flit, the bailiffs watched his every move very carefully. He had allowed Lady Byron to keep the carriage, and it was necessary to have some conveyance for the long journey ahead. In the summer of 1815 he had become fascinated by the spectacle of Napoleon's coach that had taken him across the continent from one defeat to another. This had been captured after Waterloo, and was on display at the Egyptian Hall built by William Bullock in 1812, and only yards from Byron in Piccadilly. More than 10,000 visitors a month came to stare at it, thus giving Rowlandson and Cruikshank wonderful opportunities to caricature the mob gawking and climbing all over it. Byron gave orders to Charles Baxter, a famous coachmaker in Long Acre, to build him a replica of his hero's coach. It was puzzling that Baxter agreed to make it, considering

that the cost was £500, and Byron already owed him money. It was
extremely large, standing rather high, painted dark green,* and on the
doors were the initials "N.B." which Byron claimed as his own after the
Milbankes acquired the name Noel. The similarity to Napoleon's initials
was not lost on him; and according to Leigh Hunt he used the monogram
because of his grandiose identification with Napoleon. The interior of the
coach was also modelled on Napoleon's. The original had been fitted out
with every conceivable utensil for a campaign, and in Byron's version there
was a bed, a library, and a chest containing necessities for dining with a
certain elegance.

Neither Hobhouse nor Byron's other friends saw any necessity for him to
flee England. His old Harrow protégé, William Harness, believed that he
should have quietly bided his time until the scandal eventually bored
London society, which was always eager for a new sensation. Harness
thought his abrupt departure confirmed the general view that he was guilty
of some unmentionable crime, but believed that he was actually driven by
his "morbid love of a bad reputation".**[11]

Byron dramatised every situation in which he played a leading part.
Venice could only be reached, as he often pointed out, if visitors left their
carriages at Mestre. He wrote a series of anonymous farewells on behalf of
Napoleon to the French nation.

> All I ask is to divide
>   Every peril he must brave;
> Sharing by the hero's side
>   His fall, his exile and his grave.

He could have retired to Newstead; but he seemed to have lost all interest
in it, only acquiescing in Hanson's dismissal of some of the tenants who
were not paying their rents regularly. His debts were enormous, but
Hanson believed that he could weather the storm because Newstead
would be sold eventually. But what an anticlimax it would have been!
If he were to be disgraced, he must play the role to the hilt.

Indeed he took a certain perverse delight in fanning scandal at this point.

---

* Napoleon's had been blue.

** Incest did not enter the criminal calendar until 1908. Sodomy was regarded as the vilest
crime possible, punishable by death, and the culprit was hanged on a separate gallows so as
not to contaminate the other criminals. The death penalty was reduced to life imprisonment
in 1861. In 1883 Henry Labouchere introduced the Criminal Law Amendment Act making
"acts of gross indecency" punishable by up to two years of hard labour.

On April 8 Hobhouse and Augusta accompanied him to a very grand party at Lady Jersey's. Augusta was by then eight months pregnant and naturally the object of intense scrutiny, particularly as it was known that Annabella was still in London. Not surprisingly, she was cut by Mrs George Lamb, whose lover Henry Brougham also turned his back on Byron. The world was only too eager to eject this strange outsider without any real connections, whose peerage could not be considered more than an accident. He had infiltrated their impenetrable barriers by talent alone and if only for this transgression, reasons must be found to humiliate him. Annabella triumphantly gloated about the incident to her mother. Mrs Lamb told Annabella that she "could almost pity her [Augusta]".[12] Annabella replied: "I am glad that you think of *her* with the feelings of pity which prevail in my mind, and surely if in *mine* there must be some cause for them. I never was nor ever can be so *mercilessly* virtuous as to admit *no* excuse for even the worst of errors."[13] Lady Jersey called on her the following day to indicate that she was not taking sides.*

There is a story, probably not apocryphal, that Miss Mercer Elphinstone – the confident young lady with the flaming red hair – approached Byron and said: "You should have married *me*, and this would not have happened to you!" She was possibly right; and that she had made some such remark seems borne out by a letter Byron wrote to her on April 11. He told her that "neither my vanity nor my wishes ever induced me at any time to suppose that I could by any chance have become more to you than I now am." He concluded by wishing her "a much happier destiny – not that *mine is* – for that is nothing – but that mine ever could have been – with a little common sense & prudence on my part."[14]

At the end of March Augusta attended a dinner at the Wilmots' where she refused to shake the hand of Selina Doyle whom she regarded as one of the people largely responsible for preventing Annabella from considering a reconciliation. Annabella used this incident to justify cutting off all communication with her. Lushington was delighted: "The termination of intercourse with Mrs Leigh gives me great satisfaction."[15] Augusta had already cleared all Annabella's things out of the drawers and cupboards at Piccadilly Terrace and sent them over to Mivart's Hotel. On Byron's behalf she asked for some receipts Annabella had taken with her, and also enclosed a ring (supposedly containing the hair of James I) which Byron wanted his daughter to have. The only response was a formal acknowl-

---

* Lady Jersey and her husband acted as sponsors at the baptism of Augusta's fifth child, Frederick, born on May 9, 1816.

edgement from Annabella's solicitor. An indignant Hobhouse recorded in his dairy: "This has terminated I believe all correspondence between *my dearest Augusta* and *my dearest Annabella*!!! such are female friendships!!"[16]

It was the first time in her life that Annabella had actually been in the limelight and she was reluctant to relinquish its glow. She told her mother that it seemed "urgent" for her to be on the scene as there were rumours that the Piccadilly crew were preparing to publish something about her in the newspapers. Her excuse to Lushington was that she was fearful that Byron would flee abroad before signing the final agreement. Lushington assured her that her continued presence in London would not affect the final outcome in any way; and besides, if she returned to Kirkby Mallory, she could see her daughter again. The child was the last thing on her mind – except as something that Byron might take away from her – and her letters are remarkable for her lack of interest or concern about her baby.

On Easter Sunday, April 14, Byron had his last tearful farewell with his sister. She gave him a Bible which accompanied him for the rest of his days. To Annabella he wrote: "I have just parted from Augusta – almost the last being you had left me to part with – & the only unshattered tie of my existence – wherever I may go – & I am going far – you & I can never meet again in this world – nor in the next – let this content or atone – If any accident occurs to me – be kind to *her*, – if she is then nothing – to her children." Such a plea would only strengthen Annabella's hostility towards her sister-in-law.

There was no farewell with Lady Melbourne. In March 1813 Byron had told her that the only consolation he had in Caroline's pursuit of him lay in the opportunity it gave him to continue their friendship and that he hoped that he would never do anything to endanger it. At the time she assured him that his was the last acquaintance she would ever want to lose. Two years later the situation had changed utterly. Lady Melbourne much preferred Byron to her prim niece Annabella and her abrasive mother, but during the separation she had been caught in a dreadful family dilemma. Annabella accused her of taking Byron's side, to which she replied that Mrs Leigh had told her of the misery she had endured.

This account shock'd me very much . . . I can truly say my heart bled for you . . . I told Mrs Leigh when she call'd upon me, yt I beg'd her to tell Ld B yt it was my decided opinion yt ye best thing for both would be to agree to an amicable Separation – to this I have had no answer & have no communication of any sort either written or Verbal. I beg at ye same time to have it understood yt if Ld B had express'd a wish to see me, I should not have refused, as I am far from thinking that seeing him necessarily implies that I blame you, or think him in ye right.[17]

But that is not how the warring parties in a separation ever view the situation: one's friends are supposed to take ardent sides, especially if one is related. After receiving her aunt's letter, however, Annabella told her mother that this communication of goodwill "would put me very much in the wrong if I were to cut her without further information – and I must appear to act still more unfairly by circulating such an opinion of her", at least, "till this arbitration is settled".[18] Once it was settled, they were free to vent their moral indignation about the part she had played in the whole sorry business. High Victorianism was rapidly taking over the moral climate of a more relaxed era.

Byron must have appreciated the delicate situation Lady Melbourne was in, and did not embarrass her further despite the depth of his affection for her. He seemed to put her very firmly behind him as part of the price he had to pay; and he seemed only momentarily affected when he heard of her death in April 1818.

By April 17 he was urging Hanson to let him sign the separation agreement because he was itching to be off. On Sunday the 21st the signing took place, with Hobhouse – who had been witness to the marriage – now acting as witness again. As Byron signed, he said dramatically, "I deliver this as Mrs Clermont's act and deed." Friends came in during the day: Lord Holland,* Rogers, Kinnaird, Scrope Davies. The following morning Hanson took the deed to Lady Byron and reported, as he put his hand to his heart, that she looked torn and wan.

Byron sent off a final note to Augusta: "My own Sweet Sis – The deeds are signed – so that is over. – All I have now to beg or desire on the subject is – that you will never mention nor allude to Lady Byron's name again in any shape – or on any occasion – except indispensable business."[19]

Benjamin Constant, Madame de Staël's former lover, dropped in to pay his respects. Isaac Nathan, who had collaborated with Byron on the *Hebrew Melodies*, expressed his deep regret that Byron was choosing to leave for ever, to which the latter replied in astonishment, "Good God! I never had it in contemplation to remain in exile – why do you ask that question?"[20] That evening Kinnaird and his mistress brought over a cake. That cake

---

* Even Lord Holland, according to Hobhouse, believed Byron had committed sodomy with his wife.

provides the most touching domestic quality of anything attached to those last bewildering days.

In the early-morning hours of the 23rd all was agitated bustle in order to get away to Dover before the bailiffs arrived. In addition to Polidori, Byron was taking with him a Swiss called Berger, the ever-loyal Fletcher, and Robert Rushton who would eventually be sent back from Geneva as he had been from Gibraltar in 1809. Byron seemed to want him as some sort of link with the past.

Hobhouse and Polidori travelled in Scrope Davies's chaise, Byron and Davies in the Napoleonic coach. As they departed a crowd had already gathered at the door, and the bailiffs were not far behind, eager to bear away everything that was left in the house. Even his birds and squirrel were taken.

There was a curious air of hilarity about their progress. At Canterbury they stopped to admire the cathedral. At Dover Hobhouse was anxious to have the coach loaded on to the packet as soon as possible lest a bailiff seize it for the unpaid rent on Piccadilly Terrace. The winds were contrary so it was impossible to leave that day. They walked out to see the grave site of Charles Churchill, whose satirical *Rosciad* had been one of the models for *English Bards and Scotch Reviewers*. Byron lay down on his grave and gave the sexton a crown to lay fresh turf on it.

That night much wine was drunk. Hobhouse had difficulty in arousing Byron the following morning and had to warn him that the captain threatened to sail without him. This first modern celebrity, taking Hobhouse's arm, had to pass through a throng of curious spectators. Until now Byron had been in artificially high spirits, but his demeanor changed once the packet glided from shore. He pulled off his cap and waved to his friends until they could no longer distinguish him in the rough seas. "God bless him for a gallant spirit and a kind one," Hobhouse wrote in his diary.

Back in London Hobhouse and Davies encountered the inevitable torrent of gossip. Kinnaird had received anonymous letters that Mrs Marden would be hissed off the stage that night, so they all went off to Drury Lane to support her, but the report proved unfounded.* However, Davies was blackballed from Brooks's on May 7.

Annabella did not return to the boredom of family life at Kirkby Mallory until she was sure Byron had left the country. Lushington went about

---

* Later, however, Mrs Marden's reputation was ruined. She was actually hissed off the stage on June 29; and Byron was sent an anonymous letter asking for some help for her.

London defending Annabella's compromising letter of January 16. On April 30 he reported to her a conversation he had with Walter Scott to whom he admitted that he had given more detail than he should have done, but apparently Scott judiciously refrained from passing judgement. Lady Holland declared herself a friend of both parties. She said what while Byron might not be a devil he was certainly an imp for leaving town without paying the Duchess of Devonshire the rent he owed her. "What an enormity!" Lushington exclaimed. "With this unheard of crime his peccadilloes against you cannot be weighed in the same scale."[21] From Rogers he heard that Byron was planning a leisurely trip through Switzerland and Italy before leaving for Albania. Annabella had warned her new confidante, Mrs George Lamb, not to discuss the marital situation. "Good God," the latter replied, "can I sit by and hear him defended when I know him to be the greatest Villain on earth, and you the most injured and excellent of human beings. I really *cannot*. As to the other person, I do not wish to reveal her faults, for I could almost pity her, when I think how unhappy she must be and I look upon her more as his victim than as his accomplice."[22]

There seemed no possibility, from all that Lushington had heard, that Byron had any intention of returning to England. Nevertheless, Annabella could never be certain of this. There were more than enough people to report the London gossip to her, but what she needed to know was the precise nature of Byron's activities. Augusta would have to be cultivated again.

18

ooooooooooooooo

Exile, August–September 1816

Is thy face like thy mother's, my fair child!
Ada! sole daughter of my house and heart?
When last I saw thy young blue eyes they smiled,
And then we parted, – not as now we part,
But with a hope. –
                Awaking with a start,
The waters heave around me; and on high
The winds lift up their voices: I depart
Whither I know not; but the hour's gone by,
When Albion's lessening shores could grieve or glad mine eye.

                               (*Childe Harold*, III, 1)

While Byron's friends were exerting every effort at damage control in England, Byron was overwhelmed by a sense of great relief – even liberation – as the shores of his country faded from view. Most of the passengers were ill, and he was pleased to find that his sea-legs were as sturdy as ever. With his extraordinary ability to compartmentalise his life, his thoughts turned to the unknown future ahead, and in a sense it promised to hold some of the adventure that he had experienced in 1809. Fletcher and Rushton were still with him, and Hobhouse had promised to follow as soon as possible. They had agreed to meet in Geneva and travel on to Venice or Rome – and then perhaps to Greece. There was no fixed destination in mind. All that mattered was the freedom to move where and when one wished.

Although they landed at two in the morning, Polidori was astonished to find that his employer's health seemed to have improved already. They settled in at an excellent inn, and Polidori recorded in his diary that "As soon as he reached his room, Lord Byron fell like a thunderbolt upon the chambermaid."¹ A typical tourist of the time, in other words.

And indeed from the moment they arrived on the continent they tended to act like any other tourists. On the 26th they set off in the Napoleonic coach (grander, of course, than most conveyances) pulled by four horses, followed by a calèche carrying their luggage. They found the flat landscape boring, and in Antwerp Byron displayed his philistine bias in art. Rubens he disliked intensely: his women all had "red gowns and red shoulders . . . it may all be very fine – and I suppose it must be Art – for – I'll swear – 'tis not Nature."² He was far more interested in Napoleon's naval basins built for the projected invasion of England. Whatever their purpose, the basins were "superb – as all his undertakings were". His admiration for Napoleon had not wavered: "Poor dear Bonaparte!!!"

In Ghent, with *Guide du Voyageur en Europe* in hand, they climbed to the top of the cathedral for a view of the surrounding countryside. By the time they reached Brussels the coach was in sore need of repair. Byron instructed Hobhouse to abuse Baxter as "a *pickpocket*", seemingly forgetful that he had never paid him the £500 he owed him for the vehicle. While waiting for it to be repaired, they put up at the best hotel in town. Here at the Hôtel d'Angleterre an old friend of Mrs Byron's, Major Pryse Lockhart Gordon, called on him. Byron was delighted to chat with the elderly gentleman about his childhood. Since the Battle of Waterloo the previous June Brussels had been bursting with British visitors eager to explore the battlefield; but Byron, with his intense loyalty to Napoleon, had had no intention of joining them.* However, when Gordon offered to act as his guide, he accepted courteously and perhaps more enthusiastically than he was willing to admit.

On May 4 the entire party set off. Gordon recalled that Byron remained silent at first, and then, after surveying the scene, turned to him: "I am not disappointed. I have seen the plains of Marathon and these are as fine."³ This is what his kindly guide would have expected him to say; but to Hobhouse he wrote: "The Plain at Waterloo is a fine one – but not much after Marathon & Troy . . . Perhaps there is some prejudice in this – but I detest the cause & the victors."⁴ His silence on the way back to town had its origin in some reflections far different from those Gordon attributed to him. Unlike his other countrymen, he did not include France on his

---

* Caroline Lamb was among the first of the tourists in 1815. She wrote to Lady Melbourne: "The great amusement at Brussels, indeed the only one except visiting the sick, is to make up large parties & go to the field of battle – & pick up a skull or a gunshot or an old shoe or a letter, and bring it home."

itinerary for he regarded it as an oppressed country, a view he would not have transmitted to Gordon.

That night Mrs Gordon asked him to record some lines in her album. He took it back to the inn with him and the following morning returned with two stanzas, beginning "Stop! – for thy tread is on an Empire's dust." The irony would have been lost on the good lady. This same night he may have written the first draft of the famous lines contrasting the gaiety of the Duchess of Richmond's ball with the carnage that was soon to follow.

> There was a sound of revelry by night,
> And Belgium's capital had gathered then
> Her Beauty and her Chivalry, and bright
> The lamps shone o'er fair women and brave men;
> A thousand hearts beat happily; and when
> Music arose with its voluptuous swell,
> Soft eyes look'd love to eyes which spake again,
> And all went merry as a marriage-bell;
> But hush! hark! a deep sound strikes like a rising knell!
>
> Did ye not hear it? – No; 'twas but the wind,
> Or the car rattling o'er the stony street;
> On with the dance! let joy be unconfined;
> No sleep till morn, when Youth and Pleasure meet
> To chase the glowing Hours with flying feet –
> But, hark! – that heavy sound breaks in once more,
> As if the clouds its echo would repeat;
> And nearer, clearer, deadlier than before!
> Arm! Arm! and out – it is – the cannon's opening roar!
> (*Childe Harold*, III, 21–2)

The novelty of new sights and experiences stirred up in him the impulse to write and, while he was on the surface a gawking tourist, his poetical self reverted to the persona of Childe Harold, the sensitive, withdrawn wanderer. In actual fact the parting words to his daughter were written during the long sixteen-hour crossing to Ostend, lines which were corrected and revised after his arrival in Ghent.

In the letters to Hobhouse which he wrote en route, describing all he saw, he always asked after the welfare of Ada. As they left the flat Flemish countryside behind them, and started up the Rhine, the sublime scenery overwhelmed him.

Where rose the mountains, there to him were friends;
Where roll'd the ocean, thereon was his home.
(*Childe Harold*, III, 13, 109–10)

Fragments of impressions were jotted down, eventually to be organised into a poetic framework reflecting the mature wanderer, who no longer felt any compunction to differentiate between the creator and his creation. When he left England as a young man of twenty-one he had no idea that Greece would make him a poet. Nor did he have any inkling now that in Italy his poetic powers, deepened by maturity and real suffering, would come to their full fruition.

'Tis to create, and in creating live
A being more intense, that we endow
With form our fancy, gaining as we give
The life we image, even as I do now.
(*Childe Harold*, III, 6, 46–50)

Hobhouse was told of a comical incident in Cologne where a furious innkeeper suspected that he was seducing his wife, only to have her innocently walk out one door, while a chambermaid scurried out of Byron's room. Byron's sense of humour was returning; and he took delight in everything he saw. *This* was reality, not bailiffs, lawyers, unforgiving spouses; *those* were all part of the nightmare from which he had awakened. He only wished that Augusta, not the tiresome, sickly Polidori, was there to share the experience with him, and he picked a bunch of violets to send to her. He also expressed gratitude to his old friend for all that he was doing for him in his absence – something unusual in Byron who had always tended to take for granted Hobhouse's efforts on his behalf. He begged for news: "except *one* subject – which I particularly beg never to have mentioned again – unless as far as regards my *child* – & my *child only*."[5]

At nightfall on May 25 they arrived at Sécheron, a mile out of Geneva, where English travellers usually put up at the Hôtel d'Angleterre. Byron registered his age as 100, a detail which Claire Clairmont, who had arrived the previous week with the Shelleys, was quick to pounce on.

I am sorry you are grown so old, indeed I suspected you were 200, from the slowness of your journey. I suppose your venerable age could not bear quicker travelling. Well, heaven send you sweet sleep – I am so happy.

Clare

direct under cover to Shelley for I do not wish to appear either in [?love] or curious.[6]

Byron was more concerned to find a suitable house than an importuning mistress, and the next morning he and Polidori went to look for one at Cologny on the southern side of the lake opposite Sécheron, where he was delighted by a handsome grey stone building surrounded on three sides by a balcony. The Villa Diodati stood on the hillside commanding a magnificent view of the lake and the snow-capped Jura Mountains beyond. Here Milton had stayed in 1639, a literary association that appealed to Byron. The house was somewhat smaller than Byron wanted and the rent rather high, so negotiations for some compromise had to be reached.

He was by now receiving agitated letters from Claire. On his second morning she begged for a meeting. "I have been in this weary hotel this fortnight & it seems so unkind, so cruel, of you to treat me with such marked indifference. Will you go straight up to the top of the house this evening at ½ past seven & I will infallibly be on the landing place & shew you the room."[7] Byron probably complied.

Two days later Byron and Polidori returned from a visit to Diodati after learning that it had been promised to an English family. Stepping out of the boat, they met Claire accompanied by Mary and Shelley. Both poets were notoriously shy, and the first meeting was slightly uncomfortable. But each recognised a gentle, almost effeminate quality in the other, and their shyness vanished as they began to chat about subjects in which they were both interested. Shelley was twenty-three at the time. The son of a baronet, he was almost Byron's equal but had none of the pride of birth that Byron vaunted. He too had led a turbulent life, but of a different sort. At Eton he had been tormented as an eccentric loner, and had been expelled from Oxford for publishing a pamphlet on atheism. He had deserted his wife and children to elope with Mary, daughter of Mary Wollstonecraft and William Godwin. At the point when Byron met him Shelley was on the verge of losing custody of his children because of his immoral life. While there were some remarkable similarities in their circumstances, Shelley had never courted London society where for a time Byron had basked in lionisation. While Byron had admired the dandies, Shelley was totally careless about his appearance. He lived completely in a world of the imagination with no hankering to impress anyone, driven only by a passionate if impractical longing to make the world a better place. Byron, who had always swanked beyond his means, was impressed by Shelley's innate simplicity; and during the three months that they spent together on Lake Geneva, he was to be profoundly influenced by the younger man. They were never to agree on politics, but there was a decency and idealism about Shelley that appealed to tender feelings in Byron that had been smothered by worldly cynicism.

The Shelleys, who were well aware of the liaison with Claire, were also delighted with Byron's unassuming manners. Early in June they both took houses within easy walking distance of each other. The Diodati house became available to Byron after all, and the Shelleys had already settled in a small house below his at Montalègre. It had its own little harbour, and Shelley persuaded Byron to share the cost of a rigged boat. They celebrated the acquisition of Diodati with an excursion on the lake, followed by one of a series of long conversations in which Shelley made some progress in interesting Byron in Wordsworth's pantheism.

Byron had been disappointed not to find any letters from Hobhouse waiting for him when he arrived at Sécheron. Eventually one arrived, dated May 26, full of puzzling gossip about Caroline Lamb and something related to her called *Glenarvon*.

> Yes, B, who would have thought that a new Lord B. should figure in a new Atlantis? and such an Atlantis!! This time she has knocked herself up – the Greys the Jerseys the Lansdownes and of course, the Princess of Madagascar have done with her – You will hardly believe it but there is not the least merit in the book in any way except in a letter beginning "I love you no more" which I suspect to be your's – Indeed she had the impudence to send a paragraph to some paper hinting that the whole novel is from the pen of Lord B. – I do not like to contradict it for fear of selling the book by propagating the lie – Her family are in a great quandry [sic] and know not what to do. I presume she is actually a personal terror to them.[8]

Byron, settling into what promised to be an idyllic summer, asked in bewilderment, "what – & who – the devil is 'Glenarvon.' I know nothing – nor ever heard of such a person."[9] He might not have heard of such a person but since May 9, the London world had been buzzing with the latest sensation, Caroline's *roman à clef.*

Caroline had been behaving outrageously once more. She had injured one of her pages by throwing a hard ball at his head in a pique, an incident that prompted the Melbournes to urge William to seek a separation. Caroline wrote her novel in a single feverish month during the family uproar (it was eventually settled by a temporary reconciliation between husband and wife). People read the book for its malicious portraits of famous London figures such as the Princess of Madagascar, a thinly disguised portrait of Lady Holland who presided over a literary salon of fawning parasites, including a yellow-skinned cadaverous poet (Rogers). Some of these caricatures were close to the mark; and, titillated as the public was by the recognition of familiar figures, it was the revelations about Caroline and Byron that made it a *cause célèbre*. The motto of the first edition was even taken from Byron's *Corsair*:

> He left a name to all succeeding times,
> Link'd with one virtue and a thousand crimes.

The heroine, Calantha, is an irresponsible *ingénue* but basically good compared to the wily hostesses amongst whom she is thrust. She marries Lord Avondale, who begins to neglect her because of her extravagant antics. She is drawn to the irresistible Glenarvon. Hints of indescribable crimes such as murder and kidnapping have been ascribed to him; but even worse (as far as Calantha was concerned) was his fickleness as displayed in fused excerpts from real letters written from Lady Oxford's (Lady Mandeville in the novel) in which Glenarvon bluntly informs his rejected lover that he no longer feels anything for her.

Byron was now so cocooned in his beautiful surroundings that he does not seem even to have been reading *Galignani's Messenger* which published all the English news for British tourists.* Byron told Kinnaird: "of what has passed in England I know but little – & have no desire to know more."[10] When Madame de Staël questioned him about *Glenarvon* a few weeks later, he replied coolly that the portrait could not be authentic since he hadn't sat long enough for it. Hobhouse reported that the novel had rendered "the vicious little author more odious if possible than ever",[11] and that she was being cut by society.**

---

* Established in Paris in 1814 by Giovanni Galignani and his English wife, Anne Parsons, it was something of a gossipy *International Herald Tribune* of its time.

** On June 27 Hobhouse should have been celebrating his thirtieth birthday; but after receiving abusive letters from Lady Caroline Lamb and her mother, he sighed: "Alas! alas! . . . I have read nothing and done nothing. Lord Byron's business has occupied an unreasonable portion of my time, and all to no good" (*Recollections of a Long Life*, I, p.346).

Annabella had been depicted as the prudish heiress whom Glenarvon marries, but she actually took a smug delight in the scandal, even commenting on the moral qualities of the book; and the other "Caro", Mrs George Lamb, found her attitude "very indulgent".[12] But the very day (May 17) that she wrote so charitably to Mrs Lamb, in her own journal she recorded that she thought Lady Caroline had painted too favourable a picture of him: "like all the false and cruel, he must have trembled during his whole career – that fear more and more his ruling principle – rendering him alternately vindictive and servile – that he stooped under the increasing burden of guilt to the vilest arts."[13]

Annabella had no intention of ever putting the past behind her. Driven by her obsessive jealousy, the infamies and indignities to which she had been subjected began to assume a permanent cast and to provide her with a *raison d'être*. Her chief objective in life developed into the quest to humiliate Augusta. If she could not harm her husband, she could at least destroy his alter ego. Forgetful of all Augusta's kindness to her, she had begun to construct a brother and sister allied in sin, probably always laughing behind her back. On March 16, 1816, she told her lawyer that she had observed "every sign of passion . . . She seemed fearful of every word he uttered and fearful of checking him."[14]

Accommodating herself readily to Lushington's advice, she had not written to Augusta since early April. However, in the interval there were endless discussions with Mrs Villiers about how best to proceed in the campaign to save Augusta's soul. Lady Byron bided her time until after Augusta's fifth child was born on May 9 (the same day as the publication of *Glenarvon*). On June 3 Annabella wrote one of her totally ambiguous letters explaining that her coolness had resulted from Augusta's rudeness.* How, Annabella asked, could she believe any of Augusta's professions of devotion to her? Augusta's reaction was eagerly awaited by the plotters. "I think her first feeling will be terror, her second pride," Annabella conjectured. "It is dreadful to remember that this disease of her mind has been increasing constantly since 1813."[15] A bewildered Augusta replied (June 6, 1816) that if she were on her death-bed she would affirm that she had considered Annabella's happiness "above everything else in the world & the tide of public opinion has turned against my brother that the least appearance of coolness on *your* part towards me would injure me most seriously."[16]

* She was referring to Augusta's refusal to shake hands with Selina Doyle at the Wilmots' dinner party since she believed that Selina was responsible for stiffening Annabella's resolve against a reconciliation.

Thus began the systematic destruction of Augusta. After hearing that Byron had arrived in Geneva, his sister told Hodgson (June 10, 1816) that "I am pretty well, only weak & nervous, & no wonder, for none can know *how much* I have suffered from this unhappy business – &, indeed, I have never known a minute's peace, & begin to despair of the future." She went on to tell him that she had agreed to act as intermediary in conveying messages about Ada to Byron, but she was sorry that she had ever become involved in "this most wretched business". "I can't, however, explain all my reasons at this distance, & must console myself by the consciousness of having done my duty, &, to the best of my judgment, all I could for the happiness of *another*." She then added a passage that revealed her fear of Annabella:

Have you by chance, dear Mr H, some letters I wrote in answer to yours, & in *favour* of Lady Byron and her family? If you have, may I request you not yet to destroy them, and to tell me fairly when you write next if you ever heard one word that could detract from *her* merits, or make you think me partial to *his* side of the question? Whatever ideas these questions may suggest pray at present keep to yourself.[7]

The excited Mrs Villiers suggested to Annabella that Augusta's tender feelings towards her brother might be totally obliterated if she were informed that Byron had betrayed her. Annabella's method, however, was shrewdly oblique. Augusta was devastated to be told that *she* had been the cause of Annabella's sufferings. "Tell me – pray – of anything in that which could by possibility atone for the past – in pity – tell it me my dearest A. that I may have one more chance of happiness."[18] If she had been aware that Annabella had entertained any "doubts" about her, she would never have entered her home, she assured her relentless tormentor: "perhaps I did wrong as it was to do so." Augusta was meekly surrendering herself as a hostage to a relentless persecutor.

She was summoned to London to attend the queen on July 11. Two days later Hobhouse, on the eve of his departure for Geneva, called on her to enquire whether she had any messages to send to her brother. This left her in a state of agitated perplexity as she confided to Annabella: "My dear A – I am perfectly unable to decide *how* to act for the best respecting *him* . . . I wish you to reflect on what I had better do – I really *must now* mistrust my own judgment."[19] She called Annabella her "Guardian Angel". It would have been more accurate to describe her as her "Avenging Fury".

What Byron did these women remember, which of his many personas emerge from the pages of their letters? Was Byron no longer Augusta's beloved "baby B", but rather the vicious fiend that his estranged wife described? He is certainly no longer the laughing companionable Byron with whom Augusta spent so many relaxed hours. Nor is he the famous poet whom the young Miss Milbanke praised for his high-minded humanitarianism. For Annabella there was a fixed, immutable memory of Satanism personified, like the unchanging image in a Hieronymous Bosch painting or the fictional immoral character in *Glenarvon*. For Augusta he was a wavering reflection in water, often obliterated by constant shifts of wind. But Byron himself was something distinct from their images. He had been through fire, he had fallen from an object of adulation to a pariah, and his own image of himself was frequently oscillating as he tried to adjust to the altered conditions of his life. This he tried to express in his new canto of *Childe Harold*:

> Thus far have I proceeded in a theme
> Renewed with no kind auspices: – to feel
> We are not what we should have been, and to deem
> We are not what we should be, – and to steel
> The heart against itself . . .
>
> (*Childe Harold*, III, III, 1031–5)

In these circumstances it is understandable that he should be particularly impressionable to the influence of the idealistic, unworldly Shelley.

The sordid intrigue conducted between Annabella, Mrs Villiers, and Annabella's lawyers, was a startling contrast to the tranquil life Byron was enjoying at the Villa Diodati. He soon abandoned his brief forays into Swiss society for the exclusive company of the Shelleys. He was aware that prurient British tourists were scrutinising him through telescopes from the other side of the lake so that he withdrew even more into his self-contained world. Absurd and exaggerated stories about the unconventional household, originating mainly with Henry Brougham then staying in Geneva, were circulated in England.* Nothing could be bad enough to satisfy his detractors.

As for the unconventional household, Polidori was an irritant with his forward ways, but for the moment Byron could tolerate him since his presence prevented Claire from constantly bothering him. She was always

---

* It was a case of people in glass houses. Brougham was involved in an intrigue with the other "Caro", Mrs George Lamb (the former Caroline St Just).

available when Byron needed someone to make fair copies of his poems or to satisfy his sexual urges. With Shelley he could carry on endless intellectual conversations, more stimulating than any he had ever experienced. Byron did not appreciate clever women, and Mary, whom Shelley had always treated as his mental equal, began to feel somewhat neglected. This feeling of exclusion was probably the beginning of the hostility Mary was gradually developing towards him.

Nevertheless, for now there were blissful excursions on the lake which they all enjoyed. The tranquillity of the glorious view that met Byron's eyes every day as he emerged from his bedroom on to the balcony was to have a profound effect on his work. In the past he had tended to hold Wordsworth in contempt, but with Shelley's influence he began to share the same feeling of elevation and serenity imparted by nature to a troubled heart. He later looked back on this period as one of restrained and simple living. His costs were far less than in England, and Douglas Kinnaird, who was now acting as his banker, had advanced him enough to live comfortably. It was years since he had enjoyed regular exercise and fresh air. He had gained considerable weight from heavy drinking during the tension of the separation proceedings, and he now put himself on one of his strict diets. Once more he reverted to a regular routine of writing. On evenings when it was too stormy to venture on the lake, the group would gather in the drawing room at Diodati where, at Byron's suggestion, they each in turn tried to make up ghost stories. On June 17 Byron related an unusual and rather clumsy account of betrayal: two friends, upon embarking together for Greece, made a curious pact. If one died, the other would not reveal his death to anyone. One apparently dies; but the other traveller, upon returning to England, finds his companion very much alive and making love to his sister. Byron jotted down his outline in a few pages but soon abandoned the story, aware that fiction was not his forte, but Polidori was later to make use of the material for *The Vampyre*.

Mary, however, became entranced with the idea of a man-made monster, an idea that haunted her night and day, and was eventually to result in her 1818 masterpiece *Frankenstein*. The subject became too agitating for the sensitive Shelley. One night Byron repeated the lines of Coleridge's *Christabel* (a poem Byron had persuaded Murray to publish), describing the witch's breast: "Hideous, deformed, and pale of hue". Byron had an enormous dramatic gift, and this time his chilling tones were more than effective. Shelley ran shrieking from the room, reviving only after they threw cold water on him. He described how he had imagined a woman whose breasts had eyes instead of nipples.

Shelley and Byron had been planning a leisurely boat trip around the lake, and on the 22nd they set off. Their plan was to visit all the places immortalised by Rousseau, idealised by both men as an independent spirit. Byron claimed to know *La Nouvelle Héloïse* almost by heart, although it is somewhat surprising that he was attracted to such a sentimental work. It was indeed a sacred literary pilgrimage, with Shelley reading the novel as they visited its various locales. Meillerie, Chillon, Clarens, all these places took on a delightful substantiality for them. In the evenings they talked for hours; and one gathers that Byron was very frank in his confidences, for Shelley developed a deep understanding of his fellow poet. Byron had shown great resilience in taking up his pen again, and Shelley must be given credit for encouraging him to defy public opinion by continuing to publish. He found himself intrigued by Byron's personality, but Byron's cynicism was enough to prevent any influence on Shelley's own work. The *Hymn to Intellectual Beauty* was written on this voyage, when Shelley needed only nature to inspire his rarefied imagination. But it was not one of his great creative periods; and Mary later observed that she believed that Shelley's genius had been blocked by his association with Byron that summer.

The voyage was not without incident. When they left Meillerie the lake was calm but suddenly a violent wind blew up, and for a time it looked as though they would be swamped. Byron stripped off his coat and told Shelley to seize an oar. Shelley calmly replied that he could not swim and, with his arms folded, begged Byron not to try to save him. It was an eerie foreboding of his tragic end by drowning in the Gulf of Spezia.

At Chillon both were fascinated by the dungeons and torture chambers in this grim building set almost into the lake. Shelley was appalled by it as a testament to human misery; and Byron fascinated by the story of François Bonnivard who in the sixteenth century had been confined to the lower dungeon where year after year he could hear the water lapping against the walls. At Ouchy where they were detained for two days because of bad weather, Byron rapidly composed *The Prisoner of Chillon* in which Bonnivard is depicted as a symbol of the imprisoned spirit crushed by an airless atmosphere. In Lausanne they also toured the garden where Gibbon had finished *The Decline and Fall of the Roman Empire*, one of Byron's favourite works. He reverently picked some acacia leaves which he later sent to Murray. On July 1 they arrived back at Montalègre after a tour of eight days.

Byron now plunged into the intense work of organising the accumulated stanzas of Canto III of *Childe Harold*, which was finished by late June. Claire was delighted to be asked to make a fair copy for him. Byron had already told Murray that the poem was longer than the other cantos: "& in some parts – it may be – better – but of course of that *I* cannot determine."[20]

On July 21 the Shelley party set off on a tour of Chamonix and Mont Blanc. Before their departure Claire sent him some pitiful entreaties: "I would have come to you tonight if I thought I could be of *any use* to you. If you *want* me or any thing of, or belonging to me I am sure Shelley would come and fetch me if you ask him."[21] But Byron didn't so want. Possibly because of his callous treatment of Claire – and possibly, too, because of things Byron had confided to him during their voyage – on July 17 Shelley wrote to his friend Thomas Love Peacock: "Lord Byron is an exceedingly interesting person, and as such is it not to be regretted that he is a slave to the vilest and most vulgar prejudices, and as mad as the winds."[22]

Byron was correct in his belief that Canto III marked a considerable advance over the earlier poem. Describing his state of mind while writing it, in January 1817 he told Thomas Moore that it was "a fine indistinct piece of poetical desolation, and my favourite. I was half mad during the time of its composition between metaphysics, mountains, lakes, love unextinguishable, thoughts unutterable, and the nightmare of my own delinquencies."[23]

The early part of the poem traces Byron's journey to Geneva, but within days after meeting Shelley, his influence – combined with the Wordsworthian pantheism preached to him by Shelley and the effect of visiting places sacred to Rousseau – began to transform the poem into something entirely new and more profound than anything Byron had ever written before. Canto III in effect has no contextual or emotional connection with the earlier self-conscious youthful outpourings. The narcissism is held in check by an embracive sense of unity with the universe. Some of the greatest and most hopeful lines Byron ever wrote were composed during this period while in daily contact with Shelley; but it is typical of Byron to doubt whether his temperament could ever achieve an indissoluble unity with nature.

> Where rose the mountains, there to him were friends;
> Where roll'd the ocean, thereon was his home;
> Where a blue sky, and glowing clime, extends,
> He had the passion and the power to roam;
> The desert, forest, cavern, breaker's foam,
> Were unto him companionship; they spake
> A mutual language, clearer than the tome
> Of his land's tongue, which he would oft forsake
> For Nature's pages glass'd by sunbeams on the lake.

Like the Chaldean, he could watch the stars,
Till he had peopled them with beings bright
As their own beams; and earth, and earth-born jars,
And human frailties, were forgotten quite:
Could he have kept his spirit to that flight
He had been happy; but this clay will sink
Its spark immortal, envying it the light
To which it mounts, as if to break the link
That keeps us from yon heaven which woos us to its brink.
(*Childe Harold*, III, 13–14)

For the remainder of the month that the Shelleys were away Byron continued to avoid his compatriots. By now Madame de Staël had been able to return to her estate at Coppet between Lausanne and Geneva. In her home territory Byron found her far more palatable and spent many evenings in her literary salon. On his first visit an English lady, Mrs Hervey, on hearing his name announced, fainted away.* Not surprisingly he felt as though he were "some outlandish beast in a rareeshow",[24] and some of the other habitués were not charmed by him. Madame de Staël's son-in-law, the duc de Broglie, found his conversation stilted and artificial; and her second husband, M. de Rocca, a young French officer, on hearing him abuse the people of Geneva, retorted drily: "*Eh! milord, pourquoi donc venez-vous* fourrer *parmi ces honnêtes gens?*" But his wife was very kind to him; and with Byron's need for an older woman in his life, he began to grow very fond of Madame de Staël. Some of the other habitués of her salon irritated him, especially Wilhelm von Schlegel, the great – and self-important – German *littérateur*, but he liked the Abbé de Brême who was the first person to interest him in the idea of Italian freedom.

After finishing *Childe Harold*, Byron's intense creativity did not wane, fuelled as it was by a need to escape from his troubled thoughts. "The Dream" was a recapitulation of his boyish love for Mary Chaworth, and a magnificent poem, "Darkness", is terrifying in its depiction of a universe deprived of light. He found it difficult, however, to write an elegiac poem to Richard Brinsley Sheridan who had died in miserable poverty on July 7. As his remarks to Lady Blessington in 1823 testify, his ability to write anything on this man whom he had loved and admired was inhibited by a strong identification with his poverty and humiliation. "Oh! it was enough

* Mrs Hervey's reaction was excessive in view of the fact that her half-brother, William Beckford, had had to flee England because of a homosexual scandal.

to disgust one with human nature, but above all with the nature of those who, professing liberality, were so little acquainted with its twin-sister generosity."[25]

The Shelley group returned on July 27. The boating parties were resumed, and they were joined in the middle of August by M.G. ("Monk") Lewis who encouraged another round of discussion on ghosts.* Lewis also gave an impressive recital of portions of the first part of Goethe's *Faust* which was to have a strong influence on Byron's own *Manfred*. Mary's journal records Byron and Shelley sitting companionably on a wall chatting. But the group was breaking up. Shelley's financial problems and Claire's pregnancy, which was now apparent, made their return to England imperative. Byron finally agreed to discuss the child's future with Claire. At first he suggested that it be put in Augusta's care. Claire objected on the grounds that a child needed its natural mother in its early years. Shelley generously offered to look after Claire during her confinement. Byron then would bring up the child in Europe, and conceded that Claire could visit it regularly, disguised as an aunt. There was a vague agreement that they would all meet in Italy in the summer of 1817.

Claire, after seeing Byron for the last time on August 25, wrote tearfully: "Farewell my dearest dear Lord Byron. Now don't laugh or smile in your little proud way for it is very wrong for you to read this merrily which I write in tears . . . dearest I shall love you to the end of my life & nobody else, think of me as one whose affection you can count on."[26] It was unfortunate that Byron could not love a woman who genuinely loved him; and even if he had, his pride would have prevented his allying himself with someone so far beneath him in birth. His subsequent treatment of her was to kill her love and eventually to estrange the Shelleys from him.

On August 26 Hobhouse and Scrope Davies finally arrived. They found Byron in low spirits, but he made a real effort to mask his melancholy thoughts. The most memorable news of their journey was their meeting in Calais with Beau Brummell, who had been forced to flee England because of his debts, and they had been astounded to find him sitting in a greatcoat in a common tavern. His fate and that of Sheridan reinforced Byron's determination to stay in Europe where he could afford to live in a reasonable way.

The unpoetic Hobhouse was shown the manuscript of the new poem; and he commented in his journal that it was "very fine in parts but I doubt whether I like it so much as his first cantos – There is an air of mystery &

---

* His nickname was derived from his Gothic novel, *The Monk* (1796).

metaphysics about it."[27] Shelley promised to deliver the manuscript to Murray. The same day as the departure of the Shelley party, Byron, Davies, and Hobhouse set off on an excursion to Mont Blanc. In one of the inns where they stayed they found a register in which Shelley had inscribed the Greek words for atheist and philanthropist opposite his name; and Byron, thinking to do him a favour, scratched out the entry. At Chamonix he collected semi-precious stones for Ada, Augusta, and the Leigh children, which he would send back to England with Scrope.

When they returned to Cologny there was greater leisure for Byron's friends to tell him frankly about the sort of stories that were circulating in England about his activities in Switzerland: to wit, that he was having relations with both Claire and Mary and with Rushton as well. To put Augusta's mind at rest about him, Hobhouse sent her a report that "your excellent relative is living with the strictest attention to decorum, and free from all offence, either to God, or man, or woman . . . A considerable change has taken place in his health; no brandy, no very late hours, no quarts of magnesia, nor deluges of soda water. Neither passion nor perverseness, even the scream has died away."[28] Byron, who had not heard from his sister for over a month, also assured her that the only liaison he had had was with "a foolish girl" who had thrown herself at him, and he couldn't very well resist her after she had travelled 600 miles in pursuit of him.[29]

Byron seemed relatively tranquil, but his heart yearned for Augusta who represented the only emotional centre he had on this earth. During those last weeks of July 1816 he poured out his desolation in "Epistle to Augusta", a poem he did *not* show to Hobhouse. The first stanza reads:

> My Sister – my sweet Sister – if a name
>   Dearer and purer were – it should be thine.
> Mountains and Seas divide us – but I claim
>   No tears – but tenderness to answer mine:
> Go where I will, to me thou art the same –
>   A loved regret which I would not resign –
> There yet are two things in my destiny
> A world to roam through – and a home with thee.
>
> (*Works*, IV, p. 35)

This poem Shelley also carried with him to England, but with instructions that it was to be published only with Mrs Leigh's permission.*

---

* It was first printed in Moore's *Life* in 1830.

The visits to Coppet continued, with Hobhouse now accompanying him. Byron did not deter Madame de Staël from making some gestures towards effecting a reconciliation with Annabella, but she could not have chosen a worse emissary than Lady Romilly, wife of Sir Samuel Romilly, who had betrayed Byron in not honouring his retainer during the separation proceedings. Madame de Staël heard that Annabella was ill and suggested that it might be helpful if Byron could send her some lines saying how sorry he was to hear this.* Byron replied: "To say that I am merely *sorry* to hear of Lady B's illness is to say nothing – but she has herself deprived me of the right to express more. – The separation may have been *my fault* – but it was *her* choice. – I tried all means to prevent – and would do as much & more to end it, – a word would do so – but it does not rest with me to pronounce it."[30] He added that he still loved her – but apart from bitterness, and a sense of having been humiliated, it is unlikely that he had any idea how he felt about her any more. Brougham, who ran into him one night at Madame de Staël's, warned Annabella:

I think it very possible it may only be another device to put you if possible in the wrong & make people believe that the separation rests with you. But it is also possible that he may be feeling the annoyance attending his situation, & may wish to regain some footing of esteem in Society. He may find reports spreading and wish to give them a refutation by having once more your countenance. Whatever his motive may be, I cannot fancy for a moment that it is a good one.[31]

At the time Annabella was staying at Lowestoft, and the letter was directed to Kirkby Mallory where Lady Noel opened and read it. She then warned her daughter not to confide in Augusta: "You know my Love, that I am naturally of an apprehensive disposition, and We have so much *wicked cunning* to encounter that You cannot be *too cautious*. Once more take care of + [Augusta] – if I know any thing of human nature, She *does* and must *hate You*."[32]

After receiving the letter from Madame de Staël, in September Annabella reported to Colonel Doyle that she felt it was a cynical act on Madame de Staël's part, since both authors were puffing each other in their works. When it was made clear that Annabella remained absolutely adamant that no reconciliation was possible, Byron poured his fury into

---

* A great hypochondriac, Annabella had nothing worse than a bilious attack.

"Lines on Hearing That Lady Byron Was Ill", in which he described her as "a moral Clytemnestra".

> I am too well avenged! – but 'twas my right;
> Whate'er my sins might be, *thou* wert not sent
> To be the Nemesis who should requite –
> Nor did Heaven choose so near an instrument.
>
> *(Works*, IV, p. 44)

Byron had no idea how close he was to the mark.

On September 5 Davies departed for England, taking Rushton with him. (It is possible that Rushton's disappearance from the scene was an attempt to dispel gossip.) Byron and Hobhouse were planning an ambitious journey over the Bernese Oberland, an endeavour in a way to recapture the spirit of adventure they had shared in Epirus in 1809. Before leaving, Byron finally discharged Polidori, who had been hired as a physician and ended up as a nuisance. From Augusta Byron had heard that Murray's wages at Newstead had been cut off by the Claughton negotiations, and he instructed Hanson that they be reinstated immediately – "poor old Man". He assured Hanson that he could not be easy in his mind until he knew this had been done. Concern for his retainers, bitterness towards his wife, longing for Augusta – these made up the amalgam of Byron's feelings.

He continued to be puzzled by Augusta's incoherent letters, and he attributed her apparent distress to Caroline Lamb's trouble-making. On August 27 he pleaded with her: "do not be uneasy – do not hate yourself – if you hate either let it be *me* – but do not – it would kill me – we are the last persons in the world – who ought – or could cease to love one another." On September 8, in reply to her comment that Lady Byron had been very kind to her, Byron remarked tersely, "I am glad she has the heart & the discernment to be still *your* friend – you was ever so to her."

Byron's faith in Augusta was so unshakeable that he still did not suspect the truth. By the time Augusta received this letter, Annabella's triumph seemed complete. If Byron had known what was transpiring, *his* devastation would have been complete.

As early as July Annabella had informed her supporter Colonel Doyle of her intention of extracting a confession from Augusta. Doyle warned her that her undertaking was "attended with gt risk", but if she could secure "an acknowledgement of the fact, even prior to your marriage, I shall be most happy that it has taken place".[33] Annabella was urging Augusta to promise never to see Byron again. She tried to poison her mind against him even further by reminding her that Byron apparently had designs on her daughter Georgy. (Her only evidence was a remark Byron had made in jest.) Surely Augusta must see, Annabella argued, that Byron, by betraying her, was not to be trusted? The miserable woman, torn between her affection for her brother and her fear of Annabella, replied (August 5, 1816) that she had "*long* felt that he has not been my friend – but from my heart I forgive him . . . nothing should induce me to see him again so frequently or in the way I have done." Nevertheless, she could not bring herself to say "*I will never see you again.*"[34]

Annabella realised that she must have a direct confrontation in order to achieve total capitulation.

19

○○○○○○○○○○○○○

To Italy, 1816

Byron's indolent nature was roused to adventure by Hobhouse who was eager for an excursion into the high Alps. Early in the morning of September 17 they set off in two carriages for the Bernese Oberland. Accompanied by their servants, they followed the winding lakeside road past Coppet and Lausanne to Ouchy where Byron stayed for a second time at l'Hôtel de l'Ancre. While Hobhouse went out for dinner, Byron remained in his room and wrote to Augusta. He was feeling desolate. Unable to resist breaking his own resolution not to speak of his wife, he could not restrain himself from pouring out his bitterness. No one, he asserted dramatically, could have inflicted more torture on another human being than she had done to him. Augusta was the only one he could count on. Could she not think of some way of bringing one or two of her children on a short tour of France the following spring? If she could manage it, he would return from any distance to join her. In a passage that would cause Augusta only further grief from Annabella he cried:

> What a fool I was to marry – and *you* not very wise – my dear – we might have lived so single and so happy – as old maids and bachelors; I shall never find any one like you – nor you (vain as it might seem) like me. We are just formed to pass our lives together, and therefore – we – at least – I – am by a crowd of circumstances removed from the only being who could ever have loved me, or whom I can unmixedly feel attached to.
>
> Had you been a Nun – and I a Monk – that we might have talked through a grate instead of across the sea – no matter – my voice and my heart are
>
> ever thine
B¹

But Byron could move swiftly from one mood to another. The next day was exceptionally fine, the lake calm, and Mont Blanc clearly visible against the dazzling sky. As they moved through sublime scenery, his spirits lifted. At Chillon they were amused, in passing an English carriage, to notice its female occupant sound asleep – typical of British insensitivity, Byron muttered.

He started keeping an Alpine journal for Augusta, but in the evenings, drowsy from the mountain air, he could hardly keep his eyes open. He was re-peopling his mind with nature, banishing for the moment the sombre thoughts that had been disturbing him. They climbed the Dent de Jaman to find a lake, "the very nipple in the bosom of the mountain". They were impressed by the air of freedom with which the people carried themselves. On the 22nd they were caught in a fierce storm reminiscent of their experience passing into Albania in 1809. The savage peaks and Alpine valleys were "wonderful – & indescribable". By horseback, mule, and on foot they travelled on, totally enveloped in their surroundings. Byron was moved to write some of the most wonderful prose of his life when confronted with the sublimity of the Jungfrau, and the impressions he was absorbing were to be incorporated into a long poetic drama, *Manfred*, which he had started the previous month. On the 29th, as they started back, Byron's elation evaporated and he sank back into the old feelings of desolation which he believed he would carry with him through life. There was no way he could divest himself of his "wretched identity", a creature doomed to wander the earth like the tormented heroes of his oriental tales. Life was imitating art. He bought a very ugly mongrel for company. His love of animals was rooted in their unwavering constancy. Non-judgemental and uncomplicated, they could love and be loved, something Byron found rather difficult in his relations with women.

At Diodati letters from England awaited them. Douglas Kinnaird had become not only Byron's banker, but his literary agent. In the past, Byron had airily passed over the copyrights of his works to Dallas or had left them in Murray's hands, but now with the hard-headed Kinnaird in charge, the two Scots negotiated a wary agreement. Kinnaird rejected Murray's original offer of £1,500 for *Childe Harold* and *The Prisoner of Chillon*, finally settling for £2,000. Murray had been delighted to receive Canto III from Shelley, and had been even more pleased to hear from Gifford that it was the best thing Byron had written to date.

Shelley wrote that he had also talked with Kinnaird. He heard from him that Lady Byron had recovered her health and was living with Augusta, which disproved "the only important calumny that ever was advanced against you" (apparently Byron had not confided completely in Shelley). As for the calumnies spread by Caroline Lamb, they were both extravagant and silly. It was only to be expected that a superior being such as Byron should be the victim of "the fickle multitude". In an attempt to encourage Byron, Shelley urged him to undertake some great subject like the French Revolution. "I do not know how great an intellectual compass you are destined to fill. I only know that your powers are astonishingly great, and that they ought to be exerted to the full extent."[2]

Shelley at this point made a will, in which Byron was appointed one of the trustees. He and Mary were now living in Bath with Claire who had taken the name Mrs Clairmont as she waited for the birth of the child. To her former lover she wrote: "Don't look cross at this letter because perhaps by the same post you expected one from Mrs Leigh & have not got it."[3]

The misinformation about Augusta living with Annabella was based on the fact that it was generally known that they were seeing each other frequently in London where Lady Byron had arrived at the end of August. It was more than ironical and only slightly less than tragic that Byron was compiling his Alpine journal during the very period when Augusta was capitulating completely to the woman whom he regarded as his greatest enemy. Byron's need to see Augusta as his alter ego was a narcissistic projection; in reality she was goodhearted but shallow and wavering, a puppet on a string. The crucial meeting between the two women took place on September 1 when apparently Lady Byron bullied the erring woman into some kind of confession. It is curious that Annabella did not draw up some kind of *aide-mémoire* as she had done during her interview with Caroline Lamb; but that Augusta actually admitted a sexual relationship seems incontrovertible from the subsequent letters Annabella wrote to her lawyers and to her partner in conspiracy, Mrs Villiers. Lushington now believed that they had sufficient evidence to frighten Byron if he attempted, for example, to assume custody of Ada.

There was also a new note of terror in Augusta's letters. She revealed that the only time Byron had shown real remorse was at their final parting. During the year of the marriage, she said, she had often expressed her anxiety that his wife must suspect something, but, Lady Byron told Lushington, "He reassured her when these doubts occurred – & she seems ["both seem" crossed out] to have acted upon the principle that what could be concealed from me was no injury."[4]

On September 17, three days after Augusta's return to Six Mile Bottom, she abjectly thanked her "Guardian Angel" for all her kind thoughts: "God knows – I trust – that I am anxious to make every atonement."[5] She was terrified that Byron would return in the spring, as he had hinted, and even more terrified that he would discover that she had been showing his letters to his wife: "don't for heaven's sake," she begged Annabella, "in *any* way let it travel around to *him* that you have seen his letters – you can't be *too* cautious for it's certain he would never forgive me – & [she added disingenuously] perhaps laying a trap for me." Augusta admitted that she had replied to his letter in a kindly way. "I hope & think that *whatever* happened this feeling towards him will never forsake him." It would, she argued, have more effect on him than reproaches would. "Now dear A – I hope all this was not wrong – but I beg you to advise me as to my next letter . . . Tell me what I can say best for *you* & for *myself*."[6]

Augusta's attitude wasn't at all satisfactory to the "Guardian Angel". As Annabella told Mrs Villiers, it was abundantly clear that Byron and his sister still harboured criminal feelings for each other, and Augusta must learn to hate Byron as fiercely as she herself now hated him. Augusta's mentor sternly lectured her that she must be absolutely determined never to be on affectionate terms with her brother again. "Whenever you have any communication you question your own heart most scrupulously whether there be simply your objects – whether you are not deceived by the wish of still being dear to him, or by the dread of those consequences for *his* displeasure, which led you to receive God's anger."[7]

What a task Annabella had set for herself! In addition to her nest of vipers – Mrs Villiers, Mrs George Lamb, Selina Doyle, and other sundry females – there was a whole network of people with whom she had to keep open the lines of communication in order to obtain news of Byron: Hobhouse and Davies through her intermediary, Augusta; Murray; Doyle and Lushington; and any British visitors returning from the continent who might have picked up some gossip. People praised the injured wife for her commendable silence about the separation, but the truth of the matter was that she never stopped talking about it. Even she was sometimes exhausted by her holy war. "It requires more than ordinary exertion to keep up the character of a saint," she lamented to Mrs Villiers.[8]

Meanwhile Byron in Switzerland, totally unaware of all this intrigue, was turning his head towards an entirely new life. Shortly before he and Hobhouse set off on their tour of the Bernese Oberland two young Greek brothers from the island of Zante, who had been studying at the University of Padua, came to dine with them. Nicolas and Francis Karvellas talked to them enthusiastically about the coming revolution in Greece. Byron was interested; and he conceived a rather vague plan of travelling to Greece after staying in Venice for a time.

On October 3 he dined with Madame de Staël and bade her an affectionate and grateful farewell. Two days later the Napoleonic coach moved out of the forecourt of the Villa Diodati and up the hill to the road leading along the southern shore of the lake. When the owner arrived later in the day he was disappointed to find that his famous tenant had burned all the scraps of paper on which he had been writing.

Both Hobhouse and Byron were eager to see the famous military road Napoleon had built over the Simplon Pass into Italy. As always they were impressed by his amazing engineering skills. Skirting innumerable precipices, this extraordinary road was constructed by 3,000 men over a period of nearly four years. It would have been dangerous to cross any later in the month as it could be blanketed by sudden falls of snow.

On the 10th they descended into Italy. They were on the alert for *banditti*, disbanded soldiers who were roaming the countryside, demanding money from travellers. It added a little *frisson* to their trip. After the cleanliness of Switzerland they were struck by the immediate difference in the shabby inn where they spent their first night at Ornavasso. Here Berger, the Swiss servant, slept in the coach in order to watch the luggage, and Hobhouse and Byron had their loaded pistols beside them. It was almost like the old days in Greece.

Expecting – even hoping – any minute to be waylaid, the following morning they set out for Lago Maggiore, where the principal attraction for the travellers was not the enchanting scenery – it was too artificial for Byron's taste – but the sight of the room in which Napoleon had slept in the lovely little Borromean Isola Bella, and a tree on which, just before the Battle of Marengo, Napoleon had carved with his knife the word "Battaglia". On the 12th they crossed the Lombardy plain, at that time not enveloped in smog, but covered by stands of acacia and tulip trees. Nevertheless, it was flat, very flat, so Byron dozed until they came within sight of Milan where they were distressed to find a triumphal entry arch to Napoleon left unfinished. This magnificent structure had been intended as the culmination of the Simplon route.

At first glance, Milan did not look like a city of 130,000 people. They grumbled, too, at the discomfort of the hotel. However, within a day or so Byron's view of the city changed dramatically. He wrote to Murray that it was a slightly inferior version of Seville, and the wedding-cake cathedral he found superb. What really disposed Byron favourably to the city was his experience at La Scala where he and Hobhouse took a box. The opera was, they discovered, even more of an opportunity for socialising than in London. People never stopped talking, even played cards, and visited from box to box. On their first evening at the opera they were visited by the Karvellas brothers who had preceded them from Geneva, but the visitor they were most delighted to see was Monsignore Ludovico dc Brême whom Byron had met at Coppet. De Brême, it was clear, was determined that their visit should be pleasant and was eager to introduce them to all the interesting people in the city. It was soon clear to both Hobhouse and Byron that in Italy Byron would receive the sort of respect he had never been able to elicit in England. Exile began to assume a certain curious allure.

Dutifully he looked at the pictures in the Brera but admitted "of painting I know nothing." The Ambrosian Library offered the most interest to him although the keepers were disappointed that they could not induce him to inspect treasures such as manuscripts by Leonardo da Vinci. Again and again he returned to read the love letters exchanged between Lucretia Borgia and Cardinal Bembo. To see their actual handwriting revivified their relationship for Byron – any biographer knows how remarkable this experience of immediacy is – and he tried unsuccessfully to persuade the curators to give him some copies. To Augusta he conveyed his excitement. The letters, he said, were "so pretty & so loving that it makes one wretched not to have been born sooner to have at least seen her. And pray what do you think is one of her *signatures*? – why this + a Cross – which she says 'is to stand for her name &c.' Is not this amusing? I suppose you know that she was a famous beauty; & famous for the use she made of it."[9] Byron was totally unaware that letters such as these would inflame his wife to such a degree that they would only succeed in making Augusta withdraw further and further from him. As for his fascination with Lucretia – which reminded him of another passion – he secretly went off with one of her golden hairs.

Most of his evenings were spent discussing politics and literature. Di Breme* introduced him to the most famous Italian man of letters of the time, the poet Vincenzo Monti, but Byron was also warned that Monti was notorious for being a political opportunist. An even more famous literary figure – although yet still relatively unknown – was Henri Beyle, later to be known as Stendhal. After a brief military career in the French army, Beyle had retired on half pay to Milan where people found him interesting because he had been close to Napoleon on his retreat from Moscow. A passionate admirer of *Lara*, Beyle was thrilled to meet Byron in di Breme's box one evening. A close observer of men, Beyle's recollections of Byron

---

* In France, he was known as de Brême; in Italy di Breme.

reveal both admiration and envy. It was clear to him that Byron preferred male company and made no attempt to pursue the ladies. He delighted in his enthusiastic discussions about literature and Italian freedom which formed a running colloquy in di Breme's box; but Beyle was also disappointed by Byron's personal vanity (clearly Beau Brummell was one of his heroes) and his excessive pride in his rank. Beyle realised that Byron did not appreciate being compared to Rousseau because Rousseau was the son of a clock-maker. Byron shared Beyle's adulation of Napoleon and encouraged him to talk of his idol. Beyle detected a strong sense of identification with the fallen titan.

Beyle believed that this was a man whose true self could never be developed because of his self-importance. Byron's perpetual self-absorption, Beyle believed, insulated him from a real understanding of the human heart. He noticed, too, the swift changes in mood and his sensitivity about his deformed foot. One evening as he was forced to drag his foot across a large room, his dark countenance convinced the onlookers that he had indeed committed some terrible crime about which he was constantly dropping hints. In later years, when people recalled their memories of Byron, they were inclined to exaggerate the length of time they had known him. According to Beyle, their acquaintance lasted "several months", whereas Byron was in Milan for only three weeks.

Byron continued to write to Augusta more frequently than ever and was puzzled when he did not hear from her. He knew that it could not have been because the post was impeded, since he was receiving other letters regularly from England, and "my unfortunate circumstances perhaps make me feel more keenly anything which looks like neglect" (October 26, 1816). The reason for the silence was, of course, Annabella's menacing presence in the background. By October 18 Lady Byron was telling her unpleasant ally that "I entirely agree with you in thinking that a little rousing of fear will occasionally be necessary – I have caused her to write to him in such a manner as to prove it impossible for her to accompany him abroad . . . anger may follow."[10]

On October 28 Byron was totally bewildered at last to receive a letter from Augusta (dated October 12) in which she intimated that it would be impossible for her to see him if he returned to England in the spring.

> I really do not & cannot understand [Byron wrote] all the mysteries & alarms in your letters & more particularly in the last. All I know is – that no human power short of destruction – shall prevent me from seeing you when – where – & how – I may please – according to time

& circumstance; that you are the only comfort (except the remote possibility of my daughter's being so) left me in prospect in existence, and that I can bear the rest – so that you remain; but anything which is to divide us would drive me quite out of my senses."

In this same letter he remarked, "Miss Milbanke appears in all respects to have been formed for my destruction." Believing totally in Augusta's loyalty, he still had no inkling that the agent of his destruction would read this. On November 1, the day before his departure from Milan, he also wrote to his wife himself. He assured her that "if there were a means of becoming reunited to you I would embrace it – and that I am very wretched." One might wonder why Byron suddenly put his pride aside to plead for a reconciliation. He sensed that his destination, Venice, would mark a decisive turning-point in his life, and that once there his course would be irrevocably altered. In a panic he reached out to grasp once more some link with familiarity. Annabella could not resist writing a draft reply recounting the horrors of her marriage, and a defence of her steadfastness: "The heart of hope was withered, but Forgiveness towards the man who had triumphed in my ruin became my passion, the vital principle of my love."[12] The letter was never sent, but her various correspondents benefited from quoted extracts.

If Annabella had Mrs Villiers as a confidante, Augusta had Francis Hodgson. After seeing Annabella and her daughter, Augusta told him that while Ada resembled her mother more than Byron, "still there is a look. I never saw a more healthy little thing. It was a melancholy pleasure to see Lady B for I had suffered great uneasiness of which I had given you hints."[13] Murray had shown Annabella Canto III of *Childe Harold* which he intended to publish in mid-November and Augusta trembled lest it contain any embarrassing domestic details. Another letter from Augusta to Hodgson was clearly contrived as protection if Annabella appeared menacing again.

in his own *mind* there *were* and *are* recollections, fatal to his peace, and which would have prevented his being happy with any woman whose excellence equalled or approached that of Lady B, from the consciousness of being unworthy of it. Nothing could or can remedy this fatal cause but the consolation to be derived from religion, of which, alas! dear Mr H, our beloved B, is, I fear, destitute . . . His friends (who for the most part are more or less deceived about him) argue thus: "Oh! had he married a woman of the world, she would have let him have his own way, and have had hers – and they would have done very well"; and this is worldly reasoning. I happen to know that dear Lady B would have sacrificed all her own tastes and pursuits, everything but her *duty*, to make him happy; but all was in vain; it is indeed a heart-breaking thought! And worse than all, not all my affection or anxiety can be of either use or comfort to him . . . I am sure it is very useless to express my feelings towards him – I *never* could. Pray read over the 17th, 18th, and 19th stanzas of "Lara"; they are quite wonderfully *resemblant*. Sometimes it strikes me he must be of *two* minds. Such a mixture of blindness and perception!*[14]

While Byron might have been feeling bereft, once the travellers set off on November 2, they were soon absorbed in new sights and impressions. From Verona he wrote to Augusta again: "just to keep you out of (or *in*) a fuss about baby B."[15] He and Hobhouse inspected the amphitheatre and a tomb which they were assured was that of the Capulets. In Vicenza and the surrounding area they visited the great Palladian villas, Rotondo and Barbaro. They had intended to spend some time in Padua where Hobhouse was eager to inspect the famous university, but Byron could not wait to get to Venice. On the 10th they drove along the Brenta to Mestre where they left the carriages at an inn. Pouring rain was not the most romantic introduction to Venice and for two hours they could see nothing from the hearse-like black box of their gondola except stakes in the water. And then suddenly they stopped at the landing of the Gran-Bretagna and were shown up a magnificent flight of stairs into great rooms whose chipped gilding and faded silk indicated marks of better days.

The following day Byron fell completely under the spell of the magical

---

* Stanza 18 begins:
> There was in him a vital scorn of all:
> As if the worst had fall'n which could befall
> He stood a stranger in this breathing world,
> An erring spirit from another hurled;
> A thing of dark imaginings, that shaped
> By choice the perils he by chance escaped;
> But 'scaped in vain, for in their memory yet
> His mind would half exult and half regret:
> With more capacity for love than earth
> Bestows on most of mortal mould and birth,
> His early dreams of good outstripp'd the truth,
> And troubled manhood followed baffled youth . . .

city, gliding through its silent canals, exploring its tucked-away little squares. It was pure theatre, and Byron, who had always preferred drama to life, knew that this would be his exquisite stage. There was something sad and dilapidated about the city, now once again under the control of the Austrians, but Byron rather liked seediness, certainly far preferable to the staid prosperity of Geneva.

If distorted stories about him were received in England, Byron too was beginning to hear disturbing rumours. He was told by someone who had heard from Lady Melbourne that his wife was planning to take Ada to the continent for the winter. Byron was mortified that he had humiliated himself by seeking a reconciliation; and now wrote furiously to Augusta that under no conditions was his daughter to leave England: "I trust I shall not be obliged to take *legal measures* to prevent such an occurrence."[6] Augusta in turn reported his instructions to Annabella, a proposal "which he *perverts* as he always does *every* thing – I've always found it so."[7] She also remarked that she found it strange that he should object to females travelling, after enthusiastically urging her and her daughters to join him on the continent. Augusta was to be his ultimate betrayer.

20

ooooooooooooooo

Anteroom to the East, 1816–17

The British public was anticipating the third canto of *Childe Harold* with avid curiosity. Under the circumstances Murray felt compelled to submit this new poem as well as the miscellaneous poetry Byron had written in Geneva to Lady Byron for secret inspection. One of the poems was the "Epistle to Augusta" beginning "My sister, my sweet sister". Murray wanted Annabella to examine the poetry, not because of the allusions to Augusta, but because of Byron's lament about his wife's unforgiving nature and his fear that Ada might be brought up to hate him. Annabella found the lines about herself "cruel and cold, but with such a semblance to make *me* appear so, and to attract all sympathy to himself".[1]

Actually the final decision about the removal of the "Epistle" remained with Augusta. (Byron, of course, was in total ignorance of the fact that Murray was consulting these women.) Murray called upon Augusta at St James's Palace; and while she thought the poem beautiful, she expressed uncertainty about what decision to take. After hearing from "some lady" (Annabella) that the "Lines" confirmed "the atrocious things" that were being said of her, she consulted Scrope Davies who then wrote to Murray requesting that the poem be suppressed.

As for the new canto of *Childe Harold*, Augusta decided that publication was desirable, especially as Byron had sent emphatic warnings that nothing was to be omitted. It is doubtful if Murray could have been induced to remove anything within the canto itself since he was a very shrewd businessman who knew full well what sort of salacious detail would attract the public.

Canto III was published on November 18, 1816, and Murray soon reported gleefully that he had sold 7,000 copies.* Byron fulfilled his

---

* On December 5 a slim volume, *The Prisoner of Chillon, and Other Poems*, was published. This volume included the "Stanzas to Augusta", but the "Epistle to Augusta" did not appear until Moore published his posthumous life of Byron in 1830.

readers' expectations by a complete disclosure of a broken heart and an account of his emotional pilgrimage to re-create himself. He seemed totally unaware of what distress stanza 55 might cause his sister.

> And there was one soft breast, as hath been said,
> Which unto his was bound by stronger ties
> Than the church links withal; and, though unwed,
> *That* love was pure, and, far above disguise,
> Had stood the test of mortal enmities
> Still undivided, and cemented more
> By peril, dreaded most in female eyes;
> But this was firm, and from a foreign shore
> Well to that heart might his these absent greetings pour!

Just before publication, on November 14, Augusta confided to Hodgson: "I *quite dread* the *Poems* – so afraid of their renewing unpleasant recollections in the public mind, and containing bitterness towards her who has already suffered so much."[2] The unsuspecting Byron, meanwhile, was asking her: "I want to know if you don't think them very fine & all that – Goosey my love – don't they make you 'put your finger in eye'? You have no idea of my thorough wretchedness from the day of my parting from you till nearly a month ago – though I struggled against it with some strength – at present I am better" (December 18, 1816).

Why, one might ask, did Augusta not simply write to her brother and ask him not to publish such affectionate outpourings that permitted the public to put the worst possible construction on them? The answer might be that she was flattered by his devotion, and took a certain malicious pleasure in fomenting jealousy in Annabella. The ambivalence of her feelings (as she reveals in her more forthright letters to Hodgson) was such that she seemed willing to pay the price of Annabella's animosity as well as suffer the anxiety about how she could handle Byron's possible return.

Annabella of course seized on stanza 55 to try to terrorise Augusta. On December 22 Augusta assured her that she had heard nothing but praise for the poem, and no one had even mentioned stanza 55. "Depend on one thing – dearest A – there are those who – for what reasons I know not – will make out every thing in an ill natured way against me."[3]

To Lady Anne Barnard, Annabella wrote:

Nothing has contributed more to the misunderstanding of his real character than the lonely grandeur in which he poetically invests it –

and his affectation of being *above* mankind, when in fact he exists almost in their voice and begs from them the daily bread of his vanity . . . he has bound himself to those he most despises and by the servile ties of fear.[4]

While the women in England were twittering with *Schadenfreude* or fear, Byron was beginning to make a pleasant new life for himself: "thank Heaven above & woman beneath". His only irritation was Sir Ralph Noel's evasive answer to Hanson that there were no plans "at present" to take Ada abroad, a reply Byron found "insolent & equivocal".[5] He might be compelled to take *measures*, Byron warned Augusta. He had no idea that the decision to make his child a Ward of Chancery, which had been instigated secretly during the separation proceedings, had already been implemented. As for his other imminent progeny, he continued to ignore Claire's pleas that he assure her that he would be "very pleased to have a little baby of which you will take great care".[6] The ever-solicitous Shelley felt impelled to ask him at least to send a kind message to her through him – but this too was ignored.

A critical article on Coleridge's *Christabel* appeared in the October *Edinburgh Review* in which Byron was berated for his admiration of the poem. "Great as the noble bard's merits undoubtedly are in poetry, some of his latest *publications* dispose us to distrust his authority, where the question is what ought to meet the public eye; and the works before us afford an additional proof, that his judgment on such matters is not absolutely to be relied on." Byron, so unlike his old self, brushed off the attack on him, concerned only about Coleridge: "I am very sorry that J[effrey] has attacked him, because, poor fellow, it will hurt his mind and pocket. As for me, he's welcome – I shall never think less of J[effrey] for any thing he may say against me or mine in future."[7]

Walter Scott, on the other hand, wrote a highly favourable anonymous review of *Childe Harold*. Lady Byron immediately turned to Murray to enquire if he knew who the reviewer was. She asked Joanna Baillie if she would write to Scott, who was a close friend, emphasising to Scott how painful the poem had been to Lady Byron. Scott refused to become implicated in the domestic situation. It was unfortunate that he and Byron never had the opportunity to get to know each other better, for, as Scott explained to Murray, "No one can honour Lord Byron's poems more than I do and no one has so great a wish to love him personally though personally we had not the means of becoming very intimate."[8]

Byron did not receive the *Quarterly* until the beginning of March 1817, and its review it was a splendid confirmation that the new canto was, as he believed, the best work he had done to date, and also reassurance that his poetry had survived the scandal of the separation. This renewed sense of confidence was to play no small part in his prodigious output during his Venice period, particularly in the risks he took with fresh experimentation.

Venice provided him with a wealth of new sensations, all of which he poured into his work, for with Byron life and poetry were interchangeable. Venice and Byron seemed made for each other, both symbols of decayed grandeur. He had loved Newstead Abbey because it was a ruin, something on which to exert his imaginative powers, seeing it as it once must have been. Venice, the great power celebrated in *Othello* and *The Merchant of Venice*, was a stage setting of decaying palazzi. It had long since become a dissolute playhouse where young men during the days of the Grand Tour were dazzled by the discarded concubines of the nobility who thronged St Mark's Square as semi-clad prostitutes. Their concerned tutors let them sow a few wild oats and then hurried them away to examine classical antiquities.

Until the middle of the sixteenth century Venice had exerted hegemony over the territory past Bergamo in the west, northwards to the borders of the Hapsburg Empire, and a sweep down the Adriatic to encompass Istria and Dalmatia. Further afield the Venetians controlled the Morea, Crete, and Cyprus. But decline was inevitable after their defeat by the Turks at the Battle of Lepanto in 1571 when they had to surrender the entire eastern Mediterranean. The Venetian Republic had come to an end in 1797 by the Treaty of Campoformio when it was ceded to Austria – in effect, to Napoleon.

Napoleon had appeared as a saviour after his defeat of the Austrians at the Battle of Lodi in May 1796. A strong movement towards liberty and democracy spread across northern Italy, and there was dancing in the squares of Milan and Venice. But after December 1804 when Napoleon was crowned emperor, his early avowals of liberty began to appear to have been entirely spurious. Following his victory over the Austro-Russian armies at Austerlitz in 1805, he became king of Italy. "I want no more inquisitors, no more Senate. I will be the Attila of the Venetian state," he announced. Venetian art treasures were carted off to adorn the Louvre. All that he seemed to bequeath to Venice was a road to Padua. After his final defeat at Waterloo in 1815, Venice and Lombardy were again ceded to Austria and ruled through a viceroy of the emperor. Spies were everywhere; and in Milan Byron had been convinced he was under surveillance since he had been seen constantly in the company of di Breme and other liberals.

But politics were the last thing on his mind in the late autumn of 1816. He had the feeling that he had entered the true anteroom of the East, with its exoticism and lax morality. Byron's reaction was unlike that of the average British tourist of 1816 who might spend a day or two in the city and then press on to more serious destinations: Florence, particularly Rome, and perhaps a visit to Naples. Venice was considered the city of sin and carnival, entirely frivolous. The Venetians also had the reputation for producing the most sinuous spies in Europe, not surprising for people who lived in a city offering concealment at every bend. Decayed aristocrats, demi-mondains, and Austrian officers made up a population of about 100,000 people. In such a place an English milord – especially an eccentric and famous one – was accepted and treated as he thought he should be. Byron loved the lisping Venetian dialect, he loved the late hours of social activity when Florian's opened its doors on the Piazza San Marco, and people flocked to the opera at La Fenice, which "beats *our* theatres hollow in beauty & scenery".[9]

With Hobhouse Byron visited the famous Marciana Library, once the council room of the doges. Always fascinated by the bizarre, he was particularly struck by the portrait of Marino Faliero, over which was painted a black veil. In 1355 the disgraced doge had been beheaded on the nearby stairs for conspiracy against the state, a subject whose possibilities occurred to Byron immediately; and in turn was to inspire Delacroix. Byron soon became friendly with Dr Francesco Aglietti (a friend of Lady Holland's) who spoke to them of the sad state of his country. They also attended *conversazioni* at the apartments of the Countess Albrizzi, who was the centre of social life among the upper classes. She had been described to them as the Italian Madame de Staël, but Hobhouse found her "a very poor copy indeed, though she seems a very good natured woman".[10] They were struck by the fact that the women sat in a semicircle at one end of the room, the men at the other.

Byron and his friend took a two-hour gondola ride to the island of San Lazzaro beyond the Lido. Here they visited the Armenian monastery established in 1717 by Father Peter Mekhitar who had fled from Turkish oppression. Byron was always impressed by simple goodness, and he found himself deeply moved by these gentle monks, busy with their printing press and their students. He made arrangements to visit the monastery every morning to learn Armenian. He needed something craggy on which to exercise his mind, he said, and he offered to help one of the priests compile an English–Armenian vocabulary.*

Shortly after their arrival, the friends moved out of the hotel into lodgings. Hobhouse chose rooms in the Calle degli Avvocati near the Campo San Angelo and continued to take his meals at the Gran-Bretagna. Byron, meanwhile, rented quarters above the shop of a draper, Pietro Segati, in the Frezzeria, one of the warren of narrow lanes, with their odd similarity to an Arab medina. Hobhouse was now left to his own devices.

Three days after moving into his new rooms, Byron wrote joyously to Moore that he had fallen rapturously in love with the draper's wife, Marianna. He tried to describe his *amorosa* who reminded him of an antelope.**

> She has large, black, oriental eyes, with that peculiar expression in them which is seen rarely among *Europeans* – even the Italians . . . I cannot describe the effect of this kind of eye, – at least upon me. Her features are regular, and rather aquiline – mouth small – skin clear and soft, and with a kind of hectic colour – forehead remarkably good: her hair is of the dark gloss, curl, and colour of Lady J[ersey]'s: her figure is light and pretty, and she is a famous songstress – scientifically so; her natural voice (in conversation, I mean) is very sweet; and the naiveté of the Venetian dialect is always pleasing in the mouth of a woman."

The Venetians would have taken a very tolerant view of their arrangement. It would have been a different matter if he had become her *cavaliere servente*, a common Italian custom whereby the lover was recognised by the world at large, including the husband, who had arrangements of his own. Marianna would have liked Byron to have entered into such an agreement, but it reminded him too much of the servitude of marriage, and besides, even in his exhilarated state, he would not allow himself to become permanently attached to someone of such humble birth.

Byron had fallen so frantically in love because he was swept along by a sudden taste of freedom. He was in that manic state when he wanted to proclaim his love from the rooftops. In Geneva he had still felt the weight of

---

* It is often referred to as a "grammar", but it is not at all as ambitious as that.

** This was the animal to which he had compared Augusta's friend, Lady Charlotte Leveson-Gower, who had rejected his proposal before he tried Annabella.

British opinion, and was careful to correct misconceptions about his relationship with the Shelley household. But in Venice – the British public be damned! Indeed his mood was one of impertinent defiance. He was now convinced that he never wanted to see England again. He knew that Moore, a notorious gossip, would spread the word of his activities at Bowood House and the other great country seats he frequented. He knew too that Murray would read aloud his letters to the assembled literati who gathered every morning in his premises in Albemarle Street. Byron was done with trailing his bleeding heart across Europe; now he would boast that he had never been happier. If the world saw him as a libertine, his projected image would surmount all expectations.

Augusta had written that she had "hope" for him – hope for his salvation, presumably; and she was puzzled and even rather nonplussed to hear that he was now "sick of sorrow – & must even content myself as well as I can – so here goes – I won't be woeful again if I can help it."[12] This was not at all the kind of letter that would please Annabella. Best to delay communicating to her that her erring husband was now in "fathomless love". Augusta's own "sposo", George Leigh, had returned from London with stories that Byron was using his affairs in Venice as a "blind". "One hears," she told Annabella on January 20, "that it is the *only* point on which he is afraid."[13] Surely he must have a streak of madness! As for the people he was associating with in Venice, "The taste for low society is *hereditary* in him, & was dreadfully encouraged by his poor Mother's ill Education. It is impossible to be more wretched than I am about him, yet hitherto *events* have not been worse than *anticipations*. Poor fellow!"[14] Augusta had been cruelly deceitful, but she was still genuinely concerned about Byron; and indeed, her low spirits were not exaggerated since the family finances were now in an absolutely desperate state, and Six Mile Bottom had been put up for sale.

Byron was actually talking of paying off his debts, but was as ignorant as ever about their enormity. He was anxious, he said, to relieve himself of their burden because then there would be no necessity to return to England at all. However, the debts, he insisted, would not be paid out of his literary earnings, "the produce of my *brain*".[15] Surely Hanson could make another effort to sell Newstead so that he might continue living comfortably in Venice? How pleasant to live in this world of fantasy, far from the strains that had plagued him for the past years. He boasted that he never looked at an English newspaper. And so began a whole series of letters echoing the theme of his first exile in 1809–11: his feeling of total estrangement from

England and his reluctance to return. The only difference was that in the earlier period he had vowed he would never part with Newstead. Now he simply wanted it disposed of "even at almost any price".[16] To sell Newstead seemed crucial, not only as a means of paying off his debts but, more important, by divesting himself of it he would be cutting off a crucial tie with England.

On December 5 Hobhouse left on an extended tour of Italy with plans to return in March. Byron could not be induced to leave either Marianna or Carnival which began the day after Christmas. His anticipation of excesses was like the excitement of a child at being allowed to do something unbelievably wicked. To Thomas Moore he wrote exuberantly:

> But the Carnival's coming,
>   Oh Thomas Moore,
> The Carnival's coming,
>   Oh Thomas Moore,
>
> Masking and humming,
> Fifing and drumming,
> Guitarring and strumming,
>   Oh Thomas Moore.[17]

Carnival opened with a series of balls around the Piazza San Marco and continued, with wild abandonment in gaming and carousing, until the middle of February. How different from his staid countrymen who avoided the city during this period of dissipation! How wonderful to don a white mask and a tricorn hat and to be *"nau"* constantly without any threat of penalty.

Carnival would not have suited the serious Hobhouse or the earnest Shelley who was bedevilled with troubles. His wife Harriet had thrown herself into the Serpentine, and a Chancery suit was about to deprive him of his children because of his allegedly immoral life. He had now married Mary, and was also responsible for the welfare of Claire who in Bath on January 12 gave birth to a daughter whom she named Alba, after Albé, the name the Shelley family had assigned to Byron while in Geneva. Curiously enough, shortly before hearing of the birth (January 20, 1817) Byron asked Kinnaird rhetorically: "is the brat *mine? –* I have reason to think so – for I know as much as one can know of such a thing – that she had *not lived* with S[helley] during the time of our acquaintance."

Hobhouse was urging him to join him in Rome, but again Byron used the carnival as an excuse not to leave Venice – yet. Carnival had left him exhausted and listless. To Thomas Moore he wrote that even though he had just turned twenty-nine, he felt drained by the festivities. He assured him that he was convinced that he would still do something outstanding with his life – although not in literature because he did not consider it his true vocation – yet "I doubt whether my constitution will hold out."[18]

> So we'll go no more a roving
> So late into the night,
> Though the heart be still as loving,
> And the moon be still as bright.
>
> For the sword outwears its sheath,
> And the soul wears out the breast,
> And the heart must pause to breathe,
> And Love itself have rest.
>
> Though the night was made for loving,
> And the day returns too soon,
> Yet we'll go no more a roving
> By the light of the moon.[19]

He lapsed into a fever – perhaps a recurrence of the malaria he had suffered in Patras – but refused to allow a doctor to examine him. His recovery was interrupted by the shocking news that Ada had been made a Ward of Chancery. Annabella's lawyer, Lushington, agreed with her that it was "expedient" to reveal this information to him in order to silence his complaints about the possibility of Ada leaving England. A year earlier Annabella's lawyers had conceived an ingenious scheme for accomplishing this: Sir Ralph would instigate a suit against him over some small piece of property, a device to prevent his gaining custody of his daughter. Furiously Byron poured out his sense of total betrayal by Annabella, predicting that the day would come when "Nemesis will do that which I would not." Augusta was told that "I curse her from the bottom of my heart – & in the bitterness of my soul – & I only hope she may one day feel what she made me suffer; – they will break my heart or drive me mad one day or the other – but she is a wretch & will end ill – she was born to be my destruction" (March 25, 1817).

To Annabella herself he wrote (March 5, 1817) a long letter protesting that it was apparent that making Ada a Ward of Chancery was a device to deprive him of his paternal rights. How could she stoop to making their daughter "the inheritor of our bitterness"? Annabella replied that she had never injured him as he persistently claimed and that he had firm assurances that Ada would not be taken out of the country. She concluded: "Seek not a pretext for aggression – and as I trust you will never find a just one, I shall the more firmly, and by every means in my power, resist those injustices which only malice could design – yet I cannot conclude without a wish that this may never be my afflicting duty."[20] If Byron was going to make threats to return to England to reclaim his child, she could wreak even greater devastation, she implied.

Augusta considered it "fortunate", she told Hodgson, that the child had been made a Ward of Chancery, "as things are at present".[21] To her everlasting shame, she showed Byron's furious letters to Annabella; and to Hodgson, she wrote: "I can neither do or say anything for his comfort. Indeed, dear Mr H, I don't know *who* can in his very unhappy state of feeling and perverted way of thinking."[22]

Byron's Venetian mistress was beginning to exert pressure on Byron to elope with her; and while he was still in love, Marianna's possessiveness only increased his sense of being once more entrapped by circumstances beyond his control. Perhaps the feeling of being in motion again would relieve his heavy heart. After a series of procrastinating excuses to Hobhouse, on April 17 he set off for Rome after dispatching a first draft of the poetic drama, *Manfred*, to Murray. The recent shock had drained his confidence, and he was full of apprehensions about its worth.

Proceeding by way of Ferrara, Bologna, and Florence, new sights and impressions revitalised his poetic impulse. He wrote the last lines of *The Lament of Tasso* as he crossed the Apennines. He arrived in Rome on the 29th to be greeted by a delighted Hobhouse who had secured lodgings for him at 66 Piazza di Spagna, almost directly opposite the house where Keats would die four years later.

He found the city superb, and as well as the usual sightseeing, he spent hours on horseback exploring the Alban Hills with his friend. One of the pleasures of the city was the absence of English visitors who had left with the onset of warm weather, but he did encounter a party at the top of St Peter's. This group included Lady Lovell, a friend of Lady Byron's family, who warned her daughter, "Don't look at him, he is dangerous to look at."

Together he and Hobhouse attended an execution of three robbers. Byron was drawn to the gruesome spectacle by his fascination with the macabre. He described the occasion in horrifying detail to Murray, and rationalised his attendance with his assertion that everyone should "see every thing once".[23] Would this also include *experiencing* everything once?

Hobhouse arranged to have Byron's bust carved by the distinguished Dane, Bertel Thorwaldsen. It was considered a remarkable likeness by everyone except Byron who claimed that his real expression was far more unhappy. Hobhouse also wanted to have it crowned with laurel, but Byron refused to be "garnished like a Xmas pie" (June 20, 1817).

He found himself longing for Marianna; and after only three weeks turned northwards again while Hobhouse's party set off for Naples, which Byron was determined to avoid because it was said to be full of English visitors. By now he had decided that he would not return to England for at least another year; indeed, "if I could expatriate myself altogether I would and will."[24] But what was he to do with the child Claire had produced? For the moment – nothing; but eventually a convent might provide the solution. "I must love something in my old age," he told Augusta (May 27, 1817). Who knows? Perhaps she might prove more of a comfort than his legitimate child by the woman who "bears & disgraces my name".

Venice was already shimmering with heat, so he followed the Venetian habit, the *Villeggiatura*, of escaping in mid-June to the Brenta Canal where he took a Palladian villa on a six-month lease. The Villa Foscarini at Mira, a former convent, had been taken over by a Jew from an impecunious aristocrat. It was not a particularly beautiful building, situated as it was directly on the dusty road to Padua, but it had a pleasant garden, agreeable neighbours, and he was able to ride in the evenings. He was joined by Marianna, whose husband's visit every weekend was combined with an assignation with his own mistress.

The final draft of *Manfred* had been sent off to Murray, from whom Byron asked only 300 guineas. He had professed himself uneasy about its metaphysical nature, filled with spirits of the Alps, and originally inspired one evening by "Monk" Lewis's recitation of *Faust* at Villa Diodati. Repeatedly Byron warned everyone that it was a closet drama, and under no conditions could it be enacted on the stage. He professed himself concerned about its structure, but surely he knew that its content would make it another *cause célèbre*.

Manfred is a Prometheus-like character whose gift to humanity has been an unconquerable individual will. Summoning the spirits of nature, he asks not for eternal life, power, or wisdom, but simply for forgetfulness. In the second act (in which Byron incorporated the magnificent scenery of the journey through the Bernese Oberland) he stands on the brink of the Jungfrau contemplating suicide, but is rescued by a chamois hunter who takes him back to his cottage where he offers him wine, but Manfred recoils at the sight of blood on the rim:

> I say 'tis blood – my blood! the pure warm stream
> Which ran in the veins of my fathers, and in ours
> When we were in our youth, and had one heart,
> And loved each other as we should not love,
> And this was shed . . .
> (II, i, 24–8)

Manfred then summons up the Witch of the Alps to whom he speaks of the love of one who was his spiritual twin:

> She was like me in lineaments – her eyes,
> Her hair, her features, all, to the very tone
> Even of her voice, they said were like to mine;
> But soften'd all, and temper'd into beauty;
> She had the same lone thoughts and wanderings . . .
> Pity, and smiles, and tears – which I had not;
> And tenderness – but that I had for her;
> Humility – and that I never had.
> Her faults were mine – her virtues were her own –
> I loved her, and destroy'd her!
> (II, ii, 105–17)

This wonderful creature is Astarte who appears briefly before him:

> Astarte! my beloved! speak to me:
> I have so much endured – so much endure . . .
>   Thou lovedst me
> Too much, as I loved thee: we were not made
> To torture thus each other, though it were
> The deadliest sin to love as we have loved.
> Say that thou loath'st me not . . .
> Speak to me! though it be in wrath . . .
> (II, iv, 118–48)

Astarte refuses to utter words of love or forgiveness before disappearing. She has predicted that Manfred will die; and in defying death, he proclaims his own indomitable spirit:

What I have done is done; I bear within
A torture . . .
The mind which is immortal makes itself
Requital for its good or evil thoughts –
Is its own origin of ill and end –
And its own place and time . . .

(III, iv, 127–32)

After the poem appeared on June 16, Byron eagerly enquired of Augusta if it had created a "pucker" in England. From Rome he had complained of her mysterious allusions and regrets: "I know nothing of what you are in the doldrums about at present – I should – think all that could affect *you* – must have been over long ago – & as for me – leave me to take care of myself . . . I can battle my way through – better than your exquisite piece of helplessness G[eorge] L[eigh]."[25]

It is hard to credit that Byron could not have had any conception of the humiliation to which he was subjecting his sister. "I should think all that could affect *you* must have been over long ago . . ." Did he never stop to think how he was harming her reputation? On June 23 a London newspaper, the *Day and New Times*, referred very openly to the incest theme of the poem: "*Manfred* has exiled himself from society, and what is to be the ground of our compassion for the exile? Simply the commission of one of the most revolting of crimes. He has committed incest! Lord Byron has coloured *Manfred* into his own personal features."

Augusta's relatives were appalled. Her half-sister, Lady Chichester, showed the item to Mrs Villiers who eagerly communicated its contents to Annabella: "the allusions to Augusta are dreadfully clear."[26] A distraught Augusta turned to her "Guardian Angel" for advice on how to handle the situation in her next letter to Byron. Annabella replied: "You can only speak of *Manfred* . . . with the most decided expressions of disapprobation. He practically gives you away, and implies you were guilty *after* marriage."[27] The gossip eventually died down; but from now on Augusta was to live in terror of everything her brother wrote, and people noticed how her beauty was fading into an expression of permanent anxiety.

What was Byron up to? The poem provided him with a medium to express his own suffering; and feeling that no worse scandal could touch him (except perhaps homosexuality), he felt comfortably remote in Venice. He made the most of the rumours that were circulating, with apparently no thought of how they might affect Augusta. When Manfred asked the spirits for forgetfulness, Byron was thinking only of the forgetfulness of his marriage, but he knew that incest would make the theme more dramatic. He was punishing his wife, but also punishing Augusta whom he could no longer see as his ever-supportive staff since she appeared so vague and uninterested in his life. In his narcissistic self-enclosure, he lacked the empathy to imagine the problems that were besetting her. On June 19, in his last letter for what would be almost a year, he seemed to guess at her anxiety: "What is there known? or can be known? which *you* & I do not know much better? . . . they had no business with anything previous to my marriage with that infernal fiend – whose destruction I shall yet see." Still he could not conceive that she would have allowed herself to be put in Annabella's power. Vowing vengeance against the whole Noel tribe, he abruptly stopped writing to Augusta since she persisted in "this absurd obscure hinting mode of writing". In cutting himself off from her, his exile seemed complete.

21

oooooooooooooo

A New Life, 1817–18

When Hobhouse arrived at La Mira at the end of July 1817, he was somewhat nonplussed to find "Monk" Lewis staying with Byron, so that instead of having his friend's exclusive company as he had hoped, he had to board with the family of a neighbouring physician. He was even more irritated by the possessive presence of Byron's mistress, Marianna Segati, and shocked to discover that the local priest condoned the adultery. This did not look at all like the visit he had anticipated, in which he would discuss the historical prose notes he was writing for the fourth canto of *Childe Harold*.

What Hobhouse found particularly disturbing was the fact that Byron had been discussing his domestic problems with Lewis, and had concocted a document which Byron instructed him to publicise in England on Lewis's return. In his journal on August 9 Hobhouse wrote crossly:

> find that Byron has given [Lewis] a sort of document by which he asserts that if Lady Byron's counsellors say that their lips are sealed – the sealing has not been his – he wishes them to speak & has always wished it – & regrets that he did not insist on Lady Byron's bringing her case & complaint before the public – I disapprove of this document because it will gratify Lady Byron's friends to think that Byron is annoyed and because I should think no one can suppose that Lady Byron's counsellors meant that their lips were sealed on Lord Byron's account or at his desire – but merely because they were her counsellors in a private & delicate affair.[1]

Lewis, too, apparently felt it unwise to stir things up; and the original statement was found among his papers at his death from suicide in 1818, although somehow a copy of it reached Lushington who forwarded it to Annabella in October.

Hobhouse was only too happy to see the departure of Lewis whom he described as "the greatest egoist I ever encountered".[2] Now he and his friend could revert to their easy familiarity. On the evening of August 5 they went riding together and came upon two pretty young women. One of them, unusually tall, was particularly striking. In a provocatively impertinent way, she called out to Byron in the local dialect, "Darling, you are so generous to others, why don't you help us also?" Byron replied that she was too pretty to need help, whereupon her tart reply was that he would think differently if he could see where she lived.

The truth was that Byron was beginning to tire of Marianna's constant demands and jealous tantrums. He told Hobhouse that he had spent an enormous amount of money on her; and with his increasing concern about his finances he was beginning to resent the way she was draining him. His new infatuation, Margarita Cogni, was a baker's wife, and was soon referred to as La Fornarina.* It was not long before Marianna learned of his midnight trysts and she rushed off to threaten her new rival. Byron was delighted by La Fornarina's spirited reply: "*You* are *not* his *wife*: *I* am *not* his *wife* – *you* are his *Donna*, – *I* am his *Donna* – *your* husband is a cuckold – and *mine* is another; for the rest, what *right* have you to reproach me? – if he prefers what is mine – to what is yours – is it my fault?"[3]

Hobhouse had not been so successful in his amours, but he actually began to enjoy the visits of Marianna's husband who regaled them with local gossip. On one occasion he told them the tale of a man who had been presumed lost at sea and who returned unexpectedly, and finding his wife now accompanied by a *cavaliere servente*, presented her with several generous alternatives. Byron listened attentively; and soon he began to adapt the story to a mock-heroic measure, modelled on John Hookham Frere's recently published *The Monks and the Giants*. Frere, under the pseudonym Whistlecraft, adapting the *ottava rima* from the fifteenth-century Italian poet Luigi Pulci, made of what would become *Beppo* a wonderfully appropriate means of catching the conversational ease of Byron's letters. The final rhyming couplets of each stanza enabled Byron to add a clinching cynical epigram.

As for the new canto of *Childe Harold*, Hobhouse was extremely pleased with it not only because it abandoned the metaphysical tone of Byron's

---

* Curiously enough, only five years before this, Ingres had done a painting of Raphael with his mistress, La Fornarina, sitting on his lap (Fogg Museum, Harvard).

Swiss period, but also because he felt almost like a collaborator since Byron would frequently incorporate material they had discussed or sights they had seen – such as a magnificent sunset – during their evening rides. They seemed to have achieved an even greater understanding than they had experienced as very young men, and in dedicating the poem to Hobhouse, Byron described his friend as one "whom I have found wakeful over my sickness and kind in my sorrow, glad in my prosperity and firm in my adversity, true in counsel and trusty in peril – to a friend often tried and never found wanting". The poem was substantially finished by October 10.

They did not move back to Venice until the middle of November: "a strange life – very comfortable & tranquil", Hobhouse recorded. Once again in the city he took up rooms opposite Byron's in the Frezzeria. Another pleasant routine was established. In the evenings they took Byron's gondola to the Lido where Byron had ferried his horses. Here they galloped along the hard stretch of sand, deserted because no one else in the city possessed horses. Later they might attend the opera or view one of Goldoni's comedies in the San Benedetto Theatre.

Occasionally the outside world impinged itself upon them. They heard that Madame de Staël had died, and Byron remembered her fondly as one of the few people who had befriended him after he had gone into exile. He was also very affected by the news of the death on November 6 of Princess Charlotte, whose tears he had once commemorated. The arrival of the Kinnairds – Douglas, Byron's banker, and his brother, Lord Kinnaird – meant that they spent a good deal of time in Venice during September. A young American admirer, George Ticknor, who had visited Byron in London, now called upon him once more. He found the poet exactly the same – an exception to the description his enemies sent home of a bloated, dishevelled creature.

On November 2 Byron was highly embarrassed to receive a letter from the Duchess of Devonshire reminding him that he had paid only £200 of the £700 rent he had contracted to pay in 1815 on the house in Piccadilly Terrace. Byron replied apologetically – and unconvincingly – that he had been unaware that the debt had not been paid and that while he had little control over his finances, he truly hoped that those acting for him would soon liquidate the outstanding amount.

Then suddenly he heard that Newstead had been bought by an old Harrow school-friend, Major Thomas Wildman. And he had actually paid the princely sum of £94,500, which meant that Byron could begin paying off his staggering debts. To Hanson he sent a list of all the creditors he could recollect (including the Duchess of Devonshire and Baxter, who had built his Napoleonic coach). But was it absolutely necessary for him to go to England to sign the papers?

Byron indicated no regret at the loss of the abbey. Augusta, however, found it painful to realise that it was no longer in family hands, for she seemed to have developed a greater attachment to it than Byron himself. For Annabella, too, the sale of the house, to which Byron had never once suggested taking her, signified the loss of her fantasised persona as the châtelaine of the noble poet. She made a point of secretly visiting Newstead before the new owner occupied it. In her journal at Mansfield she recorded on May 22:

> Just come from Newstead. The sunshine, the blue lakes, the re-appearing foliage of the remaining woods, the yellow gorse over the wild wastes gave a cheerful effect to the surrounding scenes. My feelings were altogether those of gratification. In becoming famil-iarised with the scene I seemed to contemplate the portrait of a friend.
>
> I entered the hall – and saw the Dog; then walked into the dining-room – not used by Ld. B. as such. He was wont to exercise there. His fencing-sword and single-sticks – beneath the table on which they stood, a stone coffin, containing the four skulls which he used to have set before him, till (as he told me himself) he fancied them animated.
>
> I saw the old flags which he used to hang up on the "Castle walls" on his birthday. The apartments which he inhabited were in every respect the same – he might have walked in. They looked not deserted. The Woman who has lived in his service regretted that the property was transferred. He should have lived there, particularly after he was married – but his Lady had never come there, and "she, poor thing! is not likely to come there now," compassionately & mysteriously. She said that he was "very fond of Mrs L–, very loving to her indeed," as if this were the only part of his character on which she could dwell with commendation, for she drew a very unfavour-able comparison between him and G.B. [George Byron] in regard to charity.
>
> Ld. B. "never gave a thought that way." . . . The parapet & steps where he sat – the halls where he walked. His room – where I was rooted having involuntarily returned.[4]

Annabella realised that this expression of strong feelings might be interpreted as weakness by her friends, but she felt compelled to reveal the visit to Augusta. The latter replied ecstatically on May 27: "My dearest

A – only think of your having seen poor Newstead – I almost cried to think of it – but I feel glad you have & that your opinion of it justifies all I have said."[5]

During the summer of 1817 Annabella also went on an extended journey to Scotland with the main object of winning Walter Scott to her side. The visit was made in somewhat nervous defiance of her mother, who was furious with Scott for the favourable review he had given Canto III of *Childe Harold*. At his home, Abbotsford, Scott was warmly hospitable, but he refused to commit himself one way or another although his sympathies were aroused, as he wrote to Joanna Baillie:

> Now, one would suppose Lady Byron, young, beautiful, with birth, and rank, and fortune, and taste, and high accomplishments, and admirable good sense, qualified to have made happy one whose talents are so high as Lord Byron's, and whose marked propensity it is to like those who are qualified to admire and understand his talents, yet it has proved otherwise . . . I can safely say, my heart ached for her all the time we were together . . . to me she was one of the most interesting creatures I had seen for this score of years.[6]

Annabella was beginning to experience the loneliness of a young woman living on her own. Self-absorbed as she was, she lacked a strong maternal feeling, and to Mrs Villiers she confessed, "Ada loves me as well as I wish and better than I expected, for I had a strange prepossession that she would never be fond of me."[7] That summer she dismissed a nurse because the child seemed too attached to her, and burst into tears when her mother put in an appearance. Nor did Annabella's estranged husband fret for her. On September 14, 1817, Hobhouse recorded in his diary: "Byron talked to me about family affairs tonight – he does not care about his wife now – that is certain"; and on hearing from Byron that Annabella had never liked him, he remarked generously, "Poor dear contradictory thing."[8]

Annabella had always used her diary as a continuous letter to herself, and in October 1817, she wrote: "I feel as if in a desert – and did not like passing through the day alone."[9] Later in the month Lushington sent her a copy of the document Byron had prepared at La Mira. Her reaction was: "A blight in the evening. Received from Dr Lushington the copy of a paper written by Lord B. Date Venice Aug 9th, 1817. I could not read it – heart heavy."[10] Her overwhelming feeling towards her husband was still that of a bitterness almost to match his own. On November 7, on hearing of Princess Charlotte's death, she recorded: "Lord B. will write verses on this public event – touching allusions to his own situation – an opportunity perhaps of cancelling his offences towards the P.R."[11]

On Hobhouse's last evening with Byron (January 7, 1818), the poet made some final alterations to Canto IV which Hobhouse was to bear back with him to England the next day. "A little before my going he told me he was originally a man of a great deal of feeling but it had been absorbed – I believe the first part of what he said – literally – God bless him."[12]

Once back in England, Hobhouse, accompanied by Scrope Davies, made a point of calling on Augusta, who by now realised that her brother was not angry with her, simply exasperated by her vague letters. Always grateful for news to satisfy Annabella's curiosity, she wrote a series of letters reporting what she had learned: Byron spoke often of Ada but had no intention of returning to England to be humiliated by people staring at him "coolly"; the sale of Newstead delighted him because it was the first time he had had a settled income; and that "the state of mind was not happy – rode every day ate meat & drank temperately – was in as good spirits as 'one who had had so many rubs' could be".[13]

Byron only gradually became aware that the sale of Newstead marked a decisive turning-point in his life. He attended Carnival, but not with the manic enthusiasm of the previous year, although he caught a dose of gonorrhoea. He missed Hobhouse a great deal, and as a companion for his evening rides he substituted the British consul, Richard Hoppner, son of the celebrated portrait painter John Hoppner*. He still attended the *conversazioni* at Countess Albrizzi's, and here on January 22 he met the teenage bride of Count Guiccioli from Ravenna. He offered her his arm to view Canova's statue of Helen of Troy, but neither made much of an impression on the other at the time. Teresa, a girl hardly out of the convent, had been married only three days, and Byron was more interested in a ravishingly pretty girl from Padua. He was now also attending the evening gatherings at the palazzo of the Countess Benzoni, who had been away when he first arrived in Venice and who now proceeded to make a great fuss over him. He was tired of his cramped quarters in the Frezzeria, and tired of Marianna. Since he planned to settle permanently in Italy, he began looking for larger accommodation. A plan to rent Count Gritti's palazzo on the Grand Canal did not materialise, but in May he agreed on a three-year lease for the Mocenigo family's massive building within sight of the Rialto Bridge.

---

* John Hoppner had painted Annabella as a child, and also Lady Melbourne and Lady Oxford, as well as Byron's young Harrow friend, Lord Dorset.

Larger accommodation was necessary because he believed the time had come to send for his illegitimate daughter. Letters were exchanged with the Shelleys about arrangements to bring her to Italy. Hobhouse was instructed to tell Shelley that he was also to bring tooth powder and brushes. Byron continued to refuse to communicate with Claire, and she did nothing to placate him by expressing her distress about confining the child to his care:

> Poor little angel! in your great house, left perhaps to servants while you are drowning sense & feeling in wine & striving all you can to ruin the natural goodness of your nature who will be there to watch her. She is peculiarly delicate – her indigestions are frequent & dangerous if neglected . . . a moment might create for me memories long & dread too terrible even in this instant's conception.[14]

Byron was deaf to the mother's concerned pleas, far more concerned as he was that Hanson or an appointed agent come to Venice with the Newstead papers; and for what would lengthen into months his letters were filled with furious complaints about Hanson's alternative proposal that they meet in Geneva.

Another tie with England was broken when he heard that Lady Melbourne had died on April 6: "the best & kindest & ablest female I ever knew", he described her to Murray.[15] In response to Annabella's condolences to her daughter-in-law, Mrs George Lamb, the latter replied that "it is impossible to see a person so loved & agreeable & not to feel that they must have had great merits to condone their faults." She added an indignant note:

> Hobhouse wrote yesterday [April 7] a most disgusting letter, asking for Lord Byron's letters, really one of the most unfeeling letters I have ever read, saying he was desired by Lord Byron to apply the moment of Lady Melbourne's demise and no expression of sorrow or Kindness to the family – I always had the worst possible opinion of that man – but I believe they are all in a fright; I do not believe that she kept any, indeed the probability is that they were all burnt.[16]

Claire, before leaving England, on March 9 took her little girl to St Giles-in-the-Fields, where she was baptised "Clara Allegra Byron, born of Rt. Hon. George Gordon Lord Byron ye reputed Father by Clara Mary Jane Clairmont". The Shelley party, accompanied by Elise, a Swiss maid who had joined their household in Geneva two years before, arrived in Milan on April 4. They tried to rent a large dilapidated villa on Lake Como, and Shelley begged Byron to visit them before taking Allegra back to Venice. If Byron was loath to travel to Geneva to meet Hanson, he was even more reluctant ever to see Claire again – anywhere. Unfortunately his letters to Shelley during this period have not survived, but his negative reply must have been as peremptory as those written to Hanson when his torpid routine was threatened. Byron complained bitterly that his life was being made a burden. Shelley's response suggested that Byron had implied that Allegra was now his property to be disposed of as he thought appropriate.

Shelley was deeply moved by Claire's agony at the prospect of being separated from her daughter for ever. He sent a long impassioned plea to Byron for some understanding of a mother's feelings.

> You write as if from the instant of its departure all future intercourse were to cease between Clare and her child. This I cannot think you ought to have expected or even to have desired. Let us estimate our own sensations, and consider, if those of a father be acute, what must be those of a mother? What should we think of a woman who should resign her infant child with no prospect of ever seeing it again, even to a father in whose tenderness she entirely confided?[17]

Shelley found himself "in the invidious position of mediator", and he indignantly refused Byron's offer to recompense him for the expenses of looking after Allegra.

Byron failed to see the irony of the fact that he was identifying with Annabella in her determination to keep Ada, and his own self-pity had not softened his feelings towards another parent caught in much the same situation of exclusion. His identification with the aggressor was an unconscious means of revenging himself on his wife. Nevertheless, his next letter appeased the Shelley group in its apparent agreement that Claire could see the child during the summer, and Shelley assured Byron that he considered the girl "the most lovely and engaging child I ever beheld".[18] Byron sent Francis Merryweather, a British merchant residing in Venice, to act as the escort for Allegra and Elise. On May 27 he reported to Kinnaird in a postscript that "*My* bastard came here a month ago – a very fine child – & much admired by the Venetian public. – Hobhouse can tell you her history. – I have broke my old liaison with la Segati – & have taken a dozen in stead."

For the time being Allegra was another pet to be regarded as part of the menagerie of assorted animals Byron was collecting for his amusement. However, Allegra was not an animal, but a confused little girl of a year and a half, suddenly separated from her mother; and if Byron and the Hoppners – with whom she was frequently sent to stay – at times found her sullen or hot-tempered – whereas Shelley had spoken of the sweetness of her disposition – it is not to be wondered at. But for the moment he was very pleased with the attractive child and professed to find a greater resemblance to Lady Byron than to her biological mother.

He seemed relatively contented with the new life he was carving out for himself. By the beginning of June he had moved into the Palazzo Mocenigo, a magnificent sixteenth-century building with a large barn-like ground area from which he would step into his gondola. Of the three floors rising above he occupied the *piano nobile* reached by a wide staircase. Here he could lean over the balcony, where he had a magnificent view of the Grand Canal. He had always loved the sight and sound of water: the lake at Newstead, the sea in which he immersed himself in the East, and now the lapping of the waters beneath him as he sat writing until he could see dawn unshadowing the Rialto.

Reverting to a mannerism of 1809–11, to his correspondents Byron repeatedly referred to England as "your country", usually in the context of relief at finding himself so far from the shores of his former home and of contentment with his new life. But there was not a day in which England was not in his thoughts; and one of the disadvantages of being so far away was that when he sent off his poems they disappeared, as it were, into the void. Hobhouse had left early in January with the manuscript of Canto IV of *Childe Harold*; it was published on April 28; and not until June did Byron receive a letter from Moore telling him of its success. Murray had decided to publish Hobhouse's notes separately as he felt that otherwise it would be too long a volume. *Beppo* had appeared anonymously on February 28 and London drawing rooms (unbeknownst to Byron) were buzzing because it didn't take people long to guess its author. On March 19 Annabella told her friend Lady Barnard that its levity convinced her of "the turbid state of his mind".[19]

It was only natural that Byron would take up the story of his pilgrim once more. Canto III, set in Switzerland, revealed the bewildered feelings of the hero in a state of transition, stopping briefly for rest and reflection before continuing to his destination, the fairy city that had haunted his dreams since childhood. Italy in a sense was the promised land beyond the Alps but at the same time he begins to recognise its fall from greatness, and identifies with its destiny: "a ruin amidst ruins" (IV, 25, 219). Weaving together the history and the arts of the country with his own lot, the narrator seems to gain some sort of personal resolution in his awareness that he, like the country in which he finds himself, can have no knowledge of the future, that only the immediate moment – such as a magnificent sunset over Venice – can offer one some satisfaction.

While Byron often stated that he wrote because he must, that poetry offered him a form of cathartic release, he also was never unaware of his audience. By Canto IV he has cast aside all pretence that he and his pilgrim are separate beings; and he uses the poem partly as a polemic to the public about the sufferings that have been inflicted upon him by venomous enemies and the calm disdain with which he has learned to absorb their attacks. He was also defiant of the very public he was addressing in his overt disgust of the decay of liberty in England. The poem ends with a redemptive vision of his own future fame which will be entwined with that of his adopted country.

Jerome McGann argues that the reader must not be repelled by the "gigantic egoism" of the poet.[20] He is right because somehow Byron the poet – the "orphan of the heart" – manages to pull it off. He is successful because he was finally creating a persona whose sensitivity to beauty and freedom convince us by the sheer magic of the poetry.

> There is a pleasure in the pathless woods,
> There is a rapture on the lonely shore,
> There is society, where none intrudes,
> By the deep Sea, and music in its roar:
> I love not Man the less, but Nature more,
> From these our interviews, in which I steal
> From all I may be, or have been before,
> To mingle with the Universe, and feel
> What I can ne'er express, yet can not all conceal.
> *Childe Harold* (IV, 178)

The poem is as autobiographical as anything he ever wrote. McGann has pointed out that Byron began the poem on the very day (June 19, 1817) that he sent Augusta a furious letter about Ada being made a Ward of Chancery, and he vowed that Time and Nemesis would destroy the Milbanke party.

> . . . let me not have worn
> This iron in my soul in vain – shall *they* not mourn?
> (*Childe Harold*, IV, 131, 1178–9)

Annabella rightly guessed that the passage was "probably intended to make a great impression on *me*. Whilst I am so free from disordered brains, this will at least be postponed."[21] In actuality his sufferings amounted to intense mortification at having been deserted. Nevertheless Byron, like Rousseau before him, was validating humiliation; and the intense appeal of the poem lay in the responsive chord of narcissism it elicited. If the Promethean character of the poem is somewhat at variance with the Byron who could treat Claire Clairmont so callously, one must suspend judgement – or indeed even biographical knowledge of the poet's life – to savour its greatness. Apart from the *ad hominem* attacks on his wife, what Byron inserted into the poem was a natural magnanimity sometimes lacking in his daily life.

If he had to wait impatiently for news of the reception of *Childe Harold*, in very short order he heard that Hobhouse's literary notes had caused a furore with Italian men of letters. In London Hobhouse had met an Italian exile, the writer Ugo Foscolo, who agreed to write the section on contemporary Italian writing so long as his contribution would remain anonymous. Poor Hobhouse failed to suspect that Foscolo was using his book for his own ends. Byron received a furious letter from Di Breme in Milan complaining that his own name had been omitted and that there was far too much emphasis on Foscolo's achievements. Byron was amused and somewhat malicious about his friend's embarrassment.

The most exciting event of the summer for Byron was the third of his famous swims. Dining at the Hoppners' on March 27 he had met a Cavalier Angelo Mengaldo, who had served in Napoleon's army and who boasted of swimming across the Berezina while under enemy fire during one of Napoleon's great defeats. Byron was not to be outdone, and suggested a swimming contest. While at La Mira he often went over to swim at the Lido, and once the water was warm enough he was also swimming in the Grand Canal.

The two contestants were joined by Alexander Scott, a young Englishman residing in Venice. There was a preliminary swim on June 15; then ten days later the three set off from the Lido, the wind and tide being with them. The swim covered a distance of four and a half miles across the lagoon and down the stretch of the Grand Canal, with Byron soon easily outdistancing the others. Mengaldo gave up before reaching the canal and Scott managed to persevere as far as the Rialto. That same day (June 25, 1818) Byron boasted to Hobhouse that "I was in the sea from half past 4 – till a quarter past 8 – without touching or resting. – I could not be much fatigued having had a *piece* in the forenoon – & taking another in the evening at ten of the Clock."

He was not always so pleased with life. He was furious with Murray for not having paid him, with Hanson for postponing his trip with the Newstead papers, and with Kinnaird and Hobhouse for being so pre-occupied with their reformist politics that he claimed they were neglecting his interests. He complained of a want of ready cash, and Kinnaird reassured him (July 7, 1818) that all he had to do was write for a letter of credit and one would always be sent by return post.

Augusta meanwhile was having grave money worries of her own. After Six Mile Bottom was sold early in the year the family had moved to London and the whole family squeezed into her apartment at St James's Palace. For some time she was uncertain about whether she would be permitted to keep it after Queen Charlotte's death on September 21. She was also promised a small pension which she did not receive until 1820. She began to turn to Byron's publisher, John Murray, with requests for loans. She could not ask her brother for help since he was offended by her empty, evasive letters.

For the time being her only news of him was through Murray or Hobhouse. On July 24 she reported to Annabella that she had had a visit from Hobhouse:

> he told me Byron was in the worst humour & quarrelling with him & "everybody" which comprised I fancy Douglas Kinnaird, Hobhouse, Hanson, & Murray – that he kept counting his money – & that at last it was become a "disease of the mind" – "a positive malady" – "quite like a Miser" & with a constant idea he was to be left there without a farthing – & all the time large sums had been sent . . . I think this sounds alarming for many reasons – Hobhouse said he ate & *drank* & was become very large – "poor man . . . poor fellow!"[22]

The Palazzo Mocenigo was filled with animals, squabbling servants, and jealous women, La Fornarina exhibiting much the same demeanour as her predecessor. Claire, who was with the Shelleys in Bagni di Lucca, received a letter from Allegra's nurse Elise, reporting the fact that the child had been sent to stay with the Hoppners. Claire and Shelley were so alarmed about Allegra's welfare that they set off for Venice on August 17. Byron's state of mind was not the most propitious for the personal confrontation Claire was determined to have.

22

ooooooooooooo

Decadence in Venice, 1818–19

O ne of the saddest episodes in the extraordinary saga that comprised Byron's life was about to be played out. The amazing alacrity with which Shelley jumped into a one-horse cabriolet to travel across Italy in the heat of August requires some explanation. Mary's feelings were not consulted in his impetuosity to act the knight in shining armour to the tremulous Claire. It must not be forgotten that at this point he was as much under Albé's spell as Claire was. He looked forward eagerly to a resumption of the conversations they had shared on Lake Geneva in 1816, and he was still optimistic about converting Byron to an espousal of a benevolent life-force. It is possible, too, that there was an element of homosexuality in the attraction Byron exerted. That summer Shelley had been translating Plato's *Ion* and *Phaedo*, and in his commentaries he had argued that the practice of the Greeks could not be compared to the degradation of modern prostitution.

As they jolted along, Claire and Shelley discussed plans as to how they were going to persuade Byron to let Claire have Allegra for a time. The distraught mother was in favour of direct confrontation, but Shelley realised that nothing would antagonise Byron more than seeing her again; and for once the impulsive Shelley urged caution. He persuaded Claire that she should stay in Padua until he had had an initial discussion with her former lover. The proposal they planned to present to Byron was that he send Allegra to Florence where she could stay for a time with her mother.

When they reached Padua, Claire complained of the fleas in the inn and begged to be taken along to Venice. Within limits, Shelley found it difficult to refuse her anything. From Fusina they embarked for Venice on Saturday night, August 22. It was rash to set off at all as a great storm was blowing up, and the gondola was tossed about like a fragile toy while flashes of lightning rent the sky. Shelley was in state of exhilaration. Without any prompting from them, the gondolier began to speak of a *"giovinetto Inglese* with a *nome stravagante* who lived very luxuriously & spent great sums of money". He added the puzzling information that he had lately had "two of his daughters over from England & one looked nearly as old as himself".[1]

They knew from Elise's letters that Allegra was staying with the Hoppners. Shelley remained tactfully in the gondola while Claire went into the consular building to make enquiries. Within a few minutes a servant appeared to invite him to enter as well. Elise brought in Allegra, and mother and child were happily reunited. Shelley found the child paler than when he had last seen her, but still very beautiful. A warm invitation was extended to stay to dinner and the Hoppners, who were delighted to be at the centre of a drama, entered eagerly into a discussion about how best to approach the moody milord.

Shelley was familiar with Byron's pattern of rising late. There was every expectation that there would be a woman in the background. Would Byron take offence if Shelley made a sudden appearance? It was a chance he had to take. Fletcher showed him into the lofty drawing room; Byron was surprised but greeted him warmly, and was naturally curious about why he was in Venice. Shelley explained that he and his family had been touring Italy. He had left them in Padua – even this white lie caused him some discomfort – and felt that he and Byron should have some private talk about Claire, who was anxious about the health of her child. Byron made it clear that he had no intention of sending Allegra to Florence because with his reputation for caprice, the Venetians might think he had already grown tired of her. He could never divest himself of his preoccupation with his public image.

However, Byron was so pleased to see Shelley that he reacted with surprising reasonableness. He could see no objection, he said, why Claire shouldn't have Allegra for a week in Padua. After a bit he had another idea: he had rented a summer villa at Este from the Hoppners but with his usual indolence had never stirred himself to use it. Why didn't the Shelleys all stay there for the remainder of the hot weather? It was a splendid solution, as Byron thought further on it, because Claire would be at a still greater distance from him, and he might see Shelley from time to time. By now the afternoon had lengthened into evening and Byron wanted Shelley to accompany him on his daily ride on the Lido. Shelley was anxious to get back to Claire, but having created the fiction about the family group in

Padua, he had no alternative but to accede. Borne along by Byron's gondola, and after mounting horses at the Lido, the talk continued. Shelley reported to Mary that "Our conversation consisted in histories of his wounded feelings, and great professions of friendship and regard for me. He said that if he had been in England at the time of the Chancery affair, he would have moved Heaven & Earth to have prevented such a decision."[2]

They returned to the Palazzo Mocenigo and it was five in the morning when they finally parted, after fourteen hours of uninterrupted conversation. A certain amount of it was taken up with Byron's reading Canto IV of *Childe Harold* to Shelley. When Shelley finally returned to his inn he immediately sat down and wrote, a letter with a report of all the events to Mary. Since Byron believed that she was in Padua, it was imperative that Mary give truth to the fiction. Without apology, Shelley listed precisely the route she was to take, urging her to leave her pleasant refuge in Bagna di Lucca and bear her two children – one of them ailing – with all possible speed (and discomfort) to Padua.

Apparently Shelley returned once more to the Palazzo Mocenigo after Byron sent to the Hoppners for Allegra, with whom Shelley played.

> A lovelier toy sweet Nature never made,
> A serious, subtle, wild, yet gentle being,
> Graceful without design and unforeseeing,
> With eyes – Oh, speak not of her eyes!
> (*Julian and Maddalo*, 144–7)

Shelley and Claire then departed for Este, accompanied by Allegra and Elise. They were delighted with I Cappucini, a former monastery in the Euganean Hills with a summerhouse at the end of the garden where Shelley began to write a long poem incorporating his conversations with Byron, heightened by the dramatically solitary setting of the Lido.

Mary meanwhile set off reluctantly to join her husband. By the time they reached Lucca, Mary's little daughter Clara had become alarmingly ill. Eventually the weary woman reached Este. Shelley wrote apologetically to Byron on September 13 that he had been about to set off several times to visit him, but had been prevented by the illness of his daughter. He finally insisted that the child be seen by Byron's physician, Dr Aglietti, rather than by a local medical man. When they arrived unannounced in Venice, the doctor was not at home. Clara was now having convulsions and, leaving Mary holding her in her arms at an inn, Shelley went in search of Aglietti.

The child was dead within an hour of their arrival in what Byron described in *Childe Harold* (IV, 18, 155) as "a fairy city of the heart". With the kind help of the Hoppners, she was buried the following morning.

A stunned Mary could not help feeling that Shelley had put Claire's interests before those of his own family. Before they returned to Este, Byron told the grief-stricken woman that he would consider it a great favour if she could make fair copies of two of his recent poems, "Mazeppa" and the "Ode to Venice". By the middle of October Shelley decided that his wife needed the distractions of Venice, but it was really he who craved distraction from her reproachful eyes. Leaving her often in the company of the loquacious Mengaldo – who professed a desire to meet the author of *Frankenstein* – he frequently slipped off to resume his long conversations with Byron.

Shelley's delight in both Venice and his friend began to sour as he viewed the scene with closer attention. Mary was equally concerned about Byron, and lamented to Leigh Hunt that he would be a "lost man" unless he escaped soon from the dissipations of Venice.[3] To Thomas Love Peacock, Shelley poured out his indignation:

I entirely agree with what you say about Childe Harold [Canto IV]. The spirit in which it is written is, if insane, the most wicked & mischievous insanity that ever was given forth. It is a kind of obstinate & self-willed folly in which he hardens himself. I remonstrated with him in vain on the tone of mind from which such a view of things alone arises. For its real root is very different from its apparent one, & nothing can be less sublime than the true source of these expressions of contempt & desperation. The fact is, that first, the Italian women are perhaps the most contemptible of all who exist under the moon; the most ignorant the most disgusting, the most bigotted, the most filthy. Countesses smell so of garlick that an ordinary Englishman cannot approach them. Well, LB is familiar with the lowest sort of these women, the people his gondolieri pick up in the streets. He allows fathers & mothers to bargain with him for their daughters, & though this is common enough in Italy, yet for an Englishman to encourage such sickening vice is a melancholy thing. He associates with wretches who seem almost to have lost the gait and physionomy of man, & who do not scruple to avow practices which are not only not named but I believe seldom even conceived in England . . . He is not yet an Italian & is heartily & deeply discontented with himself.[4]

Nevertheless, Shelley was enormously impressed by a poem Byron had begun to write. This was *Don Juan* of which Byron had just finished the first canto, and Shelley envisaged it becoming one of the greatest of satirical poems. Ironically enough, he was to adopt towards its morality a totally different view from what Byron would hear from his friends in England. Late in October Shelley returned to Este where he completed *Julian and Maddalo*, a record of his conflicting feelings about Byron.

In the prose Preface he tried to bring Byron's good qualities into sharper relief than the views he has Count Maddalo, a Venetian nobleman, express in the poem.

> He is a person of the most consummate genius, if he would direct his energies to such an end, of becoming the redeemer of his degraded country. But it is his weakness to be proud: he derives from a comparison of his own extraordinary mind with the dwarfish intellects that surround him, an intense apprehension of the nothingness of life . . . but . . . in social life no human being can be more gentle, patient, and unassuming than Maddalo. He is cheerful, frank, and witty. His more serious conversation is a sort of intoxication; men are held by it as by a spell.

As they ride along the lonely beach, Julian expounds his views on the perfectibility of man, to which Maddalo replies dismissively, "You talk Utopia." Julian never quite abandons hope that "I might reclaim him from his dark estate." The poem ends with Julian's return many years later. Maddalo is now far away in the mountains of Armenia, his dog is dead, but his little girl has grown into a splendid woman – tragically ironical in view of later events.

On October 31 Mary and Shelley took leave of Byron. Elise begged to return with the Shelley party as she had fallen in love with Paolo Foggi, a servant Mary had hired in Bagna di Lucca. This must have been another bewildering parting for little Allegra, and although Mary extracted a promise from Byron that Claire might see her again, this was to be their last meeting. The Hoppners later said that they had never been particularly fond of the child. Byron's mistress, La Fornarina, fussed over her when the mood possessed her. The fiery petrel finally had a tempestuous dismissal preceded by various histrionics such as throwing herself into the Grand Canal. Allegra was the bewildered witness to these strange and changeable events.

As early as July 17 Byron informed Murray that he was writing his memoirs. That they were written in conjunction with the opening of Canto

IV of *Don Juan* must be borne in mind. When Murray enquired eagerly about their progress, Byron replied (August 26, 1818): "I shall not publish at present. – It is nearly finished – but will be too long – and there are so many things which out of regard to the living cannot be mentioned . . . I shall keep it among my papers – it will be a kind of Guide post in case of death – and prevent some of the lies which would otherwise be told – and destroy some which have been told already." He had completed about sixty large sheets, but they were still in very rough form, and he was doubtful if it would serve any end to publish the memoir since "it is full of many passions & prejudices of which it has been impossible for me to keep clear – I have not the patience."

Some of these passions and prejudices were to be subjected to mock-heroic treatment in the new poem which was written in the *ottava rima* of *Beppo*. Byron had missed the English première of Mozart's *Don Giovanni* in April 1817, and unfortunately it was never produced at La Fenice when he was in Venice. The don, however, was certainly a mythic figure with whom he was familiar; and since he knew he himself was widely regarded as a rake, he was aware that his readers would immediately read *Don Juan* as a *poème à clef*. However, he was totally unaware that his audience was changing and that the British middle classes were undergoing a period of revulsion towards the loose morality of the Regency.

Byron had again begun writing Augusta rather frivolous letters. He had guessed by now that she was in Lady Byron's confidence, and the first letter was occasioned by the triumphant news that he now had a child of his own. "It is the first one I have had free from discontents and repinings," Augusta told Annabella.[5] Then she heard from Murray that Hanson had actually left for Venice; and that Byron "*was going to write his Life!*"[6]. Annabella enquired if she had heard anything more about the Life, for she was concerned about "the difficulties it will present", to which Augusta replied disingenuously, "do you mean to the Author as well as others – We must trust all to Providence my dearest A."[7]

Before Byron heard the reaction of his first readers to *Don Juan* which he had sent back to England in the hands of Lord Lauderdale, he finally received the long-awaited visit of Hanson and his son bearing the Newstead papers. On November 11 they were shown into the great reception room. Hanson's son Newton left a narrative account of this visit. At first Byron had difficulty controlling his tears since the sight of these familiar faces brought back memories of his childhood, but he soon made it clear that he had no desire to have their visit prolonged once business was transacted. In addition to signing the Newstead papers, he made a codicil to his 1815 will, leaving £5,000 to

Allegra, "providing she does not marry a native of Great Britain". He also gave them a joint letter to take back to Kinnaird and Hobhouse to whom he was assigning the responsibility for handling his business affairs. Hanson soon realised that any hope of a reconciliation with his wife was impossible when he saw Byron's reaction to the news that Sir Samuel Romilly had slit his throat after the death of his wife. Byron raged bitterly how this man had supported the Milbankes despite having been on his retainer. He felt exonerated for "the mountain of my curse" he had pronounced in the Coliseum in Canto IV of *Childe Harold*. Byron also gave the Hansons a letter to Lady Byron in which he poured out the bitterness that had been nourished in the two years since the separation.

> Sir Samuel Romilly has cut his throat for the loss of his wife. – It is now nearly three years since he became in the face of his compact (by a retainer – previous, and I believe general), the advocate of the measures and the Approver of the proceedings which deprived me of mine . . . This Man little thought when he was lacerating according to law – while he was poisoning my life at it's sources . . . that a domestic Affliction would lay him in the Earth – with the meanest of Malefactors.[8]

The Hansons were shocked by his appearance. Newton recalled that "Lord Byron could not have been more than 30, but he looked 40. His face had become pale, bloated, and sallow. He had grown very fat, his shoulders broad and round, and the knuckles of his hands were lost in fat."[9]

The Shelleys had been right: the fact was that Byron had almost hit rock bottom. He had gone native with a vengeance, and he pursued his sexual conquests with a cold, pleasureless monotony. Whom did he think he could impress with his boast that he had slept with over 200 women since his arrival in Venice? Once so disciplined about his weight, he had even allowed himself to look like his mother. His only sense of himself had been formed by the impression he made on other people; he had noted at the age of ten the difference it made at school when it was announced that he was now a lord. Since there was no one now to mirror back to him his self-importance, the only way he could keep in touch with his genuine feelings was through the medium of poetry when he was entirely alone.

Yet his friends remained loyal to him. When Kinnaird received Byron's letter authorising him to act for him, he immediately set about trying to put Byron's financial affairs in order. "You may *rely* on the most unremitting attention to your interest on my part," Kinnaird assured him.[10] He and

Hobhouse had long been suspicious of Hanson's probity, and they were especially suspicious of his proposal that Byron make some compromise arrangement with his creditors. Hanson had submitted a partial bill of between £9,000 and £10,000, and Kinnaird did not believe that a penny should be paid until Hanson proffered a complete itemised bill and that, in any case, Byron's creditors must be paid first. Of the £94,500 from the sale of the abbey he and Hobhouse proposed putting £66,200 in 3 per cent government bonds, and the remaining £28,300 towards paying off Byron's debts. On December 28 they had a meeting with Hanson who insisted that what had now become £12,000 on his account should be paid. Kinnaird and Hobhouse balked at this. Byron, once so careless about money when he had none, had now become obsessional on the subject. Kinnaird had to reassure him constantly about the safety of his government bonds. As to the amount owing to Hanson, however, Byron argued that he should be paid according to the promise made in Venice.

It was only natural that Kinnaird, as Byron's banker, should be the one to manage his money affairs rather than Hobhouse who from time to time had tried to straighten them out. By now Hobhouse was preoccupied with politics. He was seeking election to the House of Commons to fill the seat left vacant by Sir Samuel Romilly's suicide. Kinnaird, who had been seeking the same seat, eventually withdrew and for a time it looked as though Hobhouse might become a Radical member. On hearing the news, Byron wrote approvingly to Kinnaird: "You may depend upon it, that Hobhouse has talents very much beyond his *present rate* – even beyond his own opinion – He is too *fidgetty*, but he has the elements of Greatness, if he can but keep his nerves in order." [11] Scrope Davies pleaded with him to return: "in God's name do your duty to your friend your principles and yourself";[12] but not even his regard for Hobhouse could move Byron to return to England. Hobhouse was defeated in February 1819 by George Lamb who was enthusiastically helped in his campaign by his sister-in-law, Caroline Lamb, whose husband had now become Lord Melbourne.

Byron was not quite so approving of Hobhouse when he heard his reaction to Canto I of *Don Juan* which had reached him when he was in the middle of his political campaign. When Kinnaird first read the poem he pronounced it "exquisite", Murray was entranced although somewhat nervous, but Hobhouse was absolutely adamant that it was unfit for publication. In his diary he wrote: "the blasphemies & facetiae and the domestica facta overpower even the great genius it displays – of Mazeppa and the ode [to Venice] I do not think much."[13] One must remember that Hobhouse knew so much about Byron's life that he could not fail to be shocked by the indiscretions he thought he was revealing to the world.

For those of us reading it today the poem is a delight, but Hobhouse was absolutely correct that its attacks on living people shattered all bounds of good taste. The dedication to the poet laureate, Robert Southey, was a savage attack on a man who he had heard had been spreading stories that he had been living in an "incestuous" relationship with the Shelleys in Geneva. There is also an unnecessary baiting of Wordsworth and the other Lake poets. In many other ways Byron used the poem to settle old scores. While the action takes place in Spain, one can read the poem as another rendering of the memoirs in its account of the troubled childhood and adolescence of a guileless young man who becomes a rake *malgré lui*. His mother, Donna Inez, is a prude and a hypocrite, and contemporary readers immediately recognised her resemblance to Lady Byron. There are some elements of his own mother as well. Donna Inez connives in the seduction of the sixteen-year-old Juan by the twenty-three-year-old Donna Julia, and one wonders if this is a veiled reference to Byron's relationship with Lord Grey, especially as it ends with a chastisement to Plato. There are perhaps elements, too, of his relationship with Augusta, particularly in the description of Donna Julia with her glossy hair clustered on her brow.

> 'Twas surely very wrong in Juan's mother
>   To leave together this imprudent pair,
> She who for many years had watch'd her son so –
> I'm very certain *mine* would not have done so.
>   (I, 110, 877–80)

The scandal of their affair sends the don on his travels. The rollicking tale, filled with puns and self-mockery, leaves the reader in expectation of more (and perhaps worse) to come. The narrator purports to be an old bachelor sitting at the door of a pousada, but the reader would not be deceived that he is any the less the author than the don himself:

> But now at thirty years my hair is gray –
>   (I wonder what it will be like at forty?
> I thought of a peruke the other day)
>   My heart is not much greener; and, in short, I
> Have squander'd my whole summer while 'twas May,
>   And feel no more the spirit to retort; I
> Have spent my life, both interest and principal,
> And deem not, what I deem'd, my soul invincible.
>   (I, 213)

Hobhouse sat down and wrote a long letter to Byron in an attempt to be tactful, flattering, and firm. He described how he and Scrope Davies had read the poem together, each of them exclaiming from time to time, "*it will be impossible to publish this.*" The *ad hominem* attacks would be damaging in every respect, Byron would undoubtedly be identified with the hero, and as a result "it will be impossible for any lady to allow *Don Juan* to be seen on her table."[4] After receiving this response, Byron briefly considered suppressing the poem, but soon changed his mind. In letter after letter he expressed his stubborn determination to publish. He knew the poem to be good; he was indifferent to the moral objections they raised; and he wanted the money for the copyright. "If you suppose I don't want the money – you are mistaken," he told Hobhouse. "I do mind it most damnably – it is the only thing I ever saw worth minding."[5] As to its alleged immorality, "I maintain that it is the most moral of poems – but if people won't discover the moral that it is their fault not mine."[6] He suggested the solution he had used with *The Curse of Minerva* and *Fare Thee Well*: namely, that 500 copies be printed for private circulation.

By now Kinnaird agreed with Byron's other friends that the poem should be suppressed. Hobhouse's misery was compounded by the arrival of Canto II in mid-January 1819. This one contained the shipwreck episode with the disturbing account of cannibalism and the idyllic love story of Juan and Haidee, the pirate's daughter. Byron instructed that the two cantos be published together – anonymously – and that nothing was to be omitted beyond the dedication to Southey and a savage reference to Castlereagh.

Hobhouse was beside himself. To Murray he said that he hoped that the world wouldn't see as much of the "domestic *facts*" as he did; but once it was clear that Byron would not accept his suggested corrections, he sighed resignedly, "It cannot be helped." The poem itself would probably escape censure, "but I am sure the outcry against *him* will be very great".[7]

London was buzzing with speculation about its projected publication, and agitated letters passed between Augusta and Annabella about what Augusta referred to as "the vile poem". When Scrope Davies called on Augusta he told her that he feared that Byron, after living long in Venice, had lost all sense of decorum. On April 12 she described a long visit by Hobhouse:

> I confess I felt very anxious to hear what he would say about the new *Work* – he talked of little else but that & its author – & appeared vexed & worried to death . . . *Nothing could be worse* – he had to write to *insist* on the Publication – & they suppose it must be *anonymously* – & with

considerable *omissions* – Hobhouse said he should still do all he could
. . . *He had his own character to preserve* – Actually dear A – he spoke as if
sincerely vexed & hurt about it – he had only that day given it [Canto
II] to Murray to read & consult his Oracles upon it – one's fear is if
they are peremptory in refusing that it may be transferred to those
who will not have the same regard for the consequences – I ventured
to say to Hobhouse – I thought *he* could do more in the way of
persuasion than any one else – his reply was, if I was *there* I could – but
not *here* – "I would not hesitate to burn it before his face but I can't
behind his back" – I replied he had better go to him – He told me he
thought his chief reason for persisting was the *Money* – that on *that*
subject he was quite *insane* & gave me certainly very strong instances
which look very like it – I thought that he spoke very rationally & as
really interested in his welfare – begged me not to write on this subject
– as the idea of everybody joining in an opinion against him had so
enraged him . . . God knows what is to come of it all.[18]

As the date of publication drew near Augusta was almost desperate with
anxiety. In a letter filled with blots and erasures (July 3, 1819), she confessed
to being close to despair in her apprehension, and on July 6 she asserted
that "it is disgrace to him & his whole family. I dread all the questions &
remarks it will bring upon me."[19] Once the poem was published on July 15,
she found it less bad than she had feared. Annabella too found nothing to
ruffle her composure. She recognised herself in Donna Inez, but felt it
painted a distorted picture of her: "I must however confess that the
quizzing in one or two passages was so good as to make me smile at
myself – therefore others are heartily welcome to laugh . . . I do not feel
inclined to continue the perusal. It is always a task to me now to read his
works, in which, through all the levity, I discern enough to awaken very
painful feelings."[20]

On August 2 Augusta had another visit from Hobhouse who told her
"*Don Juan had failed completely* & did not sell . . . which he thought a most
fortunate circumstance – he added that he heard there were not to be any
more Cantos – I suppose something worse will be undertaken – he says he
thinks Byron can't possibly continue his present way of life."[21]

When Hobhouse said it was a failure he was exaggerating. What he
meant was that of the 1,500 expensive quarto copies (priced at £1.11.6),
Murray could not dispose of 150 copies, but the poem continued to sell in
cheaper, pirated editions. The *Edinburgh Review* maintained a stony silence,
but *Blackwood's* had a field day. They admitted the genius of "the vile

poem" but went on to describe the poet as "Impiously railing against his God – madly and meanly disloyal to his Sovereign and his country – and brutally outraging all the best feelings of family honour, affection, and confidence . . . it appears . . . as if this miserable man . . . were resolved to show us that he is no longer a human being, even in his frailties; – but a cool unconcerned fiend."[22]

Not unexpectedly, Wordsworth's verdict on the "infamous publication" was that it "will do more harm to the English character, than anything of our time".[23] Byron was satisfied: his work was still being talked about. Probably he still also courted gossip about himself. But his mind was now occupied elsewhere – with what he would describe as the last great passion of his life.

23

○○○○○○○○○○○○○

Next-to-Last Love, 1819

No more – no more – Oh! never more on me
   The freshness of the heart can fall like dew,
Which out of all the lovely things we see
   Extracts emotions beautiful and new,
Hived in our bosoms like the bag o' the bee:
   Think'st thou the honey with those objects grew?
Alas! 'twas not in them, but in thy power
To double even the sweetness of a flower.

No more – no more – Oh! never more, my heart,
   Canst thou be my sole world, my universe!
Once all in all, but now a thing apart,
   Thou canst not be my blessing or my curse:
The illusion's gone for ever, and thou art
   Insensible, I trust, but none the worse,
And in thy stead I've got a deal of judgment,
Though heaven knows how it ever found a lodgement.

Stanzas 214 and 215 of *Don Juan* were added to the last section of Canto I in the late summer of 1818. They captured a mood of hopelessness and world-weariness that pervaded Byron at the time. How ironical they seem in view of his emotional state eight months later!

On the evening of April 2, 1819, Byron accompanied his friend Alexander Scott to Countess Benzoni's. They placed themselves on a sofa opposite the entrance where the guests were beginning to arrive after attending the theatre. He did not at first recognise the Countess Guiccioli to whom he had been introduced the year before. She had come to the gathering as reluctantly as Byron. She was pregnant and wanted to go to bed, but her strong-willed husband insisted, only yielding to her plea that they stay but a few minutes. She was small and voluptuous, very feminine, with a mass of auburn curls. She was almost a beauty, but what one noticed about her were her large luminous eyes and general air of youthful freshness.

Countess Benzoni approached Byron and asked him if she could present him to the young matron from Ravenna. Perhaps he was striking a pose in front of his friend Scott, but he refused, protesting that he did not want to meet ugly women or beautiful women either for that matter. Was he perhaps unconsciously trying to avert his fate? Countess Benzoni and Scott eventually prevailed on him, and he smiled charmingly when his hostess described him as "Peer of England and its greatest poet".

Conversation was easy. Perhaps Byron should have remembered a maxim of one of his favourite writers, La Rochefoucauld: "If it were not for poetry, few men would ever fall in love." The attraction of Teresa was enhanced by the fact that she came from Ravenna where Dante was buried. Teresa had been given an education superior to that of most Italian women of her generation in the Convent of Santa Chiara at Faenza, and she began to speak enthusiastically of Dante and Petrarch. This was no empty-headed provincial, Byron soon realised, but a sensitive, cultivated woman with whom he could have a real conversation.

Before they parted that evening, Byron made an assignation to meet her the following day. Her absence she explained to her husband by the fact that she was slipping off quietly with her former governess-companion, Fanny Silvestrini (a sort of Mrs Clermont), to practise her French. At some point she transferred into Byron's gondola and he conducted her to his little house near S. Maria Zobenigo. He had taken the casino for sexual assignations in order to escape the jealous wrath of La Fornarina, and here his innumerable dalliances had shocked the worldly Angelo Mengaldo. There were also excursions to the lagoon where Teresa noticed that Byron sometimes relapsed into a melancholy mood.

Whether Byron at first regarded her as only another of his innumerable conquests is hard to say, but what is certain is that he was soon in fathomless love. For ten days they were lost in a passion such as neither of them had ever experienced before, while the loyal Fanny waited patiently as the afternoon shadows lengthened. It is astounding that Teresa's daily absences did not arouse the wily count's suspicions, since their affair was soon the talk of Venice. Teresa for her part was delighted with her conquest, and caused a flutter at Countess Benzoni's one evening when she called to "mio Byron". Probably the count caught wind of the scandal for he announced abruptly that they would be leaving two days later for one of his estates on the River Po. Close to hysteria, Teresa rushed off to La Fenice where Byron was attending Rossini's *Otello*. Breaking all the rules of etiquette, she slipped into his box to break the news.

On April 6 Byron sent Hobhouse an account of his new infatuation. He started out cynically enough with the statement that "She seems disposed to qualify the first year of marriage being just over. – I knew her a little last year at her starting, but they always wait a year – at least generally." But Hobhouse would have been unsettled by the ending: "What shall I do! I am in love – and tired of promiscuous concubinage – & have now an opportunity of settling for life." Hobhouse, already concerned about the fate of *Don Juan*, was equally worried by this turn of events.

> Dont you go after that terra firma lady: they are very vixens, in those parts especially, and I recollect when I was at Ferrara seeing or hearing of two women in the hospital who had stabbed one another in the guts and all *por gelosia* – take a fool's advice for once and be content with your *Naids* – your amphibious fry – you make a very pretty splashing with them in the Lagune and I recommend constancy to the neighbourhood – go to Romagna indeed! Go to old Nick. You'll never be heard of afterwards . . .[1]

But Byron was not to be reasoned with. He had lost almost every vestige of self-esteem, and he envisaged salvation with this exquisite girl of nineteen. His rash impulsiveness in entering into marriage with Annabella had been a device to save himself from the damnation of his relationship with Augusta. Now he needed another woman to save him from himself. He had not put any thought to the responsibilities that marriage entailed, but he had now been in Italy long enough to be aware exactly of the implications of *serventissimo*. In *Beppo* he had already ridiculed the custom for the hypocrisy of its pretence that the relationship between the woman and her *cisisbeo* was strictly platonic. It was a form of servitude even more exigent than marriage, and the fact that Byron was rushing towards it was a measure of his desperation. Nevertheless, he experienced a certain nervousness at Teresa's resemblance to Caroline Lamb in her disdain of public opinion, but he was "damnably in love".[2] His very choice of words is significant.

From the dreary marshland estate Teresa wrote long lovesick letters under cover to Fanny. On April 19 Fanny reported that Byron had sworn to her that his love was genuine, "that you have made on him an impression that can *never* be erased".*[3] His first surviving letter to Teresa is dated April 22. After telling her that she was his "only and last love", he went on to say that "you vowed to be true to me and I will make no vows to you; let us see which of us will be the more faithful." Nevertheless, "there is no other woman in the world for me." On April 25 he committed himself even more strongly:

> My Treasure – my life has become the most monotonous and sad; neither books, nor music, nor *Horses* (rare things in Venice – but you know that mine are at the Lido) – nor dogs – give me any pleasure; the society of women does not attract me; I won't speak of the society of men, for that I have always despised. For some years I have been trying systematically to avoid strong passions, having suffered too much from the tyranny of Love. *Never to feel admiration* – and to enjoy myself without giving too much importance to the enjoyment in itself – to feel indifference towards human affairs – contempt for many, but hatred for none, – this was the basis of my philosophy. I did not mean to love any more, nor did I hope to receive Love. You have put to flight all my resolutions – now I am all yours – I will become what you wish – perhaps happy in your love, but never at peace again. You should not have re-awakened my heart – for (at least in my own country) my love has been fatal to those I love – and to myself. But these reflections come too late. You have been mine – and whatever the outcome – I am, and eternally shall be, entirely yours.

Teresa had already had a son, Achille, who had been born on November 7, 1818, and had died a few days later. Both husband and wife seemed anxious for another child. Byron was beside himself when he heard that she had suffered a miscarriage, possibly brought on by their violent love-making. But what was he to do? While he was waiting impatiently for instructions from Teresa, he read in *Galignani's Messenger* that Polidori had published a tale, *The Vampyre*, lifted from a ghost story Byron had told at Villa Diodati. With his mind on more immediate concerns, Byron's letter to the editor was relatively mild. He denied the rumour that he was the author, and went on to say: "If the book is clever it would be base to deprive the real writer – whoever he may be – of his honours; – and if stupid – I desire the responsibility of nobody's dullness but my own."[4]

* Iris Origo has translated all these letters into English.

At the time that Byron met Teresa he was dallying with an eighteen-year-old Venetian of good birth. On hurrying to an assignation with her, he tumbled into the Grand Canal, and completed the transaction on a balcony while dripping wet. Venice was accustomed to his vagaries, but to confess the incident to Murray (who would have repeated it to his literary cronies) made him appear an absolute buffoon. Perhaps Byron, about to embark on an irrevocable step, reverted to such infantile antics to reassure himself that he was still master of his actions.

There was an even more curious letter written to Augusta the previous day (May 17, 1819). His renewed correspondence with her had been confined to brief, trivial notes. Now she was startled to receive an impassioned declaration that his love for her was as deep as the ocean. Augusta was his sheet-anchor, a Byron, and by falling in love with Teresa, he felt that in some sense he was betraying his lover, his mother, and his own deepest self. If only Augusta would send him a word of love, a sign that nothing had changed between them, he might yet be saved.

> I have never ceased nor can cease to feel for a moment that perfect & boundless attachment which bounds & binds me to you – which renders me utterly incapable of *real* love for any other human being – what could they be to me after *you*? My own xxxx [short word crossed out] we may have been very wrong – but I repent of nothing except that cursed marriage – & your refusing to continue to love me as you had loved me . . . whenever I love anything it is because it reminds me in some way or other of yourself.

He mentioned that he had been recently attached to a Venetian because her name had some secret significance associated with Augusta. (No mention of Teresa!) If he returned to England, it would be only to see her. He spoke of his wife as "that infamous fiend" who drove him from the country. "They say absence destroys weak passions – & confirms strong ones – Alas! *mine* for you is the union of all passions & of all affections."

Augusta was in a state of total bewilderment as to what to do about the letter, informing Annabella that she had received a disturbing letter from her brother, but hesitated to show it to her. On June 25, after coming to no conclusion about how it should be answered, she decided finally to send it to Annabella who was staying in Tunbridge Wells. Surely now, she suggested, Annabella could see that her brother was a maniac? "I do not believe any feelings expressed are by any means permanent – only occasioned by ye passing & present reflection & occupation of writing to the unfortunate Being to whom they are addressed."[5] What advice did Annabella have for her?

If Augusta had even a flicker of a desire to arouse her jealousy, Annabella was determined to disabuse her. "Incapable as he is of the true attachment, which is devoted to the welfare of the object, I have before observed to you that in the intervals of every pursuit which engaged him by its novelty, this most dreadful fever of the heart returned."[6] She should either break off all communication, Annabella warned her sternly, or ignore the letter.

One is stunned by the perspicacity of Annabella's observation. To Mrs Villiers, however, she spoke somewhat differently: "It is the most open avowal of unextinguishable passion – which he says will drive him mad – that *she* was the only object throughout which cost him a tear – With such a letter in my hand I should have had ample means of repelling the attacks which I expect – but I returned it – It would not have been honourable to do otherwise."[7] Nevertheless, she emphasised, the letter proved beyond a doubt that the reformation in Augusta's behaviour occurred after the marriage; and it was proof positive of the past relationship.

While these women were twittering excitedly, Byron was deeply pre-occupied with other concerns. At the beginning of June when he set off to visit Ravenna, despite his protestations to Teresa, he was still struggling against committing himself fully to her, telling himself that he would be back in Venice within a month. Just before his departure he redrafted a poem he had been working on, "To the Po".

> My heart is all meridian, were it not
>   I had not suffered now, nor should I be—
> Despite of tortures ne'er to be forgot—
>   The Slave again, Oh Love! at least of thee!
> 'Tis vain to struggle, I have struggled long
>   To love again no more as once I loved.
> Oh! Time! why leave this earliest Passion strong?
>   To tear a heart which pants to be unmoved?
>
>   (45–52)

Both Hoppner and Scott thought he was making a fool of himself. From Padua on June 2 he himself began to wonder. To Hoppner he wrote: "I am proceeding in no very good humour – for La G's instructions are rather calculated to produce an éclat – and perhaps a scene – than any decent iniquity." Teresa had irritated him by telling him that she had to go to

Bologna in the middle of June. "Why the devil then drag me to Ravenna? . . . The Charmer forgets that a man may be whistled any where *before* – but that *after* – a Journey in an Italian June is a Conscription – and therefore She should have been less liberal in Venice – or less exigent in Ravenna."

He was also a little nervous about Count Guiccioli, the husband he was going to cuckold, particularly in view of Teresa's rash impetuosity. The count was a cultivated man with a passion for the theatre, but a good deal of sinister gossip circulated about him. He had supported Napoleon and had attended his coronation in Milan cathedral, but after the papal government re-established itself in Romagna, he was soon cultivating the two Cardinal Legates presiding in Ravenna. He loved to play to the gallery with his coach and six, and he had purchased more land than he could afford. He had lost a lawsuit with a rich landowner at Forli, Domenico Manzoni, and as a result was imprisoned for several months in the Castel Sant'Angelo in Rome. Manzoni was later mysteriously murdered.

While married to his first wife, Countess Placidia, Guiccioli seduced a series of her maids, and when the countess raised objections, he banished her to one of his remote estates. She returned shortly before her death in time to make a will in her husband's favour. There were rumours of poison. Guiccioli then proceeded to marry the reigning favourite among the maids, but she too died in 1817, leaving him with seven children. Her inconsolable husband attended the theatre on the night of her death.

Another wife was required. One autumn evening in 1817 the fifty-eight-year-old count visited the Palazzo Gamba. Teresa was summoned to meet a gentleman with red hair and whiskers, a man even older than her father. With a candle in his hand, the count circled the delectable commodity fresh out of the convent. Count Gamba had an ailing wife (soon to die) and five daughters to marry off, so it probably seemed a good match. Teresa was pronounced satisfactory by this rather sinister-looking man, and the marriage took place on January 28, 1818. The inexperienced girl found her stepchildren sullen, and her husband parsimonious about the household accounts, but there seems to have been a genuine sexual passion between them which gave Teresa some power over him. Nevertheless, she chafed under the restraints imposed upon her, and was soon only too ready for an exciting liaison.

This was the domestic situation to which Byron was making his uncomfortable journey. By the time he reached Bologna the heat was unbearable, and he was thoroughly put out to find no letter waiting for him at the Pellegrino inn; and he sent word to Hoppner to prepare for his return, but the next morning scribbled on the envelope: "I am just setting off for Ravenna, June 8th 1819. I changed my mind this morning, & decided to go on." It was a combination of curiosity, passion and the heat of Bologna that was to pull him to Ravenna. Byron's geography was a little shaky as he expected to cross the Rubicon on his journey; but the actual river flowed further to the south-east of the road he was to traverse several times in the future.

The great coach rolled into Ravenna on the Feast of Corpus Christi when the whole population of the sleepy little town had spilled out into the narrow streets hung with banners and tapestries. Naturally a curious crowd gathered around the outlandish vehicle, and Byron asked a pretty young woman if she would point the way to the nearest inn. She happened to be a friend of Teresa's, and rushed over to the Palazzo Guiccioli to announce that the great poet had arrived. That evening he was invited by Count Giuseppe Alborghetti, the secretary-general of the province, to join him in his box at the theatre. Byron mentioned that he was a friend of the Guiccioli family; and on hearing that Teresa was near death, his reaction was so intense that he startled his host. Count Guiccioli, however, caught sight of him and was able to reassure him that Teresa was weak but recovering. That night Byron sent her a note from his cramped little inn only yards from her home: "I would sacrifice all my hopes for this world and all that we believe we may find in the other – to see you happy. I cannot think of the state of your health without sorrow and tears."[8] Many such notes were to be exchanged, slipped in by a compliant priest, a maid, or a black page.

The next day Byron was to see Teresa lying pale and thin, surrounded by her numerous relatives. As if in a dream he dutifully visited the sights hospitable people thought he would be interested in viewing: Dante's tomb, the magnificent Byzantine mosaics in the Rotonda and S. Appolinare in Classe. He inspected the manuscripts of Aristophanes and Dante in the Biblioteca Classense. By June 16 Teresa had recovered sufficiently to drive with Byron to the cool pine woods south of the town, with her husband following in his own coach. Byron suggested that they elope, for he had not yet absorbed the essence of *serventissimo*, although he was already caught in its bondage: "A slave is not more humble in the presence of his master – than I am in yours, – but do not abuse your power, for you have too much."[9]

As Teresa grew stronger, Byron sent for his horses and in the evenings they began riding together in the Pineta. As the days passed there were tears, quarrels, jealousy – Teresa detected him pinching her friend's thigh, he suspected that she was stealing glances at another man at the theatre, he was offended when she lost a ring he had given her. But why did the count always seem so pleasant? As events transpired, he was cultivating their visitor because he believed that Byron could be of some use to him. Having been a political turncoat, he was always alert to the presence of papal spies and fearful that his status might change at any moment. He approached Byron about the possibility of being appointed a British vice-consul which he believed would ensure his protection by a foreign government. Byron enquired first of Hoppner and then asked Murray if he could obtain assistance "amongst your many splendid Government Connections" (August 12, 1819). Murray was unlikely to have been surprised by the request because he had already been required to send everything from reviews to corn plasters and condoms.

Then Teresa again took a turn for the worse. Byron was so concerned that he sent for Dr Aglietti in Venice and his ministrations proved so efficacious that Byron won the gratitude of all her relatives. It was just as well because the count had received a nasty anonymous letter informing him that he was being cuckolded, but the ingenious Teresa managed to soothe him. Then *she* received a letter from her brother Pietro who was studying in Rome. He had been disturbed to hear the gossip about her liaison with a man who was said to have shut up his wife in a castle and was even rumoured to have been a pirate. Teresa indignantly refused to believe such stories, and as for Byron's purported treatment of his wife, "I do not believe it. I have had constant proofs of the extreme goodness of his Heart! Tears of mental or physical suffering make him almost ill – the dread of treading on an ant makes him go out of his way – a scene at the play, a sad story or a melodious tune brings tears to his eyes."[10]

Fanny Silvestrini seems to have been the only person in favour of the affair. To Hoppner (July 2, 1819) Byron spoke of the "disgust which Venice excites when fairly compared with any other city in this part of Italy – when I say *Venice* I mean the *Venetians* – the City itself is superb as it's History – but the people are what – I never thought them until they taught me to think so." Hoppner was reporting that there were all sorts of unpleasant stories about him circulating in Venice, and spoke his mind in a way that could only enrage Byron:

> I am very sorry for the distress you feel on the G's account not only
> because I think in almost every such case they are good feelings

thrown away on an unworthy object; but because I have reason to think it is particularly so in the present instance . . . to hear you talking of a serious attachment to a woman, who under her circumstances would be unworthy of it, . . . and who in the present instance is reported avowedly not to return it, but to have entangled you in her nets merely from vanity, is what the friendship you have honoured me with does not allow me to witness without a remonstrance."[11]

Byron was greatly stung by the whole letter, and particularly by the insinuation that Teresa might drop him. Alexander Scott also tried to reason with him: "Give up your horses! discharge your servants! Oibò! I will wait for your second thoughts."[12]

Apart from Kinnaird and Hobhouse, Byron was careful about what he told friends in England about Teresa. In his first letter to Augusta from Ravenna he did not mention his new attachment, but asked her to tell Lady Byron that he wished to marry again and to enquire whether there was any possibility of obtaining a Scottish divorce. (Augusta does not seem to have passed on this information.) Finally – on July 26 – he asked Augusta if her very neutral letter was a reply to his impassioned declaration on May 17: "What? Is it come to *this*? Have you no memory? or no heart? – You *had* both and I have *both* – at least for *you*. – I write this presuming that you received *that* letter – is it that you fear? do not be afraid of the post – the World has it's own affairs without thinking of *ours* and you may write safely." He then expressed a rare concern for a pain in her side which she had complained about. Would she like him to come to her? Or would she consider bringing her family, "including that precious baggage your Husband", to a warmer climate? He then revealed to her the reason he was in Ravenna, but depicted Teresa as a vain little charmer, and proceeded to give a comic description of her equestrian antics, ending, "I can't tell how long or short may be my stay – write to me – love me – as ever."

At the beginning of August, Count Guiccioli – a man as subject to sudden impulses as Byron himself – announced that Teresa must accompany him on a visit to Bologna. First they would stay at his estate at Forli. He sent Byron a warm invitation to join them in the country. Byron refused, but promised to join them in Bologna where he arrived almost two months to the day after his fateful departure for Ravenna. In his transitional life, he was moved about now by the whims of a capricious man and wife. In *Don Juan* he had Donna Julia say:

> 'Man's love is of his life a thing apart,
> 'Tis woman's whole existence . . .
>
> (I, 194, 1545–6)

But who could dispute that, possessed by passion, he had lost all sense of identity and the capacity to make decisions for himself? This was highly ironical in view of the fact that he was finally finding his authentic voice as a poet in a fusion of the lyrical and the satirical.

After a few days in the Locanda del Pellegrino, Byron took some rooms in an eighteenth-century palace, but the amiable count insisted that he use the ground floor of his palazzo which had a much prettier garden with a fountain and a pergola of vines. But once more the count insisted that Teresa accompany him to another estate near Ferrara. In the stifling heat of August Byron was left alone in Bologna, except for the spies watching his every movement. Ever since he had associated with liberals in Milan he had become as a dangerous intruder, and his growing paranoia about public surveillance was not imaginary.

To Kinnaird and Hobhouse he admitted frankly that he was frittering away his life:

> I feel it bitterly – that a man should not consume his life at the side and on the bosom – of a woman – and a stranger – that even the recompense and it is much – is not enough – and that this Cisisbean existence is to be condemned. – But I have neither the strength of mind to break my chain, nor the insensibility which would deaden it's weight. – I cannot tell what will become of me – to leave or to be left would at present drive me quite out of my senses – and yet to what have I conducted myself? – I have luckily or unluckily no ambition left – it would be better if I had – it would at least awake me – whereas at present I merely start in my sleep.[13]

In a letter three days prior to this he had expressed an eagerness to go to South America; and had Hobhouse responded with enthusiasm – as he had done for other travel suggestions in the past – Byron's fate might have been different. But to Murray, Hobhouse wrote that "it is impossible that Ld Byron should seriously contemplate – or, even if he does, he must not expect us to encourage this mad scheme."[14]

Yet Byron continued to mope about Teresa in her absence. On August 23 – on the same day as he complained to Hobhouse about the indignity of his situation – he wrote in her copy of Madame de Staël's *Corinne*:

17. *Above* Dr. Stephen Lushington, Lady Byron's legal counsel in the separation proceedings (*Pierpont Morgan Library*)

18. *Above right* John Cam Hobhouse, Byron's most steadfast friend, engraving by Charles Turner after James Hayter (© *British Museum*)

19. John Hanson, Byron's often exasperating solicitor, by James Halls (*Newstead Abbey*)

20. Napoleon's coach captured at Waterloo in 1815. Byron had an almost exact duplicate made to convey him into exile, George Cruikshank (© *British Museum*)

21. *Above* Lady Noel
Byron whose face is now
marked with adamantine
determination, engraved
by William Henry Mote
after Sir William John
Newton (*Newstead Abbey*)

22. *Above right* Claire
Clairmont, Byron's
importunate mistress by
Amelia Curran (*Newstead
Abbey*)

23. Thomas Moore to
whom Byron entrusted
the controversial
Memoirs (*NPG*)

24. Countess Teresa Guicciolo,
Byron's last attachment

25. Count Alessandro
Guiccioli, Teresa's sinister
husband

26. Percy Bysshe Shelley, whose feelings towards Byron were extremely ambivalent, by E.E. Williams (*Pierpont Morgan Library*)

27. Leigh Hunt who joined Byron in Italy but felt that he was treated badly (*NPG*)

28. Edward John Trelawny, a real-life version of Byron's Corsair, by Joseph Severn (*Courtesy of Anthea Mander Lahr*)

29. Douglas Kinnaird, Byron's supportive banker (*Courtesy of Lord Kinnaird*)

30. Lord Byron (1822) in Pisa
by William Edward West.
Many people remarked on how
fat he had become (*Scottish
National Portrait Gallery*)

31. A thin Byron (1823) drawn
by Count d'Orsay shortly
before his departure for Greece
(*Victoria and Albert Museum*)

32. *Above* Byron and a vain Teresa who apparently scratched out her face (*Biblioteca Classense, Ravenna*)

33. *Below* Byron's house at Missolonghi, the scene of his final ordeal.

my destiny rests with you – & you are a woman [nineteen?] years of age – and two years out of a Convent. – I wish that you had staid there with all my heart – or at least that I had never met you in your married state, – but all this is too late – I love you – and you love me – at least you *say* so – and act as if you *did* so – which last is a great consolation in all events. – But *I* more than love you – and cannot cease to love you. – Think of me sometimes when the Alps and the Ocean divide us – but they never will – unless you wish it.

It was at this point that he decided to send for his three-year-old daughter Allegra to keep him company. In his preoccupation with Teresa, she had seemed to slip his mind. Mrs Hoppner told Mary Shelley that the child "*est devenue tranquille et Sérieuse comme une petite vieille, ce qui nous peine beaucoup*".[5] In May a well-to-do Englishwoman living in Geneva, Mrs Vavassour, had taken a fancy to Allegra while visiting in Venice. She suggested to the Hoppners that she bring up the girl as long as Byron agreed to renounce all claim to her. When Claire heard of this possibility, she wrote to Byron: "do you think she is the destined third person to take care of Allegra? . . . It is impossible that you can live as you now do – therefore before you do any thing decided think and do not throw away the greatest treasure you have to strangers."[6] Byron refused to consider Mrs Vavassour's offer; and when the Hoppners left Venice for Switzerland for the summer, Hoppner suggested taking the girl with them since the Italian climate was clearly not beneficial to her health. Byron would not agree to this either, and so she was left this time with the wife of the Danish consul.

Alexander Scott was strongly opposed to Allegra being sent to join her father: "Allow me to tell you what I think on the subject – Allegra, once in the hands of your 'Dama' (you will not keep her at a hotel) will be a hostage for your future conduct, and if she should be taken to Ravenna, and if she should there be put in a convent, it will be no easy matter to get her out again."[7]

Byron, however, was determined to have her with him: "I wish her here instantly – as I now return to Ravenna – shortly" (August 28, 1819). After her arrival, for a few days he delighted in watching her play in the garden; and on September 10 he reported to Augusta:

Allegra is here with me – in good health – & very amiable and pretty at least thought so. – She is English – but speaks nothing but Venetian – "Bon *di* papa" &c. &c. she is very droll – and has a good deal of the

Byron – can't articulate the letter **r** at all – frowns and pouts quite in our way – blue eyes – light hair growing *darker* daily – and a dimple in the chin – a scowl on the brow – white skin – sweet voice – and a particular liking of Music – and of her own way in every thing – is not that B. all over?

The Guicciolis seem to have returned a day or so later. The count had already borrowed a considerable sum of money from Byron, and now, when he asked him for another loan, was refused because Byron's banker warned him that he was not a good risk. This decision was to be the beginning of serious tension between them. Teresa resolved the crisis by having another relapse and insisting that she must consult Dr Aglietti once more.

On September 12 Teresa set off in her husband's coach and six for Venice, with Byron following in his own coach. This arrangement probably lasted only so long as the count could see them. Where they stored Allegra is anybody's guess.

24

ooooooooooooo

Opera Bouffa, 1819–20

W
hen the lovers reached the Euganean Hills, they made a sentimental excursion to Arqua, the resting-place of Petrarch. It was one of the most romantic incidents in their relationship; and Teresa made the most of it when she later related to Moore how they drank water from the poet's fountain and she recited one of Petrarch's sonnets. "I cannot linger over these recollections of happiness. The contrast with the present is too dreadful. If a blessed spirit, while in the full enjoyment of heavenly happiness, were sent down to this earth to suffer all its miseries, the contrast could not be more dreadful between the past and the present."[1] By the time they reached Padua, they were discussing eloping, perhaps to France or America. Byron's common sense, however, eventually prevailed; and he showed Teresa around La Mira before travelling on to Venice where they arrived on September 15. Count Guiccioli's steward, Lega Zambelli, had prepared quarters for Teresa; but the following day, without mentioning that she was actually in the Palazzo Mocenigo, she wrote her husband a most extraordinary letter:

> My dear Alessandro: I arrived yesterday evening in Venice, in excellent condition, because the two days' journey had done me more good than any medicine . . . This morning Aglietti came, and having examined me, ordered me no drugs, but instead advised another journey and change of air. Your affairs, I feel sure, would not allow you to come with me, so Byron having offered to take me with him to the lakes of Garda and Como – a journey suitable to the season, and which he is now thinking of taking, not being much pleased with Venice, – I ask for your permission, and await its speedy arrival with the greatest anxiety.[2]

Byron was stunned by the count's easy compliance which reached them after they had moved back to La Mira. The speed with which they left the city was probably precipitated by the scandal their arrival had caused. To reinforce her point that she was still far from well, Teresa again wrote that Dr Aglietti had reassured her that she did not have a prolapsed uterus as feared, but she was uncomfortable with piles and still had a cough that gave them cause for anxiety. Meanwhile she and Byron were going for pleasant strolls and reading poetry together. Their idyll was disturbed by an angry letter from her father, Count Gamba, expostulating with her for her lack of prudence.

> You have hardly entered the world but it will make no allowance for your youth, the purity of your heart, the innocence of your journey, or for all the circumstances which may justify your present position. The most seductive young man is by your side, protecting you – no doubt in a manner honourable and worthy to you both. That may be enough to convince me, and your husband, and your own conscience, but the world will not be satisfied with your arguments. The retired life that you are leading will only provide further weapons for those who may wish to criticize your position.[3]

Teresa reluctantly abandoned the excursion to the lakes, and agreed to wait patiently for her husband's arrival. Within a fortnight Byron was chafing at this enforced domesticity. On October 3 he again raised the South American scheme with Hobhouse. He rejected the United States because the climate was too cold and the people "a little too coarse for me". He would take Allegra with him "and pitch my tent for good and all. – I am not tired of Italy – but a man must be a Cisisbeo and a singer in duets and a Connoisseur of operas – or nothing here – I have made some progress in all these accomplishments – but I can't say that I don't feel the degradation." He was feeling utterly humiliated in this role of something that amounted to little more than a gigolo. Hobhouse pleaded with him: "Pray do come home – or come somewhere where I can join you and take care of you."[4]

But England was out of the question – there was no point in Hobhouse trying to convince him to the contrary: "Yet I want a country – and a home – and if possible – a free one – I am not yet thirty two years of age – I might still be a decent citizen and found a *house* and a family, – as good – or better than the former."[5]

Hoppner teased him about how long the evenings at La Mira must seem, and Byron replied with a remark someone had made to Thomas Moore when he heard that Moore had married a pretty woman, " 'a very good creature too – an excellent creature – pray – *how do you pass your evenings?*' It is a devil of a question that – and perhaps as easy to answer with a wife as with a mistress – but surely they are longer than the nights."[6]

If Teresa suspected he was chafing under this unfamiliar servitude, she tried to ignore it, and strenuously denied such allegations after his death. She would not have been particularly happy if she knew the lines he was writing in *Don Juan* that had been inspired by the visit to Arqua:

> Think you, if Laura had been Petrarch's wife,
> He would have written sonnets all his life?
>
> (III, 8, 63–4)

Byron was feeling altogether subdued; and while he had begun another canto of *Don Juan*, he was somewhat constrained as a result of the fuss the first two had caused in England. Nevertheless, he knew his poem was good, and to Kinnaird he put the famous question:

confess – confess – you dog – and be candid – that it is the sublime of *that there* sort of writing – it may be bawdy – but is it not good English – it may be profligate – but is it not *life*, is it not *the thing*? – Could any man have written it – who had not lived in the world? – and tooled in a post-chaise? in a hackney coach? in a Gondola? against a wall? in a court carriage? in a vis a vis? – on a table? – and under it? – I have written about a hundred stanzas of a third Canto – but it is damned modest – the outcry has frightened me. – I had such projects for the Don – but the *Cant* is so much stronger than *Cunt* . . .[7]

He was only too delighted to see Tom Moore who arrived on October 7. Moore was introduced to Teresa whom he found amiable and intelligent, but not particularly pretty. As Byron bustled about in Fusina easing his friend's entry into Venice, Moore was struck by the fact that his lame foot did not seem to hinder or embarrass him as it had done in the past. With his gondolier, the muscular Tita, rowing them towards Venice, Byron was in high spirits, roaring with laughter over memories of scrapes they had shared in England. Moore had planned to stay at the Gran Bretagne, but Byron insisted that he put him up at his own palazzo. In his life of Byron, Moore recalled: "As we now turned into the dismal canal, and stopped before his damp-looking mansion, my predilection for the Gran Bretagne returned in full force."[8] He was scarcely reassured when he found the landing stage filled with all manner of animals who barked and snapped at him.

Moore was delighted, however, when he saw the spacious, comfortable apartments. Byron sent for Alexander Scott to join them, and as they stood on the balcony they noticed what appeared to be two Englishmen in an approaching gondola. Byron struck a comical pose: "Ah, if you John Bulls knew who the two fellows are, now standing up here, I think you *would* stare!"[9]

Dinner having been sent for from a nearby trattoria, Byron talked about his affair and the fact that Count Guiccioli had approached him for another large loan. He made a wager that he would be able to keep the woman and the money as well, an incident that reveals that he was fully aware why the count was being so cooperative about the relationship. Scott and Moore then went off to the theatre while Byron dutifully made his way back to La Mira. On the 10th, the eve of Moore's departure, Byron arrived at the palazzo like a gleeful schoolboy, announcing that Teresa had given him permission to spend the whole evening with his friend. He took advantage of the occasion to read the 300 lines of *Don Juan* he had written, including a satirical introduction on the Duke of Wellington which was later transferred to another canto.

Moore stopped off at La Mira before departing for Rome. Here he saw Allegra; and Byron remarked: "Have you any notion – but I suppose *you* have – of what they call the parental feeling? For myself I have not the least."[10] It was one of those swaggering Byronic remarks, since only a month later, he reported proudly to Hoppner: "Allegrina is flourishing like a pome-granate blossom."[11] Perhaps it was Teresa who lacked parental feeling, for in her gushy account of their earthly paradise, there is no reference to the presence of the child.

Just as Moore was about to leave Byron handed him a white leather bag. According to Moore's account, this was the first Byron had spoken of the memoirs, something very hard to credit. "Look here," Byron is supposed to have said, "this would be worth something to Murray, though *you*, I dare say, would not give sixpence for it." "What is it?" the puzzled Moore claims to have asked. "My Life and Adventures," was the reply. "It is not a thing that can be published during my lifetime, but you may have it – there, do whatever you please with it."[12]

During Moore's visit he had been quizzed by Byron about the gossip that was still circulating about his marriage. Now he viewed Moore as the agent for his side of the story. While he claimed that the memoir could not be published during his lifetime, he encouraged Moore to allow anyone to read it. He knew that he could not have chosen a better emissary. Moore was an enormous snob, and he would use the memoir to further his social ambitions just as he would later extract a considerable sum of money from Murray for its eventual publication.

Late in October a feverish infection swept through the household which was now ensconced in the Palazzo Mocenigo. Byron succumbed to it after being soaked to the skin in a thunderstorm, and became so delirious that Teresa and Fletcher were seriously alarmed. At this point Count Guiccioli chose to arrive to fetch his wife back to Ravenna. While Byron struggled to recover, fearful rows were erupting between husband and wife. Accustomed as the count was to demanding obedience from his former wives, he now drew up a list of stringent instructions to which Teresa had to adhere. Teresa refused to comply.

The count came weeping to Byron to help them out of their operatic impasse. Byron, who flinched from any sort of decision if he could avoid it, agreed to make the supreme sacrifice of leaving Italy altogether if this meant that husband and wife might be reconciled on their original terms. The only way he could persuade Teresa to agree to return to Ravenna was to leave her with the belief that he would eventually rejoin her.

While this solution also offered an escape from his tedium, to Kinnaird he ascribed the most mature and noble reasons for his conduct.

What could I do? – on one hand to sacrifice a woman whom I loved for life – leaving her destitute and divided from all ties in case of my death – on the other hand to give up an "amicizia" which had been my pleasure my pride and my passion. – At twenty I should have taken her away – at thirty with the experience of *ten such years*! – I sacrificed myself only – and counselled – and persuaded her with the greatest difficulty to return with her husband to Ravenna – not absolutely denying – that I might come there again – else she refused to go. – But I shall quit Italy – I have done my duty – but the Country has become sad to me, – I feel alone in it – and as I left England on account of my own wife – I now quit Italy for the wife of another.[13]

Whatever promises he had made to Teresa, for the moment he was resigned to returning to England. But if he did so, he would be faced with having to challenge Henry Brougham to a duel for spreading scandalous stories about him in Geneva. He would bring Allegra with him: "but I know not where to go – I have nobody to receive me – but my sister – and I must conform to circumstances – and live accordingly, – this is meanly in London & difficultly – on that which affords splendour & ease in Italy. – But I hope to get out to America – if I don't take a much longer voyage."[14] It was at this moment that Allegra became seriously ill. Any move from his vigil at her bedside, he declared, was impossible, and he succumbed completely to self-pity: "Alas! here I am in a gloomy Venetian palace – never *more* alone than when alone – unhappy in the retrospect – & at least as much so in the prospect."[15]

Byron was telling Teresa that she was "my destiny . . . but where I shall direct my steps is, alas, uncertain" (November 25, 1819), while Augusta was being told (November 28, 1819) that he would depart for England as soon as Allegra had recovered. Teresa was in hysterics at the thought of his leaving Italy, Augusta in despair at the prospect of his arrival in England. When he wrote to his sister that he loved Teresa better than himself, Augusta remarked tartly to Annabella that this was hard to reconcile with his "late precious declarations" of love for her.[16] Annabella warned her that his "criminal desires" for her were still active and that undoubtedly she was his major reason for wanting to return to England. She warned Augusta that if she agreed to see him, he would corrupt the morals of her children and public opinion would be raised against her. On the other hand, Lady Byron added maliciously, if Augusta refused to see him he could always change his will, now in her favour.[17] Augusta replied that perhaps it would be a greater misfortune if, instead of returning to England, he fell into the hands of "that most *detestable* Woman".[18]

Also in England, Murray had applied to the Lord Chancellor for an injunction to prevent the piracy of *Don Juan*. When Byron heard this he wrote in alarm that if Lord Eldon pronounced it "*indecent & blasphemous . . . I* lose all right in my daughter's *guardianship* and *education* – in short all paternal authority – and every thing concerning her – except the pleasure I may have chanced to have had in begetting her."[19] He was thinking of how Shelley in 1817 had been divested of all rights over his children by Harriet Westbrook because of the celebration of atheism and free love in *Queen Mab*. In the end the Lord Chancellor unexpectedly granted the injunction.

Finally Byron was actually on the point of departure. His gondola was filled with his luggage, he was dressed for the journey, and then suddenly he announced that if the clock struck one and he was still there, it was an omen that he was to stay. Naturally that was exactly what happened. The rest of the script was predictable as well. Teresa had another relapse. Both her husband and father were persuaded that her illness was due to her misery over Byron and also (possibly) they believed her protestations that her relations with him were platonic. This time it was Count Gamba who wrote to Byron urging him to return to Ravenna. As so often happened, someone else was deciding Byron's fate for him and he set off once more on December 21.

Three days later he was given a warm welcome by all his old Ravenna acquaintances, although he still assured Hoppner (January 10, 1820) that "I have not decided anything about remaining at Ravenna – I may stay a day – a week – a year – all my life – but all this depends upon what I can neither see nor foresee." Teresa had made a miraculous recovery and was able to attend the seasonal parties, hanging on Byron's arm with the undisguised air of a victor. The count, concerned that the Albergo Imperiale was far too small for their friend, suggested that Byron take the first floor of their palazzo. Byron was delighted to leave the cramped inn where he now lodged his servants. He took a box at the opera and resigned himself to the provincial obscurity fate had decreed for him. Now that his relationship with Teresa had reverted to its old clandestine nature with love-making confined to periods when the count was napping or at the theatre, its romance returned. There was the usual flutter of notes of jealous accusations and counter-accusations. On hearing that her brother was in Ravenna again, Augusta expressed her dismay to Lady Byron: "Surely if not *insanity*, it is akin to it! I begin to think South America would be the best thing for I see no peace in *this* quarter of the globe – perhaps time & change would be of use – God knows! it is *very* melancholy!"[20] To Murray, Hobhouse lamented: "Bad news from Ravenna – a great pity indeed."[21]

On the last day of 1819 Byron again wrote to his wife "as it were from another world". He reminded her that five years before he had been on his way to their "funeral marriage". The main purpose for writing to her was to inform her that Moore possessed his memoirs. He was offering her the option of reading the manuscript and marking what she thought erroneous.

I have omitted the most important & decisive events and passions of my existence not to compromise others. – But it is not so with the part you occupy – which is long and minute – and I could wish you to see, read and mark any part or parts that do not appear to coincide with the truth. – The truth I have always stated – but there are two ways of looking at it – and your way may be not mine. – I have never revised the papers since they were written. – You may read them – and mark what you please – I wish you to know what I think and say of you & yours. – You will find nothing to flatter you – nothing to lead you to the most remote supposition that we could ever have been – or be happy together. – But I do not choose to give another generation statements which we cannot arise from the dust to prove or disprove – without letting you see fairly & fully what I look upon you to have been – and what I depict you as being. – If seeing this – you can detect what is false – or answer what is charged – do so – *your mark* shall not be erased.[22]

Of course Lady Byron consulted Doyle and Lushington as soon as she read the letter. Both advisers more or less dictated her reply. It was Lushington's opinion that Mrs Leigh should be made aware that the publication of the memoirs would inevitably result in a rebuttal which would entail "the disclosure of everything which she was most desirous to conceal". He went on to say: "I think the great point is that Lord Byron should be *aware* of the *extent* of the *information* you possess, and be made to believe that the consequence of commencing an attack which would lead necessarily from one thing to another, would be the ultimate disclosure of everything." Lushington suggested the insertion of an additional paragraph in her reply: "Lord Byron is probably by no means aware of the extent of the information of which I was possessed before our separation, nor of the additional proofs as well as new facts which have since come to my knowledge."[23]

Finally on March 10 Annabella wrote only a brief note declining to read the memoirs, expressing the opinion that their publication might harm Ada. She ended with a veiled threat: "For my own part I have no reason to shrink from publicity, but notwithstanding the injuries which I have suffered, I should lament some of the *consequences*."[24]

Byron was making mischief in England as his only means of maintaining contact with his roots. He was greatly embarrassed about his soft incarceration where he was sentenced to be "a piece of female property",[25] carrying a lady's fan or folding her shawl in the prescribed manner. In Venice he had been a relatively free man. While he had attended various *conversazioni*, he had never allowed himself to be fully absorbed into the Italian community, since he spent a good deal of his leisure time with Hoppner and Scott. In Ravenna he had not another single Englishman for company, and he seldom had an opportunity of speaking his own language. Ravenna was considered a backwater by tourists of the time; and it was only for Byron's sake that his homosexual Cambridge friend, William Bankes, came for a few days in February. Once he was gone, Byron was left to make some sort of sense out of the confusing labyrinth of an alien culture. "Their moral is not your moral," he told Murray, "their life is not your life" (February 21, 1820).

Nothing reveals Byron's status as an alien more than his attitude to the changing political scene in Britain. Hobhouse sent him long letters describing the tumultuous events, but all Byron heard was that the country was on the brink of revolution and this meant that his government bonds were not safe. Kinnaird was instructed repeatedly to transfer them to an Irish mortgage until his banker advised him that 6 per cent in Ireland really amounted to 5 per cent. Byron simply could not grasp that the Whigs had become as much a party of reaction as the Tories. With the exception of Hobhouse, Kinnaird, and Burdett, he regarded the rest of the radical reformers as *canaille*. He might once have spoken passionately in defence of Catholic emancipation and the striking Nottinghamshire weavers, but with his reverence for rank, he was profoundly conservative, viewing the best government as an enlightened oligarchy. His friends pleaded in vain for him to return to England to help them in their struggle to achieve a broader and more representative electorate.

Byron's only reaction to Hobhouse's moving letters about the starving mill-workers was that he was being needlessly impetuous, and indeed he found it all rather amusing. One can only consider the possibility that Byron's attitude to his friend's concern about the state of England was a defensive posture of defiance from the standpoint of his own hedonistic existence. Early in December 1819 Hobhouse was found guilty of contempt by the House of Commons for a pamphlet he had written against the government. He was thrown into Newgate, where he languished, "cursedly ill", until February 28, 1820. To Hoppner (January 10, 1820) Byron wrote: "I see Hobhouse has got into a Scrape – which does not please me – he should not have gone so deep among those men – without calculating the consequences."

But worse was to follow. On March 23, 1820, Byron sent Murray a doggerel of eight stanzas to the tune of "Where hae ye been a'day/My boy Tommy O?" of which the following are stanzas 4–7:

> You hate the House – why canvass, then?
>   My boy Hobbie O?
> Because I would reform the den
>   As member for the Mobby O.
>
> Wherefore do you hate the Whigs
>   My boy Hobbie O?
> Because they want to run their rigs
>   As under Walpole's Bobby O.

> But when we at Cambridge were
> > My boy Hobbie O,
> If my memory don't err
> > You founded a Whig Clubbie O.
>
> When to the mob you make a speech
> > My boy Hobbie O,
> How do you keep without their reach
> > The watch within your fobby O? –

Byron knew full well what the consequences would be: "tell him I know he will never forgive me – but I could not help it – I am so provoked with him and his ragamuffins for putting him in *guod*." He told Murray to show the squib to Hobhouse, but he knew full well that Murray would circulate it among his friends, and indeed a version of it was published in the *Morning Post* on April 15, 1820, before Murray had condescended to send Hobhouse the offensive verses.

It is impossible to view Byron's action as less than malicious and treacherous – at best thoughtless – to the man who had been more loyal to him than any of his friends. Hobhouse was struck to the heart. On April 16 he recorded in his diary:

> I am exceedingly unwilling to record this proof of the bad nature of my friend – he thought me in prison – he knew me attacked by all parties & pens – he resolved to get his kick too . . . for a man to give way to such a mere pruriency & itch of writing against one who has stood by him in all his battles & never refused a single friendly office – is a melancholy proof of want of feeling & I fear of principle."[26]

Hobhouse feared that he could never feel the same towards Byron again, but he did not want to cause an irrevocable rupture in the relationship, and summoning up all his magnanimity he wrote:

> Oh you shabby fellow – so you strike a man when he is down do you? I do not think, however, that you intended your filthy ballad to be read in the reading room at number fifty nor to find its way into the Morning Post before I saw it myself . . . You have now, I believe, lampooned your friends all round, & I was a ninny not to know that I should be entered upon your poetical lists at the first convenient opportunity.[27]

He had put a more serious remonstrance into the fire, and now bygones would be bygones.

To Murray, however, Hobhouse spoke his mind:

> I think you have not treated me as I deserved, nor as might have been expected from that friendly intercourse which has existed between us for so many years . . . had Lord Byron transmitted to me a lampoon on you, I should, if I know myself at all, either have put it into the fire without delivery or should have sent it at once to you – I should not have given it a circulation for the gratification of all the small wits at the great & little houses where no treat is so agreeable as to find a man laughing at his friend.

He went on to say that he had received a letter from Byron that indicated he was ashamed of what he had done: "he was very wanton & you were very indiscreet – but I trust neither one nor the other meant mischief – and there's an end to it."[28]

Byron's letter of April 22, 1820, seemed to Hobhouse as much of an apology as he could expect:

> Upon reform you have long known my opinion – but *radical* is a new word since my time – it was not in the political vocabulary in 1816 – when I left England – and I don't know what it means – is it uprooting? – As to yourself it is not in the power of political events to change my sentiments – I am rejoiced to see you in parliament because I am sure you will make a splendid figure in it, and have fought hard to arrive there . . . [but] the persons calling themselves *reformers, radicals,* and such other names, – I should look upon being free with such men, as much the same as being in bonds with felons.

However, by the time Byron had received Hobhouse's letter of expostulation, he deeply regretted what he had done: "it was buffoonery – and this you know has been all along our mutual privilege" (May 11). He also again expressed delight that Hobhouse had been elected member for Westminster.

Byron was aware that he himself didn't cut a very noble figure in Ravenna. By mid-April, however, he was predicting an Italian uprising against the Austrians. "I shall stay to see what turns up."[29] Perhaps his redemption might yet be found in Italy.

25

○○○○○○○○○○○○○

Limbo in Ravenna, 1820

Byron was caught in the spider's web. He was not sure if he appeared a figure of fun to the society of Ravenna, but he knew how comical his friends and enemies in England would regard the predicament into which he had allowed himself to become entangled. He suspected that Count Guiccioli might have some plot in mind when he invited him to share his palazzo (if not his wife), and he began to detect intimations of deceit in Teresa herself. It was a curious coincidence that in April he sat down to write a tragedy of betrayal.

His poetry had always provided him with his strongest grip on reality, but now he had begun to doubt its value. Repeatedly he told Murray that he was aware that Cantos III and IV of *Don Juan* were not up to the standard of the earlier cantos and that he was under no obligation to publish them if he considered them inferior. Byron was really pleading for some reassurance. With his confidence waning he abandoned *Don Juan*, where he was beginning to find his true poetic voice, for a series of closet dramas. In July – after many interruptions – he finished *Marino Faliero*, a rendering of the story of the treacherous doge whose veiled portrait had caught Byron's eye when he and Hobhouse had visited the ducal palace shortly after their arrival in Venice in November 1816. Its theme, a man who is destroyed because he will not accept the futility of action, was to preoccupy him for the next year or so. In his rejection of the city that had once been magical to him, he now described Venice as "Gehenna of the waters! thou sea Sodom" (*Works*, IV, p. 444). The historical background could not be faulted, he insisted defensively, and the action was gripping because it was an unprecedented act for a doge to conspire against his own state. "I don't know what your parlour boarders will think of the drama I have founded upon this extraordinary event" (July 17, 1820). Byron was

364

more nervous of the opinion of Gifford, Rogers, Campbell, and the other *habitués* of Murray's literary drawing room than he would confess.

He was aware that he was now in a situation where there were only a few areas where he could exert control over his life. One of these was money. Both Hobhouse and Moore have testified how he would pore over his money box like an old miser. When Kinnaird took over his finances the previous year he found that the debts were considerably larger than Byron had estimated – some £34,162. There were about six large claims and a considerable number of smaller ones. Kinnaird advised paying off the smaller ones, and reducing the rest by instalments. This he proposed to do with Byron's wine merchant, and with Baxter, who had not yet been paid for the Napoleonic coach. A year later these debts had still not been paid. Kinnaird begged Byron to send him a letter that he could show to his creditors (May 16, 1820). It was important, Kinnaird argued, that "no man should be able to say that you were staying abroad to avoid settling with your creditors". By signing such a promissory letter, if Byron returned to England he would not then be pestered by duns, and "it is right that I acquit myself towards respectable men of having misled them."[1] It seems unlikely that Byron ever sent Kinnaird such a letter. He was far more interested in converting his government bonds into a mortgage and in the fate of a lawsuit over the section of Rochdale which his great-uncle had leased illegally. He agreed that "the payment of debts must be now my only object" (July 27, 1820), but in order to effect this, he ordered Kinnaird to make renewed efforts to sell Rochdale. He still refused to pay his creditors out of his literary earnings, although he insisted that Murray be reimbursed if he had lost any money through publishing his work.

He could, however, exert control over another piece of property – Allegra. Once he had moved into the Palazzo Guiccioli, she was sent for from Venice. There are references to Teresa's taking her with her in her coach, comments on the child's good looks and her obstinacy. Indeed, Byron mentions her so often that it is clear that he was very proud of her.

By now Claire seemed cured of her infatuation for Byron. After reading *Don Juan* on February 1, she noted in her journal: "Hints for Don J – which appears to me a soliloquy upon his own ill-luck – Ungraceful & selfish – like a beggar hawking his own sores about and which create disgust instead of Pity."[2] She had moved to Pisa with the Shelleys, and had received word from the Hoppners that Byron was in Ravenna. The first intimation she had that Allegra had joined her father appeared in a letter received from Mrs Hoppner on March 15, 1820. The following day Claire sat down again to write to Byron, reminding him that she had not seen her daughter in two years and requesting that he send Allegra on a visit to Pisa as she did not have the money to travel across Italy to Ravenna. She proposed taking the child to Bagna da Lucca, "a very cool place which may prove of service to her health as she is delicate".[3] When she received no reply, Claire again wrote on April 23, offering to go as far as Bologna to meet her daughter. She pointed out to Byron that Allegra had suffered various ailments as a result of the Venetian climate, and "Ravenna is equally objectionable and nothing must induce me to venture her life a third time."[4]

Only a day earlier Byron commented on her first letter in a postscript to Hoppner in a letter dealing mainly with problems with a servant he had employed at the Palazzo Mocenigo:

> About Allegra – I can only say to Claire – that I so totally disapprove of the mode of Children's treatment in their family – that I should look upon the Child as going into a hospital. – Is it not so? Have they *reared* one? – Her health here has hitherto been excellent – and her temper not bad – she is sometimes vain and obstinate – but always clean and cheerful – and as in a year or two I shall either send her to England – or put her in a Convent for education – these defects will be remedied as far as they can in human nature. – But the Child shall not quit me again – to perish of Starvation, and green fruit – or to be taught to believe that there is no Deity. – Whenever there is convenience of vicinity and access – her Mother can always have her with her – otherwise no. – It was so stipulated from the beginning. – The Girl is not so well off as with *you* – but far better than with them; – the fact is she is spoilt – being a great favourite with every body on account of the fairness of her Skin – which shines among their dusky children like the milky way, but there is no comparison of her situation now – and that under Elise – or with them. – She has grown considerably – is very clean – and lively. – She has plenty of air and exercise at home – and goes out daily with M Guiccioli in her carriage to the Corso.[5]

On May 1 an agitated Claire wrote again. As for Byron's stipulation that she could see Allegra only if she were in the vicinity, she pointed out that such a situation was impossible unless one lived in a city like London. She defended the Shelleys as parents, but if Byron objected to them she offered to take Allegra on her own to Livorno. Byron must have snorted with sceptical disgust when she also promised to instil her with religious principles.

Despite their initial friendliness to Claire in Venice in 1818, the Hoppners were now behaving in a thoroughly dishonourable manner. They were reporting all the gossip about Byron to the Shelley group, and yet on April 28 Hoppner wrote obsequiously to Byron:

> Mrs Hoppner has copied & sent to Claire your sentence respecting Allegra, so I hope you will not be troubled with any more applications from that quarter. She likewise recommended her to submit to your decree, but whether she will, or will resort to a personal application, you who are better acquainted than I with this voluntary little lady will be best able to judge.[6]

In a letter written shortly after this, Hoppner added:

> I hoped you would not again have been troubled on this matter, at least that we should not be made the Vehicle of annoying you. Why indeed we have been selected by Clara as the means of communicating with you, I know not: but though I could not take upon myself to keep back the letter I now enclose, I promise you it will be the last you will receive from its author through me.[7]

It had become clear from Mrs Hoppner's letters that she and her husband could no longer be seen as sympathetic intermediaries. On May 8 Mary Shelley told her friend Maria Gisborne that "the Ravenna journey does not take place. He has written to say the child shall not quit him. The Hoppners have behaved shamefully."[8]

All Claire's surviving letters to Byron are reasonable in tone and request, but Byron described her to Shelley as "irrational & provoking" (August 25, 1820). The Hoppners did not hear anything further about Allegra until they received a letter from Byron dated September 10 in reply to some gossip Hoppner had relayed about Shelley.*

Apparently by now Claire was writing directly to Byron.

> Claire writes me the most insolent letters about Allegra – see what a man gets by taking care of natural children! – Were it not for the poor little child's sake – I am almost tempted to send her back to her atheistical mother – but that would be too bad; – you cannot conceive the excess of her insolence and I know not why – for I have been at

---

* See Chapter 26.

great care and expence – taking a house in the country on purpose for her – she has *two* maids & every possible attention. – If Claire thinks that she shall ever interfere with the child's morals or education – she mistakes – she never shall – The girl shall be a Christian and a married woman – if possible. – As to seeing her – she may see her – under proper restrictions – but She is not to throw every thing into confusion with her Bedlam behaviour. – To express it delicately – I think Madame Clare [sic] is a damned bitch – what think you?[9]

Byron was probably feeling somewhat uncomfortable because he had been seriously concerned, if not downright frightened, about Allegra – something he doesn't mention to Hoppner. The child had fulfilled Claire's worst fears by developing a high fever in early August and this lasted well into September. Unlike everyone else in Ravenna, Byron had made no attempt to rent a summer villa to escape the stifling summer heat, which was notoriously dangerous because of the malaria-infested marshes around the town. Teresa had left for the country in mid-July; and Byron had teased her when she had attempted to find him a country villa so that she could have him near her, but once Allegra became ill he suddenly secured the Villa Bacinetti six miles away from Ravenna on the road to the Villa Gamba at Filetto.

Claire was not wrong in charging Byron with breaking his word about allowing her access to Allegra on a regular basis. That he had found Claire tiresome in the past bears no relevance to his promise or to the issue of Allegra's welfare. He had neglected to take a summer place mainly out of indolence, but also partially because he was anxious not to provoke the suspicions of Count Guiccioli from whom Teresa had by now secured a legal separation.

The precarious triangle in the Palazzo Guiccioli had survived for a very brief period. In the middle of May the count seems to have caught the lovers in *flagrante delicto*. (Byron is rather vague about the circumstances.) It is possible that the count had lured Byron to live in his house in order to extract money from him – or to have the previous loans forgiven because he was living rent-free – but when Byron refused to lend him any more money, he was determined to have his revenge. Tremendous rows erupted between husband and wife, and the count broke into Teresa's writing-desk in an attempt to discover incriminating letters. Byron told Teresa that they must now seriously consider a separation because if she deliberately deserted her husband her life would be intolerable. This might be construed as Byron's final bid for freedom, but he must also have realised that his argument would be totally unconvincing to the tenacious Teresa.

On Byron's advice she then turned to her father for guidance. Gamba had developed a genuine affection for Byron with whom he shared liberal sympathies, and he too was coming to detest his son-in-law. After listening sympathetically to Teresa's account of her abusive husband, he proceeded to petition the Pope for a separation. The combination of family influence and papal distrust of Guiccioli facilitated the granting of the petition on condition that Teresa reside in her father's house "in such a laudable manner as befits a respectable and noble Lady separated from her Husband".[10] On July 15 Count Gamba spirited her away to his country villa. Byron continued to occupy the apartments above those of the deserted husband, although Guiccioli had ordered him to leave the premises.

During the course of the summer Teresa inundated Byron with letters, only a few of which have survived. Byron's brief notes are far different in tone from those written in the first flush of passion. They are affectionate, relaxed, dashed off with the amused indulgence with which one would treat a wilful child. During Teresa's absence Byron swam in the Adriatic and rode in the Pineta Classe. He always carried pistols with him, a wise precaution as on August 7 he apprehended one of Guiccioli's spies following him in the woods. He had not forgotten that rumour had it that two wives and a hostile neighbour had been murdered by the count. But it wasn't too unpleasant a life, and he now had time to get down to some serious writing.

At the end of July he finally met Teresa's brother Pietro who discovered that Byron wasn't at all the monster he had heard him to be. "My Love ++++ I like your little brother very much – he shows character and talent – Big eyebrows! and a stature which he has enriched, I think, at your expense – at least in those – do you understand me? His head is a little too hot for revolutions – he must not be too rash."[11]

They were soon riding and practising marksmanship together. Above everything else, they talked insurrection against the Austrians. Through the Gambas, Byron was initiated into a branch of the Carbonari, the disaffected rebels who were springing up all over Italy (some of them associated with the Freemasons) who wanted a democratic constitution and the chance to break free from Austrian domination.*

Byron was given an honorary position as captain of a troop called the

---

* The name Carbonari signifies "makers of charcoal", symbolically the purifiers, carriers of liberty, morality and progress.

Cacciatori Americani, but we have no way of knowing how many secret meetings he attended in the Pineta. He sometimes caused offence when he expressed irritation at their impetuosity and the alarming lack of liaison with other groups around the country. Still, it was a cause in which he believed, although not with the excited ardour of youth. It was also some compensation for the fact that he was unable to attend the coronation of George IV on July 19. There would be no way that Byron could accompany "My dearest Duck", his wife down the aisle of Westminster Abbey. Nor could Byron listen to the pleas of his friends to return to England to support Queen Caroline in the divorce suit brought against her by the king, particularly as she was being defended by two of his arch-enemies, Brougham and Lushington, who had been propelled into prominence by his own separation, "like crows on carrion".[12] On August 18 the *Morning Chronicle* announced that Byron had been seen in London, and rumours spread like wildfire. Caroline Lamb was in a state of great excitement in her enquiries to Murray, but the person who would have found his arrival the most embarrassing – Augusta – didn't believe it for a moment.

At the moment that Byron was supposed to be in England he was in Filetto where he had joined Teresa's family after depositing Allegra at the Villa Bacinetti with an unfamiliar nurse whom he had recently hired. (There had been a delay in finding a suitable one because Byron had to reject even a passably pretty woman because of Teresa's jealousy.) He was warmly welcomed at the Villa Gamba where he talked politics or rode with the men of the family. The easy informality of their country life delighted him. Their bedrooms were situated around an open interior balcony from which they chatted with each other after retiring. One day in early September Byron arrived to find the family sitting silently, peering through optical instruments at an eclipse. Once the sun was visible again, he joined them in a game of bowls.

It was idyllic, except for the care he had to take in his relations with Teresa lest Guiccioli find grounds for not paying the allowance decreed by the Pope. There was also the matter of Teresa's volatile feelings. On one of his August visits to Filetto, Byron left with her a copy of Benjamin Constant's novel, *Adolphe*, which depicted the consequences of an illicit love affair, a thinly veiled account of Constant's restless weariness in his relationship with Madame de Staël. It was not the most tactful of gifts. Teresa was stunned by his insensitivity.

> *Adolphe!* Byron – how much this book has hurt me! You cannot imagine! From the beginning, alas, I foresaw the end – but I read it

with the greatest speed – thinking I might thus, at least in part, avoid the too violent impression it made on me . . . my mind, my heart, are deeply wounded. Byron – why did you send me this book? . . . To be able to enjoy that story one must be more remote from the condition of Eleonore *than I am* – and to give it to one's mistress to read, one must be *either very near to* the state of Adolphe, or very far away from it! Either you, my Byron, did not know this book (terrifying mirror of the truth) or you are not yet acquainted with your friend's heart – or you are aware in yourself of a greater or lesser strength than I think you have. How much harm, I repeat, reading this book has done to me! How much! For pity's sake, Byron, if you have other books like it, don't send them to me![13]

Byron replied soothingly, if unconvincingly: "My Love+++ The circumstances of Adolphe are very different. Ellinore was not married, she was many years older than Adolphe – she was not amiable – etc., etc. – Don't think any more about things so dissimilar in every way."[14] But were they really so disimilar?

Ferdinando, Count Guiccioli's oldest son, died on September 14, and Teresa wrote her husband a letter of condolence. She also warned him against making a journey to Milan, a very indiscreet thing to do in view of the Gamba family's subversive activities. The very fact that she would do something so rash as to jeopardise their safety indicates a bond between husband and wife that has never been fully understood. Byron did not know the contents of the letter; but the very fact that she had written to her husband at all so infuriated him that he refused to communicate with her for a fortnight. By the time they resumed their correspondence he had already succumbed to the melancholy he always experienced as the year drew to an end. The autumnal mists of Emilia-Romagna reflected his mood.

As to my *sadness* – you know that it is in my character – particularly in certain seasons. It is truly a temperamental illness – which sometimes makes me fear the approach of madness – and for this reason, and at these times, I keep away from everyone – not wanting to make others unhappy. – Is this true or not? Is this the first time you have seen me in this condition? (September 29, 1820).

But only the day before he had sent Murray a nasty poem on Samuel Rogers, beginning "Nose and chin that make a knocker", in the acid style of *English Bards and Scotch Reviewers*. He warned Murray to show it only to a very few people – the same warning he had given about the squib on Hobhouse – "but don't betray *it*, or me, else you are the worst of men."[5] His experience with Hobhouse earlier in the year had not cured him of his impetuous habit of lashing out at people – and then blaming Murray for sharing the malice (which was Byron's intention from the beginning).

The great Italian uprising, to which such high hopes had been attached, had not yet occurred. At the beginning of July 1820, a handful of Carbonari had managed to gain entry to the terrified King of Naples who immediately granted their demand for a constitution. A sympathetic revolt had been planned in the north for early September, but once word spread that Bologna, the central link in the chain, had defected, the conspirators fled to the woods or remained nervously indoors. In Ravenna the cardinal thundered against the liberals from his pulpit. Letters were scrutinised by the authorities. Byron and the Gambas were under constant police surveillance, but for the moment there were no arrests or expulsions, but "both sides watching each other like hunting leopards".[6]

Teresa was still in the country, and Byron became even more discreet in his visits to her. If he had made a mistake in showing her *Adolphe,* he made an even greater error by sending her a French edition of his poetry. She turned first to the poems written in the bitterness of his separation: the tearful "Farewell" and "A Sketch from Private Life", the cruel satire on Mrs Clermont. What on earth did he think her reaction would be? He soon learned.

The character of Teresa unfolds itself very gradually to us. If our first introduction to her character is through reading her *Vie de Lord Byron*, written many years later when she had become the wife of the Marquis de Boissy, we encounter a vain, silly, sentimental woman. Iris Origo has substantiated this view with her disclosure of Teresa's attempts to erase or change words in the correspondence which she felt did not convey the image she wished to create. We know from her relationship with her husband that she was manipulative. That she was also clearly deceitful is apparent in that she managed to persuade her father that her relationship with Byron was purely platonic. With Byron she was jealous and possessive. But her reaction to these poems, as Origo rightly remarks, shows us a woman of spirit with an independent mind of her own who was sensitive to what was hurtful or unfair. On October 10 she wrote:

> My only Love for ever!!!+++ I was infinitely glad to get your works –
> I have read one or two of them – *but how astounded I am*! One must

know them to know you. The experience of a year and a half did not tell me as much about you as reading *two of your pages*. I must however confess to you that this increase of light on the subject is to your disadvantage; I do not mean to your genius, for that must be adored in silence, but as to *morals*, of which it is permissible even for a simple mind like mine to speak, and must indeed be spoken of without reserve between Friends.

Here then are my reflections. – I believed you to be sincere; now I shall not be able to affirm it with such assurance. – I believed you to be sensitive to misfortune, but *never* affected by it; this opinion I still have and must have, in order to esteem and love you; but you have written one thing that, in my opinion, might give the impression that in some moments of your life you showed a certain weakness of character. It is your *Farewell* and the *A Sketch from Private Life* that makes me think so. In these there is more than talent, tenderness and Love; more than was proper towards a woman who had offended you; and besides it is completely in contradiction with all that you have told me about your feelings towards your wife. – I do not blame you for having felt such tenderness, it only hurts me that you should have concealed the truth from me; or if indeed you did not feel it, that you should have so deceived the World. Believe me, Byron, your *Farewell* in particular does not give any idea of your independence of character. It gives the impression of a guilty man *asking for pity*; or at least, too proud to ask for it openly, but hoping that his prayer for it will be understood; and this is a situation which should never be yours![17]

Byron was clearly stunned and subdued by this letter. "Perhaps you are right – we will talk about it when we are together" (October 12, 1820). He probably did manage to persuade Teresa of the justice of his side of the story because it was so essential to her – as she herself admits with amazing frankness – that she idealise him. Certainly Byron needed uncritical love. Perhaps the scales had fallen from both their eyes, but what could they do about it? They had sacrificed everything for a great passion. There was no question of parting simply because they now saw each other as real people, yet they must continue to act the role of ideal lovers, a fiction nourished by Teresa after Byron's death. What they actually seemed to do was to lapse gradually into an affectionate and comfortable domesticity.

If there was anything Byron disliked it was the delivery of home truths. He was tired of hearing about the agitated political involvement of his friends in England when his own political ambitions had been aborted so early. His defence was to sneer at the British parliament. In a letter from Hobhouse that does not seem to have survived, his friend made some remark about Byron's inactive life which stung him to the quick. While he retorted (Nov. 9) that it was true that "yours is now a more active life", he was relatively restrained in contrast to a letter he wrote to Murray the same day. He went on at great length about his own whoring and endurance in contrast to that of his friend – in the past. He blamed Hobhouse's remark on the fact that he was still smarting from Byron's unpleasant poem about him.

During that autumn Byron wrote a series of long reminiscences of his life at Harrow and Cambridge for his publisher, at the same time as he was taking up his memoirs again. These letters were in a sense an *apologia pro vita sua*, but they were also a means of reliving what had been the most pleasurable days of his life. Murray was chosen as the recipient because Hobhouse, Drury, and Bankes were participants in this period of youthful high jinks and there would be little point in retelling what they already knew.

When he wrote to Francis Hodgson for the first time since he left England (at the request of Augusta who corresponded with Hodgson regularly) they had been out of touch for so long that there was little to say. The letters to Murray were also occasioned by his coming upon an allusion to Hobhouse as "a young man" whereas he was actually two years older than he; and Byron was becoming abnormally sensitive about the passage of the years and the prospect of a continuing life of relative boredom and indolence. He was also irritated to read praise of the younger Keats, a poet whom he always referred to with the most insulting contempt, describing his poetry as "a sort of mental masturbation".[18] He held tenaciously to the view of himself as one of the only poets who adhered to the model of his beloved Pope – but who would acknowledge this?

Teresa moved back to her father's palazzo in Ravenna late in November. At this point, one is struck by the number of notes in which Byron excuses himself from visiting – he didn't feel well, he had important business letters to write, and so forth. Now that Teresa was separated from her husband he did not have to go through the charade of a "Cavalier Schiavo".[19] It is interesting that at this point – mid-October – he resumed the adventures of *Don Juan*.

Augusta received a few letters, one in which he told her that "I always loved you better than any earthly existence, and I always shall unless I go mad";[20] and he renewed his pleas to Annabella to promise that his sister and her children would be cared for in case of his death. Annabella replied in what was to be her last letter to her husband (December 10, 1820): "The past shall not prevent me from befriending Augusta Leigh and her children in any future circumstances which may call for my assistance – I promise to do so. – She knows nothing of this."²¹ Byron replied (December 28, 1820): "Whatever She is or may have been – *you* have never had reason to complain of her – on the contrary – you are not aware of the obligations under which you have been to her. – Her life and mine – & yours & mine were two things perfectly distinct from each other – when one ceased the other began – and now both are closed." This seems the closest admission Byron ever made to her about the true nature of his relationship to his sister.

The fact that it would soon be five years since he left England lay heavy on his heart. From Augusta he learned that his old servant Murray had died. He confessed to her that he probably would not have parted with Newstead if Ada had been a boy. That there was no alternative was irrelevant when one is indulging in what-might-have-been.

On December 9 an incident occurred that gave Byron hope that he might be living in stirring and dangerous times. As he was putting on his greatcoat to visit Teresa, he heard a tremendous commotion outside in the narrow street and his servants rushed to the balcony to see what had happened. Byron, accompanied by his former gondolier Tita, hurried down the stairs to find an officer lying in the dark street, felled by five bullets. They carried him into the house as he murmured "O Dio!" and "Gesú!" and then he was dead. He turned out to have been Captain Luigi Dal Pinto, the commander of the papal troops in Ravenna. He was laid out on Fletcher's bed for the night before the authorities came to fetch him in the morning. The assassin could not be found, but the incident, followed by three murders in Forli and Faenza, indicated that trouble was imminent. "They are a fierce people," Byron told Murray (December 14, 1820), "and at present roused and the end no one can tell."

But uneasy silence descended upon the town once more. Again Byron's thoughts turned to England. On Christmas Day he suggested to Tom Moore that they consider setting up a weekly newspaper together, perhaps with the title *I Carbonari*. Such schemes suggest how little real satisfaction or value Byron took in his role of great poet. On December 28 he sent Kinnaird the fifth canto of *Don Juan*: "Acknowledge the receipt," was his only comment. Confined indoors because of wind and rain he was unable to take his daily ride. On January 4, 1821, mainly out of boredom, he began a journal, totally unlike any he had kept before.

375

His first journal, apparently full of youthful indiscretions, Hobhouse had persuaded him to destroy in Greece. The journal of the tour of the Bernese Alps in 1816 had been written up as a means of sharing a transcendent experience with Augusta. The memoir which he had given to Moore was an act of self-justification. In his present state of suspended animation, he used this new journal as a rare exercise in introspection. On the 6th he reflected:

> What is the reason that I have been, all my lifetime, more or less *ennuyé*? and that, if any thing, I am rather less so now than I was at twenty, as far as my recollection serves? I do not know how to answer this, but presume that it is constitutional, – as well as the waking in low spirits, which I have invariably done for many years. Temperance and exercise, which I have practiced at times, and for a long time together vigorously and violently, made little or no difference. Violent passions did; – when under their immediate influence – it is odd, but – I was in agitated, but *not* in depressed spirits.

On January 13 he sketched out an outline for a tragedy based on the legendary Assyrian despot Sardanapulus, who has tasted all pleasures and all have lost their savour. Of Byron's various protagonists, Sardanapulus was the one who most reflected his state of mind while writing the drama. On the eve of his birthday Byron recorded in his journal: "I go to my bed with a heaviness of heart at having lived so long, and to so little purpose."[22]

26

∞∞∞∞∞∞∞∞∞∞

The Reluctant Departure, 1821

The Ravenna Journal is an extraordinary document. In it a sobered Byron came as close perhaps as he ever would to confronting his inner self, whereas other aspects of his personality were flights from that encounter. People meeting him in person for the first time and expecting to find a duplicate of one of his fraught poetic figures were surprised to discover a courteous man of the world. As he remarked to Thomas Moore after receiving a call from a gentleman from Boston:

> I suspect that he did not take quite so much to me, from his having expected to meet a misanthropical gentleman, in wolf-skin breeches, and answering in fierce monosyllables, instead of a man of this world. I can never get people to understand that poetry is the expression of *excited passion*, and that there is no such thing as a life of passion any more than a continuous earthquake, or an eternal fever. Besides, who would ever *shave* themselves in such a state?[1]

His poetry was written quickly, usually in a state of concentrated intensity. He might later add or cross out a line, but seldom made any significant alterations. Painstaking, laborious work only bored him. As he explained to Moore, he regarded the writing of poetry as a kind of catharsis: "if I don't write to empty my mind, I go mad. As to that regular, uninterrupted love of writing, which you describe in your friend, I do not understand it. I feel it as a torture, which I must get rid of, but never as a pleasure. On the contrary, I think composition a great pain."[2]

There is also Byron the letter-writer in the persona of the dandy – cynical, witty, ebullient – an aspect of his personality he was using in *Don Juan*. In his letters, as in his poetry, his pen sped across the page, often

377

spontaneously generous, sometimes thoughtlessly caustic. These were usually written when he was in high, occasionally manic, spirits, such as the letters from Venice recounting his amorous adventures.

But in the Ravenna Journal he actually seems to be caught in a state of self-reflection, unaware of any other audience. In this period of hiatus, between the onset of a new year and another birthday – the close connection between the two is significant – he is almost trying to understand his tormented self, why he is where he is, and where he might be going. On his birthday he composed an epitaph for himself:

1821
Here lies
interred in the Eternity
of the Past,
from whence there is no
Resurrection
for the Days – whatever there may be
for the Dust –
the Thirty-Third Year
of an ill-spent Life,
Which, after
a lingering disease of many months
sunk into a lethargy,
and expired,
January 22nd, 1821, A.D.
Leaving a successor
Inconsolable
for the very loss which
occasioned its
Existence.

Byron loved the sunshine of Greece and Italy, but this miserable Ravenna winter was "a sad thing".[3] Weather had seldom been mentioned in his letters, but now it became a vital preoccupation. Confined to the house, he moped, read fitfully, ate copiously. "This morning I gat me up late, as usual – weather bad – bad as England – worse. The snow of last week melting to the sirocco of to-day, so that there were two d—d things at once. Could not even get to ride on horseback in the forest. Stayed at home all morning – looked at the fire – wondered when the post would come" (January 4, 1821). "Mist – thaw–slop–rain. No stirring out on horseback" (January 6, 1821).

"The weather still so humid and impracticable, that London, in its most oppressive fogs, were a summer-bower to this mist and sirocco, which now has lasted (but with one day's interval), chequered with snow or heavy rain only, since the 30th of December, 1820" (January 12, 1821).

Aware that his own future might well be linked to that of a new regime in Italy, he berates the Carbonari for dilatoriness and indecision, only half-aware that their behaviour was only too similar to his own indolence. The last entry in the journal is written on February 27 after a night of terrible indigestion. It ends at a moment when all the grand plans for an uprising seem to have miscarried. The Neapolitans, who were supposed to signal the general insurrection, were acting treacherously, disclaiming any connection with the groups in the north. "Thus the world goes; and thus the Italians are always lost for lack of union among themselves. What is to be done *here*, between the two fires, and cut off from the N[orther]n frontier, is not decided . . . I always had an idea that it would be *bungled*; but was willing to hope, and am so still" (February 26, 1821).

Prior to this he had given money to the Carbonari (and was willing to give more), he stored arms for them, and had a series of discussions with them as to using the Palazzo Guiccioli as a fortress. What is puzzling is the lack of any mention of Count Guiccioli, who would have been suspicious of the frequency of his visitors. The only explanation one can think of is that he was away visiting his estates.

The entries about the insurgents in the journal reflect their wavering indecisiveness. One moment there was high optimism, the next despair. Byron was filled with indignation when the Gambas went off on a shooting party, and bemused by Carnival continuing as usual. "The Car[bonar]i seem to have no plan – nothing fixed among themselves, how, when, or what to do."[4] They were waiting for the Neapolitans to give some sort of lead. In early February the weak Bourbon King of Naples appealed to the great powers – Austria, Germany, and Russia – for help in suppressing the revolt. As a result 70,000 Austrian troops crossed the border of Lombardy. On hearing this, the Carbonari scuttled for shelter. The Austrians steadily marched southwards. On March 7 on the plain of Rieti north-east of Rome they finally encountered an undisciplined Neapolitan rabble which turned tail ignominiously with hardly a shot being fired. By the 23rd the Austrians occupied Naples and the constitutional regime came to a farcical end.

During those first months of 1821 Byron himself wavered between throwing himself into the ferment of an insurrection and a distaste for disturbing the familiar pattern of his life. "And yet, there are materials in this people, and a noble energy, if well directed. But who is to direct them?

No matter."[5] He knew that he himself could attract followers, but the will was lacking. The paralysis of energy is reflected in his tragic hero Sardanapulus whose humanitarian instincts have been stifled within an extinct volcano. It could be either Byron or Sardanapulus speaking in the journal entry of February 2: "What I feel most growing upon me are laziness, and a disrelish more powerful than indifference. If I rouse, it is into fury."

Even before the defeat of the Neapolitans, there seemed every chance that the Gambas would be banished from Romagna. If this happened, Byron would probably have to follow them. Some sort of decision was called for. Allegra provided him with the excuse that he was doing something. He had become disturbed over the disposal of his possessions: "I am somewhat puzzled what to do with my little daughter, and my effects, which are of some quantity and value, – and neither of them [will] do in the seat of war, where I think of going. But there is an elderly lady who will take charge of *her*, and T. says that the Marchese C. will undertake to hold the chattels in safe keeping."[6] On February 10, in a postscript to Hoppner, he announced: "Allegra is well – but not well disposed – her disposition is perverse to a degree. – I am going to place her in a Convent for education." Years later Teresa would say that Byron developed an intense dislike for the child; and whenever she entered the room, he turned away in disgust: "Take her away! She reminds me too much of her mother."[7] This has the ring of truth because, according to his mood, at various periods he detected a strong resemblance to Lady Byron, and again to Augusta and himself. The only problem with Teresa's story is that during this period in Ravenna, she was living in Count Gamba's palazzo where she would have had few opportunities of seeing father and daughter together.

What is undoubtedly true is that Allegra was spoilt, wilful, and undisciplined – very much the sort of child Byron had been. He had tired of her, but he had to make some kind of provision for her in case he was forced to leave Ravenna. Teresa's grandparents were patrons of a Capucine convent at Bagnacavallo, twelve miles away. On March 1 Byron's banker, Pellegrino Ghigi, escorted the girl to the school where his own daughter was enrolled. Barely four, she was the youngest child the sisters had received. The following day one of the nuns wrote to her father to reassure him that she had slept well and had already chosen a favourite playmate.

Byron grumbled about the half-yearly fees of seventy *scudi*, but the little girl arrived with beautiful dolls, exquisite dresses, and a little coral necklace. Byron later sent the nuns his peer's robe with instructions that it was to provide material for a dress for Allegra. It was very confusing for the little girl to find that she had to wear a thick cotton chemise when being bathed and she objected to wearing sandals "like a poor person". At first she thought the nuns were her servants and told them to stand behind her. But it was a world of routine and stability – things she had never known – and we can assume that she might have been content, especially as for the first time in her life she had playmates.

Claire, then in Florence, received a letter on March 15 from Mary Shelley telling her what had happened to Allegra. She recorded in her journal: "The child in the convent of Bagnacavallo. Spent a miserable day."[8] On the 24th she wrote Byron a letter in which she destroyed her arguments by lapsing into rant. She reminded him that in Geneva when she had objected to his suggestion that he place the child in Mrs Leigh's custody, Byron had promised her that the child would always remain under one parent's care. Putting Allegra into a convent "is to me a serious & deep affliction". She then proceeded to vilify Italian convents which she described as notoriously miserable educational institutions. Not content with this, she went on to describe the women who emerged from them in terms that would only weaken her case with Byron. "They are bad wives & most unnatural mothers, licentious & ignorant, they are the dishonour & unhappiness of society."[9] How Lady Byron must gloat that she had done the best for her child in keeping her away from her father! But she, Claire, on the other hand, had surrendered Allegra to Byron so that the child could receive the advantages she couldn't provide. Claire's proposal was that Allegra be put in an English school which she would pay for – even though she had no money. While one might sympathise with Claire, one can see from this letter why Byron found her so exasperating.

He forwarded this communication to the Hoppners with a defence of his actions. He described Allegra as so naughty that the servants couldn't control her; and he had sent her to a place "where the air is good and where she will at least have her learning advanced – & her morals and religion inculcated. – I had also another reason – things were and are in such a state here – that I had no reason to look upon my personal safety as particularly insurable."[10] How he knew about the salubrious air and the quality of the education at the convent is puzzling since he never set foot in the place. He took it for granted that the Hoppners would agree with him that it would be "insanity" to put Allegra in Claire's hands; and as for an English education, it would be useless to her since her illegitimacy would preclude her from making a good English marriage. As for the alleged broken promise with which Claire taxed him, he had no recollection of it, "nor can I conceive it possible to have been entered into – when the child was yet unborn – & might never have been born at all". He then referred to the gossip that Hoppner had relayed to him the previous year, that Shelley and Claire had had a child which they placed in a foundling home in Naples. Byron had been inclined to believe the story, but he was aware that there was an element of doubt since it emanated from the dismissed maid Elise (whose husband had been blackmailing the Shelleys, although Byron did not as yet know this).*

The unctuous Hoppner of course approved of the measure Byron had taken, although he abhorred Catholicism. He suggested that he and his wife take Allegra with them to Geneva where they could place the child in the home of a Protestant minister (May 2, 1821). Such a scheme would be advantageous, especially "if there is any truth in the objections suggested by Clara [sic]; if there is any likelihood of the world taking up and talking of the affair in the manner she describes, such a plan must remove them, and deprive even your bitterest enemies of any argument against you."[11] Byron liked the idea, but was reluctant to undo what had already been settled.

Meanwhile Shelley wrote from Pisa that he and Mary approved of what Byron had done since it seemed the only alternative under the circumstances. Claire's opposition to it was "the result of a misguided maternal affection" (April 17, 1821).[12] He also informed him that Keats had recently died in Rome (February 21); and Shelley attributed his death not to tuberculosis but to the cruel criticism he had suffered at the hands of the *Quarterly*. "Is it *actually* true?" Byron asked.[13] When the *Edinburgh Review* had attacked *Hours of Idleness* he described himself as furious but not despondent. (He had forgotten his threat never to write again.) Shelley had reminded him that he had now reached an age when "the eternal poets" began their supreme work: "Oh, that you would subdue yourself to the great task of building up a poem containing within itself the germs of a permanent relation to the present, and to all succeeding ages!"[14] Byron replied that he had neither the inclination nor the power. "As I grow older, indifferent – *not* to life, for we love it by instinct – but to the stimuli of life increases." Was there any possibility of their meeting during the summer – "alone?"[15]

Byron heard that there was a plan afoot to stage *Marino Faliero* at Drury

---

* For a splendid summary of the "Neapolitan mystery" and an informed speculation about the identity of the mother of this child, see Marion Kingston Stocking, *The Clairmont Correspondence*, vol. II, Appendix B (Baltimore: Johns Hopkins, 1995).

Lane. He wrote frantically to Murray and all his friends to try to prevent it, but Hobhouse replied that there was no way it could be stopped, and "I think it would take mightily."[16] He was wrong. The closet drama was published on April 21; and although Murray tried to obtain an injunction against its performance on the stage, it opened on April 27 and closed after seven performances. A Milan newspaper reported erroneously that it was hissed off the stage. Byron told Hobhouse (May 20, 1821): "Ten years ago I should have gone crazy – at present I lived on as usual."[17] None the less, he became obsessional about having the Milan report contradicted.

Sardanapulus meanwhile was finished on May 27, and two weeks later he began another closet drama of conspiracy, *The Two Foscari*, drawing again on Venice for inspiration. The Foscari father plots against the state that has wrongly banished his son – and again we have the themes of exile, imprisonment, and isolation. There is a close connection, too, between Byron's own confined spatial sense and the rigidly contained unities of these dramas written in Ravenna. Visiting the city fifty years later, Henry James was stunned by the realisation that Byron had spent "two long years in this stagnant city"; and he describes "the deadly provincial vista" as one gazes down the narrow street from the Guiccioli palazzo. "The hour one spends with Byron's memory then is almost compassionate"; and James felt a renewal of faith in the power of his inner creative drive for he saw nothing in these surroundings from which he could have drawn inspiration.[18]

Byron planned to continue the adventures of Don Juan, but Teresa, after reading an article in the Milan *Gazetta* quoting the attacks on Byron's morals in the English papers, insisted that he promise to abandon the poem. Despite his arguments to her that it was only a burlesque satire, she managed to prevail upon him to write to Murray (July 6, 1821) that Cantos 3–5 were to be his last: "it arises from the wish of all women to exalt the *sentiment* of the passions – & to keep up the illusion which is their empire. – Now D. J. strips off this illusion – & laughs at that & most other things." It was the first time Hobhouse found himself in agreement with Teresa: "Take Doctor's advice . . . La Signora to be sure, knows her sex & resembles her sex."[19]

The authorities were watching Byron more carefully than ever, especially after Tita (his former gondolier) was arrested for drawing a knife during a quarrel on the street with a soldier; and only after considerable difficulty was Byron able to have his servant released. Then on July 10 Pietro Gamba was arrested as he was returning home from the theatre. He was immediately escorted to the frontier of the Papal States and the next morning his rooms were searched, although Teresa had already destroyed any compromising papers. A few days later Count Ruggero Gamba was then also arrested; and when Teresa realised that she must accompany her father into exile, she became hysterical at the thought of leaving Byron.

She persuaded Byron to ask her father if she could stay on in Ravenna for a short time. This was the indiscretion her husband had been waiting for. Guiccioli appealed to the Pope that she be returned to him. He asked that she be placed in a convent if she failed to do so. Byron ordered Teresa to depart immediately to join her family in Florence. She left Ravenna on the 24th, and the following day from Bologna sent a tearful plea to be allowed to return. Byron was adamant; he reminded her that her duty was to her father, but she could not tear herself away from Bologna until August 2.

The plan was that the family would proceed to Switzerland which Pietro viewed as the land of freedom. Byron, having agreed to join them, wrote to his Geneva banker, Charles Hensch, for aid in securing them suitable accommodation. Meanwhile Teresa was sending Byron wild letters accusing him of refusing to follow her because he was having affairs with the maids: "a thousand insults", as he described them to Pietro. From the outset he advised the family to remain quietly in Florence until plans for a more permanent residence could be arranged. From the beginning, also, he hoped against hope that the Gambas would be allowed to return to Ravenna and that they could get on with the regular routine of quiet living. With this purpose in mind he wrote to the owner of his former home in Piccadilly Terrace, the Duchess of Devonshire, who had been residing in Rome, to ask her if she could use her influence at the Vatican to allow the Gambas to return to their home; but the Duchess had moved to Spa in Belgium, and there seemed no one else to whom he could turn.

Left alone, Byron was able to finish his drama, *The Two Foscari*, and to begin another, *Cain*, as well as completing *The Vision of Judgment* and *Heaven and Earth*. His output – with Teresa out of the way – was prodigious compared to the paucity of work he had produced the previous year. Between writing and his solitary rides in the Pineta he was content enough to let the days pass without taking any measures to join the Gambas.

Shelley's visit to Ravenna in August provided him with a possible alternative for the future. Shelley had accepted Byron's invitation, and arrived about ten o'clock on the night of the 6th. As usual they sat up talking until after dawn. Shelley was astounded by the difference a regular life had made to Byron, no longer the dissolute rake who had shocked him in Venice but rather a steady, amiable fellow.

Shelley also found himself totally bemused by the animal kingdom he encountered in Byron's residence. He described the scene to Thomas Love Peacock: "eight enormous dogs, three monkeys, five cats, an eagle, a crow, and a falcon: and all these, except the horses, walk about the house, which every now and then resounds with their unarbitrated quarrels, as if they were masters of it."[20] Just before sending off his letter he discovered more livestock on the stairs: five peacocks, two guinea hens, and an Egyptian crane. This kingdom of dependent creatures seemed to provide Byron with some kind of reassurance that he was lord of the manor. He could feel generous in providing for them, and yet they were far more disposable than human beings.

Shelley now learned the full extent of Hoppner's calumny based on Elise's gossip. He wrote indignantly to Mary that Hoppner had also told Byron that Shelley had treated Mary cruelly, a charge that seemed to upset him more than the gossip that he had had a child by Claire. Shelley suggested that Mary write a letter to the Hoppners, "in case you believe & know & can prove that it is false".[21] It was a curious way to word this to his own wife; and he also instructed her to send the letter first to him in Ravenna so that he could show it to Byron. During this visit Byron read to him Canto V of *Don Juan*; and Shelley, with his usual generosity, pronounced it "astonishingly fine. – It sets him not above but far above all the poets of the day: every word has the stamp of immortality. – I despair of rivalling Lord Byron, as well I may: and there is no other with whom it is worth contending."[22]

Shelley received the letter he wanted from Mary for the Hoppners on the 16th. "Repair – I conjure you," she pleaded, "the evil you have done by retracting your confidence in one so vile as Elise, and by writing to me that you now reject as false every circumstance of her infamous tale."[23] Shelley left this letter with Byron, who never did forward it to Venice as he promised. One obvious explanation for this oversight was simply indolence. The other (and possibly, more probable) might have been that Byron wanted the Hoppners to be left with the worst possible impression of Claire.

Shelley had always been immensely fond of Allegra, and made a point of visiting her in Bagnacavallo. He found her still beautiful but she had become shy and serious. She grew more playful after he gave her a gift of a little gold chain. He asked her if she had a message for her father, and she replied: "*Che venga farmi un visitino, e che porta seco la mammina*" ("I wish he'd pay me a little visit and bring Mama along") – the *mammina*, of course, being Teresa. Shelley found that she resembled her father in that "her predominant foible seems the love of distinction & vanity."[24] He imagined that she was well treated, but was sceptical that she was receiving an adequate education.

During his lengthy talks with Byron, Shelley began to conceive a plan for forming an interesting expatriate colony in Pisa. He knew that he would have to present some rather strong arguments to Mary for the possibility of having Byron once more in their midst: "Our roots were never struck so deep as at Pisa & the transplanted tree flourishes not. – People who lead the lives which we led until last winter are like a family of Wahabee Arabs pitching their tent in the midst of London. – We must do one thing or the other: for yourself for our child, for our existence."[25]

Exhilarating as Shelley found Byron's conversation, he was never free from the realisation that the difference in rank imposed a certain constraint on their relations.

> Lord Byron & I are excellent friends, & were I reduced to poverty, or were I a writer who had no claims to a higher station than I possess – or did I possess a higher than I deserve, we would appear in all things as such, & I would freely ask him any favour. Such is not now the case – The demon of mistrust & of pride lurks between two persons in our situation poisoning the freedom of their intercourse.[26]

This sense of the divide between them was to intensify in Pisa; but, at this point, it was only Shelley who seemed aware of it, and Byron had no hesitation in asking him to do a favour for him. His enthusiasms were so volatile that Shelley was somewhat surprised when Byron announced on August 11 that he had definitely decided on moving to Pisa. Part of his reluctance to make any plans had been his aversion to returning to Geneva. He now enlisted Shelley to plead his case with Teresa.

Shelley always delighted in the role of intermediary. He wrote the contessa a long letter describing the indignities to which Byron had been subjected in 1816 by the English visitors who spied upon his every movement. There was no reason to believe that if he now moved back to Geneva the situation would change.

> Do not delude yourself, Madam, with the idea that the English people – accepting Lord Byron as the greatest poet of our time – would on that account abstain from troubling him and from persecuting him in so far as they were able. Their admiration for his works is involuntary and they slander him in consequence of their immoderate prejudices, as much as they read him, for their pleasure.[27]

He assured her that Byron was so eager to join her that he had instructed him to find a palazzo in Pisa as soon as possible.

Teresa was very much touched by this letter, and, in thanking him, begged him not to leave Ravenna without "Mylord".[28] The agitated tone of her letters was an expression of her suspicions that Byron had no intention of leaving Ravenna. Only a week before she had written to his steward, Lega Zambelli: "Lega, write me the truth. Is Mylord pretending? Or does he really mean to leave Ravenna? Tell me, Lega, I beseech you. This uncertainty is an unbearable torment for me."[29]

After a pleasant ten-day visit of daily rides and good conversation Shelley left for Florence where he called on the contessa with further reassurance. She liked him immensely, but was concerned about his emaciated appearance. As soon as he reached Florence he sent her another comforting letter (August 22, 1821), assuring her that everything would be done to speed Byron on his way.

Once Shelley found accommodation for the family, Teresa managed to convince her father and brother that Pisa was their most feasible solution. They arrived in the city on September 1, and after taking temporary lodgings, moved into a large house on the south bank of the Arno. In Florence they had obtained temporary passports, and spies in Pisa were instructed to watch their every movement. Shelley also leased for Byron the splendid Casa Lanfranchi, a sixteenth-century palace with a small but pleasant garden on the north side of the river. He found additional stables for Byron's eight horses. All that was needed was a tenant to occupy the empty house.

Shelley became more and more excited at the prospect of a literary community. While in Ravenna he and Byron had discussed the possibility of founding a journal, and it seemed desirable to enlist the help of Leigh Hunt with his experience as editor of the *Examiner*. Would Hunt, Shelley asked, bring his family and settle in Italy? He had hesitated to ask Byron if he would finance the journey. As for Byron himself, Shelley assured Hunt that he was "reformed, as far as gallantry goes . . . I trust greatly to his intercourse with you, for his creed to become as pure as he thinks his conduct is. He has many generous and exalted qualities, but the canker of aristocracy wants to be cut out."[30]

Hunt immediately responded enthusiastically to the plan, and on September 21 wrote that he, his wife, and six children would set off in a month. He was more sanguine than Shelley about Byron's generosity. "With regard to the proposed publication of Lord Byron, about which you talk so modestly, he has it in his power, I believe, to set up not only myself and family in our finances again, but one of the best-hearted men in the world, my brother, in his."[31] All they could talk about was Italy, Italy, Italy.

Once the Gambas had settled in Pisa, Teresa could not understand why Byron did not set out immediately. He had asked Shelley to send eight wagons to Ravenna to convey his household effects. His autumnal depression of spirits assailed him with particular intensity this year so that his only expenditures of energy were his daily ride and mammoth bouts of poetry-writing. He turned again to keeping a sort of diary of "Detached Thoughts" in which he speculated on life and the hereafter. Reflecting that no one would wish to live his life over again, he was finding that he could no longer doubt the immortality of the soul. "How far our future life will be *individual* – or rather – how far it will at all resemble our *present* existence, is another question – but that the *Mind* is *eternal* – seems as possible as that the body is not so."[32]

The prospect of Pisa began to appear more distasteful with every passing day. Teresa had good cause to complain about the brevity and infrequency of his letters. Never did a lover appear less eager. Any terms of endearment were completely perfunctory, and he never failed to remind her that he was leaving Ravenna with the greatest reluctance. Shelley might have found it "a miserable place", but Byron was a creature of habit, and he resented anything that disturbed his routine.

Shelley had offered to teach Teresa English, but Byron warned her that she was only courting gossip. "You do not know the state of the factions in England – and the horrible things that are said about Shelley and me – and if you are not careful the English in Pisa and Florence will say that, *being tired of you*, I handed you on to him. I say this frankly and openly, in so many words. So, having been warned – it depends on you to behave as you think best."[33] Teresa reluctantly abandoned the idea of the English lessons.

Byron also told her that if there was any possibility that her father might be recalled to Ravenna before his own departure, he had no intention of leaving the town, and would willingly pay the costs incurred in renting the palazzo rather than have the trouble of moving. To friends such as Moore he said that he was going to Pisa for the winter only. He had time to scold Murray for printing mistakes – something he dearly loved to do. On hearing reports of an uprising against the Turks, his thoughts were again turning to Greece.

In Ravenna, Shelley had tried to extract from him a promise that he would bring Allegra with him to Pisa. Teresa had expressed the opinion that she thought it wiser to leave the child in the convent. Whether this view was dictated by possessiveness or concern for the child is hard to say. After his return Shelley continued to press her father to bring Allegra to Pisa where he assured him that he could find an appropriate school for her, and he gave his solemn word that there would be no interference from Claire. When the Mother Superior of Allegra's convent heard of Byron's intended departure, she wrote asking him to visit his daughter; and on the opposite side of the letter Allegra had written: "My dear Papa – It being fair-time I should so much like a visit from my Papa, as I have many desires to satisfy, will you not please your Allegrina who loves you so?"[34] Byron sent the note on to Hoppner, obviously proud of her, but remarking gruffly that she probably wanted him to buy her gingerbread. Having waited so long to visit her, he couldn't stir himself now to see her; and it seemed easier to leave her in the convent than to make arrangements to take her to Pisa.

He had not forgotten his other daughter. To Augusta he sent a lock of his hair and asked her to place it in a gold locket that she was to forward to Ada. It was also to have the inscription "*Il Sangue non e mai Acqua*" (blood is never water). Augusta was in a state of anxiety about gossip over the memoirs. Murray had paid Moore £2,000 for the copyright, and Byron was astounded by his generosity. He suggested to his publisher that perhaps Augusta might let him have the Alpine Journal of 1816 to add to his recollections:

> but her nerves have been in such a state since 1815 – that there is no knowing. – Lady Byron's people and Ly. Caroline Lamb's people – and a parcel of that set – got about her, & frightened her with all sorts of hints & menaces – so that she has never since been able to write to *me* a *Clear common letter* – and is so full of mysteries and miseries – that I can only sympathize – without always understanding her.[35]

This is his first declaration of knowledge about Lady Byron's influence over his sister.

Yet he wrote to Augusta to tell her of his plans for going to Pisa – for the winter. He spoke to her more frankly about Teresa than he had ever done. He described her as resembling the rest of his loves in her proclivity for making scenes. Nevertheless, he was surprised, he admitted, that his attachment, if not his passion, had lasted as long as three years; and he would never leave her, "for you know when a woman is separated from her husband for her Amant – he is bound both by honour (and inclination at least I am) to live with her all his days, as long as there is no misconduct. – So you see that I have closed as papa *begun* – and you will probably never see me again as long as you live."[36]

But October came, and still he lingered.* When Teresa protested, he told her to complain to the dilatory Lega who he claimed was responsible for the delay. Shelley told Byron that the contessa "seems apprehensive that you will *never* leave Ravenna" (October 21, 1821). In Pisa Shelley had an opportunity to observe Byron's *amica* more closely. To his friend John Gisborne he wrote: "La Guiccioli his cara sposa who attends him impatiently, is a very pretty sentimental [stupid *deleted*] innocent, super-ficial Italian, who has sacrifized an immense fortune to live [with *deleted*] for Lord Byron; and who, if I know any thing of my friend of her, or of human nature will hereafter have plenty of leisure & opportunity to repent of her rashness."[37]

On October 28 Byron was sitting in a vast, empty apartment at midnight waiting to depart in three hours. The wagons bearing his household effects had already arrived in Pisa. He was still in Ravenna all the next day. Finally – on the 30th – he climbed into the big coach to proceed to one more phase of his life. The great conveyance had become his only real home, a visibly solid object that carried him, its passive occupant, from one unfamiliarity to another.

It was a journey not without incident. He did not take the short detour to Bagnacavallo for a glimpse of his daughter, but as the coach passed Imola and proceeded towards Bologna Byron noticed the occupants of an approaching coach. The face that caught his attention was that of his beloved Lord Clare, the younger boy to whom he had been so attached at Harrow. They scrambled to the road and threw their arms around each other; and for Byron it was one of those occasions he had already written about in his "Detached Thoughts": "there are probably *moments* in most men's lives – which they would live over the rest of life to *regain*."[38] Byron felt that Clare was as moved by their meeting as he was. Clare was on his way to Rome with some friends, and had already left a note for Byron in Bologna. They arranged to meet in Pisa on Clare's return journey in the spring.

On November 1, as Byron climbed again into the great coach at Florence for the final leg of his journey, the windows of the piazza were filled with English visitors craning to catch a glimpse of the notorious figure. Thirty miles along the road, just past Empoli, Byron passed another

---

* Byron wrote *Heaven and Earth* during his last fortnight in Ravenna. For an interesting discussion of Japhet's reluctance to embark on the Ark, see Anthony B. England, "Byron and the Emergence of Japhet in *Heaven and Earth*", *English Studies in Canada*, vol. 21, December. 1995, 433–54.

coach travelling from Pisa, but showed no curiosity about its occupant as he was busy writing. It was Claire Clairmont travelling to Florence, her journey timed so that she would avoid Byron. It was curious that his journey began and ended with the name Clare, the man most loved and the woman most abhorred.

27

oooooooooooooo

The Singing Birds, 1821–2

Byron was somewhat astonished to find that his situation in Pisa was an improvement on Ravenna. Palazzo Lanfranchi was a splendid Renaissance building, with a noble staircase attributed (wrongly) to Michelangelo. Instead of being confined to a narrow dark street, he now had a splendid view of the Arno, not unlike the prospect from the Palazzo Mocenigo in Venice. Byron was delighted to hear that his new home had ghosts, but Fletcher nervously kept changing his room. There was a small pleasant garden where oranges could still be picked from the trees in November. Byron's only complaint was the noisy traffic on the road – today magnified a hundredfold. The Gambas were settled in the Casa Parra, only a short distance away.

Within days of his arrival Byron applied for permission to practise pistol-shooting in the garden, but was informed that this was forbidden within the city walls. As an alternative he initiated a pleasant routine of riding out to the *campagna* every afternoon with a group of the local British expatriates. Foremost amongst these of course was Shelley, who had taken the third floor of the Tre Palazzi in Chiesa, a building Byron could see to his left only a few hundred yards away across the river. Shelley soon introduced Byron to the nucleus of the rest of the circle. Most of them had literary ambitions. There was a well-connected Irishman, John Taaffe, who had gone into exile in 1815 after becoming involved in a scandal with a married woman. He was working on a *Commentary on Dante* which Byron was soon recommending to Murray. Some of the group had served as officers together in India and were now living on half-pay. These included Shelley's cousin Thomas Medwin, who very early conceived the idea of becoming Byron's Boswell, and was soon assiduously recording his conversations. Medwin had been living in Geneva near his friend Edward

Williams whom he had persuaded to join him in Pisa. Williams had run off with a fellow officer's wife, and this couple were now living in the same house as the Shelleys. He too became fascinated by Byron, and recorded many of his impressions of him in his journal. The group were enthusiastically expecting the arrival of Leigh Hunt and his family. As Mary Shelley told her friend Maria Gisborne: "So Pisa, you see, has become a little nest of singing birds."[1]

The Byron-watchers in England were soon apprised of his new situation. Hobhouse was again deeply distressed. He had told Byron in no uncertain terms that the world would consider *Cain* blasphemous and that he thought it had been very unwise to entrust the Memoirs to Moore (whose friendship with Byron had always irritated him) because it looked as though he had "purchased" his own biographer.

Byron complained angrily to Kinnaird who tried to pacify him: "You have too many proofs of Hobhouse's integrity of character and of sincere Friendship for you to make it necessary to me to observe that whatever Hobhouse wrote to you came from the pen of a real friend."[2] Hanson had informed Kinnaird that there were still more outstanding debts. A butcher near Newstead had never been paid, nor had Owen Mealey, the steward whom Hanson had appointed so many years ago, and Kinnaird believed that he had earned an honest wage. Byron exploded that he was a scoundrel and £10 would be enough for him. But what about Baxter, the long-suffering coach-maker? Byron replied (December 18, 1821) that only the interest on debts was to be paid: "surely I have paid debt enough for one year." His moving expenses, after all, had been considerable. "You really must not pay any body – I can't afford it." After announcing that he had been laying in some choice wines, he silenced Kinnaird for the time being with the admonition: "But don't speak to me of *paying* – it makes me so very unwell."

Shortly after his arrival in Pisa, Byron wrote a temperate letter (November 17) to his wife which unfortunately he never sent to her. He had been delighted to receive a note from her enclosing a lock of Ada's hair, light brown like his own at that age. He was particularly happy, he told her, to see Annabella's handwriting because the only sample of it he had was the single word "Household" from an old accounts book. They had both made a bitter mistake, he remarked philosophically, "but now it is over". He had long given up all hope of a reconciliation, but hoped that in future they could treat each other courteously.

Almost as soon as he arrived in Pisa he assured Augusta that he was living quite *alone* in his immense house (November 4). Wouldn't she consider the idea of paying him a visit? He was willing to put up with "your drone of a husband", it would be good for the children, and he would pay for their journey. His sister felt it tactful not to mention this invitation to Annabella, but she passed on the information that Murray had purchased the memoirs. She understood that Byron had written

> most violently and disgracefully about the *late* and *present* K[ing] – things for which any Publisher would be prevented – *altogether* the accounts are most depressing and heart breaking to those who have any heart left – I begin to think mine will soon be turned to stone . . . I hear that Leigh Hunt and that infamous *Shelley* are going out to live with him and publish an *Atheistical* Newspaper . . . it is all very bad.[3]

Cain, which was published together with *Sardanapulus* and *The Two Foscari*, on December 19, 1821, was to cause almost as much of an uproar as *Don Juan* had done. When Byron sent it off to Kinnaird, he described the three-act drama as "in my very fiercest Metaphysical manner – like *Manfred* and all that".[4] Byron offended orthodox religious sentiments by subscribing to a catastrophic theory of the universe, in which the world is successively re-populated after a series of pulverising upheavals. Worse than that, Byron depicted Cain's murder of his brother as having been provoked by the cruel tyranny of an unloving God. His resentment towards the cruel Calvinistic God of May Gray's religion was finally given an outlet.

By dedicating the poem to Walter Scott, Byron was risking jeopardising the goodwill of the one literary figure who had stood by him consistently. Ever generous, Scott, in a letter of November 2, 1821, to Murray, accepted Byron's dedication: "I do not know that his Muse has ever taken so lofty a flight amid her former soarings. He has certainly matched Milton on his own ground. Some of part of the language is bold, and may shock one class of readers, whose line will be adopted by others out of affectation or envy. But then they must condemn the *Paradise Lost*, if they have a mind to be consistent."[5]

Nevertheless, the Tory press thundered against its wickedness and blasphemy. Annabella and Augusta were outraged. Augusta found it "one of the most disagreeable productions I ever *tried* to read – I skimmed the greatest part fearfully – I really grew so afraid of thinking like Cain – I so dislike the sort of thing to read beyond all I can express."[6]

Busy settling into his new routine, Byron only gradually heard of the English reaction to the poem. In addition to the target-practice excursions, he had installed a billiard table where his new friends gathered frequently, and he initiated a series of weekly Wednesday dinners, for which the men deserted their ladies even at Christmas. It was a rather lonely time for Teresa, confined for the most part to the company of her family. Mary Shelley and Jane Williams she found pleasant, and they sometimes accompanied her in her carriage to meet the gentlemen returning from the *campagna*. As for Mary, in Geneva there had been boating parties and evenings of ghost stories, but now she found herself excluded from this male circle. Nor did she and Teresa have much in common. Her intellect was far superior to the little convent girl's, and Teresa was somewhat in awe of her. On hearing that Mary was learning Greek, Teresa asked Byron if he would love her more if she knew about Lake Trasimene. Byron had been talking of staging *Othello* with himself as Iago and Mary as Desdemona. There were a few rehearsals, and everyone was impressed by Byron's acting. However, the plan was suddenly abandoned, apparently under pressure from Teresa who would have been left out since she could not speak English.

The behaviour of the *stravaganti* did not go unnoticed by the Pisan spies. The appearance of these strange Englishmen who never socialised with the Italians (other than the exiled Gambas) led to a good deal of speculation. Byron was supposed to be a great milord, yet on his riding expeditions he looked more like a bohemian in a braided tartan jacket, loose nankeen trousers, and a jaunty blue velvet cap. The tall, bent Shelley attracted attention by wandering about reading aloud, dressed in a short boy's jacket and scruffy shoes. But none of them could hold a candle to the strange figure who appeared in mid-January, a man who modelled himself on Byron's Corsair.

This was Edward Trelawny, who had met Edward Williams in Geneva. He was a large, genial fellow, a teller of tall tales; the group was fascinated but a little sceptical of his stories of having been a pirate after deserting from the navy. Mary described him to Maria Gisborne as having "raven black hair which curls thickly & shortly like a Moor's dark, grey – expressive eyes – overhanging brows upturned lips & a smile which expresses good nature & kindheartedness . . . His company is delightful."[7]

Trelawny was equally bemused by Byron whose conversation, to his surprise, seemed confined to anecdotes about boxers and gamblers in Regency London. But he brought out the romantic streak in the poet, encouraging him to build a yacht. On February 5 Trelawny wrote to his friend, Captain Daniel Roberts, then in Genoa, to commence building the boat immediately, and no expense was to be spared. Shelley and Williams had already been exploring the waterways around Pisa in a flat-bottomed boat, the kind used by local huntsmen when navigating the canals of the *maremma*. They had ordered a thirty-foot skiff in Livorno, and were now busy making plans to find a house in the bay of La Spezia, north of Viareggio, with a view to spending the summer in a spot from which they could sail along the beautiful Ligurian coast.

Meanwhile they were all concerned about the whereabouts of the Hunts. Byron had provided Mary Shelley with the funds to furnish the ground floor of the Palazzo Lanfranchi; but not until the end of January did they hear that they had been unable to embark because of terrible winter storms. Since the journal which Hunt was to launch in conjunction with Byron and Shelley had been deferred until Hunt's arrival, incipient competitive tension between the two poets began to emerge. At shooting practice both men were excellent. Byron's hand shook but everyone agreed that he was the superior marksman. Byron was older than the rest – the only one over thirty – and was treated with seniority for his reputation and his rank. Both poets seemed to compete for dominance at the dinner table, but Byron did not have the depth or range of Shelley's mind. Privately Shelley complained that it was difficult to prevent Byron from skittering from topic to topic, and one never knew when he was in earnest. Medwin was fascinated by his soft voice and radiant smile, but after leaving him could scarcely remember anything of substance he had said.

As in Geneva, Shelley's creativity was stifled by Byron's presence; and one evening the group was made uneasy when after Byron handed Shelley the manuscript of a poem he was working on, "The Deformed Transformed", Shelley returned it with the remark that he liked it less than any of his other work. It owed too much to *Faust*, he said bluntly, and two lines were taken directly from Southey. Byron paled, seized the manuscript, and threw it in the fire. He actually had another copy in his desk which he was later to revise.

Poor Shelley had not prepared himself for his jealousy of Byron. In Geneva he was well aware that Mary, as well as Claire, had been fascinated by Byron;* and now his male friends seemed to regard Byron as their leader, a place previously occupied by Shelley. Shelley extravagantly – and genuinely – admired Byron's poetry. He considered him the greatest English poet since Milton. There is no indication of comparable magnanimity on Byron's part, although in the Appendix to *The Two Foscari*, while

---

* I find myself in disagreement with Ernest J. Lovell Jr's argument that Mary was infatuated with Byron, especially as his article contains a number of factual errors. See *Keats–Shelley Journal*, January 1953, II, 35–49.

he objected to the "metaphysical portion" of *Queen Mab*, he expressed his admiration for its poetry.*

Byron often declared that Shelley's utopian tendencies undermined the impact of his genius. If we are to believe Trelawny, when he urged Byron to praise Shelley publicly, he replied, "If we introduced Shelley to our readers, they might draw comparisons, and they are *'odorous'*."[8] Was Byron, then, secretly a little in awe of Shelley's poetic powers?

Shelley refused to allow himself to become embroiled in Byron's feud with Robert Southey because although he had been named as a member of the "Satanic School" by the poet laureate, his reputation was not secure enough to risk getting into a public altercation. Not so Byron. He had been persuaded by Hobhouse to omit some crass lines about Southey from *The Vision of Judgment*, but even so Murray refused to publish the poem, and it only appeared in the first edition of the *Liberal* in October 1822. However, in a long intemperate note to *The Two Foscari* Byron referred to Southey's "cowardly ferocity" in spreading calumnies about him. Not surprisingly, Byron's remarks were taken amiss by Southey; and on February 5 Byron was thrown into a rage by Southey's bitter reply in the *Courier* of January 5. Byron could never grasp that if he attacked people, they were bound to retaliate. He threatened to challenge Southey to a duel, but was talked out of it by Kinnaird.

Shelley had neither the temperament nor the power to get implicated in *ad hominem* altercations of this kind; but the incident brought home to him the enormous gulf between them. Byron's notoriety was just as great as Shelley's, but exile had made him a pariah only in his own eyes. The public remained curious about anything he might write, whereas Shelley's publisher, Charles Ollier, seemed to do little to advance his work; and while Byron encouraged him to change publishers, he apparently did not suggest the possibility of Murray as an alternative, although he had once begged Murray to help Coleridge and now was promoting the cause of the second-rate Taaffe.

Money proved the decisive factor in driving a wedge between Byron and Shelley. Over a period of months in 1821 Byron heard numerous reports that Lady Noel was seriously ill; but he often jocularly remarked that it was his luck that she would live for ever: "old ailing women are eternal."[9] On Christmas Day he made a wager of £1,000 with Shelley that Lady Noel would outlive Shelley's father, Sir Timothy. Then on January 28 Byron's

---

* Charles Robinson has given a persuasive account of Byron's attitude to Shelley in *Shelley and Byron. The Snake and the Eagle Writhed in Flight* (Baltimore: Johns Hopkins, 1976).

mother-in-law died and when the news reached him on February 15, his first reaction was concern for Annabella's loss.

Lady Noel's estate was to be divided, according to the separation agreement, by arbitrators, Sir Francis Burdett acting for Byron. Lushington expected great difficulties from Byron's advisers; and when Kinnaird heard this he made a point of telling Lushington: "I do not attach more value to this stuff than to other Gossip . . . I feel confident I can answer both on the part of Lord Byron & his friends for their anxious hope & confident expectation of every thing being settled in the most amicable & honourable footing."[10] Byron now took the name of Noel Byron, thrilled that his initials were the same as Napoleon Bonaparte's. With his respect for convention, he dressed his servants in mourning black despite the fact that he had loathed his mother-in-law. Lady Byron continued to live at Kirkby Mallory, and Byron, in inheriting £6,000, was to be comfortably off for the rest of his life. However, since his income was only a marital life-interest, he began to have nightmares about what would happen to him if Lady Byron died before him, and began pushing Kinnaird to take out an insurance policy on her life.

All the Pisan circle quickly heard the news. On the very day Byron received word of Lady Noel's death, Shelley sent him a note enquiring nervously whether Byron could advance any money to Hunt who had already written Byron a rather impertinently worded letter asking for financial help. "As it has come to this in spite of my exertions," Shelley wrote, "I will not conceal from you the low ebb of my own money affairs in the present moment, – that is, my absolute incapacity of assisting Hunt farther."[11] If this was a hint to Byron that he should settle the wager made on Christmas Day, Byron ignored it. Byron's apologists have brushed this off with the excuse that the wager was probably not seriously meant, just as they have dismissed the fact that there was certain indignation in 1815 when Byron failed to pay up on a wager made in Brighton that he would never marry. The only difference was that this time he had the means to honour his obligation.

Two days later Shelley informed Hunt that with Lady Noel's death "Lord B is a rich, a still richer man."[12] Shelley of course had no way of knowing the exact state of Byron's finances – or of his many unpaid debts. What he could see was that Byron lived in relative splendour, whereas he and Mary were constantly worried about money. When Shelley visited Byron on February 16, Byron agreed to lend Hunt £250 – after insisting that Shelley act as guarantor and return the money after his father's death. After their meeting Shelley was still quivering with indignation when he told Hunt that "Many circumstances have occurred between myself & Lord B. which make the intercourse painful to me, & this last discussion about money particularly so." But he assured Hunt that Byron was still enthusiastic about launching their journal, and "I will take care to preserve the little influence I may have over this Proteus in whom such strange extremes are reconciled until we meet."[3]

That Shelley had heard that Byron had been gossiping about his alleged relationship with Claire seems apparent in an angry letter he sent to her some time during February shortly before she made a secret visit to Pisa.

It is of vital importance both to me and to yourself, to Allegra even, that I should put a period to my intimacy with L B, and that without *éclat*. No sentiments of honour or justice restrain him (as I strongly suspect) from the basest insinuations, and the only mode in which I could effectually silence him I am reluctant (even if I had proof) to employ during my father's life. But for your immediate feelings I would suddenly and irrevocably leave this country which he inhabits, nor ever enter it but as an enemy to determine our differences *without words*.[14]

By April 10 Shelley had begun to feel remorseful that his jealousy of Byron had complicated his attempts to obtain a loan for Hunt. To his friend he confessed: "Certain it is, that Lord Byron has made me bitterly feel the inferiority which the world has presumed to place between us and which subsists nowhere in reality but in our talents, which are not our own but Nature's – or in our rank, which is not our own but Fortune's."[5] Shelley, who rather relished his reputation among his friends as a superior moral being, was sad that he must have fallen in Hunt's estimation: "Alas, how am I fallen from the boasted purity in which you knew me once exulting!"

Byron seemed unaware of Shelley's seething emotions. While Shelley seldom attended the Wednesday dinners any longer, the shooting expeditions continued until an incident occurred on March 24 which was to alter irretrievably the lives of the expatriates living in Pisa. Late on a Sunday afternoon the group left their regular haunt at Cisanello to make the two-mile return journey to Pisa. The party included Byron, Shelley, Trelawny, a Captain Hay, and Pietro Gamba. (Medwin had left for Rome two weeks earlier.) About half a mile from the Porta alla Piagge, they encountered Taaffe who was walking his horse. Mary and Teresa were riding ahead in Teresa's small carriage. The riders, arranged in two rows, had spread themselves completely across the road. Suddenly a horseman came galloping up behind them, passing between Taaffe and the ditch so that his horse reared up and jostled Byron's steed. Taaffe cried out indignantly to Byron, "Have you ever seen the like of that?"

Byron's immediate reaction was that he had been rudely insulted by someone whom he took to be an officer, and he set off in pursuit of the galloping figure. The man was actually Stefani Masi, a sergeant-major in the Tuscan Royal Light Horse, who had been dining with a friend in the country and was hurrying because he was fearful that he would be late for roll-call. Shelley, who was the first to reach the rider, asked him, "Please explain what you mean by your conduct." Masi replied that he had as much right to the road as they did. Insults were exchanged, Masi threatened to arrest them, and Pietro slashed at the soldier with his whip. Shelley was knocked to the ground where he lay senseless for a few minutes. Masi galloped off.

Byron ordered Pietro to hurry to the Palazzo Lanfranchi and order Lega to go immediately to the police to make a report. As Byron made his way back, he encountered Masi riding close to the river near his residence. By now a large crowd had gathered, and in the fading light one of Byron's servants was seen to run out and attack Masi with a pitchfork. Masi screamed, "Alas, I am killed!" and fell from his saddle on to the street. Bystanders picked him up and carried him to the hospital.

All was confusion. Teresa was in hysterics, and had to be bled by the surgeon, Dr André Vacca, who clearly did not feel much sympathy for the foreigners, especially as there were reports that Masi could not survive the night. By Wednesday he seemed to be recovering. Everyone was being interviewed and filing reports. The authorities then arrested Tita and Byron's coachman, Vincenzo Papi, who had apparently stabbed Masi. Tita was widely disliked in the town for his arrogant behaviour, and there was no lack of bystanders to testify that he was the assailant. A servant of the Gambas, Antonio Maluchielli, was also incarcerated. Byron then wrote to Edward Dawkins, the British chargé d'affaires at Florence, enclosing the various depositions and asking for his aid in obtaining the release of his servants. The coachman was released; but after languishing in jail for a month, Tita was ordered to leave the Grand Duchy. Byron heard this news on April 22, the same day he received word from Bagnacavallo of the death of Allegra.

In Florence Claire was studying German with the intention of eventually joining her brother Charles who was working as a tutor in Vienna. She was distraught at the thought of moving so far away from Allegra, but she could see no other way of earning her living except as a governess. Then in early February she encountered Elise Foggi. Now repentant, Elise confessed to having told scandalous stories about her and Shelley to Mrs Hoppner. Claire persuaded Elise to write to Venice contradicting the story of this alleged affair. Having decided by now that she must leave Italy, Claire wrote a final letter (February 18, 1822) to Byron, begging to see Allegra: "I assure you I can no longer resist the internal inexplicable feeling which haunts me that I shall never see her any more. I entreat you to destroy this feeling by allowing me to see her."[16]

The Shelleys were shocked when Claire raised the mad idea of kidnapping Allegra. Thoroughly alarmed, they responded in a joint letter (March 20, 1822). They agreed with her that Allegra should be taken out of the hands of "one as remorseless as he is unprincipled". Nevertheless, it would be next to impossible to remove Allegra from the convent; and Claire must accept that she was powerless against a man who had vowed that if she bothered him any more, he would place Allegra in a secret convent where she could never find her. Besides, it was always possible that Byron might be reconciled to his wife, and then he would be only too relieved to get Allegra off his hands. Shelley added in a postscript that he had endeavoured to persuade Byron to place the child in a convent in Lucca, but to no avail. He urged her to come and discuss the situation with them. Perhaps she would help them find a house for the summer. "I shall certainly take our house *far* from Lord Byron's, although it may be impossible suddenly to put an end to his detested intimacy."[17] They sent the letter by special messenger, and the next day Claire set out for Pisa for a four-day visit.

After returning to Florence, Claire again succumbed to despair. She begged Shelley to write a letter (imitating Byron's hand) to the nuns ordering them to release Allegra. Shelley was horrified that she could suggest such a thing, and again emphasised to her that Byron was both powerful and inflexible. There was no way she could possibly reach Allegra; and any of these madcap schemes would only "plunge you and all that is connected with you in irremediable ruin".[18] Shelley urged her to join them for the summer which they intended to spend in the Bay of Spezia; and he assured her that there was no chance of her encountering Byron who had rented an unfurnished country villa at Montenero, about seven kilometres from Ligorno.

Claire returned to Pisa on April 15, and while she could see Byron's palazzo very clearly from the windows of the Shelleys' apartment, her presence in the city was carefully concealed, although Trelawny and the

Williams saw her frequently. Unknown to her, by then Byron was receiving a series of letters from Pellegrino Ghigi, his banker in Ravenna, who had originally taken Allegra to the convent. Ghigi's letters were very grave accounts of consumptive attacks Allegra was suffering. On the very day Claire arrived in Pisa, Ghigi wrote that while the child seemed to be out of danger, "I assure you that she has been very ill of a dangerous illness."[19] Byron then sent off a courier to Bagnacavallo authorising the nuns to call in Professor Tommasini from Bologna if necessary.

On April 21 Allegra was dead, to the profound grief of the nuns who considered her a very special child. Ghigi's reaction was furious indignation. He told Lega Zambelli that "I am so upset by this misfortune that I wish I had never met the noble Lord."[20] According to Teresa's *Vie* it was she who broke the news to Byron. He turned pale, sank into a chair, and asked her to leave him by himself. On the 23rd he sent Shelley a note that the blow was "stunning and unexpected". He continued:

> But I have borne up against it as I best can, and so far successfully, that I can go about the usual business of life with the same appearance of composure, and even greater. There is nothing to prevent your coming to-morrow; but, perhaps, to-day, and yester-evening, it was better not to have met. I do not know that I have any thing to reproach in my conduct, and certainly not in my feelings and intentions toward the dead. But it is a moment when we are apt to think that, if this or that had been done, such event might have been prevented, – though every day and hour shows us that they are the most natural and inevitable. I suppose that Time will do his usual work – Death has done his.

Three years later he was to speak to Lady Blessington about his daughter. "While she lived, her existence never seemed necessary to my happiness; but no sooner did I lose her than it appeared to me as if I could not live without her. Even now the recollection is bitter."[21] This was exactly the reaction Annabella had attributed to him after she had left him.

When Shelley heard the news, Claire was away with the Williamses looking for a summer house. On their return, two days later, an anguished Shelley tried his utmost to hide his feelings from Claire whom they did not dare to tell so long as she was in close proximity to Byron. As soon as possible they spirited her away to Casa Magni, a whitewashed house they had rented in San Terenzo on the shore near Lerici. As the group sat debating how they would break the news to her, Claire entered the room and on seeing their faces, immediately grasped the truth. The worst had now happened, and she withdrew into numb paralysis.

The next day (May 3, 1822) Shelley wrote to Byron.

> I will not describe her grief to you; you have already suffered too much; and, indeed, the only object of this letter is to convey her last requests to you, which, melancholy as one of them is, I could not refuse to ask, and I am sure you will readily grant. She wishes to see the coffin before it is sent to England, and I have ventured to assure her that this consolation, since she thinks it such, will not be denied her.[22]

Claire apparently sent Byron a hysterical letter full of reproaches. Shelley dissuaded Claire from visiting the coffin; and on the 9th he told Byron that she was now relatively calm. He was sorry, he said, that Claire had written so intemperately; but he lacked the courage to express his anger at Byron's indifference to a mother's suffering.

Byron intended to send the body back to England to be buried at Harrow Church near the Peachey Stone where he had spent so many hours as a boy. The body had to be embalmed and sent to Livorno. When the priest and Ghigi's brother-in-law (who had overseen the arrangements) arrived in Pisa to report to Byron, he refused to see them. To Lega Zambelli, Ghigi wrote indignantly that he was much mortified by Byron's action. "I too believe that Mylord is very sensitive and much grieved, but I am also aware that every man has his pride – and one must not, on account of one's own grief, forget what is due to others."[23] Lega apologised lamely, and asked if Ghigi could procure some Romagnole truffles for his master.

Byron refused also to pay the embalmer's bill because he believed that he had been overcharged because of his rank. Nor would he pay for the coffin or the undertaker. Ghigi was totally disgusted: "If he will not pay the 300 *scudi* which are due, let him pay whatever sum he pleases. I must not and cannot believe in such baseness in the noble lord. I am not an Englishman, but in my sentiments I am as noble as any of them."[24] He paid the bills himself, and was not reimbursed until after Byron's death when Hobhouse settled both these bills, as well as the cost of maintaining all the animals that had been left in Ghigi's care when Byron left Ravenna.

But the tragic story was not yet over. Byron had proposed a tablet with the words:

In memory of
Allegra
daughter of G.G. Lord Byron,
who died at Bagnacavallo,
in Italy, April 20th, 1822,
aged five years and three months
"I shall go to her, but she shall not return to me."
2nd Samuel, XII, 23.

The rector at Harrow refused to erect such a tablet, and the child was buried just inside the threshold of the church. Shuttled around all her short life, in death she was treated with the same disregard. Unknown to Byron, one of the convenient objections raised to her burial at Harrow was the fact that Lady Byron sometimes attended services there.

When Byron finally heard the full story, he exclaimed to Augusta:

The story of this Child's burial is the epitome or miniature of the Story of my life.— My regard for her – & my attachment for the spot where she is buried – made me wish that she should be buried *where* – though I never was *happy* – I was once less miserable as a boy – in thinking that I should be buried – and you see how they have distorted this as they do every thing into some story about Lady B. – of whom Heaven knows – I have thought much less than perhaps I should have done in these last four or five years.[25]

28

ooooooooooooooo

The Wren, the Eagle,
and the Skylark, 1822

Byron's guilt over Allegra was submerged during the next months by a series of crises. The aftermath of the wounded officer, Masi, was prolonged and irritating. The coachman who had been freed actually secretly confessed to being the assailant, but, despite Teresa's pleas, Byron concealed this knowledge from Dawkins, the British chargé d'affaires in Florence. In his obsessive determination to have Tita freed, he laid the entire blame for the incident on Masi.

The servants were taken to Florence. Maluchielli (who had been in the employ of the Gambas) was kept in prison for many months and eventually banished. Tita, through the influence of Dawkins and a lawyer hired by Byron, was freed after suffering the humiliation of having his beard shaved off. He was not allowed to return to Pisa, but managed to make his way to the Shelley household near Lerici in early May, and eventually rejoined Byron after his move to Genoa.

To the relief of the Shelleys there had been no large house available in the vicinity of Lerici, so Byron had rented a villa in Montenero near Livorno for the summer, but with his usual reluctance to disturb his daily routine he did not move his household to the coast until the last week in May. The unimposing house – Trelawny described it as "not unlike the suburban verandahed cockney boxes on the Thames"[1] – belonged to a local banker, Francesco Dupuy, and Byron was soon involved in a lawsuit with him because the water supply gave out. There was a lovely garden and a view of Elba and Corsica, but the heat was so intense that they had to hang damp green boughs against the windows. They would have been much cooler if they had stayed within the thick stone walls and airy salons of the Palazzo Lanfranchi.

Teresa characteristically describes this period in idyllic terms, but in addition to the discomfort of the weather, Byron spent most of his time in his room. Teresa had placed herself in a very vulnerable position by cohabiting with him, an indisputable breach of the terms by which the Pope had granted the separation. Early in the year Count Guiccioli had reluctantly paid his wife the first six-month allowance ordered by the Pope. He then wrote to Teresa asking her to return to him. Teresa replied impertinently (February 25, 1822): "I must repeat to you that I am perfectly happy in my present situation and I think that no other would ever again suit me. When one has attained the tranquillity I now enjoy, at the cost of so many sacrifices and so much suffering, it is not easy to renounce it."[2]

Guiccioli was understandably furious and began petitioning the Pope to rescind the order for the allowance. By moving into the same house as Byron, Teresa played right into her husband's hands. Her father and brother had gone to Florence for the Masi trial. They were eventually allowed to rejoin Byron, but only on a provisional basis. On July 11 the Pope was persuaded to suspend Teresa's allowance. All was uncertainty and disarray as the Gambas had no idea when they would be allowed to return either to Pisa or to Ravenna.

Byron managed to evade these problems by shutting himself in his room to write. He had resumed *Don Juan's* adventures secretly before receiving official permission from Teresa in July. There were occasional pleasant breaks during those long smouldering days. The Mediterranean squadron of the American navy was at anchor off Livorno, and on May 21 Byron was invited aboard the *Constitution*. He was delighted with his warm welcome and his thoughts turned again towards the prospect of a new life in America.

Early in June, Byron's "earliest and dearest" friend, Lord Clare, managed to slip away from his travelling companions in Genoa to spend a day with him. To Thomas Moore Byron wrote (June 8): "As I have always loved him (since I was thirteen, at Harrow) better than any (*male*) thing in the world, I need hardly say what a melancholy pleasure it was to see him for a *day* only; for he was obliged to resume his journey immediately." Clare found him much older, defensive, and with diminished expectations about the future. Byron had a premonition that they would never meet again, and after his departure was plunged into even greater melancholy than before Clare's visit.

Meanwhile, in Lerici, Shelley and his friend Edward Williams were delighted on May 12 to greet the arrival of the little craft they had ordered from Genoa. For some time past Shelley had insisted that its name be changed from the original *Don Juan* (suggested by Trelawny) to *Ariel*. His joy in his new plaything was darkened by the discovery that *Don Juan* had been painted aggressively on the mainsail – the product of Byron's "contemptible vanity", according to Shelley. Shelley could not bring himself to sail in it so long as it bore the offensive name, and hours were spent trying to scrub it off with turpentine. Their efforts were unavailing, and finally they cut out the section of the sail altogether, replacing it with a patch of new sail, with reefs installed to disguise the disfigurement. To Mrs Gisborne, Mary remarked acidly: "I do not know what Ld Byron will say, but Lord and Poet as he is, he could not be allowed to make a coal barge of our boat."[3]

On June 13 the *Bolivar*, Byron's magnificent craft manned by Trelawny and his friend Roberts, was sighted. Its arrival was announced by a salute from Byron's crested cannon. It was, of course, a far more splendid boat than Shelley's; and after a trip in Shelley's frail craft, Trelawny was concerned by the careless way he steered with his hair over his eyes and a book on his lap. It was particularly disturbing that he did not know how to swim.

The *Bolivar* arrived in Livorno later in the week. Byron admired the boat although he grumbled about the cost, despite the fact that he had encouraged Trelawny to spare no expense in equipping it. He showed little interest in it, and Trelawny could not persuade him to take a cruise. Although Byron loved swimming and it was important to him to have a view of water, he did not share Shelley's passion for boats, and admitted to Trelawny that all the nautical terms in his work had been taken from books. In any case, the authorities informed him that he was not allowed to cruise in sight of Livorno, another indignity to exacerbate his growing dislike of Tuscany.

The long-awaited Hunt family finally turned up. Hunt's arrival had been delayed so long that Byron had lost all interest in the project that had brought him to Italy: the liberal journal to be produced by Hunt, Shelley and Byron. Pisa was no longer the nest of singing birds Mary had described after Byron's arrival, and Shelley expressed his concern to his friend Horace Smith: "I greatly fear that this alliance will not succeed, for I, who could never have been regarded as more than the link of the two thunderbolts, cannot now consent to be even that, – & how long the alliance between the wren & the eagle may continue, I will not prophesy."[4]

The wren and the eagle did not meet under the most propitious circumstances on that sultry July 1 morning when Hunt arrived in Livorno. Directed by Trelawny, whom he found aboard the *Bolivar* in the harbour, he made his way along a dusty road to a flaming salmon house, "the hottest looking house I ever saw".[5] Byron greeted him cordially enough although Hunt was shocked at how fat he had become. The household was in an uproar. The Byron and Gamba servants had got into a row and Pietro, in attempting to intervene, had been cut on the arm. Teresa was dishevelled and tearful, but Byron could not be persuaded to abandon his afternoon ride.

The Gambas by now had returned from Florence, and were ordered to appear before a tribunal in Livorno on July 2 where they were informed that they must leave Tuscany within four days. Shelley then arrived to accompany the Hunts back to Pisa where he took them to their new apartments on the ground floor of the Palazzo Lanfranchi. Mrs Hunt had been spitting blood and Shelley brought Dr Vacca to examine her. He pronounced her in grave condition, and did not believe she could live more than a year. When judging the actions of the various protagonists, one must remember that the Hunts' view of Italy was coloured by anxiety from the outset.

Byron and the Gambas arrived back in Pisa the following day. The Gambas were totally preoccupied with their impending exile, so that it was fortunate that Shelley was there to look after his English friends. From a letter to his sister-in-law, dated July 8, 1822, it is clear that Hunt was eager to make the best of the situation. "The Gambas have left for temporary refuge in Lucca, leaving Teresa behind with Byron – so you see how lightly the Italians think of certain heavy English matters."[6] (Actually Pietro had warned Teresa that there would be grave consequences if she remained alone with Byron, but she obstinately refused to leave her lover.) The Hunts' spacious apartments weren't as well furnished as they had been led to expect, but their six children had the garden in which to play. Lord Byron looked forward to the new journal "with great ardour", and had suggested the name *Hesperides* for it. He had also given Hunt a satire on Southey, entitled *The Vision of Judgment*, which was to be printed in the first issue. Despite Hunt's attempt at optimism, Shelley told Mary that in actual fact "Every body is in despair & everything in confusion."[7]

There were later complaints that Byron had been callous in his attitude towards the ailing Mrs Hunt, and that Teresa had not deigned to extend their acquaintance beyond a brief introduction. Teresa, however, could not speak English; and she and Byron could think of nothing but their uncertain future. Marianne Hunt, however, prided herself on her scorn of the aristocracy, and seemed to relish opportunities to insult Byron, although Hunt and Byron had pleasant literary conversations. Byron would come to his study window and make some joking remark. Hunt then joined him in the garden, and Teresa soon appeared. Hunt found her handsome in a buxom way, and very much aware that she was the companion of a great poet. He later remembered how Teresa would glow when Byron spoke kindly to her, but at some point Hunt decided that Byron had tired of the relationship.

This was a brief period of quiescence before all their lives were shattered by tragedy. On the evening of July 7, Shelley returned to Livorno because Williams was concerned to get back to his wife. The *Don Juan* (for so the boat continued to be called) cast off in the early afternoon of July 8. Captain Roberts was anxious about threatening clouds gathering on the horizon, and climbed to the tower where he could see the boat tossing about and pulling in its topsails near Viareggio. A summer squall erupted, and when the sky had cleared, the little vessel had disappeared from sight.

Trelawny and Roberts waited anxiously for some word of the amateur sailors; and when nothing was heard after two days, Trelawny returned to Pisa to tell Byron of his fears. Byron listened tremulously. They were soon joined by Hunt who despatched a note to Casa Magni begging for reassurance. After Mary Shelley and Jane Williams read Hunt's letter, they anxiously set off immediately for Livorno. About midnight their carriage pulled up in front of the Palazzo Lanfranchi where Teresa was standing with her maid on the balcony. When Mary told her who she was, Teresa hurried down to let her in. "*Sapete alcuna cosa di Shelley?*" But of course they had no news, and the two terrified women continued on their desperate drive south to Livorno.

Trelawny then accompanied them back to the Casa Magni, and the long fruitless search along the shore began. On the 16th Byron received a note from Roberts that two bodies had been washed ashore above Viareggio, and these were later discovered to be those of Williams and the young deck-hand, Charles Vivian. By the time the searchers reached the beach, the authorities had buried the bodies in the sand. Then on the 18th, another body appeared closer to Viareggio before it was covered with lime, and Trelawny was able to identify it only through a copy of Keats's *Lamia* still open in Shelley's pocket.

With Trelawny's help the newly widowed women moved back to their old quarters in Pisa, and Mary Shelley was touched by the kindness of Byron who was deeply moved by Shelley's death. To Murray he wrote (August 3, 1822): "You are all brutally mistaken about Shelley who was without exception – the *best* and least selfish man I ever knew. – I never knew one who was not a beast in comparison." The indefatigable

Trelawny managed to fulfil Mary's wishes that Shelley's body be removed to the Protestant Cemetery in Rome next to the grave of his son William. Through Dawkins he succeeded in obtaining permits to cremate the bodies on the beach and remove the ashes. On the 15th Byron joined the group at a spot about four and a half miles from Viareggio. While Byron and Hunt sat in the carriage under a fierce sun, Trelawny had Williams's body pulled from the sand with boathooks. Although it was in a loathsome state, Byron immediately recognised Williams's teeth. According to Trelawny, Byron looked thoughtfully at it and asked, "Is that a human body? – why it's more like the carcase of a sheep, or any other animal, than a man: this is a satire on our pride and folly."[8] Trelawny lit the fire and in a pagan ceremony of their own, the group threw incense, salt, sugar, and wine on the flames. Byron then impetuously flung himself into the sea and swam out in the direction in which his friend had drowned. When he was about a mile from shore he became violently ill, but refused to return until the grim business was completed.

The following day they met again at Massa, closer to Viareggio, where Shelley's body had been buried on a desolate beach. They had difficulty finding the body, which was in an even worse state of putrefaction than that of Williams. Hunt huddled miserably in the carriage.

Burning sun, sand too hot to walk on, silence except for the flames soaring high into the sky – it was a gruesome, hellish sight. Trelawny felt that they were "no better than a herd of wolves or a pack of wild dogs, in tearing out his battered and naked body from the pure yellow sand that lay so lightly over it, to drag him back to the light of day".[9] Ethereal during his lifetime, Shelley's body resisted destruction, and for four long hours the funeral pyre was kept alight. Byron repeated the pattern of the previous day, this time swimming out to the *Bolivar* which was anchored nearby.

Much scornful criticism has been poured on Trelawny's braggadocio, but no one can dispute that in this time of crisis he behaved in a more responsible and mature way than any of the others. He later claimed that he refused Byron's request for the skull because he knew that he had once used one as a drinking-cup. After Trelawny had gathered the ashes, Byron joined Hunt in the carriage, and they made for Viareggio where they dined sparingly and drank heavily. By now close to hysteria, Hunt recalled his behaviour and that of Byron with a feeling of shame.

Lord Byron had not shone that day even in his cups, which usually brought out his best qualities. As for myself, I had bordered upon emotions which I have never suffered myself to indulge, and which, foolishly as well as impatiently, render calamity, as somebody termed it, "an affront, and not a misfortune." The barouche drove rapidly through the forest of Pisa. We sang, we laughed, we shouted. I even felt a gayety the more shocking, because it was real and a relief.[10]

Byron had become seriously sunburnt and had to spend several days in penitential agony. One would have thought that the loss they had endured together might have brought Hunt and Byron closer together, but such was not to be the case. Even if Shelley had lived, the collaboration would not have succeeded, given Shelley's bitter feelings towards Byron. But perhaps a mutual embarrassment about their behaviour after his cremation caused a distance to be placed between Hunt and Byron. Hunt and his wife became sensitive to every slight they sensed on Byron's part; and Byron was nearly driven to distraction by the uncontrolled Hunt children whose parents did not believe in any form of restraint, and were offended when Byron complained about their writing on the walls. He trained his bulldog to growl at them from the head of the stairs if there was any indication that they were going to approach his private apartments.

Yet Byron assured Hunt that he must consider him as supportive of the *Liberal* (as the journal was now called) as Shelley had been. He probably felt that he meant the words as he said them, especially as Hunt was to remark later Byron half-hoped that it could re-establish his name in England, and also possibly generate some income. However, he wanted the Hunts out of his life, especially as some momentous decisions had to be made. For nearly three months the inharmonious group continued to occupy the same building. Despite Byron's vain hopes, the Gambas were not allowed to return to Pisa, and it was made clear to them that they could no longer linger in Lucca either. Mr Hill, the British minister in Genoa, advised them to move there. For some months Byron had been considering various exotic possibilities. At one point, he told Kinnaird that he needed to accumulate money in order to settle on an estate in South America, having named his boat after the liberator of Venezuela. On August 27 he told Thomas Moore, just before Genoa was decided upon:

I had, and still have, thought of South America, but am fluctuating between it and Greece. I should have gone, long ago, to one of them, but for my liaison with the Countess G[uicciol]i; for love, in these days, is little compatible with glory. *She* would be delighted to go too; but I do not choose to expose her to a long voyage, and a residence in an unsettled country, where I shall probably take a part of some sort.

The Gambas finally decided upon Genoa as their only safe haven. Just as Byron heard that the move was inevitable, from Milan he received a letter from Hobhouse, who was travelling through Italy with his sisters and wished very much to see him. Byron did not reply with much enthusiasm. They were packing; everything was in a state of confusion – perhaps they might meet in Genoa? Then he expressed the real reason for his reluctance to see his old friend: "These transient glimpses of old friends are very painful – as I found out the other day after Lord Clare was gone again – however agreeable they make the moment. – They are like a dose of Laudanum – and it's subsequent languor."[11]

But then Byron thought of the good times they had shared in the past. Perhaps Hobhouse could accompany him to Genoa, and Teresa could travel separately with her father. "We could confabulate in the old *imperial* Carriage as heretofore – and squabble away as usual. – I don't know whether your temper is improved – I hear that the hustings have made you somewhat haughty – but that is natural . . . my own temper is about the same – which is not saying much for it."[12]

Nevertheless, Hobhouse arrived on September 15. The friends had not seen each other for four years, and inevitably there was a certain constraint between them at first, although Byron embraced his friend with tears in his eyes. Byron he found much fatter (and probably told him so), and Teresa tolerably good-looking. Hobhouse was not prepared to like her, since he saw her as the main obstacle to Byron's return to England. However, she went out of her way to charm him with letters of introduction to friends in Florence and Rome.

He was polite but constrained with Hunt, whose association with Byron he considered infra dig and partly responsible for Hobhouse having been blackballed by several London clubs. On one occasion Byron accused him of stealing glances at his bad foot. However, as the days passed, Byron thawed, and he began to speak frankly to the man who had always been his most loyal friend. He described the Carbonari as high-minded but absurd, and admitted that he wanted to escape from his sexual liaison. During this period Byron was visited by the young Greek patriot, Nicolas Karvellas, one of the brothers who had talked passionately to them of a possible uprising when Hobhouse was staying with Byron in Geneva in 1816. This visit was to be significant in the awakening of both men's interest in the Greek cause.

On the 21st Hobhouse left Pisa, and Byron remarked to Kinnaird that "These glimpses of old friends for a moment are sad remembrancers."[13] Partings were in the air. Mary Shelley and Jane Williams left Pisa on the

11th, Mary for Genoa, Jane for England. Claire set off a week later for Florence, and was soon to join her brother in Vienna where he had found her a position as a governess. Trelawny escaped to Livorno with the pretext that he had to prepare the flotilla, because "If the Casa Lanfranchi had been on fire at midnight it could not have been worse."[4] Byron had found the move from Ravenna chaotic, but it was nothing to this. He now had Teresa with her wardrobe and her hysterics on his hands, as well as all the household goods of the Gamba establishment to be packed.

The Hunts moved out of the Palazzo Lanfranchi into a cramped inn. Byron told Hunt to apply to his steward, Lega Zambelli, if he needed any ready cash. This was a perfectly reasonable request, given the confusion of the packing, but the Hunts were ready to view it as an insult. Marianne noted in her diary: "What a pity it is the good actions of *noblemen* are not done in a *noble manner*! Aye princely I would have them be. How Mr Shelley knew how to do a favour! As *well* as my Henry. Actions really admirable, are often spoilt in the doing, from mere manner."[5] Byron wanted to leave the Hunts behind in Pisa, but Hunt argued that this would be impractical for their collaboration on the *Liberal*.

Trelawny's friend Captain Daniel Roberts had collected some of the things salvaged from the *Don Juan*. Most of these he had turned over to Byron, but gave Williams's journal to Hunt because it contained some severe strictures on Byron.

The whole party finally set off on September 28. The quantity of things Byron took with him was immense: furniture, clothes, animals, even three geese swinging in a cage behind the Napoleonic coach. At Lucca they were joined by Teresa's father and brother. The journey was so uncomfortable that they decided to stop at Lerici and continue by sea. The Hunts arrived in a state of exhaustion. Trelawny took Hunt on a tour of the desolate Casa Magni with the ocean lapping close to its verandah, a sea that looked to Hunt deceptively benign.

While at Lerici, Byron proposed a swimming contest to Trelawny. They were to head for the *Bolivar* anchored about three miles from shore, dine in the sea beside the boat as they trod water, and then return to shore. Trelawny arrived first; they ate; Trelawny stuck his usual cigar in his mouth; Byron tried to extinguish it. They then started back and after about a hundred yards Byron began to retch violently. With difficulty Trelawny persuaded him to return to the *Bolivar*; but very soon after swallowing a glass of brandy, he insisted stubbornly on returning without the aid of a boat. As a result he was close to collapse by the time they reached shore and had to be confined to bed for some days. But he was pleased to have lost so much weight and he decided to resume one of his starvation diets. While they were in Lerici, the town was struck by an earthquake which frightened the Hunts half to death, but Byron slept through it.

Curiously, Byron still did not board the *Bolivar* but another boat, as did the Hunts, even though Mrs Hunt had hoped she would never have to take another sea journey. The little flotilla as it started out, with the sails sketched against the dazzling sky, had a strangely festive appearance in contrast to the emotions of most of its occupants. These rootless people, again in a state of transition, had no inkling of what their final destinies would be. When Byron had first gone into exile in 1816, Greece had been his vague destination. Six years later his adventures had traced an arc bringing him to the west coast of Italy. He now looked seaward across the Mediterranean, fantasising about the possibility of beginning some sort of new life, perhaps in South America, where he would finally find himself free from harassment. Once he had envisaged Allegra accompanying him. Now his fate seemed completely tied to that of the unfortunate Gamba family.

Landing at Sestri, the group made the final brief journey to Genoa. It was October 1, only three months after the arrival of the Hunts in Italy. Mary Shelley had found for Byron a large pink palazzo on a hill in Albaro, a southern suburb of the city, on a year's lease. Byron liked to believe (mistakenly) that it had been the home of Andrea Doria, the doge of Genoa. Teresa later made much of the fact that it was large enough to enable her family and Byron to maintain separate living quarters. The Hunts appeared a day later and took up residence with Mary Shelley in the large Casa Negroto, about a mile up the hill from Byron's Casa Saluzzo. So began Byron's final sojourn in Italy.

29

○○○○○○○○○○○○○○

Genoa, 1822–3

D uring Byron's first months in Genoa he was busily preoccupied with business affairs. There were great pronouncements on retrenchment. The *Bolivar* was put into dry dock, and a lot of time was wasted in justifying his demand that some of the dismissed crew return their uniforms. The number of horses was reduced from nine to five.

Kinnaird was instructed to increase the insurance policy on Lady Byron's life. His banker continued to press for some payment to the widow of Owen Mealey, the steward at Newstead, and Byron agreed to give her £100 quarterly on the grounds that he might leave himself short if he paid her a lump sum. He actually remembered the existence of Baxter, the coach-maker, and expressed astonishment that the amount owing him was only £1,000, not £2,000 as he had thought. (The Napoleonic coach had cost £500, but Byron owed him money long before he had ordered it to be built.) Nevertheless, Baxter was still not paid.

Byron believed that all his debts could be liquidated if Murray ceased dragging his feet with timidity over the seven remaining cantos of *Don Juan* that were completed before the end of 1822. Byron was highly excited about the prospect of taking the don on a tour of Europe, involving him in a divorce case, acting as a witness at the French Revolution, becoming the lover of Catherine the Great, and finally invading England in what would be an exposure of current cant. Murray shuddered at how his Tory friends would react. When he received the new cantos in the autumn of 1822, he cried: "I declare to you they were so outrageously shocking that I would not publish them if you were to give me your Estate – title and Genius – for Heaven's sake revise them."[1] Byron not only refused to revise them, but demanded the return of the stanzas attacking the Duke of Wellington which had prudently been removed from Canto III. These he revised and defiantly placed at the beginning of Canto IX. He was furious when he learned that Murray had failed to deliver the correct copy of *The Vision of Judgment* to John Hunt, and Kinnaird was instructed to look for another publisher.

Meanwhile Leigh Hunt and his brother were busy with the *Liberal*, the first number of which appeared on October 15, 1822. The outcry was to be expected. Byron's attack on Southey, *The Vision of Judgment*, was the main target of abuse; and the *Literary Gazette* fulminated against its "impiety, vulgarity, inhumanity, and heartlessness" (November 2, 1822). Although the contributions to the journal were anonymous, it would not have been difficult to detect Byron's hand. John Hunt made matters worse by advertising Byron's name publicly and was served with a writ for publishing a poem defaming George III and George IV, but the case did not come to trial until after Byron's death, on June 19, 1824. Byron did, however, engage a lawyer to represent Hunt, who was eventually fined £100.

Byron's long association with Murray was drawing to an undignified close. Murray admitted that he had cut certain objectionable lines in *Cain*: "I even hoped that when their omission should be discovered, you would feel surprise rather than dissatisfaction."[2] Murray was insulted by what he claimed was John Hunt's impertinent manner when he arrived to demand the return of Byron's remaining manuscripts – so different from the manner of "your most gentlemanly friend" Lord Clare when he delivered the Ravenna Journal.[3] He wrote Byron a series of letters, pleading, offended, obsequious, outraged.

> My company used to be courted for the pleasure of talking about you [he complained]; it is totally the reverse now – and by a reaction even your former works are considerably deteriorated in sale. It is impossible for you to have a more purely attached friend than I am – My name is connected with your Fame and I beseech you to take care of it even for your sister's sake – for we are in constant alarm that she should be deprived of her situation at Court – Do let us have your good humour again and put Juan in the tone of Beppo.[4]

Augusta was deeply sympathetic to Murray, especially as she was still borrowing money from him and trying to sell some of the manuscripts Byron had given her. Byron explained that he was sacrificing himself for the sake of the Hunts who were honest and poor, and that in worldly affairs Hunt was only a child.[5] Murray repeated this – probably embellishing it – and word got back to Leigh Hunt who confronted Byron with the gossip.

Byron admitted that he might have told Murray that Mrs Hunt was ill and his children uncontrolled, but he could not remember having said that Hunt was a bore. Hunt, although still offended, was willing to put the matter behind him, espccially as his brother now had Byron's manuscripts in his hands.

The *Liberal* was a miscellany of disconnected writings without any coordinating tone to unify them in some way. It is not surprising that, after an initial success, it ceased publication after four issues. In the second number Byron published *Heaven and Earth*, in the third *The Blues* (his attack on intellectual women); and the fourth contained his translation of Pulci's *Morgante Maggiore*. Murray had also refused to publish *Heaven and Earth* because he feared he would have another *Cain* on his hands. After months of procrastination he printed 2,000 copies of *Werner* and *Heaven and Earth* together, but in a fright dropped the latter and published 5,000 copies of *Werner* alone on November 22, 1822. It was Byron's last collaboration with Murray.

In *Heaven and Earth* Byron again takes up the story of Cain. In March 1817 Lady Byron had remarked that Byron's "Imagination dwelt so much upon the idea that he was a *fallen angel* that I thought it amounted nearly to derangement, and the tradition that Angels, having fallen from Heaven, had become enamoured of mortal women, struck him particularly and he said that he should compose upon it, and that *I* should be the woman, who was all perfection."[6] The reaction of the *Quarterly Review* was predictable. Byron was described as "the professed and systematic poet of seduction, adultery, and incest: the contemner of patriotism, the insulter of piety, the raker into every sink of vice and wretchedness to disgust and degrade and harden the hearts of his fellow-creatures".[7] Rather maliciously Murray forwarded an earlier review by the same author, Bishop Heber (July 1822), with strictures on *Don Juan*. Byron returned the issue after reading only half of it. "A review," he replied mildly, "may and will direct or 'turn away' the Currents of opinion – but it will not directly oppose them. – D. Juan will be known by and bye for what it is intended a *satire* on *abuses* of the present *states* of Society – and not an eulogy of Vice" (December 25, 1822). Granted that the poem might be somewhat voluptuous, but what about Ariosto, Smollett, Fielding? "No Girl will ever be seduced by reading D[on] J[uan] – no – no – she will go to Little's poems – and Rousseau's romans – for that – or even to the immaculate De Stael – they will encourage her – and not the Don – who laughs at that – and – and – most other things. – But never mind – 'Ça ira!'"

As he had done in the past Byron completely ignored Murray's warnings about the harm his poetry might do to Augusta. He again suggested that she and her whole family move to Nice and he would pay the expenses of the journey. He could settle in a house nearby if she liked. Lest she harbour any misgivings about Teresa, he assured her that the two households were completely separate, and he related how Teresa had indignantly refused his offer to draw up a will in her favour, in which the money that would have been left to Allegra would be transferred to her. As for his association with the Hunts, he assured her that he seldom saw them. It never occurred to him that the whole idea of abandoning her roots would be abhorrent to Augusta, who would become thereby the subject of scandal she had so scrupulously tried to avoid. She left it to Hobhouse to explain her situation:

> Mrs Leigh is exceedingly obliged for your kind offers to her respecting her journey and talked to me a great deal of her great anxiety to be able to accept them – But you know she has appointments in St James which it is of very great consequence to her to retain which she will not be able to do if she comes abroad – This consideration would I should think change your view of the subject – You say something to her of meeting in England – you might perhaps come for a month or two, without being much annoyed – all your old friends would sing jubilate and go out before you.[8]

During the first months of his sojourn in Genoa, Byron established an epistolary friendship which approached nearer than any other in his life that with Lady Melbourne. His correspondent, Lady Hardy, was the wife of Nelson's Admiral Hardy who was away on an expedition in America while his wife was ostensibly taking their three daughters to Livorno for their health. She was being pursued by the ever-absurd James Wedder-burn Webster, now separated from Lady Frances with whom Byron had almost had an affair in 1813. A friendly tone between Byron and his new friend was established immediately because they were distant cousins.

> I have always laid it down as a maxim [Byron told her], and found it justified by experience – that a man and a woman – make far better friendships than can exist between two of the same sex, – but *then* with the condition – that they never have made – or are to make love with each other . . . Indeed I rather look upon Love altogether as a sort of hostile transaction – very necessary to make – or to break – in order to keep the world a-going – but by no means a sinecure to the parties concerned. – Now – as *my* Love perils are – I believe pretty well over

– and yours by all accounts are never to begin; – we shall be the best friends imaginable.[9]

During this period Byron also entered into a correspondence with a young woman in London, Isabel Harvey, who professed undying devotion to him. It was the sort of correspondence that had landed Byron in trouble with Claire Clairmont, but flattery and boredom were stronger elements than prudence. Nor had Byron heard the last of Claire, even though she had by now joined her brother Charles in Vienna. In December 1822 Charles was denounced to the Foreigners' Commission in an anonymous letter. Both he and his sister were described as undesirable aliens, the children of the infamous revolutionary William Godwin, associates of the atheist Shelley, and "intimate" with Lord Byron. Claire, never strong, was said to be ill in bed, presumably with shock.

Claire's close friend in Pisa had been a "Mrs Mason", who undertook to intervene with Byron on her behalf. The lady was really Lady Mountcashell who had run off with a certain George William Tighe. The friendship with Claire and Mary Shelley was the outcome of Mary Wollstonecraft having been a governess in the Mountcashell home in Ireland. Mrs Mason, hearing that Claire was in difficulties in Vienna, wrote to Byron on December 28, 1822: "Your Lordship intended to make a provision for the Child, of which a small part would redeem your honour, by giving sufficient independence to the Mother, whose claim on you is undeniable – I am aware that you have had cause of irritation; but surely a mind like yours must soon forget such offences."[10]

At first Mary Shelley had the impression that Byron would accede to Mrs Mason's request, but after brooding upon the matter, he wrote a long letter of refusal (unfortunately, not extant). If Mary wanted to send money to Claire, he was willing to lend it to her. In February 1823 Mary told Jane Williams that the offer was a sop to his conscience: "it will be a peculiar & most temporary necessity indeed that would make me *borrow* from him – For there after all is the sting – it is a *loan* to me, a *gift* to C."[11] Claire, after learning that she could not obtain a licence to teach in Vienna, in late March left for a position as a governess in St Petersburg – and Byron had no reason ever to think of her again.

He continued to brood about what was going to happen to his money if there were a war or if there were a decline in the currency. And why was he not receiving any income from Kirkby? He had lent Wedderburn Webster money about ten years before. Was there any way of collecting the interest that must have accrued on it? Kinnaird assured him that "*You cannot be better off*",[12] and in letter after letter begged to be allowed to pay off Baxter. Byron referred to most of his creditors as "scoundrels". He was known for his generosity to beggars and those with whom he had immediate contact, but he had great aversion to paying debts belonging to the distant past, and there was a stubborn refusal about this particular debt that seemed to have some symbolic meaning for him. Did it have something to do with his identification with Napoleon, and did he associate it with his ignominious retreat from his own Moscow? On February 27 he raised the same arguments Kinnaird had so often heard before.

> I should be very willing to *pay* Baxter off – but how? – I cannot leave myself bare . . . I can not pay Baxter – till after Kirkby produces something less aerial than is furnished by these Sylphlike trustees . . . If Baxter were paid *now* -- I should not have a sixpence hardly in your bank . . . It is well to have a sum in hand; but I have paid largely enough this half year already to desire to hear no more of Baxter.

His main preoccupation was in writing – poetry and letters. He was as interested in Kinnaird finding an alternative publisher for *Don Juan* as he was in its composition. He was reluctant to hand the last stanzas over to John Hunt until all other sources had been exhausted. The Hunts had little money, and as Byron was often heard to remark, it was lucre he was interested in.

He tried unsuccessfully to persuade the Hunts that the failure of the *Liberal* was due to prejudice against him, and that they would be better off without his participation. He regretted the day he had ever allowed himself to become associated with it, and, as he saw it, he had allowed his humanitarian feelings to prevail over his better judgement. To Thomas Moore (to whom he had first suggested the idea of founding a journal of the sort) he wrote on April 2, 1823: "I cannot describe to you the despairing sensation of trying to do something for a man who seems incapable or unwilling to do any thing further for himself, – at least, to the purpose. It is like pulling a man out of a river who directly throws himself in again." Why would Hunt simply not return to England? he constantly asked. Mary Shelley complained that she did not think he was treating Hunt with the warmth that friendship required.[13] Byron replied [n.d.], "As to friendship, it is a propensity in which my genius is very limited, I do not know the *male* human being, except Lord Clare, the friend of my infancy, for whom I feel any thing that deserves the name. All my others are men-of-the-world friendships. I did not even feel it for Shelley, however much I admired and esteemed him."

He was growing increasingly remote from Teresa, and they had a tacit agreement that she should never venture into his quarters. A visitor from Ravenna found a palpable sense of pervasive boredom in the Casa Saluzzo. "The G &. he are as ill together as may be," Mary told Jane Williams.[14] After the balmy climate of Pisa, they were experiencing a chilly, gusty winter. The Casa Saluzzo might have been ideal for an Italian summer, but in the winter it was equipped with only one fireplace, and Byron developed chilblains. He got into the habit of sending notes to Teresa; and when she received word that her sister had died in Ravenna, he did not go immediately to comfort her, but sent a note:

> I cannot express to you my sorrow over your sister's death – but She is happy – it is the living who deserve compassion and sympathy – I have not come to you because I know – by sad experience – that in the first moments sorrow shrinks alike from comfort – from society – and even from friendship itself. And words – what are they? I pity you in silence – and recommend you to Heaven and to Time.[15]

Teresa turned to Mary Shelley for comfort when after four more days Byron still did not appear.

> The G. – has just lost her sister Carolina, the flower of the family, by a consumption – she appears much grieved – I saw her yesterday – she had heard the news 4 days before & she told me she was so unhappy that she had not seen LB once during that time – Strange between lovers – for that which is the flower of love is the consolation one receives in misfortune. – I have not a good opinion of her or I shd pity her – but her unamiable jealousies & falsehoods have destroyed what remained of affection in his heart, though he clings to her as two birds of opposite breed in one cage – there they are – & what is there better to do?[16]

For Byron what was "better to do" was to fly away from his gilded cage.

Mary had been persuaded by Byron not to return to England, and he had assured her that he would do everything in his power as one of Shelley's executors to help her. While she had been very angry with him before Shelley's death, she was now grateful for any kindness he could show her. She saw little of him and this did not trouble her because his beautiful voice reminded her that she had always heard it in the past in the presence of Shelley.

But life was hard for the grieving widow confined in a house with the Hunts. She was thankful for the stanzas of *Don Juan* and the revised *The Deformed Transformed* which Byron sent up the hill for her to make fair copies. He tried also to secure some sort of settlement from Shelley's father for her and her son. When Hanson failed to be of any help, Byron agreed to write to Sir Timothy himself, and his letter is a model of good sense and honourable feeling. However, Shelley's father agreed to look after the boy only if Mary surrendered custody to him. Byron urged her to accept the offer. Mary was devastated; and to Byron she wrote that "there is no law to help me with a man who could make that insolent & hardhearted proposition about my poor boy."[7] She was referring not only to Sir Timothy; and Byron's suggestion was the beginning of her total disillusionment with him. To Jane Williams she expressed her feelings: "I differed from LB. entirely; in the worldly as well as the moral view of this question; but I literally writhed under the idea that one so near me should advise me to a mode of conduct which appeared little short of madness & nothing short of death."[8]

But Byron was little interested in Mary's opinion of him. Visitors from England were of far more consequence. On March 31 he was delighted by a visit from Henry Fox, the son of Lord Holland. He had always been very fond of the young man; and to Thomas Moore he admitted that part of the attraction was that he was also lame (April 2, 1823). "But there is this difference, that *he* appears a halting angel, who has tripped against a star; whilst I am *Le Diable Boiteux*."

Fox's visit was succeeded the following day by the arrival of the Blessington entourage. This included Lord Blessington, his wife and her sister, and a young French dandy, the Count d'Orsay. Lady Blessington was an extraordinarily interesting character. A year younger than Byron, she was entrancingly beautiful; and even more important, worldly and highly intelligent despite her humble Irish background. At a very early age she had been sold by her father to a local farmer and had been rescued by a Captain Jenkins who in 1816 relinquished her to Lord Blessington, who married her two years later after Jenkins's death. She held court in a house in St James's Square frequented by all the literary men of the day. Women, of course, would not enter her door because of her reputation as an adventuress.

Lady Blessington's *Conversations with Lord Byron* has come under a good deal of criticism (particularly from Teresa) as being inaccurate and exaggerating the length of time (ten weeks) she spent talking with the poet. If one compares her recollections with those of other independent observers, such as Thomas Medwin, one will find that the subjects on which he conversed are remarkably similar, and her descriptions of his appearance and views are among the best records we have. She was a shrewd and sympathetic woman, and her appearance on the scene was a breath of fresh air in Byron's life. A little heightening of reality in her reminiscences seems to be the worst one can accuse her of.

The Blessington party had been travelling for some months through Europe, and Lady Blessington's principal reason for alighting for a time at Genoa was in order to meet Byron. Her first impression of him was disappointing. She had imagined him taller and with a more commanding air. As she observed him closely, she was impressed by his wide forehead, grey expressive eyes, one of which was noticeably larger than the other; the nose perhaps a little too thick and best seen in profile. The mouth she found his most remarkable feature: the lips were full and turned down at the corners in a slightly scornful way; his teeth white and the chin large and well shaped. By then he was extremely thin from purgatives and a near-starvation diet. His hair was curly and dark brown, and he smothered it with oil to disguise the grey. His expression changed frequently as he talked. He smiled in order to be agreeable, but his prevailing expression struck her as one of melancholy. His voice was harmonious and rather "effeminate". His clothes were ill-fitting as he had not bought any new ones since he was in Venice and a good deal heavier. Lady Blessington was aware that he made efforts to disguise his deformed foot, but after their first meeting she could not be sure which one it was.

Of the party Byron seemed most enthralled by the elegant and handsome young French count. D'Orsay's relationship with Lady Blessington was somewhat ambiguous, but the good-natured husband seemed very fond of him. At first Byron dined with them fairly frequently at the Albergo della Villa, but began to beg off when he realised that he was regaining weight. He offered to conduct them to the most scenic views, and Lady Blessington was struck by the fact that he did not comment on their beauty.

Within a fortnight of their arrival Byron asked permission to present Count Pietro to their party. Teresa had erupted in a jealous tantrum and had insisted that Byron see the beautiful Englishwoman only when accompanied by her brother. Byron had spoken frankly to Lady Blessington about Teresa's jealousy; and on May 7, his new friend wrote: "Did you get scolded yesterday? And how are you today? I have smiled more than once at the grave face of fear you put on before we parted, and I could have told you all that was at that moment passing your mind."[9] Teresa was quick to realise that Lady Blessington brought with her what she could never give Byron: gossip about mutual acquaintances, the breath of London drawing rooms whose cant he professed to despise but which he had always missed, so much so that he had taken the don to England in order to re-create that fashionable world.

It did not take long for Byron to talk frankly about his wife. He continued to blame Mrs Clermont as the evil genius behind the separation. He spoke often of Augusta whom he described as the most faultless person he had ever known. On hearing that Colonel Montgomery, the brother of Annabella's old friend Mary Millicent Montgomery, was in Genoa, he became nervous that Montgomery would turn the Blessingtons against him. Lady Blessington tried to soften Montgomery's attitude; and on Byron's behalf asked him if he could procure a portrait of his wife for him since he did not possess a single one.

It is difficult to gauge what Byron's feelings towards his wife were at this point. Since he had already begun to consider leaving Italy – and was also convinced that he would never return – he might have been feeling slightly sentimental. When Hobhouse had visited him in Pisa, he had recorded in his diary that any feelings Byron had for his wife were now entirely dead, but Byron's emotions varied with circumstances. As Teresa became increasingly irksome, it is even possible that he began to consider a reconciliation as a way out of his present dilemma. After Montgomery's apparent refusal, Lady Blessington resolved the situation by suggesting that she herself write to Annabella requesting the portrait, and (on Byron's instructions) assuring her that Byron had no intention of ever interfering with Ada's upbringing. On being apprised of this, Montgomery wrote acidly to Annabella that her estranged husband

> speaks of you and your virtues with tears of your disgust and hatred of him – and only supposes your aversion to have been the work of ill intentioned persons who have calumniated his character and conduct ... he appears to think himself a very innocent and injured personage – but I am disposed to believe all this tenderness is directed to the £3500 per annum which in case of a reconciliation would return to his possession.[20]

A few days after the arrival of the Blessingtons, Byron had an interesting visitor sent by John Cam Hobhouse. This was a young Irishman, Edward Blaquiere, who had been energetically travelling around Europe encouraging support for the Greeks who had risen up against their Turkish masters in 1821. Greece had been subjected to a veritable blood-bath in the past year. The struggle had commenced in 1820 when Byron's old friend Ali Pasha had defied the Turks and was subsequently killed, his head ignominiously displayed outside the Seraglio in Constantinople. Paradoxically, his defiance had sparked off the revolutionary fervour of the Greek patriots.

Greece had been the subject of many discussions between Shelley and Byron; and some months before Byron arrived in Pisa, Prince Mavrocordato, the Greek patriot who had been living in exile in Italy, had left to join the battle for freedom in his homeland. Shelley was one of the first European poets to write a paean to the regeneration of Greece in *Hellas* (1821), dedicated to Mavrocordato with whom he had become friendly in Pisa.

> The world's great age begins anew,
>   The golden years return,
> The earth doth like a snake renew
>   Her winter weeds outworn:
> Heaven smiles, and faiths and empires gleam
> Like wrecks of a dissolving dream.

In the third canto of *Don Juan*, written in 1819 (not published until 1821), Byron inserted the immortal lines to "the isles of Greece" that were to be translated all over Europe, and were to help disseminate a concern over the fate of Greece.

> The isles of Greece, the isles of Greece!
>   Where burning Sappho loved and sung,
> Where grew the arts of war and peace,–
>   Where Delos rose, and Phoebe sprung!
> Eternal summer gilds them yet,
> But all, except their sun, is set.
>
> The Scian and the Teian muse,
>   The hero's harp, the lover's lute,
> Have found the fame your shores refuse;
>   Their place of birth alone is mute
> To sounds which echo further west
> Than your sires' 'Islands of the Blest.'

The mountains look on Marathon—
  And Marathon looks on the sea;
And musing there an hour alone,
  I dream'd that Greece might still be free;
For standing on the Persian's grave,
I could not deem myself a slave.

(III, 86, 689–706)

The British were relatively late in involving themselves in the Greek struggle. Since the Ionian Islands were a British protectorate, Britain endeavoured to maintain a strict neutrality; but turned a blind eye on the activities of the London Greek Committee which first met at the Crown and Anchor Tavern in the Strand on March 3, 1823. The original group consisted almost entirely of radical members of parliament such as Sir Francis Burdett and Hobhouse. When Blaquiere called on Byron he came with the blessing of the committee, although it was still very small and had no political clout whatsoever. Nevertheless, Blaquiere had been sent to deal with agents of the Greek government and encouraged to drop strong hints that substantial British aid would be forthcoming. Blaquiere was also instructed to emphasise to Byron that his presence on the scene could be decisive.

On April 28 from Rome, Blaquiere sent Byron the following letter:

From all that I have heard, it would be criminal in me to leave this without urging your Lordship to come up as soon as possible: – your presence will operate as a talisman and the field is too glorious, too closely associated with all that you hold dear to be any longer abandoned . . . The cause is in a most flourishing state . . . the effect produced by my mentioning the fact of *your* intention to join it, has been quite electric: need I say one word on the result to *yourself* of being *mainly instrumental* in resuscitating the land already so happily illustrated by your sublime and energetic Muse . . . Anxious to see your Lordship in this land of heroes, I remain most truly and devotedly yours, Edward Blaquiere.[21]

This was the first of a series of flattering letters assuring Byron of the importance of his presence on the scene. A month after Blaquiere's visit, two German Philhellenes arrived at his door. These two young men had participated in the Greek defeat by the Turks at Peta, near Arta, an area of Epirus well-known to Byron. They had made their way painfully back as far as Genoa after having been refused entry through Trieste by the Austrians. Byron provided them with money and clothes. His vague plans about a South American estate were being abandoned. It now seemed possible that he could return to the land that had always beckoned him and where he might be able to make a substantial contribution of money and advice. Meanwhile Kinnaird was instructed not to make any payments: "on Baxter or anybody else" (April 24, 1823).

Pietro Gamba was beside himself with excitement at the thought of going to Greece – "a thorough Liberty boy"[22] – but Byron was well aware of how Teresa would react. To Hobhouse (April 7, 1823), he explained the difficulty, even though nothing had been said to her as yet: "Madame Guiccioli is of course – and naturally enough opposed to my quitting her – though but for a few months – and as she had influence enough to prevent my return to England in 1819 – she may be not less successful in detaining me from Greece in 1823." Byron might have been stirred by the idea, but from the beginning his natural reluctance to make a major decision caused him to fluctuate in his enthusiasm. In the long run, however, the circumstances of the Gamba family made the decision easier.

As the days passed his resolve strengthened. Usually so stingy, he promised Hobhouse almost unlimited funds. Here was a chance not only of gaining real glory but of breaking the irksome cord to Teresa. By mid-April he had almost made up his mind, and the prospect was bringing out the best in him. He told Hobhouse: "If I go there – I shall do my best to civilize their mode of treating their prisoners – and could I only save a single life – whether Turk or Greek – I should live 'mihi carior' – and I trust not less so to my friends."[23] Yet he begged the Blessingtons to delay their departure for Rome until he had actually sailed, urging them to rent a beautiful villa with a view over the sea.

Mary Shelley certainly knew what was in the wind and confided to Jane Williams: "I think he will go – because he hates Genoa – because Pierino is half mad with joy at the idea – because Greece has many charms for him, – his pride also will be gratified."[24]

As far as Byron was concerned, there was no turning back after May 12 when he received word that he had been elected a member of the London Greek Committee. He was given to understand that this was a very great honour, little realising that the committee represented only a handful of enthusiasts. On May 31 Mary Shelley again wrote to Jane Williams: "LB. is fixed on Greece – he gets rid of two burthens; the G- & the Liberal – the first is natural, though I pity her – the second ought not be, & need not be, but so it is."[25] By now Byron was assuring the committee that he was very keen to go to Greece to obtain first-hand information on the situation; and added that his knowledge of Italian (widely spoken in Greece) and his recollection of Romaic would be helpful: "To this project the only objection is of a domestic nature – and I shall try to get over it, – if I fail in this – I must do what I can where I am – but it will be always a source of regret to me – to think – that I might perhaps have done more for the cause on the spot."[26]

This state of high excitement was conducive to Byron's creativity, and the stanzas of *Don Juan* continued to flow from his pen. By the middle of April he had sent Canto XV to his banker-agent. Was Kinnaird, Byron demanded, dragging his feet about finding a publisher out of cowardice? And there was absolutely no way he would consider resuming *Childe Harold* as had been suggested. Kinnaird replied that he had wanted to delay the publication of the latest batch of the Don's adventures until John Hunt's prosecution for *The Vision of Judgment* had been settled. As for his own opinion of them, "I certainly could wish there were some fewer or less loose expressions – I think them abounding in first-rate talent . . . It is to be recollected that if the Juans be voted improper for the female part of the public you lose a large sale."[27]

Meanwhile Byron instructed John Hunt to print the cantos so that he would be able to correct them – without committing himself to Hunt as the publisher. It is surprising that Hunt agreed to this rather humiliating request, but he was probably counting on Byron's eventual capitulation. After sending off Canto XVI, by May 21 Byron had accepted the fact that Hunt was to be the publisher, and warned him not to overprint the eleven cantos now in his possession. Kinnaird still advised him to exert a little patience over hasty publication, but he knew that his advice fell on deaf ears. His bantering man-of-the-world comments on Canto X evince the double standard of the time:

> with regard to the new Cantos I am delighted with them – the Political reflections, the address to Wellington and the Preface are admirable – but why call the *Catherine* a whore? She hired or whored others – She was never hired or whored herself – Why blame her for liking fucking? if she canted as well as cunted, then call her names for as long as you please – But it is hard to blame her for following her natural inclinations – She dared do it – others are afraid . . . I looked for more liberality from you – you must not turn against rogering – even tho' you practise it seldomer.[28]

The uneasy relationship with Leigh Hunt continued. Hunt was uncomfortable in Byron's presence, and as a consequence addressed him with a good deal of bluster. He knew that Byron was at his best when he had something to drink, and he made a point of inviting himself to dinner at the Casa Saluzzo shortly before Byron's departure for Greece. When he rose to go, Byron detained him for further conversation – but the following day the cordiality was gone.

By mid-May the plans could no longer be concealed from Teresa. She suspected that something was in the air when she caught him gazing at her sadly. On one occasion when she followed him into the garden he told her that he wanted to be alone. Afraid that he had hurt her, he quickly joined her. "How worried you look," she said, "what is the matter?" He almost brought himself to tell her, but his courage failed him.

He begged Pietro to break the news to her gradually. But there was no such thing as a "gradual" revelation, and storms of tears and bitter recriminations followed. Byron would stalk away from the tantrums, only to be followed by tear-stained notes. For the first time he began to complain about her to his friends. Kinnaird was told (May 21, 1823) that

> She wants to go up to Greece too! forsooth – a precious place to go at present! of course the idea is ridiculous – as every thing must be sacrificed to seeing *her* out of harm's way. – It is a case too in which interest does not enter, and therefore hard to deal with – for I have no kind of control – in that way – and if she makes a scene – (and she has a turn that way) we shall have another romance – and tale of ill usage and abandonment – and Lady Caroling – and Lady Byroning – and Glenarvoning – all cut and dry; – there never was a man who gave up so much to women – and all I have gained by it – has been the character of treating them harshly.

The parting was made a little less inconvenient for Byron by the fact that Count Gamba's exile from Ravenna was finally revoked. There was one stipulation: Teresa must accompany her father. Count Guiccioli was still insisting that she return to him; and the Pope would restore her allowance only if she were living apart from Byron and in Ravenna.

To humour her, Byron explored the possibility of other alternatives for Teresa's future. He wrote to a Comtesse d'Yson to ask whether Teresa might stay with her in Genoa, but the Comtesse replied that unfortunately she had to look after an ailing mother in Chambéry. He even wrote to the Superior of the Convent of the Visitation in Nice, but since it was a cloistered order Teresa would be unable to bathe in the sea, something she considered essential for her health.

To Lady Blessington Byron confided that "*liaisons*, that are not cemented by marriage must produce unhappiness, when there is refinement of mind, and that honourable *fierté* which accompanies it. The humiliations and vexations a woman, under such circumstances, is exposed to, cannot fail to have a certain effect on her temper and spirits, which robs her of the charms that won affection."[29] In other words, Byron was finding his mistress an absolute nuisance.

The Blessingtons were due to leave for Rome on June 2. There was a certain constraint towards Byron during their last days in Genoa owing to his avarice. He longed for Lady Blessington's Arabian steed, Mameluke, from whom she eventually agreed to part. However, she was shocked when Byron insisted that he could afford no more than £80 when she had paid a hundred guineas for him. Lord Blessington also suggested buying the *Bolivar*; and it was agreed that Byron's banker in Genoa, Charles Barry, would negotiate a fair price. Byron had originally planned to take the vessel to Greece, but the offer of ready cash – even 400 guineas which was far less than he had lavished on her – prevailed to induce him to part with the boat.* Byron had often said to Lady Blessington that he had a presentiment that he would never return from the Greek expedition, and on their last evening together he seemed particularly gloomy. They exchanged gifts, and all were weeping, although Byron made some ironical remark to disguise his feelings. Lady Blessington was startled the next morning to receive a note from him requesting that she return the small cameo pin of Napoleon he had impulsively given her in exchange for a locket. He also expressed the hope that her nerves were better. A few days later he told Lady Hardy that "I saw very little of them especially latterly – and now they are gone."[30] One of the recurring patterns in his behaviour was his ability to dismiss people from his mind once they had disappeared from his life unless it was a case of obsessional fixation.

The Blessingtons claimed to have been taken aback by his bickering over the horse and the boat in light of the elaborate and expensive preparations he was making for the Greek expedition. If he were going under official government sanction, there would have been more point to the splendid uniforms and dramatic plumed helmets he ordered for himself and Pietro, his flaunting the family motto "Crede Byron".

---

* Lady Blessington fails to mention that her husband's cheque for the *Bolivar* was rejected by Barry for want of sufficient funds.

Barry and Trelawny's friend, Captain Roberts, were looking for a suitable boat to convey the party which now also included a young physician, Dr Franceso Bruno. Byron had also written to Trelawny who had been in Rome attending to placing a gravestone over Shelley's ashes in the Protestant Cemetery. Byron urged him to join the party; and Trelawny naturally was very excited about the possibility of adventure, but when he arrived back in Genoa, he was somewhat alarmed to find that the *Hercules* was not much more than a coal barge of 120 tons. When he protested to Byron that what they needed to move swiftly around Greek waters was a fast clipper, Byron's reply was "They say I got her on very easy terms."[31]

Byron had promised Mary Shelley the money for her passage to England, and until the end of June she had every expectation that he would keep his word. Apparently Hunt approached Byron about this, and Byron exploded in exasperation. Hunt reminded him that he actually owed Mary the £1,000 of the wager he had made Shelley in Pisa. Unfortunately Byron appears to have made some unpleasant remarks about the Shelleys which Hunt maliciously repeated to Mary. On June 28 Byron wrote Hunt a note in which he said that he would advance the money to Hunt who in turn was to give it to Mary as a loan, so that she would be spared "any fancied humiliation". He also suggested that Hunt give him a note for the same. That he was very angry indeed can be inferred from the fact that he now refused to act any longer as one of Shelley's executors. Hunt also accused him of deserting his own extensive family after bringing them to Italy.

In situations of this kind no one sees clearly. People become easily offended, and it is difficult to disentangle the truth. What we do know is that there was general anger, and that Teresa tried to act as a peace-maker to Mary.

> I feel that I can be of little use [she told Mary]; that L.B. will not take advice, that he is much irritated. But I also feel so much friendship for you, and so much gratitude – for I shall never in my life forget the goodness you showed me during a very trying time for me – and I venture to offer, if I can do so, to be of help to you. If only my usefulness and my circumstances were as strong as my good will![32]

Mary was so angry that she turned to Trelawny for help; and although he could ill afford it, he immediately came to her aid. After Byron's death Hobhouse was told by Barry that Hunt had pocketed the money that was to go to Mary to finance his family's move to Florence, and certainly she eventually left for England believing that Byron had totally deserted her. Teresa apparently tried to effect a reconciliation between Byron and Mary; and in a response to one of her notes Mary wrote:

> I am too poor to lose my friends as well – and if I lost the friendship of LB the rest would not be worth much – and I could not accept it. I propose with all my heart a conciliation between us and if Ld Byron is willing to forget anything painful he may have endured from me and on account of me, if he recognises what Shelley deserves, it will be with real pleasure that I will wish him in person what I express now in writing, a good voyage and all the success I feel certain his plans will have in Greece.[33]

But Byron did not respond to this overture directly. A jarring cacophony was the last note heard among the discordance of the singing birds.

30

ooooooooooooooo

Cephalonia, 1823

In the busy days prior to the departure, Teresa saw little of Byron. In their brief encounters, he seemed worried and preoccupied. He had already begun to develop doubts about the feasibility of cooperation with the Greeks, and what had started out as a great adventure might have all sorts of irritating difficulties connected with it. He told John Bowring, the honorary secretary of the London Greek Committee, that he was planning to sail on July 12 since the Greek government "expects me without delay" (July 7, 1823). He intended to stay as long as his presence could be useful. Blaquiere was already in the Morea in discussions with the Greek officials, and Byron was anxious to join him and apprise himself of the situation.

On the 10th the lonely Italian mistress sought solace with Mary Shelley, but she was not at home. When Teresa returned to the Casa Saluzzo, she wrote Mary a note: "Perhaps it was better for you, my dear, my company was never worth much, and now must be unbearable. My feelings are such as cannot be described, and at best can only arouse compassion."[1] According to her version, as she was writing these words, Byron entered the room and told her to add a message for Hunt and one for Mary. To Hunt he explained that he knew he would excuse him for not bidding farewell to him personally, and that he had left detailed orders with Barry about business matters; as for Mary, he wanted her to know that he bore her no enmity.

In response to Teresa's note, Mary wrote anxiously to Byron that his message had still left her with "an uneasy sense of vagueness in my mind, will you do me the favour to state . . . & what is it's [sic] precise nature."[2] A subsequent letter sent to Jane Williams on July 23 indicates beyond doubt that Byron never replied to this note: "His unconquerable avarice prevented his supplying me with money, & a remnant of shame caused him to avoid me."[3]

According to Trelawny, once they were at sea Byron was overcome with embarrassment at the way he had treated Mary Shelley. "Tre," he said, "you did what I should have done, let us square accounts tomorrow; I must pay my debts." To this Trelawny replied, "Money is of no use at sea, and when you get on shore you will find you have nothing to spare."[4] And that was the last that was said of the matter.

Mary's letter to Jane Williams also seems to provide some negative evidence of another sort. If Byron were trying to avoid Mary, as the letter suggests, it seems highly improbable that he would have asked her to stay and comfort Teresa after he had taken leave of her. According to Teresa's *Vie*, Byron stayed with her from three to five o'clock on the afternoon of the 13th. She adds that "He did not wish to leave her alone at the moment of his departure and he had asked Mrs Shelley to come and stay with her at 5, so that she should not be alone after he had gone."[5] Teresa's romanticised version is highly distorted in her attempt to paint their relationship in the best possible light. It is far more probable that Byron tore himself from the clinging arms of his tearful mistress, and that she then sent a hysterical note to the Villa Negrotto pleading with Mary to come to her.

Teresa also says that it was very strange that the superstitious Byron chose to leave on the 13th. Possibly he wanted to sail on the 2nd, fourteen years to the day since he and Hobhouse had left Falmouth on the Lisbon packet *Princess Elizabeth* for their first great adventure, but there was far too much to attend to. Plans were made for a departure on the 12th, but the *Hercules* was becalmed in the harbour. Byron had told Teresa that he had to sleep on board on the 13th so that they could sail at dawn. But it was Teresa, not Byron, who left at dawn on the 14th when Barry came to see her off with her father as their carriage turned towards Romagna. Half-crazed with grief she wrote Byron a series of pleading notes from the side of the road: "With every step that brings me nearer to Bologna, I feel my grief increasing. My God, help me! Come and fetch me, Byron, if you still want to see me alive, or let me run away and join you at any cost."[6] These notes never reached him; but he must have been fully aware of how she was suffering.

Meanwhile Byron was immobile in his ludicrous old tub with her grandiloquent title. On the 15th some American naval vessels attempted to tow her out of the bay, but to no avail. At midnight a wind blew up, so strong that the horses kicked down their flimsy partitions. Byron remained indifferent to whatever was happening; and when Trelawny told him that they would have to return to port lest they lose their cattle, he replied, "Do as you like." Like his own Don, he allowed himself to be borne along by events. Barry later told Hobhouse that when Byron went ashore that evening he confessed that the only thing that ensured his continuing on the expedition was the thought that Hobhouse and the others would laugh at him if he withdrew.

On the morning of the 16th Byron and Pietro returned to the abandoned Casa Saluzzo. As they wandered through the empty rooms, he talked gloomily of the future, wondering where they might find themselves in a year's time. That evening just before they set sail, Pietro sent a hurried note to his sister: "Byron is well in health, but tired by the activities of the night and day, and by a hot bath – he begs you to excuse him from writing . . . wait for our letters – try to find in your friendship some consolation for your present sufferings, though I fully imagine how great they are."[7]

At last they were on their way. Crammed into the small vessel in addition to the crew were Byron, Pietro, Trelawny, young Dr Bruno, and a kinsman of Mavrocordato, Prince Schilizzi, to whom they had promised passage. There were five servants, and Byron also managed to persuade Trelawny to let him have his black American groom as he knew black servants made a great impression in the East. In addition to the livestock and four horses, Byron brought along his bulldog, Moretto – if he could frighten the Hunt children he could frighten a Greek chieftain – and an additional large Newfoundland, Lyon. There were chests of medicine to provide for a thousand men for a year. Byron had removed a one-pounder cannon from the *Bolivar* despite Barry's protest that it might be considered unethical, since Lord Blessington had contracted to buy the boat. Byron was carrying 10,000 Spanish dollars and bills of exchange provided by Kinnaird for 40,000 more.

The sailing conditions were now fine, but the unwieldy barge – built like a cradle, Trelawny sneered – wallowing along with its heavy cargo, took five days to reach Livorno. Here there was news to report back to the London Greek Committee. Several Greek "patriots" persuaded Byron to allow them to cram themselves into the boat, and soon fierce quarrels broke out. Byron received word from the Archbishop of Arta who was exiled in Pisa that the leader he should trust was Marco Botzaris. Why didn't these people go to Greece rather than accept the charity of a foreign country? he asked crossly. He reported to Bowring (July 24, 1823) that he was disturbed to find how divided the Greeks were amongst themselves. "What they most seem to want or desire is – Money – Money – Money."

Just before they sailed Pietro sent off an affectionately concerned letter to his sister in Bologna, and apparently induced Byron to add a quick note (July 22, 1823):

My dearest Teresa –
I have but a few moments to say that we are all well – and thus far on our way to the Levant – Believe that I always *love* you – and that a thousand words could only express the same idea.

ever dearest yrs
NB

The brevity of this and all his subsequent notes reveal just how little real feeling was left between them.

Once under way, Byron quickly became friendly with a fellow Scot, James Hamilton Browne, one of the innumerable figures who had some vague connection with Greece. He persuaded Byron that he had been dismissed from service in the Ionian Islands because of his Hellenic sympathies, but in actuality he was under a cloud for having passed official information to a member of the opposition in parliament. On the voyage Browne acted as an observer somewhat in the way John Galt had done when the *Townshen* packet left Gibraltar in 1809. Byron spent much of his time in his cabin, reading Montaigne, La Rochefoucauld, Swift, or a travel book.

The *Hercules* sailed close to the coast. When they neared the island of Ponza, on which many of the insurgents of the Neapolitan rebellion had been imprisoned, Byron gave vent to his hatred of the Austrians. Trelawny urged him to express these feelings in poetry, but he was in no mood to write, and justified his refusal with the statement: "You might as well ask me to describe an earthquake, whilst the ground was trembling under my feet."[8] He went on to say that he reflected on a subject for many years before starting to write, which was certainly true of *Don Juan*, although once begun, he would write rapidly. But it was the prospect of action, not poetry, that preoccupied him now.

In many ways his daily habits followed much the same pattern as in 1809. He dined at twelve, usually on vegetables, especially quantities of red cabbage, downed with cider or hock. (Browne considered this a very unwholesome way of living in the Mediterranean in July.) He still practised pistol-shooting, and his aversion to killing birds apparently did not apply to domestic fowl. He boxed with Trelawny, fenced with Pietro, and jumped in for a swim with Trelawny, even reverting to boyish horseplay, such as letting the fowl loose into the sea. Then he and Trelawny leapt in after them, shouting hilariously, each with an arm in the sleeve of the corpulent captain's new uniform while he shouted indignantly from the deck.

Blaquiere had recommended that he land in Zante, but, persuaded as he usually was by the most recent person he had spoken to, Byron followed Browne's advice to make for Cephalonia, even though the wind was blowing them towards Zante. Byron's spirits lifted considerably once they sighted the coast of the Morea on August 12. "I don't know why it is," he remarked, "but I feel as if the eleven long years of bitterness I have passed through since I was here, were taken off my shoulders, and I was scudding through the Greek Archipelago with Bathurst* in his frigate."9 The following morning they anchored at Argostoli, the capital of the island.

The parallels and contrasts between these two famous expeditions to the East are curious. In 1809 he and Hobhouse had set out with youthful buoyancy, and in a totally irresponsible spirit. (To what degree he was escaping from a scandal with Edelston we shall probably never know.) Byron was fleeing his creditors and had left his friend Scrope Davies holding a considerable promissory note for him. He was also leaving under something of a cloud since his *Hours of Idleness* (1807) and the recently published *English Bards and Scotch Reviewers* had created a wide circle of literary enemies. His mother had been left to look after Newstead Abbey and his menagerie, and it was her responsibility to keep his creditors at bay. As the *Princess Elizabeth* glided away from Falmouth harbour, he could not have dreamed that only two years later, with the publication of *Childe Harold*, he would awake to find himself famous. Poignantly aware of the unexpectedness of life, it is understandable that as he and Pietro climbed the hill to the Casa Saluzzo for that last time two weeks earlier, he should indulge in reflections on what the future might hold.

On this occasion he was also seeking flight, this time from an emotional entanglement. By now he was a European celebrity and possessed coffers of lucre. Hobhouse had become an ambitious radical member of parliament, and was indirectly controlling Byron's movements from London. He was still accompanied by the faithful Fletcher who was reluctantly following his master to a country he never liked. Byron's entourage now included the re-bearded Tita (a memento of Venice), and the avaricious Lega Zambelli, who had been lured away from the service of Count Guiccioli in Ravenna. These were the visible representatives of the long years of exile. Byron was

* Captain of the *Salsette*, which they had boarded at Malta after his romance with Mrs Constance Spencer Smith.

perhaps a good deal more cynical than the young man of twenty-one, but basically he was the same mercurial character.

This time Charles Barry, his banker in Genoa, was left in charge of the menagerie. Also in his keeping was the Napoleonic coach. Byron now spoke as passionately about his refusal ever to part from the coach as he had once spoken about Newstead. Byron was now a rich man; and while Newstead had been disposed of without a regret, he was still harping on the sale of Rochdale.

Byron had told the Blessingtons that while he would have liked to have returned once more to England, he feared a cool reception. Perhaps Greece would provide an opportunity for glory – not notoriety – and he could hold his head high amongst his countrymen once more. Yet he had an uncanny feeling that he might never return alive. Possibly what he really wanted was a glorious death, which would mean both personal oblivion and posthumous fame. Yet this whole last interval of his life was *odd*. Odd in that he tried to replicate the routine he had re-established so often in the past, but the role-playing – even in the most responsible moments – broke down in the effort to believe and to behave as though everything were real, that he actually had a role to play although it was never to be revealed to him. Poor Byron never really knew what he wanted from life. Excitement or reassuring routine was eventually bound to pall.

A couple of days after their arrival in Cephalonia the loyal Pietro sent off a letter to Teresa explaining that she had received no letters because they had not stopped at Messina and that they had decided to stay where they were for the time being. "My lord is in excellent health – and good humour. If only you could be, too!" To this Byron added: "My dearest Teresa: I cannot write long letters as you know – but you also know or ought to know how much and entirely I am ever your A.A. in E. [*Amico Amante in Eterno*]."[10] No word of concern about her well-being, no curiosity about her activities in Bologna where she was staying with the family of a former tutor, no anxiety about her father who had been stopped at the frontier of Romagna and was to be detained in Ferrara for many months.

Byron was actually in a very irritable mood on learning that Blaquiere, who had urged him to come to Greece as quickly as possible, was now in Corfu on his way back to England. Byron was only gradually beginning to realise that the London Greek Committee, composed of a small group of doctrinaire Benthamites, viewed him as essential only for his ornamental value. But he was determined not to have come all this way for nothing; and he waited expectantly for an eventuality that would allow him to exert some influence.

He found an intelligent ally in the British Resident, Colonel Napier, who warmly urged him to take up quarters in his own home, but for the time being Byron decided to stay aboard the *Hercules*. Byron knew Napier by repute as having distinguished himself in the Peninsular Wars; and while Napier was determined to maintain a strict policy of official neutrality, he had great sympathy for the Greek cause, although he had no illusions about the foibles of the Greeks.

Actually Byron could not have found a better source to give him a realistic evaluation of the political situation. Since early 1822 a provisional government had existed in Hellas which on paper looked like that of a liberally administered European nation. Greece, like Italy, was a divided country. What had united the Carbonari was the desire to rid themselves of the Austrians, and all that united the multifarious factions in Greece was the desire to eject the Turks. While the country was still dotted with Turkish fortresses in 1823, Greek independence had largely been achieved – but for whom? Local leaders wanted semi-autonomous principalities little different from those that the Turks had established. On the other hand, the Greeks who had been imbibing European ideas of democracy while in exile wanted a strong central government. When Byron appeared on the scene the energies of the leaders were mainly devoted to an internal power struggle. The military party was led by colourful chieftains: Kolokotrones, Ipsilantes, and Odysseus; the other party, composed of the civil leaders, was led by Andreas Londos (whom Byron had met in 1809) and Mavrocordato. Tripolitza, in the centre of the Morea, was decided upon as the seat of government; but only a month after Byron's arrival when Mavrocordato was about to preside over the legislative council, Mavrocordato allowed himself to be so frightened by the threats of Kolokotrones that he fled to the island of Hydra.

In Cephalonia Byron's first weeks were spent in meeting the English community, and he was much flattered by the attention they paid him. Dr James Kennedy, the physician to the British garrison, saw himself as appointed to convert him to the truth of Christian doctrine. In a series of meetings – eagerly attended by the curious – Byron and Kennedy in effect engaged in a debate. To his surprise Kennedy did not find the scoffer he had expected, but a man deeply versed in the Bible who was even able to correct him in quoting Scripture on occasion. Augusta had given him a parting gift of a Bible which he said he read every day. He respected those who had true religious faith, and he himself had wrestled with spiritual problems in *Cain* and *Heaven and Earth*. Kennedy found himself at a loss when Byron asked him if he believed that there was less misery and slaughter in the world than there had been before the advent of Christianity.

Byron, with his love of Homer, expressed a great desire to visit nearby Ithaca. It proved a hot, arduous journey. The party rose at dawn on August 11 and spent nine hours on muleback before crossing the narrow channel to the island. The principal town was six miles away so they spent the first night in a merchant's house. At daylight they started off for Vathni where they were greeted warmly by the governor.

Byron could not accept that he no longer had the energy of which he was so proud on his first great adventure. There had been warning signs when he had to take to his bed in Italy after attempting swims that were now beyond his endurance. He did not look well the following morning as they started off for the Fountain of Arethusa, five miles away. It was a pleasant day, but the sun was broiling and Dr Bruno pleaded with him to refrain from swimming. After crossing the isthmus back to Cephalonia late in the afternoon, they prepared to spend the night at a nearby monastery. The monks were waiting to greet them with lighted pine torches, and the abbot launched into a long speech of welcome. Fumes of incense arose around them. Byron suddenly went berserk, screaming, "My head is burning – will no one relieve me from the pestilential presence of this madman?"

The shocked monks and his alarmed companions had an unsettled night. When Dr Bruno attempted to give him medicine, Byron blockaded the door of his room, tore his bedding, and threw furniture against the wall. Everyone waited apprehensively for his appearance the following morning. He eventually emerged from his room quite composed, and greeted the abbot courteously as though nothing had happened. As they rode back across the mountains to Argostoli, he broke into song. What is one to make of this curious incident? Byron was undoubtedly exhausted and probably had a touch of sunstroke. Yet his behaviour was so similar to what Annabella had described during their marriage that one wonders if these fits of uncontrollable temper might have happened more often than we know, and were not recorded because neither a Browne nor a Trelawny was present as a witness. His tutor at Trinity College, Cambridge, had warned Matthews when he occupied his rooms to be careful of Byron's things because His Lordship was a young man of "tumultuous passions".

Another sort of scene greeted the party on their return. Despite Napier's cautionary advice, Byron had given a warm welcome to the Suliote warriors whom the Turks had expelled from the mainland. He had nostalgic memories of their dancing around a blazing campfire while chanting wild songs of their piratical prowess. Encouraged by his welcome, the wily mob regarded him as an inexhaustible treasure-chest, and Captain Scott had to beat them back from the ship with grappling-hooks.

On August 22 Byron received a letter from their leader, Marco Botzaris, who was repelling the Ottoman forces pressing down through the mountain valleys above Missolonghi. Botzaris urged him to join him, but the day before the letter arrived in Cephalonia, his brain was pierced by a bullet. With the death of Botzaris and the flight of Mavrocordato to Hydra, Byron could not see any pressing need for leaving Cephalonia for the moment. He had resumed a journal in which he wrote that "I did not come here to join a faction but a nation", and that it would require great circumspection to deal with "such damned liars".[11] Pietro had already come to the conclusion that the Greeks were "scum". And so Byron rationalised moving into a little house in the village of Metaxata and resuming his old routine. Trelawny, who knew him well, recalled, "I well knew that once on shore Byron would fall back on his old routine of dawdling habits, plotting – planning – shilly-shallying – and doing nothing."[12] Byron told Trelawny to write to John Hunt that he wanted Cantos XV and XVI of *Don Juan* published "without *delay*", but while he had written fourteen stanzas of Canto XVII before he left Italy, he never touched the poem again.

Such inactivity was not agreeable to the restless Trelawny who set off for eastern Greece where he joined the insurgent leader, Odysseus, then living in a romantic cave. After Byron's death, Trelawny told Jane Williams that he had left Byron because "he was past hope – nothing could move or excite him . . . Could I then longer waste my life – in union with such imbecility – amidst such scenes as are here – where the excitement is enough to wake the dead?"[13] Mavrocordato and the other Greek leaders tried to enlist Byron's aid (which meant money), but, caught between congenital laziness, uncertainty about what the London Greek Committee expected of him, and the demands of the warring Greeks, Byron did nothing. In a postscript to a letter of Pietro's to Teresa in early October, he wrote: "I was a fool to come here but being here I must see what is to be done."[14]

One thing that could be done was to help the more unfortunate. In Ithaca Byron had been moved by the plight of a once affluent family in the Morea, Chalandritsanos by name. He provided the mother (then thought widowed) and her daughters with a dwelling in Argostoli. They were soon joined by a fifteen-year-old brother, Loukas, whose beauty immediately attracted Byron. He took him into his service as a page, lavished beautiful clothes on him, and soon seemed obsessed by him.

The days passed tranquilly enough in the whitewashed house amid a sweep of vines and olive groves, with its view of the sea beyond and the contours of Zante breaking the horizon. There were good tidings from England: Kinnaird had finally managed to sell Rochdale for £11,225. But Byron was concerned to hear that Ada had been ill. Would he lose yet another daughter? It was a great relief when Augusta reassured him of her recovery. He was also pleased by the visit of George Finlay, one of the young Philhellenes who were flocking to Greece. At first his resemblance to Shelley was so remarkable that Byron felt as though he had seen a ghost. They had many conversations, and Byron told him frankly that while he believed the Greeks deserved their freedom, "The Turks, however, are far better fellows, far more gentlemanly, and I used to like them better when amongst them."[15]

The serenity of the daily routine was frequently broken by vulturous emissaries from the various factions in Greece, with a single request – money. When Byron received pleas to come to the mainland, it was simply because it would be more opportune to have the money-chest within reach. There had long been talk of negotiating a loan from London. Hamilton Browne, who had been on a foray to Tripolitza, returned to Cephalonia at the end of October, accompanied by two deputies who were to proceed with him to London to negotiate a loan which would amount to £800,000. The Greeks begged Byron to advance them 300,000 piastres so that they could put fourteen vessels to sea against the Turks. Byron agreed to let them have £4,000 out of his private purse, expecting eventually to be repaid by the London Committee.

On November 22, Pietro Gamba, who had ridden down to Argostoli, sent back the following note to Byron:

Urgente

Mio Caro Byron,
Questa notte e arrivato da Ancona in sette giorni un bastimento papale con a bordo 20 passageri e due colonelli, uno inglese e l'altro prussiano. Il primo si chiama Canop, il secondo Dylon.

The "Canop" to whom Pietro referred was actually Colonel the Hon. Leicester Stanhope, an ardent Benthamite, who saw Greece as a convenient laboratory for creating the ideal utilitarian society by means of a free press and universal education. Their first meeting was not auspicious. Byron asked Stanhope if he had brought any new publications with him, to which Stanhope, as though proffering a precious gift, produced Jeremy Bentham's *A Table of the Springs of Action. Showing the Species of Pleasures and Pains of which Man's Nature is Susceptible.* "What does the old fool know of springs of action?" Byron shouted. "My — has more spring in it." Later he asked to borrow the book.

Byron found himself admiring Stanhope's honesty and energetic decisiveness, and with his encouragement wrote a letter to the Greek government intimating that no loan would be forthcoming until civil dissensions ceased (November 30, 1823). He then wrote personally to Mavrocordato (December 2, 1823), and Stanhope carried the letter with him when he crossed over to Missolonghi. Byron loftily informed John Bowring (December 26, 1823) that he and Napier had set Stanhope straight: "He came (as they all do who have not been in the country before) with some high-flown notions of the sixth form at Harrow or Eton, etc."

In Missolonghi Mavrocordato had established a provisional government, and even the unruly Suliotes seemed willing to serve under him. With its wide harbour, Missolonghi had been chosen as an obvious base from which an attack could be launched on Lepanto and Patras, the two remaining Turkish fortresses, both situated on the Ambracian Gulf. Stanhope's report back to London does not indicate that Byron had had much influence on him:

Your agent has now been at Missolonghi one week. During that period a free press has been established, a corps of artillery has been decided on, the funds furnished for its maintenance during nine months, and a person despatched to assemble it; means have been furnished to prevent the Greek fleet from dispersing, and a proper house and grounds have been procured for the establishment of a laboratory. This is a very encouraging commencement of our labours.[16]

But Stanhope could see that what the Greeks really wanted was Byron himself. On December 29 he reported to Byron: "I walked along the street this evening, and the people asked after Lord Byron!!!"[17]

After Mavrocordato landed at Missolonghi on December 11, he sent Byron a series of letters emphasising the necessity of his presence on the scene. It was fully expected that the Greek loan must arrive shortly and Byron would be expected to administer it. It was hard to resist pleas when one was told that "you will be received as a saviour. Be assured, My Lord, that it depends only on yourself to secure the destiny of Greece."[18]

Again: "your presence will do the greatest good: our forces will be electrified; the enthusiasm of all will be kindled to follow the impulsion which you will give them."[19] Mavrocordato even sent a brig to Cephalonia to fetch him, but since it wasn't allowed to anchor in the port, it returned to Missolonghi after cruising forlornly in front of the island for a couple of days. Few of the people who were crying for Byron had ever read his poetry or even knew really who he was. He was viewed as some kind of *deus ex machina* who would descend in a glow of radiating light to create a shining new world.

Byron had attempted to emulate Napier's attitude of neutrality to the various leaders, but he always leaned towards the Europeanised Mavrocordato whom he could visualise as a responsible leader for the country. Byron had taken fifty Suliotes into his service. The man who had always professed to hate war was now planning to return to Greece as a military commander. "I am passing 'the Rubicon'," Byron told Kinnaird; "recollect that for God's sake – and the sake of Greece. – You must let me have all the means and credit of mine that we can *muster* or *master*."[20] By now he had decided that he must stir himself to participate in events on the mainland.

On December 14th he actually sent Teresa almost a proper letter in which he very carefully avoided any reference to his projected plans. He tried to quiet her fears for the moment with the hint that they might see each other within a few months. "Perhaps in the Spring – we shall be able to invite you to Zante . . . and then I could come over and see you from the Morea or elsewhere. Or Pietro or I could run down to Ancona to convey you hither – so you see – we think of your Excellency – and of your sentimental projects."

A new sense of urgency and excitement appeared in the letters to his London correspondents. The possibility of purpose and action actually beckoned. Two boats were chartered: a large one, a bombard, for conveying Pietro, the servants, and the luggage, and a light one called a mistico for Byron's personal use. There was the usual problem with winds. They embarked on the 27th but were driven back to Argostoli. On the afternoon of the 29th, as he was sitting reading Scott's novel *Quentin Durward*, Byron was informed that they must be off immediately. He was in riotous spirits as they rowed out to the mistico, chaffing Fletcher who was being drenched by the spray. The following day they landed briefly at

Zante where Byron managed to secure more money through the local banker. The two boats again set off, the passengers all singing patriotic songs across the water to each other; and when their voices could no longer be heard, they fired off pistols. "Tomorrow we meet at Missolonghi — tomorrow."

31

ooooooooooooooo

Missolonghi, 1824

Mavrocordato, in his entreaties to Byron, made no reference to the danger lurking in the waters between Cephalonia and Missolonghi. As he described the situation, if a Greek flotilla could be launched by a British loan, the Ottoman strongholds would fall like ninepins. It is hard to credit that he was not fully aware that the Turks were constantly slipping out of the Gulf of Patras, but certainly his first priority was to secure the presence of Byron in Missolonghi as soon as possible.

On the afternoon of December 30, 1823, several enemy ships appeared off Missolonghi, and the Greek ships in a panic weighed anchor and fled, leaving the Turks in full control of the waters around the port. At two o'clock in the morning of the 31st a large ship suddenly loomed up out of the darkness in the path of Byron's mistico. The captain immediately recognised the ship bearing down on them as Turkish, and everyone on board, even the dogs, remained mute and terrified. Then, totally unexpectedly, the ship veered away. The only explanation for their escape might have been that the Turks feared they had encountered a fireboat.

At daybreak the mistico sighted two large vessels: one which was clearly blockading the port of Missolonghi, and another which was pursuing the bombard carrying Pietro Gamba and the rest of Byron's retinue. The latter was by now in neutral waters and quickly raised the Ionian flag at the approach of a large ship, only to be dismayed by the sight of the Ottoman crescent being hoisted directly afterwards. Pietro reacted in a remarkably collected way. The Turks were shouting at them to send their captain aboard with his papers. Gamba instructed the skipper, Spiro Valsamaki, to tell the Turks that they were an Ionian vessel in the employ of an English lord and were proceeding to the island of Kalamos.

After the captain disappeared up the gangway to recount this unlikely story, Gamba bundled together Byron's compromising correspondence with the Greek chieftains, as well as his own diary, and weighing the bundle down with fifty pounds of shot, dropped it into the sea. The sudden splash might have raised suspicions were it not for the fact that almost simultaneously the Turks, sighting another ship which they took to be Greek, turned towards Patras, ordering the bombard to follow.

Now there was real cause for alarm. Pietro Gamba had the responsibility for 8,000 dollars, as well as Tita, Lega Zambelli, and the horses. Suddenly the figure of Valsamaki appeared on the deck of the Turkish frigate, waving supportively. When they arrived in Patras they learned that the Turkish commander had been saved from shipwreck some years before by their very own captain. It was like an episode out of one of Byron's oriental tales. Pietro was summoned for an interview with the pasha; he turned to the British vice-consul for help; and for three days, while waiting for the ruler's decision, he shot woodcock. These he presented to the pasha, and on January 4 the ship was released. This was the sort of adventure for which Pietro had come to Greece; and one can only admire the coolness and courage with which he handled every detail of the incident.

The bombard arrived in Missolonghi at noon, and the passengers were alarmed to learn that Byron's mistico had not yet appeared. After its mysterious encounter in the dark with the Turkish vessel, it had moved silently into shallow waters, scuttling from creek to creek along the coast. Byron was very uneasy, particularly about Loukas, and told him that if the Turks appeared, they would jump into the water and he would swim to land with the page clinging to his neck. He had played this same game with the worshipful young Henry Long at Worthing many years before. Byron's first thought was not the fate of Pietro on the bombard, but what might happen to Loukas if the Turks caught the delectable youth. The page and a sailor scrambled on to the rocks near Anatolica with instructions to hurry overland to Missolonghi to ask for help from Stanhope. In the note, Byron wrote: "I am uneasy at being here; not so much on my own account as on that of a Greek boy with me, for you know what his fate would be; and I would sooner cut him in pieces, and myself too, than have him taken out by those barbarians."[1]

That night the mistico reached Dragomestre just up the coast. Byron was eager to travel overland to Missolonghi, but Mavrocordato sent word by Loukas that he must stay where he was. Loukas apparently rejoined the mistico in Dragomestre where they were detained for three days because of strong winds. They finally set out on January 3, but were twice driven on to the rocks. Anchoring for the night between two small islets, Byron decided to take a swim. Since he hadn't been able to change his clothes for five days, he claimed that it would be a means of getting rid of fleas, but it was more likely that he was showing off in front of Loukas. Fletcher pleaded with him not to enter the icy waters where he swam about for half an hour accompanied by his excited Newfoundland, Lyon. He boasted to everyone about his ebullient health, but Fletcher later recalled that within days he was complaining of aching bones which continued to plague him until his death.

On the morning of January 5 Byron donned the scarlet regimentals he had borrowed from an officer in Argostoli. A little canoe (called a monoxila) had been sent to convey him across the marshy lagoon to the town of Missolonghi. There was wild cheering, a twenty-one-gun salute, and at the door of the house that had been allotted to him, he finally met Mavrocordato accompanied by a long line of dignitaries. The squat leader of the Greeks hardly presented a heroic figure. Peering near-sightedly at the world through large glasses, with his over-sized head and dark European clothes, he looked rather like a pedantic schoolmaster. But it was clear that Byron was deeply moved by the tumultuous welcome, and Pietro believed that it was one of the most thrilling days in his life. In his own journal Pietro wrote: "I cannot easily describe the emotions which such a scene excited: I could scarcely refrain from tears; whether moved by the noise and signs of joy and delight, I know not; or whether from gladness that we now met each other safe on the Grecian soil, after encountering, in the space of a few days, so many dangers."[2]

The feeling of exultation was to be short-lived. In 1809 Byron and Hobhouse had paid off their Albanian servants here; as they pulled away on that rainy day, November 23, Hobhouse recorded that the dismal huts "seemed the more wretched to us, as we passed them on a rainy day and saw the waves washing over them with every gust of wind".[3] The miserable place with its stagnant lagoons and decaying houses had not improved in the intervening years. A town of some 3,000 fishermen living in dire poverty, its population was now increased by about 1,000 foreigners. The narrow lanes were stinking pastures of mud mixed with human excrement. The houses were built on stilts, scarcely above the level of the water.

Nevertheless, Byron's gradual disenchantment had little to do with his dismal surroundings, although the cold, persistent rains that now set in did nothing to improve the situation. He was given the top floor of a house belonging to Apolostoli Capsali, the primate of Argostoli. For years he had been accustomed to living in large empty rooms. Here the only furniture seemed to be a collection of battered divans, and he decorated the walls with his collection of firearms. Colonel Stanhope and the owner of the house occupied the second floor. The house eventually became even more crowded than the Casa Lanfranchi in Pisa after the invasion of the Hunt family. Lega, Fletcher, and the rest of Byron's household made do on the ground floor which was soon to be invaded at all hours by rancorous Suliotes. Pietro Gamba lodged elsewhere in the town, but generally spent his days with Byron.

Meetings on strategy began with Mavrocordato almost immediately. It was taken for granted that the Turks would try to regain Missolonghi once the winter rains had let up; and the Greek leader convinced Byron that it was therefore imperative that Lepanto be captured. With the loan from London this could be accomplished, and Greece would in time become independent and perhaps united. But money had to appear quickly if these grand schemes were to be effected. Nine Greek vessels had already returned to Hydra after the crew had given up hope of being paid; and Byron was able to prevent the five remaining brigs from following their example only by paying them out of his own pocket in the expectation that he would be repaid when the loan was floated in London.

These last months of Byron's life were to be the most stressful he had ever experienced. He had spent a lifetime evading responsibility and now, ironically, he was to be presented with a challenge no human being could have measured up to. Single-handedly he was to be the saviour of Greece and he knew, as Stanhope acidly remarked to the London Committee, that the eyes of the world were upon him. He had set out under the delusion that unlimited reserves of money could solve everything; but now he was to find that he needed unlimited reserves of wisdom, patience, tactical skills, and the ability to make quick, correct decisions. The London Greek Committee cannot be blamed for his predicament entirely, although Blaquiere had probably left the Greeks with unreal expectations. It was not in Byron's mandate to engage actively in military operations; and as William St Clair has pointed out, the Foreign Enlistment Act made it a crime for any British subject to join the armed forces of a foreign country.[4] Hobhouse wrote pleading with him not to put himself at risk, and emphasised that "you are not called upon to make great pecuniary sacrifices – do no such thing. You have done a great deal in going at all – the moral influence is more than any money which any individual can advance."[5] But Hobhouse and the other members of the committee were far from the scene and did not realise that Byron not only craved military glory, but because he found himself in the centre of operations, was also forced into a military role. No one had clearly thought through the implications of Byron's presence on the scene.

They were all nursing the illusion that Lepanto would fall with a little bribery. But at least there had to be the semblance of an army to storm it; and all Mavrocordato possessed was a rabble of squabbling Greeks and some disaffected European volunteers, but not a single well-trained commander or even the wherewithal (apart from some rusty cannon) to arm the unruly mob thronging the slushy streets of Missolonghi.

The Greek Committee in London had assured Byron that they had despatched a director of artillery and a staff which Byron hoped would be able to establish some sort of military order. This in itself was a violation of the neutrality which the British were professing, but both Byron and the Greeks pinned high hopes on the arrival of the man from Woolwich. However, the days passed into weeks, and William Parry still did not appear, although he had left London on November 9.

Without any military experience himself, Byron assembled the nucleus of a brigade who were to be billeted in a crumbling building which had once been a seraglio. Napier had advised Byron not to pay any money to the chiefs, but to form a personal bodyguard of the most trustworthy of the soldiers.[6] But how was he to judge who were the most trustworthy? He took 600 of them into his own pay. The so-called government was to be responsible for another hundred; and the various chieftains, whom Napier had rightly predicted would regard Byron as a "mine of gold", made it clear that they preferred to serve directly under him. If it was not money, it was rank that would cause trouble as the chieftains refused to allow any of those whom they considered their equals to assume command over them. Harold Nicolson believes that Byron's stubborn idealisation of the devious and intractable Suliotes was his biggest tactical error.[7] Byron had difficulty divesting himself of that youthful memory of noble savages roasting a goat on a beach, while in the light of the flickering flames they sang wild songs of glory and revenge.

Somehow a scruffy artillery group straggled out every morning in front of the Seraglio to practise gun drill without guns; and Byron's own bodyguard of Suliotes drilled daily in the courtyard beside his house. These activities gave some semblance of military order. One of Byron's major hopes of accomplishment in Greece was the humanitarian treatment of prisoners. He felt he was doing something positive on January 11 when he asked Mavrocordato to hand over to him a Turk who had been taken prisoner by a Greek privateer. The following evening the Turk's captors burst into the house demanding his return, and Byron was able to force them out only by drawing his own pistols.

Throughout this incident Mavrocordato sat silent, blinking in bewilderment behind his glasses. Byron rounded on him for failing to use his authority; and in order to instil some backbone into him, demanded that he hand over three more Turkish prisoners, all of whom he planned to send back to Yussuf Pasha at Patras.

Mavrocordato did not want the prisoners returned, and there was some speculation that he was fomenting dissension among the Suliotes. He had begun to suspect that Byron was planning to supplant him, and Byron was beginning to resent his devious procrastination. People were aware of a coolness developing between the two leaders. One evening when Mavrocordato dropped in while Byron was entertaining his companions, Byron pointedly ignored him and spoke contemptuously of him in English although he was fully aware that the Greek politician understood the language. Mavrocordato gave no indication that he understood what was being said, and had the tact to slip quietly away.

Throughout this entire period the rain poured down, grey and remorseless. In order to get some exercise, Byron and Pietro rowed about the lagoons, while discussing plans for the proposed expedition to Lepanto. Byron seemed in a relatively optimistic mood, although he admitted that he did not have much confidence in his troops. Not a day passed without some noisy incident. That very evening an altercation between the arrogant Suliotes and the sullen townspeople broke out. Later still that night there was even graver news. Turkish ships were reported blockading the port, and the so-called Greek fleet had fled. A crazy plan to attempt to destroy the rigging of the Turkish ships was precipitately devised, and it was all everyone could do to prevent Byron from leading the expedition. Stanhope reported to London that Byron was "chivalrous even to Quixotism".[8]

With all the tension of the situation Byron's temper flared up even against Pietro when he discovered from Lega's accounts that his young friend had ordered yards of cloth without his permission. The itemised accounts are interesting from another point of view. Throughout January Lega recorded numerous expenditures and purchases for Loukas, the beautiful page. Byron was so besotted with the boy that he did not realise it might incite envy when he placed thirty soldiers under the fifteen-year-old's command. On February 2, however, Byron reacted against his excessive demands in an instruction to Lega: "Tea is not a Greek beverage – therefore Master Lukas may drink Coffee instead – or water – or nothing. –

The pay of the said Lukas will be five dollars a month paid like the others of the household. He will eat with the Suliots – or where he pleases."9

The note of petulance indicates retaliation for favours bestowed without any mark of gratitude in return. The previous October Byron had written to Charles Barry in Genoa that he had confidence in the Greek adventure so long as the Greeks did not discover "my weak side – viz. – a propensity to be governed – and were [they] to set a pretty woman, or a clever woman about me – with a turn for political or any other sort of intrigue – why – they would make a fool of me . . ."10 Byron had allowed himself to be made a fool of by a wily, greedy, attractive boy. He had ceased writing poetry, but on his birthday he came into the room where Gamba, Stanhope, and some others were sitting, and read to them a poem written for the occasion, "On This Day I Complete My Thirty-Sixth Year". It is extraordinary that Byron could have been so indiscreet, and his listeners must have been stunned, particularly by the opening lines:

> 'T is time this heart should be unmoved
>   Since others it hath ceased to move,
> Yet though I cannot be beloved
>   Still let me love.
>
> My days are in the yellow leaf
>   The flowers and fruits of Love are gone –
> The worm, the canker and the grief
>   Are mine alone.
>
> The fire that on my bosom preys
>   Is lone as some Volcanic Isle,
> No torch is kindled at its blaze –
>   A funeral pile!
>
> The hope, the fear, the jealous care
>   The exalted portion of the pain
> And power of Love I cannot share
>   But wear the chain.
>
> But 't is not *thus* – and 't is not *here*
>   Such thoughts should shake my soul, nor *now*
> Where glory decks the hero's bier
>   Or binds his brow.

The Sword – the Banner – and the Field,
    Glory and Greece around us see!
The Spartan borne upon his shield
    Was not more free!

Awake! (*not* Greece – she *is* awake!)
    Awake my spirit – ! Think through *whom*
Thy Life blood tracks its parent lake
    And then strike home!

Tread those reviving passions down
    Unworthy Manhood; – unto thee
Indifferent should the smile or frown
    Of Beauty be.

If thou regret'st thy youth, why *live?*
    The Land of honourable Death
Is here – up to the Field! and give
    Away thy Breath.

Seek out – less often sought than found,
    A Soldier's Grave – for thee the best,
Then look around and choose thy ground
    And take thy Rest.

                     (*Works*, VII, pp. 79–81)

What the others must have heard was his open declaration of his determination to break an unworthy bond which had been embarrassing all of them. Whether they also heard Byron's solution is more problematic: that he must resolutely seek death, which he saw as the only alternative to his passion. As for the glory and worthiness of the Greek cause, it is doubtful if Byron really meant his romantically expressed views about Greece, given the babble of quarrelling Suliotes serving as a Chorus on the ground floor beneath them. It was becoming a black comic opera.

But in many respects Byron was far more realistic about the Greek situation than Stanhope, with his fixed aim of applying a theoretical programme to an unruly group of people, many of them illiterate. Following Stanhope's mandate from the London Greek Committee, a newspaper expressing democratic views, the Romaic *Hellenica Chronica*, was first published on January 14. Byron disapproved of a foreign country imposing its views on the Greeks. Stanhope was appalled, he reported to the committee in London, that Byron also believed that some sort of censorship should be imposed. Knowing the Greeks far better than Stanhope, Byron was aware that blood feuds and assassinations could be the result of unrestrained reporting.

Stanhope's ill-concealed envy of Byron is apparent in the wording of his reports to Bowring. He seemed determined to undermine Byron's credibility with the committee. The hostility between the two men erupted on January 26 when a British officer, Captain Yorke, of the English brig *Alacrity*, came ashore at Missolonghi to protest against the seizure of an Ionian boat by a Greek privateer. Byron was in total agreement that the neutrality of the British be respected; and he invited the officers to dine with him. The curious and bewildered men were ushered in by the colourful Tita, and Loukas served them attired in his elegant finery but on a table without a cloth "to deliver us from plague and pestilence".*[11] They were entertained by Byron's harum–scarum conversation, and took note of the fact that he had a slight Scottish accent. Glancing at his foot, he remarked jokingly that however the situation turned out in Greece, he could not run away.

Naturally they stared at this famous figure and, fortunately for us, the ship's surgeon, Daniel Forrester, recorded his recollections. Despite a receding hairline, Byron was still remarkably handsome. Forrester was startled to see that he had a moustache; and even more surprised that it was white.[12] He was wearing a dark green hussar's jacket, adorned with a great deal of braid. His trousers were blue with a broad red stripe running down the sides, and on his head was perched a blue foraging cap. After dining, Byron suggested that they shoot at glass bottles as targets. Forrester was impressed by Byron's skill, particularly since his hand shook as though he had the ague. Byron knew, of course, that he would impress his visitors.

Captain Yorke was demanding 400 dollars in compensation; Mavrocordato demurred; but Byron saw to it that Yorke secretly got the money. Byron also persuaded the officers of the *Alacrity* to convey the Turkish prisoners back to their homes. That evening Stanhope upbraided Byron for his conciliatory attitude, objecting that the matter had not been conducted "according to the principles of equity and the law of nations". Angered by this talk of abstractions, Byron shouted that law, justice, and equity had nothing to do with politics. What Stanhope was

---

* There was a belief that plague could be spread by clothing, but there was no knowledge at this date of the nature of micro-organisms. In 1882 a German, Robert Koch, was the first to discover that bacteria caused tuberculosis, thus disseminating the idea of infection (I am indebted to Professor Edward Shorter for this information).

really aggrieved about was Byron's attitude towards his printing press. Byron began abusing Stanhope's idol, Jeremy Bentham. Stanhope objected heatedly, and Byron assured him that he was not attacking Bentham personally but rather his abstract principles which he believed calculated to cause great problems in Greece. Tempers rose; and Stanhope accused Byron of being a secret Turk. Byron said he would be judged by his acts. But they parted peaceably on Byron's part; and when Stanhope took the light to conduct him up the stairs, Byron exclaimed laughingly, "What! Hold up a light to a Turk!"[3]

On January 27 they received word that the elusive Parry, the fire-master from Woolwich, was in Ithaca awaiting orders from Stanhope and Byron. The fledgling Greek government had promised that the seraglio building would be designated for Parry's arsenal, but Byron's 600 Suliotes were already using it as a barracks. Gamba and Stanhope somehow persuaded them to leave, but the wily Suliotes extracted a heavy price. They made it clear that Byron had to continue providing habitation for their families and livestock. When they stubbornly refused to vacate the Seraglio until their demands were met, Byron threatened to discharge them from his service. By now he was beginning to realise that tough measures like these were the only instructions they understood.

The loan from the London Greek Committee had still not arrived. Mavrocordato informed Byron that the Resurrection Knights of Malta had offered the Greeks a loan on condition that they cede Rhodes and some other islands to the Knights. Perhaps using this as a ploy, Mavrocordato sent an anxious letter to Blaquiere who suggested that he come to England for discussions. To Mavrocordato's reply declining the invitation, Byron added a forceful note: "Certainly *not*, unless P. Mavrocordato wishes to risk his influence – and the hopes of Greece for the present."[4]

On February 1 word was received that Parry had reached Dragomestre. This was welcome news and came just as a marine party comprising Byron, Mavrocordato, Gamba, and Loukas were setting out for a visit to Anatolica which had heroically resisted a siege by the Turks the previous summer. The expedition was instigated by an invitation from the town's leaders and on their arrival they were greeted ecstatically. Resisting a pressing invitation to stay overnight, Byron insisted on making the two-hour return journey to Missolonghi even though a squall was blowing up. All of them were soaked to the skin, and both Pietro and Loukas developed high fevers. Byron put the page in his own bed and became his vigilant nurse.

Louis Crompton argues persuasively that a posthumously published poem, entitled "Last Words on Greece", was written during Loukas's illness, and another, "Love and Death", some time after an earthquake that struck Missolonghi on February 21.[5] The autobiographical details are so clear that there is no disputing his argument.*

> I watched thee when the foe was at our side –
>   Ready to strike at him, – or thee and me –
> Were safety hopeless – rather than divide
>   Aught with one loved – save love and liberty.
>
> I watched thee in the breakers – when the rock
>   Received our prow – and all was storm and fear,
> And bade thee cling to me through every shock –
>   This arm would be thy bark – or breast thy bier.
>
> I watched thee when the fever glazed thine eyes –
>   Yielding my couch – and stretched me on the ground –
> When overworn with watching – ne'er to rise
>   From thence – if thou an early grave hadst found.
>
> The Earthquake came and rocked the quivering wall –
>   And men and Nature reeled as if with wine –
> Whom did I seek around the tottering Hall –
>   For *thee* – whose safety first provide for – thine.
>
> And when convulsive throes denied my breath
>   The faintest utterance to my fading thought –
> To thee – to thee – even in the grasp of death
>   My Spirit turned – Ah! oftener than it ought.
>
> Thus much and more – and yet thou lov'st me not,
>   And never wilt – Love dwells not in our will –
> Nor can I blame thee – though it be my lot
>   To strongly – wrongly – vainly – love thee still. –

(Works, VII, pp. 81–2)

Byron's tormented feelings for Loukas must be borne in mind during February when external pressures on him became even more intense. Boats from Dragomestre were arriving bearing the long-awaited supplies. The

---

* That there were other more explicit poems which were destroyed by Hobhouse after Byron's death is suggested by Crompton, p.332, based on Stanhope, p.534.

proud Suliotes refused to act as porters and Byron had to hire some local folk to carry the stores. Even they refused to work on the 4th which was a holiday. The rain was coming down in sheets; and lest the precious cargo be ruined, Byron ran down to the beach and began pulling the crates to shelter so that the Greeks were finally shamed into helping. As a consequence of his labours Byron came down with a bad cold.

Once the crates were opened, there was great disappointment. They contained plenty of Bibles and religious tracts, but no Congreve rockets or the possibility of their being produced for the next couple of months, although Bowring and Stanhope had promised that Parry would make "Congreve rockets – Greek fire – and a variety of other mischievous things that will inspire terror into the Greeks".*[16]

More puzzling than the absence of the rockets was the fact that the London Greek Committee had not provided Parry with the funds to pay his men, and neither Mavrocordato nor Colonel Stanhope had any money for them. It had simply been assumed that Byron would act as banker until the Greek loan was floated. (It was actually oversubscribed that very month.) Parry claims that he approached Byron with great embarrassment, but all Byron replied was: "Is that all? – I was afraid it was something else. Do not let that give you any uneasiness; you will have only to tell me all your wants, for I like candour, and, as far as I can, I will assist you."[17]

Parry was a rough diamond, but Byron took to him at once. Byron chaffed him about taking so long to reach Greece, and Parry then provided him with an explanation which only increased his irritation. Parry had urged the committee to send him on a fast vessel that would stop at only one port for supplies. Ignoring his advice, they sent him on a boat with government supplies that were to be unloaded at Malta and Corfu. When he had finally arrived at Dragomestre, he received a letter from Stanhope urging him to give priority to the printing materials which he was to send immediately to Missolonghi. After absorbing all this information, Byron "seemed almost to despair of success, but said he would see the contest out".[18] It was becoming very clear that the final responsibility for any

---

* The rocket had been invented by General Congreve, Comptroller of the Royal Laboratory at Woolwich, and had been used effectively against Copenhagen in 1807. The rockets fired by the British during the siege of Fort McHenry in 1812, "the rocket's red glare" of the United States national anthem, were also Congreve rockets. Byron wrote about them in *Don Juan*, I, 129, 1029–30:

> But vaccination certainly has been
> A kind antithesis to Congreve's rockets, . . .

military expedition that would be undertaken was to fall on Byron's shoulders. Parry concluded that "he felt himself deceived and abandoned, I had almost said betrayed."[19]

It is not surprising that Byron came to rely on Parry as a practical man of action. Parry undertook to have an artillery corps ready in sixteen days, and after that Byron was prepared to give the order to march, especially as there were reports that Lepanto would fall easily. Byron had by now put so much faith in this bluff figure that he appointed him as his paymaster, and they met every morning to go over the accounts. They chuckled together over Parry's story of his meeting with Jeremy Bentham, and made fun of Stanhope behind his back. There was something engaging in the intimacy that grew between them. Parry, what novels have you read? Do you like poetry? Byron gradually realised that Parry was something of a buffoon. Even in these awful conditions, Byron was capable of carrying out practical jokes. Aware that Parry was terrified of earthquakes, one night he gathered together fifty Suliotes in his quarters above the room of Parry who was now living in the communal house. When Byron gave the order, they all jumped on the floor with all their might, and Byron himself rushed around banging doors. Parry burst from his room begging for the mercy of heaven.

Neither Byron then nor anyone else has given sufficient credit to another colleague, Pietro Gamba, whom Byron regarded more as his *protégé* than a comrade-in-arms. Totally devoted to Byron, Pietro played an important role in trying to rescue this disastrous undertaking in which they had become embroiled. He tried to keep Teresa reassured. He spent hours writing to Byron's dictation. After a careful examination of the list of the Suliotes, he discovered that they had padded their rolls extravagantly, just as they had done when serving under Ali Pasha. The whole corps were called together so that a firm understanding would be established before they set out for Lepanto. The Suliotes demanded that more of them be made officers (150 out of 300–400 men), which meant in effect a considerable increase in pay to them. On hearing this, Byron flew into a rage and sent Pietro to the mutinous crew of chieftains with the message that he would have nothing more to do with them, and that any prior agreement between them was now null and void. After much haggling the Suliotes finally agreed to become part of a new corps, but it was now too late to consider an immediate march on Lepanto.

At seven that evening Pietro entered Byron's room where he found him lying on the sofa. He called out: "I am not asleep – come in – I am not well."[20] About an hour later Byron went downstairs to join Stanhope and Parry. They started to discuss the possibility of another newspaper with articles written largely in Italian as few of the foreigners in Greece could understand Romaic. Byron agreed to contribute something to it. Parry noticed that he was very flushed. He complained of thirst and called for some cider. Parry begged him not to drink it after imbibing a good deal of spirits. As soon as he had swallowed a little of the cider, a great change came over his countenance. He tried to stand up, staggered forward, and fell into Parry's arms. Some brandy was poured into his mouth, and he was then seized with violent convulsions, and his mouth was pulled down at one side. Dr Bruno and a young English physician, Julius Millingen, were summoned. Millingen later recorded that he "foamed at the mouth, gnashed his teeth, and rolled his eyes like one in an epilepsy".[21] After a few minutes he recovered his speech enough to enquire, "Is it not Sunday?" On being told that it was, he replied, "I should have thought it most strange if it were not."

As soon as he had recovered sufficiently, Byron called for Stanhope to issue instructions in the event that he did not recover. He assured them that he was not afraid to die. He had been told that his convulsions were akin to epilepsy, which was enough to convince him that he was suffering from the disease, but he recorded firmly in his journal of February 15 that he had *not* been foaming at the mouth. It is possible that saliva was running down his chin, but more explicable than epilepsy would be convulsions brought on by a high fever. Undoubtedly, too, the constant pressure of his circumstances and his erratic and abstemious diet had left him totally debilitated. Stanhope believed that "the provoking conduct" of the Suliotes had caused the attack. "The mind of Byron is like a volcano," he told Bowring, "it is full of fire, wealth, and combustibles; and, when this matter comes to be strongly agitated, the explosion is dreadful."[22]

He was not to find peace even in illness. Within half an hour of his attack there was another fright. News arrived that the Suliotes were on their way to seize the arms which were stored in the seraglio building. Pietro, Stanhope, and Parry ran out to control the situation, leaving Byron alone in the house. It proved to be a false alarm, but as he lay there, weak and helpless, two drunken Germans burst into his room, waving their arms and shouting that they had come to protect him. It was a waking nightmare. The following day he felt extremely weak and complained of a sensation of weight on his head. Bruno, supported by Millingen, was now determined that he must be bled.*

---

* It was thought that fever was caused by an excess of blood. The use of leeches and the opening of veins was continued well into the nineteenth century. I am indebted for this information to Professor Edward Shorter.

They applied eight leeches to his forehead, but placed them too close to his temporal lobe, so that they could not stop the blood pouring from his head. Parry was beside himself as he saw Byron lying pale and senseless, a victim of medical obsessionalism. Parry tore bands off his clothes which he ordered Fletcher to burn under his master's nose,* while he rubbed Byron's temples and attempted to pour some brandy into his mouth.

As Byron grew a little stronger he asked the young Italian physician to prepare a memorandum on epilepsy for him. He wanted to understand all he could about his supposed ailment, although he was puzzled about the possibility that he was suffering from epilepsy since it would have been his first attack. Even though his eyes were inflamed, on February 15 he resumed the journal he had been keeping in Cephalonia in an attempt to understand what had brought on the attack.

> With regard to the presumed cause of this attack – as far as I know there might be several – the state of the place and of the weather permits little exercise at present; — I have been violently agitated with more than one passion recently – and a good deal occupied politically as well as privately – and amidst conflicting parties – politics – and (as far as regards public matters) circumstances; – I have also been in an anxious state with regard to things which may be only interesting to my own private feelings – and perhaps not uniformly so temperate as I may generally affirm that I was wont to be – how far any or all of these may have acted on the body of One who had already undergone many previous changes of place and passion during a life of thirty six years I cannot tell – nor – but I am interrupted by the arrival of a report from a party returned from reconnoitering a Turkish Brig of War just stranded on the Coast – and which is to be attacked the moment we can get some guns to bear upon her. – I shall hear what Parry says about it – here he comes.[23]

He actually wanted to join the expedition which, as one might expect in this totally unreal situation, miscarried in a most humiliating way. Parry and his group were unable to prevent the Turks either from removing the stores from the brig or blowing her up. Byron's faith in Parry began to waver after this mishap. When Gamba returned to the house on the morning of the 19th, he was astonished to find two cannon pointed towards

---

* This was based on the idea that noxious emanations could control fits. Burning feathers under a hysterical woman's nose was very common (Professor Edward Shorter).

the gate. Climbing hurriedly up the stairs, he found the place eerily quiet. A Swedish volunteer, an artillery officer by the name of Sass, who had come out to Greece with Parry's party, had been killed while attempting to break up a fracas in which a Suliotc was forcing his way into the Seraglio. The culprit had been arrested immediately, and the inevitable followed: the rest of the Suliotes gathered around the building, threatening to burn it down unless the murderer was released. It was now clear that the Suliotes, upon whom Byron had fastened such high hopes, must be banished from the town. This could be accomplished only by a bribe of 3,000 dollars which Byron was now only too willing to pay in order to get rid of them. He summoned the chieftains to his house; and, weak as he was, subdued them by his dignified demeanour. It was the end of an association created from an illusion.

Stanhope reported to London that "Lord Byron . . . is much shaken by his fit, and will, probably, be obliged to retire from Greece."[24] For a brief time he did consider retiring to one of the Ionian Islands, but as his health deteriorated he became more stubborn about not budging from where he was. His thoughts turned frequently to Ada, and he wrote to Augusta (February 23, 1824) that it was a "great comfort" to hear about her; and from what Augusta had told him about her (relayed from Lady Byron), he thought she must be much like himself at the same age. He also told Augusta that he had taken a shine to a little Turkish girl of nine (the same age as Ada and of Allegra, if she had lived). Her name was Hato or Hatagee. She had been among the Turkish prisoners, but "expressed a strong wish to remain with me".* Byron lavished pretty clothes on her, and clearly she reminded him of Allegra for she "seems to have a decided character for her age". Like Allegra, with constant spoiling she grew pert and saucy.

For a time Byron actually entertained the fantasy that Lady Byron might bring her up as a companion to Ada. After realising the impracticality of the scheme, he wrote to Dr Kennedy in Cephalonia who agreed to take her into his houschold. When the arrangement was explained to the child's mother, she refused to be separated from her daughter, "which is quite natural, and I have not the heart to refuse it" (March 10, 1824). Apparently Claire Clairmont was the one exception to this tender-hearted view.

While Byron could not bring himself to accept Kennedy's religious views, he was also very grateful for his offer of a place of convalescence. He

* This was a remarkable example of life imitating art. In *Don Juan*, Canto VIII, 94ff. the don rescues a young girl during the battle with the Russians.

thanked him for his kind suggestion, but declined since he felt "it is proper that I should remain in Greece; and it were better to die doing something than nothing. My presence here has been supposed so far useful as to have prevented confusion from becoming worse confounded, at least for the present."[25]

There was a break in the weather on the 20th, and Byron was able to go riding with Pietro who found him in a mood of deep melancholy. "I begin to fear," he said, "that I have done nothing but lose time, money, patience, and health; but I was prepared for it; I knew that ours was not a path of roses, and that I ought to make up my mind to meet with deception, and calumny, and ingratitude." Gamba urged him to retire to Athens, but he said no, there would be no more tranquillity there than in Missolonghi. "Besides, I did not come in search of tranquillity; I am neither undeceived nor discouraged."[26]

Tranquillity was not to be. The town was seized by a rumour of the plague, and people carried sticks with which to hit anyone who came near them. Then on February 21 there was a violent earthquake. The following day Byron had one of his strange convulsions. He told Parry that his life was becoming unbearable. He complained frequently of dizziness; and, more frightening still, severe anxiety attacks. He had fled from boredom only to be engulfed in chaos. Since childhood he had had forebodings of doom, and now here in Missolonghi his fears were confirmed. His only comfort seemed to be in Lyon, his faithful Newfoundland dog.

The rest of the month was spent simply marking time. Lepanto was there for the taking, but there were no trained troops, and the German volunteers refused to serve under the non-commissioned Parry. Towards the end of February George Finlay arrived from Athens carrying a letter from Odysseus, the strongest leader in the eastern part of the country. Odysseus invited Byron and Mavrocordato to meet with him at Salona in an attempt to create some kind of unity among the various factions. Trelawny, who had thrown in his lot with Odysseus months before, also wrote urging Byron to consider handing over some of the committee's stores to the chieftain. Stanhope, who was now in Athens, had become enraptured with Odysseus, and was in effect transferring his support from Mavrocordato, whom he had never fully trusted. On March 6 he wrote to Byron: "I implore your Lordship and the president, as you love Greece and her sacred cause, to attend at Salona." [27]

Byron had reason to have strong reservations about the unscrupulous Odysseus whom he saw as out only for his own ends. Nevertheless, Odysseus had a force of between 3,000 and 4,000 men, which was something to be considered since a Turkish army was said to be assembling near Larissa. While Byron reluctantly agreed to attend a meeting at the end of the month, he had no intention of handing over any munitions. On the outside chance that something positive might emerge from the discussions, he saw a small possibility of doing some measure of good. He now certainly had no delusions that he might be the saviour of Greece.

32

oooooooooooooo

Death in Greece, 1824

On March 17 Byron added a note to one of Pietro Gamba's letters to his sister Teresa: "My dearest T. – The Spring is come – I have seen a Swallow to-day – and it was time – for we have had but a wet winter hitherto – even in Greece. – We are all very well, which will I hope – keep up your hopes and Spirits." A few more commonplace remarks about their situation in this last – and only – letter from Missolonghi he ever wrote to her. We can only feel pity for the woman whose tears must have flowed when she remembered bitterly his promise to send for her in the spring.

In Missolonghi there was a perpetual crisis. On the same day as Byron wrote to Teresa, he was approached by a delegation of the citizens begging for help with the crumbling fortifications of the town. The townspeople and the soldiers quarrelled; the soldiers quarrelled among themselves. Everyone quarrelled with Parry; or, perhaps more accurately, Parry seems to have quarrelled with everyone. Byron fell into a deep gloom, and was peevish and irascible with anyone who approached him. He became obsessed with his health. He flew into a rage with Fletcher, and would allow only Tita and Loukas to be near him. Even Pietro fell into disgrace about having paid the artillery soldiers out of Byron's personal account, an error that was reported to Byron by Parry.*

In a dignified letter of March 24, Pietro Gamba apologised for his mistaken judgement:

> For such delinquencies I beg your forgiveness; and whatever punishment you may decide to inflict upon me, I shall accept it willingly, not

---

* Unfortunately Parry was probably motivated by malice. His comments on Gamba in his book, *The Last Days of Lord Byron*, are unnecessarily mean-spirited.

so much from a superior officer, as from one who is to me as a father. I must confess, however, that the reproaches that you made to me last night caused me no little pain . . . It is true that I have accomplished little, since circumstances have offered me little to accomplish. But should God give me the occasion, I feel that I possess a sufficiency of intelligence and character to prove to you that the most devoted of your friends will not be the least useful of your servants."[1]

Byron was projecting on to Pietro his own frustration at having accomplished nothing. Locked in his own self-dissatisfaction, he banished Gamba from his sight for several days. The disgraced Suliotes continued to plague him. They wandered around the countryside, even threatening the town because of some minor insult to one of their chieftains, Karaiskakis. Then the Turkish fleet suddenly appeared, blocking the port. Mavrocordato was convinced that Karaiskakis had betrayed the town through an accomplice, and was planning to open the gates to the Turks. Shops were closed, the bazaars shut down, and soldiers rushed around arresting people indiscriminately. Eventually the Turkish fleet withdrew, and Karaiskakis was captured. All this happened during the first week of April when Byron and Mavrocordato were supposed to be in Salona.

They had been unable to leave Missolonghi because rain made the roads impassable and a high wind had blown up. While their delay could be blamed on the weather, Byron was also relieved to have an excuse not to stir himself from Missolonghi, disagreeable as it was. One of the deputies of the Greek Executive Body was leaving for London in an attempt to speed up the loan. Overwhelmed by a flood of nostalgia, Byron seized a pen and wrote a letter of introduction which the Greek could present to Lord Clare. It provided him with an excuse to say, "I hope that you do not forget that I always regard you as my dearest friend – and love you as when we were Harrow boys together – and if I do not repeat this as often as I ought – it is that I may not tire you with what you so well know" (March 31, 1824). Byron began to fret that his failure to reach Salona and rumours of a possible civil war might jeopardise the loan. He told Parry that he was glad at least that he bore no personal responsibility for people being asked to subscribe to it. He was beginning to lose all hope that he could accomplish anything.

Byron had always been very irritable when he was confined to the house and could not ride. On April 9 he scrawled his last letter. On a note to Charles Barry in Genoa, he instructed him to dispose of all his possessions except "the Green travelling Chariot". This must have been tossed off just as the rain let up, and although the sky was overcast, he insisted on taking his ride. He was feeling more cheerful than usual that morning because he had finally received word that the negotiations for the Greek loan were proceeding satisfactorily.

Since the road through the town gate was impassable because of the mud, he and Pietro took a small boat across the bay to an olive grove where they mounted their horses. Within half an hour a downpour descended. By the time they returned to the canoe they were perspiring and soaked to the skin. Gamba argued that it would be the height of folly to return by boat in their condition and that they must somehow make their way back on their horses. Byron replied stubbornly: "I should make a pretty soldier indeed if I were to care for such a trifle." When they finally reached the house he was shivering and feverish. Later that evening when Gamba came to visit him, he said: "I suffer a great deal of pain; I do not care for death; but these agonies I cannot bear."[2]

Nevertheless, the following morning with pathetic bravado he went out again with Gamba and his Suliote bodyguard, but on his return he scolded his black groom, Benjamin Lewis, for having given him the same wet saddle he had used the day before.

Finlay, who was about to return to Athens, called on him that evening and found him complaining of rheumatic pains. Although he was relatively cheerful at first, he became pensive and silent, suddenly remarking that years before in Cheltenham a famous fortune-teller had told his mother that he should beware of disaster in his thirty-seventh year.*

Later that night he called for Bruno who found him shaking violently. Bruno pleaded to be allowed to bleed him, but Byron refused categorically. His speech had begun to slur. Parry tried to convince him that in Zante he would receive more experienced medical treatment. By the 13th the fever had increased; and while all the arrangements had been made to transfer the patient to Zante, it was impossible to venture into the gulf as a veritable hurricane had blown up. And this was the climate of cloudless skies for which Byron had pined all those years.

He wandered in and out of lucidity. Afraid that he was losing his memory, he made himself repeat some Latin verses he had learned at school, and found that he was able to summon up all of them apart from one word. Millingen had by now joined the scene around the bedside, and the two novice doctors resumed their pleas for the bleeding but, remem-

---

* Was he confusing this with his twenty-seventh year which was the year of his marriage, a story he had so often repeated to friends?

bering how horrible the experience had been in February, he agreed only to take some currant tea which caused him to vomit. He finally fell into a fretful sleep. He was terrified that he was not getting sufficient sleep, crying out that people died if they did not have sleep. He slept more than he realised, but he was always exhausted.

Parry was right to be so suspicious of Byron's medical attendants. Byron by now regretted having saved money by hiring someone right out of medical school. He told Fletcher that they had tried to reassure him that he had only a cold, and Fletcher agreed with him: "I am sure, my Lord, that you never had one of so serious a nature."

Each day brought new symptoms. On the 15th he was assailed by a raging thirst. The wind howled around the house and he cowered in a corner of his bed, beset by superstitious fears. He began to think that he had been cursed by an evil eye, and he asked Millingen to find a witch who could exorcise the curse. Millingen, in order to humour him, scoured the town for one, but by evening Byron seemed to have forgotten about her and talked in a quiet but rambling way to Parry. He suggested that they build a schooner and visit America together. He described his life as having been "like the ocean in a storm", and expressed the wish to live quietly in retirement in England with his wife and daughter.

On the night of the 15th, after a violent spasm of coughing, Bruno extracted the promise that Byron would allow himself to be bled the following morning. In three fumbling attempts the well-meaning pair of doctors opened his veins, followed by the application of leeches. At one point Byron accused Fletcher of being part of a plot to assassinate him.

The elements – remorseless rain and howling wind – seemed to collaborate in the dismal atmosphere of those final days. Without Byron's presiding authority, the household fell into total shambles. There was everlasting noise within as well as without: the sobs of Pietro and Fletcher, the polyglot voices in Italian, Greek, and English. Byron was drifting off into a world of his own, murmuring of the past, rising up to shout battle commands, and then falling back exhausted. Tita was so alarmed by some of the things he said that he quietly removed his pistols and the stiletto which were always kept beside his bed.

Moaning, shivering, delirious – was any death ever more terrifying? On the 18th – Easter Sunday – the artillery brigade marched out of the town as a means of drawing the citizens away from the streets when on such occasions it was their custom to fire off muskets. By now Byron was aware that his life was drawing to a close. He muttered constantly, sometimes in English, sometimes in Italian. He wanted to die. He described himself as "a young old man", who had "exhausted all the nectar contained in the cup of life". His great fear was of slowly dying in a state of torture or of becoming a grinning idiot like Swift. He pleaded that his body not be hacked to pieces nor sent back to England. From the accounts of the various witnesses – and how many deaths have had such a quantity of witnesses? – the ordeal can be reconstructed with a certain reliability. Millingen recalled that his only reference to religion was a ruminative "Shall I sue for mercy?" Then, after a pause, he answered himself: "Come, come, no weakness! Let's be a man to the last."[3]

Stanhope wrote on April 17 from Salona where a large group was anxiously awaiting his arrival: "As for you, you are a sort of Wilberforce, a saint whom all parties are endeavouring to seduce; it's a pity that you are not divisible, that every prefecture might have a fraction of your person."[4] He begged Byron to leave Missolonghi where he was sure the climate and the unending anxiety were destroying Byron's health. "Once more, I implore you to quit Missolonghi," Stanhope concluded, "and not to sacrifice your health and, perhaps, your life in that Bog."[5]

There were also letters from England, some of which he roused himself to look at. One from Hobhouse (March 15, 1824) announced that the Greek loan had finally been successfully floated, and that Byron and Stanhope were to administer it. One section from his cheerful friend was particularly ironical:

> Your monied matters Kinnaird will tell you, are going on swimmingly. You will have, indeed you have, a very handsome fortune – and if you have health, I do not see what earthly advantage you can wish for that you have not got. Your present endeavour is certainly the most glorious ever undertaken by man – Campbell said to me yesterday that he envied what you were now doing (and you may believe him, for he is a very envious man) even more than all your laurels, blooming as they are – Go on and prosper.[6]

Kinnaird (March 19, 1824) wanted his signature on the Rochdale deed to finalise the sale. He also made what was to be a final plea to pay Baxter for the Napoleonic coach, and also to make some settlement to Owen Mealey's widow since there was talk in the neighbourhood of Newstead that Byron had left her destitute.

Late on that Sunday afternoon Byron summoned Fletcher. He told him that he knew the end was near, and there were some things he was urgent to communicate to him. When Fletcher asked if he should fetch pen and paper, Byron replied that there was not time. The man who had served him faithfully for over fifteen years was not provided for in the will, but Byron assured him that Hobhouse would look after him. Fletcher begged him to speak of more important things. "Oh, my poor child!" he cried. "My dear Ada! My God! could I but have seen her! Give her my blessing, and my dear sister Augusta and her children – and you will go to Lady Byron and say – tell her everything – you are friends with her." His voice then failed him and he continued muttering inaudibly, every now and then raising his head to instruct Fletcher to follow his orders faithfully. Fletcher replied that he had not been able to hear a word.

> "Oh, my God! then all is lost, for it is now too late! Can it be possible you have not understood me?" – "No, my Lord," said I; "but I pray you to try and inform me once more." "How can I?" rejoined my master; "it is now too late, and all is over!" I said, "Not our will, but God's be done!" and he answered, "Yes, not mine be done – but I will try –" His Lordship did indeed make several efforts to speak, but could only repeat two or three words at a time – such as "My wife! my child! my sister! – you know all – you must say all – you know my wishes!"[7]

The rest was quite unintelligible.

The doctors then induced him to take a little Peruvian bark (which contains quinine). Tita and Parry rubbed his hands, and Parry removed the bandages from his head which seemed to give him some relief. "Ah, Christi!" and the tears flowed down his cheeks. Parry encouraged him to weep, telling him that it would bring the sleep he craved. He uttered a faint goodnight, and fell into a deep slumber. Occasionally they could catch names – Augusta, Ada, Kinnaird, Hobhouse – sums of money; and once, "Why was I not made aware of this sooner? Why did I not go home before I left here?" There is no recorded reference to Teresa. All that night they kept watch. "Poor Greece – poor town – my poor servants. *Io lascio qualche cosa di caro nel mondo.*" He called out, "Clare." (Mary Shelley later thought he meant "Claire".) There is no mention of Loukas (perhaps for reasons of discretion), but he couldn't bear to have Tita out of his sight. One wonders at this point: is there a possibility that as a handsome young gondolier in Venice, Tita had replaced Rushton who in turn had replaced Edelston and the Harrow favourites as deep emotional necessities in Byron's life? Fletcher, Tita, Bruno, Millingen, Gamba, Parry – these were the witnesses to the end of the turbulent life. All the following day they maintained the vigil. His breathing was irregular, but by now he did not seem to be suffering greatly. There was a rattling and choking in his throat every half-hour. Just after six he opened his eyes briefly and then closed them again. "Oh, my God," Fletcher cried, "I fear his Lordship is gone." The doctors felt his pulse. "You are right – he is gone."

That night a fearsome thunderstorm broke over the town. The super-stitious Greeks told each other that it was a sign that a great man had died.

Four days after his death, Augusta wrote anxiously: "I have been in a sad fret My dearest B. having read in the n.papers of a Scurvi . . . & God knows what – I have made every enquiry of Mr Kinnaird & Mr Hobhouse, who have promised me all the intelligence they may receive . . ." She had heard that Colonel Stanhope had confirmed that he had been ill. "*Pray* write – I hope you will when you consider the distance – & the anxiety such reports & accounts on that subject – Fletcher promised me *faithfully* he would write to me if ever you were ill – remind him of this dearest B. – let me hear of you & that you are well – I daresay you have been fagging yourself to death as you never could do any thing in Moderation." She enclosed a bulletin on Ada received from Lady Byron. Augusta herself had seen the child recently, and could report a strong family likeness. "I hope you have received all my letters & that this will also reach you – & above all that I shall soon hear from you as well – Ever my dearest B. your affectionate Augusta."[8]

Epilogue

Most biographies end with the death of the subject. But Byron was no ordinary hero, and it was inevitable that there would be messes to be cleared up, loose ends to untangle, unresolved relationships to be played out.

Had he, as he feared during those final days, accomplished nothing by coming to Greece? In actuality his death apotheosised him into myth, and in consequence alerted the European powers to assist the Greeks in their bid for freedom. The man himself was absorbed within the myth. From the moment of his death, his own wishes were disregarded in the service of his reputation. The last time he had expressed any desire to be buried in England was when his dog Boatswain died in 1808 and he had said that he was determined to be buried in the garden of Newstead beside his pet. Then in the bitterness of exile, he did not want to return to England, dead or alive. To Hoppner, as they rode along the Lido, he uttered the longing to be buried on that lonely strand. After his arrival in Greece, he repeatedly pleaded to be left there undisturbed.

Only Leicester Stanhope argued for his interment on top of the Parthenon. The English authorities in Zante insisted that the body be brought back to England. The body had to be embalmed, but first the doctors present could not resist the opportunity of an autopsy. Millingen has left us a rhapsodic account of the five physicians standing in awe gazing at the beautiful form before attacking it with their saws – again, a promise broken within days after a solemn vow had been given that his body would be left undisturbed.

Their methods were so crude that we have no way of knowing how reliable their reports were. Millingen seemed most impressed by the state of the bones in the head which struck him as those of an old man. Certainly by then Byron's hair was white. The intestines were preserved in four separate jars (the lungs have never been found), and the corpse spliced together and placed in a tin coffin. It was then carried to the recently arrived ship *Florida* which had brought the long-awaited Greek loan. On May 4 she sailed from Missolonghi to the sound of the cannon that had greeted Byron's arrival the previous year.

Dr Bruno, Stanhope, the servants, and Byron's dogs accompanied what Augusta would describe as "the dear Remains" on the doleful voyage which ended in the Thames Estuary on June 29, 1824. Pietro Gamba, concerned lest gossip arise about Byron's relationship with Teresa, tactfully sailed on another vessel. He could not bring himself to break the news to his sister, but left it to their father, Count Gamba, whom the authorities allowed to travel from the fortress in Ferrara to Bologna to comfort his daughter.

News of Byron's death arrived at Kinnaird's home in Pall Mall on May 14, and he immediately sent for Hobhouse. Hobhouse recorded in his diary: "In an agony of grief such as I have experienced only twice before in life, once when I lost my dear friend Charles Skinner Matthews in 1811 and afterwards at Paris when I heard my brother Benjamin had been killed at Waterloo, Quatre Bras – I opened the despatches from Corfu and there saw the details of the fatal event."[1]

On July 2 Hobhouse went aboard the *Florida* just after her arrival, and was distressed by the sight of Byron's dogs playing on the deck. He forced himself to look at the body when it was laid out ceremoniously in Great George Street. The parts had been assembled so clumsily that Hobhouse did not recognise his friend, and to the end of his life his most vivid memory was of Byron's laugh. On July 8 Augusta wrote to Francis Hodgson of her agonised visit two days before: "It was awful to behold what I parted with convulsed with grief, now cold and inanimate, and so altered that I could scarcely persuade myself it was him – not a vestige of what he was. But God's will be done!"[2]

The carcass was not the real Byron. The vital Byron – recorder of his own life – had already been destroyed in Murray's parlour on May 17. Hobhouse was determined on the destruction of the memoirs even though he had never read them. He had already persuaded Augusta to be discreet about a letter from Fletcher in which he had referred to the fact that Byron had had a Bible with him during his last days. He had also persuaded her that the memoirs must never see the light of day, even though Kinnaird, Caroline Lamb, Lord and Lady Holland,

and a host of others had read them without being shocked.

It is strange that Hobhouse showed no curiosity about reading the memoirs. A possible reason for this is that, remembering how Byron had behaved treacherously to him on at least one occasion, he feared that he might read something that might hurt him once again. The memoirs must be destroyed, he argued, because he had heard that the manuscript contained graphic accounts of Byron's sexual adventures, and the publication of these would destroy a reputation that had recently been enhanced by Byron's death in a noble cause.

On May 17 Hobhouse, Murray, and Moore met in Hobhouse's rooms in Albany. To Hobhouse's surprise, Murray agreed that publication was impossible (even though he claimed that he had not read the memoirs). They then adjourned to Albemarle Street where they were joined by Colonel Francis Doyle in his capacity as a watching brief for Lady Byron, and Wilmot Horton* representing Mrs Leigh, although still actually a tacit ally of Lady Byron's as he had been during the separation proceedings. A heated argument broke out, with Moore making many alternative suggestions for the preservation of the document Byron had given him at La Mira in 1819. He was inevitably overruled. Wilmot Horton and Doyle started tearing up the pages and hurriedly thrusting them into the fire. At one point Hobhouse was offered a batch, but he nervously refused. Was he reproaching himself that in these last emotional moments he had allowed his friend to be seized by the enemy?[3]

The burning of the memoirs reignited the sensationalism of Byron's death, and possibly played some part in the refusal to permit his body to be buried in Westminster Abbey. On July 9 and 10 the body was accessible to the public, and immense numbers of people applied to view it. Augusta wished it to be interred in the Byron family vault in Hucknall Torkard. As the funeral cortège wound its way through the crowded streets of London, the hearse was followed by a bizarre procession of empty carriages belonging to the great families who were reluctant to express more than the mere formality of mourning.

Mary Shelley viewed the ascent of the hearse up Highgate Hill, and was flooded with a wave of affection for the aggravating figure of whom she had so many memories. As the procession approached Welwyn, William Lamb, who had just ridden out of the gates of Brocket with Caroline following in a carriage, enquired whose funeral it was. Caroline was not told until the following day when she wrote to Murray that

---

* Robert Wilmot had recently added Horton to his name because of an inheritance.

"I am very sorry I ever said one unkind word against him."[4] Caroline herself was dead four years later.

By the time the coffin reached Nottingham, the black plumes were covered with dust. For four days the curious thronged to view it. On the 16th the procession, now joined by Hobhouse and Colonel Wildman, set off for Hucknall Torkard. There are many accounts of the undignified scene of the noisy, jostling crowd who made it difficult to carry the coffin into the church. When Hobhouse went down into the vault to see where his friend had been laid, he was told that the coffin had been placed on top of that of the fifth lord. Noticing that it had been put next to that of Byron's mother, he requested that it be moved above hers but was told that it would crush the coffin underneath.

Byron's friends flocked to commiserate on the death with Augusta. The heir, Captain George Byron, had broken the news to Annabella; and reported to Hobhouse that she was in a distressed state: she said she had no right to be considered by Lord Byron's friends, but she had her feelings.[5] How deep her feelings were can be gauged by a remark to Hugh Montgomery: "I do not like the *unkin*-like action of all the Lambs, except William, being mourners at Lord Byron's funeral."[6] She sent for Fletcher; and Mary Shelley reported to Trelawny that "he found her in a fit of passionate grief, but perfectly implacable, and as much resolved never to have united herself again to him as she was when she first signed their separation."[7] Mrs Villiers was told that Ada wept on hearing of her father's death, but it was Annabella's view that "I believe more from the sight of my agitation, and from the thought that she might have lost *me*, than from any other cause, for what could an unseen being be to a child like her? It is a great comfort to me that I have never had to give her a painful impression of her father."[8]

The end of the uneasy alliance between Annabella and Augusta was to be precipitated by Byron's death. The underlying cause was money, although Annabella would never admit such a sordid reason to herself. For over two years there had been rumours that Byron had made a new will in Genoa: and Augusta, with her usual burdensome financial problems, was in a state of anxiety until Byron's banker, Barry, after a thorough examination of his papers, could assure Hobhouse that no will was to be found. This left the 1815 will – in which Augusta was made the sole heir – as the binding one. Augusta was genuinely embarrassed that nothing except the title was left to George Byron. When she expressed her feelings to Annabella, the latter replied with a barbed undercurrent of malice:

I am . . . very far from wishing to deny now what I have more than once said to my husband – that it was his duty to provide for you and yours. How far *exclusively* is a question which I am relieved to be under no necessity of discussing – & therefore certainly shall say nothing about the matter, whatever may be said *for* me. I am sure you would not consider it as a kindness on my part to *congratulate* you on that accession – but I sincerely hope your cares may be lightened.[9]

But Augusta was not – nor ever would be – a rich woman since she could claim her inheritance only with Annabella's death. Annabella, who had no money problems, made over her jointure of £2,000 a year to George Byron, an act that managed to get into the newspapers. It was applauded by her supporters, and regarded by sceptics as one of her attempts to achieve sanctity. In later years she enlisted a gullible Mrs Harriet Beecher Stowe to write her *apologia pro vita sua* which appeared in 1870, ten years after Annabella's death, as *Lady Byron Vindicated*.

In 1826, Augusta had been forced to turn to Lady Byron for financial help when Georgiana married Henry Trevanion. Within a very short time the bride's younger sister Medora had borne three children to this same brother-in-law, Henry Trevanion. Eventually Annabella took control of the situation, now acting as Medora's guardian angel, and felt it her duty to inform her of her conviction that Byron was her father. Ada was then also told the alleged truth, and Annabella arranged for the two young women to meet in Paris.

As the years passed Annabella became more and more eccentric. She took it into her head that Augusta had prevented a reconciliation with Byron, and that if it hadn't been for Augusta's interference her husband would have come crawling on his knees begging for forgiveness. Perhaps she could wrest a further confession from Augusta? At the end of March 1851 the two women, both now elderly, had a final meeting in the White Hart Hotel in Reigate. Augusta stood her ground. Within a year as she lay dying, Emily, the only child from whom Augusta was not estranged, had to admit to "a pecuniary difficulty". Annabella sent money; and in a more spiritual mode Emily was instructed to whisper into her dying mama's ear the comforting words, "Dearest Augusta".

As for the child Byron had longed to see, Ada became a mathematical genius; and with Charles Babbage devised the first computer. Perhaps she had inherited her love of numbers from her papa rather than from the "Princess of Parallelograms" who had actually never demonstrated much understanding of figures. She asked to be buried next to her father when she died in 1852.

The cast of characters was widely dispersed. Pietro Gamba did not return to Italy since imprisonment awaited him. Instead, he returned to Greece, joined the army, and died of typhus in 1827. Count Ruggero Gamba was imprisoned in Ferrara until 1831, and eventually was able to end his days on his estate at Filetto in 1840.

Compared to the rest of the family, Teresa survived remarkably well. In 1826 she returned to her husband, but after five months fled to her father in Ferrara. For several years she passed the winters in Rome where she had an affair with Byron's lame friend, Henry Edward Fox, who found her as difficult to handle as Byron had done.

In 1847 – at the age of forty-seven – she married the Marquis de Boissy, two years her senior. They maintained a luxurious and hospitable Parisian salon where the marquis would boast proudly of his wife having been Byron's mistress, and Teresa would tell visitors that Byron had sacrificed his life in Greece because they could not marry.

Kinnaird succumbed to an early death from cancer in 1830. Hobhouse, as executor, undertook to sort out Byron's chaotic trail of debts. One of these was Pellegrino Ghigi, the banker in Ravenna, who was finally reimbursed for Allegra's funeral expenses.

Hobhouse's life followed a predictable course of respectability. His path and Annabella's crossed once more. In 1834 Annabella and Ada were riding on the road between Bakewell and Buxton, and through the carriage window Lady Byron recognised a portly gentleman, now Sir John Hobhouse, whom she had not laid eyes on since 1815. Concentrating on his walk, he did not appear to notice her.

John Fitzgibbon, second Earl of Clare, married in 1826. From 1830 to 1834 he served as governor of Bombay. He died without issue in 1851.

As for the humbler figures in the cast, Tita Falcieri fared better perhaps than anyone. He was employed in Greece by Henry Bulwer and Benjamin Disraeli; he married Mrs Disraeli's maid and eventually became a messenger in the India Office.

Parry died an alcoholic. Loukas died in Greece within a year of Byron's death, apparently from a combination of malnutrition and disease. Benjamin Lewis, the black groom, was also dead of unknown causes in England a year later. Dr Bruno attended Byron's funeral in Hucknall Torkard, and returned penniless to Italy. For a time Fletcher was given a small annuity by Augusta. He and Lega Zambelli started a pasta factory together, but it eventually foundered. Fletcher then pleaded with Hobhouse that Byron had left him £50 in his earlier will, but Hobhouse failed to help him, and in 1858 he died in the workhouse at the age of sixty-four.[10]

The Napoleonic coach was disposed of for a pittance in Genoa. It is to be hoped that Baxter, the coach-builder, after waiting ten years, finally received some payment.

References

BERG: The New York Public Library, Astor, Lenox and Tilden Foundations.

BLESSINGTON: Lady Blessington, *Conversations of Lord Byron with the Countess of Blessington*. London: R. Bentley, 1834.

BORST: William A. Borst, *Lord Byron's First Pilgrimage*. New Haven: Yale UP, 1948.

BP: Broughton Papers, British Library.

BROUGHTON: Lord Broughton, *Recollections of a Long Life*, 4 vols. London: John Murray, 1909.

BURNETT: T.A.J. Burnett, *The Rise and Fall of a Regency Dandy*. London: John Murray, 1981.

Byron's Bulldog: Peter W. Graham, ed., *Byron's Bulldog: The Letters of John Cam Hobhouse to Lord Byron*. Columbus: Ohio State UP, 1984.

CH: *Childe Harold's Pilgrimage, A Romaunt*.

Clairmont: Marion Kingston Stocking, ed., *The Clairmont Correspondence*, 2 vols. Baltimore: Johns Hopkins UP, 1995.

CROMPTON: Louis Crompton, *Byron and Greek Love*. London: Faber and Faber, 1985.

DALLAS: R.C. Dallas, *Recollections of the Life of Lord Byron, from the year 1808 to the end of 1814*. London: Charles Knight, 1824.

DJ: *Don Juan*.

EBSR: *English Bards and Scotch Reviewers*.

EG: Egerton Papers, British Library.

ELWIN: Malcolm Elwin, *Lord Byron's Wife*. London: Macdonald, 1962.

FOOT: Michael Foot, *The Politics of Paradise: A Vindication of Lord Byron*. London: Collins, 1988.

GALT: John Galt, *The Life of Lord Byron*. London: Henry Colburn and Richard Bentley, 1831.

GAMBA: Count Peter Gamba, *A Narrative of Lord Byron's Last Journey to Greece*. London: John Murray, 1825.

GRONOW: Captain R.H. Gronow, *The Reminiscences and Recollections of Captain Gronow, 1810–1860*, 2 vols. London: John C. Nimmo, 1900.

GROSSKURTH: Phyllis Grosskurth, ed., *The Memoirs of John Addington Symonds*. New York: Random House, 1984.

GUNN: Peter Gunn, *My Dearest Augusta: A Biography of Augusta Leigh, Lord Byron's Half-Sister*. New York: Atheneum, 1968.

HARNESS: Reverend A.G. L'Estrange, *The Literary Life of the Rev. William Harness*. London: 1871.

HEROLD: J. Christopher Herold, *Mistress to an Age: A Life of Madame de Staël*. Boston: Bobbs-Merrill, 1958.

HOBHOUSE: Broughton, Lord (John Cam Hobhouse), *A Journey through Albania and other provinces of Turkey in Europe and Asia to Constantinople*. London: J. Cawthorn, 1813.

HODGSON: Francis Hodgson, *Memoir of the Rev. Francis Hodgson, B.D.*, 2 vols. London: Macmillan, 1878.

HUNT: Leigh Hunt, *The Autobiography of Leigh Hunt*, 2 vols. New York: Harper and Brothers, 1850.

HUNT LETTERS: *The Correspondence of Leigh Hunt*, 2 vols., ed. by his Eldest Son. London: Smith Elder, 1862.

LANGLEY MOORE: Doris Langley Moore, *Lord Byron: Accounts Rendered*. London: John Murray, 1974.

Letters: Leslie A. Marchand, ed., *Byron's Letters and Journals*, 12 vols. London: John Murray, 1973–94.

LP: Lovelace Papers.

MAM: Megan Boyes, *My Amiable Mamma: A Biography of Mrs Catherine Gordon Byron*. Derby: Megan Boyes, 1991.

MARCHAND: Leslie A. Marchand, *Byron: A Biography*, 3 vols. New York: Knopf, 1957.

MAYNE: Ethel Colburn Mayne, *The Life and Letters of Anne Isabella, Lady Noel Byron*. London: Constable, 1929.

MILLINGEN: Julius Millingen, *Memoirs of the Affairs of Greece*. London: John Rodwell, 1831.

MOORE: Thomas Moore, *The Letters and Journals of Lord Byron with Notices of his Life*, 2 vols. London: John Murray, 1830.

MOORE LETTERS: Wilfred S. Dowden, ed., *The Letters of Thomas Moore*, 2 vols. Oxford: Clarendon Press, 1964.

MWS: Betty T. Bennett, ed., *The Letters of Mary Wollstonecraft Shelley*, 3 vols. Baltimore: Johns Hopkins, 1988.

NICOLSON: Harold Nicolson, *Byron, The Last Journey*. London: Constable, 1924.

ORIGO: Iris Origo, *The Last Attachment*. London: Jonathan Cape, 1949.

PARRY: William Parry, *The Last Days of Lord Byron*. London: Knight and Lacey, 1825.

Prose: Andrew Nicholson, ed., *Lord Byron: The Complete Miscellaneous Prose*. Oxford: Clarendon Press, 1991.

PROTHERO: Rowland E. Prothero, ed., *The Works of Lord Byron; Letters and Journals*, 6 vols. London: John Murray, 1902.

Queen: Megan Boyes, *Queen of a Fantastic Realm: A Biography of Mary Chaworth*. Derby: Megan Boyes, 1986.

Rogers: Edith J. Morley, ed., *Recollections of the Table-Talk of Samuel Rogers*. London: 1938.

Scott: H.J.C. Grierson, ed., *The Letters of Sir Walter Scott*, 12 vols. London: Constable, 1932.

Shelley: F.L. Jones, ed., *The Letters of Percy Bysshe Shelley*, 2 vols. Oxford: Clarendon Press, 1964.

SMILES: Samuel Smiles, *A Publisher and His Friends*. London: John Murray, 1911.

STANHOPE: Colonel Leicester Stanhope, *Greece in 1823 and 1824*. London: Sherwood, Gilbert and Piper, 1825.

TEXAS: Humanities Research Center, The University of Texas at Austin.

To Lord Byron: George Pastor and Peter Quennell, eds., *"To Lord Byron". Feminine Profiles*. London: John Murray, 1939.

TRELAWNY: E.J. Trelawny, *Recollections of the Last Days of Shelley and Byron*. London: Edward Morton, 1858.

Works: Jerome J. McGann, ed., *Lord Byron: The Complete Poetical Works*, 7 vols. Oxford: Clarendon Press, 1980–93.

PROLOGUE

1 *Letters*, 9, p.49
2 March 31, 1824. *Letters*, 11, p.148

CHAPTER 1
THE BYRONS – IMPETUOUS, BAD AND MAD

1 July 7, 1823 (to J.J. Coulmann). *Letters*, 10, p.208
2 Sept. 20, 1821. *Letters*, 8, p.217
3 Texas
4 March 25, 1788. Texas
5 *MAM*, p.30
6 *Ibid.*, p.36
7 *Ibid.*, pp.29–30
8 *Ibid.*, p.31
9 *Ibid.*
10 Langley Moore, p.25
11 Jan. 21, 1791. *Ibid.*, p.34

12 *Ibid.*
13 *MAM*, p.36
14 *Ibid.*, p.37
15 Langley Moore, p.37
16 *MAM*, p.39
17 May 1, 1821. *Letters*, 8, p.107
18 Nov. 26, 1813. *Letters*, 3, p.222
19 *MAM*, p.47
20 *Ibid.*

CHAPTER 2
A NEW LIFE BEGINS, 1798–1803

1 August 16, 1820. *Letters*, 7, p.204
2 See Moore, I, p.25
3 Marchand, I, p.50
4 *MAM*, p.59
5 March 13, 1799. *Letters*, 1, p.39
6 *MAM*, p.64
7 *Ibid.*, p.68

8 "Detached Thoughts", *Letters*, 9, p.40
9 *Ibid.*
10 *MAM*, p.72
11 *Ibid.*, p.79
12 Berg
13 "Detached Thoughts", *Letters*, 9, p.43
14 *Works*, VII, p.145
15 *MAM*, p.84
16 May 1–10, 1804. *Letters*, 1, p.49
17 *MAM*, p.86
18 April 2, 1804. *Letters*, 1, p.47
19 June 23, 1803. *Ibid.*, p.43

CHAPTER 3
SCHOOL DAYS, 1803–5

1 *Letters*, 9, p.34
2 Moore, I, p.56
3 *Ibid.*
4 *Letters*, 1, p.43
5 *MAM*, p.95
6 *Ibid.*, p.96
7 Marchand, I, p.80
8 *Letters*, 9, p.40
9 *MAM*, pp.137–8
10 Grosskurth, p.94
11 Dec. 12, 1804. *MAM*, p.101
12 Langley Moore, p.75
13 Texas
14 *Letters*, 1, p.44
15 *Ibid.*, pp.45–6
16 *Ibid.*, pp.49–50
17 *MAM*, p.102
18 Nov. 2, 1804. *Letters*, 1, p.54
19 *Ibid.*
20 *Ibid.*
21 Nov. 21, 1804. *Ibid.* p.59
22 July 25, 1805. Eg 2612
23 Gunn, p.53
24 Moore, I, p.43
25 Oct. 15, 1821–May 18, 1822 (Journal). *Letters*, 9, p.44
26 Moore, I, p.49
27 Crompton, p.49
28 *Ibid.*, p.49
29 Harness, p.4
30 *MAM*, p.107
31 June 5, 1805. *Letters*, 1, p.68
32 Moore, I, pp.57–8
33 Boyes, *Love Without Wings* (Derby: J.M. Tatter, 1988), p.13

CHAPTER 4
CAMBRIDGE, 1805–8

1 Marchand, I, p.85
2 John Moore, *Zeluco*, I (London: Harrison and Co., 1803), p.194.
3 *Letters*, 9, p.37
4 Nov. 30, 1805. *Letters*, 1, p.83
5 Nov. 6, 1805. *Ibid.*, p.80
6 Nov. 30, 1805. *Ibid.*, p.83
7 *MAM*, p.123
8 "Detached Thoughts", *Letters*, 9, p.37
9 July 5, 1807. *Letters*, 9, p.123
10 *Ibid.*, p.125
11 See Kay Redfield Jamison, *Touched with Fire: Manic Depressive Illness and the Artistic Temperament* (New York: The Free Press, 1993), pp.149–90. She has traced back the genetic transmission of this disorder more than 150 years.
12 See Jerome J. McGann, *Fiery Dust: Byron's Poetic Development* (University of Chicago Press, 1968) p.16
13 *MAM*, p.123
14 March 1807. *Letters*, 1, p.112
15 April 16, 1807 (to Edward Noel Long). *Letters*, 1, p.114
16 Nov. 19, 1820 (to John Murray). *Letters*, 7, p.230
17 Burnett, p.41
18 [Feb. 1808?] *Letters*, 1, p.150
19 Oct. 15, 1821–May 18, 1822 (Journal). *Letters*, 9, p.23
20 Feb. 29, 1808 (to Hobhouse). *Letters*, 1, p.160
21 March 12, 1808. *Byron's Bulldog*, p.29
22 March 13, 1808. *MAM*, p.136
23 *Letters*, 1, p.155
24 *Ibid.*, pp.171–2
25 Nov. 18, 1808 (to Francis Hodgson). *Ibid.*, p.176
26 *Ibid.*, p.175

CHAPTER 5
BITTER-SWEET DEPARTURE,
JANUARY–JULY 1809

1 Jan. 16, 1809 (to Hobhouse). *Letters*, 1, p.188
2 [n.d.] Eg 2611
3 Feb. 8, 1809. *Letters*, 1, p.192

4 March 6, 1809. *Ibid.*, p.195
5 April 9, 1809. Eg 2611
6 June 17, 1809. *Ibid.*
7 Dallas, p.54
8 *Works*, I, p.418n
9 April 17, 1809. Dallas, p.57
10 Dallas, p.64
11 Prothero, I, p.155
12 May 19, 1809. *Letters*, I, p.203
13 June 20, 1809. Burnett, pp.70–77
14 *Ibid.*, p.82
15 *Ibid.*, p.80
16 June 30, 1809. *Letters*, I, p.213
17 Burnett, pp.79–80
18 *Ibid.*, p.82
19 June 25, 1809. *Letters*, I, p.208
20 *Ibid.*, p.208
21 *Ibid.*, p.206
22 *Ibid.*, p.210
23 Eg 2611
24 Medwin, *The Conversations of Lord Byron* p.77

CHAPTER 6
THE GREAT ADVENTURE,
JULY–DECEMBER 1809

1 See Charles Oman, *A History of the Peninsular War*, II (1903), p.453
2 Aug. 11, 1809. *Letters*, I, p.218
3 *Ibid.*, p.220
4 Aug. 6, 1809. *Ibid.*, p.216
5 BP
6 Aug. 7, 1809. *Letters*, I, p.218
7 Galt, p.58
8 *Ibid.*, p.59
9 *Ibid.*, p.61
10 BP
11 See William St Clair, *Lord Elgin and the Marbles* (Oxford: Oxford UP, 1983), p.131
12 Sept. 15, 1812. *Letters*, 2, p.198
13 May 3, 1810. *Letters*, I, p.239
14 Hobhouse, I, p.8
15 *Ibid.*, p.52
16 Nov. 12, 1809. *Letters*, I, p.227
17 BP
18 *Ibid.*
19 *Ibid.*
20 Nov. 12, 1809. *Letters*, I, pp.230–1
21 March 20, 1814. *Letters*, 3, p.253
22 Hobhouse, II, p.46

CHAPTER 7
ATHENS, CONSTANTINOPLE,
JANUARY–JULY, 1810

1 See William St Clair, *Lord Elgin and the Marbles* (Oxford: Oxford UP, 1983), p.97
2 Jan. 29, 1810. BP
3 Jan. 26, 1810. *Ibid.*
4 March 19, 1810. *Letters*, I, p.234
5 Hobhouse, I, p.36
6 May 3, 1810. *Letters*, I, p.238
7 *Works*, 2, p.201
8 St Clair, *Lord Elgin*, p.161
9 May 3, 1810 (to Henry Drury). *Letters*, I, p.240
10 Galt, p.128
11 *MAM*, p.156
12 May 11, 1811. Eg 2611
13 *Ibid.*
14 March 18, 1810. BP
15 March 19, 1810. *Ibid.*
16 *Ibid.*
17 Jan. 11, 1821 (Journal). *Letters*, 8, p.22
18 May 10, 1810. BP
19 May 16, 1810. *Ibid.*
20 June 28, 1810. *Letters*, I, p.251
21 May 30, 1810. BP
22 July 6, 1810. *Ibid.*
23 July 4, 1810. *Letters*, I, p.256
24 June 23, 1810 (to Dallas). *Ibid.*, p.248–9
25 *Ibid.*, p.249
26 June 28, 1810. *Ibid.*, pp.251–2
27 Marchand, I, p.249
28 July 17, 1810. BP

CHAPTER 8
RELUCTANT RETURN,
1810–1811

1 Moore, I, p.242
2 July 29, 1810. *Letters*, 2, p.6
3 Aug. 16, 1810 (to Hobhouse). *Ibid.*, p.10
4 Aug. 23, 1810. *Ibid.*, p.12
5 *Ibid.*, p.14
6 Oct. 4, 1810. *Ibid.*, p.21
7 Marchand, I, p.259
8 Oct. 3, 1810. *Ibid.*, p.19
9 *Ibid.*, p.25
10 Eg 2611
11 Jan. 10, 1811 (to Hobhouse). *Letters*, 2, p.31

12 *Ibid.*, p.41
13 *To Lord Byron*, p.13
14 *Ibid.*, pp.13–14
15 Sept. 15, 1812. *Letters*, 2, p.199
16 May 22, 1811. *Ibid.*, pp.47–8
17 Murray Archives

CHAPTER 9
ENCOUNTERS WITH DEATH,
1811

1 Dallas, p.104
2 *Ibid.*, p.114
3 Broughton, I, p.35
4 July 31, 1811. *Letters*, 2, p.64
5 *Byron's Bulldog*, p.74
6 *MAM*, p.173
7 Galt, p.160
8 Aug. 3, 1811. BP
9 Aug. 7, 1811 (to Scrope Berdmore Davies). *Letters*, 2, p.68
10 *Ibid.*, p.68
11 Aug. 25, 1811. *Byron's Bulldog*, p.77
12 Aug. 12, 1811. *Letters*, 2, p.73
13 Gunn, p.73
14 *Ibid.*, p.74
15 *Ibid.*, p.76
16 *Ibid.*
17 Sept. 2, 1811. *Letters*, 2, p.85
18 *Ibid.*, p.89
19 Murray Archives
20 Dallas, p.160
21 Sept. 17, 1811. *Letters*, 2, p.101
22 Sept. 25, 1811 (to Hodgson). *Letters*, 2, p.106
23 Sept. 20, 1811. *Ibid.*, p.102
24 Oct. 11, 1811. *Ibid.*, p.110
25 *Ibid.*
26 Nov. 16, 1811. *Letters*, 2, p.130
27 Oct. 22, 1811. Moore, *Letters* I
28 *Ibid.* p.165
29 *Ibid.*
30 *Ibid.*, p.168
31 Gronow, I., p.253
32 *Ibid.*
33 *Byron's Bulldog*, p.86
34 Dec. 15, 1811 (to Harness). *Letters*, 2, p.149
35 Dec. 15, 1811. *Ibid.*, p.147
36 Jan. 15, 1812. *To Lord Byron*, p.29
37 *Letters*, II, p.158

38 Murray Archives
39 Jan. 28, 1812. *Letters*, 2, p.159
40 Dec. 17, 1811. *Ibid.*, p.151

CHAPTER 10
THE LONDON WHIRLIGIG, 1812

1 Foot, p.135
2 *Prose*, p.26
3 Lord Holland, *Further Memoirs of the Whig Party 1807–1821* (London: John Murray, 1905), p.123
4 Malcolm Kelsall, *Byron's Politics* (New York: Barnes & Noble, 1987), p.45
5 See William St Clair, "The Impact of Byron's Writings, An Evaluative Approach", in Andrew Rutherford, ed., *Byron, Augustan and Romantic* (Basingstoke: Macmillan, 1990)
6 LP
7 *Ibid.*
8 *Ibid.*
9 *Ibid.*
10 March 1812. *Byron's Bulldog*, p.99
11 Gronow, I, p.37
12 LP
13 Elwin, p.140
14 Dallas, p.233
15 *Ibid.*, p.240
16 *Ibid.*, p.241
17 April 26, 1812. Mayne, p.41
18 Margot Strickland, *The Byron Women* (London: Peter Owen, 1974), p.49
19 March 15, 1812. LP
20 Murray Archives
21 LP
22 *Ibid.*
23 *Prose*, p.43
24 Murray Archives
25 August 1812. *Letters*, 2, pp.185–6
26 Mabell, Countess of Airlie, *In Whig Society 1775–1881* (London: Hodder and Stoughton, 1921), p.121

CHAPTER 11
COMPULSIVE THRALDOM,
1812–13

1 March 26, 1813. Murray Archives
2 *Ibid.*
3 Sept. 15, 1812. *Letters*, 2, p.198

4 Sept. 18, 1812. *Ibid.*, p.199
5 Oct. 18, 1812. *Ibid.*, p.229
6 LP
7 Nov. 14, 1812 (to Lady Melbourne). *Letters*, 2, p.246
8 LP
9 Oct. 25, 1812, *Ibid.*
10 Nov. 1812?. *Letters*, 2, p.242
11 Nov.–Dec. 1812. *Lord Byron's Bulldog*, p.106
12 *Notes and Queries*, v.212, Jan.–Dec. 1967, p.298
13 Philip Ziegler, *Melbourne: A Biography of William Lamb, 2nd Viscount Melbourne* (New York: Knopf, 1976), p.53
14 Hunt *Letters*, I., p.88
15 Edward Blunden, *Leigh Hunt* (London: Cobden-Sanderson, 1930), p.78
16 Murray Archives
17 May 24, 1813. *Letters*, 3, p.51
18 March 14, 1813. *Ibid.*, p.26
19 *To Lord Byron*, p.46

CHAPTER 12
A DANGEROUS PASSION,
1813–14

1 March 26, 1813. *Letters*, 3, p.32
2 Aug. 22, 1813. *Ibid.*, p.96
3 Nov. 25, 1813 (to Lady Melbourne). *Ibid.*, p.174
4 Nov. 14, 1813 (Journal). *Ibid.*, p.204
5 Nov. 24, 1813. *Ibid.*, p.219
6 *Ibid.*, p.239
7 April 30, 1814. *Letters*, 4, p.110
8 Nov. 29, 1813 (to Annabella Milbanke). *Letters*, 3, p.178
9 LP
10 Aug. 23, 1813. *Letters*, 3, p.99
11 LP
12 *Ibid.*
13 Nov. 10, 1813. *Letters*, 3, p.160
14 Nov. 27, 1813. LP
15 Dec. 5, 1813. Elwin, p.179
16 Nov. 17, 1813. *Letters*, 3, p.212
17 Dec. 1, 1813. *Ibid.*, p.228
18 *Queen*, p.56
19 Jan. 8, 1814. *Letters*, 4, p.19
20 Sept. 1, 1813 (to Moore). *Letters*, 3, p.105
21 Feb. 11, 1814. *Letters*, 4, p.54

22 April 25, 1814. *Ibid.*, p.104
23 BP
24 Feb. 19, 1814 (Journal). *Letters*, 3, p.244
25 BP
26 *Ibid.*
27 April 25, 1814 (to Lady Melbourne). *Letters*, 4, p.104
28 Aug. 3, 1814 (to Moore). *Ibid.*, p.152
29 Feb. 27, 1814 (Journal). *Letters*, 3, p.246
30 Murray Archives
31 Aug. 1, 1814. Murray Archives

CHAPTER 13
UNEASY COMMITMENT,
1813–14

1 Nov. 29, 1813 (to Annabella Milbanke). *Letters*, 3, p.179
2 LP
3 *Ibid.*
4 Feb. 12, 1814. *Letters*, 4, pp.56–7
5 Mayne, p.84
6 Feb. 12, 1814. *Letters*, 4, p.56
7 Feb. 17, 1814. LP
8 Feb. 19, 1814 (to Annabella Milbanke). *Letters*, 4, p.66
9 March 12, 1814. LP
10 April 13, 1814. LP
11 LP
12 May 16, 1814. *Letters*, 4, p.116
13 LP
14 *Ibid.*
15 *Ibid.*
16 Aug. 13, 1814. *Ibid.*
17 Sept. 9, 1814. *Letters*, 4, p.169
18 Aug. 14, 1814. LP
19 Sept. 18, 1814. *Letters*, 4, pp.173–4
20 Sept. 18, 1814. *Ibid.*, p.175
21 Sept. 28, 1814. LP
22 BP
23 *Ibid.*
24 *Byron's Bulldog*, p.138
25 Oct. 24, 1814. LP
26 Sept. 20, 1814 (to Moore). *Letters*, 4, p.178
27 Smiles, pp.100–1
28 *Ibid.*
29 All contained in Lovelace Papers
30 Oct. 1, 1814. Elwin, p.215
31 Sept. 25, 1814. *Ibid.*, p.216
32 Sept. 24, 1814. LP

33 Oct. 1, 1814. LP
34 Oct. 7, 1814 (to Annabella Milbanke). *Letters*, 4, p.197
35 Oct. 22, 1814 (to Annabella Milbanke). *Ibid.*, p.222
36 Oct. 1, 1814. LP
37 Oct. 24, 1816 (to Mrs Villiers). LP
38 Oct. 7, 1814. *Letters*, 4, p.198
39 Oct. 7, 1814. *Ibid.*, p.199
40 Sept. 29, 1814. LP
41 Sept. 26, 1814. *Letters*, 4, p.182
42 Nov. 23, 1814. LP
43 Murray Archives
44 *Ibid.*
45 Oct. 15, 1814. LP
46 *Ibid.*
47 Broughton, II, p.49

CHAPTER 14
THE FATAL MARRIAGE, 1814–15

1 LP
2 *Ibid.*
3 Nov. 4, 1814. *Ibid.*
4 Nov. 4, 1814. *Letters*, 4, p.228
5 Jan. 26, 1815. *Ibid.*, p.259
6 Nov. 4, 1814. *Ibid.*, p.229
7 Statement L, LP
8 Hodgson, I, p.289
9 LP
10 *Ibid.*
11 Dec. 8, 1814. *Letters*, 4, p.241
12 Dec. 10, 1814. LP
13 Dec. 12, 1814. Gunn, p.120
14 BP
15 *Ibid.*
16 *Ibid.*
17 Gunn, p.121
18 LP
19 Jan. 28, 1816. LP
20 Mayne, p.172
21 Feb. 19, 1815. LP
22 Feb. 7, 1815. Elwin, p.277
23 Feb. 8, 1815. LP
24 1815. *Ibid.*
25 *Ibid.*
26 *Ibid.*
27 *Ibid.*
28 Feb. 15, 1815. Hodgson, II, pp.7–12
29 LP
30 *Ibid.*

CHAPTER 15
ANNUS HORRIBILIS, 1815

1 Statement Y, LP
2 Annabella described the experience to her daughter Ada in a letter of March 8, 1841. See Appendix 3, pp.172–3, in Doris Langley Moore, *Ada, Countess of Lovelace* (London: John Murray, 1977)
3 March 18, 1815. Hodgson, II, p.13
4 March 31, 1815. Hodgson, II, pp.16–17
5 Sept. 1815. See Vere Foster, ed., *The Two Duchesses* (London: Blackie and Son, 1898), p.408
6 April 1, 1815. BP
7 LP
8 *Ibid.*
9 July 6, 1812. *Letters*, 2, p.182
10 April 13–14?, 1815. *Letters*, 4, p.287
11 LP
12 *Ibid.*
13 *Ibid.*
14 *Ibid.*
15 *Ibid.*
16 BP
17 Gunn, p.144

CHAPTER 16
VENGEFUL WOMEN, 1816

1 Jan. 15, 1816. LP
2 *Ibid.*
3 *Ibid.*
4 Jan. 16, 1816. *Ibid.*
5 Jan. 20, 1816. *Ibid.*
6 Jan. 17, 1816. *Ibid.*
7 *Ibid.*
8 John C. Fox, *The Byron Mystery* (London: Grant Richards, 1924), p.104
9 LP
10 Jan. 18, 1816. *Ibid.*
11 Feb. 2, 1816. *Ibid.*
12 Jan. 21, 1816 (to Lady Noel). *Ibid.*
13 Jan. 22, 1816 (to Lady Noel). *Ibid.*
14 Jan. 25, 1816 (to Annabella). *Ibid.*
15 Jan. 23, 1816 (to Annabella). *Ibid.*
16 Jan. 25, 1816 (to Annabella). *Ibid.*
17 *Ibid.*
18 Jan. 26, 1816 (to Lady Noel). *Ibid.*
19 Jan. 30, 1816. Elwin, p.385
20 Feb. 7, 1816. *Letters*, 5, p.21
21 Feb. 2, 1816 (to Sir Ralph Noel).

Letters, 5, pp.20–1
22 Feb. 2, 1816. LP
23 Feb. 4, 1816. In Doris Langley Moore, *The Late Lord Byron* (London: John Murray, 1961), p.140
24 Feb. 3, 1816. LP
25 *Ibid.* LP
26 Feb. 5, 1816. *Letters*, 5, p.22
27 Feb. 7, 1816. Mayne, p.211
28 See Michael Joyce, *My Friend H* (London: John Murray, 1948), p.98
29 Feb. 11, 1816 (to Lushington). LP
30 BP
31 Feb. 15, 1816. LP
32 *Ibid.*
33 Feb. 19, 1816. *Ibid.*
34 *Ibid.*
35 Feb. 9, 1816 (to Annabella). *Ibid.*
36 *Ibid.*
37 Statement PM. *Ibid.*
38 *Ibid.*
39 Joan Pierson, *The Real Lady Byron* (London: Robert Hale, 1992), p.140
40 LP
41 Feb. 26, 1816. *Ibid.*
42 See Malcolm Elwin, *Lord Byron's Family* (London: John Murray, 1975), p.27
43 March 4, 1816. LP
44 [n.d.] *Ibid.*
45 Feb. 16, 1816. *Ibid.*
46 March 23, 1816. *Ibid.*
47 Elwin, p.456
48 [n.d.] LP
49 [n.d.] *Ibid.*
50 March 28, 1816. *Ibid.*
51 Broughton, II, p.319
52 *Ibid.*, p.320
53 *Ibid.*, p.319
54 [March 1816] Moore Letters, p.390
55 LP
56 Gunn, p.177

CHAPTER 17
ESCAPE, 1816

1 *Prose*, p.95
2 *Ibid.*, p.97
3 Elwin, p.433
4 Elwin, *Lord Byron's Family* (London: John Murray, 1975), p.21
5 April 9, 1816. BP

6 Elwin, p.462
7 Blessington, p.23
8 Elwin, p.463
9 April 13, 1816. LP
10 [March or April 1816] *Clairmont*, I, p.25
11 *Harness*, p.21
12 [n.d.] LP
13 Mayne, p.220
14 *Letters*, 5, p.64
15 April 2, 1816. LP
16 April 13, 1816. BP
17 Elwin, p.443
18 March 23, 1816. LP
19 April 22, 1816 (to Augusta Leigh). *Letters*, 5, p.69
20 Marchand, II, p.606
21 April 30, 1816. LP
22 [n.d.] *Ibid.*

CHAPTER 18
EXILE, AUGUST–SEPTEMBER
1816

1 Quoted by D.L. Macdonald, *Poor Polidori* (University of Toronto Press, 1991), p.62
2 May 1, 1816 (to Augusta Leigh). *Letters*, 5, pp.74–5
3 Marchand, II, p.611
4 May 16, 1816 (to John Cam Hobhouse). *Letters.*, 5, p.76
5 May 16, 1816. *Ibid.*, p.77
6 May 25, 1816. *Clairmont*, I, p.46
7 May 27, 1816. *Ibid.*
8 Michael Joyce, *My Friend H* (London: John Murray, 1948), p.222
9 June 23, 1816 (to Hobhouse). *Letters*, 5, p.81
10 July 20, 1816. *Ibid.*, p.83
11 June 8, 1816. Joyce, *Hobhouse*, p.226
12 Elwin, p.33
13 LP
14 *Ibid.*
15 June 3, 1816 (to Mrs Villiers). Malcolm Elwin, *Lord Byron's Family* (London: John Murray, 1975), p.42
16 *Ibid.*
17 Hodgson, II, pp.35–6
18 July 3, 1816. Gunn p.191
19 July 15, 1816. *Ibid.*
20 June 27, 1816 (to Murray). *Letters*, 5, p.82

21 July 1816. *Clairmont*, I, p.51
22 *Shelley*, I, p.491
23 Jan. 28, 1817. *Letters*, 5, p.165
24 Thomas Medwin, *Conversations of Lord Byron* (London: Henry Colburn, 1824), p.11
25 Blessington, p.242
26 August 29, 1816. *Clairmont*, I, p.70
27 Sept. 1, 1817. BP
28 Prothero, III, pp.347–8
29 Sept. 8, 1816. *Letters*, 5, p.92
30 Aug. 24, 1816. *Ibid.*, pp.87–8
31 August 23, 1816. Elwin, *Lord Byron's Family*, p.86
32 *Ibid.*, p.96
33 July 9, 1816. LP
34 *Ibid.*

CHAPTER 19
TO ITALY, 1816

1 Sept. 17, 1816 (to Augusta Leigh). *Letters*, 5, p.96
2 Sept. 29, 1816. *Shelley*, I, pp.506–7
3 Sept. 29, 1816. *Clairmont*, I, p.77
4 Statement K. LP
5 Sept. 17, 1816. LP
6 Sept. 30, 1816. *Ibid.*
7 Sept. 1816. *Ibid.*
8 Sept. 19, 1816. *Ibid.*
9 Oct. 15, 1816 (to Augusta Leigh). *Letters*, 5, p.114
10 LP
11 *Letters*, 5, p.119
12 *Ibid.* Oct. 24, 1816 (to Mrs Villiers). LP
13 Oct. 29, 1816. Hodgson, II, p.40
14 Oct. 29, 1816. *Ibid.*, pp.41–2
15 Nov. 6, 1816. *Letters*, 5, p.126
16 Nov. 11, 1816. *Ibid.*, p.128
17 Nov. 19, 1816. LP

CHAPTER 20
ANTEROOM TO THE EAST, 1816–17

1 Dec. 2, 1816 (to Lady Anne Barnard). LP
2 Hodgson, II, p.43
3 LP
4 *Ibid.*
5 Jan. 2, 1817 (to Augusta Leigh). *Letters*, 5, p.154

6 *Clairmont*, I, p.90
7 Dec. 24, 1816 (to Thomas Moore). *Letters*, 5, p.150
8 Jan. 10, 1817. *Scott*, IV, p.365
9 Dec. 27, 1816 (to John Murray). *Letters*, p.151
10 BP
11 Nov. 17, 1816 (to Thomas Moore). *Letters*, 5, p.130
12 Dec. 19, 1816 (to Augusta). *Ibid.*, p.144
13 LP
14 *Ibid.*
15 Jan. 20, 1817 (to Douglas Kinnaird). *Letters*, 5, p.161
16 *Ibid.*, p.161
17 Dec. 24, 1816. *Ibid.*, p.149
18 Feb. 28, 1817 (to Thomas Moore). *Ibid.*, p.177
19 *Ibid.*, p.176
20 LP
21 March 4, 1817. Hodgson, II, p.47
22 April 21, 1818. *Ibid.*, p.49
23 May 30, 1817 *Letters*, 5, p.230
24 May 30, 1817 (to Douglas Kinnaird). *Ibid.*, p.231
25 June 3–4, 1817 (to Augusta Leigh). *Letters*, 5, p.232
26 June 1817. LP
27 July 1817. Mayne, p.271

CHAPTER 21
A NEW LIFE, 1817–18

1 BP
2 Aug. 6, 1817. *Ibid.*
3 Aug. 1, 1819 (to Murray). *Letters*, 6, p.194
4 LP
5 *Ibid.*
6 Sept. 26, 1817. *Scott*, IV, pp.522–3
7 LP
8 BP
9 Joan Pierson, *The Real Lady Byron* (London: Robert Hale, 1992), p.142
10 LP
11 *Ibid.*
12 BP
13 Feb. 27, 1818. LP
14 Jan. 12, 1818. *Clairmont*, I, p.110
15 April 23, 1818 (to Murray). *Letters*, 6, p.34

16 April 8, 1818. LP
17 April 22, 1818. *Shelley*, II, p.410
18 April 28, 1818. *Ibid.*, p.412
19 LP
20 For a brilliant analysis of the poem see Jerome J. McGann, *Fiery Dust: Byron's Poetic Development* (University of Chicago Press, 1968)
21 Mayne, p.277
22 LP

CHAPTER 22
DECADENCE IN VENICE,
1818–19

1 Aug. 23, 1818 (to Mary). *Shelley*, II, p.35
2 Aug. 24, 1818. *Ibid.*, p.36
3 April 6, 1819. *MWS*, II, p.92
4 Dec. 17 or 18, 1818. *Shelley*, II, pp.57–8
5 Sept. 16, 1818. LP
6 Oct. 7, 1818. *Ibid.*
7 Oct. 26, 1818. *Ibid.*
8 Nov. 18, 1818. *Letters*, 6, p.80
9 Hanson Narrative. Murray Archives
10 Dec. 22, 1818. *Ibid.*
11 Dec. 9, 1818. *Letters*, 6, p.88
12 [n.d.] (Nov. 18, 1818) Burnett, p.172
13 Dec. 27, 1818. BP
14 *Byron's Bulldog*, p.259
15 Jan. 25, 1819. *Letters*, 6, p.96
16 Feb 1, 1819, *Ibid*, p.99.
17 June 22, 1819. Murray Archives
18 LP
19 *Ibid.*
20 Mayne, p.283
21 LP
22 Samuel C. Chew, *Byron in England* (London: John Murray, 1924) p.29
23 Late Jan. 1820 (to Henry Crabb Robinson). Ernest de Selincourt, ed., *The Letters of William and Dorothy Wordsworth* (Oxford: Clarendon Press, 1970), III, p.579

CHAPTER 23
NEXT-TO-LAST LOVE, 1819

1 April 27, 1819. *Byron's Bulldog*, p.266
2 April 24, 1819 (to Douglas Kinnaird). *Letters*, 6, p.115
3 Origo, p.43
4 April 27, 1819 (to editor of *Galignani's Messenger*). *Letters*, 6, p.119

5 LP
6 June 27, 1819. *Ibid.*
7 *Ibid.*
8 June 10, 1819. *Letters*, 6, p.152
9 June 17, 1819. *Ibid.*, p.161
10 Origo, p.87
11 *Ibid.*, p.89
12 *Ibid.*, p.96
13 Aug. 23, 1819 (to Hobhouse). *Letters*, 6, p.214
14 Nov. 1819. Murray Archives
15 Jan. 6, 1819. *Clairmont*, I, p.148
16 May 18, 1819. *Ibid.*, p.127
17 Origo, p.110

CHAPTER 24
OPERA BOUFFA, 1819–20

1 Origo, p.117
2 *Ibid.*, p.119
3 *Ibid.*, p.123
4 Sept. 10, 1819. *Byron's Bulldog*, p.278
5 Oct. 3, 1819. *Letters*, 6, p.226
6 Oct. 29, 1819. *Ibid.*, pp.237–8
7 Oct. 26, 1819. *Ibid.*, p.232
8 Moore, II, p.250
9 *Ibid.*, p.252
10 *Ibid.*, p.273
11 Oct. 29, 1819. *Letters*, 6, p.238
12 Moore, II, p.273
13 Nov. 16, 1819. *Letters*, 6, p.241
14 *Ibid.*, p.242
15 Nov. 21, 1819. *Ibid.*, p.245
16 Dec. 17, 1819. LP
17 Dec. 23, 1819. *Ibid.*
18 Dec. 29, 1819. *Ibid.*
19 Dec. 4, 1819 (to Murray). *Letters*, 6, p.252
20 Jan. 24, 1820. LP
21 Jan. 28, 1820. Murray Archives
22 Dec. 31, 1819. *Letters*, 6, p.261
23 Jan. 27, 1820. LP
24 Jan. 29, 1820. *Ibid.*
25 Jan. 31, 1820. *Letters*, 7, p.28
26 BP
27 April 21, 1820. *Byron's Bulldog*, p.290
28 April 1820. Murray Archives
29 April 16, 1820 (to Kinnaird). *Letters*, 7, p.76.

CHAPTER 25
LIMBO IN RAVENNA, 1820

1 May 16, 1820. Murray Archives
2 Marion Kingston Stocking, ed., *The Journals of Claire Clairmont* (Cambridge: Harvard UP, 1968), p.121
3 *Clairmont*, I, p.140
4 *Ibid.*, p.142
5 April 22, 1820 (to Hoppner). *Letters*, 7, p.80
6 *Clairmont*, I, p.143
7 *Ibid.*
8 *MWS*, I, p.145
9 Sept. 10, 1820 (to Hoppner). *Letters*, 7, p.174
10 July 14, 1820. Origo, p.188
11 July 29, 1820. *Letters*, 7, p.146
12 Oct. 18, 1820 (to Augusta Leigh). *Letters*, 7, p.208
13 Origo, p.214
14 August 26, 1820. *Letters*, 7, p.163
15 Sept. 28, 1820 (to Murray). *Ibid.*, p.181
16 Oct. 1, 1820. *Ibid.*, p.190
17 Origo, p.229
18 Nov. 9, 1820 (to Murray). *Letters*, 7, p.225
19 Oct. 8, 1820. *Ibid.*, p.195
20 Aug. 19, 1820. *Ibid.*, p.159
21 LP
22 Jan. 20, 1821 (Journal). *Letters*, 8, p.31

CHAPTER 26
THE RELUCTANT DEPARTURE, 1821

1 July 5, 1821. *Letters*, 8, p.146
2 Jan. 2, 1821. *Ibid.*, p.55
3 Jan. 6, 1821 (Journal). *Ibid.*, p.15
4 Jan. 23, 1821 (Journal). *Ibid.*, p.32
5 Jan. 8, 1821 (Journal). *Ibid.*, p.19
6 Jan. 23, 1821 (Journal). *Ibid.*, p.33
7 Hubert E.H. Jerningham, *Reminiscences of an Attaché* (William Blackwood and Sons, 1886), p.102
8 Marion Kingston Stocking, ed., *The Journals of Claire Clairmont*, (Cambridge: Harvard UP, 1968), p.216
9 *Clairmont*, I, pp.163–4
10 April 3, 1821. *Letters*, 8, p.97
11 Clairmont, I, p.167
12 Shelley, II, p.283

13 April 26, 1821. *Letters*, 8, p.103
14 April 17, 1821. *Shelley*, II, p.284
15 April 26, 1821. *Letters*, 8, p.104
16 Feb. 15, 1821. *Byron's Bulldog*, p.304
17 May 20, 1821. *Letters*, 8, p.122
18 Fred Kaplan, ed., *Travelling in Italy with Henry James* (London: Hodder and Stoughton, 1994), p.371
19 Aug. 12, 1821. *Byron's Bulldog*, p.314
20 Aug. 10, 1821. *Shelley*, II, p.330
21 Aug. 7, 1821. *Ibid.*, p.319
22 Aug. 10, 1821. *Ibid.*, p.323
23 Aug. 10, 1821 (to Isabella Hoppner). *MWS*, I, pp. 207–8
24 Aug. 15, 1821 (to Mary Shelley). *Shelley*, II, pp.334–5
25 Aug. 15, 1821. *Ibid.*, p.339
26 Aug. 8, 1821 (to Mary Shelley). *Ibid.*, p.334–5.
27 Aug. 9, 1821. *Ibid.*, p.328
28 Aug. 11, 1821. Origo, p.275
29 Aug. 22, 1821. *Ibid.*, p.278
30 Aug. 26, 1821. *Shelley*, II, p.345
31 Hunt, I, p.172
32 Oct. 15, 1821–May 18, 1822 ("Detached Thoughts"). *Letters*, 9, p.45
33 Sept. 9, 1821. *Letters*, 8, p.205
34 Sept. 28, 1821 (to Hoppner). *Ibid.*, p.226
35 Sept. 20, 1821. *Ibid.*, p.217
36 Oct. 5, 1821. *Ibid.*, p.234
37 Oct. 22, 1821. *Shelley*, II, p.363
38 Oct. 15, 1821–May 18, 1822. *Letters*, 9, p.33

CHAPTER 27
THE SINGING BIRDS, 1821–2

1 Nov. 30, 1821. *MWS*, I, p.209
2 Dec. 16, 1821. Murray Archives
3 Dec. 2, 1821. LP
4 Sept. 11, 1821. *Letters*, 8, p.205
5 *Works*, VI, p.648
6 Jan. 3, 1822 (to Lady Byron). LP
7 Feb. 9, 1822. *MWS*, I, p.218
8 Trelawny, p.40
9 Dec. 4, 1821 (to Kinnaird). *Letters*, 9, p.73
10 Feb. 20, 1822. Murray Archives
11 Feb. 15, 1822. *Shelley*, II, p.389
12 Feb. 17, 1822. *Ibid.*, p.390
13 *Ibid.*, p.394

14 Feb. 1822. *Ibid.*, pp.391–2
15 April 10, 1822. *Ibid.*, p.405
16 *Clairmont*, I, p.169
17 *Shelley*, II, p.399
18 *Ibid.*, p.403
19 Origo, p.310
20 *Ibid.*, p.311
21 Iris Origo, *A Measure of Love* (London: Jonathan Cape, 1957), p.76
22 *Shelley*, II, p.415
23 Origo, *A Measure of Love*, p.80
24 *Ibid.*, p.81
25 Dec. 12, 1822. *Letters*, 10, p.55

CHAPTER 28
THE WREN, THE EAGLE, AND
THE SKYLARK, 1822

1 Trelawny, p.105
2 Origo, p.307
3 June 2, 1822. *MWS*, I, p.236
4 June 29, 1822. *Shelley*, II, p.442
5 Hunt, II, p.124
6 Hunt Letters, I, p.188
7 July 4, 1822. *Shelley*, II, p.444
8 Trelawny, p.129
9 *Ibid.*, p.133
10 Hunt, II, p.131
11 Sept. 2, 1822. *Letters*, 9, p.201
12 *Ibid.*, p.202
13 Sept. 21, 1822. *Letters*, 9, p.211
14 Trelawny, p.150
15 *Bulletin and Review of the Keats–Shelley Memorial*. Rome, No. 2, ed. Sir Rennell Rodd and Nelson Gay (London: Macmillan, 1913)

CHAPTER 29
GENOA, 1822–3

1 Oct. 29, 1822. Murray Archives
2 Sept. 25, 1822. *Ibid.*
3 *Ibid.*
4 Oct. 29, 1822. Murray Archives
5 Oct. 9, 1822 (to John Murray). *Letters*, 10, p.13
6 Elwin, p.263
7 *Quarterly Review*, XXVII, p.477
8 March 2, 1823. *Byron's Bulldog*, pp.324–5
9 Nov. 10, 1822. *Letters*, 10, p.50

10 Marchand, p.1049
11 Feb. 20, 1823. *MWS*, I, p.312
12 Jan. 21, 1823. Murray Archives
13 Nov. 16, 1822. *MWS*, I, p.288
14 Jan. 12, 1823. *Ibid.*, p.306
15 Feb. 15, 1823. *Letters*, 10, p.100
16 Feb. 19, 1823. *MWS*, I, p.313
17 Feb. 25, 1823. *Ibid.*, p.314
18 March 7, 1823. *Ibid.*, p.320
19 Murray Archives
20 May 20, 1823. LP
21 William St Clair, *That Greece Might Still Be Free* (Oxford: Oxford UP, 1972), p.152
22 May 19, 1823 (to Hobhouse). *Letters*, 10, p.176
23 April 17, 1823. *Ibid.*, p.152
24 April 10, 1823. *MWS*, I, p.329
25 *Ibid.*, p.341
26 May 12, 1823 (to John Bowring). *Letters*, 10, p.168
27 April 19, 1823. Murray Archives
28 June 3, 1823. *Ibid.*
29 Blessington, p.142
30 June 10, 1823. *Letters*, 10, p.197
31 Trelawny, p.177
32 Origo, p.330
33 July ?2–10, 1823 (trans.). *MWS*, I, p.348

CHAPTER 30
CEPHALONIA, 1823

1 Origo, p.346
2 July 13, 1823. *MWS*, I, p.348
3 July 23, 1823 (to Jane Williams). *Ibid.*, p.349
4 Trelawny, p.152
5 Origo, p.347
6 *Ibid.*
7 *Ibid.*, p.348
8 Trelawny, p.183
9 Nicolson, p.113
10 Origo, p.353
11 Sept. 28, 1823 (Journal). *Letters*, 11, p.32
12 Trelawny, p.211
13 H. Buxton Forman, ed., *Letters of Edward John Trelawny* (Oxford: Oxford UP, 1910), p.84
14 Oct. 7, 1823. *Letters*, 11, p.43
15 Stanhope, p.512

16 Nicolson, p.170
17 *Ibid.*, p.178
18 *Ibid.*, p.174
19 *Ibid.*, p.177
20 Dec. 27, 1823. *Letters*, 11, p.85

CHAPTER 31
MISSOLONGHI, 1824

1 Dec. 1, 1823. *Letters*, 11, p.87
2 Nicolson, p.187
3 Hobhouse, I, pp.210–11
4 William St Clair, *That Greece Might Still Be Free* (Oxford UP, 1972), p.136
5 Dec. 6, 1823. *Byron's Bulldog*, p.339
6 Marchand, p.1121
7 Nicolson, p.198
8 Marchand, p.1163
9 Langley Moore, p.403
10 Oct. 25, 1823. *Letters*, 11, p.55
11 Thomas Medwin, *The Angler in Wales*, II (London: Richard Bentley, 1834), p.204
12 *Ibid.*, p.210
13 Stanhope, p.98
14 Marchand, not, p.117
15 Crompton, pp.326, 329
16 Nicolson, p.209
17 Parry, p.18
18 *Ibid.*, p.21
19 *Ibid.*, p.28
20 Gamba, p.174
21 Julius Millingen, *Memoirs of the Affairs of Greece* (London: 1831), p.118
22 Stanhope, pp.115–16
23 *Letters*, 11, pp.113–14
24 Stanhope, p.118
25 March 4, 1824 (to Kennedy). *Letters*, 11, p.126

26 Gamba, pp.192–3
27 Stanhope, p.127

CHAPTER 32
DEATH IN GREECE,
1824

1 Nicolson, p.239
2 Gamba, p.249
3 Millingen, p.141
4 Trelawny, p.220
5 *Ibid.*, p.221
6 *Byron's Bulldog*, p.352
7 Nicolson, pp.265–6
8 April 23, 1824. Murray Archives

EPILOGUE

1 BP
2 Gunn, p.220
3 An excellent account of the destruction is given in Doris Langley Moore, *The Late Lord Byron* (London: John Murray, 1961), pp.12–45
4 July 13, 1824. Murray Archives
5 Mayne, p.298
6 *Ibid.*, p.301
7 *MWS*, I, p.437
8 Malcolm Elwin, *Lord Byron's Family* (London: John Murray, 1975), p.238
9 Mayne, p.302
10 According to Moore he lived to over eighty, but I am more confident in the research of Roger Lloyd Jones who is writing a biography of Fletcher.

Index

NOTE: Works by Byron are listed directly under title; works by others appear under the author's name

Abercromby, Miss (Catherine Byron's kinswoman), 45
Aberdeen, 13, 16–17
Ada *see* Byron, Augusta Ada
Adair, Robert, 107, 109–11, 114
Aglietti, Dr Francesco, 306, 330, 348, 352–3
Alacrity, HMS, 454
Alba *see* Byron, Clara Allegra
Albania: B and Hobhouse visit, 93–5; unrest in, 122; in *Childe Harold*, 152
Albany, Piccadilly (London): B moves to, 191, 194
Alborghetti, Count Giuseppe, 347
Albrizzi, Countess Isabella Teotochi, 306, 321
Alfred Club, 141
Ali Pasha: reputation, 91, 97; in Albania, 94; meets B and Hobhouse, 95–6; captures Berat, 122; killed, 425; and Suliotes, 458
Allegra *see* Byron, Clara Allegra
Alps *see* Switzerland
Althorp, John Spencer, Viscount (*later* 31d Earl Spencer), 194
Andreas (Albanian servant), 124
Annabella *see* Byron, Annabella, Lady
Annesley Hall, Nottinghamshire, 23, 36–9, 67
Arqua, 353, 355
Athens, 98, 99–104, 112, 116, 118, 125
Augusta *see* Leigh, Augusta Mary
Austen, Jane, 131; *Persuasion*, 173
Austria: and Italian rebellion, 379

Babbage, Charles, 475
Bagnacavallo (Italy), 380–1, 385, 400, 402
Baillie, Joanna, 143, 210, 233, 242, 304, 320
Baillie, Dr Matthew, 27, 29, 242
Banff (Scotland), 17
Bankes, William, 54, 59–60, 160, 360, 374
Barnard, Anne, Lady, 303, 324
Barry, Charles, 430–1, 434–5, 438, 452, 465
Bathurst, Captain Walter, 106–7, 111, 437
Baxter, Charles, 266, 274, 318, 365, 393, 415, 420, 468, 478
Becher, Revd J.T., 51, 57–8, 64, 136, 147
Becket (land agent), 10
Beckford, William, 81, 86, 286n
Bembo, Cardinal, 297
Bentham, Jeremy, 455, 458; *A Table of Springs of Action*, 443

Benzoni, Countess Marina Querini, 321, 340–1
Beppo (B), 88, 317, 324, 333, 342
Berger (B's Swiss servant), 271, 296
Bernese Oberland, 292, 312
Bessborough, Henrietta Frances, Countess of, 161, 164, 166
Bettesworth, George, 61
Beyle, Marie-Henri *see* Stendhal
Birch (Hanson's partner), 78
Blackwood, William, 263n
Blackwood's Magazine, 260, 338
Bland, Robert, 141
Blaquiere, Edward: visits B, 424–6; and B's journey to Greece, 437–8, 449; Mavrocordato writes to, 455
Blessington, Charles John Gardiner, 1st Earl of, 422, 427, 430, 435, 438
Blessington, Marguerite, Countess of, 90, 264, 286, 402, 422–4, 427, 430, 438; *Conversations with Lord Byron*, 422–3
Blues, The (B), 417
Boatswain (B's dog), 68, 136, 471
Boissy, Marquis de (Teresa's second husband), 476
Bolivar (B's yacht), 407, 413–14, 415, 430, 435
Bologna, 349–50
Bolton, Samuel, 136
Bonnivard, François, 284
Borgia, Lucretia, 297
Botzaris, Marco, 435, 441
Bowman (Newstead tenant), 113
Bowring, John, 435, 443, 454, 457, 459
Bowser (Aberdeen schoolmaster), 16
Boyce, Susan, 238, 248, 261, 265
Breme, Ludovico di (or de Brême), Monsignore, 286, 297–8, 306, 326
Bride of Abydos, The (B), 96, 183–4, 189
Brighton, 65
Broglie, duc de, 286
Bronsted, Peter, 122
Brothers, Richard, 121
Brougham, Henry (*later* Baron), 64, 175, 264, 282, 289, 357, 370
Browne, Denis, 25n
Browne, James Hamilton, 436–7, 442
Bruce, Michael, 119–20
Brummell, George (Beau), 44, 62–3, 156, 158, 287, 298

Bruno, Dr Francesco, 431, 435, 440, 459, 466–7, 469, 472, 476

Brussels, 274

Bryant, Jacob, 107

Bullock, William, 266

Bulwer, Henry, 476

Burdett, Sir Francis, 361, 398, 426

Burgage Manor, Nottinghamshire, 34

Burnett, T.A.J., 78

Butler, Dr George, 31, 49, 57, 65, 82

Byron, Allegra (B's daughter) *see* Byron, Clara Allegra

Byron, Lady Amelia (B's father's first wife), 8

Byron, Annabella, Lady (Anne Isabella; *née* Milbanke; B's wife): on *Childe Harold*, 152–4, 326; describes B, 152, 160, 163, 168, 238–9; on Lady Holland, 157; suitors, 160–1, 188, 212; appearance and character, 161, 187, 212, 219, 230, 234; and Caroline Lamb, 161–3, 168, 255–7; relations with B, 163; B confesses attachment to, 167–8; first rejects B, 168, 212; self description, 168–9; on B and Augusta Leigh, 181; resumes contact and correspondence with B (1813), 186–9, 198–206, 211–13; and Lady Melbourne, 198–200, 202, 205, 210, 217, 236, 269–70; accepts B's marriage proposal, 206–9, 211–12; B visits in Seaham, 213–16; on B's vanity, 214, 304; marriage settlement, 215–16, 218, 257; and B's departure from Seaham, 216–17; doubts over marriage, 216; jealousy of Augusta, 216, 226, 230–1, 235, 261; proposes economical life-style, 218; and marriage date, 219; wedding and honeymoon, 219–24; suspects B's incestuous relations with Augusta, 222, 228, 235, 248, 252–3, 256–7; religious views, 223; marriage relations, 226–8, 232, 237–40, 242, 300; seeks house, 226; collects autographs, 227; stays with Augusta at Six Mile Bottom, 227–32; pregnancy, 230, 232, 237–8; friendship and intimacy with Augusta, 231–2, 236–9, 241, 244–5, 248; at Piccadilly Terrace house, 232, 235; social life and friends, 232–3; Augusta visits in London, 233; copies out B's poems, 237, 246; dislikes London, 237; birth of daughter (Augusta Ada), 240; leaves B, 240–5; suspects B of suffering from hydrocephalus, 242; initiates separation proceedings, 246–58; literary ambitions, 246; and custody of daughter, 253–4, 262, 323, 381; B's separation poem to, 260–1, 263n, 264; break with Augusta, 268–9; attitude to daughter, 269, 320; and B's departure for exile, 269, 271–2; enjoys London celebrity, 269; and separation agreement, 270; cultivates Augusta's friendship after B's exile, 272; aims to disgrace and humiliate Augusta, 280–1, 290–1, 294–5, 298–9, 303; depicted in Caroline Lamb's *Glenarvon*, 280; view of B, 282; hypochondria, 289n; and

Mme de Staëls' attempts at reconciliation with B, 289; B's "Lines" on illness, 290; Shelley reports to be living with Augusta, 293–4; Augusta admits incest to, 294; Murray shows *Childe Harold* to, 299, 302; plans to take Ada to continent, 301; and Scott's review of *Childe Harold*, 304; Augusta reports on B to, 308, 327, 394; and making daughter Ward of Chancery, 310–11; and B's statement on breaking silence, 316–17; visits Newstead after sale, 319; diary, 320; visits Scott at Abbotsford, 320; Hoppner portrait of, 321n; on *Beppo*, 324; and B's memoirs, 333, 359–60; B complains of Romilly to, 334; depicted in B's *Don Juan*, 336, 337–8; and B's letter to Augusta declaring love, 344–5, 358; B enquires about divorce from, 349; correspondence with B in Italy, 374–5; assures B of looking after Augusta and family, 375; pacific letter from B, 393; outraged at *Cain*, 394; and mother's death, 398; insurance on life of, 415; on B's preoccupation with fallen angels, 417; B requests portrait, 424; B speaks of to Lady Blessington, 424; B's later feelings towards, 424; B's dying message for, 469; and destruction of B's memoirs, 473; and B's funeral, 474; and B's will, 474; helps Augusta Leigh's children, 475; makes over jointure to George Byron, 475; sees Hobhouse in later life, 476

Byron, Augusta Ada (B's daughter): Mrs Clermont's concern for, 162; born, 240; custody question, 253–4, 262, 323; Annabella's attitude to, 269; in *Childe Harold*, 273; B enquires after, 275–6; Augusta Leigh passes on meesages about, 281; appearance, 299, 470; Annabella plans to take to continent, 301, 304; B fears being being hated by, 302; made Ward of Chancery, 304, 310–11, 325; Annabella fears effect of B's memoirs on, 360; exchanges locks of hair with B, 389, 393; illness, 442; B thinks of while in Greece, 461, 469; weeps at father's death, 474; mathematical genius, 475; meets Medora Leigh, 475; death and burial next to B, 476

Byron, Catherine (*née* Gordon; B's mother): background, 8–9; marriage, 8–9; and B's birth, 10–12; marriage relations, 13–14; moves to Aberdeen, 13, 16–17; financial anxieties, 14–15, 71, 81, 106–7, 121; and B's lame foot, 15, 25–6, 117, 134; and husband's death, 15–16; and B's upbringing and education, 16–18, 25–6, 28–9, 35; emotional nature, 18, 50; and B's inheritance, 19–20; at Newstead, 21, 24; pension and improved finances, 26–7; relations with B, 28–9, 37–8, 42, 45–6, 49–50, 55, 64, 66, 68, 72, 81–2, 134; indiscretions, 29; fortune told, 33; moves to Burgage Manor, 34; on B's being in love, 38–9; and Lord Grey, 39, 42, 46; helps finance B at Cambridge, 54–5;

anxiety over B's debts, 60; illness, 66, 131–2; and B's 21st birthday, 71; criticises Lord Carlisle, 73; in B's will, 77; and B's travels abroad, 81–2, 107; letters from B abroad, 95, 106, 110, 113, 117, 127–8, 135; B instructs Hanson to take care of, 113; opposes sale of Newstead, 122; and B's return from Greece, 131; character and qualities, 131; death and funeral, 133–6

Byron, Clara Allegra (Alba; Claire Clairmont's daughter): death and burial, 34, 400, 402–4; born, 309; B has brought to Italy, 322–4, 328–9; baptised, 322; Shelley and Claire Clairmont follow to Venice, 327–30; in B's will, 334; joins B, 351, 357, 365; illness, 358; Claire Clairmont asks B to see, 366–8, 401; B on upbringing, 367–8; fever in Ravenna, 368; B leaves with nurse, 370; B places in convent, 380–1, 389; disposition and character, 380; Shelley visits in convent, 385; Shelley wishes B to bring to Pisa, 388–9; Claire Clairmont plans to kidnap, 401

Byron, Frances, Lady (5th Baron's widow), 25

Byron, George Anson (B's uncle), 18, 72

Byron, George Anson (*later* 7th Baron; B's cousin): in B's will, 183, 216; stays with Annabella, 240; B boasts to, 248; and B's separation proceedings, 251; and B's death and funeral, 474; Annabella's generosity to, 475

Byron, George Gordon, 6th Baron:
Characteristics: appearance, 17, 67, 89, 120–1, 143n, 181, 334, 395, 423, 454; Scottish accent, 29, 32, 454; shyness, 30, 45, 51; ambitions for "grandeur", 33–4, 53; superstitiousness, 33, 224; self-indulgence, 41–2; fatness, 45, 60–1, 283, 327, 334, 408, 412, 423; depressions, 56–7, 59–60, 125, 225–6, 292–3, 371, 376; misanthropy, 76; morbid quality, 89–90, 114; romantic persona, 90; suggested bisexuality, 96n, 103; anger over perceived precedence slight, 110; sexual promiscuity, 119, 274; and vicarious feeling, 140; "Don Juan complex", 185–6; temper, 197, 261, 440; vanity and self importance, 214, 224, 298, 304, 334, 407; guilt feelings, 224; boredom in Seaham, 225; Annabella describes character, 238–9; self-aggrandisement, 248; self-image, 282; self-reflection, 377–8; conversation, 396; reputation in Greece, 444; humanitarian treatment of Turkish prisoners, 450–1, 454; moustache, 454; frustrations and irritability in Missolonghi, 464–5; posthumous myth, 471

Finances: debts and repayments, 54–5, 59–60, 62, 69, 71, 77–8, 106, 143, 164, 215, 237, 241, 267, 308, 318, 321, 365, 393, 415, 420; and maintenance of Newstead, 72; wills and codicils, 77–8, 127, 136, 183, 237, 333–4, 474; and attempted sale of Newstead, 165; literary earnings, 190–1, 197; marriage settlement, 215, 218, 257; refuses advance from Murray, 240; sells books, 266; and sale of Newstead, 308–9; repays debts after sale of Newstead, 318, 321; preoccupation with money, 365; inheritance at Lady Noel's death, 398; and Mary Shelley's passage money back to England, 431–2, 434

Health: deformed foot and lameness, 10–12, 15–16, 25–7, 29–30, 50, 116–17, 223, 234, 298, 355, 422; takes laudanum, 64, 242; fevers, 120, 310, 357; ill-health, 127; insomnia and nightmares, 184; mental condition, 194, 242–3, 245; hypochondria, 224, 266; Annabella believes suffering from hydrocephalus, 242; gonorrhea, 321; physical weakness in Greece, 440; tantrum from sun stroke, 440; suffers convulsions in Missolonghi, 459–60, 462; final illness, 466–9

Interests, activities and views: swimming, 1, 50–1, 54, 61, 87, 108–9, 116–17, 326, 410, 413, 436, 447–8; animals and pets, 47, 66, 68, 137, 293, 327, 384–5, 411, 430, 435, 462; cricket, 50, 60; early poetry, 51, 57–8; reading, 52–3; gambling, 61, 63; political convictions, 62, 64, 148–50; death of pet dog, 68; enters House of Lords, 73–4, 159; shoots eagle, 97; studies demotic Greek, 122; religious scepticism, 137–8, 223, 394, 468; and industrial unrest, 147; maiden speech in Lords, 148–50; ignorance of art and music, 158, 274, 297; attendances in Lords, 163–4, 172–3; views on incest, 184; on Drury Lane Theatre subcommittee, 237; buys pet dog in Switzerland, 293; learns Armenian, 306–7; attends execution, 311–12; view of English political scene, 361, 374; joins Carbonari and Italian revolutionary movement, 369–70, 379–80; on poetry as excited passion, 377; yacht (*Bolivar*), 395–6, 407; Blaquiere urges to support Greek cause, 426; buys Lady Blessington's horse Mameluke, 430; knowledge of Bible, 439; in Greek war, 449–50, 458–62

Personal life: background and family, 5–6; birth and christening, 10, 12; Aberdeen childhood, 13, 16–17; and father's death, 15–16; early schooling, 16–17, 25–8; boyhood infatuations, 17–18, 28, 36–9; portraits, 17, 121, 172; inherits title and estate, 19–20; arrives at Newstead, 21–3; at Harrow school, 30–3, 35, 37, 41, 45–50; asked to leave Harrow, 48–9; at Cambridge, 52–4, 59, 61–2, 65–6; dissolute activities, 61–2, 64; revisits Harrow, 65, 131; awarded Cambridge MA, 66; reoccupies and improves Newstead, 66–8; illegitimate children, 70; duelling threats, 92 & n, 397; writes to mother from abroad, 95, 106, 113, 117, 127–8; letters from Constantinople, 113–14; reluctance to sell Newstead, 121, 124, 145, 164; reviews life, 126–7; grief at death of mother and friends, 133–6, 140, 145; eating habits and dieting, 134, 142, 194, 236, 283, 436; considers marriage, 137, 184, 191, 197; life at Newstead, 139, 141, 143–6; social lionisation, 159–60; and Augusta's pregnancy (with Medora), 183; keeps journal, 184, 460; stands godfather to Medora Leigh, 192; drinking, 194, 224, 283, 429; social activities, 194; engagement to Annabella, 206–9, 211; correspondence with Annabella after engagement, 211–12; visits Annabella in Seaham, 213, 214–16; final visit to Newstead, 214; leaves Seaham, 216–17; reluctance over marriage, 218–19; wedding and honeymoon, 219–23; marriage relations, 226–9, 232, 237–40, 242; *seeks* house after marriage, 226; stays with Annabella at Six Mile Bottom, 227–32; at Piccadilly Terrace house, 232; Augusta visits in London, 233; Annabella leaves, 240, 242–4, 246; on birth of daughter (Ada), 240; separation proceedings, 246–8, 249, 258; decides on self-exile, 259, 260, 266–7; poem to Annabella on separation, 260–1; vengeful poem against Mrs Clermont, 261–4; owns coach based on Napoleon's, 266–7, 274, 347, 390, 415, 438, 478; social ostracism, 267–8; bids farewell to Augusta, 269; signs separation agreement, 270; Shelley's influence on, 278, 283, 285; in Caroline Lamb's *Glenarvon*, 279–80; tells ghost stories, 283, 343; opposes Annabella's taking Ada to continent, 301; and birth of Allegra (Claire Clairmont's daughter), 309, 312; protests at making Ada a ward of Chancery, 310–11, 325; bust by Thorwaldsen, 312; discontinues letters to Augusta, 315; arranges for Allegra to be brought to Italy, 322–3; Shelley visits in Venice to discuss Allegra, 328–30; memoirs, 332–3, 356–7, 374, 376, 389, 393, 394; letter to Augusta declaring love, 344–5; considers move to Americas, 350, 354, 359, 406, 411, 414; sends for Allegra, 351; informs Annabella of memoirs, 359–60; and Claire Clairmont's requests to see Allegra, 365–8; on Allegra's upbringing, 367–8; Hobhouse chides for inactive life, 374; writes reminiscences of Harrow and Cambridge, 374; Ravenna journal (1821), 375–80, 416; places Allegra in convent, 380–1; speaks of Annabella's hold over Augusta, 389; adopts name Noel, 398; and Allegra's death, 400, 402–4; seeks new publisher after

disagreements with Murray, 416, 420; correspondence with Lady Hardy, 418; correspondence with Isabel Harvey, 419; Lady Blessington visits and writes on, 422–4; writes last letter, 465–6; death, 470; embalmed and returned to England for burial, 471–2; memoirs destroyed, 472–3; funeral and burial, 473–4

Relationships: meets Lord Clare in Italy, 1–2, 390; relations with mother, 28–9, 37–8, 42, 45–6, 49–50, 55, 64, 66, 68, 72, 81–2, 134; relations with Lord Grey, 39–42, 44–6, 51; early correspondence with Augusta, 42–6, 198; male friends and homo-erotic attachments, 46–8, 51, 54–6, 61–2, 81, 90, 103–4, 117, 256, 442, 469; and Mary Duff's marriage, 51; and Caroline Lamb, 89, 162–5, 166–8, 170–2, 174, 176–9, 180, 185, 195–6, 209; involvement with Constance Spencer Smith, 91–2, 125–6, 168; reconciled with Augusta Leigh, 136–7; literary friends, 141–2, 175; infatuation with Susan Vaughan, 144–5; interest in Annabella, 160; attachment to Annabella, 167, 186–8, 198–206; affair with Lady Oxford, 169–72, 174, 178–9, 181, 185; relations with and possible child by Augusta Leigh (1813), 181–5, 190, 192, 194, 196, 208, 252, 256–7, 294, 314; on Dorset's death, 225–6; takes mistress (Susan Boyce), 238, 248, 261; pleads for reconciliation with Annabella, 250–2; affair with and child by Claire Clairmont, 265, 282–3, 285, 287, 304; and Mrs Marden, 265; Italian mistresses, 307–9, 311–12, 316–17, 321, 323, 331, 334, 341, 344; falls for Countess Teresa Guiccioli, 341–3, 345–51, 358; and Guicciolis' disagreement, 357; settled relationship with Teresa Guiccioli, 359, 373, 411; lampoons Hobhouse, 361–3; and Teresa's separation from Guiccioli, 368–9; gives Benjamin Constant's *Adolphe* to Teresa, 370–2; Teresa Guiccioli reads and comments on poems, 372–3; relations with Shelley, 386, 396–9, 411; confesses Teresa Guiccioli attachment to Augusta, 389; and Shelley's drowning, 409–10; relations with Leigh Hunt, 411–12, 418, 429; growing coolness towards Teresa Guiccioli, 421, 430; favours Loukas Chalandritsanos, 442, 447–8, 451–2, 455–6, 464; Stanhope's hostility to, 454–5

Travels: in Montenero, 2, 401, 405–6; first plans travel abroad, 63, 69, 72, 76–7; first departure from England (1809), 79–83, 84–5; in Portugal and Spain (1809), 84–9; travels in Mediterranean (1809), 90–4; visits Albania, 93–6; first visit to Greece, 96–104; in Turkey, 104–5, 109–15; meets Turkish Sultan, 112; Hobhouse leaves, 114–15;

second stay in Greece (1810–11), 116–25; rescues Greek woman from death, 119; returns to England from Greece (1811), 124–8, 129–31; plans second trip abroad, 176–7; departs for exile, 271; tourist behaviour, 274–6; at Cologny with Shelley, 277–89, 292–3; at Villa Diodati, 277–8, 282–3; in Italy (1816), 296–7, 300–11; life in Venice, 305–7, 309, 318, 321, 324, 331, 383; under surveillance in Italy, 350, 372, 383; travels with Teresa Guiccioli, 353–4; with Teresa Guiccioli in Ravenna, 358–60; moves to Pisa, 390–3; social life in Pisa, 394–5, 399; in scuffle with Italian sergeant major, 399–400, 405; rents Montenero villa, 401; moves to Genoa, 413–15, 418; decides to go to Greece, 427–8; departs for Greek expedition (1823), 434–8; arrives in Greece, 438–42; prefers Turks to Greeks, 442; reaches Missolonghi, 448–9; protects Turkish girl Hato (Hatagee), 461; agrees to meet Odysseus, 462–3

Byron, John Anson (B's cousin), 136

Byron, John, Baron Byron of Rochdale (B's ancestor), 6

Byron, John (B's father; "Mad Jack"): marriages and behaviour, 7–10, 13–14; debts, 9–13, 15; in France, 9, 14–15; B's relations with, 13; incest with sister Frances, 14; death and will, 15

Byron, Admiral John (B's grandfather; "Foulweather Jack"), 6–7

Byron, Sir John, of Colwyke (B's ancestor), 5

Byron, Sophie (B's aunt), 204, 227

Byron, William, 5th Baron ("the Wicked Lord"), 6–7, 18–19, 23

Byron, William (5th Baron's son), 7

Byron, William (5th Baron's grandson), 7, 18

Cadiz (Spain), 88–9, 153

Cain (B), 384, 393, 394, 416, 439

Cambridge University: B attends (Trinity College), 52–4, 59, 61–2, 65; awards MA to B, 66; B writes reminiscences of, 374

Campbell, Thomas, 75, 142–3, 233, 365, 468

Canning, Stratford (later 1st Viscount Stratford de Redcliffe), 109–10, 111n

Capsali, Apolostoli, 448

Carbonari, 369–70, 372, 379, 412, 439

Carlisle, Frederick Howard, 5th Earl of: interest in B's upbringing, 26–7, 29–30, 34, 46; and Augusta Leigh, 42, 59; B's resentment towards, 49; and B's attending Cambridge, 52; B sends Hours of Idleness to, 68; B attacks, 72–3, 75–6, 114, 137, 180; declines to sponsor B in Lords, 72–3, 159; humiliates B, 72, 75

Carlisle, Henry Howard, 4th Earl of, 26

Carlisle, Isabella, Countess of (later Lady Musgrave), 26

Carlton House (London), 156

Carmarthen, Amelia, Marchioness of (later Baroness Conyers; Augusta Leigh's mother), 181

Caroline, Queen of George IV (formerly Princess of Wales), 160, 172, 370

Castlereagh, Robert Stewart, Viscount (later 2nd Marquess of Londonderry), 337

Catholic Emancipation, 148

Cawthorne, James, 73, 106, 131, 151

Chalandritsanos family, 441

Chalandritsanos, Loukas, 442, 447–8, 451–2, 454–5, 464, 469

Champion (newspaper), 264

Charles I, King of Great Britain, 5–6

Charlotte, Princess, 148, 150, 160, 230n; death, 318, 320

Charlotte, Queen of George III, 232, 327

Chaworth family, 6

Chaworth, Mary (later Musters): B first meets, 23–4; B's infatuation with, 36–9, 58, 201; relations with Jack Musters, 36, 38; in B's poems, 38, 58, 105, 220, 286; marriage, 50, 74; B meets again (1808), 67; writes to B (1813), 189–90; announces visit to London, 197; proposed later acquaintance, 201, 220

Chaworth, William, 6–7, 23

Chichester, Mary Henrietta Juliana, Countess of (Augusta's half-sister), 314

Childe Harold's Pilgrimage (B): publication, 73, 138–9, 148, 151, 302–3, 324; celebrity and reception, 76, 151–2, 173, 185, 304–5, 320, 324, 326, 437; and B's travels, 85–9, 93, 97, 102, 103n, 104, 152–3, 276, 285, 325; writing, 96, 101, 105, 284–6, 316, 317–18; on Lusieri, 100; Dallas's disappointment with, 130; religious scepticism in, 138–9; revised, 139; B corrects proofs, 144, 148; on Lord Elgin, 151, 155; character and autobiographical element, 153–5, 186, 275, 282, 324–6; Scott praises, 234; on B's daughter Ada, 273; on Duchess of Richmond's Waterloo ball, 275; Hobhouse on, 287–8; Murray's payment for, 293; Annabella sees third canto, 299, 302; fourth canto dedicated to Hobhouse, 318; Shelley on, 331; B declines to continue, 428

Choiseul-Gouffin, Comte de, 100

Churchill, Charles, 271

Cintra (Portugal), 86, 94; Convention of, 138, 153

Clairmont, Charles Gaulis (Claire's brother), 400, 413, 419

Clairmont, Claire (Mary Jane): affair with and child by B, 265, 278; pregnancy and birth of child (Allegra), 265, 287, 294, 304, 312; in Switzerland with B, 276–7, 282–3, 285; copies B's work, 284, 331; and Allegra's departure for Italy, 322–3, 327; B's reluctance to see, 323; B's callousness towards, 326, 461; travels to Venice with Shelley, 328–30; and Mrs Vavassour's offer to adopt Allegra, 351; on B's Don Juan, 365; in Pisa with Shelleys, 365;

requests to see Allegra, 365–7, 401; objects to B placing Allegra in convent, 381; alleged affair and child with Shelley, 382, 385, 399, 401; leaves Pisa for Florence, 391; studies German in Florence, 400; Elise Foggi confesses to, 401; returns to Pisa, 401–2; learns of Allegra's death, 402–3; leaves Pisa for Vienna, 413, 419; B refuses allowance to, 419; denounced in Vienna, 419; takes governess post in St Petersburg, 419; and dying B, 469

Clare, John Fitzgibbon, 2nd Earl of: B meets on road in Italy, 1–2, 390; B's attachment to, 2–3, 46–7, 54, 76, 406, 420, 465; at Oxford, 52, 54; in B's early poetry, 58; B complains of depression to, 60; in B's will, 77, 266; declines to spend time with B, 113; Caroline Lamb and, 170; visits B in Montenero, 406, 412; delivers B's Ravenna Journal to Murray, 416; B sends letter of introduction for Greek politician, 465; and dying B, 469; marriage and death, 476

Claridge, John, 139

Clarke, Ann, 23, 36

Clarke, Hewson, 64, 132

Clarke, Revd William, 23

Claughton, Thomas, 80, 165, 171, 176–7, 180, 196–7, 205–6, 218

Clermont, Mary Anne: at B's wedding, 220; and Annabella's return from honeymoon, 224; on B's behaviour, 238; accompanies Annabella on leaving B, 242; with Lady Noel in London, 245, 247; encourages Annabella's separation, 249–50; B's vengeful poem to, 261–2, 263n, 264, 372; B blames, 424

Cockerell, Charles, 122, 124

Cocoa Tree Club, 63, 193–4

Cogni, Margarita ('La Fornarina'), 317, 327, 332, 341

Coleridge, Samuel Taylor, 143, 233, 394; *Christabel*, 283, 304

Cologne, 276

Cologny (Switzerland) *see* Diodati, Villa

Congreve, Sir William: rockets, 457 & n

Constable (publishers), 263n

Constant, Benjamin, 270; *Adolphe*, 370, 372

Constantinople, 91–2, 105, 109–13

Constitution, USS, 406

Conyers, Baroness *see* Carmarthen, Amelia, Marchioness of

"Cornelian, The" (B), 59

Corsair, The (B), 185, 189–90, 279

Courier (journal), 397

Courtenay, William, 3rd Viscount (*later* 8th Earl of Devon), 81

Criminal Law Amendment Act (1883), 267n

Crompton, Louis, 96n, 455, 456n

Cruikshank, George, 266

Curse of Minerva, The (B), 123–5, 151, 337

Dallas, Robert Charles: B confesses licentious reputation to, 57; and publication of B's works, 72–6, 130–1, 138–9; B writes to from Constantinople, 113; and B's loneliness at deaths of mother and friends, 135; B names as executor, 136, 171; and Murray's reservations over *Childe Harold*, 138–9; on B's maiden speech in Lords, 149; on lionisation of B, 159; B turns against, 174; B gives copyrights to, 189, 293; and B's disavowal of literary earnings, 191; *Recollections of the Life of Lord Byron*, 74, 139, 149, 174

"Darkness" (B), 286

Davies, Scrope Berdmore: borrows money, 59n; on B's character, 62, 64; qualities, 62–3; B accompanies to Brighton, 65; and B's financial affairs, 77–81, 121; B dines with on return from Greece, 129; and B's reaction to mother's death, 135; in B's will, 136; on Georgiana Leigh, 136–7; visits Newstead, 139; loan repaid, 171; friendship with B, 175, 260; B's debts to, 189, 194, 437; informs Hobhouse of B's engagement, 209n; and B's separation proceedings, 258, 270; blackballed at Brooks's, 271; visits B in Switzerland, 287–8; returns to England, 290; and Annabella's intrigues, 295; advises suppression of "Epistle to Augusta", 302; calls on Augusta with Hobhouse, 321; pleads with B to return to England, 335; reads B's *Don Juan*, 337; and B's first trip abroad, 437

Davy, Sir Humphry, 233

Dawkins, Edward, 400, 405

Day and New Times (newspaper), 314

de Bathe, James, 63

"Deformed Transformed, The" (B), 396, 422

Delacroix, Eugène, 306

Delawarr, George John Sackville, 4th Earl, 45–6, 51, 58, 65

Dervish (B's Albanian servant), 124

"Detached Thoughts" (B), 17, 28, 37, 40, 54, 63, 388, 390

Devonshire, Elizabeth, Duchess of, 159, 161, 227, 272, 318, 384

Diodati, Villa (Cologny, Switzerland), 277–8, 282–3, 293, 296

Disraeli, Benjamin, 476

D'Israeli, Isaac, 131, 233

Don Juan (B): recounts Admiral Byron's shipwreck, 7; on lake at Newstead, 22; high spirits, 89; on Marathon, 103; and Constantinople, 107, 110; on swimming Hellespont, 109; Shelley praises, 332; writing, 333, 340, 374, 428, 436; reactions to, 335, 337–9, 394, 417; contents, 336–7; publication and sales, 338, 420, 441; on men's and women's love, 350; B praises to Kinnaird, 355; on Laura and Petrarch, 355; piracy of, 358; B doubts standard of cantos III and IV, 364; B sends fifth canto to Kinnaird, 375; self-revelation in, 377; B abandons, 383; Shelley praises fifth canto, 385; B resumes, 406; Mary Shelley copies, 422; on Greece, 425; on Congreve rockets, 457n; episode of rescued young girl, 461n

Don Juan (Shelley's boat), 406–7, 409, 413

Dorant (hotel proprietor), 59n

Doria, Andrea, Doge of Venice, 414

D'Orsay, Count Alfred *see* Orsay, Count Alfred d'

Dorset, George John Frederick Sackville, 4th Duke of, 225, 321

Doyle, Col. Francis, 209, 247, 289, 290, 295, 360, 473

Doyle, Selina, 209, 233, 235, 243, 245, 268, 280n, 295

"Dream, The" (B), 38, 105, 220, 286

Drury, Henry, 31, 33–4, 65, 81, 92, 104, 112, 374

Drury, Dr Joseph, 29–31, 33–5, 37, 39, 48–9

Drury, Mark, 33–4, 45, 53

Drury Lane Theatre (London), 171, 237–8, 264–5, 271, 382–3

Duff, Mary, 17–18, 51

Duff, Col. Robert, 12

Dulwich Gallery (London), 157

Dupuy, Francesco, 405

Edelston, Ann, 140

Edelston, John: B's attachment to, 48, 55–6, 61, 216, 437, 469; B's poem to, 59, 151; death, 140, 145

Eden, George, 160, 163, 212

Edinburgh Review (magazine): criticises B's *Hours of Idleness*, 63–5, 75, 123, 149, 382; B rages against, 73; reviews Coleridge's *Christabel*, 304; ignores B's *Don Juan*, 338

Ekenhead, Lieut. William, 108–9

Eldon, John Scott, 1st Earl of, 36, 38, 74, 358

Elgin, Thomas Bruce, 7th Earl of: collecting activities in Greece, 91, 100–1, 104–5, 107, 110, 125; B satirises, 123–4, 151, 155; B delivers Lusieri's letter to, 127, 151

Elise (Swiss nurse) *see* Foggi, Elise

Elizabeth I, Queen of England, 5

Ellice, Edward, 114

Elliston, Robert, 171

Elphinstone, Mercer, 161, 167, 268

England, Anthony B., 390n

English Bards and Scotch Reviewers (B), 61, 64, 70, 72–3, 75–7, 101, 106, 113–14, 123, 130–2, 137, 142, 150, 152, 180, 233, 437

"Epistle to Augusta", 288, 302

Ewing, Elizabeth, 230n

Examiner (journal), 75, 260

Falcieri, Tita, 355, 375, 383, 400, 405, 437, 447, 454, 464, 467, 469, 476

Faliero, Marino, Doge of Venice, 306, 364

Falkland, Charles John Cary, 9th Viscount, 72, 74

Falkland, Christine, Lady, 74, 174

Falkner (Southwell landlord), 53

"Fare Thee Well" (B), 260–1, 263n, 264, 337, 372–3

"Farewell to Malta" (B), 126

Farquhar, James, 24

Fauvel, Louis François Sebastian, 100, 122

Fazakerly, John Nicholas, 122

Fernando VII, King of Spain, 87

Fielding, Henry, 86

Finlay, George, 442, 462, 466

Fletcher, Anne (*née* Rood), 242–3, 245, 250, 253

Fletcher, William: becomes B's valet, 66; influences Rushton, 77; accompanies B abroad, 82, 84, 90, 94, 111, 117; B sends back to England, 121; in B's will, 136; in Hastings with B, 197; marriage to Anne Rood, 243; and Annabella's separation from B, 248, 253; and B's exile, 266, 271, 273; and Shelley's arrival in Venice, 329; alarm over B's fever, 357; in Pisa, 392; with B on 1823 Greek expedition, 437, 444, 448–9, 464; and B's final illness and death, 460, 467–70, 472; Annabella sees after B's death, 474; later life and death, 476–7

Florence: Gamba and Teresa exiled to, 384, 387

Florida (ship), 472

Foggi, Elise (Swiss nurse), 322–3, 329–30, 332, 366, 382, 385, 401

Foggi, Paolo, 332

Foot, Michael, 149

Fornarina, La *see* Cogni, Margarita

Forrester, Daniel, 454

Foscarini, Villa, La Mira (Italy), 312, 316

Foscolo, Ugo, 326

Foster, Augustus, 160, 232

Foster, John, 122, 124

Fox, Charles James, 62, 148

Fox, Henry, 422

Fox, Henry Edward, 476

Frame Work Bill (1812), 148–50

France: war with Britain, 148

Frere, John Hookham ("Whistlecraft"), 88; *The Monks and the Giants*, 317

Friott, John, 122

Fugitive Pieces (B), 57

Galignani, Giovanni, 279n

Galignani's Messenger, 279, 343

Gall, Richard: "Farewell to Ayrshire", 51

Galt, John, 88n, 89–91, 103–6, 134, 436

Gamba family, 1, 370, 372, 379–80, 411–14

Gamba, Carolina (Teresa's sister), 421

Gamba, Count Pietro (Teresa Guiccioli's father): and Guiccioli's marriage to Teresa, 346; rebukes Teresa for imprudence, 354, 408; invites B to Ravenna, 359; and Teresa's separation from husband, 369; exile, 384, 406,

408, 411; moves to Pisa, 387–8, 392; in scuffle with Italian sergeant major, 399–400; arm cut in domestic quarrel, 408; meets Lady Blessington, 423; exile revoked and return to Ravenna, 434, 429, 434; informs Teresa of B's death, 472

Gamba, Count Pietro (Teresa Guiccioli's brother): alarm at sister's liaison, 348; B meets, 369; moves to Genoa, 411–12; and Greek war of independence, 427, 429–30; departs for Greece with B, 435–6; letters to Teresa, 435–6, 438, 441, 458, 464; despises Greeks, 441; activities in Greece, 444, 451, 455, 458, 460, 462, 466; intercepted by Turkish ship, 446–7; in Missolonghi, 448–9; apologises for paying soldiers from B's personal account, 464–5; and B's final illness and death, 467, 469; leaves Greece, 472; later career and death, 476

Gamba, Count Ruggero, 384, 387–8, 476

Geneva, Lake *see* Switzerland

Genoa: B moves to and stays in, 411–15, 418; Lady Blessington visits, 422–3

George III, King of Great Britain, 148, 232, 394, 416

George, Prince of Wales (*later* Prince Regent; *then* King George IV): George Leigh loses favour with, 106, 137; Whigs oppose, 148; debts, 156; and London social life, 156–8; banishes wife, 158; B meets, 160; and Lady Bessborough, 161; mocked in B's *Waltz*, 171; Hunt brothers attack, 175; B criticises in "Lines to a Lady Weeping", 191; receives Louis XVIII, 195; funeral, 370; in B's memoirs, 394; B defames, 416

Georgiori, Eustathios, 117–18

Ghigi, Pellegrino, 380, 402–3, 476

Giaour, The (B), 119, 173–4, 182, 187, 189, 191, 252

Gibbon, Edward: in Lausanne, 284

Gibbs, Sir Vickery, 132

Gibraltar, 87–9

Gifford, William, 61, 131, 139, 141, 233, 293, 365

Giraud, Nicolas (Nicolo), 103–4, 118–20, 125, 127, 136

Gisborne, John, 390

Gisborne, Maria, 367, 393, 395, 407

Glennie, Dr (schoolmaster), 28–9

Godwin, William, 265

Goethe, Johann Wolfgang von: *Faust*, 287, 312, 396

Gordon, Alexander Gordon, 4th Duke of, 12

Gordon, George, 12th Laird of Gight (B's maternal grandfather), 9

Gordon, Major Pryse Lockhart, 274–5

Gordon, Mrs Pryse Lockhart, 275

Gosford, Lady, 188, 210, 233

Graham, Peter W., 209n

Granville, Granville Leveson-Gower, 1st Earl, 161

Gray, Agnes, 53

Gray, May (Mary; B's nanny), 21–2, 27–8, 40–1, 53, 224, 394

Greece: B first visits (1809), 93, 96–103; political unrest, 97, 99–100, 122, 295; B's second stay in (1810–11), 116–25; foreign scholars in, 122; B leaves (1811), 124–5; effect on B, 128; rising against Turks (1821), 425–6; B joins independence movement, 427; B arrives in (1823), 437–42; provisional government, 439; war of independence, 441; British aid for, 442–3; money needs and loans, 442–4, 449, 455, 466, 468; B's poems in, 453, 455–6

Greek Executive Body, 465

Grey de Ruthin, Henry Edward Gould, 19th Baron, 34–5, 39–42, 44–6, 51, 336

Gritti, Count, 321

Gronow, Count Rees Howell, 142, 156

Guiccioli, Count Alessandro: marriage to Teresa, 321, 346; and B's relationship with Teresa, 341, 348, 354, 356; takes Teresa to country estates, 342, 349–50; background, 346; and Teresa's illness, 347; borrows from B, 352, 356, 368; Teresa writes to from Venice, 353; makes demands on wife, 357; B shares palazzo with, 359, 364, 368–9; Teresa separates from, 368–9; pays allowance to Teresa, 370, 406, 429; death of eldest son, 371; and revolutionary meetings at home, 379

Guiccioli, Count Ferdinando (Alessandro's eldest son), 371

Guiccioli, Countess Placidia (Guiccioli's first wife), 346

Guiccioli, Countess Teresa (*née* Gamba Ghiselli): B first meets, 321; B re-encounters and falls for, 340–3, 345–51; background and character, 341, 372; marriage, 346; illnesses, 347–8, 352, 358–9; travels with husband, 349–50, 352; proposed travels with B, 353–4; alarm over B's fever, 357; husband's demands on, 357; as B's "destiny", 358; settled relationship with B, 359, 373, 408; B suspects of deceit, 364; looks after Allegra, 365–6; leaves Ravenna for country, 368, 372; separation from Guiccioli, 368–9, 406; letters to B, 369; on Constant's *Adolphe*, 370–2; receives allowance from husband, 370; writes to husband, 371; marriage to de Boissy, 372, 476; reads B's poems, 372–3; returns to Ravenna, 374; on B's dislike of Allegra, 380; urges B to abandon *Don Juan*, 383; joins father in exile in Florence, 384; Shelley writes to and visits, 386–7; moves to Pisa, 387–8, 392; and B's reluctance to come to Pisa, 388, 390; B speaks of to Augusta, 389; life in Pisa, 395; and scuffle with Italian sergeant major, 399–400; on death of Allegra, 402; with B in Montenero, 405–6; allowance from husband suspended, 406; and Shelley's drowning, 409; and B's plan to move to South America, 411; moves to Genoa, 411–13; Augusta's attitude to, 418; B's growing coolness to, 421, 430; and Lady Blessington, 422–4; opposes B's supporting Greek cause, 427, 429; allowance from husband resumed, 429; required to accompany father on return to Ravenna, 429; attempts reconciliation between B and Mary Shelley, 432; and B's departure for Greece, 434–6, 438; letters from brother Pietro, 435–6, 438, 441, 458, 464; B writes to from Greece, 444, 464; told of B's death, 472; *Vie de Lord Byron*, 372, 402, 434

Haller von Hallerstein, Karl, 122
Halnaby, Yorkshire (country house), 221–2, 226, 229, 238
Hamilton, Douglas Hamilton, 8th Duke of, 100
Hanson, Captain (RN; John's brother), 10
Hanson, John: and B's birth, 10; and William Byron's death, 19; meets B and mother at Newstead, 22–4; and Lord Carlisle, 26–7; B stays with family, 27–9, 32; on May Gray's misbehaviour with B, 27–8; and B at Harrow, 30, 33–4, 45; and Lord Grey, 42, 46; Augusta Leigh writes to, 43; and B's leaving Harrow, 48–9; and B at Cambridge, 52, 54–5; Augusta consults over B's depression, 59; and Catherine Byron's anxiety over B's debts, 60; and B's proposed disposal of Newstead, 66; and B's finances, 69, 72, 77–9, 143, 196, 211, 393; and B's illegitimate child, 70; and B's 21st birthday, 71; and B's entry into House of Lords, 73–4; and B's plan to travel abroad, 77; in B's will, 77; reports to B while abroad, 80, 121; letters from B abroad, 90, 102, 106, 113–14, 124, 128; sends money to B in Turkey, 112; urges B to sell Newstead, 121, 124, 145, 164; and Mrs Byron's death, 133; visits Rochdale with B, 140; doubles rents of Newstead tenants, 150; persuades B to economise, 171; B requests to sell Rochdale property, 176; and B's proposed second trip abroad, 176–7; proposes suing Claughton, 177; and B's prospective marriage, 205, 211, 213; and prospective sale of Newstead, 211, 308; arranges B's marriage agreement, 215–16; as B's executor, 237; and Annabella's suspicion of B's mental condition, 242; and B's separation proceedings, 248, 253, 270; dismisses Newstead tenants, 267; B instructs to restore Joe Murray's full wages, 290; and Annabella's plans to take Ada abroad, 304; and repayment of B's debts on sale of Newstead, 318; and final sale of Newstead, 322, 335; postpones trip with Newstead papers, 327; visits B in Venice, 333; Hobhouse and Kinnaird suspect, 335; fails to help over Mary Shelley finances, 422
Hanson, Newton, 27, 333
Hardstaff, Mrs ("Lady Betty"), 7
Hardy, Anne Louise Emily, Lady (née Berkeley), 418, 430

Harness, William, 48, 57, 65, 143–4, 267
Harrow school: B attends, 2–3, 29–33, 35, 37, 41, 45–50; B revisits, 65, 131; B writes reminiscences of, 374
Harrowby, Dudley Ryder, 1st Earl of, 169, 181
Harvey, Isabel, 419
Hastings (Sussex), 196–7, 203
Hato (or Hatagee; Turkish girl), 461
Hay, Captain John, 399
Hazlitt, William, 202
Heathcote, Lady, 178
Heaven and Earth (B), 384, 390n, 417, 439
Heber, Reginald, Bishop of Calcutta, 417
Hebrew Melodies (B), 234, 270
Hellenica Chronica (newspaper), 453
Hellespont: B swims, 1, 87, 108–9
Henry VIII, King of England, 5
Hensch, Charles, 384
Herbert, Edward, 1st Baron Herbert of Cherbury, 53
Hercules (barge), 431, 434–6, 439
Hervey, Elizabeth, 286
Hesperides (proposed journal), 408
Hill (British ambassador in Cagliari), 91
Hill (British minister in Genoa), 411
Hints from Horace (B), 123, 151
Hobhouse, Benjamin (JCH's brother), 472
Hobhouse, (Sir) John Cam: on B's leg brace, 30; on Grey's influence on B, 40; friendship with B, 41, 63, 65, 73, 76–7, 177, 192, 233; on B's friendships, 47; scepticism on B's reading claims, 53; B meets at Cambridge, 61–2; rebukes B for behaviour, 64; B accompanies to Brighton, 65; in Nottingham with B, 67; on Long's death, 73; in B's will, 77; and B's finances, 79; accompanies B abroad, 81–2, 84–7, 89–100, 103–4, 109, 111–12, 116, 437, 448; on homosexual practices in Albania, 95–6; and Greek political situation, 97; on Elgin's depradations, 101–2; and B's Hellespont swim, 108; on Constantinople dancing boys, 110; attentiveness to B's welfare, 114; leaves B in Greece, 114–15, 134; letters from B in Greece and voyage to England, 117–18, 127; B describes Lady Hester Stanhope to, 120; and B's return from Greece, 128–30; father pays debts, 129, 150; joins militia, 129; and B's *Childe Harold*, 130, 155, 317–18, 321; in Ireland with regiment, 132, 135, 143n; and B's mother's death, 133, 135; and Matthews' death, 135; B names as executor, 136; B complains of Claridge to, 139; on B's literary circle, 143; and Samuel Rogers, 143n; and B's devotion to Edleston, 145; B requests IOU from, 150; on B in Lords, 163–4; and B's relations with Caroline Lamb, 164, 170; jealousy of Moore, 174; makes European tour, 176–7; helps B separate from Caroline Lamb, 177; returns from second foreign trip, 192; and

B's *Ode to Napoleon*, 193; on B's solitude, 194; B proposes further continental trip with, 206, 208; learns of B's marriage, 209; attends B's marriage, 219–21; Lady Milbanke welcomes, 222; B denigrates, 223; sends Ligne's autograph to Annabella, 227; visits France (1815), 233, 237; as B's executor, 237; Annabella attacks, 240, 250–1; on B's marriage, 240; and B's separation proceedings, 247, 250, 252, 258; joins B in Piccadilly Terrace, 259, 260, 262–3; friendship with James Perry, 264; buys books from Byron, 266; and B's departure for exile, 267, 271, 273–4; with B at Lady Jersey's party, 268; on break between Augusta Leigh and Annabella, 269; witnesses B's separation agreement, 270; letters from B in exile, 275–6; on Caroline Lamb's *Glenarvon*, 278–9; thirtieth birthday, 279n; calls on Augusta before leaving for Geneva, 281; with B in Switzerland, 287, 290, 292; visits Mme de Staël at Coppet, 289; and Annabella's intrigues, 295; in Italy with B (1816), 296–7, 300, 306–7; travels in Italy alone, 309, 311–12; meets B in Rome, 311; 1822 visit to B in Italy, 312; arranges Thorwaldsen bust of B, 312; visits B at La Mira, 316–17; B dedicates fourth canto of *Childe Harold* to, 318; on B's indifference towards Annabella, 320; calls on Augusta, 321; returns to England (1818), 321, 324; requests Byron's letters to Lady Melbourne, 322; and Foscolo, 326; B's anger at, 327; B assigns business affairs to, 334; condemns B's *Don Juan*, 335–8; political career, 335; suspects Hanson's probity, 335; and B's attachment to Teresa Guiccioli, 342, 349, 359; and B's sense of wasting life, 350; and B's South America plan, 354; invites B to return to England, 354; B lampoons, 361–3; imprisoned for radical pamphlet, 361; reports British affairs to B, 361; elected MP, 363; on B's preoccupation with money, 365; and B's reminiscences of Cambridge, 374; chides B for inactive life, 374; and B's reaction to staging of *Marino Falieri*, 383; supports Teresa Guiccioli urging abandonment of *Don Juan*, 383; and B's move to Pisa, 393; settles B's debts to Ghigi, 403; explains Augusta's reluctance to move abroad, 418; on B's lack of feelings for Annabella, 424; introduces Blaquiere to B, 424; in London Greek Committee, 426; and B's decision to go to Greece, 427; and Hunt's taking money meant for Mary Shelley, 431; and B's departure for Greece, 435, 437; and B's presence in Greece, 449; and B's final illness, 468, 470; destroys B's memoirs, 472–3; learns of B's death, 472; and B's burial, 474; later life, 476; fails to help Fletcher, 477; *Collection*, 111; *A Journey through Albania . . . to*

Constantinople, 102–3, 177; *Recollections of a Long Life*, 279

Hodgson, Francis: friendship with B, 61–2, 67, 76, 82, 102, 111, 120, 128, 130; and B's religious scepticism, 137–8, 144; and B's reaction to death of Edelston, 140; rejected by woman, 141; at Newstead, 144–5; B announces intention to quit England, 149; and B's maiden speech in Lords, 150; attends theatre with B, 192; B asks to find house in Hastings, 196–7; engagement, 197; urges B to marry, 197, 203; welcomes B's engagement to Annabella, 209, 217; on B's marriage settlement, 217; letter from Augusta Leigh on B and Annabel's visit, 231; attempts conciliation in B's separation proceedings, 251, 258; and Augusta Leigh's fears of Annabella, 281, 299; Augusta Leigh confides in and corresponds with, 299, 303, 311, 374; B writes to from Italy, 374; Augusta tells of return of B's body, 472

Holderness, Mary, Countess of (Augusta's grandmother), 10, 42

Holland, Elizabeth, Lady, 157, 161–2, 272, 279, 472

Holland, Henry (architect), 194n

Holland, Henry Richard Vassall Fox, 3rd Baron: on B's power to affect readers, 140; entertains Moore, 141; seen as C.J. Fox's successor, 148; and B's political sympathies, 149; objects to new edition of *English Bards*, 150; and Drury Lane Theatre, 171; letters from B on going abroad, 173–4; and B's *The Giaour*, 191; denies Annabella's accusations over B, 257–8; believes in B's sodomy with Annabella, 270n; and B's separation, 270; reads B's memoirs, 472; *Memoirs*, 150

Holland House (London), 157

Hoppner, Isabelle (Richard's wife): takes care of Allegra, 323, 329–30; B dines with, 326; admits not liking Allegra, 332; on change in Allegra, 351; writes to Claire Clairmont on Allegra's movements, 365; behaviour towards Claire Clairmont, 367; and alleged affair between Claire Clairmont and Shelley, 401

Hoppner, John, 321

Hoppner, Richard: friendship with B in Venice, 321, 326, 360; Allegra stays with, 323, 329–30; admits not liking Allegra, 332; and B's attachment to Teresa Guiccioli, 345, 354; and B's visit to Ravenna, 347, 359; and Count Guiccioli's attempt to secure vice-consulship, 348; and Hobhouse's imprisonment, 361; behaviour towards Claire Clairmont, 367; B reports on Allegra's condition to, 380; B informs of placing Allegra in convent, 381; calumny on Shelley's 'child' with Claire Clairmont, 382, 385; and B's burial wish, 471

Horton, Robert Wilmot, 473 & n

Hours of Idleness (B), 58, 61, 63–5, 68, 75, 132, 149, 264n, 382, 437
House of Lords *see* Lords, House of
Hucknall Torkard, Nottinghamshire, 134, 473–4
Hunt, John, 175, 416, 420, 428, 441
Hunt, Leigh: jailed, 75, 175–6, 189; friendship with B, 176, 236, 260; B sends *The Bride of Abydos* to, 189; on B's monogram, 266; Mary Shelley speaks to on B in Venice, 331; Shelley invites to Italy, 387–8, 393–4, 396; requests for financial help from B, 398–9; arrives in Livorno with family, 407–8; on Teresa Guiccioli, 408–9; and Shelley's death, 409–10; and *Liberal* (journal), 411, 413, 416–17, 420; relations with B in Italy, 411–12, 418, 429; Hobhouse and, 412; in Lerici, 413; moves from Villa Lanfranchi, 413; B gossips to Murray about, 416–17; and money for Mary Shelley's return to England, 431–2; *The Story of Rimini*, 176
Hunt, Marianne, 176, 408, 413–14
Hunter, Dr John, 12, 15
Hydra (ship), 124–5

Ibrahim Pasha, 122
incest: as crime, 267n
Ionian Islands, 93–4, 426
Ipsilantes, Prince Alexander, 439
Irving, Washington, 144
Island, The (B), 33
Italy: B travels in with Hobhouse (1816), 296–7, 300–11; revolutionary movement in, 369–70, 372, 375, 379–80, 439; *see also* individual cities
Ithaca (Greece), 440

Jackson, John ("Gentleman"), 66
James, Henry, 383
Jamison, Kay Redfield, 56
Jeffrey, Francis, 64, 75, 123, 141, 304
Jersey, Sarah, Countess of, 156, 268
Jones, Revd Thomas, 54, 62

Karaiskakis, George, 465
Karvellas, Francis, 295, 297
Karvellas, Nicholas, 295, 297, 412
Kay, John, 17
Kean, Edmund, 157, 192, 195, 214
Keats, John: death in Rome, 311, 382; B condemns, 374
Kelsall, Michael, 150
Kemble, Fanny, 143, 157
Kennedy, Dr James, 439, 461
Kinnaird, Charles, 8th Baron, 318
Kinnaird, Douglas: in Cambridge Whig Club, 62; and B's membership of Drury sub-committee, 237; friendship with B, 239, 270; denies harsh comments on Annabella, 257–8; supports Mrs Marden, 271; and B's contentment in Switzerland, 279; advances

money to B in Switzerland, 283; as B's literary agent, 293; and paternity of Allegra, 309; visits B in Venice, 318; B's anger at, 327; advises B on business affairs, 334, 361, 365, 393, 419–20; and B's *Don Juan*, 335, 337, 355, 428; and sale of Newstead, 335; B confides in about Teresa Guiccioli, 349, 357; and B's sense of wasting life, 350; B sends fifth canto of *Don Juan* to, 375; defends Hobhouse to B, 393; B sends *Cain* to, 394; dissuades B from duel with Southey, 397; and Lady Noel's estate, 398; and B's plan to move to South America, 411; increases Annabella's life insurance, 415; B instructs to find new publisher, 416, 420, 428; B instructs not to make payments, 427; funds B on departure for Greece, 435; sells Rochdale property, 442; and B's activities in Greece, 444; on B's fortune, 468; and B's final illness, 470; learns of B's death, 472; reads B's memoirs, 472; death from cancer, 476
Kirkby Mallory, Leicestershire (house), 236–7, 241, 244, 271, 398
Knight, J. Wilson, 89
Koch, Robert, 454n
Koes, George, 122
Kolokotrones, Theodore, 439

Labouchere, Henry, 267n
"Lachin Y Gair" (B), 59
Lamb, Caroline ("Caro George"; Mrs George Lamb): on B's happy marriage, 232; supports Annabella, 255, 268, 272; sends B's offensive poems to Annabella, 263–4; snubs Augusta, 268; and Caroline Lamb's *Glenarvon*, 280; intrigue with Brougham, 282n; and Annabella's intrigues, 295; and death of Lady Melbourne, 322
Lamb, Lady Caroline ("Caro William"): B's romance with, 89, 162–5, 166, 180, 183; Annabella sees B at party of, 152; interest in B, 161–2; B disengages from, 167–8, 170–1, 176–8; jealousy of Lady Oxford, 170; irrational behaviour, 172, 176; friendship with John Murray, 178; self-stabbing, 179; B continues correspondence with, 185; on B in *The Giaour*, 191; resumes relations with B, 195–6; and Lady Melbourne, 198; and Annabella's engagement to B, 209; calls on Lady Noel, 236; and Annabella's separation proceedings, 255–7; attempts to recover letters to B, 255; traduces Lady Melbourne to Annabella, 255–6; and B's offensive poems, 263; visits Brussels and Waterloo, 274n; and *Glenarvon*, 278; trouble-making, 290, 294; helps George Lamb win parliamentary seat, 335; resemblance to Countess Guiccioli, 342; hears rumours of B's return to England, 370; reads B's memoirs, 472; and B's funeral, 473–4; death, 474; *Glenarvon*, 170, 278–80, 282

Lamb, George, 335
Lamb, William *see* Melbourne, 2nd Viscount
Lament of Tasso, The (B), 311
Lanfranchi, Palazzo, Pisa, 392, 396, 405, 408, 413
Lang, Cecil Y., 96n
Lansdowne, Henry Petty-Fitzmaurice, 3rd
    Marquess of, 141, 175
Lara (B), 195, 197, 297, 300
"Last Words on Greece" (B), 455
Lauderdale, James Maitland, 8th Earl of, 333
Launders sisters, 34
Laurie, Dr Maurice, 27, 29–30
Lavender (Nottingham quack doctor), 25–6
Leacroft, Julia, 57, 104
Leake, William Martin, 93
Leeds, Catherine, Duchess of, 43
Leeds, Francis Godolphin Osborne, 5th Duke of,
    8, 10, 24
Leigh, Augusta Mary (*née* Byron; B's half-sister):
    Clare reports to on meeting B in Italy, 2;
    birth, 8; relations with B's mother, 9–10;
    father's fondness for, 13; at Castle Howard,
    26; correspondence with B, 42–6, 51, 70, 180–
    1; B invites to Harrow, 49–50; and B's
    attending Cambridge, 52; B complains of
    mother to, 55, 72; anxiety over B's spirits, 59,
    180; marriage and children, 68, 180; and B's
    finances, 69, 180; B threatens to sever relations
    with, 73; offended by B's attack on Carlisle,
    76, 114, 137, 180; in B's will, 136, 183, 237, 474;
    reconciled with B after mother's death, 136;
    financial embarrassments, 137, 180, 308, 327;
    and B's proposed second trip abroad, 177;
    appearance, 181; romantic/incestuous relations
    with B, 181–5, 188, 196, 208, 234, 252–3, 256–
    7, 314; visits B in London (1813), 181, 236;
    pregnancy and birth of Elizabeth Medora,
    182–3, 191, 194; B keeps lock of hair, 184–5;
    visits Newstead with B, 189–91, 197, 204; B
    gives money to for husband's debts, 196; urges
    B to marry, 197, 203, 205; and Lady
    Melbourne, 198, 236; and Annabella's
    acceptance of B, 207; writes to Annabella,
    210–12, 225; Annabella's jealousy of, 216, 226,
    230–1, 235, 261; dissuades B from breaking off
    engagement, 217; letter to B on wedding, 221–
    2; on B's desire for large house, 226; and B's
    marriage relations, 226–7; B and Annabella
    stay with at Six Mile Bottom, 227–32; wears
    brooch from B, 230; friendship and intimacy
    with Annabella, 231–2, 236–9, 241, 244–5, 248;
    appointed lady-in-waiting to Queen Charlotte,
    232, 418; stays with B in Piccadilly Terrace,
    232, 243–4; visits B and Annabella in London,
    233; B visits alone, 237; believes B deranged,
    240; and birth of B's daughter (Ada), 240; and
    Annabella's leaving B, 244–5, 248; attempts
    reconciliation between B and Annabella, 248–
    51, 254, 258, 268; Annabella refuses to meet,

253, 258; moves to St James's Palace, 259, 327;
    and custody of Annabella's daughter, 262; B's
    poem to, 263; acquires books from B auction,
    266; break with Annabella, 268–9; at Lady
    Jersey's party with B, 268; pregnancy and
    birth of Frederick, 268 & n, 280; snubs Selina
    Doyle, 268, 280n; and B's departure for exile,
    269–70; and B's separation agreement, 270;
    Annabella cultivates after B's departure for
    exile, 272; Annabella persecutes, 280–1, 290–1,
    294, 298–9; view of B, 282; and B's absence in
    Switzerland, 288, 290, 292–3, 295; B's
    "Epistle" to, 288, 302; reproachful letter from
    B in Switzerland, 292; Annabella rumoured to
    be living with, 293–4; admits incest to
    Annabella, 294; submits to Annabella, 294–5;
    B writes to from Italy, 297–8, 312; writes
    saying unable to meet B in England, 298–9;
    and Annabella's proposal to take Ada to
    continent, 301; and publication of *Childe
    Harold*, 302–3; and B's improved spirits in
    Venice, 308; on Ada as Ward of Chancery,
    311, 325; and incest theme of *Manfred*, 314–15;
    B suspends letters to, 315, 327; regrets sale of
    Newstead, 319–20; B resumes letters to, 333,
    344, 374; on B's *Don Juan*, 337–8; B declares
    love for, 344–5, 349, 358, 374; informs
    Annabella of B's letter declaring love, 344;
    and B's attachment to Teresa Guiccioli, 349,
    358–9, 418; disbelieves rumours of B's return,
    370; anxieties over B's memoirs, 389; forwards
    lock of B's hair to Ada, 389; B invites to Pisa,
    393–4; outraged at *Cain*, 394; and Allegra's
    death, 404; and John Murray, 416; B suggests
    moving to Nice, 418; B praises to Lady
    Blessington, 424; reassures B of Ada's recovery
    from illness, 442; B writes to from Greece,
    461; B's dying blessing on, 469; letter to B
    after death, 470; on return of B's body, 472;
    and destruction of B's memoirs, 473; pays
    annuity to Fletcher, 476
Leigh, Elizabeth Medora (Augusta's daughter):
    born, 191, 202; appearance, 218, 230;
    Annabella tells of paternity, 475; children by
    Henry Trevanion, 475
Leigh, Emily (Augusta's daughter), 475
Leigh, Frances (*née* Byron; B's aunt), 10, 12, 14,
    18
Leigh, Frederick (Augusta's fifth child), 268n, 280
Leigh, Col. George (Augusta's husband): B sends
    good wishes to, 43; parents oppose marriage
    to Augusta, 44; marriage, 68, 180; loses favour
    with Prince of Wales, 106, 137; and Augusta's
    pregnancy with Medora, 183, 191; leaves for
    Yorkshire, 191; B clears debts, 196; and B's
    marriage breakdown, 212; flu, 219; absence on
    shooting party, 230; on B in Venice, 308; B
    mocks, 314
Leigh, Georgiana (*later* Trevanion; Augusta's

daughter): born, 68; described to B, 136; B's supposed designs on, 291; marries Henry Trevanion, 475

Le Mann, Dr Francis, 242–5, 250

Lepanto, 449–50, 458, 462

Lerici, 405, 406, 413–14

Leveson-Gower, Lady Charlotte, 197, 202–5, 307n

Lewis, Benjamin, 466, 476

Lewis, Matthew Gregory ("Monk"), 287, 312, 316–17

Liberal (journal), 397, 411, 413, 416–17, 420

Ligne, Prince of, 227

Linckh, Jacob, 124

"Lines on Hearing that Lady Byron Was Ill" (B), 290

"Lines to a Lady Weeping" (B) *see* "Sympathetic Address to a Young Lady Weeping"

Lisbon, 85–7

Literary Gazette, 416

London: described, 155–9

London Greek Committee, 426–8, 435, 438, 441–2, 449–50, 453, 455, 457

Londos, Andreas, 97, 117, 439

Long, Edward Noel: with B at Harrow, 32, 46, 48; at Cambridge with B, 54, 57; drowned, 73, 135, 140

Long, Henry, 143n, 447

Lords, House of: B enters, 73–4; B's maiden speech in, 148–50; B's attendances in, 163–4, 172–3

Louis XVIII, Emperor of France, 195

"Love and Death" (B), 456

Lovell, Ernest J., Jr, 396n

Lovell, Lady, 311

Lucy (servant girl), 70, 139, 144

Luddite riots, 147–50

Lushington, Dr Stephen: advises Annabella on separation, 246–8, 250–3, 255–6, 262, 264, 268–9, 271; on B's crimes, 272; and Annabella's attitude to Augusta Leigh, 280; has evidence of B's incest, 294; and Annabella's intrigues, 295; and Ada's being made Ward of Chancery, 310; sees B's statement on breaking silence, 317, 320; Annabella consults over B's memoirs, 360; defends Queen Caroline, 370; and Lady Noel's death and estate, 398

Lusieri, Giovanni Battista, 100–1, 103–4, 118, 122–3, 125, 127, 151

Lyon (Newfoundland dog), 435, 448, 462

McGann, Jerome, 64, 325, 325

Macri, Tarsia, 99, 118

Macri, Theresa, 104

Mahmoud II, Ottoman Sultan, 112

Malta, 91–2, 125–6

Maluchielli, Antonio, 400, 405

Mameluke (horse), 430

Manfred (B), 287, 293, 311–15, 394

Manzoni, Domenico, 346

Marchand, Leslie: on B's club foot, 12; on B's "Stanzas to Jessy", 56; and B's illegitimate child, 70; on B's pederastic interests, 81; misreads word "Collection", 111n; on B's letter to Caroline Lamb, 164

Marden, Mrs (actress mistress of B), 265, 271 & n

Marianna (B's Venetian mistress) *see* Segati, Marianna

Marino Falieri (B), 364, 382

Marmaratouri (Greek patriot), 122

Marston Moor, Battle of (1643), 6

Masi, Sergeant-Major Stefani, 400, 405–6

"Mason, Mrs" *see* Mountcashell, Countess of

Massingberd, Elizabeth, 32, 59n, 80, 129, 143

Matthews, Charles Skinner: at Cambridge, 54, 61–2, 76–7, 81, 118, 440; death, 135, 140, 472

Maturin, Charles: *Bertram*, 237

Mavrocordato, Prince Alexander: in Greek war of independence, 425, 439, 441; correspondence with B, 443–4; in Missolonghi, 443–4, 447–9, 455; military actions, 449–50; and Turkish prisoners, 451; resists Captain Yorke's demands, 454; Blaquiere invites to London, 455; money shortage, 457; Odysseus invites to meeting, 462; suspects Karaiskakis, 465

"Mazeppa" (B), 331

Mealey, Owen, 24, 35, 36–7, 39, 42, 393

Mealey, Mrs Owen, 415, 468

Medwin, Thomas: and B's departure from England, 83; and B's rescuing Greek woman from death, 119; and B's affair with Caroline Lamb, 163; in Pisa, 392; leaves for Rome, 399; recollections of B, 423

Mekhitar, Father Peter, 306

Melbourne, Elizabeth, Viscountess (*née* Milbanke): and B's feelings for Mrs Spencer Smith, 92, 125; London social life, 157–9; background, 158; and B's interest in Annabella, 160; as B's confidante and correspondent, 165–72, 174, 176–9, 183, 185, 190–2, 196, 198–9, 211, 215–16, 226, 270; and B's proposed second trip abroad, 176–7; and B's relations with Augusta Leigh, 181–3, 192, 198, 203, 211; and Annabella's relations with B, 186–8, 198–200, 202–3, 205, 254n; and B's *The Giaour*, 191; B informs of Annabella's acceptance of marriage proposal, 208, 211; Lady Milbanke (Noel) discusses Annabella's engagement with, 210; taxes Annabella over B's departure from Seaham, 217; advice to Annabella after wedding, 222, 226; on Augusta's character, 222; letter from B on hopes for marriage success, 224; recommends Devonshires' house to B, 227; calls on Lady Noel, 236; Lushington decries, 247; and B's separation from Annabella, 248, 255, 269; on

Annabella as spoiled child, 254n; Caroline Lamb traduces, 255–6; and B's departure for exile, 269; Caroline Lamb writes to, 274n; and Annabella's plan to take Ada to continent, 301; Hoppner portrait of, 321; death, 322

Melbourne, Peniston Lamb, 1st Viscount, 159, 165–2

Melbourne, William Lamb, 2nd Viscount, 158, 161, 163, 172, 279, 335, 473–4

Mengaldo, Cavalier Angelo, 326, 331, 341

Merryweather, Francis, 323

Milan (Italy), 296–8

Milbanke, Annabella *see* Byron, Annabella

Milbanke, Judith, Lady *see* Noel, Judith, Lady

Milbanke, Sir Ralph *see* Noel, Sir Ralph

Miller, William, 131

Millingen, Dr Julius, 11n, 459, 466–8, 469, 471

Milner, Emily, 209

Milton, John, 277, 394

Mira, La *see* Foscarini, Villa

Missolonghi: B first *sees* (1809), 93, 97; Mavrocordato in, 443–4, 448; threatened by Turkish ships, 446, 465; B in, 448–9, 464; earthquake, 462

Mocenigo, Palazzo (Venice), 321, 324, 327, 330, 353, 356–7

Moers, Ellen: *The Dandy*, 156

Montenero, near Livorno (Italy), 2, 401, 405

Montgomery, Col. Hugh, 188, 209–10, 212, 215, 424, 474

Montgomery, Mary Millicent, 188

Monthly Monitor (magazine), 63

Monti, Vincenzo, 297

Moore, Doris Langley, 69n

Moore, John: *Zeluco*, 53

Moore, General Sir John, 68

Moore, Thomas: Lord Clare tells of detroying B's letters, 3; on Newstead, 21; and Dr Glennie, 29; on Mary Chaworth's rejection of B, 37; on B and Lord Grey, 40; interviews Elizabeth Pigot, 45; on B's friendships, 47–8; on B's illegitimate children, 70n; B criticises in *English Bards*, 75, 141; reprints B's lines on Beckford, 86; on B's departure from Constantinople, 114; on B's lame foot, 116–17; and Lord Holland's remark on B's power to arouse feelings, 140; abortive duel with Jeffrey, 141; friendship with B, 141–3, 174, 195; and B's political sympathies, 149; and Lord Holland's objection to *English Bards*, 150; and B's interest in Annabella, 160; and Caroline Lamb, 162; letter from B on romantic entanglement, 182; and B's journal, 184; B dedicates *The Corsair* to, 189; and B's *The Giaour*, 191; and B's relations with Augusta, 194; and B's social indifference, 194; poor opinion of Annabella, 209; on B's wedding night, 221; and B's complaints of married life, 225; on breakdown of B's marriage, 258; and B's exile, 266; B

describes writing *Childe Harold* to, 285; prints B's "Epistle to Augusta", 288n, 302n; writes life of B, 302n; gossip about B, 308; B describes Venice Carnival to, 309–10; on success of fourth canto of *Childe Harold*, 324; Teresa Guiccioli tells of travels with B, 353; marriage, 355; meets Teresa Guiccioli, 355; visits B in Venice, 355–6; B gives memoirs to, 356–7, 359, 376, 393; on B's preoccupation with money, 365; B suggests jointly starting weekly newspaper, 375; B writes to on visitor from Boston, 377; and B's proposed move to Pisa, 388; Murray buys copyright of B's memoirs from, 389; and B's attachment to Lord Clare, 406; and B's plan to move to South America, 411; B complains of Hunt and *Liberal* to, 420; and B's feelings for Henry Fox, 422; and destruction of B's memoirs, 473; *The Poetical Works of the Late Thomas Little*, 57

Moretto (B's bulldog), 411, 435

Morgan, Sydney Owenson, Lady, 162

Morning Chronicle (newspaper), 150, 191, 264, 370

Morning Post (newspaper), 362

Mountcashell, Margaret King, Countess of ("Mrs Mason"), 419

Mozart, Wolfgang Amadeus: *Don Giovanni*, 333

Murray, Joe: at Newstead, 22, 24, 66, 71, 144; accompanies B abroad, 82, 87; returns to England, 90; in B's will, 136; wages cut, 290; death, 375

Murray, John II: B confesses inherited melancholy to, 9; and B's recollection of Loch Leven, 21; B requests to delay collected edition of works, 113; publishes B, 131, 138–9, 151, 193, 237; on B's religious scepticism, 138; and B's *Waltz*, 171; Caroline tricks into giving miniature of B, 172; buys and publishes Mme de Staël's *De l'Allemagne*, 175n; friendship with Caroline Lamb, 178; publishes B's *Bride of Abydos*, 189–90; and success of *The Corsair*, 190–1; and B's engagement to Annabella, 209, 212; praises Annabella, 232; Byron visits offices, 233–4; B refuses advance from, 240; and B's offensive poems against Mrs Clermont, 263; acquires books and prints from B auction, 266; offer to Polidori, 266; publishes Coleridge's *Christabel*, 283; and B's *Childe Harold*, 285, 288, 293, 299, 302, 324; Kinnaird makes agreement for B with, 293; and Annabella's intrigues, 295; B writes to from Milan, 296; shows *Childe Harold* to Annabella, 299, 302; reads B's letters to literary circle, 308; B describes execution to, 311; and B's *Manfred*, 311; Augusta *seeks* loans from, 327; B's anger at for non-payment, 327; and B's memoirs, 332–3, 356–7, 389, 394; and B's *Don Juan*, 335, 337–8, 364, 383, 415; B tells of romantic accident, 344; B *seeks* help from over consular appointment for Guiccioli, 348;

and B's plan to visit South America, 350; *seeks* to prevent piracy of *Don Juan*, 358; B writes to on Italian cultural differences, 360; B sends lampoon on Hobhouse to, 361–3; B honours financial obligations to, 365; B sends poem on Rogers to, 371–2; B criticises Hobhouse to, 374; B writes to on unrest in Italy, 375; B rebukes for printing errors, 388; B recommends Taaffe to, 392, 397; refuses to publish *The Vision of Judgment*, 397; B writes to on Shelley's death, 409; B's disagreements with, 415–17; agrees to destruction of B's memoirs, 473

Murray, John III, 234

Musgrave, Isabella, Lady *see* Carlisle, Countess of

Musters, Jack, 36–8, 67, 74, 190

Musters, Mary *see* Chaworth, Mary

Musters, Mrs (Jack's mother), 236

Napier, Col. Charles James, 439–40, 444, 450

Naples: Austrians occupy, 379–80

Napoleon I (Bonaparte), Emperor of France: B admires, 85, 128, 184, 193; seizes Malta, 91; alleged assassination attempt on, 92; English supporters, 148; and treatment of Catholics, 163; exiles Mme de Staël, 175; Hobhouse relates anecdotes on, 192; downfall, 193; B's disenchantment with, 195; escapes from Elba, 232–3; Waterloo defeat, 234n; B copies coach, 266–7; exile on St Helena, 266; B admires naval basins, 274; in Italy, 296; Simplon Pass military road, 296; Stendhal and, 297–8; and Venice, 305; Guiccioli supports, 346

Nash, John, 156

Nathan, Isaac, 234, 270

Necker, Jacques, 175

Newstead Abbey, Nottinghamshire: Byrons first acquire, 5; 5th Baron Byron despoils, 7; B inherits, 18; B occupies, 21, 24–6; finances and maintenance, 24, 72, 102, 107; let to Lord Grey, 34; B visits Grey at, 35, 39; B's poems to, 59; B reoccupies and improves, 66–8, 106; Grey's lease expires, 66; B throws house party at, 76; sale prospects, 78, 80, 211–12, 215, 217, 308–9; Hanson urges B to sell, 121–2, 124, 145, 164; and Mrs Byron's death, 133; in B's will, 136; B's life at, 139, 141, 144–6; Harness spends Christmas at, 143–4; attempted auction and sale to Claughton, 165, 171, 177, 196; Augusta Leigh visits with B, 189–91, 197, 204; reverts to B, 197; Murray visits, 209; B's final visit to, 214; and B's marriage agreement, 215; George Byron inherits, 216; re-auctioned (1815), 237; tenants dismissed for non-payment of rent, 267; B's attachment to, 305; sold to Wildman, 318, 321–2, 335

Nicolson, Harold, 450

Noel, Judith, Lady (*formerly* Milbanke; Annabella's mother): criticises Lady Melbourne, 200, 227;

on Annabella's prospective marriage, 210; and B's visit to Seaham, 214–15, 225; at Annabella and B's wedding, 219–20; reservations about B, 222; B snatches wig, 225; asks B to take care of Annabella, 228; in London, 235, 240; changes name, 236; inheritance from brother Wentworth, 236; and Annabella's leaving B, 245–6; arranges separation for Annabella, 246–8, 254; suspicion of Augusta Leigh, 248; Annabella confides incest suspicions of B to, 253; and inheritance at death of, 257, 261, 398; and B's defence of behaviour towards Annabella, 258; and custody of Annabella's daughter, 262; vengefulness, 262; reads Brougham's letter to Annabella, 289; death, 397–8

Noel, Sir Ralph (*formerly* Milbanke; Annabella's father): background, 159; financial difficulties, 167, 216, 218, 239; and B's visit to Seaham, 214–15, 218, 222; and Annabella's marriage settlement, 215; B endures long stories, 215, 225; inherits brother's estate (Kirkby Mallory), 236; letters to B proposing separation from Annabella, 248–9; told of B's incest, 253; demands Perry retract conspiracy charge, 264; and plans to take Ada abroad, 304, 310

Noel, Revd Thomas, 219–20, 223

Nottingham: industrial and social unrest in, 147–8

"Ode to the Framers of the Frame Bill, An" (B), 150

Ode to Napoleon (B), 193

"Ode to Venice" (B), 331

Odysseus (Ulysses; Greek chieftain), 439, 441, 462

Ollier, Charles, 397

O'Meara, Barry, 266

"On This Day I Complete My Thirty-Sixth Year" (B), 452

Origo, Iris, 343, 372

Orsay, Count Alfred d', 422, 423

Oxford, Edward Harley, 5th Earl of, 169–70, 172, 174, 177

Oxford, Jane, Countess of: relations with B, 169–72, 174, 177–9, 181, 183, 185, 198; in Caroline Lamb's *Glenarvon*, 279; Hoppner portrait of, 321n

Pakenham, General Sir Edward Michael, 160

Papi, Vincenzo, 400, 405

Parisina (B), 237, 253

Parker, Margaret, 28

Parkyns, Ann, 25

Parry, William: in Greece with B, 450, 455, 457–62, 464–7, 469; death, 476

Parsons, Anne (Mme Galignani), 279n

Peacock, Thomas Love, 285, 331, 385

Peel, (Sir) Robert, 32

Peninsular War, 88, 152–3

Perry, James, 264

Petrarch, 353, 355

Pigot, Elizabeth, 45, 50, 51, 56, 61, 70n, 140

Pigot, John, 51, 57–8

Pinto, Captain Luigi dal, 375

Pisa: B in, 1–2, 390–2, 394–5, 399; Shelleys in, 1, 365, 382, 386, 399; Shelley's literary colony in, 387–9, 390, 392–5; Teresa and father move to, 387; Hunts arrive in, 408

Polidori, Dr John William: B engages for travel abroad, 266, 271, 276–7; on B's licentiousness, 273; at Villa Diodati, 282; B discharges, 290; *The Vampire*, 105, 283, 343

Pope, Alexander, 53, 123, 374

Portland, William Henry Cavendish Bentinck, 3rd Duke of, 27

Princess Elizabeth (ship), 82, 85, 434, 437

Prisoner of Chillon, The (B), 293, 302n

Pulci, Luigi, 317; *Morgante Maggiore*, 417

Pylades, HMS, 104–5

Quarterly Review, 131, 305, 382, 417

Radford, Ann, 36

Ralph de Burun (B's Norman ancestor), 5

Ravenna, 347, 351, 359, 363, 364, 368, 372, 378, 383–4, 388

Reform Bill (1832), 173

Rhigas, Constantine, 97

Richmond, Charlotte, Duchess of Richmond, 275

Ridge, John, 57, 65

Roberts, Capt. Daniel, 395, 407, 409, 413, 431

Robinson, Charles, 397n

Rocca, M. de, 286

Rochdale: Byron property in, 69 & n, 72, 78–9, 82, 102, 122, 135, 176, 365, 438; B visits with Hanson, 140; prospective sale, 215; property sold, 442, 468

Rogers, Drummer, 25–6

Rogers, Samuel: told of B's behaviour as child, 17; B praises poetry of, 75, 142; in London literary circle, 142–3; and B's celebrity, 159; and Caroline Lamb's interest in B, 161–3; friendship with B, 174; denies harsh comments on Annabella, 257; acquires books from B's library sale, 266; and B's separation, 270; informs Lushington of B's proposed trip abroad, 271; satirised in Caroline Lamb's *Glenarvon*, 279; B fears opinion of, 365; B's satirical poem on, 371–2; *Jacqueline*, 197

Rome, 311

Romilly, Anne, Lady, 289, 334

Romilly, Sir Samuel, 246, 334

Ross (B's childhood tutor), 16

Rousseau, Jean-Jacques, 66, 284–5, 298, 326

Rowlandson, Thomas, 266

Rushton, Miss, 113

Rushton, Robert: appointed B's page, 66; Fletcher leads astray, 77; accompanies B on first trip abroad, 82, 87; sent home, 90; appears in B portrait, 121; and B's boxing, 134; awarded annuity in B's will, 136; and Susan Vaughan, 144–5; supposed relations with B, 256, 288, 469; with B on 1816 trip to Switzerland, 271, 273; leaves for England, 290

Ruskin, John, 157

Rutland, Elizabeth, Duchess of, 192

St Clair, William, 105, 151, 449

Salsette, HMS, 106–7, 111–12, 114, 116, 437n

Sanguinetti (Portuguese guide), 87

Sardanapulus (B), 376, 383, 394

Sardinia, 90–1

Sass, Lieut. (Swedish volunteer in Greece), 461

Saunders, George, 76–7, 121

Sawbridge, Col., 78–9

Schilizzi, Prince, 435

Schlegel, Wilhelm von, 286

Schliemann, Heinrich, 107

Schoenberg, Arnold: sets B's *Ode to Napoleon* to music, 193n

Scott, Alexander, 326, 340–1, 345, 349, 351, 356, 360

Scott, John (captain of *Hercules*), 441

Scott, Sir Walter: witnesses Catherine Byron's outburst at theatre, 8; B criticises in *English Bards*, 75; Murray publishes, 131; B discusses works with Rogers, 143; romance poems, 151; hears rumours of B's engagement to Mercer Elphinstone, 167; B introduced to at Murray's, 234; Lushington talks with, 272; reviews *Childe Harold*, 304, 320; Annabella visits, 320; B dedicates *Cain* to, 394; *Quentin Durward*, 444; *Waverley*, 151

Scourge, The (magazine), 132

Sécheron (Switzerland), 277–8

Segati, Marianna (B's Venetian mistress), 307, 309, 311–12, 316–17, 321, 323

Segati, Pietro, 307, 316–17

"She Walks in Beauty" (B), 234–5

Sheldrake (bootmaker), 35

Shelley, Clara (daughter of Mary and PBS): death, 330–1

Shelley, Harriet (*née* Westbrook; PBS's first wife): suicide, 309; gains rights to children, 358

Shelley, Mary (*née* Godwin): elopement, 265, 277; in Sécheron, 276–7; excluded by B, 283; in Bath, 294; marriage to PBS, 309; travels to Venice, 328, 330; and death of daughter Clara, 330–1; in Pisa, 365, 393, 395; condemns Hoppners for treatment of Claire Clairmont, 367; approves of placing Allegra in convent, 382; told of Hoppners' calumnies, 385; and Shelley's plan for expatriate colony in Pisa, 386; Teresa likes, 395; furnishes Palazzo Lanfranchi, 396; supposed infatuation with B, 396n; and scuffle with Italian sergeant major, 399; and Claire Clairmont's plan to kidnap

Allegra, 401; and Shelley's new boat, 407; and Shelley's drowning, 409–10; leaves Pisa for Genoa, 412–14, 421–2; and "Mrs Mason", 419; criticises B's treatment of Leigh Hunt, 420; on B's cooling relations with Teresa, 421; B *seeks* financial settlement for, 422; copies work for B, 422; and B's decision to go to Greece, 427; B declines to give money for return to England, 431, 434; comforts Teresa on B's departure for Greece, 434; believes B's dying call for Claire, 469; on Annabella after B's death, 474; *Frankenstein*, 283

Shelley, Percy Bysshe: in Pisa, 1, 365, 382, 395; elopes with Mary Godwin, 265, 277; loses custody of children, 265, 277, 309, 358; in Switzerland with B, 276–8, 283–5, 287; influence on B, 277–8, 282–3, 328; temperament and ideals, 277–8; in storm on Lake Geneva, 284; delivers B's *Childe Harold* to Murray, 288; writes to B from England, 293–4; names B trustee in will, 294; and Claire Clairmont's impending child, 304; marries Mary, 309; accompanies Allegra on way to Italy, 322–4; travels to Venice to see B about Allegra, 327–30; alleged affair and child with Claire Clairmont, 382, 385, 399, 401; approves of placing Allegra in convent, 382; visits B in Ravenna, 384–6; visits Allegra in convent, 385; proposes literary colony in Pisa, 386–7, 390, 392, 407; relations with B, 386, 396–9, 411; writes to and visits Teresa on B's behalf, 386–7; sailing, 395–6, 406; B's wager unpaid, 397–8, 431; financial anxieties, 398–9; requests financial help from B for Leigh Hunt, 398; injured in scuffle with Italian sergeant major, 399–400; and Claire Clairmont's plan to kidnap Allegra, 401; and death of Allegra, 402–3; welcomes Hunts to Pisa, 408; drowned and cremated, 409–10; discusses Greece with B, 425; *Hellas*, 425; *Hymn to Intellectual Beauty*, 284; *Julian and Maddalo*, 330, 332; *Queen Mab*, 358, 397

Shelley, (Sir) Percy Florence (son of Mary and PBS), 422

Shelley, Sir Timothy, 397, 422

Shelley, William (son of Mary and PBS), 410

Shepherd, Sir Samuel, 257, 261

Sheridan, Richard Brinsley, 148, 161, 286 7

Sherwood, Neely, and Jones (London publishers), 171

Shorter, Edward, 454n, 459n, 460n

Siddons, Sarah, 8, 143, 157

Siege of Corinth, The (B), 237, 253

Silvestrini, Fanny, 341, 343, 348

Simplon Pass, 296

Six Mile Bottom: B visits alone, 219, 237–8; B and Annabella stay with Augusta in, 227–30; sold, 308, 327

"Sketch from Private Life, A" (B), 161–2, 263n, 264, 372–3

Sligo, Howe Peter Browne, 2nd Marquess of, 116–17, 119–20, 134, 176, 191

Smiles, Samuel, 163n

Smith, Constance Spencer, 91–2, 103, 125–6, 168

Smith, Horace, 407

Smith, John Spencer, 91–2

Smyrna, 104–5

"So we'll go no more a roving" (B), 310

Society of Dilettanti, 101

sodomy: as crime, 267n

Somerset, Charlotte, Duchess of, 262

Sotheby, William, 175

South America: B plans to visit, 350, 354, 359, 408, 411, 414, 427

Southey, Robert, 131, 336, 337, 396–7, 416

Spain: B travels in, 87–8

Spencer, Margaret Georgiana, Countess, 165

Spezia, La (bay), 396, 401, 409

Spider (ship), 92–3

Staël-Holstein, Germaine, Baronne de (*née* Necker): B meets, 175; Napoleon exiles, 175; advises B against warring with world, 260; relations with Benjamin Constant, 270, 370; questions B on *Glenarvon*, 279; returns to Coppet, 286; and Annabella's illness, 289; and B's departure for Italy, 296; death, 318; *Corinne*, 350

Stair, Lord (physician), 194

Stanhope, Lady Hester, 119–20

Stanhope, Col. Leicester, 442–3, 447, 449, 451, 453–5, 457–9, 461–2, 468, 470, 471–2

"Stanzas to Augusta" (B), 263, 302n

"Stanzas to Jessy" (B), 56

"Stanzas to a Lady on Leaving England" (B), 67

"Stanzas to the Po" (B), 345

Stendhal (Marie-Henri Beyle), 297–8

Sterne, Laurence: *A Sentimental Journey*, 159

Stocking, Marion Kingston, 382n

Stowe, Harriet Beecher: *Lady Byron Vindicated*, 475

Strane (British consul in Patras), 116–17

Suliotes (Greek mountain warriors), 97, 450, 452–3, 455, 458–9, 461, 465

Switzerland, 277–89, 292–3

Symonds, John Addington, 41

"Sympathetic Address to a Young Lady Weeping" (B), 150, 190, 193

Taaffe, John, 392, 397, 399–400

Tagus, River: B swims, 87

Talavera, Battle of (1809), 87

Thorwaldsen, Bertel, 312

"Thoughts Suggested by a College Examination" (B), 65

"Thyrza": identity of, 174, 223

"Thyrza" (B), 145

Ticknor, George, 318

Tighe, George William, 419

Tita *see* Falcieri, Tita

"To Mary" (B), 57–8

"To my Son!" (B), 70

Tommasini, Professor, 402

Townshend (ship), 90, 436

Trelawny, Edward: B describes Greece to, 128; appearance and character, 395; on B's view of Shelley, 397; in scuffle with Italian sergeant major, 399; sees Claire Clairmont in Pisa, 402; on B's Montenero villa, 405; and Shelley's boat, 406–7; mans B's yacht, 407; and Shelley's drowning, 409–10; leaves for Livorno, 413; swims with B, 413, 436; takes Hunt on tour of Casa Magni, 413; helps Mary Shelley with passage money back to England, 431, 434; invited onto Greek expedition, 431; places gravestone over Shelley's ashes, 431; departs with B for Greece, 434–6; on B in Greece, 441; with Odysseus in Greece, 462; Mary Shelley reports Annabella's grief to, 474

Trevanion, Henry, 475

Trinity College, Cambridge *see* Cambridge University

Tripolitza (Greece), 439, 442

Troy: site, 107

Turkey: rule in Greece, 99–100; and Greek war of independence, 439

Turner, J.M.W.: *Snowstorm* (painting), 158

Two Foscari, The (B), 383–4, 394, 396–7

Vacca, Dr Andre, 400, 408

Valenciennes, France, 9, 14

Valsamaki, Spiro, 446–7

Vaughan, Susan, 144–5

Vavassour, Mrs: offers to adopt Allegra, 351

Veli Pasha, 97, 118

Venice: B in, 266–7, 300–1, 305–8, 318, 321, 324, 331, 383; history and character, 305–6; Carnival, 309, 321; Shelley visits B in, 327–30; and B's affair with Teresa Guiccioli, 348–9; Moore visits, 355–6; B describes in *Marino Falieri*, 364

Verona, 300

Villiers, Teresa, 182, 254, 280–2, 294–5, 299, 314, 320, 345, 474

Vimiero, Battle of (1809), 87, 138n

Vision of Judgment, The (B), 384, 397, 408, 416, 428

Vivian, Charles, 409

Volage (ship), 126

Waddams, S.M., 247n

Walpole, Horace, 23

Waltz (B), 171

Waterloo, Battle of (1815), 234, 274

Watson, James, 10–11

Webster, Lady Frances, 183, 186, 188, 418

Webster, Sir Godfrey, 157, 161, 183

Webster, James Wedderburn, 76, 132, 418

"Well! Thou Art Happy" (B), 67

Wellington, Arthur Wellesley, 1st Duke of, 85, 89, 128, 153, 193, 356, 415, 428

Wentworth, Thomas, 2nd Viscount: Annabella expects to inherit from, 206, 209–10, 216, 222; leaves estate to Lady Noel, 213n, 236; travels to meet B, 213; illegitimate son, 220, 223; illness and death, 235–6

Werner (B), 417

Westmoreland, Jane, Countess of, 89, 162

Wherry, Francis, 105, 107

Whig Club (Cambridge), 62, 64

White, Payne, 101

Wildman, Col. Thomas, 318, 474

William (Catherine Byron's servant), 37

Williams, Edward: in Pisa, 392–3, 395, 402, 406; drowned with Shelley, 409–10; journal, 413

Williams, Jane, 395, 402, 409, 412–13, 419, 421, 427, 434, 441

Wilmot, Barbarina (*later* Lady Dacre), 192, 234

Wilmot, Juliana, Lady (B's aunt), 12

Wilmot, Robert, 257

Wingfield, John, 46, 135, 140

Winter, Lady Caroline, 212

Wollstonecraft, Mary, 265

Wordsworth, William: B criticises, 75, 336; Shelley praises to B, 278, 283, 285; on B's *Don Juan*, 339

Wright, Walter, 130

"Written after Swimming from Sestos to Abydos" (B), 109

York, Ernest Augustus, Duke of, 194

Yorke, Captain, RN (of *Alacrity*), 454

Yousouf Pasha, 451

Yson, Comtesse d', 429

Zambelli, Lega, 353, 387, 390, 400, 402–3, 413, 437, 447, 449, 451, 476

Zograffo, Demetrius, 99, 101, 103, 124, 136